# KNOWLEDGE AND INTERACTION

Decades of research in the cognitive and learning sciences have led to a growing recognition of the incredibly multifaceted nature of human knowing and learning. Up to now, this multifaceted nature has been visible mostly in distinct and often competing communities of researchers. From a purely scientific perspective, "siloed" science – where different traditions refuse to speak with one another, or merely ignore one another – is unacceptable. This ambitious volume attempts to kick-start a serious, new line of work that merges, or properly articulates, two different traditions with their divergent historical, theoretical, and methodological commitments that, nonetheless, both focus on the highly detailed analysis of processes of knowing and learning as they unfold in interactional contexts in real time.

*Knowledge and Interaction* puts two traditions in dialogue with one another: Knowledge Analysis (KA), which draws on intellectual roots in developmental psychology and cognitive modeling and focuses on the nature and form of individual knowledge systems, and Interaction Analysis (IA), which has been prominent in approaches that seek to understand and explain learning as a sequence of real-time moves by individuals as they interact with interlocutors, learning environments, and the world around them. The volume's four-part organization opens up space for both substantive contributions on areas of conceptual and empirical work as well as opportunities for reflection, integration, and coordination.

**Andrea A. diSessa** is Corey Professor of Education Emeritus and Professor of the Graduate School at the University of California, Berkeley, USA. He is a member of the National Academy of Education and a Fellow of the American Educational Research Association.

**Mariana Levin** is Assistant Professor of Mathematics Education in the Department of Mathematics at Western Michigan University.

**Nathaniel J. S. Brown** is Associate Research Professor of Educational Research, Measurement, and Evaluation at the Lynch School of Education, Boston College, USA.

# KNOWLEDGE AND INTERACTION

A Synthetic Agenda for the Learning Sciences

*Edited by Andrea A. diSessa,
Mariana Levin,
and Nathaniel J. S. Brown*

NEW YORK AND LONDON

First published 2016
by Routledge
711 Third Avenue, New York, NY 10017

and by Routledge
2 Park Square, Milton Park, Abingdon, Oxon OX14 4RN

*Routledge is an imprint of the Taylor & Francis Group, an informa business*

© 2016 Taylor & Francis

The right of Andrea A. diSessa, Mariana Levin, and Nathaniel J. S. Brown to be identified as the authors of the editorial material of this work, and of the authors for their individual chapters, has been asserted by them in accordance with sections 77 and 78 of the Copyright, Designs and Patents Act 1988.

All rights reserved. No part of this book may be reprinted or reproduced or utilized in any form or by any electronic, mechanical, or other means, now known or hereafter invented, including photocopying and recording, or in any information storage or retrieval system, without permission in writing from the publishers.

*Trademark notice*: Product or corporate names may be trademarks or registered trademarks, and are used only for identification and explanation without intent to infringe.

*Library of Congress Cataloging in Publication Data*
Names: DiSessa, Andrea A., editor. | Levin, Mariana, editor. |
Brown, Nathaniel J. S., editor.
Title: Knowledge and interaction : a synthetic agenda for the learning sciences / edited by Andrea A. DiSessa, Mariana Levin, Nathaniel J. S. Brown.
Description: New York ; London : Routledge, [2016] |
Includes bibliographical references and index.
Identifiers: LCCN 2015023242 | ISBN 9781138797130 (hardback) |
ISBN 9781138998292 (pbk.) | ISBN 9781315757360 (ebook)
Subjects: LCSH: Learning, Psychology of. | Knowledge, Theory of. |
Interaction analysis in educationClassification: LCC LB1060 .K625 2016 |
DDC 370.15/23–dc23
LC record available at http://lccn.loc.gov/2015023242

ISBN: 978-1-138-79713-0 (hbk)
ISBN: 978-1-138-99829-2 (pbk)
ISBN: 978-1-315-75736-0 (ebk)

Typeset in Bembo
by Out of House Publishing

# CONTENTS

| | |
|---|---|
| *Preface* | *ix* |
| *Acknowledgments* | *xii* |
| *List of contributors* | *xiv* |
| Introduction | 1 |

**PART I**
**Foundations**     **9**

1  Competence Reconceived: The Shared Enterprise of Knowledge Analysis and Interaction Analysis    11
   *Nathaniel J. S. Brown, Joshua A. Danish, Mariana Levin, and Andrea A. diSessa*

2  Knowledge Analysis: An Introduction    30
   *Andrea A. diSessa, Bruce L. Sherin, and Mariana Levin*

3  Interaction Analysis Approaches to Knowledge in Use    72
   *Rogers Hall and Reed Stevens*

## PART II
## Synthetic Analyses — 109

4 Ecologies of Knowing: Lessons From the Highly Tailored
   Practice of Hobbies — 111
   *Flávio S. Azevedo and Victor R. Lee*

5 A Microlatitudinal/Microlongitudinal Analysis of Speech,
   Gesture, and Representation Use in a Student's
   Repeated Scientific Explanations of Phase Change — 133
   *David DeLiema, Victor R. Lee, Joshua A. Danish, Noel Enyedy, and Nathaniel J. S. Brown*

6 Working Towards an Integrated Analysis of Knowledge in
   Interaction — 160
   *Joshua A. Danish, Noel Enyedy, and Orit Parnafes*

   Commentary: When Will Science Surpass Our Intuitive
   Capacities as Expert Practitioners? — 182
   *Andrea A. diSessa*

7 "Seeing" as Complex, Coordinated Performance: A
   Coordination Class Theory Lens on Disciplined Perception — 191
   *Mariana Levin and Andrea A. diSessa*

8 Working Out: Mathematics Learning as Motor Problem
   Solving in Instrumented Fields of Promoted Action — 212
   *Dor Abrahamson and Dragan Trninic*

9 Gestures, Speech, and Manipulation of Objects as a Window
   and Interface to Individual Cognition — 236
   *Shulamit Kapon*

   Commentary: "IA Lite": Capturing Some of the Explanatory
   Power of Interaction Analysis Without Committing to
   Its Ontology — 252
   *Andrew Elby*

10 Bridging Knowledge Analysis and Interaction Analysis
   Through Understanding the Dynamics of Knowledge in Use — 260
   *Ayush Gupta, Andrew Elby, and Vashti Sawtelle*

| | | |
|---|---|---|
| 11 | Ensemble Learning and Knowing: Developing a Walking Scale Geometry Dilation Strategy<br>*Jasmine Y. Ma* | 292 |
| | Commentary: From the Individual to the Ensemble and Back Again<br>*Luke D. Conlin and David Hammer* | 311 |
| 12 | Parents as Skilled Knowledge Practitioners<br>*Jessica F. Umphress* | 326 |
| 13 | Knowledge and Interaction in Clinical Interviewing: Revoicing<br>*Andrea A. diSessa, James G. Greeno, Sarah Michaels, and Catherine O'Connor* | 348 |
| 14 | The Intersection of Knowledge and Interaction: Challenges of Clinical Interviewing<br>*Rosemary S. Russ, Bruce L. Sherin, and Victor R. Lee* | 377 |
| 15 | Feedback-Relevant Places: Interpreting Shifts in Explanatory Narratives<br>*Nathaniel J. S. Brown* | 403 |

## PART III
## Theoretical, Methodological, and Meta-scientific Issues     427

| | | |
|---|---|---|
| 16 | Computational Analysis and the Importance of Interactional Detail<br>*Bruce L. Sherin* | 429 |
| | Commentary: The Need for the Participant's Perspective in a KAIA Joint Enterprise<br>*Noel Enyedy and Joshua A. Danish* | 447 |
| 17 | Navigating Turbulent Waters: Objectivity, Interpretation, and Experience in the Analysis of Interaction<br>*Ricardo Nemirovsky and Molly L. Kelton* | 458 |

18  Three Meta-Scientific Micro-Essays  480
    *Andrea A. diSessa*

19  Towards a Generous* Discussion of Interplay Between
    Natural Descriptive and Hidden Machinery Approaches
    in Knowledge and Interaction Analysis  496
    *Rogers Hall, Ricardo Nemirovsky, Jasmine Y. Ma,
    and Molly L. Kelton*

    Commentary: "Openness" as a Shared Research Aesthetic
    Between Knowledge Analysis and Interaction Analysis  520
    *Mariana Levin*

    Commentary: How Science Is Done  525
    *Andrea A. diSessa*

**PART IV**
**Reflections and Prospects**  **551**

20  Another Candidate for Relating Knowledge Analysis and
    Interaction Analysis: Mitchell's Integrative Pluralism  553
    *James G. Greeno*

21  That Old Problem of Intersubjectivity  558
    *Timothy Koschmann*

22  Reflections: The KAIA Project and Prospects  570
    *Andrea A. diSessa, Mariana Levin, and Nathaniel J. S. Brown*

*Index*  *583*

# PREFACE

In the late 1980s and through the 1990s, the Berkeley/Palo Alto axis was a swirling cauldron of intellectual activity that laid important groundwork for the Knowledge Analysis/Interaction Analysis (KAIA) project, out of which this volume grew. In 1985, the Education in Mathematics, Science, and Technology unit (EMST) at the University of California at Berkeley declared itself the first Ph.D. and research program focusing on cognitive science in the service of learning. Jim Greeno, Alan Schoenfeld, and Andy diSessa were principles of the new unit. The next year, the Institute for Research on Learning (IRL) started up in Palo Alto, initially associated with the innovative Xerox Palo Alto Research Center. John Seely Brown and Jim Greeno were co-directors and intellectual leaders of that institution; diSessa and Schoenfeld were senior consultants. IRL was instrumental in advancing the visibility of "situated cognition," which aimed to either extend or supplant, depending on the author, purely cognitive approaches to learning with anthropological, social, and interactional approaches. On the anthropological side, Jean Lave's ideas were influential, particularly in her critique of cognitive developmental approaches to understanding learning and in her promoting apprenticeship as an attractive alternative to schooling as a model for learning. IRL developed the idea of "cognitive apprenticeship," combining Lave's ideas within the larger frame of situated cognition, but also building on revised conceptions of learning and knowing, such as those advanced by Schoenfeld and diSessa. Lave worked for a time at IRL, and then moved to Berkeley (reversing Jim Greeno's move from Berkeley to Palo Alto). Brigitte Jordan ran the Interaction Lab at the hub of IRL activity, and her article on Interaction Analysis with Austin Henderson in the *Journal of Learning Sciences* (Jordan & Henderson, 1995) arguably cemented the modern version of Interaction Analysis into the core of the learning sciences.

Many contributors to KAIA, as younger students and faculty, continued the dance between traditions and institutions. Rogers Hall worked as a post-doc at IRL, and then became an assistant professor (later, associate professor) at Berkeley. Randi Engle worked as a graduate student with Jim Greeno at Stanford before becoming an assistant professor (later, associate professor) at Berkeley. A number of the next two generations of researchers that are involved with the KAIA project worked with both the interaction and knowledge perspectives at Berkeley, including Reed Stevens, Noel Enyedy, and Nathaniel Brown. Other participants in this project (David Hammer, Andrew Elby) began complementary studies – expanding from KA-inspired work to include focus on interactional elements – after they left the West Coast.

During this middle period (1990s), the public face of cross-perspective work included two American Educational Research Association (AERA) symposia (one organized as a debate between situative and cognitive perspectives, one on p-prims in everyday conversation) involving diSessa, Greeno, Sherin, Stevens, and others.

It's easily arguable that the split between traditions was much more external to the Berkeley/Palo Alto axis than internal to it. Certainly almost all these actors were more familiar with both traditions than most researchers outside these circles. In addition, collegial friendships crossed boundaries willy-nilly. Thus, intellectually and socially, the Berkeley/Palo Alto axis set the stage for this current work, even if the two ends of the frequently traveled road became better known as advocates of interaction (and "situated cognition") and knowledge ("cognitive approaches") separately. Almost all the other authors in this volume worked with one of the researchers named above, or with their students.

By the mid-2000s, Knowledge Analysis and Interaction Analysis had become more established, and articulation of perspectives was becoming a more prominent and explicit concern. In 2006–2007, diSessa organized a faculty seminar on "dialectical approaches to cognition" at Berkeley. Attendees included Abrahamson and Engle. The following year, during sabbaticals, Andy diSessa and Rogers Hall jointly organized a "dialectical" seminar at the Center for the Advanced Study of the Behavioral Sciences in Palo Alto, an institution with a long and strong tradition in hosting and fostering cross-disciplinary and cross-perspective research. In 2010, diSessa organized an AERA symposium on "dialectical approaches to cognition."

Meanwhile, Orit Parnafes, and Mariana Levin, who had both been graduate students at Berkeley, spearheaded a 2009 effort to get funding from the AERA to host a mini-conference on bridging Knowledge Analysis and Interaction Analysis approaches to studying knowing and learning (together with Andy diSessa, David Hammer, Bruce Sherin, Nathaniel Brown, Rogers Hall, Reed Stevens, and Victor Lee). The idea was that real progress on articulation of perspectives would have the best chance if it happened in cross-paradigm research projects, working out ideas collaboratively on concrete data sets.

The work of this volume grew directly out of the resulting AERA-funded workshop held in June 2011 in Marin County, California. The Marin meeting gathered 29 researchers from the Knowledge Analysis and Interaction Analysis communities, spanning methodological expertise and career stages. Charles Goodwin, a luminary in Interaction Analysis (one of few attendees not within the geography of the social history described above – but certainly in it intellectually), also participated in the workshop. At the workshop, four teams of researchers worked up analyses using tools from both KA and IA and presented these analyses. Following the workshop, additional teams and individuals began working on their own attempts at integrated analyses. Two additional workshops (Vancouver, 2012, and San Francisco, 2013) furthered development of the agenda and community. The work of the KAIA project was disseminated through conference symposia at AERA (2012: "Integrating Issues of Knowledge and Interaction in Analyses of Cognition and Learning" with Bruce Sherin and Reed Stevens, discussants) and ICLS (2014: "Is the Sum Greater than its Parts? Reflections on the Agenda of Integrating Analyses of Cognition and Learning" with Timothy Koschmann, discussant).

# ACKNOWLEDGMENTS

The efforts of many individuals and organizations helped move a research volume on the contributions of the KAIA project from a dream to a reality. We gratefully acknowledge the AERA Educational Conferences Program for funding the initial mini-conference "Integrating Knowledge Analysis and Interaction Analysis Approaches to Studying Learning and Conceptual Change," which took place June 5–7, 2011, in Marin County, CA. The following individuals, along with the editors of this volume, collaborated in writing the initial proposal to fund the workshop and also gave input in planning the meeting: Ann Edwards, Victor Lee, Jim Greeno, Rogers Hall, David Hammer, Orit Parnafes, Bruce Sherin, and Reed Stevens. Orit Parnafes and Mariana Levin were the primary organizers of the workshop, a conceptual and practical task that was accomplished skillfully and with foresight. Janet Koster van Groos videotaped and provided other logistical support.

We also thank Felice Levine and AERA for partial support for two follow-up meetings in Vancouver and San Francisco. The Evelyn Lois Corey Chair at Berkeley (A. diSessa, chair holder) provided additional support for follow-up meetings.

Alex Masulis and Dan Schwartz of Taylor & Francis provided intellectual and invaluable practical support in moving our work toward publication. Melinda diSessa provided critical and editorial feedback on several chapters. We thank the Knowledge Analysis and Patterns research groups at UC Berkeley for generative conversations as the general integrative agenda and specific analyses took shape. Leigh Kupersmith copy-edited the final volume.

Lastly, we especially owe thanks to our families and partners, Melinda diSessa, Aaron Levin, and Eve Brown.

## In Memoriam

Randi Engle: 1967–2012. She is and will be greatly missed.

**FIGURE 0.1** The participants of the KAIA workshop in Marin, CA. June 2011. Pictured in the photo: (back row, left to right) Chandra Turpen, Luke Conlin, Andy diSessa, Rogers Hall, Joshua Danish, Andy Elby, Victor Lee, Jim Greeno, David DeLiema, Ricardo Nemirovsky, Noel Enyedy; (middle row, left to right) Lama Jaber, Ann Edwards, Sarah Michaels, Ayush Gupta, Bruce Sherin, Reed Stevens, Molly Kelton, Siri Mehus, Shuly Kapon, David Hammer; (front row, left to right) Janet Koster van Groos, Mari Levin, Orit Parnafes, Jessica Umphress, Jasmine Ma, Flávio Azevedo, Randi Engle. Not pictured: Chuck Goodwin.

# CONTRIBUTORS

Dor Abrahamson
Graduate School of Education
University of California, Berkeley

Flávio S. Azevedo
Department of Curriculum and
Instruction
The University of Texas at Austin

Nathaniel J. S. Brown
Educational Research, Measurement,
and Evaluation
Lynch School of Education
Boston College

Luke D. Conlin
Graduate School of Education
Stanford University

Joshua A. Danish
Learning Sciences
Indiana University

David DeLiema
Graduate School of Education and
Information Studies
University of California, Los Angeles

Andrea A. diSessa
Graduate School of Education
University of California, Berkeley

Andrew Elby
Department of Teaching & Learning,
Policy & Leadership
University of Maryland, College Park

Noel Enyedy
Graduate School of Education and
Information Studies
University of California, Los Angeles

James G. Greeno
School of Education
University of Pittsburgh

Ayush Gupta
Department of Physics
University of Maryland, College
Park

Rogers Hall
Department of Teaching and
Learning
Vanderbilt University

David Hammer
Departments of Education and Physics & Astronomy and Center for Engineering Education & Outreach
Tufts University

Shulamit Kapon
Department of Education in Science and Technology
Technion – Israel Institute of Technology

Molly L. Kelton
Department of Mathematics and Statistics
San Diego State University

Timothy Koschmann
Department of Medical Education
Southern Illinois University

Victor R. Lee
Department of Instructional Technology & Learning Sciences
Utah State University

Mariana Levin
Department of Mathematics
Western Michigan University

Jasmine Y. Ma
Steinhardt School of Culture, Education, and Human Development
New York University

Sarah Michaels
Education Department
Clark University

Ricardo Nemirovsky
Department of Mathematics and Statistics
San Diego State University

Catherine O'Connor
School of Education
Boston University

Orit Parnafes
Department of Education
Ben Gurion University

Rosemary S. Russ
Department of Curriculum and Instruction
University of Wisconsin–Madison

Vashti Sawtelle
Lyman Briggs College and Department of Physics & Astronomy
Michigan State University

Bruce L. Sherin
School of Education and Social Policy
Northwestern University

Reed Stevens
School of Education and Social Policy
Northwestern University

Dragan Trninic
Graduate School of Education
University of California, Berkeley

Jessica F. Umphress
School of Education and Social Policy
Northwestern University

# INTRODUCTION

Decades of research in the cognitive and learning sciences have led to a growing recognition of the incredibly multifaceted nature of human knowing and learning. It is immensely sensible that different communities develop in a "divide and conquer" approach to understanding different aspects of human cognition. Still, at some point, sometimes fractious debate between diverse communities with the same overarching goal (an emblematic example is the cognitive–situative debate; see Anderson, Reder, & Simon, 1996; Greeno, 1997) must be replaced by sensible interactions among perspectives and mutual accountability.

This volume is ambitious, attempting to kick-start a serious new line of work that merges – or properly articulates – different traditions along with their divergent historical, theoretical, and methodological commitments. At the same time, we believe we are being realistic in not proposing to try to take on the task of putting all possible perspectives on knowing and learning in relation to each other at once. Rather, our approach is to focus on two lines that, while representing clearly different traditions (broadly, one socio-interactionist and one individual/cognitive), still have a great deal in common. The two traditions we put in dialogue both deal with details of knowledge in development, typical of the cognitive perspective, but they also deal with learning in interaction, typical of sociocultural or situated perspectives. Perhaps most important in terms of aligning or merging is that both lines of research focus on the intricate analysis of processes of knowing and learning as they unfold in real time. The two perspectives are Knowledge Analysis (KA) and Interaction Analysis (IA).

Knowledge Analysis draws on intellectual roots in developmental psychology and computational modeling, and it focuses on the nature and form of individual knowledge systems: what they are comprised of, how they are organized, and how this organization changes over time in interactions with the physical, social, and material world. KA has been prominent in approaches to conceptual change that – unlike most approaches to that topic – include real-time learning analysis. Interaction Analysis draws on foundational work in linguistic anthropology, ethnomethodology, and conversation analysis, and it seeks to understand and explain learning as a fine-grained and interwoven sequence of real-time moves by individuals as they interact with interlocutors, learning environments, and the world around them. Of particular interest are the social and embodied practices of communities of learners and the interactional means by which participants display and interpret meaning.

Despite this volume's agenda to join perspectives, it also recognizes deep debates and differences in points of view between KA and IA, which will not recede quickly. For example, one of the broader controversial issues is methodological: How is it sensible to model knowledge "in the head" given that we have no direct access to the inner workings of minds, and we thus construct models of knowledge only by observing actions and interactions? IA proposes a more direct approach to observation, eschewing complex inferences to underlying mechanisms. Another issue that is very much a part of conversations between KA and IA researchers concerns how and whether cognition can be studied in the lab, separately from the broader material and social context in which it is generally situated. Thus, not only progress and agreement, but also difficulties and disagreements, are reported in chapters and commentaries.

Several previous volumes, handbook chapters, and special issues have noted the diversity of perspectives on cognition and learning that exist, and they have observed that different lenses can illuminate different educational issues in a "compare and contrast" mode. However, the current volume makes the further effort to articulate perspectives and bridge across them through original and collaborative analyses. That is, this volume does not merely showcase the diversity of perspectives that could be illuminating of a particular piece of data or an issue, but rather, it involves researchers of differing perspectives working together to create a new analysis, or even in some cases a new kind of analysis.

From a purely scientific perspective, "siloed" science – where different traditions refuse to speak with one another, or merely ignore one another – is unsatisfactory. Competing accounts of the same thing, say, learning in a classroom, need to have their differences and contradictions resolved. In some cases, one or another tradition may be wrong about some particular issue. More likely, proper articulation will produce an encompassing and more powerful account. What follows is a list of progressively more intimate models of how IA and KA may come to relate to one another.

To begin, two models – global competition and complementarity – are quite common in the existing educational research literature, but they are not emphasized in this book. We aim to engage more synthetic approaches. The next three models – micro-complementarity, influencing paradigms, and deep synergy – are well represented in this book. While each chapter has a unique perspective on the relationship between KA and IA and we do not wish to pigeon-hole, we think these three models serve as a useful advance organizer for Part II: Synthetic Analyses. The final model – fusion – represents a possible far-future outcome of the present work. Fusion is clearly speculative and beyond our current grasp, but it is addressed in bits and pieces in a few empirical chapters, in some of the essays and synthetic chapters in Part III (Theoretical, Methodological, and Meta-scientific Issues), and, tangentially, in Part IV (Reflections and Prospects).

## Global Competition

In principle, one might frame IA and KA as competing perspectives between which one must choose. One perspective might be right and the other wrong. "Choice" is a common trope at the "cognitive" vs. "sociocultural" level; many researchers still act as if one must choose between them. However, we think this attitude is antiquated. Minimally, both views deserve respect and continued attention for their accomplishments and promise.

## Complementarity

One might take the view that IA and KA perspectives are complementary. They concern different phenomena. In this view, there need not be any conflict. A common way of thinking about this is that one has a variety of issues and problems to investigate concerning learning, and, depending on the problem, one or the other perspective might be more productive – "live and let live." One might frame this issue as incommensurability (and some authors have done so). Both perspectives are useful, but they have nothing to say to one another. We think this might be or has been an appropriate attitude in the historical development of IA and KA, but it is too weak a connection to support the main efforts of this volume.

## Micro-complementarity

Suppose IA and KA are not just complementary at the level of choice of problem or phenomenology to investigate, but each has a perhaps critical role in understanding particular and important issues in learning. To take an example that is developed at some length later in the volume, it might be that KA researchers, trying to identify knowledge in a clinical interview, might need the help of IA to understand optimal conditions for – and possible threats to – their enterprise of "reading out knowledge." Here, KA and IA researchers probably have to read and listen to each other, but they might still conduct their investigations within a paradigm.

KA and IA researchers already both investigate processes of knowing and learning in clinical and other "artificial" settings, but also in the real world of classrooms, workplaces, museums, gardens, and rocketry clubs. All such settings intimately involve both interaction and knowledge, hence they can serve as loci for micro-complementary analyses. But different contexts likely involve different issues and different relations of micro-complementarity, some of which might be easier to approach, at present, than others. The great diversity of contexts investigated in empirical chapters in this volume provides similarly diverse views of micro-complementarity, which are sometimes enhanced by companion commentaries.

Putting KA and IA in micro-complementary relationships also provides good grounds for investigating methodological issues. We already mentioned managing interactional optimizations or threats to Knowledge Analysis in clinical interactions. Similarly, comparative study across different contexts can enlighten the different affordances of "natural" vs. "artificial" contexts or small vs. large groups for studying thinking and learning. These and similar methodological issues are broached in many empirical chapters, and they are developed later in meta-scientific ones.

Micro-complementary analyses put IA and KA in intimate contact with one another, especially if one team of researchers does both. Such studies are also fertile ground for deeper synergy, which we take up immediately below.

## Mutually Influencing Paradigms

Different intellectual traditions identify their own families of phenomenology worthy of investigation, and they also develop methods of investigation and theorizing appropriate to their focal phenomena. Once identified and developed, however, there is no strong reason to suppose that foci of investigation or methods of investigation and theorizing need remain with the tradition in which they originated. For example, IA – having staked a claim in phenomenology that, as a matter of fact, was largely ignored by historical approaches to knowledge – might convince KA researchers to bring their methods to bear on the same focal phenomena. In a similar way, KA has methods of theorizing and model building that one doesn't see in IA, but we know of no convincing arguments that they cannot be insightful, once one begins to try to use them on different-than-traditional phenomena.

Several chapters involve very particular versions of the dialectical agenda that we would put under the rubric of "mutually influencing paradigms." Some seek to demonstrate the additional insight that complementary analyses may provide *even concerning exactly the same issues*. For example, data previously analyzed from a KA or IA point of view may be subjected to complementary analysis, resulting in reaffirmations of results, corrections, additions, or, most importantly, extensions and refinement of avenues of research originally developed only from one (KA or IA) perspective. Some chapters seek to re-situate central constructs developed in one perspective in the other perspective, resulting in changed or expanded meanings of theoretical terms, or changes in the range of applicability or the form of empirical results.

## Deep Synergy

This is the level of articulation at which things pass beyond being "interesting" to being "fundamental for the field." One can identify two grades or levels of deep synergy. First – valuable also as a working principle, rather than only as a level of accomplishment – the perspective might undertake systematic *mutual accountability*. Whatever result one obtains within one perspective, it should also be examined and found sensible in the other perspective. As mutual accountability progresses, one may expect the next substage, *deep synergy* (proper), where the intellectual support for at least some of the most important ideas comes from both perspectives. This is the regime where retaining the identity of the two perspectives begins to become questionable. Genuinely new intellectual territory has been reached that is not construable from within only one perspective.

Several chapters aim explicitly at "deep integration," articulating KA and IA at a grain size that makes it difficult or impossible to distinguish "separate perspectives."

We briefly consider two different versions of deep synergy that appear in existing literature.

*Reduction* means that one has discovered that one level of explanation seems to account for most or all phenomena at "higher" levels. For example, all of chemistry is based on the basic principles of quantum mechanics. In this case, reduction is at best "in principle," since chemistry is a very particular context for doing quantum mechanics, and puts basic quantum mechanical principles in forms (the periodic chart of elements) and with attention specificities (e.g., binding energies of particular atoms) that are relevant to certain kind of phenomena (chemistry) and not others (nuclear reactions, plasma physics).

Reduction is not division by status. It is, minimally, unclear in this modern world whether chemists (biochemists among them) are doing more to enhance civilization than physicists, or vice versa. There is no point denying the value of each. Where fields have come to equilibrium with respect to one another, physicists (for example) do not dismiss the work of chemists (for example), nor do chemists believe that physicists are arrogantly encroaching on and doing violence to their territory. Reduction is not the bugaboo that it seems popular to assume.

Reduction puts a certain kind of emphasis on the "lower" of two levels. *Subsumption* puts the same emphasis on a "higher" level. Again, physics also provides a clear example. Electromagnetism and nuclear physics were eventually subsumed by "particle exchange" and quantum field theory, where the "sciences" that are subsumed turn out to be special cases.

In the learning sciences, whether subsumption or reduction is possible is, speaking minimally, unclear. At the cognitive vs. sociocultural level, however, one can certainly find claims or hopes that border on subsumption or reduction.

Socioculturalists often give voice to the concern that cognitivists have an unproductive (imperialist) reductionist program; historically, some cognitivists have at least bordered on claiming that culture might be an unproblematic extension of cognitive principles (Newell and Simon, more so by omission rather than commission). In terms of subsumption, Lave gives the impression that social perspectives (e.g., participation) will subsume phenomena such as "knowing and learning," and Greeno projected interaction to enfold (rather than to obliterate) cognition. Even if one of these eventualities is realized, whether the lower level of reduction or the upper level of subsumption can be seen to emerge unproblematically from one of the (definitively incomplete) existing paradigms of study, or whether such levels will emerge mutually or independently, is impossible to know.

Meta-scientific chapters engage some of these issues, particularly concerning levels.

## Fusion

Finally, one might imagine a future stage of *fusion*, where distinct perspectives have become completely merged into an overarching one. We are a long way from that, so speculating about when, how, and even if, is not worth much effort.

These models represent potential outcomes of our work bringing together researchers from the KA and IA traditions, but they are equally applicable to an attempt to bring together any competing scientific paradigms. Our aim is that the analyses in this volume will illuminate how current theories and methods for studying learning and interaction, across different scholarly traditions, can be better articulated and coordinated. In this sense, by articulating KA and IA approaches, we hope to explore foundational issues emblematic of the larger cognitive–situative debate (and other such debates) in educational research, starting with a potential synergy that seems particularly likely to be immediately profitable.

## Organization of the Volume

The volume is organized into four parts, with different intentions and somewhat different styles.

### *I. Foundations*

The first part of the book provides a foundation for the rest. The first chapter lays out the "big-picture" background and intentions of this work, including the case for the compatibility between KA and IA with respect to theoretical focus, methodology, and analysis. The chapter also describes historical and current differences between the approaches, reasons for believing a joint analytical effort would be productive, and a description of the forms that such a joint effort might entail.

The two following chapters provide introductions to each of the main orientations that are articulated in this volume, Knowledge Analysis and Interaction Analysis. DiSessa, Sherin, and Levin situate KA with respect to historical and recent trends, give a description of theoretical and methodological foundations of KA, and then close by surveying the landscape of work done from a KA perspective and commenting on near-future pursuits of KA research. Hall and Stevens discuss some lines of work drawing upon IA methods, taking stock of almost 20 years of research since the publication of the fundamental IA reference by Jordan and Henderson (1995). At the same time, they identify new opportunities and problems in developing methods for Interaction Analysis that have a bearing on what counts as knowledge.

## II. Synthetic Analyses

This part may be regarded as the main set of results that have emerged from the multi-year efforts of the larger KAIA project. Empirical chapters in this section draw from two main sources: (1) research that was explicitly initiated in conjunction with the Marin conference and follow-up meetings, and (2) research conducted by individuals who have been part of the ongoing conversations in this community and which explores issues related to the conference and volume. Most empirical chapters engage the task of repositioning phenomena typically understood from either a KA or IA perspective by creating a new, joint cognitive-interactional lens on the phenomena.

## III. Theoretical, Methodological, and Meta-scientific Issues

This part aims to rise above (although sometimes enfolding) empirical work to directly reach important theoretical, methodological, and meta-scientific perspectives on a potential KAIA synthesis. Some of this effort aims to expose the essentially interactive and dialectical work (in the literal sense of people speaking directly back and forth at the original workshop or in subsequent meeting) that was done while working toward this volume. Other contributions are broader explorations of such issues, mostly occasioned by our interactive work. In several cases, the larger contributions spurred further critical, extending, or complementary commentary, which is also presented here.

## IV. Reflections and Prospects

The final part of the volume includes reflections by the editors and chapters by Jim Greeno and Timothy Koschmann on the current state of the KAIA project and where the best future possibilities may lie.

Finally, readers can find thumbnail descriptions of all the chapters (save Part I and Part IV itself) in the editors' reflections chapter. These can interpolate between the aggregated introduction here and the chapters themselves.

## References

Anderson, J. R., Reder, L. M., & Simon, H. A. (1996). Situated learning and education. *Educational Researcher*, 25(4), 5–11.

Greeno, J. G. (1997). On claims that answer the wrong questions, *Educational Researcher*, 26(1), 5–17.

Jordan, B., & Henderson, A. (1995). Interaction Analysis: Foundations and practice. *The Journal of the Learning Sciences*, 4(1), 39–103.

# PART I
# Foundations

# 1
# COMPETENCE RECONCEIVED
## The Shared Enterprise of Knowledge Analysis and Interaction Analysis

*Nathaniel J. S. Brown, Joshua A. Danish, Mariana Levin, and Andrea A. diSessa*

Knowledge Analysis (KA) and Interaction Analysis (IA)[1] are two approaches within the learning sciences that trace their primary lineage to opposite sides of the cognitive–situative divide. On the one hand, KA is deeply committed to the study of intra-mental phenomena, focused on understanding systems of knowledge. On the other hand, IA is deeply committed to the study of situated practice involving individuals, artifacts, and culture, focused on understanding systems of interaction. However, despite the apparent incompatibility implied by this history, there is much in common in their theoretical perspectives on knowing and learning and their suite of methodological and analytical tools. Over the last decade, a growing number of researchers have come to believe that these approaches are in fact deeply compatible and that a joint effort between KA and IA would represent a powerful synergy, a possible way to bridge the cognitive–situative divide and leverage the strengths of both approaches to improve education.

This volume is the result of a concerted attempt at capitalizing on synergy, bringing together researchers from both traditions to analyze data on knowing and learning while drawing on both approaches. This chapter lays out the case for the similarities between KA and IA with respect to goals, methodology, and theoretical orientation. Despite similarities, we also describe differences and points of contention between the approaches. The chapter concludes with a brief discussion of why we believe a joint effort would be particularly productive for the design of learning environments.

### Competence Reconceived: Knowing and Learning as Performance in Context

Although they emerged as independent research traditions within different paradigms, Knowledge Analysis and Interaction Analysis can both be viewed as efforts to rethink how we analyze an individual's observable performances. We use the word *performance* to capture the broad range of activities in which people engage; in the learning sciences, these performances are the observable cognitive and physical actions of learners or experts in a variety of settings, including schools, workplaces, research sites, and everyday life. Both KA and IA treat such actions as performances in the sense that they recognize their nature as dynamic and responsive to activity as it unfolds. That is, both approaches recognize that a performance is never a simple public display of a static mental state, but rather a highly contingent and continually adaptive response that is shaped by many aspects of the individual's history and by the context of action.

For the learning sciences, one crucial result of focusing on dynamic and contingent performances as a means of understanding knowing and learning is that researchers in these traditions have fundamentally transformed our conceptions of competence. Competence and its opposite – incompetence, deficiency, or naiveté – are treated not as static traits but as interpretations of performances that are situated in the immediate context, allowing the possibility for each action to be viewed (by both participants and researchers) as more or less competent based on both the physical and social context. The most poignant and likely most important cases of this reframing concern KA and IA researchers' challenging conventional characterizations of learners as systematically deficient. For example, KA researchers have challenged descriptions of students as holding fundamental and entrenched misconceptions of scientific phenomena, discovering that such students demonstrate a highly contextualized understanding, giving both normative and non-normative explanations for the same phenomenon in response to shifts in attention. As another example, IA researchers have challenged descriptions of students as being academically or behaviorally deficient, discovering that such students demonstrate a highly contextualized ability, giving both competent and deficient performances of the same academic skill in response to shifts in the interactional environment.

The root of revised conceptions of competence and incompetence lies in equally dramatic shifts away from orthodox conceptions of knowing and learning. Instead of assuming that knowledge and ability to learn are stable, KA and IA researchers began to focus on when and where (in which contexts and interactions) students are either viewed or treated as competent, and how novice competency evolves very gradually into expert competency. For both perspectives, *contextuality* became a central concern, and the term acquired a very different and deeper meaning than the ways in which it had been previously construed. Rather than expecting differences in competence depending only on broad strokes of context – such as in school vs. out of school, or English Language Arts vs. Mathematics – these perspectives came to understand contextuality as operating on a moment-by-moment basis, highly sensitive to the changing details of the situation as participants interact with the environment and people around them. Striking differences in competence can manifest within the same setting or domain as a result of subtle differences in participants' focus of attention, the social arrangement, or the materials at hand.

Reconceiving competence and accounting for the contextuality of knowing and learning was not the only impetus behind the development of KA and IA, nor even necessarily the most important. However, it represents a fundamental commitment of both approaches, deeply connecting with their theoretical perspectives, preferred methodologies, and recommendations for educational reform. Relevant to the purpose of this volume, this joint commitment is a wellspring of the convergent evolution that makes it seem possible and desirable to search for common ground between KA and IA, and to look for ways to work together.

## *Parallel Examples from Knowledge Analysis and Interaction Analysis*

To highlight the KA and IA convergence concerning contextuality, we review two chapters from edited volumes that were published in the mid-1990s, each describing the important role of this deeper sense of contextuality in understanding and explaining the competence of a student. We associate the first chapter with the cognitive tradition and argue that it is, despite appearing many years before the term Knowledge Analysis came into use, an example of the KA approach. We associate the second chapter with the situative tradition and argue that it is, despite appearing several years before the term Interaction Analysis came into common use, an example of the IA approach. The first, "What do 'just plain folk' know about physics?" was written by Andrea diSessa in 1996 and published in *The Handbook of Education and Human Development: New Models of Learning, Teaching and Schooling*, edited by Olson and Torrance. It describes apparent changes in the conceptual understanding of an undergraduate student, J, in subtly different contexts. The second, "The acquisition of a child by a learning disability," was written by Ray McDermott in 1993 and published in *Understanding Practice: Perspectives on Activity and Context*, edited by Chaiklin and Lave. It describes apparent changes in the reading ability of an elementary school student, Adam, in subtly different contexts.

Although both were and remain influential, neither of these chapters represents the first application of their respective approaches. The data underlying the argument in each chapter were collected many years prior (in the late 1970s and early 1980s), and had been previously analyzed in other published reports. Moreover, as described in the chapters in this volume on Knowledge Analysis (diSessa, Sherin, & Levin, this volume) and Interaction Analysis (Hall & Stevens, this volume), both of these traditions trace their roots even further back. Nor are these two chapters the most famous or highly cited examples of their respective approaches. Arguably, these might be the theoretical and methodological overviews provided by diSessa (1993) and Jordan and Henderson (1995). However, this pair of case studies provides a striking parallel, illustrating a common awareness of the importance of moment-by-moment contextuality, and arguing forcefully for a reimagining of the notion of competence.

### J and "What do 'just plain folk' know about physics?"

J was a female university freshman enrolled in introductory physics, participating in a series of seven one-hour clinical interviews intended to probe her understanding of physics. She enjoyed and had obtained good grades in physics classes. In the excerpts below, J exhibits an apparent inconsistency in her understanding of what happens when a ball is tossed into the air. First, she provides a normative physics account of the toss, emphasizing by asserting twice that the only force acting on the ball during the toss is gravity:

> J: Not including your hand, like if you just let it go up and come down, *the only force on that is gravity*. And so it starts off with the most speed when it leaves your hand, and the higher it goes, it slows down to the point where it stops. And then comes back down. And so, but *the whole time, the only force on that is the force of gravity*, except the force of your hand when you catch it. And, um, it ... when it starts off it has its highest speed, which is all kinetic energy, and when it stops, it has all potential energy – no kinetic energy. And then it comes back down, and it speeds up again.
>
> (diSessa, 1996, p. 720; emphasis added)

Then, after being asked what happens at the peak of the toss, J gives an incorrect but common account (after waffling about the role of air resistance) in which a second force acting on the ball is in competition with gravity, initially stronger, then fading away:

> J: Um, well air resistance, when you throw the ball up, the air ... It's not against air because air is going every way, but the air force gets stronger and stronger to the point where when it stops. *The gravity pulling down and the force pulling up are equal*, so it's like in equilibrium for a second, so it's not going anywhere. And then gravity pulls it back down. But *when you throw it, you're giving it a force upward, but the force can only last so long* against air and against gravity – actually probably more against gravity than against air. But *so you give this initial force*, and it's going up just fine, slower and slower because gravity is pulling on it and pulling on it. And it gets to the point to the top, and then it's not getting any more energy to go up. You're not giving any more forces, so the only force it has on it is gravity and it comes right back down.
>
> (p. 720; emphasis added)

Before the follow-up question about the peak of the toss, J appeared to be a competent physics student, giving a normative account of this phenomenon. Her subsequent account, however, appears to be deficient, invoking a common misconception, which was, in fact, previously documented and described as a (stable and pervasive) naive theory of mechanics (McCloskey, 1983). diSessa's (1996) analysis of J illustrates one of the central phenomena uncovered by conceptual change researchers working in the KA tradition: students can produce both normative and non-normative explanations in response to what is ostensibly the same line of questioning, in response to subtle shifts in attention to different aspects of the phenomenon. The interviewer's intervention, merely asking J to consider the top of the toss, was, in fact, designed to probe for the stability of her apparently normative model of a toss by subtly highlighting different aspects of the situation, leading to a reconfiguration of her model.

## Adam and "Acquisition of a Child by a Learning Disability"

Adam was a male nine-year-old elementary school student, participating in a multi-year study in which he was videotaped in various settings, including classroom lessons and testing sessions, an after-school cooking club, and everyday life, to record naturally occurring examples of mental activities like attending, remembering, and problem solving. He was an officially designated Learning Disabled (LD) child. In the excerpts below, Adam exhibits what appears to be an inconsistency in his level of reading competence as he prepares bread in Cooking Club. First, Adam brushes off a mistake in which he and a friend, working together, add some ingredients in the wrong order and produce green cranberry bread, a behavior that is ultimately treated as a normal level of competence for these students:

> When the others gathered around to laugh, he simply said, "So I made a goddamn mistake, so what." The issue passed.
>
> *(McDermott, 1993, p. 287)*

On a different day, when working alone, Adam once again adds some ingredients in the wrong order, giving the impression to a fellow student that he is farther along than she in preparing banana bread, a context in which she participates actively in positioning Adam as needing more than a normal level of assistance, perhaps deliberately "putting him in his place":

> The girls are screaming and Adam whimpering. The double vowels in Lucy's talk are chosen to show that she is reading to Adam as one would read to a child in a phonics lesson. The scene opens with Adam returning from the adult with the sense that he knows what to do next.

| | |
|---|---|
| **Adam:** | Finally! |
| | Where's the yogurt. Oh. |
| **Nadine:** | You're *up* to yogurt already. |
| **Adam:** | Yeah. |
| **Nadine:** | Where's the bananas. |
| **Adam:** | We, uhm, they didn't give us bananas yet. |
| **Nadine:** | Well, go get 'em. |
| **Adult:** | The bananas are here on the shelf. |
| **Adam:** | But this is our second page. |
| **Lucy:** | That is a teaspoon. That is a tablespoon. |
| **Adam:** | This is a teaspoon, and it says |
| **Lucy:** | It says tablespoons, twoo taablespooons. |
| **Adam:** | We're right here, Lawana. Lawana, we're right here. |
| **Lucy:** | That's |
| **Nadine:** | That's the ingredients, not the instructions. |
| **Lucy:** | That's baakiing powowder. |
| **Adam:** | What do you mean, baking powder? |
| **Nadine:** | You go in this order. |
| **Adam:** | (Oh my God). What do you mean, in what order? |
| **Nadine:** | Look! This is the instructions. That's what you need to do all this. |
| **Adam:** | Ai yai yai. |
| | One ... Cup ... Mashed ... Fresh |

Everyone looks away, and Adam returns to the adult for more advice.

*(pp. 288–289)*

When making cranberry bread incorrectly, Adam appeared to be a typical elementary school student, someone who makes the occasional mistake in reading but who is not marked by himself or his peers as incompetent. However, when making banana bread incorrectly, Adam appeared to be a typical LD student, someone who is expected to make mistakes in reading comprehension and who is publicly marked as incompetent. Note that both his peers ("That's baakiing powowder.") and Adam ("Ai yai yai. One ... Cup ... Mashed ... Fresh") participate in this marking. Ironically, it seems likely that his difficulty might not be his self-mocked reading, per se, but rather his missing the cultural template that separates "ingredients" and "instructions." McDermott's (1993) analysis of Adam's experiences illustrates one of the central phenomena uncovered by educational anthropologists working in the IA tradition: students can be construed to be both competent and incompetent at what is ostensibly the same task, in response to subtle shifts in the social environment and the attention of others.

### Reconceiving J's and Adam's Competence as Performance in Context

Both J and Adam look like a competent student in some contexts but like a deficient student in other, very similar contexts. Indeed, for an analyst not expecting performance to be sensitive to subtle shifts in context, it may be tempting to search for a description of their behavior that identifies their "true" level of competence, dismissing inconsistencies as the result of unusual circumstances. For example, such an analyst might hypothesize that J doesn't really understand these physical phenomena, and is only able to say the right words that she learned in physics class until her understanding is probed more deeply. Or they might hypothesize that J does understand these phenomena well enough, but is momentarily tricked by a particularly complex or misleading question. Likewise, they might hypothesize that Adam isn't really able to read as well as he should be, and that he is only able to get by when the task is simple or he has enough external support from his friends. Or they might hypothesize that Adam's reading difficulties aren't deserving of particular note, but that he is being targeted and maligned by his peers when it suits their needs.

In contrast, and in their own ways, both diSessa and McDermott reject the notion that J and Adam have a "true" and stable (mis)understanding or (in)ability that is masked or revealed under certain conditions. Instead, they offer alternative descriptions in which competency is highly situated, and in which the observable differences in J's and Adam's performance are understandably tied to subtle differences in context.

In the case of J, diSessa (1996) argues that different knowledge elements[2] are activated in response to a focus on different aspects of the ball toss. When focused on the hand pushing the ball up, J describes an upward force as existing only while the hand is in contact with the ball, having activated the *force as mover* knowledge element. When focused on the apparent stopping of the ball at the peak of the toss, J describes two forces as being in balance, having activated the *dynamic balance* knowledge element. These knowledge elements are cognitive resources that J and others deploy to their advantage in different situations. *Force as mover* allows J to explain why the ball starts moving and to predict what will happen next. *Dynamic balance* allows J to explain why the ball appears to be stationary at the peak, despite the continuing action of gravity. Shifts in focus make one knowledge element more likely than the other. What J needs to succeed in school is to learn which knowledge elements are appropriate to use in which situations. *Dynamic balance* is not useless. But it just doesn't apply at the top of a toss. One would want to deliberately restructure the learning environment so that J can face her own complex contextuality: She needs to rethink how to construe a variety of contexts; she does not need to reject dynamic balance or think more abstractly.

In the case of Adam, McDermott (1993) argues that different social positionings[3] of Adam – alternatively as unremarkable or as an LD student – emerge in response to differing forms of attention to his performance. When other students have no need to pay close attention to his performance, Adam is able to pass off mistakes without lingering consideration. When others do have need to pay close attention to his performance, such as when Nadine feels threatened that he is farther along than her, Adam is caught up in a public display of incompetence. These positionings are interactive resources that Adam and others deploy to their advantage in different situations. Positioning mistakes as no big deal allows Adam to navigate difficult tasks efficiently while maintaining dignity. Positioning Adam as LD allows Adam, his peers, and his teacher to explain away his poor performance. Shifts in the consequentiality of Adam's performance make one positioning more likely than the other. What Adam needs to succeed in school is to be positioned as unremarkable – as making mistakes that are no big deal – in more situations. That would require a deliberate restructuring of his learning environment to minimize the contexts in which he is positioned as being LD.

In both of these cases, we see how competence has been reconceived as performance in context. J and Adam are not described as having a static, inherent competence or constant relationship with others, but they are instead described as acting in ways that are sensitive to moment-by-moment shifts in systems of knowledge and/or interaction. This shared need to characterize and understand performance in context has led researchers in both KA and IA to gravitate toward similar methodologies and theoretical orientations. These are described in the following section.

## The Shared Enterprise of Knowledge Analysis and Interaction Analysis

Reconceiving competence as performance in context, and the consequent need for analysts to carefully attend to and account for moment-by-moment shifts in systems of knowledge and/or interaction, has led to a number of similarities in the preferred methodology and theoretical orientation of KA and IA.

### *Methodology*

As the brief transcripts above illustrate, both KA and IA attend closely to the details of talk on a moment-by-moment basis. To record these details, both J and Adam were videotaped. Video recordings have become common data in the learning sciences, for a variety of reasons (Derry et al., 2010; Goldman, Pea, Barron, & Derry, 2007). For one, video provides a stable, reviewable record of what occurs in educational settings. Moreover, video cameras have the potential to capture much more than human observers in terms of both quantity and quality.

These features make video recordings attractive to many researchers. However, what sets KA and IA apart from most other research in the learning sciences is an attention not only to *what* occurs in educational settings, but to *how* it occurs. Researchers working in these traditions want to know not only what a student says or does, but also why it was said or done in that particular way at that particular time. This presents an added methodological challenge, as the ways that participants attend to context on a moment-by-moment basis – how they signal their understanding of what is happening and attempt to influence what happens next – are particularly difficult for a human observer to record, for several reasons.

First, people have multiple, simultaneous, and overlapping channels by which they can interact and communicate meaning, including speech, prosody (e.g., tone and emphasis), gesture, kinesics (e.g., gaze and body positioning), the manipulation of artifacts, and the creation and use of inscriptions and representations. As participants interact with each other and their environment, it would be impossible to monitor all of the ways they attend to context without the use of video recordings.

Second, meaning is generally construed through a combination and coordination of some or all of these channels, rather than a single channel in isolation (C. Goodwin, 2000, 2013). People often rely on coordinations of speech and gesture to communicate understanding (Goldin-Meadow, 2003, 2004). Coordinations of speech, prosody, and kinesics can communicate confusion, displeasure, or sarcasm (Goffman, 1983; C. Goodwin, 2007; M. H. Goodwin, 1990; Kendon, 1990). Manipulation and creation of artifacts, inscriptions, and representations involve gesture and kinesics, and are often coordinated with speech and prosody (Danish & Enyedy, 2007; C. Goodwin, 1994; Hall, 1996). Without video recordings, which can be slowed down and repeatedly viewed, it would be impossible to analyze how participants precisely time and coordinate their actions from one moment to the next.

Third, although humans are highly sensitive and responsive to subtle shifts in context, this sensitivity is largely intuitive and often not available for conscious reflection. People often don't explicitly realize what cues they are responding to and what cues they are sending to others, and their explanations of their behavior are often inconsistent with how they are observed to behave (Garfinkel, 1967). Video recordings allow researchers to avoid relying on intuitive and potentially inaccurate explanations of participants' behavior, instead allowing them to produce analyses supported by evidence that can be shared with and critiqued by other researchers.

The multifaceted, precisely coordinated, and largely unconscious nature of interaction presents an enormous challenge to human observers in the field. Video recordings, however, are uniquely positioned to document and support the analysis of performance in context, allowing researchers to identify and describe subtle shifts in context, why such shifts occur, and what effect they have on the participants.

While this methodological interest in video data is shared by both KA and IA, it is important to note that analysts in the two traditions often make different choices in what and how to record, and how to display this information in transcripts and research reports. As a later section argues, while these differences are theory-laden and consequential for both analysis and conclusions, and while they have historically marked points of contrast between KA and IA, we do not believe they represent an irreconcilable difference between the two approaches.

## *Theoretical Orientation*

In order to account for moment-by-moment shifts in systems of knowledge and interaction, researchers in both the KA and IA traditions typically rely upon a complex-systems approach and develop theories with a smaller grain size than other traditions. Such theories propose a relatively large number of theoretical entities and processes, with the goal of explaining how and why observed behavior unfolds from one moment to the next.

KA researchers sometimes refer to their theoretical orientation as involving a process account (diSessa & Sherin, 1998) or a humble theory (Cobb, Confrey, diSessa, Lehrer, & Schauble, 2003). In a typical KA analysis, descriptions of observed behavior are accompanied by an account of which elements of an individual's complex knowledge system are likely to have been activated and how those elements shape and are shaped by the evolving context. IA researchers sometimes refer to their theoretical orientation as involving a simplest systematics (Sacks, Schegloff, & Jefferson, 1974), an ethnographically adequate account (McDermott, Gospodinoff, & Aron, 1978), or a sequential organization (Schegloff, 1968, 2007). In a typical IA analysis, descriptions of observed behavior are accompanied by an account of which aspects of the complex system of social interaction are relevant and procedurally consequential (Schegloff, 1972) and how those aspects shape and are shaped by the evolving context.

The theoretical orientations of KA and IA, involving a complex-systems approach and proposing a relatively large number of theoretical entities and processes to account for the contextuality of performance as it evolves moment to moment, stand in contrast to theories that attempt to identify a relatively small number of underlying causes that govern wide swaths of human behavior. Indeed, recognizing the differences between their theoretical orientation and that of most other researchers in their respective fields, KA and IA researchers often explicitly contrast their work against such alternative theories.

Researchers in the KA tradition have often positioned their work in contrast to alternative theories of conceptual change in developmental and cognitive psychology. As an example of such an alternative theory, Gopnik & Wellman (1994) proposed a Theory Theory that seeks to explain young children's intuitive psychology and their understanding of mind. This theory identifies a small number of concepts, such as desire, perception, and belief, and posits that all children transition from one theory involving these concepts to a more normative theory between the ages of 2 and 5, passing through one intermediate stage along the way. As another example, Carey (1991, 1999) proposed a theory of conceptual change in science involving a small number of processes, such as differentiation and coalescence, positing that children's understanding of matter, life, and other domains develops via these pathways.

Similarly, researchers in the IA tradition have often positioned their work in contrast to alternative theories of human behavior in sociology and anthropology.

As an example of such an alternative theory, Parsons (1949) proposed a Social Action Theory that seeks to explain human social action within a culture. This theory identifies a small number of motivational factors, such as ends, purposes, and ideals, and posits that a society's culture is the product of such factors. As another example, Searle (1970) proposed a Speech Act Theory that seeks to explain the function of different utterances. This theory identifies a small number of speech acts, such as assertives, directives, commissives, expressives, and declarations, and posits that these different forms of speech indicate different intentions on the part of the speaker.

The alternative theories mentioned above have several features against which the theoretical orientations of KA and IA can be contrasted. First, these alternative theories assume that human behavior can be compactly described, invoking a relatively small number of theoretical entities and processes to explain a large domain such as conceptual change in science or the culture of a society. In contrast, researchers in KA and IA assume that human behavior is much more complex, involving – and requiring a description of – many theoretical entities and processes. Second, these alternative theories presume that the behavior of an individual is relatively consistent, given their current state. Even if theories or goals are not available for conscious reflection, they are nonetheless stable cognitive structures that will produce similar behavior across multiple contexts. In contrast, researchers in KA and IA assume that human behavior is highly sensitive to context, producing differences in behavior that can appear inconsistent and unstable. Third, these alternative theories often rely upon theoretical entities that are poorly differentiated from everyday ideas used by laypeople to describe why people act the way they do, such as concepts, beliefs, theories, goals, and intentions. In contrast, researchers in KA and IA believe it is necessary to propose novel, technically precise theoretical entities that require more analytic effort to apply to data.

Together, these contrasts highlight the fundamental differences between the theoretical orientations of KA and IA and those that are more common in related fields. When analyzed on a moment-by-moment basis, knowing and learning are revealed to be complex, constantly shifting in response to subtle contextual clues, and resistant to being described using common-sense language. A proper account of performance in context demands a relatively large number of technically precise theoretical entities and processes as well as careful analytic attention to the details of interaction.

Of course, this endeavor comes with its own set of challenges, challenges that are shared by researchers in both KA and IA. One particularly notable set of challenges arises from our shared commitment to doing detailed, moment-by-moment analyses of performance in context, while retaining a commitment to understanding and impacting education more generally, which involves much longer timescales. Minimally, KA and IA researchers must attempt to relate moments of knowing and learning that occur over seconds and minutes with longer-term changes in student and teacher practices that occur over the length of a unit, course, educational career, or lifetime (e.g., Hall & Rubin, 1998). Saxe (1999) would call this coordination between microgenetic and ontogenetic processes. Moreover, some researchers (e.g., diSessa, 2000; Hall, Lehrer, Lucas, & Schauble, 2004) are also interested in long-term cultural changes, such as those brought about by changes in representational infrastructure and practices around that infrastructure, that operate on an even longer timescale and require further coordination with sociogenetic processes (Saxe, 1999).

Coordinating timescales of knowing and learning presents both practical and theoretical challenges. On the practical side, capturing learning over ontogenetic timescales produces an enormous corpus of video data for analysis. Studies of classroom learning frequently generate hundreds of hours of video data, which must be reviewed, content logged, and at least partially transcribed. Since not all the hours of data can be given equal attention, a sampling problem arises, and analysts must be wary of the extent to which moments that stand out are representative of the overall process. Transcribed examples in published reports often focus on interesting moments of insight or conflict, which suggests they may be relatively unusual. On the theoretical side, sociocultural researchers have pointed out how inextricably linked these levels of analysis are, arguing that they cannot be conveniently separated but must instead be understood and analyzed in relation to each other (Cole, 1996; Lemke, 2000; Rogoff, 1995; Saxe, 1999).[4]

The preceding sections have made the argument that KA and IA share much in terms of methodology and theoretical orientation, both in their commitments and in the challenges they face. However, a larger historical difference in theoretical paradigm represents a hurdle that must be overcome. This historical difference arises from the traditional association of KA and IA researchers with opposing sides of the cognitive–situative debate that emerged in the 1990s. This historical legacy, and the residual but very real points of contention between the KA and IA approaches, are described in the following section.

## Uneasy Bedfellows: Tensions Between Knowledge Analysis and Interaction Analysis

As has been often noted (e.g., Anderson, Greeno, Reder, & Simon, 2000; Sfard, 1998), the cognitive and situative paradigms define learning in different ways. For cognitivists, learning is best understood as involving knowledge, with a focus on the nature of how knowledge is represented in the mind and how mental representations are acquired and modified. For situativists, learning is best understood as changes in practices, with a focus on the similarities and differences between practices in different human pursuits and how practices are adopted and adapted.

Commitments to knowledge and practice are still hallmarks, respectively, of the KA and IA approaches. Knowledge analysts hold an explicit commitment to the existence and central importance of knowledge, studying its nature as a complex system or ecology of many types of mental representation of various forms and functions. Interaction analysts, on the other hand, hold an explicit commitment to the existence and central importance of human social interaction, studying how individuals and communities adopt and adapt social, cultural, and historical practices.

For some researchers in the heydays of the cognitive–situative debate, mental representations and practices were treated as incompatible perspectives on knowing and learning, with the competing perspective at best dismissed as irrelevant or at worst decried as undermining education. While the tone of this debate has softened considerably since the 1990s, the contentious history of the cognitive and situative paradigms has an enduring influence on the relationship between KA and IA. Despite the similarities in methodology and theoretical orientation described previously, consequential differences do exist in terms of the analytic approaches and research questions that researchers pursue in practice. These differences, which have historically been a source of tension between knowledge and interaction analysts, will need to be addressed in dialogue between the two perspectives. Indeed, fostering this dialogue is one of the explicit purposes of this volume, and many of these issues are discussed in later chapters. In the following sections, two particularly salient tensions are highlighted as they pertain to the analysis of performance in context: which aspects of performance are given central focus, and which settings are selected in which to observe performance.

## *Selective Focus*

As previously discussed, people have multiple, simultaneous, and overlapping channels through which they can interact, communicate meaning and intention, signal their understanding of the current context, and attempt to influence how that context evolves. For this reason, researchers from both the KA and IA perspectives rely upon video recordings to capture as much of this complexity as possible. However, not all of this complexity can be focused on simultaneously during an analysis, nor can all of it be described or represented in reports of research. Consequently, at any given time, analysts must selectively focus on certain aspects of performance while backgrounding others.

It is problematic to associate either KA or IA with a stereotypical selective focus, given that each field contains a wide variety of approaches. Moreover, individual researchers focus on different aspects of performance in different reports (for example, contrast diSessa [2007] with diSessa [1996], and McDermott, Gospodinoff, & Aron [1978] with McDermott [1993]). However, despite this within perspective variety, published KA analyses have tended to look different from published IA analyses for a variety of historical, theoretical, and analytical reasons. For example, in comparing the transcript excerpts at the beginning of this chapter, it is apparent that McDermott (1993) has chosen to represent more detail about prosody (i.e., tone and intonation) than diSessa (1996).

Differences like these have been a source of tension between KA and IA because of the relationship between how performance is represented and the researcher's theoretical and analytical commitments (Bucholtz, 2000; Hall, 2000; Jordan & Henderson, 1995; Ochs, 1979). On the one hand, if a researcher represents a particular aspect of performance in a transcript, it is straightforward to assume that they focused on that aspect in their analysis and found it to be relevant and consequential. For example, McDermott (1993) provided prosodic detail in his transcripts because key to his analysis is the claim that the participants in Cooking Club are using prosody to establish and maintain social positioning. On the other hand, if a researcher does not represent a particular aspect of performance in a transcript, it is not at all straightforward to interpret the reason. For example, diSessa (1996) did not represent prosody in his transcripts and McDermott (1993) did not represent kinesics or gesture in his transcripts, and these aspects of performance may have been omitted for any number of reasons. Perhaps they were analyzed in detail but backgrounded as not being consequential for these participants at this time. Perhaps they were attended to in broad strokes but not considered deserving of a closer analysis. Perhaps they were assumed a priori to be irrelevant for the current analysis. Perhaps they were attended to intuitively but without particular and systematic reflection. Perhaps their consideration was entirely absent, as might be the case if the video recordings were transcribed before analysis. Without a dialogue with the researcher, it is impossible to know why a particular aspect of performance may have been backgrounded.

The issue of selective focus is not unique to KA and IA. Because of the complexity of knowing and learning in context, it is unlikely that a universal, one-size-fits-all approach to analysis would ever be useful, even if it were possible. Different aspects of performance must be focused on in different settings and in service of different research questions.

Within a community with a shared history, researchers are often more willing to accept the selective focus of their colleagues, believing, perhaps too complacently, that choices were made in good faith and that a widening of focus is unlikely to undermine the researcher's conclusions. In contrast, researchers are often less willing to accept the selective focus of researchers in a different community, believing, perhaps unfairly, that choices may have been made out of ignorance and that a widening of focus may undermine or even contradict the researcher's conclusions.

Given the contentious history of the cognitive and situative paradigms, it is understandable that researchers in KA and IA might interpret salient differences in selective focus as emblematic of deep and perhaps insurmountable divisions. We, however, disagree. We believe that researchers working in both perspectives are likely to benefit from a study of how the other side operates. By challenging each other to revisit basic assumptions about analyzing and representing performance in context, we expect a dialogue between KA and IA will lead to increased sensitivity to the aspects of performance to which analysts can and should attend in order to better understand learners' activities. Indeed, we believe this is one of the great benefits of working together: learning about and leveraging the ontological and analytical innovations of both perspectives to understand more about how performance is sensitive to systems of knowledge and interaction.

## Research Settings

One of the guiding principles of both KA and IA is that, since performance is highly sensitive to context, conducting research in multiple settings is both productive and necessary for understanding processes of knowing and learning. However, because the possible range of settings that could be studied is so vast, researchers must necessarily select particular settings to observe, thereby excluding, at least temporarily, others.

Just as it was for selective focus, it is problematic to associate either KA or IA with a stereotypical research setting, given that each field has conducted research in a wide variety of settings. Moreover, there is considerable overlap, with researchers in both traditions having studied classrooms, both "as they are" and those in which the researchers have intervened. However, despite this variety and overlap, KA and IA researchers have tended to supplement classroom studies with different research settings in which knowing and learning can be seen. For example, to return to the case studies at the beginning of this chapter, diSessa (1996) studied J in a series of clinical interviews, while McDermott (1993) studied Adam in an after-school club and in other "everyday life" settings.

Differences like these have been a source of tension between KA and IA because of concerns about ecological validity. Underlying the choice of research setting is the assumption that it will reveal important and useful information about processes of knowing and learning that will be relevant to other settings, including learning environments. Non-classroom-based KA studies often involve clinical or semi-structured interviews that probe how students think about unusual phenomena or how they respond to questions they may never have considered. The benefit of these settings is that the researcher can obtain focused, nuanced information about knowledge resources that might otherwise be difficult or time-consuming to observe. Non-classroom-based IA studies often involve students in after-school programs, experts engaged in professional practice, or individuals interacting with friends or family. The benefit of these settings is that the researcher can obtain information about highly routinized patterns of interaction and how different patterns affect knowledgeable performance. What all of these studies have in common is the assumption that these knowledge resources or patterns of interaction will be relevant in other settings.

Issues of ecological validity and generalization across research settings are not unique to KA and IA. Because of the complexity, contextuality, and adaptability of human behavior, it is unlikely that researchers could ever fully plumb the depths of human performance. Particular settings must be chosen because of what they can reveal, and despite what they can obscure, about knowing and learning.

Within a community with a shared history, researchers are often more willing to accept the research settings of their colleagues, believing, perhaps too complacently, that findings will translate to other environments. In contrast, researchers are often less willing to accept the research settings of researchers in a different community, believing, perhaps unfairly, that findings will be limited to that narrow context.

Given the contentious history of the cognitive and situative paradigms, it is understandable that researchers in KA and IA might interpret salient differences in research settings as emblematic of deep and perhaps insurmountable divisions. Once again, however, we disagree. We believe that researchers working in both perspectives are likely to benefit from expanding the settings in which they conduct research. By actively comparing and contrasting performance in a wider range of settings, we expect a dialogue between KA and IA researchers will lead to increased understanding of the contextuality and adaptability of processes of knowing and learning. Indeed, we believe this is one of the great benefits of working together: learning about and leveraging what both perspectives know about the relationship between performance and setting to guide the design of novel and more effective learning environments that draw on systems of both knowledge and interaction.

## The Time for Synthesis Is Now

While it may have been unavoidable, and even prudent, for KA and IA to have evolved independently, we believe the time has come for researchers to actively investigate how these perspectives could be synthesized. No longer should we be content to set aside considerations of individual learning (as proposed by McDermott, 1993) or cognition (as proposed by Latour, 1988). Likewise, it is time to move beyond views of cognitive processes as timeless, a-cultural, and immune to deep influence by real-time social and material interaction (as implied by, e.g., Anderson, Reder, & Simon, 1997; Newell, 1980, 1990). The synthetic agenda we have set for ourselves in this volume is to tackle head-on both knowledge and interaction as they contribute to performances of knowing and learning in context.

There is every reason to believe that this agenda will be complex, that the sum of KA and IA will be greater than its parts. In fact, complexity is everywhere evident. KA has established that systems of knowledge are complex, and IA has established that systems of interaction are complex; accounting for the relations between these two complex systems will add yet another layer of complexity. Competing claims will have to be reconciled, misattributions will need to be clarified, and productive synergies will need to be identified. The chapters in this volume are a welcome start to this process, but we expect and hope that others will join us in this effort.

## Notes

1 From the outset, we want to emphasize that this ordering implies no relative value. Whenever the two approaches are listed in the text (e.g., "KA and IA") or in the structure of the volume, the reader should assume they are being discussed as equals.
2 As described in diSessa (1996), these are examples of a specific form of knowledge element called phenomenological primitives or p-prims (diSessa, 1993).
3 As described in McDermott (1993), these positionings are similar to those described by Garfinkel (1956) and Goffman (1979).
4 The problem of coordinating timescales from the KA perspective is discussed in diSessa, Sherin, and Levin (this volume).

## References

Anderson, J. R., Greeno, J. G., Reder, L. M., & Simon, H. A. (2000). Perspectives on learning, thinking, and activity. *Educational Researcher*, 29, 11–13.
Anderson, J. A., Reder, L. M., & Simon, H. A. (1997). Situative versus cognitive perspectives: Form versus substance. *Educational Researcher*, 26(1), 18–21.
Bucholtz, M. (2000). The politics of transcription. *Journal of Pragmatics*, 32, 1439–1465.
Carey, S. (1991). Knowledge acquisition: Enrichment or conceptual change? In S. Carey & R. Gelman (Eds.), *The epigenesis of mind: Essays on biology and cognition* (pp. 257–291). Hillsdale, NJ: Lawrence Erlbaum.
Carey, S. (1999). Sources of conceptual change. In E. K. Scholnick, K. Nelson, S. A. Gelman, & P. H. Miller (Eds.), *Conceptual development: Piaget's legacy* (pp. 293–326). Mahwah, NJ: Lawrence Erlbaum.
Cobb, P., Confrey, J., diSessa, A. A., Lehrer, R., & Schauble, L. (2003). Design experiments in educational research. *Educational Researcher*, 32, 9–13.
Cole, M. (1996). *Cultural psychology: A once and future discipline*. Cambridge, MA: Harvard University Press.
Danish, J. A., & Enyedy, N. (2007). Negotiated representational mediators: How young children decide what to include in their science representations. *Science Education*, 91, 1–35.
Derry, S. J., Pea, R. D., Barron, B., Engle, R. A., Erickson, F., Goldman, R., et al. (2010). Conducting video research in the learning sciences: Guidance on selection, analysis, technology, and ethics. *Journal of the Learning Sciences*, 19, 3–53.
diSessa, A. A. (1993). Toward an epistemology of physics. *Cognition and Instruction*, 10, 105–225.
diSessa, A. A. (1996). What do "just plain folk" know about physics? In D. R. Olson & N. Torrance (Eds.), *The handbook of education and human development: New models of learning, teaching and schooling* (pp. 709–730). Oxford, UK: Blackwell.
diSessa, A. A. (2000). *Changing minds: Computers, learning, and literacy*. Cambridge, MA: MIT Press.
diSessa, A. A. (2007). An interactional analysis of clinical interviewing. *Cognition and Instruction*, 25, 523–565.
diSessa, A. A., & Sherin, B. L. (1998). What changes in conceptual change? *International Journal of Science Education*, 20, 1155–1191.
Garfinkel, H. (1956). Conditions for a successful degradation ceremony. *American Journal of Sociology*, 61, 420–424.

Garfinkel, H. (1967). *Studies in ethnomethodology.* Oxford, UK: Blackwell.
Goffman, E. (1979). *Gender advertisements.* London: Macmillan.
Goffman, E. (1983). The interaction order. *American Sociological Review*, 48, 1–17.
Goldin-Meadow, S. (2003). *Hearing gesture: How our hands help us think.* Cambridge, MA: Harvard University Press.
Goldin-Meadow, S. (2004). Gesture's role in the learning process. *Theory Into Practice*, 43, 314–321.
Goldman, R., Pea, R., Barron, B., & Derry, S. J. (2007). *Video research in the learning sciences.* Mahwah, NJ: Lawrence Erlbaum.
Goodwin, C. (1994). Professional vision. *American Anthropologist*, 96, 606–633.
Goodwin, C. (2000). Action and embodiment within situated human interaction. *Journal of Pragmatics*, 32, 1489–1522.
Goodwin, C. (2007). Participation, stance and affect in the organization of activities. *Discourse Society*, 18, 53–73.
Goodwin, C. (2013). The co-operative, transformative organization of human action and knowledge. *Journal of Pragmatics*, 46, 8–23.
Goodwin, M. H. (1990). *He-said-she-said: Talk as social organization among Black children.* Bloomington, IN: Indiana University Press.
Gopnik, A., & Wellman, H. M. (1994). The theory theory. In L. A. Hirschfeld & S. A. Gelman (Eds.), *Mapping the mind: Domain specificity in cognition and culture* (pp. 257–293). Cambridge, UK: Cambridge University Press.
Hall, R. (1996). Representation as shared activity: Situated cognition and Dewey's cartography of experience. *Journal of the Learning Sciences*, 5, 209–238.
Hall, R. (2000). Video recording as theory. In D. Lesh & A. Kelley (Eds.) *Handbook of research design in mathematics and science education* (pp. 647–664). Mahwah, NJ: Lawrence Erlbaum.
Hall, R., Lehrer, R., Lucas, D., & Schauble, L. (2004, June). Of grids and jars: A comparative analysis of representational infrastructures. Paper presented at the Sixth International Conference of the Learning Sciences, Santa Monica, CA.
Hall, R., & Rubin, A. (1998). There's five little notches in here: Dilemmas in teaching and learning the conventional structure of rate. In J. G. Greeno & S. V. Goldman (Eds.), *Thinking practices in mathematics and science learning* (pp. 189–236). Mahwah, NJ: Lawrence Erlbaum.
Jordan, B., & Henderson, A. (1995). Interaction Analysis: Foundations and practice. *Journal of the Learning Sciences*, 4(1), 39–103.
Kendon, A. (1990). *Conducting interaction: Patterns of behavior in focused encounters.* Cambridge, UK: Cambridge University Press.
Latour, B. (1988). Drawing things together. In M. Lynch & S. Woolgar (Eds.), *Representation in scientific practice* (pp. 19–68). Cambridge, MA: MIT Press.
Lemke, J. L. (2000). Across the scales of time: Artifacts, activities, and meanings in ecosocial systems. *Mind, Culture, and Activity*, 7, 273–290.
McCloskey, M. (1983). Naive theories of motion. In D. Gentner & A. Stevens (Eds.), *Mental models* (pp. 299–323). Hillsdale, NJ: Lawrence Erlbaum Associates.
McDermott, R. (1993). The acquisition of a child by a learning disability. In S. Chaiklin & J. Lave (Eds.), *Understanding practice: Perspectives on activity and context* (pp. 269–305). Cambridge, UK: Cambridge University Press.
McDermott, R. P., Gospodinoff, K., & Aron, J. (1978). Criteria for an ethnographically adequate description of activities and their contexts. *Semiotica*, 24, 245–275.

Newell, A. (1980). Physical symbol systems. *Cognitive Science*, 4, 135–183.
Newell, A. (1990). *Unified theories of cognition*. Cambridge, MA: Harvard University Press.
Ochs, E. (1979). Transcription as theory. In E. Ochs & B. B. Schieffelin (Eds.), *Developmental pragmatics* (pp. 43–72). New York: Academic Press.
Parsons, T. (1949). *The structure of social action*. New York: Free Press.
Rogoff, B. (1995). Observing sociocultural activity on three planes: Participatory appropriation and apprenticeship. In J. V. Wertsch, P. D. Rio, & A. Alvarez (Eds.), *Sociocultural studies of the mind* (pp. 139–163). Cambridge, UK: Cambridge University Press.
Sacks, H., Schegloff, E. A., & Jefferson, G. (1974). A simplest systematics for the organization of turn-taking for conversation. *Language*, 50, 696–735.
Saxe, G. B. (1999). Cognition, development, and cultural practices. In E. Turiel (Ed.), *Development and cultural change: Reciprocal processes* (pp. 19–35). San Francisco, CA: Jossey-Bass.
Schegloff, E. A. (1968). Sequencing in conversational openings. *American Anthropologist*, 70, 1075–1095.
Schegloff, E. A. (1972). Notes on a conversational practice: Formulating place. In D. Sudnow (Ed.), *Studies in social interaction* (pp. 75–119). New York: Free Press.
Schegloff, E. A. (2007). *Sequence organization in interaction: A primer in conversation analysis* (Vol. 1). Cambridge, UK: Cambridge University Press.
Searle, J. R. (1970). *Speech acts: An essay in the philosophy of language*. Cambridge, UK: Cambridge University Press.
Sfard, A. (1998). On two metaphors for learning and the dangers of choosing just one. *Educational Researcher*, 27, 4–13.

# 2
# KNOWLEDGE ANALYSIS
## An Introduction

*Andrea A. diSessa, Bruce L. Sherin, and Mariana Levin*

The purpose of this chapter is to introduce one of the two perspectives that are highlighted in this volume – Knowledge Analysis (KA). Briefly, KA is the study of the content and form of knowledge for the purpose of understanding learning. Our goal is to give a relatively deep account of KA, one that articulates its core premises with some precision. At the same time, we attempt to capture some of the breadth of the work that has been carried out under the KA banner. Up to this point, principles and practices of KA have been articulated mainly in the methods sections of a diverse body of research studies on thinking and learning, across several topic areas (mechanics, statistics and probability, algebra, special relativity, etc.). Thus, in this chapter, we aim to synthesize KA in a way that allows readers to recognize the unifying methodological principles behind a large body of research, while also giving insight into the real-world practice of Knowledge Analysis.

Readers outside the community of researchers who draw upon the methods of KA might be more familiar with two connected terms, *Knowledge in Pieces* (KiP) and *phenomenological primitives* (p-prims). To help readers get grounded with respect to the methodological focus of this chapter, here is how we understand the relationships among these terms:

- *KiP* is the name for a class of theoretical models of knowledge – models in which knowledge is seen as consisting of a complex system of elements.
- *P-prim* is the name for an element in one such model, a model that was developed by diSessa to describe intuitive knowledge of the physical world.
- KA is the name for the methodological approach to studying knowledge employed by KiP and allied researchers. In principle, research programs built on the basis of KA could result in very different kinds of models of knowledge. For that reason, KA is the most encompassing of these terms.

The purpose of this chapter is to take on the most expansive and explicitly methodological category, KA. However, because of the way that theory and method are linked, we believe it is important simultaneously to address the epistemological arm of the program, which here means, for the most part, KiP. In addition, we take it to be important to exemplify the program with specific models of knowledge that have arisen from employing KA. We will use p-prims and another prominent model arising from KA, coordination classes, as leitmotivs to exemplify a number of aspects of KA work. Several other contributions to this volume employ these models in one way or another, so defining and discussing them as examples here will do double duty.

We begin the main work of this chapter by situating KA historically, as well as in relation to more recent trends. Following this situating, we describe in some detail the theoretical and methodological foundations of KA. The final two sections of the chapter give our take on the current state of KA research. We first describe the broad landscape of current and past KA work. Then, in the last section, we lay out what we see as the most important near-future pursuits for KA research.

## A Little History

There are good arguments that knowledge is among the most important concepts in education, if not the most important one. Students come into class without the knowledge that we intend them to have, and they go out (we hope) with it. However, the study of knowledge is a subtle business. What is knowledge, and what is the right language with which to characterize it in order to understand how individuals learn?

With the dawn of the cognitive revolution in education research, it seemed possible that we had a set of tools that would provide us with a solid handle on knowledge. In the cognitive perspective, knowledge is constituted in mental representations and processes of individuals – a type of mental stuff. Furthermore, knowledge is not correct information that exists outside of individuals, say, in textbooks. The cognitive revolution gave us methodologies for studying mental representations, as well as some language for describing them.

With the tools provided by the cognitive perspective came a new set of debates among educational researchers about the nature of knowledge (diSessa, 1993; Vosniadou & Brewer, 1992). While the nature of knowledge and learning has been a topic of study in several fields, many of the debates spurred by the cognitive revolution played out in the context of science teaching and learning, especially within the domain of physics. At their heart, these debates had to do with what students know about physics prior to formal instruction. It is in this context that KA was born.

Why did learning in the domain of physics play such an important role in the unfolding of the cognitive revolution in education research? To some extent, this is probably an accident of history. But there are also reasons that the learning of physics highlighted what would turn out to be extremely important issues. On the one hand, formal physics seems to encompass a collection of ideas that lies far beyond the informal understanding of the average person. However, at the same time, it is manifestly true that all humans understand a tremendous amount about the natural world simply from our everyday interactions in this world. This leads to some core questions. For example, does it make sense to say that people know any physics, per se, prior to formal instruction?

Indeed, one of the earliest advances associated with the cognitive revolution was the demonstration that students do, in fact, know a great deal about the physical world prior to any formal physics instruction, and this knowledge lingers during and after instruction. However, it was found that even successful students harbored profound and robust "misconceptions." These misconceptions were profound in the sense that they pertained to some of the most central ideas in physics. They were robust in the sense that they seemed to be extremely resistant to change with instruction.

The recognition that a "naive physics" exists led to new questions about the nature of this knowledge and its role in learning. How, for example, is naive physics like and unlike formal physics knowledge? What happens to that knowledge during instruction? From the early 1980s to the early 1990s, the state-of-the-art presumption about naive knowledge in physics was that it was, in some fundamental respects, very similar to formal knowledge. Although this naive knowledge was wrong in content, it was nonetheless theoretical, coherent, "remarkably articulate," and fairly easy to characterize (McCloskey, 1983). Attributing the status of "theory" to naive ideas is, in general, known as "the theory theory." The most widely recognized such model was that students possessed a theory, called the impetus theory, wherein objects that are impelled to move acquire an "impetus," an internal force that drives them forward, but that impetus gradually dissipates. Furthermore, because this naive theory is incorrect, it was assumed that formal instruction must confront and replace it. An early and prominent version of this view appeared in an edited volume called *Mental Models* (Gentner & Stevens, 1983).

The origins of knowledge analysis might be traced to a set of ideas articulated by diSessa around this time. In this same edited volume, diSessa contributed a chapter that argued against the view that naive physics should be viewed as theory-like. Real theories, he argued, are based on a small number of laws that are applied consistently across a wide range of circumstances. In contrast, he maintained that naive physics consists of a large number of elements of knowledge that are inarticulate, seemingly contradictory, and which are applied in a manner that depends sensitively on the context at hand (diSessa, 1983, 1988, 1993). Furthermore, he argued that far from replacing this body of intuitive knowledge, instruction in formal physics must build a new understanding of physics on the foundation it provides. diSessa called these knowledge elements *phenomenological primitives*: p-prims, for short.

The notion of p-prims was a seed out of which the larger epistemological and methodological program would grow. diSessa's turn marked a dramatic shift away from the epistemological assumptions behind the "theory theory" of naive physics. It is a shift that has implications for how we conceptualize knowledge and learning across many disciplines. The assumptions of this new program generalize those behind p-prims: (a) Prior (intuitive) knowledge will often be difficult to see, inarticulate, and will be applied in a manner that depends sensitively on context. Nonetheless, (b) even in the most abstruse of domains, learning always builds on this wealth of knowledge.

## Situating Knowledge Analysis

The early incarnation of Knowledge Analysis described above was framed as a response to the literature on physics misconceptions and naive physics. But it was built on and reflected a set of ideas that had been developed over the preceding decades, and that continued to percolate around diverse areas of the cognitive sciences. For example, Minsky (1986) argued that minds are best understood as a community of voices – a "society of mind." And, outside of research on naive physics, the majority of cognitive literature, even at this early time, adopted a view in which human knowledge was seen as consisting of a large number of elements, activated in a manner that depends on context. For example, early articulations of the notion that knowledge consists of *schemas* had this character. Similarly, a significant part of the literature on problem solving, though concerned with behavior of a somewhat different character, nonetheless saw knowledge as a large number of *productions* that were cued and employed in a context-dependent manner (Anderson, 1987; Newell & Simon, 1972). In addition, researchers in artificial intelligence, working in parallel to model how humans understand the physical world, built systems that incorporated ideas similar to those expressed in diSessa's early work on naive physics (de Kleer, 1986; Forbus, 1984).

There was another popular strand of research in the 1980s and 1990s that is important to the story of knowledge analysis, and to this volume. At the same time that the cognitive revolution was beginning to take hold in education research, there was a growing voice of research that explicitly reacted against it. This movement, known by such names as "situated cognition" and "situativity theory," was epitomized in the work of Jean Lave (1988, 1991), Lucy Suchman (1993), and James Greeno (1998). Although this work was usually framed as a reaction against the cognitive view, it was nonetheless built on many of the same observations as early Knowledge Analysis work; namely, it was built on the observation that human cognitive behavior is highly sensitive to exigencies of context (consult Brown, et al., this volume, for examples and a broader discussion of contextuality as a common concern in both Knowledge Analysis and Interaction Analysis). Suchman (1987) famously likened cognitive behavior to the experience of canoeing down rapids:

> When it really comes down to the details of responding to the current and handling a canoe, you effectively abandon the plan and fall back on whatever skills are available to you. The purpose of the plan in this case is not to get your canoe through the rapids, but rather to orient you in such a way that you can obtain the best possible position from which to use those embodied skills on which, in its final analysis, your success depends.
>
> *(p. 52)*

Researchers such as Lave and Suchman took observations of context dependence as motivation to reject core elements of the cognitive perspective on thinking and learning. Some of these researchers maintained a version of an information-processing perspective but saw representations (knowledge) as spread over people and the environment, rather than solely localized in the mind (Hutchins, 1995). Others, such as Jean Lave, rejected the information-processing metaphor entirely.

Jumping to the present day, there is much in the intellectual environment that remains the same, but there are also new developments. Researchers in science education continue to produce new examples of misconceptions across various topics. In some respects, the "theory-theory" view of naive science knowledge continues to exist, but it has gone in a number of diverse directions. Examples are Chi's work on ontological categories (Chi, 1992, 2013) and Vosniadou's (2013) continued work on mental models and framework theories. In the developmental arena, researchers such as Carey (1985, 2009) and Gopnik (2003) have proposed extensive frameworks in which theory-like systems appear.

In some respects, it is possible to see Interaction Analysis (IA) as a descendent of the situated cognition of the 1980s. But there have been important transformations. IA is not defined primarily as a reaction against traditional cognitive science, as was situated cognition. Instead, it incorporates the insights and methods of other analytic traditions, such as conversation and discourse analysis. This transformation is important for the work of this volume; it means that it might well be possible to adopt a stance in which IA and KA are seen as complementary, and not opposing, styles of work.

There are also some new theoretical trends. One example is the growing prominence of *embodied cognition* (Barsalou, 1999; Lakoff & Núñez, 2000; Varela, Rosch, & Thompson, 1992). Embodied cognition provides an interesting case for a number of reasons. On the one hand, work that describes itself as about embodied cognition has, from the start, had a strong superficial resemblance to work conducted under the Knowledge Analysis banner (see, for example, our later discussion of non-propositional encoding). One of the core aims of both traditions has been to trace the bases of disciplinary expertise in domains such as physics to the knowledge that is employed in everyday thinking and action. For example, in some of his earliest work, diSessa suggested how parts of formal physics understanding might be built, at least in part, out of elements of simple everyday knowledge, such as notions of balancing and constraint. Similarly, working in one tradition of embodied cognition, Lakoff and Núñez (2000) attempted to show how even the most abstract mathematics was built on a small number of "conceptual metaphors," themselves rooted in shared bodily experience.

Given this similarity, one might expect to see great affinity among KA researchers for embodied cognition. However, as should be evident from other contributions to this volume, researchers in IA seem to have much more strongly and explicitly embraced embodied cognition. This is likely, in part, because embodied cognition is sometimes framed as rejection of the information-processing tradition out of which KA evolved. Thus we see that, although much has changed, some of the core debates about the nature and source of knowledge that existed when Knowledge Analysis was born continue to the present day, albeit in new forms.

## Theoretical Foundations for Knowledge Analysis

In principle, KA should be of interest to a variety of theoretical perspectives on knowledge. When we can, we take such an expansive perspective. However, we illustrate more specific methodological foci using arguably the most visible theoretical orientation among those adhering to KA principles, Knowledge in Pieces (KiP). In doing so, our intention is not to marginalize other points of view but only to avoid complications and caveats while still providing helpful detail.

As stated in the introduction, KA is the methodological arm of an epistemological approach to learning. It focuses on the nature of knowledge and its transformations during learning. As an epistemological approach, it shares some concerns with philosophical approaches to knowledge, with Piaget's genetic epistemology (1972) and related educational approaches such as constructivism, and also with cognitive modeling. Cognitive modelers aim to make explicit, computer-runnable models of what knowledge people have and also how that knowledge works and develops. On the other hand, KA aims to produce a new and distinctive view of knowledge, one that is truly responsive to educational realities. It may be regarded as a more ambitious and technical version of constructivism. KA's educational focus certainly distinguishes it from philosophical orientations, probably also from Piagetian views, and, in some ways, from cognitive modeling as well. So, the knowledge relevant to KA turns out to look different from, even opposed to, that endorsed by other traditions. To remind readers of this fact, and to help ward off importing unhelpful assumptions from other perspectives, we call our focus knowledge★ (pronounced "knowledge star," meaning a variant, updated version of the conventional concept of knowledge).

## Principles

We list six principles of KA. One at a time, these principles are not unique to KA. However, as a set we believe they characterize a unique program of research.

1. *Knowledge is constituted in mental representations.* This first principle announces the focus of KA on knowledge. As mentioned, KA is essentially cognitivist in that we aim to describe knowledge and learning in terms of mental representations. One should think of this as aiming toward, but not necessarily achieving, just now, models of thinking and learning that are complete and precise enough to "run," say, on a computer.
2. *Knowledge can be non-propositional and encoded in various modes (e.g., visually encoded).* This principle, and the two that follow, characterize our assumptions about the nature of the knowledge we study; they distinguish knowledge★ from a more typical view of knowledge. Knowledge★, particularly in its early-developing forms – such as most of the intuitive and tacit foundations of cultural or individual knowledge – often seems difficult to express in words. Instead, the encoding of various ideas may be closer to that of sensory experience, such as kinesthetic experience, patterns of visual configuration, or instinctual affective reactions. In this way, as mentioned, aspects of KA are consonant with principles of embodied cognition. In parallel, knowledge★ is frequently, if not essentially, *reactive*, being called automatically into action by perceived circumstances. Reactive is in opposition to *reflective*; reflective knowledge may be discussed as an object of consideration and deliberately considered as to whether it should apply or not. Reactivity is the essential point in Suchman's canoeing metaphor.
3. *Studying the mental representations of individuals requires highly nuanced accounts of content.* KA has a strong commitment that what students (or experts!) mean by anything they say is extremely subtle while also being critical in understanding learning trajectories. Is it fair to say that the content of students' intuitive physics is equivalent to a self-aware belief that "forces impart an impetus that dies away"? KA studies often develop frameworks for describing details of the content of students' knowledge★, not just general laws of thinking or learning. See, for example, the framework for specification of aspects of the concept of force in diSessa, Gillespie, and Esterly (2004). An emphasis on the content of students' thinking makes KA studies all the more useful in the construction of plausible curricula, especially when building on naive ideas. In addition, the nuances of knowledge★ specification make micro-assessment and tracking of individuals' learning and individual differences in understanding much more tractable, even if these tasks are, at this stage, very time-consuming.
4. *Intuitive knowledge is an important target of study and forms of naive knowledge are diverse, rich, and generative.* The knowledge★ that humans possess is inherently diverse (encompassing many varieties) and rich (capable of being combined

and deployed in many different ways). In addition, time and time again one discovers that humans can quite easily adapt and extend what they know, so that any closed account of knowledge★, say, "what children know about any topic at a particular age," will necessarily have fuzzy edges and wide variability across individuals. Indeed, the seeds of later, "better" ways of knowing seem often to come from nearly invisible details in the depths of prior stages of knowing.

5. *Studying knowledge requires full accountability to data records that capture thinking and learning processes.* Our final two principles capture our focus on understanding the complexities of real-time thinking. KA is committed to producing models consistent with real-time process data; that is, data that are generated on a timescale of seconds to minutes as individuals solve problems, think out loud, or interact with other individuals. (See the discussion of microgenetic and microanalytic study, below.) Real-time accountability is rather uncommon across the existing range of cognitive or sociocultural approaches to studying learning. Even within conceptual change research, it is uncommon for researchers to attend to the thought sequences of students while learning. Instead, much conceptual change research produces "snapshots" of understanding at various points in time. Other approaches to learning look only at "factors" and their influence. The KA commitment is that one can see a lot about knowledge★ in ongoing thought and action. From a practical point of view, also, teaching requires "massaging" students' thinking in real time, so it behooves us to know how that works. Finally, and most broadly, it also seems incontestable that, eventually, we should have a scientific account of the real-time details concerning how students think and learn.

6. *Intellectual performance is highly contextual.* KA research has documented how a person's intellectual performance is highly contextual, dependent on the particular situation in which one acts (diSessa, 1996; Wagner, 2006). This contextual dependence is frequently highlighted by approaches, such as situated cognition and interaction analysis, that do not focus on identifying knowledge. However, we believe it is simply untrue that cognitive modeling has difficulty with explaining contextuality. Cognitive modeling can also involve highly reactive knowledge, which is minutely and intimately dependent on both situations and the local and long-term history of the learner. If there is a difference of orientation among KA, IA (and situative approaches), and cognitive modeling along the dimension of contextuality, it might have to do more with *how* we conceptualize the particulars on which thinking depends rather than *that* contextuality is a factor. Concerning learning, contextuality is a two-edged sword. On the one hand, it bespeaks responsiveness to circumstances and richness of possibilities. On the other hand, the broad systematicities that constitute the essence of science are inherently difficult to achieve using highly contextual ideas.

## *Counter-principles*

It helps in defining an intellectual line to delineate the things it does *not* espouse, or actively opposes. Here are some important ones for KA.

1. *Rejecting the "subset" model.* It is a natural instinct to view knowledge from an expert's point of view, listing the things s/he knows, and then trying to map the novice state in those terms. In such a view, knowledge is understood to be a subset of an expert's knowledge. "Here's what the student knows; here's what s/he doesn't know." However, as was pointed out, many naive ideas may be quite productive – both in their everyday use, but even more importantly, in contributing to "improved" ideas in learning. Yet, they may not, themselves, count as true, or even well-formed, ideas. The subset model tends toward characterizing students as thoroughly ignorant of scientific ideas, in effect opposing the basic constructivist principle that we must understand how scientific ideas arise from non-scientific ones. The basic lesson is that we must understand pre-instructional knowledge in its own terms. Once we understand how scientific knowledge comes to be, another epistemological revolution follows. Experts will not look at all like textbooks; their minds will not be filled with knowledge corresponding one-to-one with the topics and principles in books or lectures. In principle, one could start by studying how experts *really* think, and then move "backwards" toward the untrained state. In practice, most KA researchers believe it is easier and more important to approach professional techno-scientific thinking by understanding how it emerges out of naive thought.

2. *Skepticism toward common-sense knowledge terms.* In our everyday lives, we all regularly converse about knowledge. We talk about what our friends know and don't know. We talk about our own beliefs. As instructors, we might talk about the concepts to be covered in our courses. However, we believe that everyday terms such as concept, belief, and theory are vague, loaded with implicit assumptions, and not up to the task of a careful scientific analysis of knowledge. In fact, a decent high-level description of what we want from a KA point of view is a set of models of knowledge★ types that are much more specific and durable than previous theories, truly accountable to all that we can see in humans' reasoning and knowing. See diSessa and Sherin (1998) for a broader discussion of why the concept of "concept" is theoretically lacking. In addition to being cautious about drawing on everyday terminology, we must be cautious about our use of related terminology from other academic disciplines. One example is the notion of *knowledge* as it is employed by philosophers. Traditional philosophical approaches take truth as an essential characteristic of knowledge – knowledge is necessarily true; things that are false or have no truth value are just something else. But, in any

study of knowledge★, truth is neither here nor there. Much of knowledge★ – the resources for developing solid, effective scientific understanding – cannot count as true. So, they may escape our study. Instead, we need to trace the lines from perhaps inchoate, intuitive, inarticulate ideas through to the best understanding that modern science allows. We need an embracing idea of knowledge★.

3. *Skepticism toward a priori "modeling languages."* KA is skeptical of a priori approaches to defining knowledge, or ones that start, for example, with models of knowledge★ that appear to prioritize ease of mapping to computational constructs[1] (Newell, 1980). The KA program seeks refined, complete, and explicit understanding of knowledge★ and its associated processes of development and deployment, just as cognitive modeling does. But we aim for more direct empirical accountability in terms of forms of knowledge *as we discover and validate them in the thoughts and actions of our subjects.*

## An Integrative View of the Program

Distinct principles or counter-principles help define a research program, but they disassemble it, rather than creating a gestalt. This section aims at creating such a gestalt in three stages. First, we introduce an image of the encompassing program as studying the form and content of, and transformative principles behind, knowledge★ viewed as an evolving complex system. Second, we identify several modes of research that contribute to somewhat separable sub-goals to achieving the overall goal. Third, we show that identifying these modes and their relations contributes to an understanding of how apparently different kinds of studies can contribute to the same overall goal.

### *A Systems Perspective on Change and Development*

KA focuses on systems of knowledge, including many instances of many different kinds of knowledge. Think of a "conceptual ecology" involving many concepts, many beliefs, and many intuitions (assuming, for simplicity, that concepts, beliefs, and intuitions constitute a sensible partitioning of relevant kinds of knowledge★). At any point in time, we need to list all such entities, and describe their relationships. For example, one intuitive belief, a documented "misconception," might relate two concepts: Any *force* (concept 1) gives rise to a *speed* (concept 2) *in proportion to* (relation between concepts) the force's magnitude.

Over time, particular new elements arise, and even new types of elements. Some older elements may fall out of use, or, more likely, remain but be used only for everyday, rather than techno-scientific, purposes. In addition, connections change, as the knowledge system is reconfigured to achieve expertise. Figure 2.1 is static, but of course, an important part of this inquiry is the principles by which

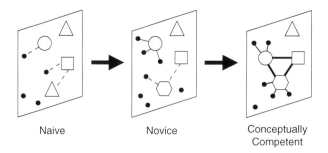

**FIGURE 2.1** Snapshots of the development of knowledge★ systems. (On-line processing and moment-by-moment change are not depicted here.)

Source: Reprinted from *Reconsidering Conceptual Change: Issues in Theory and Practice*, edited by Margarita Limón and Lucia Mason. Copyright © 2002 Kluwer Academic Publishers. Reprinted with kind permission from Springer Science and Business Media. Material excerpted from Figure 2 on page 31 in the chapter, "Why 'Conceptual Ecology' is a Good Idea," by Andrea A. diSessa.

knowledge★ works in real time, and how later states emerge gradually out of prior ones.

We can look at Figure 2.1 in terms of form (what are the types of knowledge and their relations?) or in terms of specific content. For example, "Speed is proportional to force" and "Length in inches is proportional to length in centimeters" have the same relational form but different content. Naturally, the content of expert knowledge is different from naive or incoming knowledge, but change in form might be just as important, or more so. Expert knowledge in a domain is typically assumed to show a higher degree of organization. Figure 2.1 suggests that how more and different organization comes about might be complicated, involving many changes.

One essential complication of the KA program of study is that the range of timescales is huge. On the one hand, we are committed to studying real-time thinking at the smallest observable time grain size. From classroom data or clinical videotape we probably cannot see much finer than a modest fraction of a second, say, on the order of $10^1$ seconds, at best. On the other hand, we have educational commitments on far grander timescales. We want to understand how the most important and difficult ideas in science and mathematics emerge during learning, which may take several years, in the range of $10^8$ seconds. Piaget came at this unification of very different timescales from the other direction. After focusing primarily on developmental timescales for most of his life, he came to accept the need to look at and integrate on-line thinking and local changes. His colleague, Bärbel Inhelder, spearheaded the formation of the "strategies group" at Geneva for this purpose (Inhelder et al., 1992).

## *Characterizing a Complex Knowledge System*

What follows is a compact rendering, for reference and summary, of the above characterization of the foci of KA, with some extensions for completeness.

- **Functional descriptions**: What does the system do for those who possess it? What are the functions of a system's components? (For example, p-prims provide people with a sense of naturalness and ability to predict some events, or in complementary manner, evoke surprise and inquiry as to how some "unnatural" event could have come about.)
- **Structural descriptions**: What are the various pieces of the system; how do they emerge, connect with one another, and develop over time?
  - **State of the system**: What is the system's structure at any point in time?
    - **Taxonomy**: What are the various types of elements that are involved?
    - **Distribution**: What is the variety and variation of elements, within and across types?
    - **Relationality**: What is the nature and extent of systematicity among elements?
    - **Nesting**: If the relevant system is a subsystem or supersystem of another, what is the nature of the nesting?
  - **Dynamics**: How do we describe activity in the system?
    - **Processing** (short timescale: seconds to hours).
    - **Normal operation**: How does one describe everyday use of the relevant knowledge?
    - **Changes during normal operation**: How does one describe change during normal operation? In particular, what changes accumulate into longer-term development (*microgenesis*)?
    - **Changes in elements**: emergence, change of character, extinction.
    - **Changes in relationality**: reorganization and shifts in activation priorities of elements.
  - **Development** (long-term change: months or years; *macrogenesis*)
    - **Changes in elements**: ultimate origins and evolution of individual elements toward expertise.
    - **Changes in relationality**: reorganization, and the emergence of new systems.

While the KA agenda is daunting, there are some synergies that make it more tractable. For example, knowing relevant knowledge elements – and knowing them very well – means that understanding of what happens to them during relatively short-term learning may become far clearer. diSessa (2014) shows a worked-out example of exactly this process of analysis; it shows how a few well-understood p-prims, and other ideas, come to constitute a socially shared model of thermal equilibration among a group of students. Similarly, identifying local principles of change, one can then extrapolate to thinking about how many such changes may accumulate. Conversely, knowing about long-term changes at high resolution can help us understand which local changes are the critical ones.

## Regimes of KA Study

Within the very wide range of types of studies, in terms of timescale, empirical, and theoretical focus, we identify here some "natural clusters" (we call them "regimes") that help partition and classify different types of KA study. Historically, KA studies have progressed along comprehensible trajectories, from one regime to another, capitalizing on synergistic relationships such as those suggested above.

### Microanalytic Study

In this regime, one focuses on elements and how they are used in real-time thinking. Here, the focus is primarily on short-timescale phenomena – brief segments of reasoning. For example, a person might view some physical event in the world. In response, some element of knowledge★ would be cued and provide part of the basis for interpreting the phenomenon. The microanalytical focus of our modeling may be on just this short slice of reasoning: the process of cuing to activation of the relevant element of knowledge. The cuing of the element might, of course, have longer-term consequences. It may suggest or anticipate aspects of the direction of further reasoning.

The microanalytic regime seems well adapted to generating ideas about knowledge types. That is, it may well be analytical in the theoretical sense of developing theoretical categories. A characteristic of the microanalytic regime is that, as both empirical and theoretical categories develop, many contexts may be needed to triangulate different aspects of one element or type. Contextuality, for example, is impossible to determine from one or just a few contexts of use.

Methodologically, microanalytic studies tend to select short segments of thinking for analysis out of a fuller corpus of thinking. So, more integrative and longer-termed microgenetic and micro-operational goals (below) may not be directly or fully met. Sherin (2001) provides a transparent example of the principled selection of parts of a large corpus for microanalytic purposes.

### Microgenetic Study

As educational researchers, we are of course interested in changes to knowledge (i.e., learning). Microgenetic studies step up from microanalytic ones specifically in seeking to understand the processes that underlie the achievement of recognizably new states of understanding – not just a student's finding any way to interpret a situation, but finding a *new*, and relatively *stable*, way to interpret it. In our view, changes to knowledge may be a concomitant of even the briefest and most routine instances of reasoning. Thus, there may not be a big step from microanalytic to microgenetic study. Knowing elements well (microanalytic perspective), one may be able to infer changes (microgenetic perspective) much more easily than otherwise.

We use the prefix *micro* in describing this regime since, in the larger program, we need to see how time-local (micro) changes fit into long-term (macro) changes ("development," below).

## Micro-operational Study

A substantial body of historical work has attempted to model reasoning at a timescale at which that reasoning can be seen to have a sequential, strategic quality. It is here that we begin to capture the overall flow of reasoning as it occurs over seconds, minutes, or even hours. This is the standard regime of cognitive modeling, but modeling reasoning at this level in a way that is consistent with the principles of KA poses significant challenges. The twin commitments to the complexity of knowledge and to the full details of real-time thinking result in a daunting micro-operational task. *All* the relevant elements and processes that might be involved over an extended period of time need to be described in careful detail. A KA-oriented model of extended thinking should ideally be complete and sufficient (should "run" on its own) – as opposed to affording scattered, if critical, insights (say, when one particular element is evoked), which is more typical of microanalytic or microgenetic study. In practice, this remains a long-term goal, and not a currently well-developed empirical regime.

## True Developmental Study

This is the regime occupied by developmental psychology. Traditional developmental research is concerned with changes to individuals that occur over months or years, with an emphasis on changes that are maturational and occur during childhood. Developmental studies often provide easy starting points for research, because they provide us with highly contrasting styles of thinking about which to theorize. But, the KA challenge is to connect well with shorter timescale perspectives. As suggested earlier, synergies exist between developmental and shorter-term perspectives to the extent that long- and short-duration changes provide constraints and suggestions about each other. For example, can developmental patterns be realized with the elements and local processing mechanisms specified in microanalytic and microgenetic studies? diSessa (1993) speculates on global development based on shifting the parameters that determine elements' activation, which may be determined in microanalytic study.

## Methodology

This section presents an image of KA in practice. Although a "practical guide to Knowledge Analysis" is beyond the scope of this chapter, readers are introduced to some current and characteristic methodological practices involved in doing KA.

### Overview

While KA researchers employ many practices that can be found across multiple research traditions, when viewed as a whole, KA employs a set that is recognizable and distinct. To position KA in relation to the larger field, we introduce a simple, high-level framework (Martin & Sherin, 2013), one that we believe can be used to characterize any empirical research effort focused on human activity. The framework has five parts:

1. *Empirical set-up.* What instances of thinking and learning are studied? For example, do we look at interviews, classroom discussions, or everyday conversation?
2. *Capture.* What aspects of the learning phenomena are captured and how are they captured? For example, do we videotape the interaction? Take field notes?
3. *Reduction.* What do we attend to in what is captured? For example, do we only care about whether a student gave a right or wrong answer? Do we pay attention to gestures, or just the words that are spoken? Do we reduce the data to a set of codes?
4. *Pattern finding.* How do we find patterns in the data? Do we look for statistically significant correlations in codes? Do we read transcripts to draw impressions that may be generalized? We use "patterns," here, in a very general sense, referring even to such complex patterns as theories.
5. *Reporting.* How do we report our results to other researchers? For example, how are the results of pattern finding described in journal articles?

### Empirical Set-up

KA research is concerned with the content, form, and dynamics of individual knowledge and how it develops. Such issues can be investigated in both researcher-manufactured contexts (such as clinical interviews) and in naturally occurring contexts (such as students working together in small groups on a problem). In both cases, the assumption is that what individuals say or do is a window into their thought processes. No matter the context, the KA goal is to uncover subjects' natural[2] ways of reasoning about phenomena, *not* to assess individuals' state of understanding with respect to a normative standard. The contexts that individuals are asked to reason about are often complex conceptual situations as opposed to contexts that require only the execution of a procedure or allow the assessment of factual knowledge.

As discussed in the theoretical foundations section, a characteristic concern for KA is the issue of contextuality of knowledge use. The methodological implications of making contextuality a key focus are substantial, and the means of generating opportunities to observe it can vary. Subjects may be asked to reason about multiple representations of the "same" issue, or they may have multiple opportunities to consider the same event or idea. The researcher may, at some point, deliberately prompt other ways of thinking to measure the subject's receptivity.

## *Capture*

In almost all cases, the phenomenon sampled is captured in video and audio. Concrete artifacts, such as drawings, are also collected. As KA is interested in how individuals perceive the world and how their knowledge about it is organized, it is critical for researchers to put themselves in the position to notice what subjects are focusing their attention on and what is salient to them. Thus, in many cases, care must be taken during the data-collection phase to make sure the camera is positioned so that indications such as subjects' eye gaze, gestures, and the way they interact with artifacts and materials are all available for later study. In recent years it has become common to convert all of this data to a digital form for rapid access, indexing, and annotation.

## *Reduction*

In most cases, video recordings are transcribed. Many times the work that follows is done using primarily these transcriptions; however video is also frequently consulted, especially in situations where, for example, things like eye gaze or gradual construction of a visual representation are involved. KA research is not dogmatic when it comes to the features of interactions that *must* be captured in initial transcripts. As such, standardized practices for representing events of interest have not been developed within the community. Features of the interaction or context that are thought to be relevant to the question at hand are captured and the transcript is iteratively improved as necessary for the purpose of investigating the chosen focus. This could include marking features like gestures, eye gaze, and lengths of turns and pauses. It is not common to meticulously capture details such as intonation, rhythm, and pronunciation of words, although some of these might become important to certain interpretations (e.g., evaluating level of confidence, or as indicators of careful on-line thinking).

In addition to linguistic expression, other indications in data can give clues about better or worse analyst renderings of subjects' attention and meaning. The flow of individuals' actions or their reactions within interactions can be indications of what they find salient. Evidence that a subject takes a statement to be explanatory and an adequate basis for reasoning is important information. (Does the subject react to an idea posed by the interviewer or by another participant with an implied "of course" or, conversely, with surprise?) Commitment and confidence are important features that may be implicated by pacing, prosody, and tone of speech. (Does the participant confidently – or timidly – reject formulations offered to them?) Time profile can also be of interest. What ideas about the topic at hand did the participant express first? Do some ideas appear to be generated on the spot or does the participant appear to be reasoning on the basis of ideas that are pre-compiled? On the other hand, participants may radically reformulate their ways of thinking, which is extremely important in assessing both the range of ways they can think about a situation and also the ways in which they decide how best to understand it. This contrasts markedly with studies that may take only the participant's first response into account or not allow the subject's nuanced reconsideration.

## Pattern Finding

Outside of KA, qualitative analysis of video data includes many strategies for finding patterns in reduced data (e.g., Chi, 1997). One prominent family of strategies includes hypothesis testing, in which researchers specify a hypothesis about a phenomenon at the beginning of a study, before data collection. They then code their data and perform significance testing on the results to see whether the initial hypothesis should be rejected or confirmed. Another approach outside of KA is correlational analysis, in which quantitative parameters are extracted from data through coding and related to each other.

The relationship between pattern finding and data reduction in KA generally follows neither of these approaches. Systematic coding of video by KA researchers, though not unheard of, is not a common practice. A more common type of reduction takes the form of the selection of episodes that illustrate the phenomenon at issue and the creation of theory-based narrative accounts of these episodes. Furthermore, in prototypical cases of KA practice, there is an iterative process of *theory building*, in which the researcher goes back and forth between the data and the theory. The data are examined in an open way with respect to a topic of interest, episodes illustrating a particular issue are selected, a theory is built, then reduced narrative accounts of episodes are produced employing the theory as it currently exists. The fit of the theory to the episodes is then evaluated, and the process iterates. The iterative, data-grounded approach to developing theoretical accounts shares features with grounded theory and the constant comparison method (Glaser & Strauss, 1967), as elaborated in Parnafes and diSessa (2013).

## *Reporting*

In the prototypical case, KA research articles present the theoretical frameworks that have been developed (during pattern finding) and they illustrate and establish the plausibility of the framework by drawing on selected theory-based narrative episodes. In many non-KA qualitative analyses, the rigor in the analysis comes from (a) having large numbers of subjects to guard against anomalous findings with small samples, and (b) a process of coding and measuring the agreement between multiple coders in order to demonstrate the clarity and operationalization of coding schemes. While either of these techniques could be used by researchers doing KA, there are theoretically motivated constraints on analyses that provide ways other than large numbers and objective coding to evaluate the quality of an analysis. For example, the function of p-prims is to make certain occurrences feel natural and obvious and others seem odd. The subject's consequent attitudes ought, in principle, to be observable and should be in accord with theoretical analysis of cases. In addition, properties of p-prims ought to be relatively stable across instances, unless events that might induce change are observed. See diSessa (1993) and Kapon and diSessa (2012) for discussion of these and other theoretically motivated validation principles.

We have discussed, at a high level, the methodological approaches that characterize Knowledge Analysis. To further give a sense for the methodology that is typical of KA, we now discuss two prototype instances of KA work. The first, on p-prims, is an instance of microanalytical work; the second, coordination classes, is microgenetic. In elucidating some of the concrete details of empirical set-up, capture, reduction, pattern finding, and reporting, the description of each of the examples loosely follows the general methodological framework described in the previous section.

## A Microanalytic Prototype: P-prims

P-prims, a particular type of knowledge★, are arguably the first reference model in the modern history of KA (diSessa, 1983, 1988, 1993). They are the exclusive type of element in a system called "the sense of mechanism," which accounts for (this is its function) people's feelings of naturalness or surprise concerning happenings in the world. P-prims are "phenomenological" in the sense that they are mostly seen by people directly in phenomena. They are "primitive" in the dual senses that no further explanation lies behind them and that they are quite simple mental entities which are invoked as a whole. This simplicity is in stark contrast to scientific theories, which are universally complex, involving coordinated use of many ideas over extended periods of reasoning.

A prototypical example of a p-prim is Ohm's p-prim, which specifies what happens in common circumstances where some kind of *effort* or *agency* acts through a *resistance* to achieve some sort of *result*. Ohm's p-prim entails that greater effort begets a greater result, but an increase in resistance leads to a lesser result. So, in pushing a rock, it moves more if you push harder, but a bigger rock moves less for the same effort.

As we discussed in the historical situating section, the first articles on p-prims were published at a time when studies of learning had recently taken cognizance of the striking phenomenon of naive or intuitive conceptions, mainly in science learning. The dominant view of naive conceptions was that they were part of (or constituted) a coherent and even articulate theory of the physical world, but one opposed to what is taught in school. Quite unlike "an intuitive theory," there are hundreds or thousands of p-prims, each of which serves humans in particular contexts, but not in others. Because of that contextuality, p-prims may have people drawing apparently conflicting conclusions, such as that in some circumstances, one needs an agent to cause motion (Ohm's p-prim-like situations), while in others, motion is called forth merely by spatial configuration. The latter is exemplified by the intuitive fact that balance, say of a pan balance, is automatically restored (no agency or intervention is needed) once a perturbation, such as a finger pushing on the scale, is removed.

P-prims are difficult to describe in language. They operate mostly by recognition in particular kinds of situations where they are likely apt, providing a sense of regularity in the world and also the ability to predict. Recognizing Ohm's p-prim, one's attitude is: "Of course! If you push harder, things move more!" Instrumentally, in order to get a greater effect, one tries harder. Modal encoding is consistent with the hypothesized origins of p-prims as simple mental "descriptions" of common events that have been learned, over an extended period of time, to be primitively explanatory.

The 1993 monograph that laid out p-prims theory (diSessa, 1993) documented around three dozen p-prims. It was argued that these could be seen to account, in concert, for apparent intuitive theories that other researchers described universally in a few words or sentences of text. In order to improve understanding of the key phenomenon of contextuality, p-prims theory added a simple model of the activation and deactivation of individual p-prims, involving parameters called *cuing priority* (activation) and *reliability priority* (relevant to sustaining or deactivating p-prims). Hence the rough concept of "contextuality" developed into a more precise technical language.

The study reported in the 1993 monograph took place over three years, involving about 20 undergraduate students and a total of roughly 400 hours of interview data. Clinical interviews were chosen as an open-ended approach that would allow for the possibility of focusing on whatever knowledge* emerged from the study. The study involved an evolving set of problems, specifically designed to triangulate on the meaning, contextuality, and relevant processing around focal events. Pattern finding and data reduction occurred in small and larger cycles, more or less continuously during the study. At the largest level, pattern finding resulted in a theory of intuitive knowledge in physics, centering on the particular, hypothesized-to-be-important knowledge form, the p-prim. Steps in developing theoretical description began to filter and reduce data. For example, later on, all data were excluded that did not appear to bear directly on p-prims. Characteristics of p-prims that filtered out non-relevant data included that p-prims are hypothesized to act over short periods of time, to be inarticulate (not encoded in language), and to provide students with a sense of "how things happen" – this last being an intuitive equivalent of principles of physics. Then, instances of proposed activation of a p-prim were considered specifically with respect to hypothesized properties of p-prims, whether the salient properties of subjects' thinking could be effectively mapped into the properties of p-prims, according to the theory. That is, the existing theoretical frame constituted an analytical framework for interpreting each selected episode, and reduction constituted the re-description of an episode in terms of the theory. The output of each analysis might be an improved "pattern" (theory), an improved empirical case that the pattern fit the episode, or both.

Similar cycles of pattern induction, description improvement, and refining occurred at the content level, which consisted largely of carefully describing the content of a fairly large collection of p-prims. Data were filtered and sorted according to potential p-prims, and then matched against existing descriptions of the relevant p-prim. With regard to contextuality, hypotheses concerning the circumstances in which a particular p-prim would be evoked could be tested against multiple cases and contexts. These tests often resulted in the rejection of earlier descriptions of proposed elements or their contextuality. A somewhat novel aspect of this particular study, perhaps, is that hypotheses (mainly about the content of particular p-prims) drove the development of new problems and variations (and hence the collection of more data) that could result in improved triangulation across instances.

The overall methodological process of this study could be described as a purposeful competitive argumentation concerning the viability of descriptions of both form and content, augmented by deliberate generation of data (new problems) that could differentiate hypotheses. The evolving theory was guided not only by empirical cases but by the following integrated set of concerns. This is in essence a subset of the list, above, concerning "Characterizing a complex knowledge system."

1. What is the nature (form) and content of knowledge elements involved in focal events?
2. What can be said about the local processing (cognitive mechanism) involving these elements?

3. What are the relations (systematicities) in the overall set of elements?
4. How does the overall system evolve over time?

Like many microanalytic KA studies, reporting produced a list of carefully described exemplars – p-prims – specifically with respect to their "content," complementary to theoretical and general specification of "form" (structure, encoding, activation, etc.). A relatively large set of examples was also important to begin study of the overall systematicity of the intuitive physics knowledge system. Explicit principles for identifying p-prims in data developed late in the process and required a reanalysis of most of the preliminary work, with stricter levels of accountability. Principles for observing p-prims were also reported in the final paper as a contribution supporting further work on p-prims.

There are several idiosyncratic features in the argumentation and reporting of the body of work on p-prims. The 1993 monograph placed the work on p-prims in the context of a more ambitious epistemological program. The larger goals of KA (within a KiP perspective), beyond distinctively microanalytic goals, were unusually evident in this study. We made the point, earlier, that each regime of KA study can provide ideas and constraints concerning other regimes. In this mainly microanalytic study, true developmental goals were broached, including speculating on the origins of elements and their gradual change toward expertise, although data used for that purpose were informal. Local processing was described in such a way as to anticipate possible micro-operational study, although no attempt was made to track changes in thinking over extended periods of time. More in line with typical microanalytical study, no systematic data were collected that could contribute to microgenetic goals; microgenetic speculation was comparably minimal.

In closing this section, we note two telling and related facts about the idea of p-prims. First, it is self-consciously a model, and it is a model of only one part of the naive ecology of ideas that affect learning of science; it is not a theory of all of thinking and learning. In fact, it falls far short of being what would be needed to create a runnable micro-operational model of episodes of reasoning in which p-prims figure. From the very beginning, the idea of a p-prim was expected to fail at some point, or to fail to account for some phenomena regarding the sense of mechanism. Some modes of failure and insufficiency were anticipated. For example, in the model, p-prims are always "evoked as a whole" (unlike, say, scientific theories, which are used in bits and pieces across time) and the only variation in the meaning of a p-prim across individuals was carried in the cuing and reliability priorities. Exactly how common attributes across several p-prims (e.g., agency) work was not elaborated. Similarly, no analysis was given of how people may deliberately shift attention so as to invoke different p-prims, and no empirical analysis was given to the early origins of p-prims. Still, the p-prim model has been useful, while the need for refinement appears now to be more focused and pressing (for example, see diSessa, 2014, on malleability of activation).

## A Microgenetic Prototype: Coordination Classes

Having completed our example of microanalytic study, we turn to exemplifying microgenetic study. In the case we discuss here, theory development is somewhat differently situated than in the p-prim example above. In particular, the core theoretical model (coordination class theory) had already been developed, and new theoretical contributions involved extension, refinement, and adaptation of the model to a new context. We begin by explaining the pre-existing theory, which has informative contrasting properties to the theory of p-prims. Then, we exemplify microgenetic study through a discussion of the work of Parnafes on students' conceptual development using computational representations.

### *A Contrasting Reference Model: Coordination Classes*

Coordination classes were intended to constitute a model of well-defined, well-functioning ("expert") concepts, and also of intuitive approximations to such concepts. Coordination classes are most useful as a model of conceptual organization when students are approaching expertise (on the right side of Figure 2.1), less so for the naive state (on the left). Coordination classes are, by themselves, fairly extensive and integrated systems, with some strong internal coherence constraints, quite unlike the fragmentation and independence of p-prims. As expertise always involves families of concepts, say, those involved in a theory, coordination classes typically come in clusters that interact with each other, both during development but also in expert problem solving. Thus, they are systems (as opposed to elements, like p-prims) that are nested in higher-level systems (more akin to "theories"). P-prims, themselves, are modeled mainly as elements, not systems, and the system in which they are embedded, the sense of mechanism, does not have much evident structuring, unlike coordination classes (or supposed naive theories). In short, in comparing p-prims to coordination classes, relationality is different in almost all respects.

An analysis of the internal structure of coordination classes begins with the observation that seeing scientific concepts, such as force, in the world is a complicated thing. The primary function of a coordination class, in fact, is to allow people to see the essential properties of things such as force. "Essential properties" might be things like "magnitude" and "direction." Coming to understand a concept like "force" involves being able to determine those parameters across a wide range of contexts (e.g., in cases like tossed balls, books lying on tables, and orbiting spacecraft). Since essential properties are almost never directly observable, determining them requires inferencing from what is observable, and different observations and inferences are necessary depending on the context (looking, feeling, measuring, computing ...). Thus, the coordination class system is partitioned into functional units: (1) a perceptual component (*extractions*), which is, essentially, all possible observations relevant to determining a concept's parameters, and (2) an inferential component (the *inferential net*), which is comprised of all possible inferences that lie between observations and the concept's parameters.[3]

The pathway from observations to defining parameters can be short ("I feel a force") or long (computing a force based on other coordination classes, such as mass and acceleration). The longer paths may be quite complex, unlike what happens with, say, instinctive inferences involving individual p-prims.

Contextuality shows up in the theory of coordination classes as a coherence constraint, called alignment. Many inferential pathways from various extractions to defining parameters are possible, yet they must all, in the end, determine the same concept parameters: Two ways of determining the magnitude of a force cannot yield different answers. Alignment is the source of many novice difficulties in achieving a "good" coordination class, and, in general, coordination class theory anticipates and interprets a wide range of learning problems. More about coordination class theory can be found in diSessa (1991), diSessa and Sherin (1998) and diSessa and Wagner (2005).[4]

We now use the work of Parnafes (2007) to illustrate prototypical issues that arise in microgenetic studies of knowledge in transition. Although some details of this prototype are already reported in the form of a methodological case study in Parnafes and diSessa (2013), we demonstrate here how the case illustrates each of the components of the framework for research introduced previously (empirical set-up, capture, reduction, pattern finding, and reporting).

Parnafes was interested in the general question of how representations, and, in particular, computational representations, mediate conceptual development. Her study involved data from eight pairs of high-school students in which students reasoned about simple harmonic motion (oscillation) using both computational representations and physical oscillators. The general aim was to try to understand the ways in which students' reasoning with simulations of simple harmonic motion could help build their understanding of the phenomenon. The activities in the study revolved around:

1. a purposefully rich and varied set of physical means for exploring the phenomenon (springy rods, physical pendulums, springs, etc.)
2. a dynamic and interactive simulation of harmonic motion, itself with several coordinated views that highlighted various aspects of harmonic motion.

Over the course of an open-ended session (~90 minutes), students were asked to discuss similarities and differences between various oscillators. Unlike in the microanalytic study of p-prims using clinical interviewing methods, in this microgenetic study, the researcher intervened only occasionally to ask pairs to consider certain aspects of the situation and, if they had come to a local impasse, to prompt them to continue their explorations in particular directions. The social interactions in the sessions tended towards "naturalistic" in the sense that the activities and props could easily be considered instructional in the way that a (relatively open) school lab might operate. In many cases, the students working together were acquainted with each other, and the researcher made a particular effort to make sure the students felt comfortable and in control of the situation. The design of the activity itself gave students agency to explore a reasonably complex topic in a relatively unstructured way without specific expectations for the endpoint of their investigations. To be sure, there was an expectation that they would deepen their understanding through engaging in these activities, but there was not a tightly prescribed sequence of tasks and expected learning outcomes. The students explored issues that they found puzzling or surprising about the relationship between the simulations of oscillatory motion and the physical oscillators that were made available to them. In several instances, these issues came to their attention because the simulation itself violated their expectations and this violation of expectations led them to explore further.

The empirical set-up was chosen because the researcher wanted to observe episodes of more or less spontaneous learning with representations. She needed a way to elicit how students thought about the phenomenon and also the role of the computational representation in supporting their learning. She could not be explicitly directive in her interactions if she wanted to emphasize students' personal processes of knowledge construction. Thus, she used the indirect approach of having students talk with a peer as they reasoned in combination with the introduction of a computational representation designed to be a generative support for their reasoning and learning. The students' work was videotaped with one camera. The camera was positioned so as to capture the students' faces and upper bodies as they talked with each other and played with the oscillators and, later, to capture screen and mouse movement.

As mentioned in the general description of KA methodology and illustrated in the microanalytic section, the pattern-finding process here shared features with grounded theory (Glaser & Strauss, 1967). In Parnafes and diSessa (2013), Parnafes reports that she started with a preliminary and open analysis of the data to identify segments of particular interest for understanding the processes by which interaction with representations seemed to support the development of students' understanding. Such moments and issues were briefly characterized and named, and the iterative process of describing features of such moments and schematizing their properties began. One such issue, which became core to her study, was that students seemed to use the term "fast" in different ways, without noticing. The preliminary stage was followed by a search across the data for similar occurrences. At this stage, the focus was on noticing interesting features and phenomena in the data, not on overlaying any particular theoretical framework. The next phase of analysis involved negotiating between candidate theories and the data in the corpus that exemplified the previously noted issues. Because coordination class theory highlights the perceptual processes relevant in studying the interplay between external representations and learning, it was selected as a starter theory for the analysis.

The core results of Parnafes' investigation included the appropriation and adaptation of coordination class theory to this new context. Parnafes' focus of analysis thus became "How can a computer-based representation of oscillatory motion contribute to increasing the alignment (the coherence principle that multiple paths of inferencing must lead to the same results) and span (the range of circumstances in which the concept can be use) for the coordination class for velocity ('fastness')?" To begin with, the students seemed to use an intuitive coordination class, "fast," that was, however, insufficient to capture key features of oscillation. For example, "fast" sometimes determined what a scientist would call linear speed, and sometimes it determined frequency.

In looking to see how the students came to coordinate linear speed and frequency independently, she uncovered key mechanisms of conceptual development that intimately involved representations. For example, noticing patterns in the behavior of the representations (e.g., that a distance that represented the period of oscillation did not change when the amplitude of oscillation changed) instigated inquiries that resulted in finding core inferences in the coordination class of "linear speed" (e.g., that differences in speed can compensate for differences in distance traveled, leaving a constant period). Another mechanism involved stabilizing the students' means of observing the physical world (extractions) so as to distinguish linear speed from frequency; students gained control over what, previously, had been automatic and unarticulated perceptions of "fast." Thus, Parnafes' interrelated mechanisms extended coordination class theory to the particulars of learning with computer representations, and they also illuminated the whole process of learning with representations, using existing coordination class theory as a starting framework.

## Landscape of Knowledge Analysis Work

Although it is not definitive for KA, most current researchers whose approach shares the orienting features described in the theoretical assumptions section and the practices described in the methodology section are informed by the Knowledge in Pieces epistemological perspective. In this section, we give an overview of the range of KA work drawing upon KiP in particular. We then describe a sampling of general research themes to which KA methods have contributed – many involving the theories of p-prims or coordination classes. Finally, returning to our theoretical leitmotivs, we describe the ways that the p-prim and coordination class models themselves have been adapted and extended in recent years.

### Topic Distribution

While much of the work employing KA methods had its roots in trying to understand the nature of individuals' understanding of the physical world and

**TABLE 2.1** Research Contributions to the KA Program Organized by Disciplinary Content

| | |
|---|---|
| Intuitive physics topics such as simple oscillatory motion, intuitions about the seasons and the phases of the moon, intuitive ideas about force and motion | Clark, D'Angelo, & Schleigh, 2011; diSessa, 1993; diSessa, Gillespie, & Esterly, 2004; Kapon & diSessa, 2012; Parnafes, 2007, 2012; Sherin, Krakowski, & Lee, 2012; Thaden-Koch, 2003 |
| More advanced topics in physics, including thermodynamics, wave mechanics, and special relativity | Clark, 2006; Frank & Scherr, 2012; Gupta, Hammer, & Redish, 2010; Hutchison & Hammer, 2010; Levrini & diSessa, 2008; Masson & Legendre, 2008; Sayre & Wittmann, 2008; Sherin, 2001; Wittmann, 2002 |
| Mathematics, ranging from studies of rational number, area, and algebra to studies of modeling, integration, the concept of limit, and statistical principles such as the law of large numbers | Adiredja, 2014; Izsák, 2000, 2005; Jones, 2013; Kapon, Ron, Hershkowitz, & Dreyfus, 2014; Levin, 2012; Pratt & Noss, 2002; Smith, 1995; Wagner, 2006, 2010 |
| Biology, evolution, genetics, and ecology | Duncan, 2007; Ly, 2011; Southerland, Abrams, Cummins, & Anzelmo, 2001; White, 2000 |
| Other disciplinary content, including chemistry, complex systems, and computer science | Barth-Cohen, 2012; Brown, 2009; Lewis, 2012; Taber & García-Franco, 2010 |
| Less explicitly "disciplinary" domains of knowledge, including subjects' epistemologies, and ideologies concerning race | Hammer, 1994; Hammer & Elby, 2002; Philip, 2011 |

how this relates to schooled physics (mechanics), the field has broadened significantly with respect to the topical focus of studies of cognition. Table 2.1 organizes KiP-inspired research contributions by disciplinary content. In addition to the breadth of topics, the range in age and expertise of subjects under study is notable.

## *Research Themes*

We now consider the diversity of the KA literature across strands of research related to general learning phenomena, such as transfer, analogical reasoning, explanation, and problem solving. While such general phenomena cut across disciplinary domains in their interest and applicability (see Table 2.2), existing theoretical treatments of them have often not taken into account issues that are important to KiP and KA, such as the role of individuals' prior knowledge, adequate tests of "having knowledge," and individual variation. By providing purchase on these issues, KA reformulations of these phenomena offer new perspectives and insights.

**TABLE 2.2** Contributions to the KA Program Organized by Research Theme

| | |
|---|---|
| Analogical reasoning | Kapon & diSessa, 2012 |
| Problem solving | Jeppsson, Haglund, Amin, & Strömdahl, 2013; Levin, 2012; Sherin, 2006 |
| Conceptual development | diSessa, 2014; Parnafes, 2007 |
| Explanation generation | Barth-Cohen, 2012; Parnafes, 2012; Sherin, Krakowski & Lee, 2012 |
| Misconceptions | diSessa, 1996; Smith, diSessa, & Roschelle, 1993 |
| Transfer | diSessa, 2004; diSessa & Wagner, 2005; Wagner, 2006, 2010 |

## Evolving Theories

In the social sciences, there are many orientations toward theory, and many strategies for developing it. KA's approach is unusual. On the one hand, we aim, eventually, for a comprehensive and computationally precise theory, surely a very high-end goal. On the other hand, we expect that such a grand theory will emerge only slowly and bit by bit. In the interim, we need to be modest and aim for "humble theory" (diSessa & Cobb, 2004), which is insightful, but guaranteed to go through multiple cycles of revision and extension. In this sense, we are model builders like Niels Bohr, who knew the limits of his model of the atom and expected – demanded – further developments. Indeed, rather than accepting or hiding limits in our models, we actively seek them out and pursue combining, improving, and extending the relevant models. A reasonable amount of the history of KA research can be understood as a sequence of extensions and improvements. In this section, we will catalog a few such sequences.

## Extending the P-prim Model

A canonical focus of KA research has been on exploring the nature of individuals' intuitive knowledge. We took diSessa's work on phenomenological primitives and the sense of physical mechanism as prototypical. However, the interest in the nature of intuitive knowledge extends to domains far beyond individuals' sense of physical mechanism. We present here some theoretical innovations and extensions to the construct:

- *Explanatory primitives* (e-prims) (Kapon & diSessa, 2012) are a direct abstraction of p-prims, where form is no longer considered a distinguishing factor. That is, e-prims have the same function as p-prims (explanation), but they may or may not be non-linguistically encoded. E-prims were first used in the context of explaining individual differences in accepting or rejecting analogical inferences based on students' repertoire of prior knowledge. While all

p-prims are e-prims (they all are treated as explanatory), some e-prims have characteristics (e.g., explicit connections to language and articulate learning histories) that p-prims do not have.
- *Naturalized axioms* (Philip, 2011) describe intuitions about race and racism. Philip (2011) studied the role of such intuitions in reasoning about situations in which race is salient. Naturalized axioms are similar to p-prims, and they collectively form an aesthetic system analogous to the sense of mechanism. However, in addition to the difference in content, as in the case of explanatory primitives, naturalized axioms have connections to language and social history that are not highlighted with p-prims.
- *Symbolic forms* (Sherin, 2001) are knowledge structures that encode intuitions related to symbolic expressions that represent physical situations. In terms of structure, they involve binding an explanatory schema (including p-prims) to a symbol template. Work on symbolic forms can be found in Sherin (2001), Izsák (2000), Jones (2013), Jeppsson, Haglund, Amin, and Strömdahl (2013), and Kuo, Hull, Gupta, and Elby (2013).

In the above examples, p-prims and the way they function in thinking served as reference models for theoretical innovation. In some cases, structural or functional features of p-prims were relaxed in order to get at core generalities that cover a broader range of knowledge types (e.g., explanatory primitives); the theory was specialized, adapted, or extended as appropriate for different regimes of thinking and knowing (e.g., naturalized axioms); or the theory was extended to explain genuinely new phenomena (symbolic forms).

A different but equally important reason to relax constraints is to communicate with other researchers and practitioners at a big-picture level, so that the general implications of this perspective on knowledge are more readily apparent and usable. Below we list three additional examples of how the p-prim reference model was adapted in such a way as to relax more detailed features of the model.

- *Facets* – Minstrell (1989) introduced facets as slight abstractions of what students say or do when they think about instructionally relevant physical phenomen. Although coding data of student thinking for facets is often explicitly informed by KiP and the grain size of interest for identifying facets is similarly small, there is no a priori assumed homogeneity in terms of the structure, function, developmental history, or dynamics of facets.[5]
- *Nodes-modes* – Sherin, Krakowski, and Lee (2012) propose a relatively simple and neutral framework for understanding the contextual activation and use of knowledge elements in activity. In their model, knowledge nodes do not necessarily share structural features. In addition to attending to intuitive knowledge elements, they also attended to locally stable compositions, such as "a model of seasonal temperature variations," which they called, generically, *dynamic mental constructs*.

- *Resources* – Hammer (2000) assumes that individuals' thinking involves many cognitive resources that may or may not activate in any particular context. Resources are elements of knowledge systems, but, like nodes, they are not theoretical models of particular kinds of knowledge elements. They are diverse in structure and developmental history, as well as function. Using the term "resources" to describe the "nodes" of a system serves to highlight the potentially productive nature of individual knowledge.

Common across all of the knowledge types discussed above is the assumption that knowledge elements (p-prim, symbolic form, explanatory primitive, naturalized axiom, node, resource, facet) activate depending on the context, including in response to social, material, and physical features of the environment.

Though it is not explicitly developed in relation to p-prim theory or the KiP epistemological perspective, we mention here a construct that plays a similar role to p-prim in theories of abstraction and the development of mathematical meaning – that of *situated abstraction* (Noss & Hoyles, 1996). Resonant with the assumptions of KiP, Noss & Hoyles argue against traditional views of abstraction as a hierarchical and decontextualized process. Instead, they argue that mathematical understandings are first expressed in a highly situated and contextualized form (situated abstractions), similar to p-prims. This construct has been elaborated through multiple studies in a variety of mathematical contexts (Hoyles, Bakker, Kent, & Noss, 2007; Noss, Hoyles, & Pozzi, 2002; Paparistodemou, Noss, & Pratt, 2008; Pratt & Noss, 2002; Prodromou & Pratt, 2006, 2013; Sacristan & Noss, 2008).

## Extending the Coordination Class Model

Coordination class theory has been useful for understanding issues involved in learning a wide range of scientific concepts (e.g., proper time: Levrini & diSessa, 2008; expected value: Wagner, 2006; "fastness": Parnafes, 2007; algebra: Levin, 2012; the concept of programming state in computer science: Lewis, 2012; wave mechanics: Wittmann, 2002; judgments of realism of motion: Thaden-Koch, Mestre, Dufresne, Gerace, & Leonard, 2005). In addition to conceptual scope, coordination class theory has provided a theoretical basis for diverse investigations into fundamental learning phenomena including (a) reformulating the nature and processes involved in knowledge transfer (Wagner, 2006), (b) how representations mediate conceptual development (Parnafes, 2007), and (c) the coordination of knowledge in problem solving (Levin, 2012).

Below, we discuss some of the theoretical extensions to the coordination class model that have emerged through the appropriation and adaptation of the construct into different empirical contexts.

- *Concept projections and distributed elements* (diSessa, 2004; diSessa & Wagner, 2005; Wagner, 2006) – In reformulating transfer research through a coordination class theory lens, the analytic focus on the construction of partial states of competence, how knowledge use appears different across contexts, and how this contextuality changes over time led to the articulation of the idea of a *concept projection* (the collection of knowledge and strategies used in implementing a concept in a particular context) and *distributed elements* (elements of a concept that may be used in only some concept projections).

- *Mechanisms of development* – Increasing span and improving alignment were generic processes proposed by diSessa and Sherin (1998) for describing how coordination classes become increasingly tuned as systems. These processes have been documented in several empirical studies of knowledge growth and change (diSessa, 2004; Levin, 2012; Levin & diSessa, this volume; Levrini & diSessa, 2008; Parnafes, 2007; Wagner, 2006). diSessa and Wagner (2005) introduce the terms *incorporation* and *displacement* to describe the processes by which elements of coordination classes come to play new roles in the partial encoding of new concepts. Levrini and diSessa (2008) introduced the term *articulated alignment* to describe the explicit and articulate view of the relationships between concept projections (alignment) that can be developed by students as they learn to normatively determine information across different circumstances. In addition to observing general learning processes such as increasing span and improving alignment, as mentioned briefly, Parnafes (2007) uncovered several more specific learning mechanisms (*pattern detection, anchoring, challenging, re-application*) related to the role that interacting with representations plays in building coordination classes.[6]

- *State as a coordination class* (Lewis, 2012) – Similar to Levin (below), Lewis demonstrated the usefulness of the coordination class model to an unusual domain, understanding computational state in computer science. Using clinical case studies of students' reasoning, she demonstrated typical coordination phenomena: positive and, occasionally, problematic use of intuitive inferences in the inferential net, and the gradual alignment of different concept projections. Lewis argued that getting information about a state (readout) and creating a specified state (setting) need to be separately considered in computer science. In contrast, diSessa and Sherin (1998) argued that, for mechanics, readout and setting substantially overlap, and hence need not be separately analyzed.

- *Coordination clusters* – Parnafes (2007) documented the mutual bootstrapping process between several related coordination classes, called coordination clusters. This is an example of a conjectured but undocumented component of the theory becoming exemplified, opening the possibility for theoretical and empirical refinement.

- *Determination of a different class of information – solutions to problems – as opposed to concept-characteristic classes of information* (Levin, 2012) – Explicitly building on the coordination class model, Levin's work on problem solving introduced the construct of a *strategy system*. In the case of coordination of knowledge toward problem-solving goals, there is a fairly complex set of multiple readouts (e.g., several relevant quantities) that need to be managed and coordinated over time towards the end of solving a problem. The strategy system model was developed to capture the interplay between what individuals attend to, infer, and do as they solve problems. Levin traced the development of strategy systems over multiple problem-solving trials, each of which was viewed as a *strategy projection*, in analogy with diSessa and Wagner's (2005) idea of concept projection.

Chapters in the current volume further develop coordination class theory towards understanding multiple processes of learning through social interaction (Danish, Enyedy, & Parnafes, this volume; Levin & diSessa, this volume).

## The Future of Knowledge Analysis

Where should knowledge analysis go in the future? What are the most important challenges? In describing the landscape of current knowledge analysis work, we gave a sense of current trends in KA research. To some extent, we anticipate the near future by extrapolating these trends. We can expect, for example, that KA research will be expanded to more domains. We can also expect that the core knowledge types of p-prims and coordination classes will find new applications. Other existing knowledge types may well have similar paths of development, and new types will be identified. And we can expect more work on cross-cutting themes, such as analogy and transfer.

These trends reflect important work that remains to be done. But, as we conclude our overview of Knowledge Analysis, we want to do more than just extrapolate what has been done. We want to consider what fundamentally new steps will be required to take Knowledge Analysis to the next level and to address what we see as some of the current limitations in the program. What follows is a list of potentially very substantial and, in our view, interesting new work that remains to be done.

### *Methodological Refinement and Explicitness*

Earlier, we laid out a methodological characterization of Knowledge Analysis; we attempted to provide a sense of what KA looks like in practice. But our description was far from a recipe or complete description. A more refined and explicit characterization of the methodology behind KA would serve at least two aims. First, it could help more researchers engage in programs of Knowledge Analysis. Making complex methodologies explicit and teachable is important and a high bar for *any* research method. A second aim, while still difficult, presents a lower bar for success. More explicitness about methods would make it easier for

KA researchers to report on KA programs in publications and talks; one could merely refer to generic methods and their properties, rather than always having to describe them anew.

There are some small ways in which we could make progress on these aims. It would help if KA researchers simply find consensual and better ways of describing our methods. However, it would be better still if the community reached a shared understanding of the methodological standards to which we should all aspire. For example, consider coding, which, with a few exceptions, is uncommon in KA work. But, to what extent, and under what conditions is coding necessary to confirm qualitative data? If we do code data, to what standards of reliability should we hold ourselves? The nature of Knowledge Analysis – its commitment to capturing the complexity and individual nature of knowledge – makes it difficult to code data directly in terms of theoretical constructs. However, it is worth thinking about exactly where and how coding might help.

There are other, newer methodological avenues that might be profitable to explore. The new science of *learning analytics* is producing computational methods that use methods from machine learning to analyze data, including textual and verbal data. Sherin (2013) argues that these new methods might be a better fit to programs like Knowledge Analysis than more traditional social science methods. These methods have the benefit of being objective, in the sense that a well-defined and automated procedure leads from data to results. But they have the potential to do better in capturing richness and diversity in knowledge than standard statistical methods. For example, Sherin (2013) shows how these new methods can be automated to discover knowledge elements in transcripts of interview data and how such elements are applied over time as an interview unfolds.

## *KA and Human Language*

Any discussion of methodology must lead inevitably to a discussion of language. The relationship between KA and language has always been fraught. On the one hand, researchers in KA have emphasized that the knowledge we seek to capture will typically be very difficult for people to verbalize. In fact, the knowledge need not have any straightforward representation in language at all. On the other hand, spoken language is the primary source of our data, and we spend much of our time arguing over nuances of expression. For example, does "push" mean something that differs in important ways from "press"? Does "tilt" differ from "slant"?

Answering questions of this sort will require explicit attention to the relationships that exist between language and the sort of tacit knowledge that has typically been the focus of KA research. This will not be easy and, in our view, is largely uncharted ground. One might start by thinking in this way: Some element of tacit knowledge (e.g., a springiness p-prim) gets activated, and that p-prim is in turn linked to a specific word (e.g., "springy"). But such a story is too simple; at the least, it leaves out most of the important work: How might these links between highly tacit knowledge and words get made?

It might be difficult to explore these issues without encountering some of the thorny issues around the relationship between consciousness and tacit knowledge. We might imagine that, from the point of view of conscious thought, the activation of a springiness p-prim is associated with something like a "feeling of understanding." If that is the case, then we need a model of how these "feelings" get attached to the language through which we understand them.

What this makes clear, in our view, is that a one-way story, from tacit knowledge to words, is much too simple. Some cognitive linguists, such as George Lakoff (Lakoff & Johnson, 1980/2003) have argued that the structure of language itself is a kind of data about the ideas that we are capable of expressing. Strikingly, one cognitive linguist, Talmy (1988), working independently from diSessa, identified language structures that appear very similar to a certain class of p-prims. If we follow the work of the cognitive linguists to its logical extreme, we might conclude that (at least sometimes) the arrow (genesis, influence) points from language to tacit knowledge, rather than the reverse. If this is the case, then it might be that language contains, within itself, a specific range of ideas that humans can easily express.

We believe that, at least initially, the right stance to take is a theoretically neutral one. We should see linguistic knowledge and linguistically formulated ideas as one part of the larger knowledge systems that we study, with multifarious connections to other parts of the knowledge "soup." In this view, articulate knowledge is not a type of *readout* of a non-linguistic knowledge system. It is not special in that respect; it is just one part of the knowledge systems we study. However, it *is* special in that it is the part of the system that is particularly visible to us. The same could be said about other external representational systems, such as gestures and diagrams.

### *Culture and Interaction*

Just as our discussion of methodology led to language, our discussion of language must lead us to issues of culture and interaction. As we argued above, it inappropriately diminishes the role of language if we think of the activation of non-linguistic tacit knowledge as simply triggering a search for the right word to express it. When we put things into words, whole new modes of thinking become relevant, changing the nature of "the idea." At least initially, we should adopt a more neutral stance in which language is viewed as much as a driver and determinant of conceptualization as an expression of it; the outer world of language is one of the forces shaping our understanding of the world.

What is true of language is also true of the larger physical, cultural, and social world. Here we make contact with age-old questions of nature and nurture, questions that span many research endeavors in psychology and cognitive science. To see their relevance and importance for Knowledge Analysis, we can pose some questions for the specific case of the sense of mechanism, the knowledge system that comprises p-prims. For example, how much is the sense of mechanism sensitive to physical experiences that differ from one individual to another? Is the sense of mechanism of a blacksmith different from that of a lawyer? Similarly, how much is the sense of mechanism sensitive to differences that exist across cultures? Culture might impact the sense of mechanism by influencing the range and intensity of a person's physical experiences. Systematic differences in activities and activity contexts might have consequences (see Medin & Atran, 1999, concerning differential experience and cultural differences in intuitive biology). But there are other ways to think about the issues. As in our discussion of language above, we can adopt a more neutral view, in which knowledge of all sorts, including the sense of mechanism and culturally specific knowledge, is part of a larger interconnected system. The sense of mechanism will need to be adapted and tuned for the particular roles it plays within the system – roles which might differ substantially across cultures. The question is whether these roles differ enough that they result in a sense of mechanism that differs substantially across individuals and cultures.

Real-time interpersonal interaction seems an excellent locus for KA advancement specifically connected to the principal goals of this volume. Indeed, diSessa, Greeno, Michaels, and O'Connor (this volume) begin to explore these issues. Their chapter notes that some interaction (particularly when it is a professional skill or practice) is near-articulately cognized. It thus asks the KA question, "where is the boundary between articulate and non-cognized interaction, and how can we describe the knowledge*, particularly its contextuality, that guides it (p-prims that automatically instigate action)?"

## *Where and When Is Microgenesis?*

The discussion of culture and interaction above leads to the next step in our thoughts about the future of KA. Above, we wondered whether different physical and cultural experiences might cause the sense of mechanism to be "tuned" differently. But there remain questions of microgenesis: What do the earliest moments of the formation of tacit knowledge like p-prims look like? Does microgenesis happen in the moments when a child interacts with physical objects such as toy blocks? Is the knowledge somehow communicated from parent to child? Almost certainly, the correct story involves a complex combination of multiple forces, but the core questions here are unsettled.

## *Steps Toward Refined and Even Runnable Cognitive Models*

As researchers in KA, we have seen ourselves as unapologetic cognitivists focused on the development of cognitive models. The ideal end goal of this work would be *computational* models, described with enough specificity to be run on a computer.

To date, that goal has only been an ideal. However, the goal need not be as far away as it might seem. Humble theories do not need to be grand theories in order to be computational and runnable. With some cleverness, we might be able to build computational models that encompass limited subsets of knowledge, applied in focused tasks.

Even more complex models might not be as far off as they might seem. Researchers in artificial intelligence have had a long-term agenda of building systems with knowledge of the physical world. This includes knowledge that allows an artificial system to function in the physical world. But it also includes knowledge that allows the artificial system to construct explanations of the physical world, much as humans do (Friedman, Forbus, & Sherin, 2011a, 2011b) Although the aims of this research in AI are somewhat different from our own, building on that work would almost certainly give us a substantial head start on building computational models of the sort of knowledge we care about.

## Connection to Neuroscience

No one should deny that, in the end, neural activities in the brain (and elsewhere in the body) are a central substrate for thinking and learning. So, however we understand cognition, it will behoove us as scientists, eventually, to understand neural processes underlying it. Whether, at this stage, our understanding of the brain can seriously illuminate and extend what we already know from KA and other such methods, and vice versa, remains unclear. However, some brain research that seems close to KA concerns has already started (Schwartz, Blair, & Tsang, 2012).

KiP, in particular, begins to approach phenomena that might best be understood by including something like a neural level. For example, p-prims seem connected to particular modalities, such as sight and kinesthetics, that might reside in different parts of the brain from, for example, more conscious, deliberative, and possibly linguistic processes. It seems that experimentation here might be a near-term possibility. More deeply, questions such as how to understand plasticity and permanent changes of activation of p-prims might also be understood most perspicuously at a neural level (diSessa, 2014).

KA and KiP researchers might have special contributions to make in bridging to neural research. Because of the special care taken by the community to use as much data as possible from thinking to triangulate on the nature of ideas, our models might have more to say to the neural research community, and vice versa, than other approaches. Alternatively, researchers having, for example, misconceptionist orientations may "colonize" neural results by infusing them with ready, but perhaps empirically insufficient, interpretations (Stavy, Goel, Critchley, & Dolan, 2006).

Finally, it is worth remembering that "implementing runnable models of cognition" does not assume any particular modeling language. In addition to symbolic computation, connectionist models – inspired by basic neural characteristics and processes, such as parallel processing and activation pathways – might be most suitable for some types of knowledge★, and hence bring brain science and KA closer together.

## Appendix: Coordination Class Revised Terminology 2014

### Problems and Opportunities

Coordination class terminology has meandered a bit through the years, and some early choices appear to have been counterintuitive, causing unnecessary confusion. For example, the term "readout" originally referred only to the perceptually proximal part of the process of determining concept-characteristic information. However, many people instinctively (and sensibly) referred to the overall process of determining as "readout." The term "strategy" was also appended to "readout," even though many "readout strategies" are instinctive and automatic – hardly strategic in any reflective sense. Finally, the original term for the family of inferences leading to final determination was "causal net." "Causal" is appropriate in some instances, although mainly in science (physics). "Causal" does not capture the full generality of inferencing, particularly for mathematical coordination classes.

With that background, we here propose a revised terminology, as follows. New terms are in bold; old terms are in italic.

> **Extraction** refers to the perceptually proximal first stage of the overall **readout**. **Extraction** replaces the older term *readout strategies*. One can optionally use **extraction strategies** to emphasize that there might be (or is, in some cases) a strategic character to the **extraction**.
> **Readout** refers to the whole chain of processing, from **extraction** to final determining of the concept-characteristic information. As with **extraction**, one can optionally use **readout strategy** to emphasize that there is or might be a strategic character to the process. The actual result of **readout** can also be referred to as the **readout** (as is natural in English, even if it is ambiguous). To be more precise, one can emphasize the distinction between process and result by using **readout process** and **readout result**.
> **Inferential net** refers to the full knowledge base underlying the coordination class. It includes, notably, (a) the set of all possible inferences for **readouts**, (b) the knowledge that provides a sense of relevance for **extractions**, and (c) that which manages attention during extraction.
> **Concept projection** refers to the collective of parts of the full coordination class that are active in a particular **readout**. The term may also be helpful to refer to a sub-part of the full coordination class that covers a reasonably well-defined class of situations.

Other basic terms, including **span** and **alignment**, remain unchanged.

## Notes

1. For example, the roots of coordination class theory, discussed below, lay in criticism of Newell and Simon's "physical symbol systems hypotheses." See diSessa (1991).
2. By "natural" we do not mean "pure" and free from context or interaction. We mean uncoerced and sensible-feeling.
3. This chapter uses the revised coordination class terminology, as described in the Appendix.
4. Since it seems a common misinterpretation of coordination classes, we note explicitly that they are not normative in a reductive sense. First, analysis of how students coordinate often or always reveals functions, both positive and negative, for naive knowledge like p-prims. Specific types of limits of span and alignment are also anticipated in the model. In addition, the model leaves open very substantial differences in even experts' particular ways of coordinating, while still achieving common ground in terms of determining the same concept parameters in most common cases.
5. Arguably, the idea of facets was historically developed somewhat independently of KiP, but the frameworks were taken up immediately as synergistic and mutually informative.
6. Identifying mid-level "mechanisms of learning" has received increased interest in recent years within the KiP community, whether connected to coordination classes, per se, or not. In addition to Parnafes' work, see Izsák (2000) and diSessa (2014).

## References

Adiredja, A. (2014). *Leveraging students' intuitive knowledge about the formal definition of a limit.* (Unpublished doctoral dissertation). University of California, Berkeley.

Anderson, J. R. (1987). Skill acquisition: Compilation of weak-method problem situations. *Psychological Review,* 94(2), 192–210.

Barsalou, L. W. (1999). Perceptions of perceptual symbols. *Behavioral and Brain Sciences,* 22(04), 637–660.

Barth-Cohen, L. A. (2012). *The role of prior knowledge and problem contexts in students' explanations of complex systems.* (Unpublished doctoral dissertation). University of California, Berkeley.

Brown, N. J. S. (2009). *Information performances and illative sequences: Sequential organization of explanations of chemical phase equilibrium.* (Unpublished doctoral dissertation). University of California, Berkeley.

Carey, S. (1985). *Conceptual change in childhood.* Cambridge, MA: MIT Press, Bradford Books.

Carey, S. (2009). *The origins of concepts.* Oxford, UK: Oxford University Press.

Chi, M. T. H. (1992). Conceptual change across ontological categories: Examples from learning and discovery in science. In F. Giere (Ed.), *Cognitive models of science: Minnesota studies in the philosophy of science* (pp. 129–160). Minneapolis, MN: University of Minnesota Press.

Chi, M. T. H. (1997). Quantifying qualitative analyses of verbal data: A practical guide. *Journal of the Learning Sciences,* 6(3), 271–315.

Chi, M. T. H. (2013). Two kinds and four sub-types of misconceived knowledge, ways to change it, and the learning outcomes. In S. Vosniadou (Ed.), *Handbook of conceptual change research* (2nd ed., pp. 49–70). New York: Routledge.

Clark, D. B. (2006). Longitudinal conceptual change in students' understanding of thermal equilibrium: An examination of the process of conceptual restructuring. *Cognition and Instruction,* 24, 467–563.

Clark, D. B., D'Angelo, C. M., & Schleigh, S. P. (2011). Comparison of students' knowledge structure coherence and understanding of force in the Philippines, Turkey, China, Mexico, and the United States. *Journal of the Learning Sciences*, 20(2), 207–261. doi:10.1 080/10508406.2010.508028

de Kleer, J. (1986). Qualitative physics. In S. C. Shapiro (Ed.), *Encyclopedia of artificial intelligence* (pp. 1149–1159). New York: John Wiley.

diSessa, A. A. (1983). Phenomenology and the evolution of intuition. In D. Gentner & A. Stevens (Eds.), *Mental models* (pp. 15–33). Hillsdale, NJ: Lawrence Erlbaum.

diSessa, A. A. (1988). Knowledge in pieces. In G. Forman & P. Pufall (Eds.), *Constructivism in the computer age* (pp. 49–70). Hillsdale, NJ: Lawrence Erlbaum.

diSessa, A. A. (1991). Epistemological micromodels: The case of coordination and quantities. In J. Montangero & A. Tryphon (Eds.), *Psychologie génétique et sciences cognitives* (pp. 169–194). (Volume from the Eleventh Advanced Course.) Geneva, CH: Archives Jean Piaget.

diSessa, A. A. (1993). Toward an epistemology of physics. *Cognition and Instruction*, 10(2–3), 105–225; Responses to commentary, 261–280.

diSessa, A. A. (1996). What do "just plain folk" know about physics? In D. R. Olson & N. Torrance (Eds.), *The handbook of education and human development: New models of learning, teaching, and schooling* (pp. 709–730). Oxford, UK: Blackwell.

diSessa, A. A. (2004). Contextuality and coordination in conceptual change. In E. Redish & M. Vicentini (Eds.), *Proceedings of the International School of Physics "Enrico Fermi": Research on physics education* (pp. 137–156). Amsterdam, NL: ISO Press/Italian Physics Society.

diSessa, A. A. (2014). The construction of causal schemes: Learning mechanisms at the knowledge level. *Cognitive Science*, 38(5), 795–850.

diSessa, A. A., & Cobb, P. (2004). Ontological innovation and the role of theory in design experiments. *Journal of the Learning Sciences*, 13(1), 77–103.

diSessa, A. A., & Sherin, B. (1998). What changes in conceptual change? *International Journal of Science Education*, 20(10), 1155–1191.

diSessa, A. A., & Wagner, J. F. (2005). What coordination has to say about transfer. In J. Mestre (Ed.), *Transfer of learning from a modern multi-disciplinary perspective* (pp. 121–154). Greenwich, CT: Information Age Publishing.

Duncan, R. G. (2007). The role of domain-specific knowledge in generative reasoning about complicated multileveled phenomena. *Cognition and Instruction*, 25(4), 271–336.

Frank, B. W., & Scherr, R. E. (2012). Interactional processes for stabilizing conceptual coherences in physics. *Physical Review Special Topics-Physics Education Research*, 8(2), 020101.

Forbus, K. (1984). Qualitative process theory. *Artificial Intelligence*, 24(1–3), 85–68.

Friedman, S. E., Forbus, K. D., & Sherin, B. (2011a). Constructing and revising commonsense science explanations: A metareasoning approach. In *Proceedings of the AAAI Fall Symposium on Advances in Cognitive Systems*. Arlington, VA: AAAI Press.

Friedman, S. E., Forbus, K. D., & Sherin, B. (2011b). How do the seasons change? Creating and revising explanations via model formulation and metareasoning. In *Proceedings of the 25th International Workshop on Qualitative Reasoning*. Barcelona, Spain.

Gentner, D., & Stevens, A. (1983). *Mental models*. Hillsdale, NJ: Lawrence Erlbaum Associates.

Glaser, B. G., & Strauss, A. L. (1967). *The discovery of grounded theory: Strategies for qualitative research*. Chicago, IL: Aldine.

Gopnik, A. (2003). The theory theory as an alternative to the innateness hypothesis. In L. Antony and N. Hornstein (Eds.), *Chomsky and his critics* (pp. 238–254). Oxford, UK: Blackwell.

Greeno, J. G. (1998). The situativity of knowing, learning, and research. *American Psychologist*, 53(1), 5–26.
Gupta, A., Hammer, D., & Redish, E. F. (2010). The case for dynamic models of learners' ontologies in physics. *Journal of the Learning Sciences*, 19(3), 285–321.
Hammer, D. (1994). Epistemological beliefs in introductory physics. *Cognition and Instruction*, 12(2), 151–183.
Hammer, D. (2000). Student resources for learning introductory physics. *American Journal of Physics, Physics Education Research Supplement*, 68(S1), S52–S59.
Hammer, D., & Elby, A. (2002). On the form of a personal epistemology. In B. K. Hofer & P. R. Pintrich (Eds.), *Personal epistemology: The psychology of beliefs about knowledge and knowing* (pp. 169–190). Mahwah, NJ: Lawrence Erlbaum.
Hoyles, C., Bakker, A., Kent, P., & Noss, R. (2007). Attributing meanings to representations of data: The case of statistical process control. *Mathematical Thinking and Learning*, 9(4), 331–360.
Hutchins, E. (1995). *Cognition in the wild*. Cambridge, MA: MIT Press.
Hutchison, P., & Hammer, D. (2010). Attending to student epistemological framing in a science classroom. *Science Education*, 94(3), 506–524.
Inhelder, B., Cellerier, G., Ackermann, E., Blanchet, A., Boder, A., de Caprona, D., ... Saada-Robert, M. (Eds.) (1992). *Les cheminements de découverte chez l'enfant: Recherche sur les microgenèses cognitives*. Neuchatel, CH: Delachaux et Niestlé.
Izsák, A. (2000). Inscribing the winch: Mechanisms by which students develop knowledge structures for representing the physical world with algebra. *Journal of the Learning Sciences*, 9(1), 31–74.
Izsák, A. (2005). "You have to count the squares": Applying knowledge in pieces to learning rectangular area. *Journal of the Learning Sciences*, 14(3), 361–403.
Jeppsson, F., Haglund, J., Amin, T. G., & Strömdahl, H. (2013). Exploring the use of conceptual metaphors in solving problems on entropy. *Journal of the Learning Sciences*, 22(1), 70–120.
Jones, S. R. (2013). Understanding the integral: Students' symbolic forms. *The Journal of Mathematical Behavior*, 32(2), 122–141.
Kapon, S., & diSessa, A. A. (2012). Reasoning through instructional analogies. *Cognition and Instruction*, 30(3), 261–310.
Kapon, S., Ron, G., Hershkowitz, R., & Dreyfus, T. (2014). Perceiving permutations as distinct outcomes: The accommodation of a complex knowledge system. *Educational Studies in Mathematics*, 1–22.
Kuo, E., Hull, M. M., Gupta, A., & Elby, A. (2013). How students blend conceptual and formal mathematical reasoning in solving physics problems. *Science Education*, 97(1), 32–57.
Lakoff, G., & Johnson, M. (1980/2003). *Metaphors we live by*. Chicago, IL: University of Chicago Press.
Lakoff, G., & Rafael Núñez, R. (2000). *Where mathematics comes from*. New York: Basic Books.
Lave, J. (1988). *Cognition in practice: Mind, mathematics and culture in everyday life*. Cambridge, UK: Cambridge University Press.
Lave, J. (1991). *Situated learning: Legitimate peripheral participation*. Cambridge, UK: Cambridge University Press.
Levin (Campbell), M. E. (2012). *Modeling the co-development of strategic and conceptual knowledge during mathematical problem solving*. (Unpublished doctoral dissertation). Berkeley, CA: University of California, Berkeley.

Levrini, O., & diSessa, A. A. (2008). How students learn from multiple contexts and definitions: Proper time as a coordination class. *Physical Review Special Topics: Physics Education Research*, 4, 010107.

Lewis, C. (2012). *Applications of out-of-domain knowledge in students' reasoning about computer program state.* (Unpublished doctoral dissertation). Berkeley, CA: University of California, Berkeley.

Ly, U. A. (2011). *The nature and variability of children's alternative conceptions of evolution.* (Unpublished doctoral dissertation). Berkeley, CA: University of California, Berkeley.

McCloskey, M. (1983). Naive theories of motion. In D. Gentner & A. Stevens (Eds.), *Mental models* (pp. 299–323). Hillsdale, NJ: Lawrence Erlbaum Associates.

Martin, T., & Sherin, B. (2013). Learning analytics and computational techniques for detecting and evaluating patterns in learning: An introduction to the special issue. *Journal of the Learning Sciences*, 22(4), 511–520.

Masson, S., & Legendre, M. F. (2008). Effects of using historical microworlds on conceptual change: A p-prim analysis. *International Journal of Environmental and Science Education*, 3(3), 115–130.

Medin, D., & Atran, S. (1999). *The native mind and the cultural construction of nature.* Cambridge, MA: MIT Press.

Minsky, M. (1986). *The society of mind.* New York: Simon & Schuster.

Minstrell, J. (1989). Teaching science for understanding. In L. B. Resnick & L. E. Klopfer (Eds.), *Toward the thinking curriculum: Current cognitive research* (pp. 129–149). Alexandria, VA: Association for Supervision and Curriculum Development.

Newell, A. (1980). Physical symbol systems. *Cognitive Science*, 4, 135–183.

Newell, A., & Simon, H. A. (1972). *Human problem solving.* Englewood Cliffs, NJ: Prentice Hall.

Noss, R., & Hoyles, C. (1996). *Windows on mathematical meanings: Learning cultures and computers.* Dordrecht, NL: Kluwer.

Noss, R., Hoyles, C., & Pozzi, S., 2002. Abstraction in expertise: A study of nurses' conceptions of concentration. *Journal for Research in Mathematics Education*, 33(3), 204–229.

Paparistodemou, E., Noss, R., & Pratt, D. (2008). The interplay between fairness and randomness in a spatial computer game. *International Journal of Computers for Mathematical Learning*, 13(2), 89–110.

Parnafes, O. (2007). What does fast mean? Understanding the physical world through representations. *Journal of the Learning Sciences*, 16, 415–450.

Parnafes, O. (2012). Developing explanations and developing understanding: Students explain the phases of the Moon using visual representations. *Cognition and Instruction*, 30(4), 359–403.

Parnafes, O., & diSessa, A. A. (2013). Microgenetic learning analysis: A methodology for studying knowledge in transition. *Human Development*, 56, 5–37.

Philip, T. M. (2011). An "ideology in pieces" approach to studying change in teachers' sense-making about race, racism and racial justice. *Cognition and Instruction*, 29(3), 297–329.

Piaget, J. (1972). *The principles of genetic epistemology* (W. Mays, Trans.). New York: Basic Books. (Original work published 1970.)

Pratt, D., & Noss, R. (2002). The microevolution of mathematical knowledge: The case of randomness. *Journal of the Learning Sciences*, 11(4), 455–488.

Prodromou, T., & Pratt, D. (2006). The role of causality in the coordination of two perspectives on distribution within a virtual simulation, *Statistics Education Research Journal*, 5(2), 69–88.

Prodromou, T., & Pratt, D. (2013). Making sense of stochastic variation and causality in a virtual environment. *Technology, Knowledge and Learning*, 18(3), 121–147.

Sacristan, A., & Noss, R. (2008). Computational Construction as a means to coordinate representations of infinity. *International Journal of Computers for Mathematical Learning*, 13(1), 47–70.

Sayre, E. C., & Wittmann, M. C. (2008). Plasticity of intermediate mechanics students' coordinate system choice. *Physical Review Special Topics-Physics Education Research*, 4(2), 020105.

Schwartz, D. L., Blair, K. P., & Tsang, J. M. (2012). How to build educational neuroscience: Two approaches with concrete instances. *British Journal of Educational Psychology Monograph Series II*, 8, 9–27.

Sherin, B. L. (2001). How students understand physics equations. *Cognition and Instruction*, 19(4), 479–541.

Sherin, B. L. (2006). Common sense clarified: The role of intuitive knowledge in physics problem solving. *Journal of research in science teaching*, 43(6), 535–555.

Sherin, B. L. (2013). A computational study of commonsense science: An exploration in the automated analysis of clinical interview data. *Journal of the Learning Sciences*, 22(4), 600–638.

Sherin, B. L., Krakowski, M., & Lee, V. R. (2012). Some assembly required: How scientific explanations are constructed during clinical interviews. *Journal of Research in Science Teaching*, 49(2), 166–198.

Smith, J. P. (1995). Competent reasoning with rational numbers. *Cognition and Instruction*, 13, 3–50.

Smith, J. P., diSessa, A. A., & Roschelle, J. (1993). Misconceptions reconceived: A constructivist analysis of knowledge in transition. *Journal of the Learning Sciences*, 3(2), 115–163.

Southerland, S. A., Abrams, E., Cummins, C. L., & Anzelmo, J. (2001). Understanding students' explanations of biological phenomena: Conceptual frameworks or p-prims? *Science Education*, 85, 328–348.

Stavy, R., Goel, V., Critchley, H., & Dolan, R. (2006). Intuitive interference in quantitative reasoning. *Brain Research*, 1073–1074, 383–388.

Suchman, L. (1987). *Plans and situated actions: The problem of human-machine communication*. New York: Cambridge University Press.

Suchman, L. (1993). Response to Vera and Simon's situated action: A symbolic interpretation. *Cognitive Science*, 17(1), 71–75.

Taber, K. S., & García-Franco, A. (2010). Learning processes in chemistry: Drawing upon cognitive resources to learn about the particulate structure of matter. *Journal of the Learning Sciences*, 19, 99–142.

Talmy, L. (1988). Force dynamics in language. *Cognitive Science*, 12, 49–100.

Thaden-Koch, T. (2003). *A coordination class analysis of college students' judgments about animated motion*. (Unpublished doctoral dissertation). Lincoln, NE: University of Nebraska, Lincoln.

Thaden-Koch, T., Mestre, J., Dufresne, R., Gerace, W., & Leonard, W. (2005). When transfer fails: Effect of knowledge, expectations and observations on transfer in physics. In J. Mestre (Ed.), *Transfer of learning: Research and perspectives*. Greenwich, CT: Information Age Publishing.

Varela, F. J., Rosch, E., & Thompson, E. (1992). *The embodied mind: Cognitive science and human experience*. Cambridge, MA: MIT Press.

Vosniadou, S. (2013). Conceptual change in learning and instruction: The framework theory approach. In S. Vosniadou (Ed.), *International handbook of research on conceptual change* (2nd ed., pp. 11–30). New York: Routledge.

Vosniadou, S., & Brewer, W. F. (1992). Mental models of the earth: A study of conceptual change in childhood. *Cognitive Psychology*, 24, 535–585.

Wagner, J. F. (2006). Transfer in pieces. *Cognition and Instruction*, 24(1), 1–71.

Wagner, J. F. (2010). A transfer-in-pieces consideration of the perception of structure in the transfer of learning. *Journal of the Learning Sciences*, 19(4), 443–479.

Wittmann, M. C. (2002). The object coordination class applied to wave pulses: Analyzing student reasoning in wave physics. *International Journal of Science Education*, 24(1), 97–118.

White, P. A. (2000). Naive analysis of food web dynamics: A study of causal judgment about complex physical systems. *Cognitive Science*, 24(4), 605–650.

# 3
# INTERACTION ANALYSIS APPROACHES TO KNOWLEDGE IN USE

*Rogers Hall and Reed Stevens*

A great deal of video has been recorded and analyzed in learning sciences research since the publication of Jordan & Henderson (1995), which remains one of the most frequently cited articles on methods (or any other topic) in *Journal of the Learning Sciences*. That article brought Interaction Analysis (IA) to the attention of our field, but the policies and methods proposed had been under continuous development since at least the early 1950s. Current uses of IA by learning sciences researchers draw unevenly from these earlier developments. We revisit some of that history here, particularly as a frame for studies of knowledge in use, something that is an ongoing program of research and not just a collection of methods. We then identify new opportunities and problems in developing methods for IA that have a bearing on what counts as knowledge.

The first part of our chapter focuses on assumptions about the character of knowing and learning, as these are observable in interactions shaped by what people find relevant in activity. In most research situations in our field, members' relevancies are also related in complex ways to the deliberate and hopeful designs of learning sciences researchers. We argue that these relations should always be part of Interaction Analysis of knowledge in use, particularly those that involve design. While this creates new challenges for analysts, the effort is both productive and necessary for developing new methods and advancing our understanding of knowing and learning.

### Points of Departure: From "Natural History" to an "Outdoor Psychology" of Knowledge in Use

For many readers of this volume, IA will be understood as a method, not as an approach to analysis of knowledge in use. Framing IA as an approach to the study of knowledge in use involves, from our perspective, two orienting maneuvers.

In the first move, we recommend looking for knowledge in use in the ongoing activities of people who are engaged in those activities in ways that are adequate for their own practical purposes. This is not the same as studying "experts," if we mean by "expertise" what highly educated people do when asked to solve typical school problems (e.g., the odd-numbered problems in a chapter on polynomial functions in an introductory algebra text). As an alternative, we recommend studying people who are engaging with conceptual practices (e.g., algebraic description and modeling) to get something done, accountably to their own satisfaction and to the organizational requirements of their work (e.g., two civil engineers modeling the amount of dirt to be "cut" or "filled" to design usable roadways for a multi-million-dollar residential development; see Hall & Stevens, 1995; Stevens & Hall, 1998). Learning to participate in knowledge in use is also something that can be studied when taking this first move, as learning is also an activity shaped by what members or participants take to be relevant for their practical activity (Stevens, 2010).

This first move has a number of rich historical precedents. One is the close study of communicative activity in a psychotherapeutic interview,[1] undertaken by an interdisciplinary team of linguists, anthropologists, and psychiatrists – the Natural History of an Interview (NHI) Project (Bateson, 1971; Hall, Nemirovsky, Ma, & Kelton, this volume; Leeds-Hurwitz, 2005). This early effort at what would today be called multimodal Interaction Analysis (e.g., Streeck, Goodwin, & LeBaron, 2011) deeply shaped the fields of communication studies, conversation analysis, and varied approaches to discourse analysis. For NHI analysts, there was a basic commitment to discovery within the details of naturally occurring activity:

> We start from a particular interview on a particular day between two identified persons in the presence of a child, a camera and a cameraman. Our primary data are the multitudinous details of vocal and bodily action recorded on this film. We call our treatment of such data a "natural history" because a minimum of theory guided the collection of the data.
> 
> *(Bateson, 1971, p. 6)*

The "natural history" approach was not intended to be theory-free, any more than was the development of grounded theory (Glaser & Strauss, 1969; see their discussion of theoretical sensitivity and sampling in Chapters II and III). Rather, the idea was to take scenes from social life, capture the ways participants typically went about enacting those scenes, and use these records as material for making discoveries about interaction, learning, and other phenomena.

> The natural history approach proposed the detailed description of whatever could be observed in an interaction. Since what was sought for was

> an understanding of the natural orderliness of interaction, observations must be made in terms of what there is to be observed, not in terms of pre-established category systems. To decide what will be measured and counted before this is done will prevent the very understanding that is sought.
>
> *(Kendon, 1990, p. 20)*

The sense of "natural history" used in the NHI Project also hinged on the idea that "specimens" of human communication could be captured with enough detail to support close analysis from multiple theoretical points of view. A collection of such specimens could provide a repository (a corpus) for independent lines of analysis as well as for collaborative theory building. Then as now, new technologies for recording human interaction open up new possibilities for discovery, as we consider later in this chapter.

> If we take the point of view that all aspects of observable behavior can play a role in communication ... and if we recognize that how participants interpret each other's flow of action depends upon how the various aspects of action are patterned in relation to one another, it is natural that we should require as full a description as possible of the behavior that can be observed in an interaction. This, it will be clear, can only be achieved if we have *specimens* of interaction available to us for study.... [T]he camera can be used to create specimens of interaction that do make possible the discovery of facts about behavioral organization which cannot be done by other means.... [A]ny photographic or cinematographic shot always contains far more information than can possibly be foreseen – at least if it is shot of the uncontrived world of daily life – and it provides, thus, a genuine "field" for exploration within which real discoveries can be made about what happened out in the world when the shutter was open.
>
> *(Kendon, 1990, pp. 29–31, italics in original)*

This is important for understanding the roots of Interaction Analysis, but it is also relevant to papers in this volume in two additional ways. First, when specimens are gathered and analyzed in this way, they provide a type of "boundary object" (Star & Griesemer, 1989) that may be powerful for discovery and is common in scientific practice. Specimens in the repository (objects) are captured and indexed (one could also say, conserved or curated) in a way that maintains their identity through time and across distant uses. This is important, of course, because specimens can be used in dramatically different ways (e.g., film or video recordings can be played back, repeatedly, to recover and analyze different modalities of talk and embodied action). This requires that specimens are captured and their conservation accomplished in a way that preserves details that might make a difference for analyses framed in different theoretical ways (i.e., different local uses for a durable collection of specimens, when the repository is seen as a boundary object). This possibility for a repository of specimens, particularly used as a means of discovery, is captured nicely by Griesemer (1990):

> "Remnant models,"[2] i.e., material models made from parts of the objects of interest ... are robust to some changes of theoretical perspective because they are literally embodiments of phenomena. If these embodiments are preserved, they may be studied again and again under different perspectives.... Changes of theoretical perspective about the nature of species can be taken into account by pulling the specimens back out of the drawers or off the shelves and reanalyzing the model in terms of a different set of taxonomic designations.
>
> *(pp. 80–82)*

This "natural history" perspective on a repository of specimens identified the NHI Project as one of the first examples of what we would now call "multiple analysis projects" (Derry et al., 2010; Grimshaw, 1994; see Koschmann, 2011, for a recent and lively effort). The core idea is that with an adequately conserved repository (e.g., indexed using standard forms, made accessible to a group of investigators with diverse theoretical commitments), it may be possible to compare different or competing theoretical treatments of social life (including activities of learning and teaching) using the "same" collection of specimens. While this may be attractive in principle, Hall (2011) notes that these kinds of projects are often fraught with difficulties – capture and conservation of specimens is selective in ways that always involve theory (Hall, 2000; Ochs, 1979), and latecoming contextual information can call seemingly stable findings into question.

Our second move in framing Interaction Analysis of knowledge in use concerns how we might go about locating and studying knowledge in the practical activities of people engaged together, accountably, in social and technical practices that make up what are usually called "disciplines" (e.g., the disciplines of academic mathematics, civil engineering, or museum curating all involve "learning to see" (Stevens & Hall, 1998) in distinctive ways). To say that someone who proves theorems or designs roadways is a capable member of a "discipline" hides more than it reveals. But how can we go about looking behind these conveniences of classification to find knowledge in use through Interaction Analysis?

Here again, there are rich historical precedents to help theorize knowledge in use and how it is organized as an interactional achievement. A first step is to recognize knowledge in use as a social activity or practice, something that people are doing in diverse settings and with consequences (for themselves and others) that far outstrip the walls of a laboratory or a classroom:

> It is a matter of conceiving of cognition, emotion, motivation, perception, imagination, memory ... whatever, as themselves, and directly, social affairs. How precisely to accomplish this, how to analyze symbol use as social action and write thereby an *outdoor psychology* is, of course, an

> exceedingly difficult business.... [It requires] regarding the community as the shop in which thoughts are constructed and deconstructed, history the terrain they seize and surrender, and to attend therefore to such muscular matters as the representation of authority, the marking of boundaries, the rhetoric of persuasion, the expression of commitment, and the registering of dissent.
>
> *(Geertz, 1983, p. 153, italics added)*

The project of creating such a program of studies – an "outdoor psychology" populated with social and technical practices that are changing even as people learn to participate in them – requires that we leave our offices to go see what people are doing in settings where their disciplinary understandings involve or even produce both subjects and matter (i.e., deliberately reworking a view of disciplinary knowledge as already out there, a normatively specified subject matter). The direction in which Geertz was pointing was not lost on two monographs that, we argue, have given a great deal of shape to our field. In the first, Lave (1988) took up a critical analysis of how mathematical knowledge in use in school assessments compared with what adult alumni of schools did in a variety of everyday contexts of quantitative reasoning. Her project embarked from exactly where Geertz left off:

> The problem is to invent what has recently been nicknamed "outdoor psychology" (Geertz, 1983). The book is an inquiry into conditions that would make this possible. The conclusion: that contemporary theorizing about social practice offers a means of exit from a theoretical perspective that depends upon a claustrophobic view of cognition from inside the laboratory and school. The project is a "social anthropology of cognition" rather than a "psychology" because there is reason to suspect that what we call cognition is in fact a complex social phenomenon.
>
> *(Lave, 1988, p. 1)*

In the second monograph, after weeks of tedious observation in the bowels of ship boiler rooms, Hutchins (1995) was released to invent a new approach to the distributed character of way finding on the navigation bridge of a U.S. Navy ship.

> I had been asked to write a book describing what is in cognitive anthropology for the rest of cognitive science. I began that project, but after I became disillusioned with my field I lost interest in it. The choice of naturally situated cognition as a topic came from my sense that it is what cognitive anthropology really should have been about but largely had not been. Clifford Geertz (1983) called for an "outdoor psychology," but cognitive anthropology was unable or unwilling to be that. The respondents may have

been exotic, but the methods of investigation were largely borrowed from the indoor techniques of psychology and linguistics. When cognitive and symbolic anthropology split off from social anthropology, in the mid-1950s, they left society and practice behind.

*(Hutchins, 1995, p. xii)*

In important ways, the learning sciences we pursue today would not have been possible without the "outdoor psychologies" of Lave and Hutchins.

## Interaction Analysis, Members' Relevance, and Methods

A basic commitment of an IA perspective is to an analysis of "in use," "in action," or "in practice." All of these phrasings index the idea that IA approaches to cognition and learning lean on a sense of "natural" events, as discussed in the previous section. Natural or "naturally occurring" is typically used to refer to events that the researcher has sought to capture without being a strong agent in the organization of those events. When we capture events in settings (e.g., classrooms, workplaces, museums, family homes) that are organized by and for the participants in those settings, we are working from this natural perspective.

A second basic commitment of an IA perspective is to a form of data capture that allows for close, repeated analysis and some accountability to allow for alternative interpretations of the data, either by publication to readers in the form of a transcript that accompanies an analysis or in the form of the actual recordings. Building off Sacks' (1995) original argument for using recordings, Atkinson and Heritage (1984) argued:

> [T]he use of recorded data serves as a control on the limitations and fallibilities of intuition and recollection; it exposes the observer to a wide range of interactional materials and circumstances and also provides some guarantee that analytic conclusions will not arise as artifacts of intuitive idiosyncrasy, selective attention or recollection or experimental design. The availability of a taped record enables repeated and detailed examination of particular events in interaction and hence greatly enhances the range and precision of the observations that can be made. The use of such materials has the additional advantage of providing hearers and, to a lesser extent, readers of research reports with direct access to the data about which analytic claims are being made, thereby making them available for public scrutiny in a way that further minimizes the influence of individual preconception.
> 
> *(p. 4)*

Once data of naturally occurring events are captured in recorded form, further commitments of an IA perspective involve how the data is analyzed. Perhaps the most basic answer to the "how" question is that data is analyzed *sequentially*, unfolding in time as *interaction*: as interaction among people and interaction between people and cultural artifacts (e.g., computers, cars, cookware). Nearly always, analysts prepare a transcript of recorded events that either follows an accepted standard (Jefferson, 2004) or is more selectively constructed to display relevant events in the interactional record (Ochs, 1979). Transcripts of human interaction are generally organized into speaking turns, since the turn organization of human interaction is one of the earliest basic findings in conversation analysis (Sacks, Schegloff, & Jefferson, 1974).

The issue of what to transcribe is an important one. One perspective comes from Jefferson (2004), who wrote:

> Why put all that stuff in? Well, as they say, because it's there. Of course there's a whole lot of stuff "there," i.e., in the tapes, and it doesn't all show up in my transcripts, so it's because it's there, plus I think it's interesting. Things like overlap, laughter, and "pronounciational particulars" (what others call "comic book" and/or stereotyped renderings), for example. My transcripts pay a lot of attention to those sorts of features. What good are they? I suppose that could be argued in principle, but it is also seems to me that one cannot know what one will find until one finds it.
>
> *(p. 15)*

Jefferson goes on to show, through analysis of transcripts, "some places where attention to such features turned out to be fruitful" (p. 15).

In practical work with recordings where transcripts are made, what typically happens is that analysts converge on recorded events of interest (relative to the research questions they are asking) and they work back and forth between evolving transcripts and the recordings (Pomerantz & Fehr, 1997). This poses the question of when to stop adding details to the transcript, and Jefferson (2004) provides an answer in two distinct registers: a *realist* answer that what is represented is "there" in the interaction, but also the *subjective* answer that she finds these details interesting. This is an honest admission, but we think there is perhaps a more principled way to address the "when to stop transcribing" question if we turn our attention to two of the core analytic commitments (i.e., interests) of IA work in conversation analysis: member relevance and procedural consequentiality (Schegloff, 1992).

Member relevance refers to the idea that an analysis of conduct must take, as its first line of work, questions like: What is going on for the different participants? To what are participants oriented? What is the working consensus in this interaction? How through their (varied, multimodal) actions are participants displaying and adjusting this mutually constructed orientation to an interaction (e.g., Erickson & Schultz, 1981/1997; McDermott, Gospodinoff, & Aron, 1978; Schegloff, 1992)? In conversation analysis, member relevance typically focuses on membership categories that can be shown to be relevant to a particular interaction (e.g., that a person is a "teenager"). The reason this is important, following an early insight by Sacks (1995), is that all people are potentially and legitimately categorized in many ways, but only some of these social categories can be shown to be relevant to events at hand. For example, I am a volunteer soccer coach but it would be hard to make that category relevant to my current activities ... though I just have. Procedural consequentiality is a further constraint on analysis, building on a prior establishment of relevance. It involves showing that an identity is "consequential for the trajectory of a stretch of talk, its content, its character, or for the procedures used to organize it" (Raymond & Heritage, 2006, p. 679).

In research on learning and development, avoiding extrinsic categories (e.g., teacher/student, expert/novice, motivated/unmotivated) and instead demonstrating their procedural consequentiality during moments of interaction can be a challenge (Hall, 1999). That someone is a teacher, for example, is sometimes relevant and sometimes not. In our approach to IA, people enact membership categories (Schegloff, 2007) by engaging in actions typically bound together with those categories (e.g., interactively producing a crisp initiation-response-evaluation sequence positions speakers as "teacher" and "students"), they bring forward topics or accounts of past-time activities as being in need of revision (e.g., what was good enough before will not be, here and now), and they use these accounts to orient towards future consequences of current activity. In short, people orient to their own learning in ways that show to each other (and make available for IA) a broader kind of "developmental consequentiality" (Hall, 1999, p. 190). An example showing both relevance and consequentiality in an analysis related to the knowledge and learning-centered themes of this volume can be found in Stevens (2010). Here Stevens examines an interaction involving two girls in a classroom. Neither has an official institutional designation as teacher and thereby neither would expect to take a reciprocal role as "learner" or "student" to a classmate. Yet that is precisely what happens in this classroom, which of course is occupied by an adult teacher. Stevens shows the relevance of these reciprocal roles between the girls in interaction, as they mutually position each other in these roles, beginning with a question from one student to the other about how to do something, a question that is met not with a "go ask the teacher" but an immediate demonstration. Stevens shows how these roles are sustained, thereby showing the relevance and consequentiality of "teacher" and "learner" over the course of the analyzed segment.

An IA analysis of member relevancies and consequentiality is achieved through the methods of sequential analysis. Once a recorded event is selected and transcribed to a level of sufficient detail, analysts move through the transcript turn by turn, seeking to see what one turn sets up for a subsequent turn and what those subsequent turns do with prior turns. Said in more familiar human terms, what one person does with the prior contribution of someone with whom they are interacting matters for what comes next. Moving through a transcript (and accompanying video or audio record) is how an analysis of an event gets built up as an analysis of what is going on for the participants in the interaction. If member relevance and developmental consequentiality provide constraints on analyzing interaction, they likewise suggest a constraint on when to stop adding detail to a transcript, i.e., when a transcript includes all the observable elements in a recorded event that can be shown to be relevant and consequential for the participants within that interaction.

## What Counts as Knowledge

Turning directly to one of the core constructs for this volume – knowledge – the issue of relevance and consequentiality can be framed in the following way. A typical social-scientific approach to knowledge analysis (in the broad sense, not the specific sense meant by authors in this volume, though it would include their approach) is to determine beforehand what counts as knowledge and then to devise a machinery to detect and capture it in human data (e.g., pre- and post-test, coding interview, or interactional data). What counts as knowledge might be framed in terms of concepts or skills or metacognition or p-prims, but in every case it is a pre-existing, specialized theoretical language that is largely or entirely indifferent to what participants in an interaction count as knowledge and how they handle it according to their own criteria (e.g., its reliability, durability, correctness, incorrectness). One of the primary values of an IA perspective on knowledge is that it provides an ongoing check on what is persistently a danger in the analysis of "others" (especially less powerful others), namely the production of deficit accounts of their knowledge. Attributing a lack of or faulty knowledge to someone from an "outside" perspective now can be juxtaposed to a consideration of whether the status of that apparent lack or faultiness has any meaning or relevance to the participants themselves.

Conducting an analysis of knowledge in use with the criteria of relevance and consequentiality may be especially useful for interactions involving more traditional research activities (i.e., not the sorts of natural events we are mostly interested in) in which the researcher takes a strong role in organizing and guiding events – like interviews and experiments. In these situations, certain aspects of interaction are clearly relevant to the researcher (e.g., math or physics knowledge), but it remains to be shown that they are relevant to the research participants. This is an important issue, because without establishing something like a mutual sense of relevance (e.g., that solving a problem with math or physics matters), researchers' inferences about knowledge that a participant has or does not have are equivocal. For example, if I were asked to solve a hard calculus problem, I could probably do it but my incentive for conjuring up that long distant school knowledge would be minimal. I might try for a bit, lose interest, and then stop without solving the problem. In such a situation, could an analyst say that I did not know? IA techniques furnish the means to differentiate between events in which some knowledge is demonstrably relevant to participants and those in which it is not, an issue that various chapters in this volume have explored (see Gupta, Elby, & Sawtelle, this volume).

In the first section of this chapter we presented a historical retelling of the formative "natural history of an interview," and in the second section, we explored some of the roots of the IA approach to knowledge in use within the history and commitments of conversation analysis and ethnomethodology. Education and learning have never been core concerns for studies in these traditions; it took other scholars to pick up these ideas and bring them into contact with education- and learning-related topics. Beginning in the late 1970s, a trio of scholars – Hugh Mehan, Ray McDermott, and Fred Erickson – undertook such an endeavor. Each of these scholars drew heavily on ethnomethodological ideas and conversation analytic techniques in a collection of related studies of classroom talk and social organization. For example, Mehan studied a common interactional structure of classroom talk, the initiation-response-evaluation (IRE) sequence, and showed how IRE sequences were used to ask "known-answer" questions (Mehan, 1979). McDermott (1977a) analyzed a reading lesson in a first-grade classroom to provide an exemplar of an "ethnographically adequate" account of these "concerted" activities among students and a teacher, showing in fine detail how the group moved through a series of "positionings" that were collaboratively accomplished and as a sequence produced what was mutually understood and enacted as the reading lesson. Among Erickson's (2004) classroom studies was one in which he analyzed a mixed-age classroom (composed of first graders and kindergartners) in which a teacher was asking known-answer questions to the cohort of children, showing how the students less familiar with the interactional organization of classroom talk routines (e.g., kindergartners) were susceptible to "turn sharks," "who watched for damage in other speakers' turns. When they saw blood in the water they would strike, taking the turn away from a speaker who had faltered or committed some error in appropriateness" (Erickson, 2004, p. 54–55).

Taken together, these studies established a critical point about knowledge in classrooms – that there were quite particular ways that knowledge could be displayed for it to count; as Erickson put it, contributions to classroom talk needed to be "informationally correct but socially correct as well" (Erickson 2004, p. 55). These studies also showed that when interaction is the medium for knowledge display, the available range of ways of displaying knowledge are often quite narrow and that these ways – or the opportunities to learn these ways – can be unevenly and unfairly distributed among students (Erickson, 2004; McDermott, 1977a). In sum, what these studies did was to show that appearing to "have knowledge" depended on the interactional context of its display.

## Comparative Analysis of Knowledge in Use

Another suggestive aspect of these studies is the use of comparison, a use that echoes Howard Becker's famous framing in "A School Is a Lousy Place to Learn Anything In" (1972), which argued that (a) schools might not be organized to perform their "characteristic function" (i.e., organizing learning) and that (b) other organizations of activities in contexts other than schools might perform this function more effectively. In these interactional studies, Erickson, McDermott, and Mehan compared the interactional arrangements of classrooms, and the affordances thereof, to those in which the students were otherwise engaged, like their homes. For example, Erickson's (2004) case of "turn sharking" revolves around a kindergartner named Angie, whose lack of familiarity with having to compete for turns in the competitive environment of a classroom lesson led her to participate in a number of what Erickson calls "inappropriate moments" (p. 66). Based on some visits to Angie's home, Erickson reports that Angie was an only child, who, in that home interactional context, did not need to compete for a turn at talk with other children (e.g., siblings) and could hold the floor easily (i.e., her parents did not "turn shark" her). While Angie eventually did adapt to the forms and timing of knowledge display in the classroom, Erickson reported on another child named Billy, who did not, and that this had consequences for his longer-term school career. McDermott (1977b) told a similar story about Rosa, a native Spanish speaker and first grader, who was seen by her teacher as an unreachable, failing reader. McDermott shows the value of an interactionally grounded ethnographic approach by showing that both Rosa and her teacher were behaving sensibly, though without what McDermott (1977b) calls "trusting relations" (p. 199) or a "working consensus" (McDermott, Gospodinoff & Aron, 1978, p. 268). The lack of trusting relations meant that the teacher and Rosa effectively and implicitly "conspired" in Rosa "not getting a turn to read." So Rosa "spends little time trying to read in the classroom; she will either learn to read at home or suffer school failure" (McDermott, 1977b, p. 204). Other similar comparisons highlighted the different interactional arrangements between classroom and home cultural interactional patterns. Both Erickson & Mohatt (1982) and Philips (1972) showed how classroom interactional practices, like singling out individual students to answer known-answer questions, were at odds with more cooperative and voluntary forms of adult–child communication "preferred" (in the conversation analytic sense) in Native American cultural contexts.

While this formative work used conversation analytic techniques to understand classroom interactional practices and therefore invited attention to the narrow conditions for knowledge display that counted, this work largely did not try to characterize *learning* itself (Gardner, 2013). The general point these studies made, for those looking for it, was to establish that all contexts present opportunities and constraints on what knowledge will count and who gets to count it (Stevens, 2000b); whether it be a teacher, a researcher, or other participants in the scene (e.g., Erickson's turn sharks, who knew they could interrupt faulty attempts to hold a turn in the classroom). In showing the narrowness of classroom interactional arrangements for the display of knowledge, suggestive comparisons from these foundational works in the 1970s began to invite attention to how other contexts might be organized in alternative ways for displaying a person's knowledge and, in fact, whether that knowledge should be properly treated as exclusively an individual's.

A dramatic example of how different contexts can be organized for a person to appear differentially knowledgeable is the case of Adam (McDermott, 1993; cf. Cole & Traupmann, 1981). McDermott studied video recordings of Adam, an eight-year-old boy institutionally labeled as learning disabled. These analyses compare what might be called the differential organization of Adam as observably knowledgeable (or not) for others and himself; the comparison involved four contexts of "Everyday Life, Cooking Club, Classroom Lessons, and Testing Sessions" (McDermott, 1993, p. 278). What the comparative analysis argues for is a strong alternative to the default assumption that knowledge (or lack thereof) should be understood to be the sole property of an individual, in this case a learning disabled child. Across the cases, the same child, Adam, appears in some of the contexts rather completely unknowledgeable and incapable (e.g., Testing Sessions) and in other contexts (e.g., Cooking Club, and Everyday Life) he gets along. Why the difference? Because the situations organized around him are differentially flexible and arbitrary in their task demands: the more flexible the environment for getting things done and the less arbitrary the tasks, the more capable and knowledgeable did Adam appear. Though McDermott is using a strategic case to make this relational point about knowledge in use by studying a learning disabled child, it is clear that the conceptual insight can generalize (Becker, 1990) to all contexts of knowledge display.

## *Disciplined and Disciplining Perception*

One paper did take on the question of learning directly using the techniques of Interaction Analysis (Stevens & Hall, 1998).[3] Since we have tried to give our text so far a historical as well as a conceptual basis, we will share some history of how this paper came into existence, what it was responding to, and why Interaction Analysis techniques were valuable in helping us understand the recorded events that were selected to form the two cases in the paper. Our investigations began with a shared principle of both cognitivist- and interactionist-oriented researchers using recordings – to "make sense" of the events available in the recordings. (That same principle animates all of the analyses in the current volume). Searching for ways to make sense of the video recordings, we began exploring conversation-analytic approaches. We found ourselves increasingly attending to *interactions as a primary unit*, between people (i.e., the tutor Bluma and Adam), and between Adam and Bluma's sensory modalities (i.e., looking, pointing, marking) and the various semiotic/representational materials in the environment. This represented a marked difference from the dominant focus at the time on internal cognitive processes, states, and forms.

These two key ideas about interaction animated the specific findings of the disciplined perception line of work. First, fine-grained attention to the materiality of the task and tool environment and the ways it was used by Adam brought into view what Stevens and Hall would call Adam's "grid calculus"; the grid calculus was a non-standard but locally productive way to solve some of the problems using a grid of dots that were in the task environment. This was similar to non-standard solution strategies Hall had found in his dissertation (Hall, 1990) and treated as "workarounds" (Gasser, 1986) to the demands of formal algebra instruction. This same grid of dots was of course visible to the tutor, but there was a sense that it was also invisible *for practical purposes* to the tutor, because she had other routine ways of solving the problems using linear equations. This was why, in the analysis of the recorded events, there was significant confusion in the interaction between the tutor and Adam, because her "disciplined eyes" could not quite see (at least initially) that he was using the grid of dots to solve the problems. Eventually she did come to realize this, and that was the second focus on interaction as an analytic unit in this study: the interactions between Adam and the tutor in which differences in practical action and understanding are shown to develop that are at first unseen, then recognized, then attended to explicitly in interaction. As the productive possibilities of the grid calculus "dawned" (cf. Wittgenstein on "the dawning of aspects," 1953) on the tutor Bluma, she sought, in a variety of ways, to "discipline" how Adam saw and used the semiotic resources in the environment. In the end, although this was an analysis of cognition, it was one that treated cognition as embodied and distributed, and decisively shaped through interaction, both interactions between people, and between people, tasks, and tools.

This project came to be embedded within a broader shared program of work, studying how mathematics was used "at work." Hall had studied algebraic problem solving for his dissertation and Stevens had taught mathematics in settings ranging from a school for adults, to a private high school, to a university; in all of these contexts, a common question from students was, "when are we ever going to use this"? Hall and Stevens decided to investigate this question directly, conducting initial fieldwork in a civil engineering firm. Engineers were among the professionals most commonly identified as those in need of high-level mathematics, but there were no studies at the time that detailed how mathematics was used by engineers (or other professionals) in their daily work. Based on the fieldwork, we undertook two comparative analyses; the first compared the engineering design case to the work of middle-school students doing architectural design in their project-based classroom experiences (Hall & Stevens, 1995) and the second compared the tutoring case from Stevens' prior work to the same engineering case (Stevens & Hall, 1998).

Disciplined perception is a concept grounded in close interaction analyses of video recordings of two pairs of people engaged in complex socio-technical practices.[4] As our recounting of the paper's history suggests, our interest in putting this concept into circulation was, in part, corrective, as theoretical work often is. At the time the paper was written and revised (between 1992 and 1998), prominent accounts of cognition and learning left out too much that mattered about how people learned and used knowledge together. These accounts were richly furnished with actants of the mind – schemas, concepts, sub-goals, productions, p-prims – but were anemic when it came to actants of the observable world – voices in conversation, computer screens, drawings, pointing fingers, moving hands, and noticing eyes. This focus on interaction had a basic Deweyan resonance, as written in *Art as Experience* (Dewey, 1934/2005): "The first great consideration is that life goes on in an environment, not merely in it, but because of it, through interaction with it" (p. 12). And because, informed by science and technology studies, we saw disciplinary practices as cultural practices, we sought a better account of how other people shape each other's practices and understandings through *disciplining perception*.

Borrowing techniques and principles from conversation analysis and ethnomethodology, we attended to observable actions and interactions, and, moreover, to what participants in interaction were noticing, seeing, using, and making matter to themselves and to each other. What we were studying after all were *their* interactions, and, however implicit, they themselves had their own understandings of them, which according to conversation analysis, they displayed to each other. As we described earlier, some of these understandings, both between Adam and Bluma and between the two engineers, were unaligned. That we refrained (for the most part) from looking past the observable actants (turns at talk, hands in motions, computer screens, drawings, gestures, pointing, etc.) into the world of mental actants that are so readily visible to many cognitive scientists was indeed our bias, but we held no epistemological or ontological stance (then, nor do we now) that rules out a parallel and integrated account, one that seeks to argue for durable interior resources we "acquire" and carry around with us that give shape to our actions. We do remain skeptical about how observable actants and actions can be *seen through* to provide a confident account of interior actants and processes, though many of the cases in this volume, by showing real attention to interaction, give us some of the liveliest examples in the literature.

Though we did not elaborate on how we would approach such an integrative account, it is worth exploring how we might do so. "Disciplined perception" used interaction analytic techniques and ideas from science and technologies and ethnomethodology, but it also closely aligned itself, especially in its use of the concept of coordination, with Hutchins' ideas of distributed cognition (Hutchins, 1995). Following Hutchins' heuristics (see below) would lead us, we believed, to discover how and when internal representations and processes do real work in contexts of knowledge in use and avoid the "overattribution" that Hutchins diagnoses in his critique of traditional cognitive science approaches (Hutchins, 1995).

> When one commits to the notion that all intelligence is inside the inside/outside boundary, one is forced to cram inside everything that is required to produce the observed behaviors. Much of cognitive science is an attribution problem.
>
> *(p. 355)*

In light of this attribution problem, Hutchins argues that we should first describe the representations that are observable in the analysis of any tasks. If the "propagation and transformation of representational state" (to use Hutchins' technical language) is not observable but happened, *then* it argues for positing internal knowledge entities or processes. For example, if I am asked for the square root of 121 and verbally produce an answer of "eleven," if "external" representational transformations are not observable – such as those involving the use of calculator, pen, or paper – this computation could be inferred as an internal process. In fact, in our disciplined perception cases, we implicitly attribute some "background knowledge" in both cases though we don't elaborate it. For example, in the tutoring case, we highlight Adam's "simple visual capacities" (Stevens & Hall, 1998, p. 115) as essential to his ability to deploy his grid calculus. Thus, our perspective may be like Occam's with respect to the attribution of functional internal representations (i.e., favoring parsimony), but it is by no means a principled or ideological objection. And therefore we consider it a fruitful exercise to revisit these cases in the disciplined perception analysis from the perspective of explicitly attributed internal "knowledge" (cf. Levin & diSessa, this volume).

The disciplined perception analyses (Stevens, 1999; Stevens & Hall, 1998) and others coming from the Math at Work project (Hall & Stevens, 1995; Hall, Stevens, & Torralba, 2002; Jurow, 2004; Stevens, 2000a, 2000b) employed comparison in an explicit sense, comparing the talk and embodied action of pairs or groups of people "in different contexts." For example, Stevens and Hall (1998) compared a tutoring interaction around recognizably school mathematics involving coordinate systems, graphs, and equations with interactions between two architects involving engineering-specific coordinate systems and conventional representational media of plans, sections, and profiles. These analyses also employed a less obvious form of comparison, in comparing and connecting non-contiguous events. The purpose of these comparisons was to provide accounts of learning that extend over time (see Hall [1999] on ways of following "developmental consequentiality"). While much of our work has involved comparative analysis, there are still serious methodological questions about how to make connections across non-contiguous events, a seemingly pervasive and largely ignored analytic issue.

Stevens (2010) identifies two distinct approaches to the analysis of learning – one endogenous and one exogenous. The exogenous approach dominates in formal contexts and in academic discourse, though arguably the endogenous approach dominates in almost all of the other contexts of human activity and learning, making it the primary learning phenomenon worth understanding. The conventional exogenous approach involves analysts or experts administering instruments or procedures (e.g., tests, surveys, interviews) at two (or more) points in time and using differences between (or among) performances by "subjects" to make claims for (or against) learning. An endogenous approach that treats "learning as a members' phenomenon" looks within and across events to understand how participants are initiating, managing, sustaining, and bringing to a close learning as a joint interactional achievement. Stevens' analysis showed how the techniques and principles of conversation analysis could be used to show learning endogenously when the datum is a contiguous event, but argued that there were real tensions with "pure" conversation-analytic approaches when an analysis seeks to connect non-contiguous events. Since not all learning happens only within contiguous short-term events (cf. Lemke, 2000), an endogenous approach to learning requires ways of connecting events without falling back into an exogenous approach. This elaboration is beyond the scope of the current chapter but can be found elsewhere (Stevens, 2001a, 2001b).

While much of our prior work has involved comparisons of related activity systems involving different people (e.g., middle-school students designing and professionals designing), more recent work has sought to use IA techniques to more directly explore knowledge in use questions about what psychologists called transfer (e.g., Gick & Holyoak, 1983) and what Lave called "continuity across contexts" (Lave, 1988). These ongoing studies of knowledge in use involve following the same people across contexts (Stevens, Wineburg, Herrenkohl, & Bell, 2005). These studies build on prior comparative work, such as McDermott's case study of Adam interacting with others in different contexts (McDermott, 1993), and other formative studies that highlight differences in what interactional arrangements are available for knowledge display. In this ongoing line of work (e.g., Keifert, 2012; Mehus, Stevens, & Grigholm, 2010, 2012), we have sought to explore both what counts as knowledge in different contexts (Stevens, 2000a; Stevens, O'Connor, Garrison, Jocuns, & Amos, 2008) and what interactional arrangements are in place for both learning and knowledge display (Stevens, Satwicz, & McCarthy, 2008). Not surprisingly, we have found stark differences in how social and material contexts afford ways of learning and opportunities for using and displaying knowledge. This may seem an obvious finding, though it has had little impact on the practical business of organizing formal or informal learning environments or on how we see people as knowledgeable (or not) across contexts.

We have so far discussed a range of ways that IA techniques have been combined with comparative analysis to explore knowledge in use. These include (a) comparisons of related activity systems involving different people learning and using knowledge, (b) comparisons of distinct, non-contiguous interactional events that can be analytically connected while still treating knowledge and learning as members' phenomena, and (c) comparing interactional events involving the same people across time and place to explore transfer-like questions. A newer (tacitly comparative) line of work involves using IA techniques to look at intersections between physical mobility and knowledge in use to study people literally in motion. While our work from the outset has been about forms of active movement and embodied practice (e.g., the very active hands and eyes in Stevens & Hall, 1998), these studies push us further to consider a sense of mobility that has always been with us but has been ignored, mobility that is increasingly visible due to the pervasiveness of mobile information and communication technologies (Taylor, Stevens, & Champion, 2014; Taylor, Takeuchi, & Stevens, in press). Actually, these mobilities have perhaps been understudied because recording technologies have not been up to the task of following them, but also certainly because of a bias toward studying forms of human activity that involve relatively still and boxed-up humans (Leander, Philips, & Taylor, 2010).

## Interaction Analysis, Mobility, and Studies of Knowledge in Use

For many of the things that people learn to do together, our understanding of their activity is advanced only indirectly and partially by making inferences about what an individual would need to know to participate in the activity. For some types of activity – e.g., navigating ships (Hutchins, 1995), achieving architectural designs (Stevens, 2000a), performing in team activities like a high-school marching band (Hall & Ma, 2011b), or riding bicycles as a group in an urban street grid (Taylor & Hall, 2013) – doing the activity and quite probably learning the activity would be impossible without careful attention to multiple bodies, multiple experiential modalities, and the structure of ongoing, mobile participation in ensemble performance. It is, of course, possible to see activities like mathematical modeling, engineering design, or scientific inquiry as multi-body ensemble performance and learning, but this has not been typical in our field.

A commitment to studying learning in intact activity systems recommends that we take this wider perspective on knowledge in use in efforts to integrate IA and KA. This is, of course, not entirely new. Reviewing the contribution of cultural and historical theories of mind to our understanding of how people (learners) participate in activity, Duranti (1997) notes:

> [T]hinking subjects do not just think, but they also move, build, touch, feel, and, above all, interact with other beings and material objects through both physical and semiotic activity. This perspective, which is often absent in North American cognitive psychology, is close to (and in some cases supported by) recent anthropological studies that treat culture as practices rather than simply patterns of thought.
>
> *(p. 282)*

Most research using IA to study knowledge in use and how it is learned focuses on talk and action (including use of technology) that is within reach of a stationary, often seated, group of interactional partners, typically within an enclosed space no larger than a classroom or laboratory. While early research in IA traditions has been described as limited by "talk bias" (Hak, 1999; Mondada, 2013), we could add to this "seat" and "container" bias (Leander, Phillips, & Taylor, 2010). Perhaps this is a result of philosophical traditions that treat knowledge as the contents of a (typically singular) mind that is carried around (only incidentally) by a body. With some notable exceptions (e.g., Ochs, Gonzales, & Jacoby, 1996, set hands and eyes in motion in an analysis of work by university physicists), there is still relatively little work that focuses on the modal engagements of the body in knowing and learning, much less on ways of knowing that involve or appear to require moving bodies (Hall & Nemirovsky, 2012).

Learning to participate in knowledge in use is often also "learning on the move" (Taylor, 2013), in the sense that the joint activities making up these practices regularly extend across settings (e.g., modeling architectural spaces on site and at the drafting table; see Murphy, 2005; Stevens, 2000a) or involve movement as part of the activity being learned (e.g., learning a part in a high-school marching band; see Hall & Ma, 2011b). Extending IA to study knowledge in use under these circumstances, something that we think is implied by the concept of "use" we are advancing, presents challenges and new opportunities.

## *We Have Always Been Mobile/We Have Never Been A-modal/A-mobile*

From an IA perspective on knowledge in use, mobility may be a broadly relevant but overlooked topic. In this section, we consider conceptual practices of scientific and engineering modeling, and in later sections, we describe studies of IA and mobility in a variety of quite different practices. What learning sciences researchers study as "models" rarely include people moving across sites, even though representational practices of modeling and the systems that support them (databases, graphs, tables, etc.) are predicated on (i.e., are about and enact) complex relations between activity in the world and symbols or marks on paper (Latour, 1990). Even if a modeler does not visit the world shown on paper (or a computer screen), representations in modeling are understood to be about that world. Latour (1999, pp. 68–73) describes this activity as "cycles of amplification and reduction" in a case study of soil scientists at work discovering the role that earthworms play in moving the boundary between forest and savanna ecosystems. Plants and dirt are collected, their qualities are coded by type and quantified, and these codes and numbers are arrayed in tables to show changes in soil over time and across space (i.e., soil and plants/animals are "reduced" but their qualities and quantity are "amplified" by coding for later assembly in tables and graphs). Representing or modeling required coordinated movements of people and material across settings, including: the field where samples were cut or excavated, restaurant tables over which samples were ordered and examined, university offices where papers were written, and still other offices where published papers – now in professional circulation – were read and ransacked to contest content claims and borrow methods. Though models (e.g., drawings, tables, and graphs) published in scientific articles appeared at the end of these active traversals, they were made and read as a demonstrable, reversible, and contestable relation between the world and marks on paper. In this sense, the epistemic practices of modelers – studied as working accomplishments of knowledge in use – have always been mobile.

Lots of people make and trade models for a living, of course. While discipline-specific modeling practices vary with the scale of what is modeled and what networks of modelers value, mobility across settings may be a critical and understudied aspect of how models are made and used. For example, when we set out to study uses of mathematics in design-oriented work (Hall, 1995; Hall & Jurow, in press; Hall, Stevens, & Torralba, 2002; Stevens, 2000a; Torralba, 2006), we faced the immediate problem of figuring out where that work took place and how to follow people (and material) across settings they assembled together in their modeling practices. This was made possible (both as a practical matter and in our imagination) by newly available consumer video recorders with image stabilization features and removable batteries, which allowed us to move with people within and across settings. We also took advantage of wireless microphones that enabled forms of audio sampling that were independent of the location of a moving camera.

For example, with truly separable L/R audio input to a camera or audio recorder, a collection of wireless microphones could be attached to people and places to sample conversation from different positions – both physical and personal – within unfolding activity. Figure 3.1 shows three toon strips[5] of civil engineers talking about roadways in hilly terrain. In the top panel, a senior engineer (Jake; see Levin & diSessa, this volume; Stevens & Hall, 1998) shows how to make a "profile" view of a roadway, and then, seconds later (bottom panel), he shows how to make a "section" view of the same roadway. In the center panel (recorded about an hour later), Jake finds and holds a place along an unusually steep roadway they have designed, then draws and talks through a design rationale that trades the cost of filling in dirt below the roadbed (sketch in rightmost image) against the larger cost of denuding the surrounding landscape.

By following these engineers across settings during their workday (a partial but informative sample of their activities), we learned several things about modeling in design work. First, design conversations typically waited for drawings (e.g., engineers were "rigging"[6] places for comparative analysis and talk; see de la Rocha, 1985). Second, the representational infrastructure of modeling (e.g., computer-aided drawings) amplified information about surfaces in the hilly terrain for volumetric soil calculations, but it simultaneously reduced information about landscape features that were important for a successful design (e.g., trees and other upslope vegetation in the surrounding terrain). Third, what Jake restored to the model (landscape features) in his design rationale suggested that he and (in a learning opportunity for) his junior partner Evan were thinking and acting simultaneously in the office and in the field; knowledge in use while modeling roadways in hilly terrain engaged Jake and Evan simultaneously in the world and on

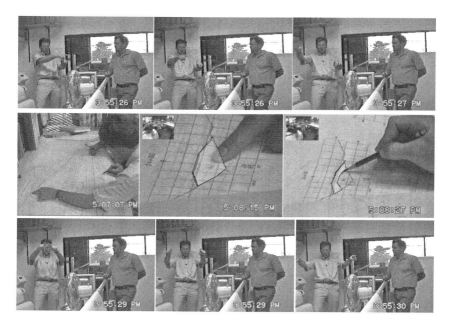

**FIGURE 3.1** Showing and doing roadway design in civil engineering: (top panel) A senior engineer shows how to make a "profile" view of a roadway; (bottom panel) The engineer shows how to make a "section" view of the roadway at a particular point along its path; (middle panel) The senior engineer creates a design rationale that trades the cost of filling in dirt against ruining landscape features in the surrounding terrain.

paper (Hall & Stevens, 1995; Stevens & Hall, 1998). Finally, as anticipated in Jake's justification for his junior partner, models that draw together the world on paper can travel and serve as settings for (sometimes contentious) conversations among design stakeholders (e.g., they become a repository for the history of a complex design project; see Henderson, 1998).

We found similar mundane but important aspects of interactive work across settings in the modeling practices of working architects, field entomologists, and habitat conservation planners (Goldstein & Hall, 2007; Stevens, 1999; Torralba, 2006). While there is not space in this chapter to examine the mobility of people and material in detail, an approach to IA that follows people across settings can be valuable for understanding knowledge in use as something that is important from the social actor's point of view (e.g., Goldstein & Hall, 2007), and it can show how stakeholders in design work hold different, sometimes incommensurable perspectives on the temporal or social scale of the "same" entities). What some KA approaches treat as a normalized collection of elements that people know more/less about may instead be seen as people engaging in conceptual practices that actively bind the world of activity together with representational media in quite different ways. To the extent that practitioners understand knowledge in use in these ways (as active assembly), we have an obligation to understand what they understand and do together while participating in these conceptual practices. This way of approaching knowledge in use is also consistent with organizational explanations for why scientific visualization is powerful – modeling practices "draw things together" (Latour, 1990) and support forms of calculation that span remarkable scales of time and space.

### *Engaging Bodies to Make Places for Learning*

Our discussion of movement across settings in modeling took for granted that people were engaged together in concerted activity in each of these settings (this is how we found and studied them at work). But working formations in place and how they arise are themselves topics for study in IA. When knowledge in use involves (or requires) people working together, how do they arrange or form themselves in ways that support this activity? What kinds of formations are possible or typical, and how do people on the move manage to create places/formations for joint work/activity? As Goffman (1983) put it near the end of his career, in a retrospective on studies of the interaction order,[7]

> What sorts of animals are to be found in the interactional zoo?… One can start with *persons as vehicular entities*, that is, with human *ambulatory units*. In public places we have "singles" (a party of one) and "withs" (a party of more than one), such parties being treated as self-contained units for the purposes of participation in the flow of pedestrian social life.
>
> *(p. 6, italics added)*

"Withs" can be understood as units of multi-party joint attention that are formed in systematic ways within the interaction order that people experience and produce on a daily basis. "Facing formations" (Ciolek & Kendon, 1980; Kendon, 1990) have been studied as systems that create proximal spaces for joint attention and action. These spaces are fitted to human perceptual capacities (e.g., creating a shared region for fine visual focus) and the center region provides a mutually visible region for physical manipulation, using tools or gesture production (e.g., each participant's "gestural stage" [McNeill, 1992] is oriented towards the center of a facing formation like slices of a pie). Facing formations are dynamic – they open as bodies and attention are recruited to a place, body placement and posture shift with topic change, they are monitored for intrusions by non-members or unwanted overhearing, and they close when interrupted or when the purpose of joint action ends.

For IA studies of knowledge in use, facing formations are an intriguing unit of analysis, since they draw our analytic attention to what people are doing with their bodies in order to have a go at working together. But they may also be overly generic, in the sense that use of past tense or managing turn boundaries in sequentially organized talk are structural aspects of almost any human communicative activity. These scenes of mutual engagement and monitoring of the surround for interruptions may be very common in human interaction, particularly when people gather around a focal object and tool-mediated joint action (C. Goodwin, 1994, 2013).

Our interest is in facing-formation systems that form joint attention for doing things that are specific to the conceptual practices we are studying. In this sense, Jake and Evan (the civil engineers we described earlier) are doing something specific to roadway design, in an interactive environment (setting) that has been rigged to make this possible (e.g., what Hall & Stevens [1995] called a "paper space" for roadway design). The same might be said of archeologists (C. Goodwin, 1994) who have rigged up a pit they are excavating as a 3D Cartesian space for precise spatial description (i.e., they act through a "structure of intentionality" [p. 609] specific to disciplined perception in archeology). And if we follow archeologists out of the pit (Hall & Ma, 2011a), we find them using their bodies in ways that establish a reversible "ground truth" (Pickles, 1995) relation between material of interest in the field (the physical remains of past-time dwellers) and remnant models of the field (in digital and material form) back in the lab. Learning to see (Stevens & Hall, 1998) like an archeologist or an engineer is also learning to move in the field, in the lab, and in the relation between them in ways that are specific to the discipline.

As a project for continuing development in IA concerned with knowledge in use, how can we animate Kendon's (1990) concept of facing-formation systems as interactional achievements in spaces traversed by people for (possibly discipline-) specific purposes? Put another way, how do people move and deploy their bodies to look at, manipulate, and talk about entities in conceptual practices in which people operate specific types of representational infrastructure? If we see "persons as vehicular entities" (Goffman, 1983, p. 6), along what paths do people constitute objects of interest, learn new things about them, and thereby make up the content of discipline-specific practices and knowledge?

Ananda Marin (Marin, 2013, 2014) has developed the concept of an "ambulatory sequence" to describe shifts in pacing and body formation as parents and children walk together in a forest park. Since her research questions concern how American Indian families relate in embodied ways with the land as a conceptual practice (i.e., consistent with our concept of knowledge in use), her analysis of these sequences provides a set of findings that begin to show how paths (mobility) and sequentially organized talk assemble ways of understanding land, water, plants, and animals that make up what cultures experience (differently) as the natural world.

In a study of paths taken by visitor groups through a cultural heritage museum (Shapiro, Hall, & Heiberger, 2015), we analyzed how visitors form "engagement contours" around exhibits they select from galleries that display the diverse history and material culture of American roots music. Similar to the ambulatory sequences described in Marin's study, family or acquaintance groups (we studied 22 visitor groups) walked through the museum gallery at a pace that slowed as one or more in the group found an exhibit that engaged their interests. Engagement had rising and falling contours (by analogy to lines of equal elevation on a topographic map), and in moments of peak engagement, movement typically stopped, distal group members were called over (using voice or hand signs), and conversation started about particularly interesting aspects of an exhibit (e.g., a musical instrument, text and images describing its history, and sometimes audible music). Most members of the visitor group (2 to 5 people) wore a camera,[8] so we could follow how engagement contours initially formed (we think of these as "arrivals"), what happened during interest-driven conversations (e.g., many visitors used smartphones to gather, annotate, and share images or film – forms of personal curation[9] that rescale the museum into social networks and make it more persistent), and how the engagement ended (on "departure," visitors resumed walking in the gallery space).

Since an analysis of multiple speakers, each moving along independent paths in a richly appointed cultural space (e.g., the gallery space of a museum) is a novel problem for IA and at the edge of (our view of) the field's capacity, we describe how Shapiro et al. (2015) have analyzed these materials in some detail. Figure 3.2 shows a map-like visual representation of a path taken by one of our visitor groups – the "Bluegrass Family" (BG; mother, daughter and two sons, and boyfriend of the daughter). All the children (and boyfriend) were active bluegrass musicians, and they produced a series of engagement contours while walking through a gallery where photographs of famous musicians were displayed beside their actual instruments. On the left in the top row of Figure 3.2, we show the gallery space in plan view (case displays for musicians are named in an arc in plan view). We superimposed paths (in gray scale[10]) in the gallery taken by each member of the BG group over a period of eight minutes. On the right in the top row, we redraw paths for group members over time (horizontal axis), while preserving location in the gallery space with the vertical dimension and varying the line quality of visitor paths.

While we trace the path of every visitor in the gallery (a painstaking operation), the units of analysis of greatest interest are engagement contours that form when individual paths intersect and ongoing movement slows to engage with what can be seen, read, or heard in an exhibit. In this transcription system (i.e., talk through time and over space), utterances by individuals are embedded along their paths, and conversations that form in engagement contours collect people (paths) and their utterances (fragments of transcript) together to make a place for engaging with the exhibits. On the left in the second row of Figure 3.2, we show a conversation about Bill Monroe's mandolin (excerpted out of the larger path diagram) between four of the five members of the BG visitor group. This transcript (embedded in overlapping paths) uses a reduced set of conventions for

IA Approaches to Knowledge in Use  95

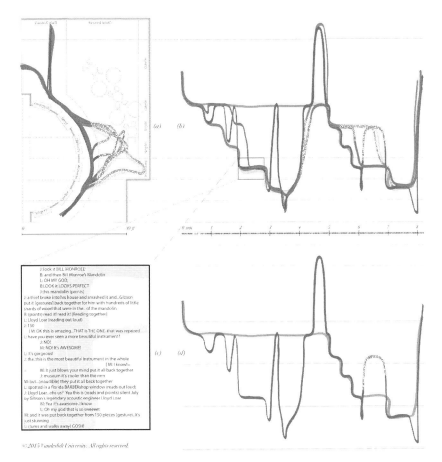

**FIGURE 3.2** Movement and conversation by visitor groups in a cultural heritage museum gallery: (top row) Superimposition of paths taken by each member of "Bluegrass Family" in floor-plan view (left image) and extended over time in a Mondrian Transcript™ (right image); (bottom row, left image) Close-up of path-embedded utterances form a conversation about a famous mandolin; (bottom row, right image) Entwined paths of Adhir (young adult) and Blake (age 9) around a display case showing Hank Williams' guitar.

Source: Copyright © 2015 by Vanderbilt University. Reprinted by permission of Vanderbilt University.

showing prosody and turn boundaries, but by locating talk in place, we can see (at various levels of zoom) how talk by identified speakers makes up engagement with particular museum exhibits.

In the second row of Figure 3.2 (on the right), we isolate the path of two BG group members – Adhir (the boyfriend) and Blake (the youngest son) – to show a lively effort to get the boyfriend to shift between engagement contours. As is evident in the lighter (shaded) path of the older Adhir, he became transfixed by an exhibit showing the guitar used by Hank Williams during the late 1940s. He remains in reverent silence at the exhibit for 5 minutes (horizontal path, minutes 0.5 to 4.5), while the younger Blake moves back and forth between him and the rest of the BG group (his mother, brother, and sister), trying to collect Adhir for looking at and talking about the other exhibits. After checking in (often without talking) on Adhir five times, Blake finally (at 5 minutes along the horizontal scale) manages to lead him on a tour of the remaining instruments (their entwined paths between minutes 5 and 8).

While there is not yet a consensus on how to analyze IA and mobility in relation to learning or knowledge in use, several observations may be helpful. First, while learning often happens *in* places, it is also the case that learning can depend on or arise from *making* places for engaging with entities or phenomena that interest learners. In our study of museum visitor groups, as in Marin's (2013) study of parent/child observations and talk during nature walks, people make places for learning as they are on the move, slowing their pace and creating forms of engagement that can produce or realize (existing) learning opportunities. Second, while it has been tempting to treat museum exhibits (or other designed environments) as stable information caches for learning, attending to mobility and interest-driven (Azevedo, 2011) engagement with these environments (e.g., engagement contours and personal curation in museum gallery spaces) reminds us that what visitors experience is always a personally edited version (Lave, Murtaugh, & de la Rocha, 1984; Ma & Munter, 2014) of what was designed. By analogy to studies of pedagogical practice, designers create an intended curriculum, but visitors produce the enacted curriculum. Developing new approaches to IA and mobility may support design practices that help to bring idealized/realized spaces for learning into more productive alignment.

### *Learning By/About Making Things Together*

A critical reader might argue that labor-intensive IA that follows mobility to find "withs" in the activities of learners will only reveal the *means* through which knowledge in use is enacted or learned, but that this tells us little about that knowledge itself (the content or *ends* from a KA perspective). In this section, we consider cases in which mobility plays a role both as the means for and the content/ends of knowledge in use. This relates to our argument at the beginning of this section that some forms of knowledge in use (e.g., modeling practices in scientific and professional disciplines) are about and appear to require activity that moves across settings, even if we rarely study that activity. More generally, the idea that what people do together with their bodies can be the content (and a central concern) of some conceptual practices is not completely unfamiliar. Dancers, people who play team sports, and ensemble musicians all deploy their bodies in ways that comprise what they learn and create. For example, Hall and Ma's (2011b) analysis of ensemble learning in a competitive high-school marching band described an arduous rehearsal process during which marchers learned to create dynamic visual and aural "chunks" that would garner high scores in juried competition. What they learned about a "chunk," how they learned it, and how they produced it in competition all involved dynamic, multi-body formations.

There may be a large variety of conceptual practices in which mobility is centrally important as means and/or ends for knowledge in use. In another example, Taylor and Hall (2013; Taylor, 2013) reported a design study in which non-driving youth living in urban neighborhoods built bicycles out of discarded or donated parts, then used these bicycles to explore their surrounding neighborhoods. These youth eventually developed "counter maps" which they presented to the city government, resulting in new bicycle lanes being marked on the city's street grid. One part of this complex intervention involved a "safety ride" through the urban street grid by a sizable formation of youth and adult riders (17 riders). That riding formation, which included youth who did not yet know how to shift gears on their bikes when climbing hills, extended over 1.6 miles in the city and crossed over 20 intersections where the riding formation would need to negotiate street signs, traffic lights, and other vehicles (e.g., cars and buses). Several youth and adults wore GoPro™ cameras attached to their bike helmets, and the resulting video and audio record could be mapped directly onto the urban street grid for further analysis.

Figure 3.3 shows two perspectives on how the riding formation produced their safety ride as an ensemble performance. The top rows show a sequence of street intersections that was part of the safety ride, captured in Street View™ using Google Maps™. Since intersections along the route of the safety ride were a stable part of the transportation infrastructure of the city, we think of them as "semiotic aggregates" (Scollon & Scollon, 2003, p. 175) that, over historical time, bring together diverse structuring resources for human activity. Intersections present riders (also drivers and pedestrians) with signage, computer-controlled signal lights, and street markings that can be used to coordinate who passes through the intersection and in which order. In just this sense, intersections are places designed to produce the sequential order of vehicle interactions while driving in the city. The parallel with studies of sequential order in conversation analysis (Sacks, Schegloff, & Jefferson, 1974) is clear once actual drivers arrive together at the intersection – intersections are sites of interaction order that any urban bike rider (adults in the riding formation, but not yet the youth on their hand-made bikes) will describe in (often vehement) depth when asked about traversing the city on a bike. Types of intersections along the safety ride are one thing to know about (in the active sense), but any particular crossing of an intersection on a bike is also an interactional achievement for riders in the ensemble. Adult riders tried to take bounding positions in the riding formation to protect younger riders, but

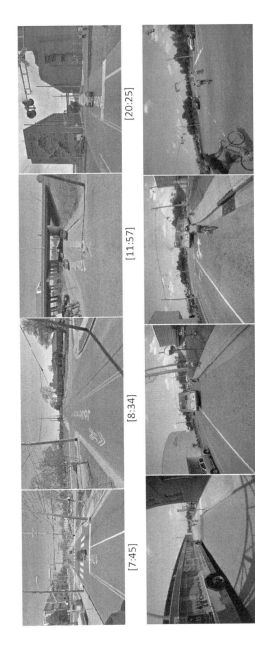

**FIGURE 3.3** Learning to be a riding formation in an urban street grid: (first row) Sequence of street intersections that operate a turn-allocation system; (bottom row) Toon strip showing a bus intrusion and an adult rider attempting to position his body (moving and then stationary) as repair.

the formation was dynamic, moving like a slinky through the city, and subject to unexpected intrusions from vehicular traffic.

The bottom row of Figure 3.3 shows a toon strip in which a city bus intruded on the riding formation as they were approaching the intersection shown at the top of the figure. As described in more depth in Taylor and Hall (2013), adults and youth announced the arrival of the bus as the episode began ([21:50]), hollering "BUS!" to riders ahead. The bus, approaching a green light at the intersection, signaled a right turn and drifted into the right lane ([22:15]), even as youth riders slowed and drove up on the sidewalk to avoid being hit (it is illegal to ride bikes on city sidewalks in this city). In an effort to block a right turn by the bus and leave space for two youth riders, one of the adults (also shown in [22:15]) rode between the right side of the bus and the curb, pulling ahead of the bus to stand his bike in the middle of the intersection. Despite the adult rider's attempt to interrupt and repair the bus's intrusion, the bus completed a right turn ([22:23]) as youth waited to enter the intersection. Finally, the adult held his position in the middle of the intersection ([22:30]) as youth and a trailing adult rider passed through the intersection, entering against a yellow light and passing through as the traffic light turned red.

Mapped onto the usual understanding of "third turn repair" (Sacks, Schegloff, & Jefferson, 1974; Schegloff, 1991) in IA traditions that led this chapter, the first turn involves youth approaching the intersection with the intention of passing straight through, the second turn involves the bus ignoring their bid for clear passing to intrude with a right turn "out of order," and the third turn repair involves the adult signaling (by body and bike position) his intention to pass through the intersection as well (he succeeded in holding the bus, but the youth did not follow). This sequence, while not a comprehensive analysis of knowledge in use required for bicycle riding formations in the urban street grid, does illustrate our idea that what people do together with their bodies can be the content (and a central concern) of particular conceptual practices. In this case, an IA plus mobility analysis makes aspects of knowledgeable riding visible, as well as illustrating what we might think of as a zone of proximal development on the move. What youth riders stand to learn by participating in this sort of mobile apprenticeship is how street intersections work, how to interact with vehicles and drivers who treat youth as if they were invisible (e.g., youth were forced into the gutter and onto the curb), and how to survive in an interaction order that remains risky even as it is touted as an opportunity for healthier living and going green – a recurring refrain in the Mayor's office that eventually inscribed these youths' desire for bike lanes into the semiotic aggregate of this and other intersections in the city (i.e., lines painted on the ground).

## Discussion

We were charged in writing this chapter to provide an overview of IA that could be read alongside the chapter on KA (diSessa, Sherin, & Levin, this volume). As we took up this task, it became quickly clear to us that IA is neither a singular tradition nor a prescribed, unitary set of methods. So, one of our goals in this paper has been to make some of that breadth and history of development accessible to readers. A good part of how we study what we have called knowledge in use is linked to different traditions for analyzing human interaction (e.g., conversation analysis and ethnomethodology) and to ethnographic studies of scientific and technical practice (e.g., Actor-Network Theory). As we have argued, our work (and many collaborative projects, hopefully more to come) has always pursued an account of knowledge in use and how it is learned, something that is not a central concern of either conversation analysis and ethnomethodology, nor of science and technology studies (Stevens, 2001b; Stevens, 2002). Since one of our early papers (Stevens & Hall, 1998) has become an object of secondary analysis in this volume (Levin & diSessa, this volume), we also included some of the social history of the line of work that produced that paper. That paper, and the ensuing conversation with proponents of KA from diSessa's group, span over 20 years of productive exchange that are made visible and furthered considerably in this edited collection.

Our ever-evolving approach to studying knowledge in use continues to invite careful attention to interaction between people and among people and things (e.g., tools, the built environment). Our approach also argues for an analysis of learning as an accountable activity – accountable in Garfinkel's (1967) sense of "observable-and-reportable" (pp. 1–2) – that is transacted in unfolding moments of time but that is often connected (as evident in participants' talk and actions) by participants themselves to broader scales of time, place, and social relationships. These studies focus on learning as a member's phenomenon (Stevens, 2010) with careful attention to developmental consequentiality (Hall, 1999).

The epistemic stance we take and the commitments we make in this approach include: (a) striving for "descriptively adequate" (McDermott et al., 1978) accounts built from recordings of human interaction during people's concerted activities, supplemented by broader ethnographic observations (cf. M. H. Goodwin, 1990), (b) giving analytic primacy to the social actor's point of view and to what is demonstrably relevant for those we study, (c) making inferences about knowledge in use that are grounded in the details of visible and audible traces of people's activity *before* appealing to hidden mental contents or mechanisms (Hutchins, 1995; Latour, 1987), (d) following the social history of changing socio-technical practices as conditions of possibility for knowledge in use (Lave, 2011), (e) maintaining an open stance towards what can be discovered in records of ongoing human activity (diSessa & Cobb, 2004; Koschmann & Zemel, 2009), and (f) offering an open account of our own desires and interests in pursuing IA approaches that we believe contribute to generous★ research in the learning sciences (Hall, Nemirovsky, Ma, & Kelton, this volume) and more just social futures (Espinoza & Vossoughi, 2014; O'Connor & Allen, 2010).

Although we have sprinkled this chapter with a fair amount of history, we did not set out to write a comprehensive history of IA approaches to knowledge in use. Instead, our primary goal has been to point forward to work currently underway in this area and to what seems to lie just ahead, at the edge of what is currently possible, in this research. We have devoted considerable space to studies that engage in comparative IA of knowledge in use, either across time within a setting or across settings (and time) as people do things and learn together on the move. An IA approach to learning and knowledge in use that includes mobility is, we think, one of the leading edges of our field. As we have argued, learning as a member's phenomenon does not always remain (or perhaps only rarely remains) within the container of physical settings (e.g., classrooms) that have been typical in learning sciences until just the past few years.

What technology allows us to capture and the ways it can support novel lines of analysis has been a recurring topic in this chapter. As technologies for recording, organizing and indexing, and visualizing human interaction advance, the kinds of data we can gather, analyze, and curate are rapidly expanding. Recordings of human interaction in and across the cultural landscape set up new opportunities and questions for knowledge in use and learning "on the move" (e.g., our brief descriptions of research by Keifert, 2012; Mehus, Stevens, & Grigholm, 2010, 2012; Marin, 2013; Shapiro et al., 2015; Taylor, 2013) show various directions forward in this landscape). As recording devices become multiple and wearable (e.g., Ma, this volume; Sherin, this volume), learning sciences research is being swept along with digital consumer culture towards massive stores of "personal data" and a growing interest in personal analytics (Lee, 2015). More so than ever, capturing, analyzing, and curating "data" about one's self and one's consociates is itself a member's phenomenon. This creates new opportunities for research.

There remain important issues for ongoing research regarding how different contexts shape the deployment and development of knowledge for use, with contexts understood both as places and as settings organized by people and things in interaction to deploy and develop knowledge. Another important issue, also made possible by innovative uses of recording technologies, is capture of the "same" event from different perspectives. This has been a metaphoric goal of ethnographic work from the beginning, especially with the injunction to study from the social actor's point of view." But this metaphor is more easily realized now, with the ubiquity of wearable cameras that provide something like a first-person perspective on unfolding events. Another use of technology for multiplying perspectives appears in studies by Stevens and colleagues, in which multiple recordings of the same event, from different perspectives, are recorded simultaneously (e.g., the view of people in a room interacting and the view of dynamic video game play they are engaged in) and then synchronized to constitute new kinds of video data (Stevens, Mehus, & Kuhl, under review; Stevens, Satwicz, & McCarthy, 2008).

Our approach to studying knowledge in use should make clear that IA is more than a method. The IA perspective informs our understandings of what counts as knowledge, where and how it is to be found, and how it is learned. It informs how we see knowledge as the same (or not) across time and place. And so, new developments in IA will continue to evolve with new theoretical ideas about how knowledge moves, changes, and settles – in bodies, places, and even minds.

## Notes

1. The NHI seminar started with several video recordings of family members involved in psychotherapy, but the recording receiving the closest scrutiny was an "interview" between Gregory Bateson and the mother (Doris) of a family seeking psychotherapy. The interview concerned the mental status of Doris' young son, who can be seen playing in and around the room during the "interview."
2. Griesemer's (1990) use of "model" refers to the entire collection of specimens (the repository), while his use of "material" refers to the idea that specimens are genuine samples from the world about which a theory is made. Video and audio recordings of human interaction are always selective (Hall, 2000), hence our focus on curation and conservation.
3. Two earlier versions of this paper were submitted as first- and second-year projects by Stevens in the UCB graduate program in Cognition & Development. The first was entitled "Through Disciplined Eyes: The Dawning of Aspects and the Evolution of Noticing," and the second was entitled "Disciplined Perception: Learning to See." diSessa was a reader for both of these papers and Hall was a reader for the second. Alan Schoenfeld was the other reader for the first paper.
4. This account was extended in Stevens' dissertation "Disciplined perception: Comparing…", which compared middle-school students doing architectural design projects in their middle-school classrooms with professional architects doing their work in their firm's offices and in the field. This study was conducted as part of Hall's NSF-funded Math at Work project.
5. What we call a "toon strip" borrows the conventions of panels, sequence, and gutters (or dialogue balloons) from cartooning (McCloud, 1993) to show unfolding details of talk in interaction among people and things.
6. By "rigging" we mean forms of "personal invention" (de la Rocha, 1985) and other ways in which people layer/make places with representational infrastructure that supports what Hall (1990, p. 88) termed "continuity of activity across settings." In our studies of design-oriented uses of mathematics at work, settings were systematically "rigged" to support the "same" ways of thinking in different places (e.g., in the lab and in the field for a group of research entomologists (Hall, Stevens, & Torralba, 2002; see Latour [1993] for a similar argument about the rise of germ theory in France).
7. Goffman's writing about the interaction order remains a central resource for IA, but different traditions (notably conversation analysis and ethnomethodology) formed and have taken a different stance towards social order since at least the middle 1960s (see Schegloff's introductory essays in Sacks [1995]). While beyond the scope of this chapter, the recent controversy over "epistemics in action" (Heritage, 2012) includes themes related to the purpose of this volume.
8. We attach GoPro™ HD cameras to CD jewel cases worn on lanyards around a consenting visitor's neck. This produces quite good sound and surprisingly detailed video records of things directly in front of the visitor, including their use of smartphones or computer tablets (brought to the museum by most visitors).
9. By "personal curation" we mean activities of gathering, annotating, and sharing images, sound, or video among members of a visitor group and their (much larger) social or professional networks available through social media platforms. We think of personal curation as a form of learning that makes places for shared interest and inquiry.

10  The Mondrian Transcripts™ we work with use color, which makes speaker/visitor paths much easier to distinguish. For the purposes of this chapter we use gray-scale shading.

## References

Atkinson, J. M., & Heritage, J. (Eds.). (1984). *Structures of social action*. Cambridge, UK: Cambridge University Press.

Azevedo, F. S. (2011). Lines of practice: A practice-centered theory of interest relationships. *Cognition and Instruction*, 29(2), 147–184.

Bateson, G. (1971). Communication. In N. A. McQuown (Ed.), *The natural history of an interview* (pp. 1–40). Microfilm Collection of Manuscripts on Cultural Anthropology, 15th Series. Chicago: University of Chicago. Joseph Regenstein Library, department of photo duplication.

Becker, H. S. (1972). A school is a lousy place to learn anything in. *American Behavioral Scientist*, 16(1), 85–105.

Becker, H. S. (1990). Generalizing from case studies. In E. Eisner & A. Peshkin (Eds.), *Qualitative inquiry in education: The continuing debate* (pp. 233–242). New York: Teachers College Press.

Ciolek, T. M., & Kendon, A. (1980). Environment and the spatial arrangement of conversational interaction. *Sociological Inquiry*, 50, 237–271.

Cole, M., & Traupmann, K. (1981). Comparative cognitive research: Learning from a learning disabled child. In W. A. Collins (Ed.), *Aspects of the development of competence* (Minnesota symposium on child psychology, Vol. 14, pp. 125–154). Hillsdale, NJ: Lawrence Erlbaum.

de la Rocha, O. (1985). The reorganization of arithmetic practices in the kitchen. *Anthropology and Education Quarterly*, 16, 193–198.

Derry, S. J., Pea, R., Barron, B., Engle, R., Erickson, F., Goldman, R. … Sherin, B. (2010). Conducting video research in the learning sciences: Guidance on selection, analysis, technology, and ethics. *Journal of the Learning Sciences*, 19, 1–51.

Dewey, J. (1934/2005). *Art as experience*. New York: Penguin.

diSessa, A. A., & Cobb, P. (2004). Ontological innovation and the role of theory in design experiments. *Journal of the Learning Sciences*, 13(1), 77–103.

Duranti, A. (1997). *Linguistic anthropology*. Cambridge, UK: Cambridge University Press.

Erickson, F. (2004). *Talk and social theory: Ecologies of speaking and listening in everyday life*. Cambridge, UK: Polity Press.

Erickson, F., & Mohatt, C. (1982). Cultural organization and participation structures in two classrooms of Indian students. In G. Spindler, (Ed.), *Doing the ethnography of schooling* (pp. 131–174). New York: Holt, Rinehart & Winston.

Erickson, F., & Schultz, J. (1981/1997). When is a context? Some issues and methods in the analysis of social competence. In M. Cole, Y. Engeström, & O. Vasquez (Eds.), *Mind, culture, and activity* (pp. 22–31). New York: Cambridge University Press.

Espinoza, M. L., & Vossoughi, S. (2014). Perceiving learning anew: Social interaction, dignity, and educational rights. *Harvard Educational Review*, 84(3), 285–313.

Gardner, R. (2013). Conversation analysis in the classroom. In J. Sidnell & T. Stivers (Eds.), *The handbook of conversation analysis* (Volume 121). Chichester, UK: John Wiley & Sons.

Garfinkel, H. (1967). *Studies in ethnomethodology*. Oxford, UK: Blackwell.

Gasser, L. (1986). The integration of computing and routine work. *ACM Transactions on Information Systems (TOIS)*, 4(3), 205–225.

Geertz, C. (1983). *Local knowledge: Further essays in interpretive anthropology*. New York: Basic Books.

Gick, M. L., & Holyoak, K. J. (1983). Schema induction and analogical transfer. *Cognitive Psychology*, 15, 1–38.

Glaser, B. G., & Strauss, A. L. (1967). *The discovery of grounded theory: Strategies for qualitative research*. Chicago, IL: Aldine.

Goffman, E. (1983). The interaction order. *American Sociological Review*, 48, 1–17.

Goldstein, B. E., & Hall, R. (2007). Modeling without end: Conflict across organizational and disciplinary boundaries in habitat conservation planning. In R. Lesh, E. Hamilton, & J. Kaput (Eds.), *Foundations for the future in mathematics education* (pp. 57–76). Mahwah, NJ: Lawrence Erlbaum.

Goodwin, C. (1994). Professional vision. *American Anthropologist*, 96(3), 606–633.

Goodwin, C. (2013). The co-operative, transformative organization of human action and knowing. *Journal of Pragmatics*, 46, 8–23.

Goodwin, M. H. (1990). *He-said-she-said: Talk as social organization among black children*. Indiana, IN: Indiana University Press.

Griesemer, J. R. (1990). Material models in biology. *Philosophy of Science Association*, 2, 79–93.

Grimshaw, A. (1994). *What's going on here? Complimentary studies of professional talk* (Vol. 2) Norwood, NJ: Ablex.

Hak, T. (1999). "Text" and "con-text": Talk bias in studies of health care work. In S. Sarangi & C. Roberts (Eds.), *Talk, work and institutional order: Discourse in medical, mediation and management settings* (pp. 427–451). Berlin: Mouton de Gruyter.

Hall, R. (1990). *Making mathematics on paper: Constructing representations of stories about related linear functions*. Dissertation, University of California, Irvine. Monograph 90-0002, Institute for Research on Learning.

Hall, R. (1995). Exploring design-oriented mathematical practices in school and work settings. *Communications of the ACM*, September, p. 62.

Hall, R. (1999). The organization and development of discursive practices for "having a theory". *Discourse Processes*, 27(2), 187–218.

Hall, R. (2000). Video recording as theory. In D. Lesh & A. Kelley (Eds.), *Handbook of research design in mathematics and science education* (pp. 647–664). Mahwah, NJ: Lawrence Erlbaum Associates.

Hall, R. (2011). Cultural forms, agency, and the discovery of invention in classroom research on learning and teaching. In T. Koschmann (Ed.), *Theories of learning and studies of instructional practice* (pp. 359–383). New York: Springer.

Hall, R., & Jurow, A. S. (in press). Changing concepts in activity: Descriptive and design studies of consequential learning in conceptual practices. *Educational Psychologist*.

Hall, R., & Ma, J. Y. (2011a). "You know, it was a pain in the ass for those people." Embodied measurements of change in archeological practices of spatial analysis and modeling. Paper presented at the *32nd Annual Ethnography in Education Research Forum*, University of Pennsylvania.

Hall, R., & Ma, J. (2011b). Learning a part together: Participant trajectories with ensemble spatial forms in a high school marching band. In *Symposium on Difference, Culture and Distribution in Mathematics and Science Learning*, at the Annual Meetings of the Jean Piaget Society, Berkeley, CA.

Hall, R., & Nemirovsky, R. (2012). Introduction to the special issue: Modalities of body engagement in mathematical activity and learning. *Journal of the Learning Sciences*, 21(2), 207–215.

Hall, R., & Stevens, R. (1995). Making space: A comparison of mathematical work in school and professional design practices. In S. L. Star (Ed.), *The cultures of computing* (118–145). London: Basil Blackwell.

Hall, R., Stevens, R., & Torralba, T. (2002). Disrupting representational infrastructure in conversations across disciplines. *Mind, Culture, and Activity*, 9(3), 179–210.

Henderson, K. (1998). *On line and on paper: Visual representations, visual culture, and computer graphics in design engineering.* Cambridge, MA: MIT Press.

Heritage, J. (2012). Epistemics in action: Action formation and territories of knowledge. *Research on Language & Social Interaction*, 45(1), 1–29.

Hutchins, E. (1995). *Cognition in the wild*. Cambridge, MA: MIT Press.

Jefferson, G. (2004). Glossary of transcript symbols with an Introduction. In G. H. Lerner (Ed.), *Conversation Analysis: Studies from the first generation*. Amsterdam, NL: John Benjamins.

Jordan, B., & Henderson, A. (1995). Interaction analysis: Foundations and practices. *Journal of the Learning Sciences*, 4(10), 39–103.

Jurow, A. S. (2004). Generalizing in interaction: Middle school mathematics students making mathematical generalizations in a population-modeling project. *Mind, Culture, and Activity*, 11(4), 279–300.

Keifert, D. (2012). Young children's everyday inquiry: A field study of a young girl's play across contexts. *Proceedings of the 10th International Conference of the Learning Sciences*, 1, 315–322.

Kendon, A. (1990). *Conducting interaction: Patterns of behavior in focused encounters*. Cambridge, UK: Cambridge University Press.

Koschmann, T. (Ed.). (2011). *Theories of learning and studies of instructional practice*. New York, NY: Springer.

Koschmann, T., & Zemel, A. (2009). Optical pulsars and black arrows: Discoveries as occasioned productions. *Journal of the Learning Sciences*, 18, 200–246.

Latour, B. (1987). *Science in action*. Cambridge, MA: Harvard University Press.

Latour, B. (1990). Visualisation and cognition: Drawing things together. In M. Lynch and S. Woolgar (Eds.), *Representation in scientific activity* (pp. 19–68). Cambridge, MA: MIT Press.

Latour, B. (1993). *The pasteurization of France*. Cambridge, MA: Harvard University Press.

Latour, B. (1999). *Pandora's hope: Essays on the reality of science studies*. Cambridge, MA: Harvard University Press.

Lave, J. (1988). *Cognition in practice: Mind, mathematics and culture in everyday life*. Cambridge, UK: Cambridge University Press.

Lave, J. (2011). *Apprenticeship in critical ethnographic practice*. Chicago, IL: University of Chicago Press.

Lave, J., Murtaugh, M., & de la Rocha, O. (1984). The dialectic of arithmetic in grocery shopping. In B. Rogoff & J. Lave (Eds.), *Everyday cognition: Its development in social context* (pp. 67–94). Cambridge, MA: Harvard University Press.

Leander, K. M., Phillips, N. C., & Taylor, K. H. (2010). The changing social spaces of learning: Mapping new mobilities. *Review of Research in Education*, 34(1), 329–394.

Lee, V. R. (2015). *Learning technologies and the body: Integration and implementation in formal and informal learning environments*. New York: Routledge.

Leeds-Hurwitz, W. (2005). The natural history approach: A Bateson legacy. *Cybernetics and Human Knowing*, 12(1, 2), 137–146.

Lemke, J. L. (2000). Across the scales of time: Artifacts, activities, and meanings in ecosocial systems. *Mind, culture, and activity*, 7(4), 273–290.

Ma, J. Y., & Munter, C. (2014). The spatial production of learning opportunities in skateboard parks. *Mind, Culture, and Activity*, 21(3), 238–258.

Marin, A. M. (2013). *Learning to attend and observe: Parent-child meaning making in the natural world*. Dissertation, Northwestern University.

Marin, A. M. (2014). Re-placing walking in the analysis of children's observational inquiry. In J. L. Polman, E. A. Kyza, D. K. O'Neill, I. Tabak, W. R. Penuel, A. Jurow, ... (Eds.), *Learning and becoming in practice: The International Conference of the Learning Sciences (ICLS) 2014*. (Vol. 3, pp. 1237–1246). Boulder, CO: International Society of the Learning Sciences.

McCloud, S. (1993). *Understanding comics: The invisible art*. New York: HarperCollins.

McDermott, R. P. (1977a). *Kids make sense: An ethnographic account of the interactional management of success and failure in one first-grade classroom*. (Unpublished Ph.D. thesis). Department of Anthropology, Stanford University.

McDermott, R. P. (1977b). Social relations as contexts for learning in school. *Harvard Educational Review*, 47(2), 198–213.

McDermott, R. P. (1993). The acquisition of a child by a learning disability. In S. Chaiklin & J. Lave (Eds.), *Understanding practice* (pp. 269–305). New York: Cambridge University Press.

McDermott, R. P., Gospodinoff, K., & Aron, J. (1978). Criteria for an ethnographically adequate description of concerted activities and their contexts. *Semiotica*, 24, 245–275.

McNeill, D. (1992). *Hand and mind: What gestures reveal about thought*. Chicago, IL: University of Chicago Press.

Mehan, H. (1979). "What time is it, Denise?": Asking known information questions in classroom discourse. *Theory into practice*, 18(4), 285–294.

Mehus, S., Stevens, R., & Grigholm, L. (2010). Doing science with others at preschool and at home: A comparison of contextually situated interactional configurations and their implications for learning. In B. Bevan, P. Bell, R. Stevens, & A. Razfa (Eds.), *LOST learning opportunities: Learning in out-of-school time*. New York: Springer.

Mehus, S., Stevens, R., & Grigholm, L. (2012). Interactional arrangements for learning about science in early childhood: A case study across preschool and home contexts. In K. Gomez, L. Lyons, & J. Radinsky (Eds.), *Learning in the disciplines: Proceedings of the 9th International Conference of the Learning Sciences (ICLS 2010)* –Vol. 1, Full Papers. Chicago, IL: International Society of the Learning Sciences.

Mondada, L. (2013). The conversation analytic approach to data collection. In T. Stivers & J. Sidnell (Eds.), *The handbook of conversation analysis* (pp. 32–56). Oxford: Wiley-Blackwell.

Murphy, K. M. (2005). Collaborative imagining: The interactive use of gestures, talk, and graphic representation in architectural practice. *Semiotica*, 156, 113–145.

Ochs, E. (1979). Transcription as theory. In E. Ochs & B. Schieffelin (Eds.), *Developmental pragmatics* (pp. 43–72). New York: Academic Press.

Ochs, E., Gonzales, P., & Jacoby, S. (1996). "When I come down I'm in the domain state": Grammar and graphic representation in the interpretive activity of physicists. *Studies in Interactional Sociolinguistics*, 13, 328–369.

O'Connor, K., & Allen, A. R. (2010). Learning as the organizing of social futures. *Yearbook of the National Society for the Study of Education*, 109(1), 160–175.

Philips, S. U. (1972). Participant structures and communicative competence: Warm Springs children in community and classroom. In C. B. Cazden, V. P. John, & D. Hymes (Eds.), *Functions of language in the classroom*. New York: Teachers College Press.

Pickles, J. (1995). *Ground truth: The social implications of geographic information systems*. New York: Guilford Press.

Pomerantz, A., & Fehr, B. J. (1997). Conversation analysis: An approach to the study of social action as sense-making practices. *Discourse as social interaction*, 2, 64–91.

Raymond, G., & Heritage, J. (2006). The epistemics of social relations: Owning grandchildren. *Language in Society*, 35(5), 677–705.

Sacks, H. (1995). *Lectures on conversation* (Vol. I, II). G. Jefferson (Ed.). Oxford: Blackwell.

Sacks, H., Schegloff, E., & Jefferson, G. (1974). A simplest systematics for the organization of turn-taking in conversation. *Language*, 50, 696–735.

Schegloff, E. A. (1991). Conversation analysis and socially shared cognition. In L. B. Resnick, J. L. Levine, & S. D. Teasley (Eds.), *Perspectives on socially shared cognition* (pp. 150–171). Washington, DC: American Psychological Association.

Schegloff, E. A. (1992). On talk and its institutional occasions. In P. Drew & J. Heritage (Eds.), *Talk at work: Interaction in institutional settings* (pp. 101–134). Cambridge, UK: Cambridge University Press.

Schegloff, E. A. (2007). A tutorial on membership categorization. *Journal of Pragmatics*, 39(3), 462–482.

Scollon, R., & Scollon, S. W. (2003). *Discourses in place: Language in the material world*. London: Routledge.

Shapiro, B., Hall, R., & Heiberger, L. (2015, April). Assembling American roots music: Visitors' micro-curation and engagement in museum gallery spaces. Paper presented at the Annual Meetings of the Association of American Geographers, Chicago, IL.

Star, S. L., & Griesemer, J. R. (1989). Institutional ecology, "translations" and boundary objects: Amateurs and professionals in Berkeley's Museum of Vertebrate Zoology, 1907–39. *Social Studies of Science*, 19(3), 387–420.

Stevens, R. (1999). *Disciplined perception: Comparing the development of embodied mathematical practices in school and at work*. Dissertation, Cognition and Development, Graduate School of Education, University of California, Berkeley.

Stevens, R. (2000a). Divisions of labor in school and in the workplace: Comparing computer and paper-supported activities across settings. *The Journal of the Learning Sciences*, 9(4), 373–401.

Stevens, R. (2000b). Who counts what as math? Emergent and assigned mathematics problems in a project-based classroom. In J. Boaler (Ed.), *Multiple perspectives on mathematics teaching and learning* (pp. 105–144). Westport, CT: Ablex Publishing.

Stevens, R. (2001a). *Documenting learning within and across moments*. AERA Presidential Invited Symposium. The American Educational Research Association Conference. Seattle, WA.

Stevens, R. (2001b). Within and across moments: The help ethnomethodology provides for respecifying "learning". *The Culture and Communication Seminar Series*. Harvard Humanities Center. Harvard University. Cambridge, MA.

Stevens, R. (2002). Technoscientists in the making. Paper presented at the Workshop on Pedagogy and Science Studies (Training Scientists, Crafting Science). Massachusetts Institute of Technology, Cambridge, MA.

Stevens, R. (2010). Learning as a members' phenomenon: Toward an ethnographically adequate science of learning. *National Society for the Study of Education*, 109(1), 82–97.

Stevens, R., & Hall, R. (1998). Disciplined perception: Learning to see in technoscience. In M. Lampert & M. Blunk (Eds.), *Talking mathematics in school: Studies of teaching and learning* (pp. 107–149). Cambridge, UK: Cambridge University Press.

Stevens, R., Mehus, S., & Kuhl, P. (under review). An interaction analysis of joint attention and joint action in a laboratory experiment with infants: Results from an interdisciplinary study.

Stevens, R., O'Connor, K., Garrison, L., Jocuns, A., & Amos, D. (2008). Becoming an engineer: Toward a three-dimensional view of engineering learning. *Journal of Engineering Education*, 97(3), 355–368.

Stevens, R., Satwicz, T., & McCarthy, L. (2008). In-game, in-room, in-world: Reconnecting video game play to the rest of kids' lives. In K. Salen (Ed.), *The ecology of games* (Vol. 9, pp. 41–66). Cambridge, MA: MIT Press.

Stevens, R., Wineburg, S., Herrenkohl, L., & Bell, P. (2005). The comparative understanding of school subjects: Past, present and future. *Review of Educational Research*, 75(2), 125–157.

Streeck, J., Goodwin, C., & LeBaron, C. (2011). *Embodied interaction: Language and body in the material world.* Cambridge, UK: Cambridge University Press.

Taylor, K. H. (2013). *Counter-mapping the neighborhood: A social design experiment for spatial justice.* Dissertation, Vanderbilt University.

Taylor, K. H., & Hall, R. (2013). Counter-mapping the neighborhood on bicycles: Mobilizing youth to reimagine the city. *Technology, Knowledge and Learning*, 18, 65–93.

Taylor, K. H., Stevens, R., & Champion, D. (2014, June). Constructing the daily media round of children: Methodological innovations and issues. Presented at the International Conference of the Learning Sciences, Boulder, CO.

Taylor, K. H., Takeuchi, L., & Stevens, R. (in press) Mapping the daily media round: Methodological innovations for understanding families' mobile technology use. *International Journal of Learning and Media.*

Torralba, J. A. (2006). *Learning to speak for nature: A case study of the development of scientists and their representational practices.* Dissertation, University of California, Berkeley.

Wittgenstein, L. (1953). *Philosophical investigations.* Oxford, UK: Blackwell.

# PART II
# Synthetic Analyses

# 4
# ECOLOGIES OF KNOWING

## Lessons From the Highly Tailored Practice of Hobbies

*Flávio S. Azevedo and Victor R. Lee*

In this chapter, we draw on concepts, methods, and foundations of both Knowledge Analysis (KA) and Interaction Analysis (IA) to hone our understanding of knowing and learning in activity and to advance theory that informs both KA (diSessa, 1993) and IA (Jordan & Henderson, 1995) pursuits. Our project, therefore, seeks synergies among these research traditions and we hope it will inspire new lines of research that productively "blend" these approaches to the study of knowing and learning.

We begin with the central KA tenet of *conceptual ecology* – the idea that knowledge elements are multiple (i.e., there are numerous knowledge elements, rather than a few monolithic entities, involved in reasoning conceptually in a domain) and diverse (i.e., there are numerous types of knowledge, rather than one or two). In the domain of physics, for instance, diSessa (1996) listed such knowledge types as *narratives*, *nominal* and *committed facts*, *p-prims*, and *mental models*, each of which potentially is made up of hundreds or thousands of distinct elements. To that, others have added such constructs as *symbolic forms* and *devices* (Sherin, 2001), *coordination classes* (Danish, Enyedy, & Parnafes, this volume; diSessa & Sherin, 1998), and *epistemological frames* (DeLiema, Lee, Danish, Enyedy, & Brown, this volume; Hammer, Elby, Scherr, & Redish, 2005; Hammer & Elby, 2003). As a whole, research taking the KA perspective has sought to articulate how the varied and multiple knowledge elements can account for complex, dynamic, and moment-to-moment reasoning in complex tasks (diSessa, 1996, 2006; diSessa & Sherin, 1998) – a stance we also adopt here.

To those, we add IA's methodological and epistemological tenet that knowing and learning are produced in the complex, "real-world" interactions between members of communities, as they go about their daily chores and shared goals (e.g., Hall & Stevens, this volume; Greeno, 2006; Greeno, Collins, & Resnick, 1996; Lave & Wenger, 1991; Rogoff, Paradise, Arauz, Correa-Chávez, & Angelillo, 2003) and explore how conceptual ecologies are manifested in the interactional context of the hobby of model rocketry – rather than, say, the more "engineered" context of clinical interviews often favored by KA pursuits (e.g., diSessa, Greeno, Michaels, & O'Connor, this volume; Parnafes, 2007; Russ, Sherin, & Lee, this volume; Sherin, 2001; Wagner, 2006). By pursuing this demonstration, we are beginning an exploration of the relationship between the *nature of a practice* and the *ecologies of knowing* that are within the practice's immediate purview. By ecologies of knowing, we mean to encompass KA's idea of conceptual ecologies but also to highlight the larger social and cultural processes through which conceptual ecologies emerge and are used. In line with the tradition of IA, then, we seek to make more visible how "knowledge and action are fundamentally social in origin, organization, and use, and are situated in particular social and material ecologies" and "in the interactions among members of a particular community engaged with the material world" (Jordan & Henderson, 1995, p. 41). As we will see, doing so provides us with means to see how conceptual ecologies are simultaneously individual and communal achievements (e.g., Hutchins, 1995a, 1995b).

To further elaborate, our overarching hypothesis is that different kinds of practice bear directly on the overall nature of the ecologies of knowing that people develop in that practice as well as the processes that underlie knowing and learning in such a practice. For example, if we consider knowing and doing within a physics classroom, one's ecology of knowing might consist of ways of recognizing and talking about "force," what kinds of explanations or problem solutions are considered acceptable, how to represent relationships between quantities, and forms of visualization and mental simulation of idealized problems. However, if we consider an alternate situation that should involve the same domain of knowledge, we could reasonably expect the ecology of knowing to differ in a number of ways. For instance, for a hobbyist engaged in building and optimizing a robot car for a soapbox derby, canonical physics knowledge may still be consequential, but we may expect the conceptual emphasis of the active ecology to be somewhere other than on formal means for talking about forces or the equations relating force and acceleration. Indeed, these differences in knowing that are brought to bear given seemingly comparable domains have been well documented in extant literature (e.g., Lave, Murtaugh, & de la Rocha, 1984; Lave, 1988). However, while such work has functioned as a critique of cognitive modeling approaches that emphasize individual knowledge, we do maintain that individual knowledge is present and important. Yet, to that we add that the boundaries around collections of knowledge that contribute to an act of "knowing" must be more inclusive. In other words, as we will show, the ecology of knowing in particular practices spans more than the conceptual ecology associated with one's mind.

As we have mentioned, the empirical domain we consider is the hobby of model rocketry. Hobbies are prototypical of open-ended, interest-driven practices, and thus they offer practitioners much leeway in terms of *what* and *how* to learn about their hobby – that is, the ecology of knowing that they might develop in the practice, how model rocketeer communities create and propagate such an ecology, and so on. Given the character of hobbies, therefore, we expect that issues regarding the relationship between the nature of a practice and ecologies of knowing will be made prominent in our ethnographic records of the collective practice of model rocketry communities.

At the same time, because rocketeers may learn such a variety of topics and concepts in the hobby (e.g., motors, parachutes, rules of participation, painting techniques), we focus our inquiry on problems of knowing a single "concept" in the hobby – namely, model rocket *stability*. Knowing stability is potentially complex, given the rich conceptual space of physics in which it rests. Given these conditions, we pursue three questions as a means to our goals: What is the ecology of knowing that rocketeers and rocketry communities typically develop in the hobby? What are the ecology's characteristics and what are the processes underlying its functioning? More generally, what do these tell us about the relationship between the open-ended, interest-driven nature of model rocketry practice and the ecology of knowing stability that develops in it?

## A Short Introduction to Model Rocket Stability

As it appeared in the fields of practice and the specialized literature (Stine & National Association of Rocketry, 1983; Stine & Stine, 2004), the stability of a model rocket is determined by a relationship between its *center of gravity* (CG, or center of mass) and *center of pressure* (CP). Yaw, pitch, and roll axes of rotation also bear on the problem of model rocket stability, but for practical purposes they can be ignored (and indeed were never mentioned by rocketeers).

The center of gravity is the point at which the entire weight of the rocket may be considered as concentrated, and if supported at that point the rocket would balance. A flying rocket or any free body in space rotates about its center of gravity.

The center of pressure is a point where all pressure forces due to the flowing air can be said to act on a flying rocket (Stine & Stine, 2004). To more easily explicate this idea, consider a weather vane as a two-dimensional model of a rocket (Figure 4.1). In a well-functioning vane, its support can be said to divide the vane into two sections of different surface areas; the tail section has a larger area than the front section, which results in a larger air pressure in the vane's tail section. In turn, this leads to a larger torque on the tail than on the front, which turns the vane into the wind (i.e., weathercocks it).

If we now slide the vane's support towards its tail we will eventually reach a point in which the total surface area on each side of the support is the same. If supported at this point, the pressure exerted by the air flowing past the vane would be the same on both tail and front sections, the resulting torque would be

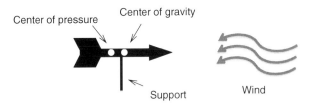

**FIGURE 4.1** A weather vane and its centers of gravity and pressure.

Source: Reprinted from *Cognition and Instruction*, Volume 31, Issue 3. Copyright © 2013 Taylor & Francis LLC. Reprinted by permission of Taylor & Francis LLC. Material excerpted from Figure 1 on page 348 in the article, "Knowing the Stability of Model Rockets: A Study of Learning in Interest-Based Practices," by Flávio S. Azevedo.

nil, and the vane would not point in the wind's direction. This point is the vane's center of pressure.

With this basic understanding, we now return to model rockets and the more complex situation of stability in flight (see Figure 4.2 for a schema of a stable model in flight). When flying, a rocket may wobble relative to its flight path due to wind gusts or other phenomena (e.g., thrust variations in the motor). The rocket will thus begin rotating about its center of gravity, which will cause its axis to be inclined at an angle $a$ (technically called angle of attack) relative to the flight path. In this case, a lift force ($L$) is generated by the rocket's body and fins, while the aerodynamic drag ($D$) remains relatively constant (at least for small angles of inclination). Lift ($L$) and drag ($D$) forces both act through the rocket's center of pressure. (It should be noted that the vane model introduces an important simplification – namely, that the CP of a flying model is not a fixed point, but rather varies with the angle of attack. As will be shown, however, this does not preclude rocketeers from correctly assessing stability.)

In Figure 4.2, the rocket's nose has been perturbed to the left (say, the pitch direction) and the lift force that is generated is also directed to the left (or downwind) side of the rocket. Both lift and drag forces will thus produce clockwise torques about the rocket's center of gravity. In terms of behavior, this means the rocket's tail will swing to the left under the action of the resultant force $L + D$ and the nose will move to the right, thus restoring the model to its initial (correct) path.

Conversely, were the center of pressure located *ahead* of the center of gravity (say, due to very heavy fins), the air pressure on the nose cone would be larger than the air pressure on the rocket's fins, and the resulting torque would make it rotate even further. The rocket would thus behave unpredictably.

To summarize, a rocket is stable if its center of pressure is located "behind" (i.e., towards the tail) its center of gravity, and unstable if the CP is ahead of the CG. A borderline case, in which the centers of gravity and pressure overlap or are too close together also exists, and safety considerations suggest the rocket should not be flown.

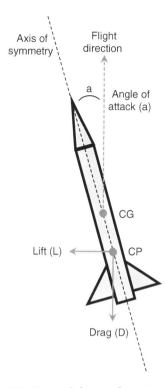

**FIGURE 4.2** Schema of a rocket in flight.
Source: Reprinted from *Cognition and Instruction*, Volume 31, Issue 3. Copyright © 2013 Taylor & Francis LLC. Reprinted by permission of Taylor & Francis LLC. Material excerpted from Figure 2 on page 349 in the article, "Knowing the Stability of Model Rockets: A Study of Learning in Interest-Based Practices," by Flávio S. Azevedo.

Still, how far behind the CG should the CP be located? In other words, what can be said about the relative distance between CG and CP? Both empirical evidence and mathematical models suggest that the CP should be at least one body diameter behind the CG – technically known as one-caliber stability. Thus, if the rocket's body tube is 1.34 inches in diameter – a common industry standard available in hobby stores – its CP should be no less than 1.34 inches behind the CG. If the model has more than 2 or 3 calibers stability, it may be over-stable and weathercock excessively, but it is usually safe to fly.

## Empirical Context and Methods

The first author (FA) carried out a 3½-year-long ethnography of two distinct model rocketry communities, each of which had its specific sets of norms and values, sites of practice, etc. The original goal of the research was to investigate the structure of long-term, interest-driven participation in a STEM (science, technology, engineering, and mathematics) practice and the learning that resulted from this mode of practice participation. As such, issues of knowing and learning were expected to organically emerge in the daily routines of rocketry communities, as rocketeers plied their trade in the fields.

In ethnographic fashion, between 2000 and 2003 FA documented (in videotapes and field notes) the naturally unfolding activities of Club-1 and Club-2.[1] Overall, the data-collection strategy focused first on following the process of flying a rocket in the field and the sites through which participants had to pass in the process. For example, as we will see, rocketeers wishing to fly a rocket had to stand in line to have their models inspected for safety. Both the line and the inspection desk are sites in which interactions among participants might lead to conversations around issues of stability, and therefore are richly represented in the data.

At the same time, because of the open-ended nature of model rocketry, we know that practitioners develop widely different, tailored pursuits in the practice (Azevedo, 2011). For instance, one may specialize in low-powered rockets and perhaps painting and decoration, whereas another may prefer medium- and high-powered models that have counterparts in real life. In this regard, FA also documented the idiosyncratic activities of several individual rocketeers, most prominently David, Bill, and George, but also Allan and others. In all, this sought to capture possible differences in ecologies of knowing stability and their contextual features.

Finally, in the course of this ethnographic research, FA also designed a "task" to elicit understandings about stability in the context of an actual activity encountered in model rocketry practice (see Saxe, 1991). The task materials consisted of three scratch-built rockets (Figure 4.3), each of which represented a prototypical case of stability along a continuum of model rocket stability–instability (Stine & Stine, 2004). Rocket 1 was a prototypical case of a stable rocket (i.e., positive stability), with the CG clearly ahead of the CP. Rocket 2 was a borderline case (neutral stability) because it had a long body tube but very small fins – a design that puts the CG and CP dangerously close or, worse, perhaps overlaps them. Lastly, rocket 3 had its CP ahead of its CG and thus it was clearly unstable (negative stability), both because of its large fins near the nosecone and the bottom fins relatively far up the body tube.

As part of the normal flow of field practice, FA asked practitioners and rocket inspection personnel whether each of the rockets would pass inspection, especially as it related to stability issues. The "task" was administered during routine field practice and so it was constituted as a real problem to be solved, given that the rockets would be (and were) flown that day. Furthermore, because of the nature of rocketry field practice, subjects freely exchanged ideas about the rockets' features and engaged in somewhat extended conversations about them.

All activities were videotaped and recording flowed organically between documenting collective work and that of three foci rocketeers (David, Bill, and

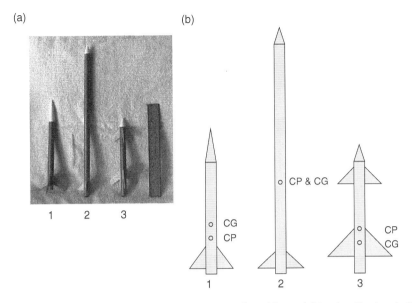

**FIGURE 4.3** (a) From left to right: a prototypically stable model (rocket 1), a borderline case (rocket 2), and an unstable model (rocket 3). The foot-long ruler on the right affords an estimate of the overall dimensions of the models; (b) From left to right, the schemas of rockets 1, 2, and 3, respectively, with center of gravity (CG) and center of pressure (CP) shown.

Source: Reprinted from *Cognition and Instruction*, Volume 31, Issue 3. Copyright © 2013 Taylor & Francis LLC. Reprinted by permission of Taylor & Francis LLC. Material excerpted from Figure 3 on page 353 in the article, "Knowing the Stability of Model Rockets: A Study of Learning in Interest-Based Practices," by Flávio S. Azevedo.

George). As we will see, other rocketeers also spontaneously volunteered information and we will use them here. In all, the data corpus totals about 20 hours of videotapes of collective and individuals' activities, selected transcriptions of video records, several pages of field notes, and some artifacts produced by rocketeers (e.g., rocket drawings).

## Data

We provide a short summary account of model rocketry practice in two distinct communities (Club-1 and Club-2), as well as some of the specifics of David, Bill, and George's practices (see Azevedo, 2011, for details). Additional data will be presented in the analysis section.

At Club-1 and Club-2 people flew a variety of scratch-built rockets and off-the-shelf models (i.e., kit-ready rockets designed, built, and marketed by specialized companies and easily found in hobby stores). Off-the-shelf rockets run the gamut of assembly complexity, ranging from "plug-and-play" to those requiring machining of parts and long-term construction. Commercial, kit-ready models come labeled with a number indicating the kit's level of assembly difficulty, ranging from 1 to 4, in ascending scale of difficulty, and step-by-step instructions come as standard.

Club-1 allowed flights with motors of up to $E$ power – in the scale ¼$A$, ½$A$, $A$, $B$, $C$... $H$, $I$, $J$, each letter representing double the total impulse of its predecessor. Club-2, on the other hand, allowed for motors up to $H$ power. Club-1's practice site was a large parking lot surrounded by other open areas, but also trees and low-rise buildings that were known to trap rockets. As such, people tended to fly mostly low- to medium-powered motors. In contrast, Club-2 was located in a large and remote soccer field, also surrounded by open grass fields, and high-powered flights were very common and encouraged.

Routines of field practice at both Club-1 and Club-2 were very similar and participants at any launch event generally divided their day between actively preparing and flying rockets and socializing with family, friends, and peers. The physical arrangement of the fields and surrounding space facilitated these processes, and so did the communities' practices. Take Club-1 as an example.

When arriving at the site, practitioners set up tables that served as both work area and picnic grounds (Figure 4.4). They circulated through social areas and launch grounds, in the process chatting about all things within and beyond model rocketry. If flying a rocket, a typical rocketeer would first prepare the rocket at his/her table – i.e., load the desired motor into the rocket (or its stages, in case of a multi-stage model) and attach to it the launch lugs, roll the parachute (or streamer) and fit it into the cavity below the nosecone, place the nosecone, etc. The rocketeer would then fill out the rocket's flight card, which contained some basic information on the rocket (e.g., scratch-built or off-the-shelf, motor power, whether it had been flown before). Inspection was done at the inspection desk and it was performed by one or two experienced rocketeers who were usually old-time members of the community.

The work of inspectors was to detect any problems that would make a rocket unsafe to fly (e.g., cracked fins, loose motors, and misplaced lugs). It was at the inspection desk that problems of rocket stability arose most commonly, but also many others of a more practical nature which therefore could be treated on site. To illustrate, take the following exchange between Michael (an inspector) and a first-time visitor who was attempting to fly a well-known kit.[2]

28:34 (LocalNAR, 11/24/2002)
1    Michael:    ((speaking to rocketeer)) Do you have a bit of sandpaper with you? 'Cause you gotta:: there's some paint here ((points to the nosecone rim of the rocket)) that's ... that's hanging up to this nosecone and you don't want to do that.
2    Rocketeer:    Okay, I'll pop it off.

Ecologies of Knowing 119

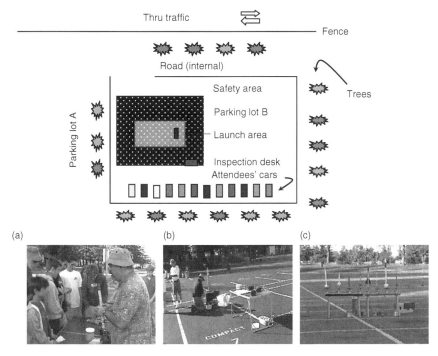

**FIGURE 4.4** A schema of the Club-1 practice site. Insets: (a) the inspection desk and the inspector (right) busy at work; (b) the launch desk; (c) rockets placed on the launch pad and ready for takeoff.

3   Michael:    Yeah … just clean that off ((scratching spot on the rocket's nosecone with finger)) because this nosecone has a tendency to not want to come out anyway.
4   Rocketeer:  OH, okay.

Rocketeers with models that passed inspection would then move into the launch area (to await flight) and then the launch pad area (to set up the rocket on numbered pads for actual launch). On each round, some 12 models were launched, each with its countdown routines announced on loudspeakers by either the Launch Control Officer (LCO) or the rocket owner. (Club-1, 11/24/2002): "The sky is clear, the range is clear… Going up in five, four, three, two, one ((button push))." After launch, retrieving landing rockets was an animated affair sometimes done in groups that exchanged experiences.

## *Some Details on the Practice of David, Bill, and George*

Within the shared aspects of culture that David, Bill, and George encountered in their visits to Club-1 and Club-2, the varieties of practice participation that they developed were quite illustrative of the open-ended nature of hobbies.

David is a Caucasian who was 14 when we met in June 2000 and he had started participating in the hobby at the age of six. As with many youngsters, David came to the field with his father and sometimes with his extended family and friends. While he had budget limitations, he had developed a rich and varied practice, populated by a number of kit-ready and scratch-built or modified models. To begin, David had two Mosquitoes (off-the-shelf, small, plastic-molded, low-powered models that fly out of sight and deploy a streamer for recovery); a high-powered, off-the-shelf LOC IV (which he flew exclusively at Club-2); a Lunar Lander (an off-the-shelf, saucer-like, low-powered rocket); and an Ugly Boy (off-the-shelf, low- to medium-powered rocket).

David also had a preference for design and he mastered techniques that allowed him to produce some innovative models. For instance, he had a line of cheap and wacky rockets that were creative in design and made from cheap (or free) materials, which were very well adapted to the treacherous conditions of Club-1. These rockets included a Bottle rocket, a Paper Cup rocket, three Shuttlecock rockets, and plans for building a two-stage version of Shuttlecocks. He also had a line of tall and mighty rockets, which he built by extending the body tubes of off-the-shelf models and refitting them with higher-powered motors, which he flew exclusively at Club-2.

Contrasting with David, Bill (also a Caucasian) did not care for design aspects of the hobby: "I don't do any design of my own" (Club-1, 6/5/2000). Instead, he concentrated on building high-powered kits, which always involved complex assembly and sometimes machining, both of which were aspects of the hobby that appealed to him very much. Because Bill also had budget limitations, at any given time he only had two or three such high-powered models. As it turns out, Bill was a video store manager in his late twenties, and he too had started the hobby with the help of his father. While growing up, his conditions of hobby practice naturally changed, but Bill always managed to maintain the hobby along stable lines, connecting the hobby to other important interests in his life. First, his rockets always found counterparts in full-scale rocketry, which fascinated him. In this regard, Bill knew many technical details of both model and full-scale rockets, as seen in his spontaneous, almost endless elaborations of rocket specs. Second, his job at the video store afforded him the opportunity to freely watch movies and to further cultivate his interest in the hobby. In particular, Bill watched movies that were rocketry related but which also strongly connected with American cultural symbols, history of achievements, and identity:

> You would… they could never land it on a commercial airport. There's… they just don't have an airport they're gonna ((inaudible)) so you fl… so it lands at Edwards Air Force base or a special launch pad at Cape Canaveral, uh:: a special landing strip. I even have a book, uh:: The Dream is Alive about uh:: about that uh:: Imax film I got to see, uh, over at Paramount Great America in '86 and that that's a spectacular movie.

Finally, George was an Asian American in his early thirties who had a successful career as a software engineer. He also had a prolific "career" as a model rocketeer and during the ethnographic period he had some 30 to 40 rockets flying a range of motor configurations. Because he was deeply engaged in the design aspects of the practice, essentially all of his rockets were built from scratch or stemmed from modifications to existing models. As an example, he had created a low-powered Funnel Rocket by simply attaching a standard kitchen funnel to a spare body tube and nosecone. His design was not meant to fly very high but rather to create a "cool cloud of concentrated smoke right behind the rocket's motor," as he described it (Club-1, 9/22/2002).

Stemming from his technical background, George also had about eight night rockets – i.e., models fitted with light-emitting devices and which he flew at special night launch events at Club-2. He had also tried video rocketry, which consists in installing a video or still camera as rocket payload. George suspended this pursuit upon finding the images of low quality (due to the range of cameras that he could afford), but vowed to return to it once things improved.

## Analysis

Few rocketeers we met in the fields could advance an explanation of rocket stability that approached the one presented earlier. And yet, almost no rockets ever failed inspection due to design problems that affected stability. How do rocketeers and communities do it, collectively and individually?

In this section, we present a list of observed ways for rocketeers to know model rocket stability. Similar to the conceptual ecology metaphor, this list contains a set of productive knowledge elements and resources – i.e., an ecology of knowing – that contribute to observed reasoning and action. However, this ecology is clearly reflexively linked to participation in a community that is actively involved in processes of conceiving, building, and flying model rockets. The list is not exhaustive; rather, we present it to show the diversity within the ecology of knowing stability as it is used in rocketry practice. Here and in the subsequent section, we fold into the narrative many details of the processes through which these ways of knowing are coordinated in use.

### *A Visual Rocket Schema*

Stable rockets – i.e., those ubiquitously present in the fields of practice – have a look and feel that is known by both newcomers and old-timers to the practice. Roughly, this schema describes the rocket component parts, their relative measures and relationships, and so on. Thus, a rocket has a pointy or round nosecone, which sits atop an elongated, tubular body, and at the bottom it has a set of fins that are placed symmetrically (i.e., equidistant from one another, rather than bunched up on one "side" of the body). Further, fins are generally not too big or too small, relative to the total length of the model; rockets certainly range in length, but there is a rough relative proportion between fin "size" and overall body length.

Evidence for this rough description comes from many sources. For instance, while David and George had evolved alternatives to the standard nosecone + body tube + fins design – i.e., David's Shuttlecock somewhat avoids the problem of fins and George's Funnel Rocket relied on a continuous fin – by and large their models preserved the overall "shape gestalt" observed in the fields. More tellingly, throughout the long ethnographic period and across all rocketeers attending those events, we never saw a standard body-tube-and-fin rocket with a single fin or even two fins, nor did we document fins placed asymmetrically or shaped in different sizes. Instead, 3- and 4-fin designs were the norm, with identical fins arranged symmetrically along the bottom edge of the model. Fins were most often made from balsa wood sold in hobby stores.

As further evidence, model rocketeers also talked about stability in terms of such a visual schema. This is captured, for instance, in George's explanation of the stability of one of his models: "Well, ((to start with)) it looks just like the Big Bertha." The Big Bertha™ is an off-the-shelf model that is very popular at both Club-1 and Club-2 and it is widely available at hobby stores. Time-tested, stable-by-design models were thus a handy way of knowing stability used even by old-timers in the hobby.

Beyond a schema for roughly describing stable models, more experienced rocketeers also seemed to know that "violations" to this basic visual schema signaled specific cases of stability problems. This is most readily illustrated by Michael's (an inspector at Club-1) quick reaction to FA showing him rocket 3 (a prototypical case of negative stability) in the stability "task" (11/24/02): "This is not gonna fly, no way." By the same token, Michael quickly assessed rocket 2 (neutral stability) as a borderline case and stated: "It doesn't look terribly bad… although the fins look a little small." After more careful consideration, he allowed FA to fly the rocket but using the farther launch pads as a precaution.

To summarize, rocketeers seem to know the sketch of a stable rocket – i.e., what it should look like, the patterns in rockets' overall shapes, their component parts, and their interrelationships, etc. This visual/perceptual inspection process recurred in social interactions in the field and thus was shared by participants, making the use of a visual schema both an individual and collective activity to judge stability. Further, this visual/perceptual way of knowing stability is structured around prototypical rocket shapes that fall along a continuum of stability–instability. Note, however, that perceptual ways of knowing stability alone cannot guarantee a correct assessment or design and thus must be coordinated with other elements and processes in the ecology of knowing stability. Briefly put, a rocket may well look stable, but upon further inspection one may find its fins to be made of a heavy material, thereby shifting its CP too far down the rocket body. Given that the models in the stability task were made of standard, commercially available balsa wood, body tubes, and nosecones, rocketeers' and inspectors' judgments stood as valid (and likely took these issues into account).

## Fact-Like Ways of Knowing

A second set of elements in the ecology of knowing stability regards *fact-like* forms that capture and articulate correct relationships between the centers of gravity and pressure and thus guarantee a good design. As a whole, these forms are very similar to *nominal* or *committed facts* that have been documented in students' reasoning in physics and mathematics (Sherin & Fuson, 2005; diSessa, 1996).

To illustrate, let us use an episode involving David and which took place during field practice at Club-2. On that occasion, a friend had gifted David a used, but fully functional, two-stage rocket. In line with David's style of modifying existing designs – say, to make them "go extra high," as he remarked – he started to fiddle with the possibility of fitting a spare, and more powerful rocket stage (a remnant of a long-lost multi-stage model) to the just-inherited model. He considered two possibilities, the first consisting of substituting the larger stage for one of the original ones and the second consisting of simply adding the extra stage to the existing configuration, thus making it a three-stage model. Regarding the latter, the following interaction ensued:

3:46 (Club-2, 9/15/2002, tape 2/3)
| | | |
|---|---|---|
| 1 | David: | I was thinking about uh like uh ((unint, 1s)) taping this ((the motor he is holding on his left hand)) onto this ((the stage he is holding on his right hand)) like this ((slides motor into the spare stage)). |
| 2 | Flávio: | Uh huh. |
| 3 | David: | And then here make it a third stage ((unint))… I haven't tried that yet, I was thinking about that ((unint)) probably too much weight. |
| 4 | Flávio: | Right. |
| 5 | David: | I'd have to uh:: extend the tube which I don't want to since I:: already got ((unint)) and everything. |
| 6 | Flávio: | I see. |
| | | ((17 seconds interruption)) |
| 7 | Flávio: | So why do you say if you added a third thing you'd have to extend the tube? |
| 8 | David: | I might have to extend the tube yeah because there'd be so much weight down here ((points to the bottom of the second, large stage))… it might it might go haywire. |
| 9 | Flávio: | So right so by extending it you'd be // |
| 10 | David: | //You'd be counteracting the weight ((unint)) you'd have to add weight up here in the nose. |
| 11 | Flávio: | Right. |
| 12 | David: | ((unint)) |
| 13 | Flávio: | Right. |

14  David:  ((David attempts to locate the rocket's CG by equilibrating it on his indicator finger and finds that it falls very near the fins.)) 'Cause right now I think it's… it probably just barely makes it.

On turns 1 and 3, David demonstrated how to simply plug the three stages in sequence, turning the original design into a 3-stage rocket. But at the end of turn 3, he stated that there was "probably too much weight" somewhere in the rocket, which signified a problem ("it might go haywire," turn 8). Indeed, supporting this inference, immediately on turn 5 David sought a way to fix the excess weight problem by extending the body tube. He would go on to further elaborate his strategy for correcting the problem on turns 8 and 10.

Still on turn 8, David effectively identified the problem by concluding that the addition of the large third stage + motor amounted to excess weight at the bottom of the rocket. Importantly, in turn 14 we see that he further saw this excess rear weight as impacting the rocket's center of gravity. In fact, after balancing the rocket on his right indicator finger, he concluded that the center of gravity had moved dangerously down the rocket's body tube and stated: "Cause right now I think it's… it probably barely makes it." This also points to David's understanding that the CG stands in relation to some other imaginary point (i.e., the center of pressure) along the rocket's body tube. In all, he was not sure whether the resulting configuration was stable and thus flyable.

To explain David's reasoning and how it embodies ways of knowing stability that were present in many of his designs, we list a minimal set of stability-centered *facts*, which together and in coordinated use can account for his performance. By facts we mean to refer to correct propositions/information regarding key theoretical constructs and relationships involved in determining the stability of a rocket.

(*Fact* a) A rocket has something called a *center of gravity* (CG), which is the point where the rocket balances on a finger. While David did not mention the technical term in the previous exchange, he did so on other occasions.

(*Fact* b) There is another point involved in determining stability, and in a properly functioning model, this point sits somewhere near the fins. This can be seen in David's assertion that "… right now it barely makes it," in reaction to finding the CG to fall too close to the fins.

(*Fact* c) Stability involves a relationship between the center of gravity and the point-near-the-fins. The two points should not be too close together (again, as seen in David's stating that "… right now it barely makes it") or the rocket "may go haywire." How far apart these points should be is not necessarily specified.

In all, the coordinated use of these stability *facts* afforded David and others the possibility of producing a wealth of stable models or assessing the stability of existing ones. That said, facts were only functionally efficient because the commercially existing material infrastructure (such as standard-sized body tubes, nosecones, and fins) were made to hold constant some important parameters in a rocket. Here as elsewhere (e.g., Hutchins, 1995b), therefore, ways of knowing in a specific practice rely on the knowledge embedded in the artifacts that commonly circulate in the practice – here, the stability built by design into rocket parts, which is an integral part of the ecology of knowing.

## *Heuristics*

In the last excerpted episode, we saw that David made several considerations to determine the stability of a model, in the process articulating procedures for correcting emergent problems of stability. Such procedures are heuristics that are well known in the rocketry communities visited and they can be used when designing a new rocket, modifying existing ones, or fixing unstable models.

To illustrate the range of heuristics for knowing stability found in the fields, let us consider Allan's explanation of the stability of his scratch-built Blazer-4 – a rocket with a central body tube, two lateral hollow tubes extending from the bottom to about one-third of the rocket's length, and three fins symmetrically placed along the tube system.

2:23 (Club-1, 9/10/2000)
| | | |
|---|---|---|
| 1 | Flávio: | So how do you know this is stable? |
| 2 | Allan: | Uh:: when it was built I don't. There isn't a ((computer)) simulator to date that will do tube fins ((points simultaneously at both lateral tubes)) or offset fins ((swings right hand back and forth between the two opposing hollow tubes)). Uh: I just basically figured out roughly what the center of pressure would be, which I'm assuming will be about here ((points to the body tube at the height of the hollow tubes)) the center of most resistance … being here ((points again to the body tube at the height of the hollow tubes)). |
| 3 | Flávio: | Your assumption is based on? |
| 4 | Allan: | Drag. Yeah just where it's gonna create the most drag. This ((points to the top half of the rocket)) is gonna cut through pretty clearly I'd say … and the drag … the pressure is probably gonna build right about here ((indicates a middle point in the body tube)). So I figured my center of pressure is here ((touches that same point)). So I weighed my nosecone to get the center of gravity right about here ((indicates a point ahead of the purported center of pressure)). |
| 5 | Flávio: | Okay:: |
| 6 | Allan: | And I figured, if my center of gravity were here ((the same point he had previously identified as CG)) … as long as my center of pressure were anywhere between here and here ((one or two fingers down the body tube)) … and back ((i.e., even farther down the body tube)) I'd be okay. So I just overcompensated for a little bit of weight in the nosecone than I normally would have. |

| 7 | Flávio: | Okay. |
|---|---|---|
| 8 | Allan: | Basically with rocketry ... with rocketry the primary thing is to keep the center of gravity forward ... ahead of the center of pressure ... having enough fin surface to get the rocket to fly stable ... and having a powerful enough motor to get it up to speed. |

To begin with, we see that Allan knew key terms and "concepts" (e.g., center of gravity and pressure) involved in determining a rocket's stability (turns 2 and 8). In fact, on turn 8 we see that he was comfortable with the same set of fact-like ways of knowing stability considered above. But his understanding of stability was also shaky and somewhat inarticulate. For example, he confused the center of pressure with ideas about a purported "center of most resistance" (turn 2) and never really managed to state a convincing explanation of rocket stability.

And yet, the procedure that he outlined on turns 4 and 6 amounts to a heuristic that can be used to guarantee designing stable models. Basically, starting from knowledge of the positions of the rocket's CG and CP and the correct relationship between these (turn 8), Allan took measures to ensure that the CG was high enough in the body tube so as to be safely away from the CP (turn 6, last utterance) – i.e., he added weight to the nosecone, just like David had suggested when considering his 3-stage improvement (above). Notice that rather than simply adding an arbitrary amount of weight, Allan showed knowledge of overstability problems by stating (turn 6): "So I just overcompensated for a little bit of weight in the nosecone than I normally would have."

In a complementary heuristic, one might work to shift the CP down by increasing the area of the fins rather than attempting to shift the CG up the body tube. George synthesized both approaches: "So you can either compensate by making the fins bigger or putting more weight in the nose" (Club-1, 9/22/2002).

Lastly, extending the length of stable models – say, by attaching a spare body tube to the existing one – does not significantly alter the relationship between the CG and CP and therefore preserves the model's stability. This heuristic was foundational to David's implementation of design modifications seen in his line of tall and mighty rockets. The complementary heuristic – i.e., shortening the body tube – may eventually move the CG too close to the CP and was never seen in the fields.

As before, note that the heuristic procedures considered here always operated in conjunction with other elements in the ecology of knowing. For example, heuristics always appeared articulated around fact-like ways of knowing and were also dependent upon knowledge embedded in the standard materials for building rockets.

## *The Inherent Properties of Objects*

Like off-the-shelf rockets, some objects may fly straight and stably by design, although they might not have been originally conceived to function as model rockets. This is the case of David's Shuttlecock rockets, which derive from an object that is designed to travel in space in a manner similar to flying, but which stems from an entirely different practice and domain (i.e., badminton or children's games). The observation that objects lying outside the practice of model rocketry may easily travel into its fields of collective practice suggests that many other objects – e.g., plastic darts and arrows, and an array of children's products – may potentially be transformed into model rockets, and thus, ways of knowing rocket stability may originate from many domains other than rocketry proper.

## *A Procedural Way of Knowing Stability*

Fully assembled models can be assessed for stability through the use of a simple and well-known procedure. The procedure consists in tying a string to the rocket's CG, then swinging it in a circle above the head. A properly designed rocket will fly straight and an unstable one will tumble.

## *Histories*

Individual rocketeers and rockets develop a history of participation in the communities that they frequent and these are factored into judgments of stability. For example, both rocketeers and inspectors at Club-1 knew David's Shuttlecocks for their successful, long-term "career." So while these rockets were always rigorously inspected, they were most likely stable.

Moreover, information regarding a rocket's stability is available, in part, in the rocket's flight card. As we saw, a flight card is a form that contains some basic information on the rocket, such as its origins (e.g., whether it has been flown before), whether it was made from an original kit or scratch-built, and so on. From the perspective of the rocket inspector, then, judging the stability status of any model involved triangulating historical information and various forms of technical assessments.

## *Processes of Distribution of Work and Knowing*

In characterizing the knowledge elements in the ecology of knowing stability, we have hinted at processes of coordinated use of these elements as critical means through which rocket stability can effectively be known. In fact, many ways of knowing stability were only functional because they rested on other ways of knowing "designed" into the materials and practices of the community. This is the most basic mechanism through which knowing stability is a distributed achievement (Hutchins, 1995a, 1995b). For example, fact-based ways of knowing stability were effective because they relied on a material infrastructure designed with the knowledge of holding constant important parameters of rocket stability.

The distribution of the work of knowing stability is even more obvious when we stretch the timeframe of description to encompass the entire process of successfully flying a rocket (i.e., from conception to design to building, flying, and retrieving the rocket). In this context, we see that guaranteeing the stability of a model often relies on the collective work of various actors, including the rocketeer, inspectors, and manufacturers of rocketry parts – a process distributed across time, people, and space. For example, as just mentioned, the model rocketry industry produces stable models of various types, as well as parts structured for the building of stable models. The rocketeer may then buy the necessary parts and pattern a design after some creative scaling of existing models or through modifying existing kits according to some heuristic principles. Books and resources appearing online may be consulted to guide design and construction decisions. Finally and importantly, prior to flying, inspectors perform a final check on the model, perhaps helping correct any problems of stability or explaining principles behind it (see Azevedo, 2013 for details). We will return to these points in the discussion below.

## Discussion

We have examined the knowing of a "concept" in an interactional space that differs in a number of substantive ways from interviews and classroom interactions. We took as a starting point that the analysis of knowledge (KA) would benefit from considering the broader multiplicity and diversity of knowledge resources brought to bear on a given practice because the conceptual ecology of a practice is reflexively related to the nature of such a practice. Our empirical choice of the hobby of model rocketry was key to our pursuit because the practice embodies complex conceptual spaces, yet it is shaped by goals very different from those of schooling and other formal and informal learning spaces.

As we have seen, ways of knowing model rocket stability amount to various knowledge types, which together form an ecology of knowing that both the community and its participants deploy across phases of designing, building, and flying rockets. In line with the KA program, this ecology of knowing included such knowledge forms as facts, visual/perceptual schemas, heuristics, histories of participation (both of individual rocketeers and rockets), and others, each of them with markedly different character. Yet, in line with IA, these ways of knowing were manifest through, and identifiable within, specific interactions, such as formal rocket inspection. Bringing these two approaches together provides a richer view of how knowing appears in situ.

This integrative approach also reveals that there is no single way of determining stability (such as the canonical form considered earlier) that is universally used by all participants in a practice. Instead, multiple ways of knowing stability are quite obviously deployed by different rocketeers, in different times and contexts.

For instance, when reasoning about the stability of his Shuttlecock rockets, David relied on the well-known properties of that object as a way to determine the model's suitability for flying. When judging the stability of his tall and mighty rockets, on the other hand, he resorted to time-tested, domain-dependent heuristics for modifying rockets that were known to preserve CG–CP relationships.

Focusing more explicitly on the character of the ecology of knowing stability and its component elements reveals additional insights. For example, the conceptual ecologies appearing in KA studies of classroom interactions and clinical interviews typically highlight knowledge elements that are directly tied to the domain under consideration. In physics classrooms, for instance, knowing a "concept" would involve coordinating p-prims, nominal facts of physics and physics-based narratives (diSessa, 1996, 2002). But in the open-ended, interest-driven practice of model rocketry, knowing a complex "concept" often includes knowledge elements not necessarily tied to the technicalities of the domain within its immediate purview (e.g., a rocketeer's history of successful participation in the hobby).

Furthermore, note that none of the elements in the ecology of knowing stability approximates the canonical explanation introduced earlier (though they do anticipate canonical understandings in many ways). Instead, by formal physics standards, they are "sketchier," somewhat "less articulate" and "less elaborate." Yet, together and in coordinated use, the ecology of knowing stability of rocketeers and their communities does the real "conceptual work" of determining model rocket stability. Here, too, we see clearly the link between practice nature and the ecology of knowing that emerges in the practice. Specifically, as in Scribner's (1985) study of the mathematical problem-solving strategies of dairy workers and the *practical* nature of the *knowledge* they develop, the ecology of knowing that rocketeers and communities develop is directly tied to the practical problem of generating stable rocket designs. Even George – a software engineer who was knowledgeable about many formal means of calculating stability and canonical explanations of stability phenomena – never used such methods in designing and building his many rockets. Instead, he relied on the practical means for determining stability considered above. In all, given the interest-based nature of hobbies, the practice of model rocketry was organized such that rocketeers achieved full participation – relative to the concept of stability – very quickly and at a very low learning cost.

In contrast, in classrooms and other formal learning arrangements, conceptual achievements of this kind are more complex and protracted. Under these conditions, the ecology of knowing is built through a very long-term, cumulative process. Model rocketry is interestingly different in that practitioners must master, at least in action, a notion that is conceptually complex before their designs will fly safely (i.e., a theoretically steep threshold). But as a reflection of its open-ended nature, the hobby of model rocketry – conceived as a system composed of rocketeers, rocketry clubs, larger societal actors (e.g., manufacturers of tools, rockets, and rocket parts), and the practices that bind them together – has evolved many mechanisms for establishing rocket stability and these make it possible for even newcomers to get beyond that threshold relatively rapidly. By stepping outside of classroom walls we see more clearly how the learnability of a "concept" is a feature of the ecology of knowing that emerges in the practice.

By the same token, we see that there are no "clean breaks" to be found between what knowledge an individual rocketeer possesses and how that individual participates in the practice. This is so because the ecology of knowing stability is "comfortably" distributed across people (individual rocketeers, their peers, and inspectors) and materials (e.g., off-the-shelf, stable rockets and standard rocket parts). For instance, David's tall and mighty rockets are founded on heuristic procedures that operate on stable-by-design models produced by professional designers/manufacturers who are not immediately present when judgments of stability are being made, but whose influence is still felt. The existence of, and familiarity with, stable-by-design models is an important part of David's knowing and it comprises an important part within his ecology of knowing stability for that specific rocket type. From an integrative perspective, then, the distribution of work and knowing is a critical aspect of the ecology of knowing a "concept" in actual practice.

Finally, the ecology of knowing stability in model rocketry is also distributed across time and it operates in somewhat overlapping, redundant, mutually reinforcing ways tied to the critical nature of determining stability (i.e., getting it wrong may have bad consequences). For example, the rocketeer builds a model according to specs or assembles one from scratch following some time-tested procedures. Later in the field, stability is checked and perhaps corrected by the inspectors, as seen previously. In some kinds of practice, then, the ecology of knowing a concept is tied to social routines that necessarily stretch the knowing of a concept across space and over long time spans. Analytically, this suggests that those interested in knowledge analysis through an integrative KA/IA approach would benefit from studying knowing and learning phenomena of relatively long duration.

## Conclusion

In closing, our analysis illustrates how a KA/IA integrative approach can shed light on phenomena of STEM knowing and learning that would not necessarily be gleaned from any program alone. In this regard, we started from some central KA tenets on the nature of knowledge and knowing, and onto that we overlaid IA principles and methods to stretch our understanding of cognitive activity in different STEM practices. Doing so has afforded us several insights on issues at the intersection of KA and IA research programs. Most centrally, it allowed us to productively theorize the forms of knowledge making up the ecology of knowing a "concept" (namely, model rocket stability) and the processes through which such knowledge emerges and is used. At the same time, by attending to how knowing stability is actually performed in the open-ended practice of rocketry, we have shown that the ecology of knowing the "concept" is distributed across people, materials, space, and time and cannot be confined to mental activity alone. As we move forward, we hope our approach will spur similar analytical efforts that both continue to sharpen the theoretical constructs of each individual program and further develop intersections between these programs.

## Acknowledgments

This work was supported in part by a dissertation year fellowship from the Spencer Foundation to the first author. The opinions expressed here are those of the authors and not the Foundation's. We thank the editors for the invaluable feedback throughout the preparation of the manuscript.

## Notes

1. Clubs' and rocketeers' names are pseudonyms.
2. We use the following conventions when transcribing participants' talk (adapted from Hall & Stevens, 1995):

| | |
|---|---|
| . . . | Ellipses show pauses of less than three seconds |
| :: | Extended vowel sound (e.g., No::) |
| (( )) | Authors' comments |
| [ | Beginning of overlapping talk |
| unint | Unintelligible talk, seconds indicated if > 1 sec. |
| caps | EMPHATIC talk |

## References

Azevedo, F. S. (2011). Lines of practice: A practice-centered theory of interest relationships. *Cognition and Instruction*, 29(2), 147–184.

Azevedo, F. S. (2013). Knowing the stability of model rockets: An investigation of learning in interest-based practices. *Cognition and Instruction*, 31(3), 345–374.

diSessa, A. A. (1993). Toward an epistemology of physics. *Cognition and Instruction*, 10(2–3), 105–225.

diSessa, A. A. (1996). What do "just plain folk" know about physics? In D. R. Olson & N. Torrance (Eds.), *Handbook of education and human development: new models of learning, teaching and schooling* (pp. 709–730). Oxford, UK: Blackwell.

diSessa, A. A. (2002). Why "conceptual ecology" is a good idea. In M. Limón & L. Mason (Eds.), *Reconsidering conceptual change. Issues in theory and practice* (pp. 29–60). Boston, MA: Kluwer Academic.

diSessa, A. A. (2006). A history of conceptual change research: Threads and fault lines. In R. K. Sawyer (Ed.), *Cambridge handbook of the learning sciences* (pp. 265–282). Cambridge, UK: Cambridge University Press.

diSessa, A. A., & Sherin, B. L. (1998). What changes in conceptual change? *International Journal of Science Education*, 20(10), 1155–1191.

Greeno, J. G. (2006). Learning in activity. In R. K. Sawyer (Ed.), *The Cambridge handbook of the learning sciences* (pp. 79–96). New York: Cambridge University Press.

Greeno, J. G., Collins, A., & Resnick, L. B. (1996). Cognition in learning. In D. C. Berliner & R. C. Calfee (Eds.), *Handbook of educational psychology* (pp. 15–46). New York: Macmillan.

Hall, R., & Stevens, R. (1995). Making space: A comparison of mathematical work in school and professional design practice. In S. L. Star (Ed.), *The cultures of computing* (pp. 118–145). London: Basil Blackwell.

Hammer, D. M., & Elby, A. (2003). Tapping epistemological resources for learning physics. *Journal of the Learning Sciences*, 12(1), 53–90.

Hammer, D., Elby, A., Scherr, R. E., & Redish, E. F. (2005). Resources, framing, and transfer. In J. Mestre (Ed.), *Transfer of learning from a modern multidisciplinary perspective* (pp. 89–120). Greenwich, CT: Information Age Publishing.

Hutchins, E. (1995a). *Cognition in the wild*. Cambridge, MA: MIT Press.

Hutchins, E. (1995b). How a cockpit remembers its speed. *Cognitive Science*, 19, 265–288.

Jordan, B., & Henderson, A. (1995). Interaction analysis: Foundations and practices. *Journal of the Learning Sciences*, 4(10), 39–103.

Lave, J. (1988). *Cognition in practice*. New York: Cambridge University Press.

Lave, J., Murtaught, M., & de la Rocha, O. (1984). The dialectics of arithmetic in grocery shopping. In B. Rogoff & J. Lave (Eds.), *Everyday cognition: Its development in social context* (pp. 67–94). Cambridge, MA: Cambridge University Press.

Lave, J., & Wenger, E. (1991). *Situated learning: Legitimate peripheral participation*. Cambridge, UK: Cambridge University Press.

Parnafes, O. (2007). What does "fast" mean? Understanding the physical world through computational representations. *Journal of the Learning Sciences*, 16(3), 415–450.

Rogoff, B., Paradise, R., Arauz, R. M., Correa-Chávez, M., & Angelillo, C. (2003). Firsthand learning through intent participation. *Annual Review of Psychology*, 54, 175–203.

Saxe, G. B. (1991). *Culture and cognitive development: Studies in mathematical understanding*. Hillsdale, NJ: Lawrence Erlbaum Associates.

Scribner, S. (1985). Thinking in action: Some characteristics of practical thought. *Anthropology & Education Quarterly*, 16(3), 199–206.

Sherin, B. L. (2001). How students understand physics equations. *Cognition and Instruction*, 19(4), 479–541.

Sherin, B. L., & Fuson, K. (2005). Multiplication strategies and the appropriation of computational resources. *Journal for Research in Mathematical Education*, 36(4), 347–395.

Stine, G. H., & National Association of Rocketry. (1983). *Handbook of model rocketry*. New York: Prentice Hall.

Stine, G. H., & Stine, B. (2004). *Handbook of model rocketry*. Hoboken, NJ: John Wiley & Sons.

Wagner, J. (2006). Transfer in pieces. *Cognition and Instruction*, 24(1), 1–71.

# 5

# A MICROLATITUDINAL/ MICROLONGITUDINAL ANALYSIS OF SPEECH, GESTURE, AND REPRESENTATION USE IN A STUDENT'S REPEATED SCIENTIFIC EXPLANATIONS OF PHASE CHANGE

*David DeLiema, Victor R. Lee, Joshua A. Danish, Noel Enyedy, and Nathaniel J. S. Brown*

Students who are asked to explain natural phenomena often exhibit variations in their answers, offering conflicting ideas only moments apart in the same conversation (Clark, D'Angelo, & Schleigh, 2011; diSessa, Gillespie, & Esterly, 2004; Sherin, Krakowski, & Lee, 2012). For example, a student may characterize the motion of a ball tossed into the air as being an exclusive product of gravity, only to change her description a few seconds later and suggest that this motion is in fact the product of both upward and downward forces and states of momentary balance between forces (e.g., Brown et al., this volume; diSessa & Sherin, 1998). These changes in explanation range from the subtle to the dramatic, and have led to the suggestion that they represent weakly organized knowledge structures. However, we argue that students' changing explanations could also be attributed to properties of the interaction between interviewer and interviewee that are not typically analyzed in conceptual change research. The questions that drive this chapter are: What factors contribute to the variation or stability of an explanation over time? And what value is there in teasing apart the different causes of variability and stability?

Our tentative answer is that part of the reason for students' novel explanations lies in their social interactions, such as the way participants frame the interaction and make connections between spoken, drawn, and gestured representations. In the analysis described in this chapter, we document the changes that occur in a single student's explanation of a chemical phenomenon when variations occur in interactional context. This allows us to explore how efforts to explain the same phenomenon change or stay the same when the framing of the conversation changes, when variations in a drawn representation offer new affordances, and when prior knowledge becomes repurposed for a new context.

Our research approach involves a process of data collection and analysis that we call *microlatitudinal/microlongitudinal*. Microlatitudinal is intended to indicate that we compare moments of interaction across similar episodes in an effort to see what results from slight changes to each interaction. There are several ways in which the conversations were designed to be similar to one another. Specifically, the topic, the setting, the depictive tools in the environment, and the general task remained the same. The case student, an undergraduate to whom we have given the pseudonym Colin, was involved in each interaction. Over four days, Colin was tasked with explaining to another individual how molecules in a liquid state change to a gaseous state during the process of evaporation, as part of a larger discussion of different aspects of phase equilibrium. The interactions were also designed to be slightly different, allowing us to explore the influence of context on Colin's explanations. Specifically, Colin's interlocutor (researcher, friend, confederate student) shifted each day against the backdrop of different frames (searching for an explanation versus a right answer).

Our use of the term microlongitudinal is partly a play on the implied spatial coordinate system terminology but also an acknowledgment that time and reiteration play important roles in Colin's evolving understanding and his related explanation. Longitudinal research is generally understood as focusing on change over time – typically on the scale of years (e.g., Clark, 2006). Thus, microlongitudinal for us means change over time, but at a far smaller timescale. In this case, we examine change within and across four interactions occurring over the course of about three weeks. The episodes we describe vary slightly in the design of the interaction (microlatitudinal) but take place sequentially and involve a task done multiple times by the same student (microlongitudinal).

The overarching argument we make in this chapter is that explanations produced in interactions are ultimately caught between two processes. One of these is a trend toward stability, as a student repeatedly attempts to clarify his own understanding. The other is a pull toward addressing the particulars of the immediate situation – so that an explanation is properly customized for the given context. Following a review of our theoretical perspective, which is informed by both Interaction Analysis (IA) and Knowledge Analysis (KA), we present fine-grained analyses of Colin in interaction with different conversation partners. Taken together, the series of excerpts that we present show how competing stabilization and customization forces are at work over time. Furthermore, we also show that this competition does not play out only in the presence of dramatic changes to contexts; rather, this tension is in play at all times in the interaction, capable of occurring even during the smallest variations to the semiotic fields.

## Theoretical Perspective

We consider three aspects of social interaction and knowledge that give us purchase in understanding how and why an explanation can stabilize and change.

We examine the connection between (1) framing, (2) prior knowledge, and (3) lamination of semiotic fields, arguing that each concept helps explain the changing form of the student's explanation. Here, we summarize existing research on each concept with the goal of defining terms and setting the stage for our research questions and analysis.

## *Framing*

One of our base assumptions is that social encounters invoke tacit social frames that organize participants' expectations for how to interact (e.g., Goffman, 1974). A definition of framing can be found in Hammer, Elby, Scherr, and Redish (2005): "phenomenologically, a set of expectations an individual has about the situation in which she finds herself that affect what she notices and how she thinks to act" (p. 98). In line with sociolinguistic approaches (Goffman, 1974), we consider framing to be ubiquitous across moments of interaction and subject to subtle variations over time (Erickson & Schultz, 1981; Kendon, 1990). For example, a frame helps people to determine whether a potentially insulting comment is intended to be either a friendly act of teasing as might happen with friends or a deliberately hurtful statement as might happen in an unfriendly argument.

Frames are the product of complex negotiations, but there is some agreement that they can be understood as having at least two important dimensions: *social* and *epistemic* (Hammer et al., 2005). The social aspect of framing, often called a participation framework (Erickson, 1992; Goffman, 1981), captures how participants expect to interact, such as through turn-taking (e.g., in interviews, whole-class discourse), synchronous action (e.g., carrying a large couch, harmonizing), modeling (e.g., demonstrating to teach), performing (e.g., performing to entertain), etc. Social frames determine who should partake in the interaction, who should be responsible for certain tasks, and how and when participants should be expected to accomplish those tasks.

The epistemic[1] aspect of framing refers to how participants expect to treat knowledge and knowing. Greeno (2009) describes epistemic framing as expectations "regarding the kind(s) of knowledge that are relevant to and expected to be constructed in order to succeed in the task" (p. 271). One way that participants achieve epistemic framing is by setting a knowledge goal. In this way, participants adopt socially relevant epistemic aims (Chinn, Buckland, & Samarapungavan, 2011) in their interaction. For example, participants may agree to pursue knowledge, understanding, or truth, among other possibilities. Epistemic aims function as frames for how other dimensions of epistemic cognition are enacted, such as what sources of knowledge to use or how to justify knowledge claims (Chinn et al., 2011).

Together, social and epistemic frames in interaction govern participants' senses of the rules for how to engage with one another and how to infer meaning from the talk, gesture, and drawings of others, in addition to the knowledge – such as truth, understanding, or explanation – that should be pursued. As we argue later, frame changes are consequential for how Colin explains the phenomenon of phase change.

## Prior Knowledge

Another of our assumptions is that when students are in a situation that demands they present an explanation, they draw upon a rich pool of prior knowledge. This store of knowledge is diverse and complex – it may involve coherent models, factoids, generalized schemata, specific episodic memories, narratives, or other structures (diSessa, 2002). In many cases, explanations that students provide based on that body of knowledge will be emergent depending on what knowledge has been made relevant by the interaction. For example, when asked about the cause of the seasons, it is not at all unusual for students to explain temperature variation as being due to the overall distance of the Earth from the sun. When an interviewer reminds the student how different locations on the Earth can experience summer and winter simultaneously, many students will adapt to this new cue by changing their explanation to state that one side of the Earth is facing the sun while the other is facing away from the sun (the axial rotation that actually causes the day and night cycle). When asked about how night and day are involved, students will often shift their explanation again and mention axial tilt, and how the greater distance of one hemisphere from the sun leads to differences in temperature for different parts of the Earth (Sherin et al., 2012). These explanations are also often responsive to the material context of the interaction (e.g., to what sort of drawing is provided or made) (e.g., Parnafes, 2012).

In the previous example with the seasons, an important feature to note about the use of prior knowledge is that substantial moment-to-moment continuities exist with respect to what knowledge is used. When posed with a challenge or presented with new information, students do not abandon the entire set of resources with which they have assembled an explanation, but rather they examine different pieces of the current *assemblage* to see which parts are inadequate given the current circumstances. Many of the same core knowledge resources are involved in the new assemblage. For instance, students might draw on the same generalized schema or phenomenological primitive (diSessa, 1993), such as how distance from a source (e.g., the sun) changes the experienced heat, in different circumstances. This is evident when students initially reason that seasons are the product of orbital distance and then reason that seasons are explained in terms of a particular hemisphere being closer or farther from the sun due to tilt. Indeed, this continuity in thinking is posited as being central to the eventual development of expertise in the subject area (Smith, diSessa, & Roschelle, 1993). Yet, while many bits of knowledge in talk, gesture, and image are expected to carry over, some new knowledge elements that were not initially made relevant can play a more prominent role later in the interaction. Such is the case when students are reminded about different, co-occurring seasons, which adds an imperative to include more specific knowledge about hemispheres.

This view of prior knowledge as involving a diverse pool of resources, parts of which are assembled in response to immediate explanatory demands suggests three things about how we understand stabilization and customization at the microlatitudinal/microlongitudinal scale. First, we should expect some continuities in cued knowledge over time such that many of the same knowledge elements appear across explanations, albeit in different configurations. Second, as the same explanation is reproduced over time, the assemblage should become more routine and automatic as the search and construction process associated with presenting an explanation becomes more rehearsed. Third, the immediate material and semiotic resources, in addition to the epistemic frame, play an important role in that they can and do privilege different ways of explaining phenomena. Changes in diagrams or representations are very likely to lead to new ways of thinking, even when an individual draws on the same knowledge resources over time.

## *Laminating Semiotic Fields in Interaction*

The previous two sections suggest that attention to verbal utterances, drawing, and how an interaction is framed should figure prominently in our work. Additionally, gestures are central to our analysis as they are both intra-mental and inter-mental. From the intra-mental perspective, gesture can serve as a window into and catalyst for individual thinking processes (e.g., Goldin-Meadow, Alibali, & Church, 1993; Goldin-Meadow, Cook, & Mitchell, 2009). From the inter-mental perspective, gestures are often communicative and laden with meaning derived from the social interaction. Gestures like the peace sign are culturally defined, and coordinating gestures have been shown as a way to establish inter-subjectivity and to establish the current frame (Kendon, 2000).

Central to our analysis is the observation that many gestures, especially those that accompany demonstratives such as *this* or *that*, cannot be understood without reference to the visual objects they demarcate in the local referential field (Clark, Schreuder, & Buttrick, 1983). That is, gestures can be *environmentally coupled*, interleaving the body, speech, and environmental structures into a single action, as in the case of pointing to different features of a kitchen appliance while saying, "So she sold me this – But she didn't sell me this or that" (Goodwin, 2007). Gestures are one focus of our analysis in part because they bridge the divide between conceptual and interactional analyses, and because they are often grounded in the material circumstances (e.g., drawings on a whiteboard) that dynamically shape thought and interaction. Stated another way, gestures can be an important means by which stabilization is reached and maintained, but they can also change quickly in response to the demands of the situation.

The integration between gesture and the visual world warrants an analysis that takes into account both resources (see also Kapon, this volume). Permanent or semi-permanent external representations (such as drawings), in contrast to transitory gestural representations, frequently remain present in the interactional context, providing an ongoing site for reflection and discussion. In our view, these representations are most productively examined as artifacts that are actively used in conjunction with speech and gesture to communicate meaning (e.g., Danish & Enyedy, 2007). This is in contrast to more static analyses of representations as objects inherently laden with meaning (e.g., Heiser & Tversky, 2006).

In summary, language, gesture, and material artifacts have been noted in the literature as important to the expression, reflection, and modification of ideas (e.g., Goldin-Meadow & Beilock, 2010; Parnafes, 2012). Moreover, when gesture, speech, and representation intersect, they act cooperatively to establish an intended meaning (Hutchins & Palen, 1997), an interactional process that *laminates* multiple semiotic fields (e.g., lexical structure, prosody, gesture, visual diagrams) into a stream of action (Goodwin, 2013). The metaphor of lamination, in Goodwin's words,

> provides a simple and vivid way to look clearly at how a variety of semiotic fields with quite different properties work co-operatively with each other simultaneously to build evanescent actions that might endure for only a few seconds, but which have rich, analytically interesting complex internal structure.
>
> (p. 12)

Lamination is a process we expect to vary subtly as an explanation is initially presented and then re-presented several times later. That is, "the laminated structure of action, the way in which it is composed of layers of different kinds of semiotic materials, is something that participants in interaction can disassemble and reorganize in order to build subsequent action" (Goodwin, 2013, p. 12). Given different demands of the learning environment and different social and epistemic frames, laminated resources in the setting can be deconstructed and relaminated to produce new configurations, in a manner similar to our discussion above of how prior knowledge changes in response to new demands.

In an effort to be comprehensible, conversation participants select features to emphasize and combine from various semiotic fields in order to get an intended meaning across – drawing on the public display of other participants' semiotic contributions. Interlocutors rely upon established and negotiated frames to help infer each other's meaning. One major point we will stress below is that while participants may have certain intentions associated with a given arrangement of laminated fields, residual features of that lamination can be taken up and renegotiated in the context of a new frame to create new meaning. In one of the episodes we discuss below, the student expresses his "stabilized" explanation through a drawing that the tutor and student then reuse in ways not originally intended. This transformation is made possible because participants reframe the interaction as one in which the focal student, Colin, is not considered the sole expert but rather a participant in a process where the correct answer still needs to be uncovered. In the episode, this leads to the joint construction of a new and unanticipated explanation, customized to the demands of the situation.

## Data Sources and Empirical Base

The data in this study come from four video-recorded sessions involving Colin, the undergraduate student. Colin was enrolled in an introductory-level general chemistry course at a large, public, urban university. Colin was recruited by one of the authors (Brown) to participate in a series of conversations, during which he was always present and Colin worked to explain the same set of chemistry phenomena (Brown, 2009, this volume). In the discussion that follows, Brown is referred to as the Researcher. In the first session, the Researcher conducted a clinical interview with Colin about the chemistry phenomena. In the second, Colin brought a personal friend and was asked to explain the same phenomena that were covered in the clinical interview, responding to follow-up questions from the friend. In the third interaction, Colin was asked to explain the phenomena to a stranger (a confederate graduate student in education who was a novice in the content domain being discussed). Finally, in the fourth interaction, the Researcher served as a tutor to Colin on the same topics discussed the three times prior. However, at the beginning of that meeting, the Researcher began by asking Colin to first provide explanations like he had done before. Then, the Researcher intervened and helped to correct inaccuracies in Colin's explanations.

The interactions raised a number of questions about equilibrium in chemistry. For this chapter, we focus on episodes where Colin was asked to explain why liquid methanol in a closed flask would partly evaporate (see Figure 5.1), first decreasing in amount (lowering the visible level of liquid present) and then stopping after a period of time (so that the level of liquid appears to stay the same from then on). Briefly, a normative explanation of this phenomenon describes the eventual attainment of a dynamic equilibrium in which the rate at which liquid methanol is evaporating is equal to the rate at which methanol vapor is recondensing back into liquid. Such an explanation would invoke processes and motion occurring on the molecular scale and bridge that with the observed changes in the level of the liquid.

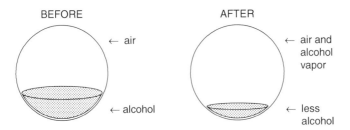

**FIGURE 5.1** The chemical phenomenon presented to and explained by Colin (Brown, 2009).

For all of the interactions, Colin was provided with a small whiteboard, markers, and an eraser. Two video cameras were active. One camera was positioned such that the participants, seated at a table, and the whiteboard could all be seen in the frame. The other camera was positioned beside Colin and zoomed into the whiteboard so that the drawings he made could be better seen. We use images from both recordings in our analysis.

## Colin's Explanations

The argument we make relies heavily on multimodal transcripts as a source of evidence (produced in a style comparable to Goodwin, 2013), in which moments of talk are anchored to gestural acts and drawn diagrams. We mark conversation pauses in seconds (e.g., (2.0) refers to a 2-second pause). The portions of the recordings that we discuss in Section 1, below, all relate to a brief narration (on the scale of a few seconds to up to a minute) that Colin provides, uninterrupted, in some form during the first six minutes of the four interactions.[2] In this narrative, Colin describes a single molecule of liquid methanol that, in his words, "escapes" the other molecules and becomes part of the gas above the liquid. We identified segments of the recordings in which Colin first uses language associated with the escape of the molecule. In all of the segments, the words *escape*, *intermolecular*, and *molecule* appear, and some verbal or gestural references are made to the drawings that Colin creates (Section 1).

This is a period of time in which stabilization is visible in light of only minor shifts in framing, although, as we discuss, some customization takes place with each interlocutor. Following that analysis, we then discuss how these terms are reconfigured in the fourth and final interaction such that Colin appears to shift in his reasoning, stating that liquid molecules are not separated by space but exist in contiguous clumps (see Figure 5.7). We describe how a reframing of the type of interaction Colin and the Researcher have in the final session, a change in the diagram, and the selective use of gesture lead to Colin's custom explanation of molecular arrangement (Section 2).

## Section 1: Stabilizing an Escape Narrative

In this first section, our intent is to show how Colin, responding to the prompt to explain the chemical phenomenon, largely stabilizes (across talk, gesture, and drawing) how to represent a molecule escaping from liquid state to gas state. In addition, we discuss the stability of the epistemic and social frames across the first four sessions. Note that because the data samples provided in this section focus on relatively brief, uninterrupted utterances by Colin, we only present images of Colin and not his interlocutors in these transcripts (Figures 5.2, 5.3, 5.4, & 5.5).

From these four segments, there are two key features that we wish to highlight. The first feature is that Colin generates a stable interpretation of intermolecular attraction. We focus on this feature because mention of intermolecular attraction makes its way into all four interactions and plays an especially important role when Colin later revises his explanation. In the incipient moments of all four sessions (Figures 5.2, 5.3, 5.4, & 5.5), Colin depicts attraction between molecules, which he calls "intermolecular attractions," "intermolecular pull," and "pull on the intermolecular forces." With his hands, Colin displays attraction through fists bumping into each other three consecutive times (Figure 5.2, line 6) and through pen movements that thrust down toward the liquid (Figure 5.5, line 12). Colin couples his gestures to the visual scene, tying the movement of pulling/attracting specifically to the visible liquid area of the drawing. Laminated together, the talk, gesture, and diagram present a multimodal narrative in which a molecule escaping

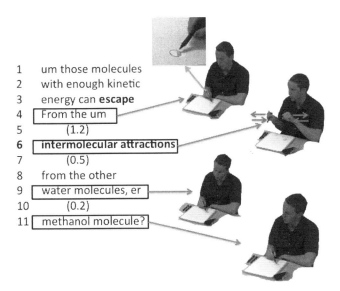

| | |
|---|---|
| 1 | um those molecules |
| 2 | with enough kinetic |
| 3 | energy can **escape** |
| 4 | From the um |
| 5 | (1.2) |
| 6 | intermolecular attractions |
| 7 | (0.5) |
| 8 | from the other |
| 9 | water molecules, er |
| 10 | (0.2) |
| 11 | methanol molecule? |

**FIGURE 5.2** The escape narrative from the clinical interview between Colin and the Researcher on their first day. White arrows originating from Colin or the whiteboard show the path of his gestures.

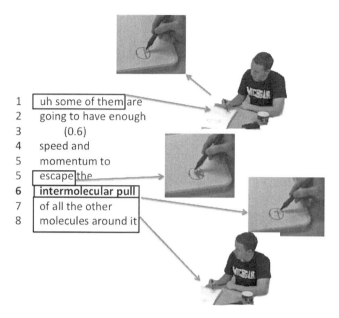

**FIGURE 5.3** The escape narrative from the second interview, conducted in the form of a tutoring session with Colin explaining phase changes to his personal friend.

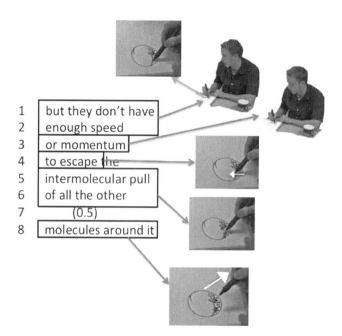

**FIGURE 5.4** A first statement related to the escape narrative when Colin was tutoring the confederate graduate student.

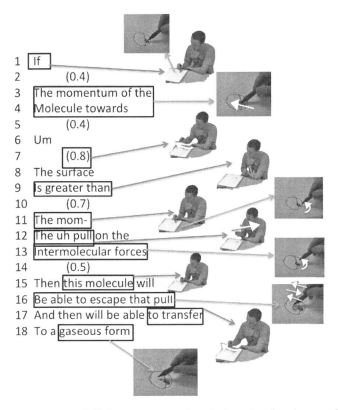

```
1   If
2        (0.4)
3   The momentum of the
4   Molecule towards
5        (0.4)
6   Um
7        (0.8)
8   The surface
9   Is greater than
10       (0.7)
11  The mom-
12  The uh pull on the
13  Intermolecular forces
14       (0.5)
15  Then this molecule will
16  Be able to escape that pull
17  And then will be able to transfer
18  To a gaseous form
```

**FIGURE 5.5** Colin's escape narrative during the fourth recorded interaction in which he was explaining phase change immediately prior to being tutored by the Researcher.

liquid to become gas must first overpower the attraction between molecules in the liquid state.

From a microlongitudinal vantage point, the laminated semiotic fields have stabilized. The use of the words intermolecular "attraction," "pull," and "force" occurs alongside gestures and drawings that consistently show molecules held down in the liquid. With this baseline of intermolecular attraction, Colin's conception of molecular escape also stabilizes. Laminating gesture and image, Colin simulates the word *escape* with a composite outward flick gesture over the drawing in the opposite direction from the pulling motion (Figures 5.3, line 5; Figure 5.4, line 4). That is, in order to escape, the molecule must break away from its attraction to other liquid molecules. These observations suggest not only that Colin's narrative has stabilized, but also that his idea of intermolecular attraction is situated in terms of how a single molecule moves from liquid to gaseous state. In other words, the purpose of presenting the background condition of intermolecular attraction is to describe some of the constraints on how a molecule escapes.

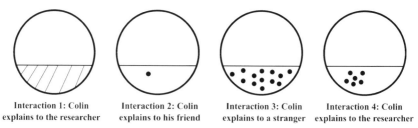

**FIGURE 5.6** A reproduction of the initial drawings of molecules that Colin prepared early into each of the four conversations.

But even within a stable narrative there is some variability. This is the second feature of these interactions that we wish to highlight, noting how the drawn representation changes (Figure 5.6). Colin's first drawing of liquid, which has angled hash marks and no initial markings for molecules (Figure 5.2, line 4), parallels the form of the representation given to Colin on a sheet of paper at the beginning of the interview (Figure 5.1). This is done presumably just to distinguish the liquid and gas regions in the first conversation, at a time when Colin did not know that he would eventually be focusing on and needing to represent molecules individually. In the second through fourth drawings, Colin moves from a lone molecule-as-dot drawing to small groupings of molecules-as-dots, the latter of which allows him to add and point to specific molecules when talking about intermolecular forces. In a sense, the transition to multiple molecules-as-dots suggests the increased relevance for Colin of talking about dynamics between molecules. Even in Colin's first interview with the Researcher, he relies on descriptions of molecules, suggesting that he views their inclusion as necessary for producing a sufficient explanation for how liquid changes to gas. However, each of the drawings retains the line that marks the boundary between the liquid and gas state. This line does not make normative sense, as the line should be comprised of molecules. The position of the molecules in the drawing, both in relation to the line and in relation to each other, becomes consequential during the explanation change in the reframed fourth interaction (discussed later).

The overall stability of Colin's explanation can be credited in part to the microlatitudinal similarities across the four sessions. The first three interactions, and the beginning of the fourth, were all similar to one another in terms of content (same phenomena), material resources (whiteboard and pens), and framing. With respect to framing, Colin is told to present his own version of the molecular escape narrative in a context in which his co-participant is positioned as needing to understand Colin; the frame is a mix of Colin expressing his own view and teaching that view to another person.

Here, in a manner similar to Russ, Lee, and Sherin (2012), we provide a few examples of the verbal activation of the frame. The Researcher's publicly stated interest, "How people explain chemical phenomena" (Session 1), is broad and aligns with the Researcher's allowance that Colin can take "as long as he wants" (Session 1). In response to Colin's question about whether he can draw, the Researcher says, "You can do whatever you want!" (Session 1). In session 2, the Researcher states, "He (*pointing to Colin*) is going to try to explain to you (*pointing at the friend*) what happened" and "if you think he's wrong, you can probe him, you can ask whatever you want." Colin responds: "It should be said that I don't necessarily know what I'm talking about," after which both he and the Researcher laugh. At the beginning of Session 3, the Researcher says that the chemistry phenomena, "which Colin has seen many times before," will be explained by Colin, and that the confederate graduate student should "see if you can understand what he's saying, and, uh, if it seems like it's at least plausible. And if it's not, you can press him on it." In all three episodes, and at the beginning of the fourth, the Researcher asks Colin to address the chemistry phenomena in his own way, to make his explanation comprehensible and plausible in the eyes of his interlocutor, and to respond to his interlocutor's questions.

These frames are publicly stated and reinforced throughout the discourse. The epistemic aims of plausibility and comprehensibility – not truth or accuracy – allow Colin to articulate his understanding of the chemical phenomena, but not without Colin recognizing publicly that he does not necessarily know what he is talking about. That is, the epistemic frame of providing a plausible and comprehensible solution is already balanced specifically against the inactive epistemic frame of truth – and Colin's own admission that he does not have access to that normative model. In this way, we are studying a particular situation in which the student and Researcher both frame the student's knowledge as tentative, giving us a window into how a student uncertain about the content manages conceptual change. On the social side, the frame consistently gives Colin the lead as the explanation starter and his interlocutor the allowance to break into that explanation to ask questions. The general stability of these frames across episodes gives Colin the warrant to provide a consistent narrative about molecular escape, while simultaneously recognizing the lack of knowledge or accuracy in his explanation.

To summarize, the content of Colin's explanation largely stabilizes under the same epistemic and social frames, with the same materials and chemical phenomena, and with different interlocutors. Colin's narrative laminates multiple semiotic fields. The physical actions of pulling and attracting are coupled to the visual diagram and take on a precise meaning alongside the talk. What can we conclude, then, about Colin's knowledge? Colin makes known at least the following ideas about the chemistry phenomenon: (1) Molecules are thought of as small and numerous discrete entities; (2) A single molecule can demonstrate an instance of escaping; and (3) Attractions between molecules are particularly strong in the liquid state and create resistance for an escaping molecule. In the coming section, we examine how Colin and the Researcher focus on a new aspect of the escape narrative: the space out of which the molecule escapes. Instead of seeing the molecules as entities separated by space in the liquid, Colin states that the molecules would "clump" together. Why and how does Colin change his mind?

## Section 2: The Emergence of Clumps

In this section, we focus on how and why Colin's escape narrative becomes disrupted. The change in his explanation takes place after the Researcher introduces a new way to draw molecules and asks a series of pointed questions. After a few minutes, Colin arrives at a characterization of molecules in the liquid state as clumps (Figure 5.7). As Colin describes them, clumps are groups of molecules separated in space and capable of moving in different directions. The prospect of clumping marks a significant departure both from Colin's original narrative and from the normative account of molecules in a liquid state.

The goal of our analysis in this section is to understand the engine behind a rather routine explanation shift. How do framing, properties of semiotic fields, prior knowledge, and sequences in interaction produce the explanation shift? Our main contention is that Colin did not think of molecules as existing in clumps prior to the Researcher's sequence of pointed questions. Rather, clumps represent a custom explanation that emerges from the shift in interactional framing, the shift in attention to a new property of the diagram, the reuse of knowledge resources that had been useful in his earlier narrative of escape, and a wave of pointed questions.

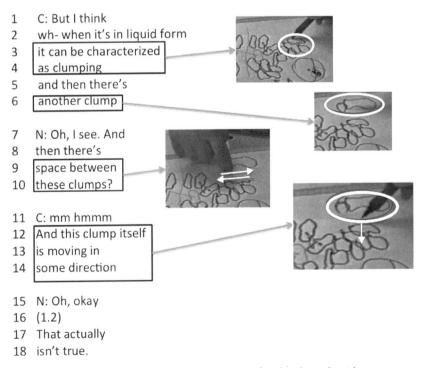

1  C: But I think
2  wh- when it's in liquid form
3  it can be characterized
4  as clumping
5  and then there's
6  another clump

7  N: Oh, I see. And
8  then there's
9  space between
10 these clumps?

11 C: mm hmmm
12 And this clump itself
13 is moving in
14 some direction

15 N: Oh, okay
16 (1.2)
17 That actually
18 isn't true.

**FIGURE 5.7** Colin states the existence of clumps of molecules in liquid state.

## Explicit Changes to the Social and Epistemic Frames

In seeking an understanding of why Colin talks about clumping, we reviewed video footage preceding the first mention of clumps to help us understand what Colin expects of the fourth and final interaction. Our review of the preceding video indicated that a critical frame shift could be traced to the preceding session's conversation between Colin and the confederate graduate student. Despite the Researcher having positioned himself as a passive observer and neutral interviewer in the first three sessions, the following discussion at the end of the third interaction reframes that role. What is important about this transaction is that the participants, for the first time, activate as their goal an epistemic frame of normative or accurate knowledge:

| | |
|---|---|
| **Colin:** | What's next time? |
| **Researcher:** | Next time, it's you and me and we're actually going to talk about what the right answers are. |
| **Colin:** | (2.0) Oh. |
| **Confederate:** | The right answers? I didn't realize there were answers. |
| **Researcher:** | OH YES! |
| **Confederate:** | This is science. There are no right answers. |
| **Researcher:** | Ah, ya know…I…all day, I have been good about not using the word right, and then, but today I use it with you and you call me out on it. |
| **Colin:** | (*laughs*) |

In the above conversation, largely involving a transaction between the Researcher and the confederate, the Researcher launches a new epistemic frame for the fourth episode: The Researcher and Colin will actually discuss the normative explanation of the chemistry phenomena, a tweak to the past frame that gives Colin pause, for exactly 2 seconds, before he responds with a flat "Oh." We understand this as a frame shift that creates a distinction between Colin's explanation so far and the "right answer" that will be coming next. Colin's long pause before "Oh" and his laughter in the final turn reflect his recognition of the frame change. In many ways, the preceding frames and Colin's earlier allusions to "not necessarily knowing what I'm talking about," equally set the stage for the final session; the right answer will be in contrast to some elements of Colin's earlier explanation. At this point, the frame for the fourth interaction contains only an epistemic aim, one of seeking *right* answers (with the built-in caveat that science does not really offer those types of answers). The participants have not yet negotiated a social frame to provide contours for how to pursue the epistemic aim.

When the Researcher and Colin meet again in the subsequent and final session, Colin begins by reinforcing his expectation to pursue the epistemic aim of truth. At the same time, details begin to emerge about the social frame:

| | |
|---|---|
| **Researcher:** | So, um, I think what we'll do, um, is…uh…you'll just start up the explanation again… |
| **Colin:** | (*nods*) |
| **Researcher:** | And…I'll just keep stopping you and keep stopping you. |
| **Colin:** | (*smiling*) Are you really going to tell me what is the – |
| **Researcher:** | Yeah. |
| **Colin:** | Okay. |
| **Researcher:** | Right. So if you say something – so, I'll – um…yeah, I mean I'll be asking – I'll ask questions, but they'll be like… |
| **Colin:** | (*laughing audibly*) |
| **Researcher:** | Pointed questions (*laughing audibly now also*). And we won't leave until we've got it got it down. |

This jocular but candid discussion between Colin and the Researcher ultimately serves to confirm explicit epistemic and social frames for the final session. Without ever saying the words "right" or "truthful" – in fact by avoiding completing sentences about the knowledge goal – Colin and the Researcher reinforce the epistemic frame of pursuing the correct solution. More specifically, Colin's harkening back to his and the Researcher's prior contract ("Are you really going to tell me…") and the Researcher's affirmation ("Yeah") strengthens the epistemic aim. A second epistemic aim is also interleaved in the frame, one of reaching understanding, or not stopping until Colin has the new knowledge figured out.

In addition, the Researcher lays out the social frame, specifying roles the two should play and what discourse patterns they should follow to achieve the goal. The Researcher and Colin establish that in the upcoming session, a naive speaker (Colin) will start an explanation and then react to an expert tutor (the Researcher) who asks pointed questions. The smiles and laughter indicate the participants' visceral reaction to the frame change. The message is that what Colin said earlier (what had been laminated and stabilized) was not entirely correct and should be open to revision. In publicly committing to this way of interacting with one another, both participants can proceed to interact with multiple media (body, diagrams, words) to collaborate in the assembly of a new – both normative and comprehensible – narrative about molecular phase transition.

### *Incidental Features of a Drawing Become the Central Focus*

As much as the frame constrains the actions of participants in discourse, the media (talk, gesture, drawing) through which interlocutors create representations give specific shape to the approach, opening up select routes for how to achieve explanation change. In short, the frame governs expectations, but the representational landscape governs how those expectations are instantiated in specific next turns at talk, gesture, and drawing.

**FIGURE 5.8** The Researcher presents a new version of Colin's drawing. The image on the left is a close-up version of the whiteboard pictured in the wide-angle image at the right.

Episodes 1 through 3 showed Colin settling into a stable version of the escape narrative, rooted in similar language, similar hand and pen gestures, and similar drawings of entities at the same scale (Figures 5.2, 5.3, 5.4, and 5.5). Colin's escape narrative laminated a set of semiotic fields into a relatively stable explanation. However, these actions can become *delaminated*. That is, participants can "disassemble and reorganize [them] in order to build subsequent action" (Goodwin, 2013, p. 12). The public delamination of past representational configurations is one of the mechanisms that facilitate explanation change in interaction, and we see exactly this process in Episode 4.

Colin begins by re-enacting the configuration of semiotic resources that made up his escape narrative in earlier episodes (e.g., Colin's utterance and gestures in Figure 5.5 over the circle with just a few dots representing molecules from Figure 5.6), and then stops as the Researcher interrupts, takes the floor (and a marker), and proposes a new, zoomed-in visual perspective on the scene (Figure 5.8). The Researcher draws a larger surface line and an isolated molecule, simultaneously uttering the following:

**Researcher:** I'll start you out. Say this is the surface and here is the molecule that is gonna leave. Um, draw what's around it.

The Researcher's drawing performs three major transformations to Colin's original. The new drawing (1) blows up the scale of the drawing, (2) changes Colin's molecules-as-dots representation into a new molecules-as-blobs representation, and (3) conspicuously leaves out the molecules surrounding the escape molecule. The new drawing visually reshapes much of what Colin had established with dots in his escape narrative previously; the new scale and lone molecule strip away the surrounding visual clutter while enhancing the focus on the escape molecule, forcing Colin to return to the beginning of his narrative and proceed more transparently. Maybe somewhat paradoxically, in *not* drawing the molecules surrounding the escape molecule, the Researcher is drawing attention to them. From the perspective of lamination, the change to the drawn semiotic field contains new affordances. That is, the upcoming gestures and talk will now be laminated on a new visual resource, one at a much higher zoom level. The change to one semiotic field affords the possibility of change to other semiotic fields.

As part of the Researcher's first pointed question, the drawing can also be understood as setting up an expectation for Colin that the surroundings of the molecule are meaningful. The talk, "What's around it," clarifies that expectation. In light of how the framing of the interaction has changed, Colin would be well warranted to interpret the Researcher's re-presentation of the molecule as a signal that Colin should reconsider (relative to his past explanation) how to construe space around the molecule.

Colin, invoking parts of the explanation he had stabilized previously and which worked in the area of talking about how a molecule escapes, follows the Researcher's lead and draws other molecules scattered around the escape molecule. If we accept that Colin is trying to reuse as much as possible from his earlier explanation, and yet still follow the Researcher's lead, we can understand his additions to the drawing as accepting the Researcher's proposal to use the new molecule-as-blob shape but preserving the placement of molecules from his original diagram (Figure 5.6). In the new drawing, Colin draws a visible gap between the escaping molecule and the surface (Figure 5.9), completes the path of the molecule escaping to the surface, and looks up at the Researcher. Even though Colin has been given license to revise his explanation, he revises it only so much as to accept the Researcher's substitution of blobs for dots.

### Reinterpreting the Drawing: The Researcher's Second Wave of Questions

Working from Colin's additions to the blob-as-molecule drawing, the Researcher's second question focuses attention on gaps between molecules. The multiple pointing gestures, laminated on the whiteboard drawing, are possible because of the diagram's new scale; tips of fingers can now fit in the gaps between drawn molecules. The Researcher, in singling out a specific visual property of the diagram – empty space – reifies that gaps between molecules are part of Colin's narrative.

Researcher: You've drawn space between the molecules *(the Researcher uses his finger to gesturally trace gaps between several molecules; see Figure 5.10).*
Colin: (1.0) Yeah.
Researcher: So, what's in that space? Is that – Is that just nothingness?
[…The Researcher and Colin talk for a few turns to rule out that no foreign material separate from the ethanol is present in the glass sphere…]
Colin: …so, uh, yeah, just…the grand degree of nothingness.

Speech, Gesture, and Representation Use   **151**

**FIGURE 5.9**   In black, Colin draws six molecules surrounding the escape molecule and leaves an opening above the escape molecule.

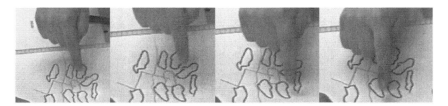

**FIGURE 5.10**   Over the course of two seconds, the Researcher points to four different gaps between molecules.

Colin agrees that gaps of "nothingness" exist between liquid molecules. However, we can interpret the brief hesitations and halting speech in his final turn as suggesting that he is in the process of considering a new explanation or at least doubting his current version. Taking into account the epistemic aim of the conversation, that Colin reformulate his thinking with help from an epistemic authority, the Researcher's gestural privileging of space between molecules can be seen as a cue that Colin needs to be more attentive to gaps.

### *Reinterpreting the Drawing: The Researcher's Third Wave of Questions*

In the third wave of questions, the Researcher clarifies the direction of the expected explanation change. The Researcher's earlier questions about space *around* the molecule and about space *between* molecules have now become even more pointed, focusing on *movement* between molecules. Instead of producing a static portrait of gaps between molecules, the Researcher now questions actions between molecules. The Researcher wiggles his finger back and forth between the drawn molecules, questioning the notion of attraction (Figure 5.11):

**Researcher:** Are these two attracted to each other? *(the Researcher moves his finger back and forth between two specific molecules; see Figure 5.11)*
**Colin:** Yes.
**Researcher:** So, why wouldn't they come together until they touch?
**Colin:** (1.0) Well, they just might have *(flicking hand toward the molecule the Researcher referenced)* a frame *(points with pen toward molecule)* before this picture was taken. They might have hit each other *(hovers pen above drawing and moves it from one molecule to the other)* and now they're flying away again *(hovers pen to draw the same line but in the opposite direction)*.

The focus of attention shifts from space around and between molecules to movement between molecules, and Colin readily agrees that the molecules would be attracted to each other. The transaction is noteworthy because attraction resonates with Colin's prior knowledge of intermolecular attraction (e.g., Figures 5.2 and 5.3). In those earlier episodes, Colin had progressed to talking about intermolecular attraction as a resistant pull against another molecule's escape in his stabilized explanation. Now, the notion of intermolecular attractions is recruited in a new context, to question movement between non-escaping molecules.

Colin's agreement that intermolecular attraction is involved leads him to revise his account of the molecule scene once the Researcher poses the next question in this wave: "Why wouldn't they come together until they touch?" The Researcher's expected direction of explanation change is now publicly charted. The Researcher is asking for change not only with respect to space around and between molecules, but also with respect to movement between molecules. If true, the question would conflict with how Colin previously depicted space between molecules in both his drawings and gestures (Figures 5.2, 5.3, and 5.4).

Colin, in committing publicly and thoroughly in the previous three sessions to intermolecular attractions between molecules – and then again just now after the Researcher's first question of the third wave – makes a concession. He suggests that the drawing is but a snapshot in time; the molecules may very well have been touching a frame earlier. The concession at once saves the appearance of the drawing and recognizes the validity of intermolecular attraction. Colin is suggesting that the drawing is only partially accurate, representing the *now* but not the *just before now*. As Colin builds time into his diagram of molecular behavior, space between molecules takes on new meaning, correctly representing Colin's depiction of the present but also recognizing the possibility that the molecules could have been touching. Colin draws on what seem to be suggestions from the Researcher and begins to construct a new way of talking about liquid molecules – they have attractions to one another that *sometimes* leave spaces between molecules.

Speech, Gesture, and Representation Use    **153**

FIGURE 5.11   The Researcher hovers his finger over the page and moves it back and forth in the space between two molecules (left) and he then looks up at Colin (right).

## *Reinterpreting the Drawing: The Researcher's Fourth Wave of Questions*

The fourth wave of questioning extends the reconstruction of the molecule scene to a new hypothetical. The first three pointed questions probe space around a single molecule, space between a group of molecules, and attraction between two particular molecules. Now, the Researcher ropes in a third molecule, exploring movement (intermolecular attractions) in a molecule *group*. Building on the premise that the molecules touch at points in time, even if not currently shown in the diagram, the interaction proceeds as follows:

**Researcher:**   Okay, so, um (4.5) so if this one came over and, and was nestled up next to it.
**Colin:**   Mhmmm.
**Researcher:**   In the process of bouncing off.
**Colin:**   Mhmmm.
**Researcher:**   Um (1.5) would that, like, leave a space behind it over here *(the Researcher drags his finger back and forth above the space where a gap might appear between molecules)*, or would this one also come to try and be closer also *(the Researcher hovers finger above drawing and traces multiple connections between molecules)*?
**Colin:**   (2.0) Ummmm...

After the above exchange, just as Colin begins to respond further, the Researcher interrupts, leans away from the diagram, draws his eyes away from the diagram, and presents an analogy. He asks if the molecules are more "like you take ball bearings and shake 'em and there's always space between them...like they're always bouncing off each other" (while gesturing two fists repeatedly smashing into each

**FIGURE 5.12** The Researcher hovers his finger over the page, moving it back and forth referencing a gap that may or may not open up between molecules.

other) or more like "something [that] all sticks together so that it's all like mushed up next to each other" (while gesturing the motion of patting dough into a ball). The analogy contrasts two models. Does Colin endorse his original gap model or the new smashed-together model? When the Researcher finishes the analogy, Colin offers the following:

> **Colin:** I'd say it's probably a little more toward the latter than the former. Ummm, I mean I think drawing it like this probably isn't quite accurate. It would probably be more like you're going to have clumping.

Following this statement, Colin draws additional molecules adjacent to one another and labels the new configuration "clumping" (see Figure 5.7). The new version of how molecules are arranged allows for some molecules to be in contact with one another yet also recognizes space between groups of molecules. In summary, as a result of the Researcher's new laminations of gesture and talk on the zoomed-in visual diagram, and against the backdrop of a frame that organizes the expectation that the Researcher will lead Colin to an accurate and comprehensible model, Colin reuses his conception of intermolecular attractions to reconfigure space between molecules.

In this analysis, we have not been concerned with the move that takes place several turns later, when the Researcher tells Colin that his way of thinking and talking about molecules as clumps "actually isn't true" (see Figure 5.7). Instead, we focused on how pointed questions corral attention to new aspects of the explanation, how laminated and delaminated semiotic fields make that process possible, how frames dictate expectations and understandings of specific moments of interaction, and how the history of the interaction, including prior knowledge, shapes the ongoing explanation change.

## Summary of Results

In our analysis, we have offered an account of the mechanisms that guide a student's explanation change. The answer begins with Colin stabilizing a narrative about molecular escape under constant frames, material resources, and knowledge elements. Under these conditions, Colin provides a repeated account of molecular escape, but acknowledges his own uncertainty about its accuracy. In the final session, several new and co-occurring processes – changes to the frame, delaminations of semiotic fields, and waves of pointed questions – lead Colin to apply his knowledge of intermolecular attractions in a novel way. In short, the tendency toward preserving his explanation caves beneath multiple interactional signals that explanation change is needed.

### *Frame Change*

The frame shift is the first event to signal the potential for explanation change. On the epistemic side of the frame, the interaction in the fourth session changes in focus from *plausible* and comprehensible explanations to *correct* and comprehensible explanations. On the social side of the frame, the interaction changes from one of Colin providing explanations and receiving *clarifying* questions to one of Colin providing explanations and receiving *pointed* questions. The shift in frames from plausible to correct explanations and from clarifying to pointed questions provides a generic expectation for how the Researcher will guide Colin toward the right answer.

### *Delamination*

The frame shift allows Colin and the Researcher, working together, to understand what they are doing and pursuing when they start to disassemble Colin's laminated explanation. A shift in the viewpoint of the diagram to a zoomed-in drawing affords a new set of gestural laminations (e.g., pointing between molecules-as-blobs, wiggling the finger back and forth between molecules-as-blobs, and touching three specific molecules in sequence) and a new set of verbal laminations (asking questions about specific molecules in the diagram). Phrased more generally, the process of isolating and changing a single semiotic field affords new laminations with other semiotic fields. The result is the highlighting of a previously unremarkable aspect of the material inscription – gaps between molecules. The transformations that focus attention on gaps cannot be explained as random acts of delamination; they are pointed efforts to guide explanation change.

### *Pointed Questioning*

Through focused acts of delamination, the Researcher and Colin narrow down the possibilities for explanation change, specifying what should be done with gaps.

The process occurs through waves of pointed questions that progress from drawing attention to (1) static space around one escaping molecule and (2) static space between pairs of non-escaping molecules to (3) dynamic movement between pairs of non-escaping molecules, and finally (4) dynamic attractions between groups of non-escaping molecules. With each pointed question, and with the final analogy that juxtaposes two versions of space between molecules, the Researcher charts a clear expectation for Colin's explanation change. The history of past pointed actions from the Researcher makes the next pointed actions even sharper (see also Russ, Sherin, & Lee, this volume). That is, by the time the last question arrives about movement between a group of molecules, Colin is already well aware of the sequence of earlier pointed questions that have focused attention on gaps.

The result is a new explanation: distinct clumps of touching molecules. The explanation preserves knowledge of intermolecular attractions, but applies that knowledge in a new way to non-escaping molecules. The successful disassembly and relamination of Colin's explanation relies on the establishment of new social and epistemic frames, in addition to purposeful actions on the Researcher's part to foreground parts of the escape narrative that could be productively unpacked. Moreover, the purpose of discussing intermolecular attractions gradually changes over the course of the interaction. Colin's diagrams and gestures in the first three interactions were intended to highlight how molecules escape, not whether or not space exists between molecules. In fact, the space originally depicted between dots might have arisen as a consequence of the constraints built into the visual representation (it is hard, if not impossible, to draw small, connected dots without making them look like one mass). However, attention was drawn to what may have been an incidental property of Colin's diagram, and more focused directions for change were charted.

While still non-normative, this new explanation is one step closer, and over the next half-hour of recorded interaction, Colin and the Researcher did successfully construct the normative explanation. The success of this process, resulting in seemingly sudden conceptual change, depended on the careful disassembly and relamination of the explanation. Colin's original, stable lamination was not rejected wholesale, nor picked apart arbitrarily. Previously unremarked aspects of the lamination were highlighted, revealing to Colin implicit inconsistencies between the various aspects of the representations and his knowledge resources. Importantly, these inconsistencies were highlighted because the Researcher felt they were possible to resolve using the existing set of material and knowledge resources with which Colin was working. Indeed, Colin was able to reorganize these resources and relaminate them into a new, better explanation.

## Discussion and Conclusions

Because this chapter is part of a larger volume focused on the integration between Knowledge Analysis and Interaction Analysis, we position the discussion of our findings relative to that dialogue. Both KA and IA have ways of describing why explanations sometimes change, in the way we have documented for Colin. From a KA perspective, this change might be described as the result of a different activation and organization of knowledge elements. From an IA perspective, this change might be described as the result of repeated, pointed questions from an authority figure. Both perspectives would highlight the importance of representations in prompting this case of change. Therefore, a simplistic combination of the two perspectives might describe changes in explanation as the result of differences in activation and organization of knowledge elements, prompted by repeated questioning from an authority figure and shifts in representation. In a general sense, we believe a statement like this is accurate. But we believe that a more sophisticated integration of the two perspectives permits and demands a more nuanced, process-level description of how prior knowledge, epistemic and social frames, and multiple modes of representation interact with each other on a moment-to-moment basis to produce change.

Both KA and IA approaches contribute to the more complete story of how and why a student changes his explanation about liquid molecules. From a KA standpoint, the recognition that the student can deploy knowledge of attraction between molecules helps explain *how* he applies that knowledge in a new way to non-escaping molecules. Without the knowledge, the tutor's pointed questions could have fallen on deaf ears; with the knowledge, the student can rapidly formulate a new hypothesis. But *why* the student makes that concession cannot be divorced from the particulars of the interaction. The microlongitudinal and microlatitudinal history of the interaction in frame shifts and in sequences of pointed questions guide how Colin redeploys the knowledge resource of intermolecular attraction. Transformations in the properties of and laminations between semiotic fields make it possible for the researcher to ask pointed questions and for the student to search for solutions.

Such a nuanced description of the process of change – the process of disassembly and relamination – allows for a deeper understanding of how moments of change occur, which in turn opens up the possibility of better designing such moments. Given time and repeated opportunities, students will tend to stabilize their explanations of a phenomenon. This stability can provide a barrier to conceptual change. Within each iteration, however, there is the potential for change, as students adapt and customize their explanations to the particular demands of each social context that defines what an adequate explanation will be. Through this interplay of stabilization and customization, we see explanations generated and regenerated. At times, these two forces create tension, yet we can use these to our advantage. In line with a long tradition of KA and IA, we should be thinking about the material and knowledge resources students draw upon when responding to a socially defined epistemic aim. Educators should be attuned to these resources and to the range of interactional or instructional moves they can make that will lead students to transform and relaminate representations into new explanations. It is within these momentary adaptions of an explanation that the potential for new, stable, and normative explanations resides.

## Notes

1 Some scholars, including Hammer et al. (2005), use the term *epistemological*, but we support Kitchener's (2002) argument that *epistemic* is more precise. The frames we discuss are ones that set expectations about what knowledge (epistemic) is appropriate in the interaction, not expectations about what *theories of knowledge* (epistemology) participants should adopt.
2 Many of the first few recorded minutes involved setting up cameras and microphones, explaining the roles of each participant, and re-describing the phenomenon.

## References

Brown, N. J. S. (2009). *Information performances and illative sequences: Sequential organization of explanations of chemical phase equilibrium* (Doctoral dissertation). Retrieved from https://escholarship.org/uc/item/9zw1p1ps.

Chinn, C. A., Buckland, L. A., & Samarapungavan, A. L. A. (2011). Expanding the dimensions of epistemic cognition: Arguments from philosophy and psychology. *Educational Psychologist*, 46(3), 141–167.

Clark, D. B. (2006). Longitudinal conceptual change in students' understanding of thermal equilibrium: An examination of the process of conceptual restructuring. *Cognition and Instruction*, 24(4), 467–463.

Clark, D. B., D'Angelo, C. M., & Schleigh, S. P. (2011). Comparison of students' knowledge structure coherence and understanding of force in the Philippines, Turkey, China, Mexico, and the United States. *The Journal of the Learning Sciences*, 20(2), 207–261.

Clark, H. H., Schreuder, R., & Buttrick, S. (1983). Common ground at the understanding of demonstrative reference. *Journal of Verbal Learning and Verbal Behavior*, 22(2), 245–258.

Danish, J. A., & Enyedy, N. (2007). Negotiated representational mediators: How young children decide what to include in their science representations. *Science Education*, 91(1), 1–35.

diSessa, A. A. (1993). Toward an epistemology of physics. *Cognition and Instruction*, 10, 165–255.

diSessa, A. A. (2002). Why "conceptual ecology" is a good idea. In M. Limón & L. Mason (Eds.), *Reconsidering conceptual change: Issues in theory and practice* (pp. 29–60). Dordrecht: Kluwer.

diSessa, A. A., Gillespie, N., & Esterly, J. (2004). Coherence versus fragmentation in the development of the concept of force. *Cognitive Science*, 28, 843–900.

diSessa, A. A., & Sherin, B. (1998). What changes in conceptual change? *International Journal of Science Education*, 20, 1155–1191.

Erickson, F. (1992). They know all the lines: Rhythmic organization and contextualization in a conversational listing. In P. Auer & A. D. Luzio (Eds.), *The contextualization of language* (pp. 365–397). Amsterdam, NL: John Benjamins.

Erickson, F., & Schultz, J. (1981). When is a context? Some issues and methods in the analysis of social competence. In J. L. Green & C. Wallat (Eds.), *Ethnography and language in educational settings* (pp. 147–160). Norwood, NJ: Ablex.

Goffman, E. (1974). *Frame analysis: An essay on the organization of experience*. Cambridge, MA: Harvard University Press.
Goffman, E. (1981). *Forms of talk*. Philadelphia, PA: University of Pennsylvania Press.
Goldin-Meadow, S., Alibali, M. W., & Church, R. B. (1993). Transitions in concept acquisition: Using the hand to read the mind. *Psychological Review*, 100(2), 279–297.
Goldin-Meadow, S., & Beilock, S. (2010). Action's influence on thought: The case of gesture. *Perspectives on Psychological Science*, 5(6), 664–674.
Goldin-Meadow, S., Cook, S. W., & Mitchell, Z. A. (2009). Gesturing gives children new ideas about math. *Psychological Science*, 20(3), 267–272.
Goodwin, C. (2007). Environmentally coupled gestures. In S. D. Duncan, J. Cassell, & E. T. Levy (Eds.), *Gesture and the dynamic dimension of language* (pp. 195–212). Amsterdam, NL: John Benjamins.
Goodwin, C. (2013). The co-operative, transformative organization of human action and knowledge. *Journal of Pragmatics*, 46, 8–23.
Greeno, J. (2009). A theory bite on contextualizing, framing, and positioning: A companion to Son and Goldstone. *Cognition and Instruction*, 27(3), 269–275.
Hammer, D., Elby, A., Scherr, R. E., & Redish, E. F. (2005). Resources, framing, and transfer. In J. Mestre (Ed.), *Transfer of learning from a modern multidisciplinary perspective* (pp. 89–120). Greenwich, CT: Information Age Publishing.
Heiser, J., & Tversky, B. (2006). Arrows in comprehending and producing mechanical diagrams. *Cognitive Science*, 30(3), 581–592.
Hutchins, E., & Palen, L. (1997). Constructing meaning from space, gesture, and speech. In L. B. Resnick, R. Säljö, C. Pontecorvo, & B. Burge (Eds.), *Discourse, tools, and reasoning: Essays on situated cognition* (pp. 24–40). Berlin: Springer-Verlag.
Kendon, A. (1990). *Conducting interaction: Patterns of behavior in focused encounters*. Cambridge, UK: Cambridge University Press.
Kendon, A. (2000). Language and gesture: Unity or duality. In D. McNeill (Ed.), *Language and gesture* (pp. 47–63). Cambridge, UK: Cambridge University Press.
Kitchener, R. F. (2002). Folk epistemology: An introduction. *New Ideas in Psychology*, 20, 89–105.
Parnafes, O. (2012). Developing explanations and developing understanding: Students explain the phases of the moon using visual representations. *Cognition and Instruction*, 30(4), 359–403.
Russ, R. S., Lee, V. R., & Sherin, B. L. (2012). Framing in cognitive clinical interviews about intuitive science knowledge: Dynamic student understandings of the discourse interaction. *Science Education*, 96(4), 537–599.
Sherin, B., Krakowski, M., & Lee, V. R. (2012). Some assembly required: How scientific explanations are constructed in clinical interviews. *Journal of Research in Science Teaching*, 49(2), 166–198.
Smith, J. P., diSessa, A. A., & Roschelle, J. (1993). Misconceptions reconceived: A constructivist analysis of knowledge in transition. *Journal of the Learning Sciences*, 3, 115–63.

# 6

# WORKING TOWARDS AN INTEGRATED ANALYSIS OF KNOWLEDGE IN INTERACTION

*Joshua A. Danish, Noel Enyedy, and Orit Parnafes*

This chapter proposes that there is great value in explicitly integrating Knowledge Analysis and Interaction Analysis in service of understanding student learning. Our work is grounded in the assumption that knowledge and interaction are inseparable in practice. Knowledge is not only seen through interaction, but drives interaction and is in turn shaped by interaction in a continuous and dynamic manner. Similarly, interaction originates in, displays, and leads to the transformation of an individual's knowledge. This suggests that there is value in considering how analyzing interaction constitutes an analysis of knowledge, and how an understanding of interlocutors' knowledge always implies an analysis of interaction.

Other chapters in this volume have attempted to explore the relationship between Knowledge Analysis (KA) and Interaction Analysis (IA) by examining how each might introduce new insights into an existing analysis using the alternative approach. For example, Levin and diSessa (this volume) have reanalyzed the data presented by Stevens and Hall (1998) in order to indicate how a clearer KA focus might shed additional light on the prior discussion, which was grounded in IA. In contrast, we hope to complement those contributions by demonstrating how a single integrated analysis might reveal important aspects of a phenomenon that would not be visible through either individual analytic lens. In doing so we hope to dispel the fiction that analysts from either tradition make such a clean distinction in their work. Instead, by providing caricatures of strict analyses we hope to show that analysts are always integrating the two foci, but often intuitively instead of programmatically. We will attempt to identify some of the advantages of explicit integration of the two approaches, not the least of which is to move us beyond theory wars and towards a joint enterprise to better understand learning and knowing in its complexity so that we can improve the lives of learners.

Prior approaches to analyzing knowledge have frequently ignored social context and interactional features, or analyzed only those interactional features that appeared immediately consequential for the analysis of students' conceptual structures. As Parnafes (2014) notes, efforts are often made to account for the influence of each interlocutor on their peers' knowledge in a step-wise sequential manner. This is in contrast with the IA approach, which usually treats a dyad as a combined unit co-constructing knowledge in interaction (Erickson, 2006). That is, in KA, interaction is not typically analyzed systematically, nor is it explicitly explored in an effort to examine the learning context.

In contrast with the KA focus on knowledge over interaction, IA aims to understand how people simultaneously make, and make sense of, the social context that they are co-constructing with others (Erickson, 2004; Jordan & Henderson, 1995). In IA analyses, knowledge is analyzed only when it is explicitly displayed within interaction, and is typically viewed only in terms of how it sheds light on the interaction, and is thus is rarely considered programmatically and in depth. As Sacks put it when describing a specific form of IA, conversation analysis, "the idea is to take singular sequences of conversation and tear them apart in such a way as to find rules, techniques, procedures, methods, maxims [...] that can be used to generate the orderly features we find in the conversations we examine" (Sacks, 1984, p. 411). Thus, when knowledge is explored, the analysis tends to focus solely on how that knowledge is made visible in interaction. Typically, no effort is made to understand the central topics of KA – the content and structure of knowledge, nor how it relates to the normative explanations of the domain.

Our goal in this chapter is to explore the implications of explicitly and intentionally combining KA with IA. This integrated analysis will allow us to describe the process through which multiple participants may co-construct knowledge while simultaneously exploring the structure of students' knowledge. We will analyze the role of interaction in producing, shaping, and revealing students' knowledge, while at the same time examining how knowledge helps to structure, promote, and necessitate new interactive components. In particular, we attempt to complement Parnafes' (2007) prior KA of students' engagement with the concept of speed in the context of an oscillating pendulum by creating a synthesized account that we believe extends beyond what either KA or IA would accomplish individually. Specifically, we focus on a brief episode where two students are working together with a computer simulation to jointly develop and produce a way of reasoning and making inferences about the interrelations of speed, time, and distance in the context of simple harmonic oscillation.

In analyzing the same episode as presented by Parnafes (2007), our intention is to articulate the distinctive contributions of a separate KA and a separate IA, and demonstrate the value of integrating the two approaches. By contrasting this synthesis with the prior analysis, it also becomes possible to articulate how the one builds explicitly upon the other and to attend to the strengths and weaknesses of both approaches. While it would have been possible to identify new data for this analysis, we felt that working with data that had previously been analyzed by a member of our team complemented other attempts at integration (see Levin & diSessa, this volume), and it has the advantage of relying upon that team member's voice to clarify and challenge our collective assumptions.

It is important to note that our goal is not to provide a more robust KA or IA in the terms that those prior analytic approaches have previously been conducted. That is, a practitioner of KA should not expect to see that the introduction of IA would help them to identify new knowledge structures, but rather a more robust account of how they are employed in interaction. While it is possible, it is neither our goal nor do we expect that it will happen with every analysis. Rather, our goal in conducting an integrated analysis is to provide a new form of account that builds on both KA and IA to produce something unique that provides productive insights into students' participation and developing conceptual understanding within learning environments.

We will now briefly describe both KA and IA before reporting on our efforts to integrate the two.

## Knowledge Analysis and Coordination Class Theory

While the term KA refers broadly to analytical approaches whose goal is to identify the content and structure of students' conceptual understanding, we have elected to use Coordination Class (CC) theory (diSessa & Sherin, 1998) because it was the theory used in the original analysis of our data (Parnafes, 2007). In addition, we believe that CC theory focuses on relating knowledge to observation and perception and is well suited to integrating this theory with IA. CC theory was developed as a means of describing and explaining some properties of well-developed knowledge in individuals. It builds on a knowledge system approach in which knowledge of concepts includes the ability to coordinate sensory input with actions to construct "information from the world" (diSessa, 2002; diSessa, Sherin, & Levin, this volume; diSessa & Sherin, 1998).

Conceptual understanding, viewed from CC theory, consists of knowing how to read out a specific type of information from the world (the key characteristics of a "concept") across different contexts and situations. For example, to understand the scientific concept of velocity means that the student should know how to "see" velocity and how to read out information about velocity (comparing velocities, estimating and calculating the amount of velocities, etc.) in many different contexts: in linear uniform motion, in falling objects, in circular motion, at rest, in oscillation, etc.

A Coordination Class is a particular type of concept that includes the full set of processes that allow one to perceive and make sense of a concept. At the heart of the CC is a knowledge base, called the *inferential net*. The inferential net includes the set of relations that allow an individual to build on available information and construct meaningful inferences. As students perceive the world, their inferential net allows them to connect information from their observations to their existing knowledge base through a process of *extraction*, where they perceive relevant information, and a *readout* where they connect that information to their prior knowledge and generate inferences about it. In this way, CC theory accounts for not only the "structure" of individuals' knowledge but how they connect that knowledge to their perceptual experiences in the world.

Broadly speaking, CC theory answers the question: "how do we read out specific information we need from our immediate context in order to better understand the world at large?" Thus our analysis of the video data attempts to answer this question by focusing on what students indicate they are attending to (e.g., what their extraction strategies are), and how they connect their observations to domain knowledge (e.g., their readout strategies and inferential net). By looking at students' interactions in a learning environment, it then becomes possible to see how students' CCs change over time and what role the designed environment plays in supporting those changes.

## Interaction Analysis

IA (Jordan & Henderson, 1995) emerged as an approach to making sense of learning in rich social contexts. Its popularity was driven in part by the increasing ease of collecting rich video data of students' learning opportunities. However, as Erickson (2006) points out, there are many ways that analysts have used video data to examine the nature of interaction in educational contexts. These include approaches that build on pedagogical and content expertise to analyze specific aspects of the phenomena of interest (e.g., evidence of content understanding and how it relates to instruction) and those that focus more broadly on the nature or technology (Sacks, 1984) of the interaction. Analyses that are focused more explicitly on the nature of interaction often inadvertently or programmatically ignore some key issues of interest to educators, such as the content being studied.

For the purposes of this project, guided by our understanding of the intended instructional activity, we aim to develop a reconstruction of the participants' experience of the interaction. That is, our IA attempts to identify how the participants constructed a shared understanding of the task they were presented with, including their understanding of the phenomena under study, and how these two shared understandings changed over time as they continued to interact with each other and the material environment. Specifically, our use of IA focuses our attention on how the students *publicly* construct epistemic aims (Chinn, Buckland, & Samarapungavan, 2011) and then work together to reach them by manipulating the signs and symbols and material world around them.

This focus on the public construction of intersubjectivity and shared aims is valuable in that it helps to highlight the aspects of the rich context to which the interlocutors are actually attending. As Goodwin (2000) notes, individuals are always interacting within a semiotic ecology that contains an abundance of "information" in the environment. This information comes in multiple forms, including talk, objects, and the spatial layout. These interactional cues help individuals to foreground aspects of the environment as they interact. As individuals learn to consistently foreground certain aspects of the environment, they effectively learn to see the world differently, often in a manner that is viewed as normative or appropriate by a given community (Goodwin, 1994; Stevens & Hall, 1998).

This focus on how learners influence each other's perception of the environment also parallels the focus on extraction strategies within CC theory, providing a possible site of overlap between the two approaches. It is important to note that this approach to exploring changes in perception and practice that arise in interaction is often associated with situative or sociocultural theories of learning (Greeno, 2011; John-Steiner & Mahn, 1996). CC theory, in contrast, is typically associated with more "cognitive" and individual-focused theories of learning, but its fit with IA makes joint analysis easier and allows us to better situate students' knowledge within rich social contexts and interactions.

Another idea that is central to our approach is the assumption that talk is produced sequentially in interaction (Schegloff, 2007). Simply put, this principle argues that individuals do not prepare all of their speech in their heads and then simply produce it. Rather, they begin to speak while observing the meaning of their speech as well as the impact that it has upon the interlocutors in the environment. They then adjust their production accordingly. In the context of examining students' CCs, an attention to the sequential production of talk can reveal how interactional cues appear to intersect with individual knowledge as it is revealed.

An explicit focus on how interaction is built up sequentially might lead to the inference that a semiotic ecology is built up in a step-by-step manner, with elements added in an easily delineated manner as the conversation progresses. Rather, Goodwin, Goodwin, and Yaeger-Dor (2002) suggest, all of the interlocutors operate on and respond to elements in the semiotic ecology concurrently and are continually adjusting their understanding of the changing situation. IA researchers have pointed out on numerous occasions that the other parties in a conversation don't freeze while one person is talking (Goodwin, 2000). Instead, they continue to move, act, and even talk while the first party has the floor. More importantly, the person that has the floor is not blind and deaf to the actions and talk of the other parties. The active interlocutor often incorporates their back-channel directly or indirectly by using it to change what they are saying or how they are talking. Our interaction analyses thus attempt to account for this rich and simultaneous flow of information in interaction. In particular, we have attempted to avoid attending solely to how each turn at talk appears to build upon the immediately prior turn. Instead, we have found it productive to attend to the simultaneity across turns of talk and to focus on how interlocutors act and react to each other at the same time.

## Methods

### Process

The goal of our analytic approach was to explore the value of using both IA and KA to make sense of students' interactions as they learned new science content. In doing so, we hoped to provide an integrated account of how the students' knowledge played a role in their interaction while also being shaped by their interaction. To describe students' knowledge, we used Coordination Class theory. Our approach to this analysis was iterative, building on each of these theoretical and methodological approaches as we aimed to articulate the unique insights provided by each, as well as the ways in which they might be integrated. Our analytical process can generally be divided into four steps.

### Step 1: Looking at the Overall System's Accomplishment

We began by reviewing the video data with a goal of exploring how the system (the two students and the computer simulation) engaged in the task at hand. We wanted to develop hypotheses about what made this an interesting segment of interaction, both in terms of interaction and knowledge. We could then revisit these hypotheses in our subsequent analysis and continue to refine them. In this step, we wanted to determine what the system accomplished as a whole and what made this accomplishment difficult and interesting before exploring the different elements of the system in our subsequent steps. We used this opportunity to explore both knowledge and interaction without attempting to disentangle them because we wanted to remain open to how the integration of the two might reveal unique insights.

### Step 2: Identifying Critical Points of Change and System Self-Correction

While the episode we are studying is quite short, it is also rich. Our goal in the second step was to parse the interaction into sub-parts, delimited by key visible transitions in the students' knowledge, the nature of their interaction, or both. We focused on identifying ways to divide this data that we could then use across all three subsequent analyses, allowing us to more easily contrast the individual analyses. This approach yielded three general sub-parts of the episode that respected the concerns of both analytic frames. This is not entirely surprising, as shifts in students' knowledge often motivate changes in interaction, and vice versa.

### Step 3: Separate Passes at KA and IA

Our goal in the third step was to develop separate analyses of the episode to see how they each presented unique insights into the phenomena represented in the data. One researcher drafted a strict KA while a second researcher drafted a strict IA. We refer to these analyses as "strict" because our goal was to adhere as closely as possible to the focus of the analysis (knowledge or interaction, respectively) without introducing casual and common-sense analyses into the mix. Such common-sense analyses can be quite productive but may obscure the unique character of the analytic approaches. For example, colleagues who practice KA often pointed out that they would likely have noticed certain interactional cues without needing to do a full IA, and vice versa. In a sense, these observations suggest that all knowledge or interaction analyses are, in some sense, integrated. However, the varying degrees of integration muddy the waters and thus make it difficult to see how the different approaches each enhance the overall enterprise. Thus our goal at this stage was to attempt to be as strict in our analyses as possible in order to help tease out these contributions.

## Step 4: Integrating Analyses

Concurrent with the individual analyses, the third member of our team drafted an integrated analysis. The goal of this pass was to construct an analysis that attempted to synthesize approaches holistically, so that any insights that might have arisen from looking explicitly for a synthesis of ideas would not be lost by focusing solely on building a synthesis from the two independent analyses. We then compared this integrated analysis to the two individual analyses, incorporating ideas from each to refine the final integrated analysis. Thus the integrated analysis represents the combination of our attempts to develop a synthesized analysis from scratch and to build a synthesis from the individual more focused analyses.

## Data Source

The selected episode is relatively simple in terms of the interactional dynamics – a dyad working at a computer – as well as relatively constrained in terms of the semiotic fields available. It was collected with a focus on analyzing knowledge rather than interaction, and thus does not always provide a clear view of the students in interaction. For example, while the interaction with representations in a computer simulation is captured by the video camera, gestures, body movements, and facial expressions are not always visible. This episode was a successful piece of collaboration. Over the 44 seconds of the interaction, the students clearly achieved intersubjectivity around something they did not understand before the interaction began. The combination of achieving intersubjectivity and successful learning make the interaction analytically interesting. The relatively short period of time and the constrained context make it analytically tractable.

The downside to our choice is that the interaction is not as dramatic as other cases we might have chosen. The students seem to be "in sync" with one another, in that converging on intersubjectivity doesn't require much time or effort. That intersubjectivity was so easy to achieve raises the question of whether a collective unit of analysis is really necessary. However, we argue that understanding these small, well-constrained, and perhaps even mundane occurrences of learning and interaction cases *in detail* actually provides the basis for beginning to develop a theory that will effectively combine KA with IA for longer interactions. Furthermore, if our approach provides insights in a case such as this, which was intentionally focused on examining knowledge, it should provide even more robust results in future work where we can collect new data with an eye towards examining both knowledge and interaction.

## The Selected Episode

Sue and Robin, two Grade 10 students, participated in a study on simple harmonic oscillation (for additional detail, see Parnafes, 2007). The session from which the episode is extracted included two main parts: interaction with physical oscillators and an interaction with a simulation that has multiple representations of simple harmonic oscillation (Figure 6.1). Like many other students in the research, Sue and Robin used the word "fast" inconsistently and thus were referring to a range of different things: frequency, average velocity, instantaneous velocity, and duration of the motion until it dies out. In the episode, Sue and Robin are 10 minutes into working with the simulation (the second part of the session), exploring its various functions, and referring to the assignment: "make the oscillator go fast. What does 'fast' mean?"

The simulation (see Figure 6.1) includes three linked representations: (1) an animation of an oscillating object that goes back and forth and leaves visual traces behind; (2) the "bar representation," produced by the depiction of one bar on a timeline every time the oscillating object begins a new cycle. It thus represents the periods and the frequency of the oscillator; and (3) a velocity versus time graph.

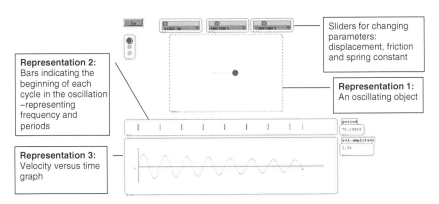

**FIGURE 6.1** The natural harmonic oscillation simulation.

Source: Reprinted from *The Journal of the Learning Sciences*, Volume 16, Issue 3. Copyright © 2007 Taylor & Francis LLC. Reprinted by permission of Taylor & Francis LLC. Material excerpted from Figure 1 on page 422 in the article, "What Does 'Fast' Mean? Understanding the Physical World Through Computational Representations," by Orit Parnafes.

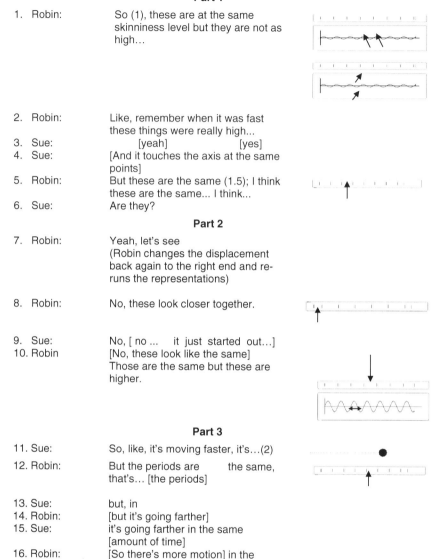

**Part 1**

| | | |
|---|---|---|
| 1. | Robin: | So (1), these are at the same skinniness level but they are not as high... |
| 2. | Robin: | Like, remember when it was fast these things were really high... |
| 3. | Sue: | [yeah] [yes] |
| 4. | Sue: | [And it touches the axis at the same points] |
| 5. | Robin: | But these are the same (1.5); I think these are the same... I think... |
| 6. | Sue: | Are they? |

**Part 2**

| | | |
|---|---|---|
| 7. | Robin: | Yeah, let's see (Robin changes the displacement back again to the right end and re-runs the representations) |
| 8. | Robin: | No, these look closer together. |
| 9. | Sue: | No, [ no ... it just started out...] |
| 10. | Robin | [No, these look like the same] Those are the same but these are higher. |

**Part 3**

| | | |
|---|---|---|
| 11. | Sue: | So, like, it's moving faster, it's...(2) |
| 12. | Robin: | But the periods are    the same, that's... [the periods] |
| 13. | Sue: | but, in |
| 14. | Robin: | [but it's going farther] |
| 15. | Sue: | it's going farther in the same [amount of time] |
| 16. | Robin: | [So there's more motion] in the [same amount of time.] |
| 17. | Sue: | [so, it's going...yeah] |

**FIGURE 6.2** Episode transcript divided into three analytic parts. Arrows are used to indicate where the students are gesturing with the mouse while discussing their interpretation of the representation. Brackets represent overlapping speech and numbers in parentheses indicate pauses.

Students can change the amount of displacement, the friction, and the spring constant of the oscillator and thus explore some of the causality in oscillatory motion.

The episode starts when Robin points out something she has noticed in the patterns of the representations: compared to a previous run, the "hills" of the graph in the present run are the same width, but they are not as high as before. They negotiate this observation, until in line 9 they are in agreement regarding this observation, when Robin concludes in line 10: "those are the same but these are higher." From here, they move on to explore the meaning of this representational pattern: What does it mean in terms of the phenomenon represented that "those are the same" and "these are higher," and does it make sense? It turns out that it doesn't make sense immediately and requires some work on their part, which they do in the last section of the episode. See Figure 6.2 for a transcript of this interaction, which was designed to include key information necessary for both our KA and IA (e.g., in order to ease the process of comparing analyses, we included some features such as overlapping talk that might be present in IA but not KA).

## Analysis

### Knowledge Analysis

The objective of our KA is to focus on the content and form of a student's individual knowledge system: what it is comprised of, how it is organized, and how this organization changes throughout the activity. In particular, our analysis aims to describe the students' knowledge using the framework of CC to identify its content and structure. We focus on the CC that is related to the scientific notion of "fast." Note that, building from Parnafes' (2007) original analysis of this data, we present a single analysis, which treats the students as having a similar knowledge structure unless otherwise indicated.

In the episode under consideration, Sue and Robin vary the initial displacement (distance) of the oscillation, and explore the notion of fast – which they take as the ratio of distance covered to the time it takes. This exploration leads to a moment of confusion as they attempt to explain why two different runs of the simulation at two different speeds would have the same period (time). As they attempt to reconcile this, they continue to explore the details of the representations, which allow them to engage with several relevant aspects of oscillation and to relate time, distance, and velocity in a way that solves the puzzle. In this process, they expand the span of the CC of "velocity" (which the students know how to use in a variety of contexts of motion) to include the special and, it turns out, slightly challenging, case of oscillation.

### Part 1

This episode begins when Robin recognizes a pattern of variation in the graph representation (line 1). She compares two situations: their previous run (with lower initial displacement) and the current run (with higher initial displacement) and notices that the "width" (the skinniness) of the graph remains the same across these situations, whereas the height of the peaks of the graph changes. The width and the height are both seen to be relevant to a discussion of "fast," thus Robin's focus on them may indicate that her inferential net contains productive relations to begin this exploration as she is attending to two dimensions (velocity and time) that are central to a normative account of "fast" in this environment. However, what is not yet clear is *how* she sees these features as relevant to fast. We cannot yet determine whether Robin has a normative understanding of the relationship between velocity, time, and speed or simply recognizes that these attributes are important to attend to, which would still be a valuable starting point for this exploration.

Robin continues to elaborate by relating to the history and noting that the graph was really high in the previous exploration, "when it was fast" (line 2). Up until this point, we assume that Sue shares Robin's interpretation. Sue then notices that the line touches the axis at the same points, a different and perceived-to-be relevant extraction that she does not explicitly connect to Robin's description. Robin further explores the pattern by focusing on whether or not the intervals in the bar representation are also the same. Robin sounds a little puzzled in line 5 when she says, "I think…," which may indicate that she expects to have both measures (width or interval, and height) co-vary with fastness, which would be an inferential relation (in the developing inferential net) that "faster implies less time." It is important to note here that while the potential reasoning behind Robin's confusion is well within the domain of KA, the feature that helped us notice this ("I think…") is an epistemic marker that is viewed as important in both KA and IA because of how it positions her relative to her claims.

## Part 2

The episode continues with Sue echoing Robin's uncertainty that the intervals are indeed the same, indicated by her query, "are they?" (line 6). Our casual attention to this element of the interactional space helps once again to see how Robin's decision to check by changing the initial displacement to its setting in the previous run (a bigger displacement) is at least partially bolstered by her interaction with Sue. The students are then carefully evaluating information from the simulation (an extraction strategy) to see whether the intervals in the bars are the same or not. Robin initially notes that the starting point shows a different interval, which would have led to a different readout of the situation (line 7). However, Sue recognizes this as being due to the simulation just beginning, and explains that to Robin (line 9): "no… it just started out…." As the simulation plays out, Robin then sees the expected pattern and agrees that the intervals are the same as in the recently completed run. The students then conclude that "Those are the same, but these are higher" (line 10), referring to the periods being the same and yet with greater amplitude, which they interpret (properly) as speed. This observation confirms the tentative observation that began the episode. It is important to note here that it is sensible for the students to expect that if the oscillation is faster, other dimensions also change rather than remaining constant. For example, this might be an extension of the observation that if we run faster, the time we need to complete the race is shorter. In the final part of the episode, the two students solve this puzzle by separating the CCs of velocity and frequency, which are overlapping, if not fused, in their naive understanding.

## Part 3

In the last section of the episode, the students attempt to make sense of the idea that the graphs have the same "skinniness" (the intervals in the bar representation are the same) and yet the graphs now are higher than in the previous case (with lower displacement). The students appear to be using an inferential relation that is commonly used to make inferences about simple motion situations, such as a race: different velocities mean different times (we know that children do that in many cases; see Bamberger, 1990; Inhelder & Piaget, 1958; Levin & Gardosh, 1993). However, applying this inferential relation for speed and time ("more speed implies less time") is inconsistent with what they see in the representations, which might instead be described as "more speed is accompanied by the same time." This inferential relation does not work in this specific context, and the difficulty in its application creates a momentary conceptual challenge. It is important to note that the notion that the students' experienced this as a "challenge" comes in part from our noticing the hesitation in their utterances in lines 11–12: "it's moving faster, it's..." and "But the periods are the same, that's..." We view this as another case where a constructive KA necessarily attends to elements of the interaction to highlight aspects of the knowledge state.

As soon as they realize that in this particular situation the distances traveled by the oscillating ball are different ("it's going farther"), they immediately resolve the conceptual challenge. Noticing that in this context the distance also varies, they re-apply a different inferential relation of a CC of velocity that applies to many other motion situations: that speed/velocity is the relationship between time and distance. Applying this inferential relation helps them make sense of the fact that the time stays the same because an increase in distance may be compensated for by an increase in speed. They articulate these ideas clearly: "it's going farther in the same amount of time" (line 15) and "there is more motion (speed) in the same amount of time" (line 16). The important notion that the analysis highlights here is that through the exploration of "fastness" the evolving CCs of velocity and frequency that the students may apply in simple contexts of motion have been refined and extended to work in one more context of oscillatory motion. In other words, the span of the CC of velocity and frequency has increased to include an additional context.

## Summary of Knowledge Analysis

The value of this analysis is in its ability to illuminate the critical moments where students experience delicate but substantial changes in their CC structure. The change in the conceptual system is motivated by a conceptual challenge the students face, and the analysis demonstrates how the students are able to overcome this challenge as they refine the notion of "fastness" and begin to differentiate frequency and velocity.

The students were usually in agreement, and it seemed that they were focusing together on the same issues. Each of them contributed different observations or ideas, but those were picked up by the other student most of the time. Therefore, for the sake of simplicity, the two students were frequently treated as one conceptual entity in this KA, and the interaction between the two is de-emphasized. In fact, because the students appeared to be consistently in sync, we were able to model the situation as a single, evolving conceptual system which largely ignored the differences between the students' individual conceptions and hence avoided the complexity of a dual model. The choice of modeling the situation as a common conceptual system prepares us for the next section, where we attempt to highlight the possible contribution of an IA in analyzing the work that the students did to get and keep aligned.

## Interactional Analysis

Our IA focuses on how the students construct their shared activity: articulating what "fast" is through the use of the computer simulation. We then explore the transformation of the students' public alignment regarding how particular graphic elements in a simulation related to the use of the term "fast." Our analysis looks at how knowing is constructed in interaction and how the students' public talk may have consequences for themselves and their peers. Our IA focuses in greater detail on the social interactions and context, with fewer observations about the content and structure of knowledge than the individual KA included.

### Part 1

Prior to the beginning of this episode, the instructor framed the activity as one of exploring the notion of "fast" in a dyad, using the simulation, which includes several visual representations. In part 1 of the episode, we see the students building upon this frame to establish intersubjectivity around what the representation is showing, and how this relates to the task at hand. That is, the students are simultaneously noting the key relationships in the representation and determining that observations of these relations are shared between them as relevant to the problem at hand.

We can see that Robin and Sue share an initial framing of the activity, because Robin speaks in shorthand descriptions, such as using the phrase "skinniness level" to refer to the width of the hills of the graphs, and does not explicitly state why those are relevant. Sue's understanding of these shorthand moves is evident in her quick acceptance of Robin's claims as relevant and the lack of any explicit push-back or attempt to clarify. Furthermore, it is worth noting that both Sue and Robin appear content to work with the representation of the motion (the graph) rather than the actual simulation (the animation of the pendulum swinging). Thus they are demonstrating a shared orientation towards this representation as a core tool for this practice, and they avoid observing directly the motion of the pendulum that might be appropriate in other contexts.

Robin moves beyond indicating a shared frame, though, to begin indicating which aspects of the representation are relevant to that frame. Robin takes advantage of the shared representational space to make those aspects of the representation and how she interprets them public and visible by speaking and pointing with the mouse to establish a shared frame of reference. That is, Robin draws Sue's attention to aspects in the semiotic fields that she views as relevant to their current exploration, effectively foregrounding them and backgrounding all of the other features of the representation (line 1).

In addition to noting features of the physically present representation, Robin evokes the pair's shared history in which they associated high with fast. In doing so, she also explicitly invites Sue to participate, with the phrase: "like, remember when…" (line 2). Sue now not only has an opportunity to respond, but there is also a social expectation that she will acknowledge the reference, which she does by indicating a similar recollection. She confirms her agreement twice by saying "Yeah," and "Yes" (line 3). In doing so, Sue effectively indicates not only that she remembers, but that this is relevant to the current investigation.

Sue further indicates that she shares Robin's framing of the activity by building upon it to add a new observation with the use of the word "and" to indicate that she is explicitly building upon Robin's observation. Sue's new contribution – "and it touches the axis at the same points" (line 4) – suggests an interpretation of a new aspect of the semiotic field. Robin does not explicitly acknowledge this and continues with her own exploration. She uses the marker "but" to contrast her previous observation that the peaks of the graph "were really high" with her more recent observation regarding the spacing between the peaks. The comment, "but these are the same" (line 5) indicates that the intervals in the bar representations are the same as the previous run. She then repeats this observation to get Sue's attention, a move that helps the students converge on the same problem rather than pursuing potentially disparate lines of investigation.

Robin's contribution that the intervals between the bars are the same is made in a hesitant way (line 5: "I think… I think…"), making it easier for Sue to express doubt with the premise as alignment with Robin's public uncertainty. Sue's response is to align with Robin's affect but question the factual status of the statement by asking, "Are they?" (line 6). This query confirms that she shares Robin's focus of attention (even though she was just making a different contribution). She recognizes the claim Robin is making and calls for an investigation to determine if the claim is in fact true.

These interactions can be seen as a "semiotic challenge" (Wertsch, 1985), a language game that is often used to create a shared situation definition. The game is to make public observations that create a shared interpretation and simultaneously test if the interpretation is indeed shared – where the evidence for intersubjectivity is either explicit agreement or taking action in a way that demonstrates one's shared understanding.

*Part 2*

As the episode continues, the students' joint activity appears to shift from creating a shared interpretation of what is known to a shared inquiry into something they are both uncertain of. Now they are focused on a new epistemic aim they intend to pursue together. Robin changes a parameter on the simulation and runs it again. She then begins to comment about the bar representation as it is produced, indicating how her attention is directed toward certain features of the graph and inviting Sue to attend to those same features. Robin notices that the first period of the graph is smaller than the intervals they have seen before, and she makes this observation public. The public observation again presents an opportunity for Sue to share her identification of the relevant features of the representation as well as her interpretation of them. While Sue appears to direct her attention similarly, she does not, in this case, align her interpretation with Robin's, a first in the current episode.

Because Sue speaks somewhat later in the generation of the graph, she also has access to more information. That is reflected in her statement: "No, no it just started out." This observation in essence makes the first period an unusual case that does not provide generalizable information. Almost immediately, the two students realign and agree that the intervals are similar to the ones before, a realignment echoed by the fact that their speech overlaps. Robin reassures herself and Sue that "those are the same and these are higher" (line 10), thus establishing a shared understanding of the graphs as having the same period but different heights, a confirmation in response to the previously shared question of whether or not this was the case in part 1 of the episode. While IA tends to focus on the presentation of intersubjectivity, our use of the term "understanding" here highlights our inclination to attempt intuitive analyses of knowledge states when completing an IA.

*Part 3*

This part immediately follows the interaction above and Robin's conclusion that "[t]hose are the same and these are higher." After clearly stating the joint observation, the epistemic aim shifts from creating a shared interpretation of the semiotic fields to making sense of the meaning of those semiotic fields. Sue says, "So, it's like moving faster, it's…" (line 11). The "so" indicates that a new idea based on the previously established information is being introduced. However, Sue leaves her sentence unfinished. This provides Robin an opportunity to step in and provide a different yet relevant observation (line 12). The fact that Robin can relate to Sue's observation with a relevant observation demonstrates that they understand the subject at hand in similar ways.

It's useful to ask why Sue returns to the first premise. It might be that she wants to return to their first epistemic aim of listing what is known. Her use of the marker "so" tells us that she is trying to make sense of the observations they already have and explain how the two observations that they had publicly produced fit together. Robin takes her turn and juxtaposes the two observations in the construction of a new epistemic aim. Robin then adds a third observation (line 14): "it is going farther." Sue immediately aligns with this statement and elaborates by placing it in juxtaposition with time (line 15): "it's going farther in the same amount of time." Robin is simultaneously doing the same thing, saying (line 16): "so there's more motion in the same amount of time." The turn ends with explicit agreement.

From this point forward, the students' overlapping speech patterns echo overlapping ideas. At first glance, the two students talking at the same time might suggest that they are ignoring each other. However, we see the parallel construction of their ideas and borrowed terminology as evidence that they are hearing each other, and building upon each other's ideas as they attempt to construct an explanation of what is happening.

## Summary of Interaction Analysis

Despite focusing on the same data, our IA differs from our prior KA by focusing far more explicitly on the shared nature of the students' enterprise. By focusing on the nature of their interaction, it is possible both to establish that the students are in alignment and to describe what kind of work they do to reach that alignment (intersubjectivity). Specifically, our analysis indicates how the students build on (1) the shared prior framing of the activity, (2) the physical and social organization of the space, which facilitates the use of indexical gestures over the representation, and (3) their ongoing talk to indicate that they are noticing and interpreting similar aspects of the situation and then building upon this to explain what they are seeing (e.g., how "fast" is evident in the system). This analysis answers a different question than the KA by indicating how the students go about reaching consensus on the explanation that they articulate at the end of the episode. At the same time, while this analysis implicitly tracks knowledge in the sense of tracking conceptual lines, puzzles, and potential disagreements, it is far less explicit about the content and structure of the students' knowledge and how it relates to normative explanations of "fast." Thus we can see some of the trade-offs inherent in pursuing one of these analyses over the other.

## Integrated Analysis

Our objective in the integrated analysis is to identify a shared "conceptual space" which describes the students' jointly produced understanding of their activity, along with the process through which the individual students created this space and how it changed. We use the term conceptual space here to identify the intersection of the knowledge structures that were explored in the KA with the shared social frame that was explored in our IA. Our focus is on explicitly identifying how changes in the knowledge that students demonstrate are organized by interactional features such as the interactional cues, epistemic aims, and social framing. The social framing of this episode is rather distinctive, though common in school activities: The students are expected to work together to create an explanation of a concept (fast) using the tools that were made available to them. Throughout the episode, we see the students' ongoing efforts to construct intersubjectivity in the form of a mutually understood explanation where they both have buy-in. This social framing is constructed throughout the session through the task formulation and the students' mutual orientation toward sense-making. This specific social framing also organizes the activity in certain ways. As we will see below, the students necessarily share some prior knowledge of the context and content, which allows them to interact meaningfully as they work together to construct their agreed-upon understanding.

## Part 1

The episode begins, as noted in the IA above, with the students establishing intersubjectivity around what the representation is showing, and how this relates to the framed activity of exploring the notion of "fast." This begins when Robin recognizes a pattern of variation in the graph representation that she finds relevant for the exploration of the "fastness" (line 1). The peaks of the graph are at the same "skinniness" as in the previous run, but they are not as high as before. The logic implied here is that something is noteworthy about the fact that one is the same and the other is not. Sue indicates tacit buy-in by not challenging or contradicting Robin.

Over the next few moments, the students work to confirm Robin's initial observation. This confirmation is a critical point in the process, after which they explore the meaning of this shared observation. This in turn leads to progress in their understanding of the situation, because the students simultaneously reach intersubjectivity regarding both the framing of the ongoing activity as a joint interpretive exercise focused on the representation and the underlying conceptual meaning of the representation in the domain of fastness. In fact, our integrated analysis suggests that this intersubjectivity is driven by both elements (activity framing and conceptual meaning), indicating the value of combining an analysis of interaction with one focused on knowledge.

Through the interaction, Robin does some substantial work to establish intersubjectivity around these topics. She starts by foregrounding specific aspects of the representation (the height and the skinniness) to make those aspects visible to Sue. She orients Sue to some aspects of the semiotic field, ignoring others, by pointing with the mouse and verbally referring to those aspects. She also explicitly refers Sue back to their shared history by calling her attention to a previous run in which the peaks were higher than now ("like, remember...," line 2). Finally, she makes an explicit connection between "fast" and "high peaks." While this happens so seamlessly that it appears to be trivial, this is actually an important point of the joint analysis. It demonstrates the work done by the students to facilitate this joint attention through shared prior experience and shared tools, and at the same time it provides a context for us to analyze the students' understanding and how it develops. To exemplify, Robin's use of the shorthand in quickly pointing out these details effectively treats Sue as having similar background information, which Sue then confirms in her response. In analyzing knowledge, it appears that Robin has a developing CC of velocity which allows her to read out information and make inferences that facilitate her judgment that the current graph is anomalous.

Sue reacts to Robin by confirming these observations (line 3). She then adds something new: "and it touches the axis at the same points" (line 4). Her contribution starts with the marker "and" to indicate a direct relationship to Robin's prior utterance, as another act of confirmation. But it is also a new contribution, bringing a new inference and new aspects of the semiotic field to the fore. At the same time, labeling these aspects of the graph in this manner may also make visible other aspects of Sue's CC for reading and interpreting graphs, and her knowledge that the points where the graph intersects the line are important.

Consider a hypothetical alternative interaction in which Robin then questions why the intersection with the axis is relevant. The students would then be in a position to discuss how the axis describes a key element of the motion of the pendulum, making that knowledge visible for both interrogation by the students and analysis by researchers. However, rather than respond to Sue's new contribution, Robin moves on and continues her own exploration. Specifically, Robin notes that the intervals in the bar representations are the same as the previous run. To get Sue to dedicate more attention to this new observation, Robin repeats: "I think these are the same..." (line 5).

Robin sounds a little puzzled (line 5: "I think, [...] I think..."), perhaps because she expects heights (interpreted as "fast") to co-vary with intervals (interpreted as time duration). Sue, who was just drawn into this momentarily (recall that she was just making her own observation), is attuned to Robin's hesitation and she follows up by challenging Robin's observation that the intervals are the same as before: "are they?" (line 6). This confirms that Sue shares Robin's focus of attention as well as her epistemic aim, recognizes the claim she is making, and wants to investigate whether the claim is in fact true. Thus, while there are multiple directions in which Sue and Robin might have proceeded, they have now chosen together to pursue the question of whether or not the spacing of the lines is similar despite a difference in height.

It is valuable to note here that Robin and Sue effectively shut down one possible line of inquiry in favor of another before Robin completed her analysis in line 5. That is, they pursue a version of the problem as formulated by Robin and appear to ignore the potential importance of Sue's observations. Thus, the final shared understanding that is constructed doesn't necessarily incorporate all of the knowledge that was suggested, and it is shaped by social choices the two students make. Had Sue insisted on having her idea addressed and had Robin consented to that, the resulting discussion and explanation might have diverged. We view this as a key contribution of a combined analysis in that it helps to highlight the process through which interactional choices both shut down and open up various explorations of knowledge.

## Part 2

Robin and Sue's shared hesitation around their recent observation is attributed in our joint analysis to both knowledge consideration, and interactional considerations. From a knowledge perspective, it becomes evident through their line of reasoning that they expect time to co-vary with "fast", hence the observation of "same intervals" and varied height is surprising to them. This observation is supported by interactional inferences about the students' expressions of surprise. Indeed, their next collective move is to revisit their recollection to determine whether or not they remember correctly or saw the details in sufficient resolution. Thus they re-run the simulation with the previous parameters and check if the intervals are the same with small and big displacements, beginning in line 7.

The students are now focused on reading information from the representation to see whether the intervals are the same or not. There is a moment of confusion around the starting point that showed a different, shorter, interval than the students had recalled (line 8). Sue immediately notes that the anomaly appears only at the beginning of the oscillation and that the next intervals appear to be similar. After Robin acknowledges this, she concludes: "Those are the same, but these are higher" (line 10). A hypothetical can again help us to see the value in the integrated analysis here. We can imagine a situation in which Robin might have been rather confused by the difference but not noted it, or one in which she pauses the simulation at that moment and then proceeds with the mistaken assumption that the intervals were now shorter (closer together). However, because Robin makes her confusion public while allowing the simulation to continue running, Sue is able to offer an explanation that allows the students to effectively ignore this early anomalous data and focus instead on the regular intervals that appear later in the graph. In other words, students' choices, whether conscious or not, about what to make visible in the shared interactional space clearly have an impact on how their knowledge influences and is influenced by the interaction.

Through this short checking of the simulation, a shared public focus of attention is established around the secondary representations. There is a strong indication that intersubjectivity is indeed forming throughout this interaction. We see a great deal of overlap in the students' talk in lines 9–10. They both say "no" at nearly the same time: "no, no… it just started out…" and "no, these look like the same." This overlap regarding the anomalous beginning indicates that they both notice the same things at the same time. In other words, they share the same focus of attention and the same inferences, which enables them to react similarly. The simultaneity of their comments is important because it helps to rule out any explanations which might rely on one student having the observations and the other simply agreeing or repeating the idea without understanding. Rather, we see here some evidence that the students are in fact producing similar observations at the same time.

A key result of this exchange is that the students return full circle to the observation in line 1 with some sense of confidence that: (1) the observation is right and the intervals are the same despite different heights, (2) they are in agreement with regard to it, and (3) they seem to share the same conceptual challenge of explaining these representational differences.

## Part 3

The students end up with a confirmed observation that the graphs have the same "skinniness" (and the intervals in the bars are the same) and yet the graphs now are higher (more speed) than in the previous case (with lower displacement). They are puzzled because they presumably both use an inferential relation that applies to simple motion situations, such as a race between two objects: different speeds mean different times. However, this is inconsistent with what they see in the representations. More speed does not necessarily translate to less time, which creates a conceptual challenge.

Sue makes a new contribution: "so, like it's moving faster, it's…" (line 11). The "so" marks a new epistemic goal, namely, once the observation is confirmed (previous epistemic goal), they now move to make sense of it. In line with this epistemic goal, Sue makes an explicit reference to how fast the animated ball is moving. This is a new focus of attention and a new explicit inference about the "fastness" of the ball that is possibly intended to put the puzzle they need to solve in focus.

Robin's coordinated action – moving the mouse to the same spot as Sue moves her hand and saying "So, like it's moving faster" – implies that Robin is in sync with Sue. Robin's contribution in line 12 supports this. The "but" suggests that Robin relates to what Sue has just said, but also indicates an additional meaning that stands in some contrast to what Sue had said. Having these two sentences together, one right after the other, highlights the conflict and makes it apparent: "it's moving faster" "but the periods are the same."

Robin, still puzzled, then introduces a new idea in line 14: "but it's going *farther*." The notion of distance is introduced here for the first time. More importantly, distance, as a new parameter in their discussion, produces new opportunities to make sense of the situation. Whereas prior to this exchange more speed was assumed to necessitate less time, now by considering distance to compensate for time the students can solve their puzzle of how something could be moving faster but take the same amount of time to do so. Sue articulates clearly: "it's going farther in the same amount of time" (line 15) and Robin complements this with "there is more motion in the same amount of time" (line 16). As they reach this point they are both in perfect alignment as they are constantly speaking at the same time, overlapping their talk and ideas. They are hearing each other, and building upon each other's ideas as they attempt to construct an explanation of what is happening. Through these moves, the CC of "velocity" that the students know how to use in a variety of contexts of motion is extended to work also in one more context of oscillatory motion. In other words, the span of the CC of velocity is increased to include an additional context.

*Summary of Integrated Analysis*

Our integrated analysis helps to illustrate the ongoing relationship between the social moves, which are used to build intersubjectivity, and the conceptual underpinnings of that intersubjectivity. The students continually notice and point out features of the semiotic field, making the features they attend to visible to the other, while the other becomes attuned to those aspects and gradually shares the focus of attention. Their understanding is not identical, and some of these differences appear both in the timing and expression of their understanding. Nonetheless, their understanding appears to be well enough aligned to coordinate shared constructions. The alignment of their sequential observations helps to construct an account of similar understanding, grounding the intuitive assumption behind the "one conceptual system" model adopted by the KA report.

The integrated analysis looks closely at how joint attention is being established, rather than assuming joint attention based on apparent alignment. The analysis exposes the interactional process by which this joint attention is established, with particular attention to how the students are building on their prior knowledge. Furthermore, this analysis highlights the nature of the students' knowledge structures and the explicit interactional moves that they use to foreground those aspects and make them visible to their peer.

## Conclusion

We began this paper by noting that we believe knowledge and interaction are inseparable. In fact, we have found that when analysts attempt to complete an analysis that only focuses on one dimension (knowledge or interaction), they necessarily rely upon common-sense casual interpretations of the other dimension. Furthermore, these casual or common-sense interpretations are not always made explicit in those cases and thus cannot be easily interrogated or addressed.

In our own efforts to strictly adhere to a plan of analyzing knowledge and interaction individually in our first pass, we found that it was challenging not to stray in these common-sense ways, further highlighting the importance of both elements in either analysis. Nonetheless, we still find these close-to-strict analyses to be productive, shedding light on different aspects of what the students we have observed are accomplishing. Using Coordination Class theory, the KA provides some new insights into the students' understanding of the developing concepts of speed/velocity and frequency in the context of oscillatory motion. At the same time, the IA illustrates how the students in this context formulated their questions about speed with relation to the interface and to each other.

We also found that the explicit attempt to integrate the analyses helped to highlight new and important aspects of the episode we were studying. We found that the integrated analysis provided new insights into how the nature of the interaction may have influenced the production of the students' shared understanding and how the nature of their understanding may have driven their ongoing interaction. The contribution of this integrated analysis can be phrased in terms of two key ideas. First, knowledge includes both the nuances of the phenomena being studied (the KA focus), and an awareness of the social context surrounding how and when to explore and utilize that knowledge in interaction (IA). In other words, by integrating analyses, we make visible how the students' knowledge of the task, context, and norms all influence their articulation of the science-related ideas that are also of interest to us and which are the primary focus of prior KA efforts. Second, interaction is necessarily driven by knowledge. In particular, we see here how the students often worked to construct intersubjectivity around issues, such as the meaning of fastness, that can be productively illuminated by examining not only what they students demonstrate in interaction but how that knowledge might be tied to a cohesive knowledge structure. In many ways, the KA helped to expand upon our understanding of what the goal of intersubjectivity was, and helped to make visible the nature of the breakdowns which drove interaction forward (e.g., not understanding why the intervals were the same).

We want to reiterate that our goal was not to suggest that an integrated analysis would provide insight into "more" of what the individual analyses already focused on. For example, we don't expect that analysts interested in how students structure their understanding of "fast" will see new dimensions of fast in this analysis. Rather, we believe that the integrated analysis necessarily expands our notion of what both knowledge and interaction are and thus reveals added nuance into our understanding of how students such as Robin and Sue make sense of the world through interactions in real, idiosyncratically organized, and structured learning environments. We also believe that a systematic and conscious effort to complete both individual and integrated analyses helped to make visible both our assumptions about the phenomena under study and the very nature of those phenomena in ways that a holistic analysis did not, on its own.

# Commentary

## WHEN WILL SCIENCE SURPASS OUR INTUITIVE CAPACITIES AS EXPERT PRACTITIONERS?

*Andrea A. diSessa*

In this commentary, I aim to draw out, frame, and explain what I take to be the larger significance of one of the main points that emerged from Danish, Enyedy, and Parnafes' work. And then I would like to explain why I thought an alternative path that was contemplated by these authors, while worthwhile, might have been difficult in its best form, and would not have contributed as much to the agenda of this volume.

### Tipping Points

Danish, Enyedy, and Parnafes make the casual-seeming remark that it was difficult to accomplish a Knowledge Analysis (KA) without simultaneously doing some Interaction Analysis (IA), carried out, probably, at an intuitive level. The complementary point was also made: Doing an analysis of interaction without paying at least some attention to knowledge seems unnecessarily constrained and unnatural, especially when the analyst's goal is to understand learning. I'm very happy that they chose to emphasize those points, and I encouraged them to do so during the volume's editorial review process. I believe these general issues have fairly far-reaching ramifications, especially concerning the KAIA agenda.

In order to frame this point in a larger context, I need a concept. Here's the nub of the idea. We know that science, engineering, and technology can be great helps in accomplishing practical goals. Wireless long-distance communication came to exist on the basis of understanding electromagnetic waves. Nuclear energy came to exist, for better or worse, on the basis of some excellent science. Prospectively, I don't expect cancer to be effectively handled in all its forms on anything but scientific advance.

So, we ask the central question: *When in the course of development of civilization do we experience a tipping point where science and its related infrastructure make possible things that are cleanly beyond even the most expert (but intuitive) practitioner without them?*

In phrasing the question in this way, I've deliberately invoked a professional class, "experts." The question could be stated in other ways. For example, we could be talking about accomplishments that "everyone" or "anyone" might reach. These are independently fine questions, but "experts" best fits the line of thought that I am going to pursue. I also need a name to compactly reference this tipping point, and I'll call it a *STEP* (a rough acronym for scientifically/technologically enabled tipping point). Incidentally, excellent practical knowledge, know-how, has long been referred to as *techne*, and philosophical debates about its nature have swirled since ancient times.

Let me briefly exemplify and elaborate the STEP concept – and some of its complications – before applying it to the present context. An example that I used myself in early thinking about STEPs is sword making. The ancient world was replete with excellent swords long before materials science, metallurgy in particular, came to exist. Expert practitioners (sword makers) set a high standard for a STEP. I don't doubt that today we could (and probably do) make superior swords: lighter, stronger, sharper, and with better ergonomics. When the STEP actually occurred is probably not of much significance now. It is even plausible that the goal of making the best sword possible became obsolete before the STEP in sword manufacture occurred. In this way, the goal of making better swords might have been subsumed by the goal of making better hand weapons in general, so the focus for practical STEPs might have shifted (a sideSTEP?) to guns.

A famous STEP in the history of artificial intelligence is the Turing Test. Can a mechanical system be created such that an intelligent person "conversing" with it could not tell the difference between the machine and a person? The Turing Test involves a STEP that might be an ideal type in that it set a relevantly high goal, and one that plausibly opens up a very wide range of practical applications. We know that people are really "useful" in a general sense, and being able to create "more of them" is likely to have profound societal implications. The Turing STEP was also formulated at a time when the infrastructure for achieving it was just beginning to appear, both scientifically and technologically. We were beginning to understand the mind and to master what computers can do, probably a really good start on a relevant technological infrastructure for achieving human simulacra. So, in sum, the Turing STEP set a high bar, but one that was beginning to be plausible, and one that would most likely have concomitant widespread impact, if achieved. A STEP of this sort (call it a *Turing STEP*) constitutes an important goal, and also an important landmark.

STEPs may be scientifically important, practically important, or both. For example, I've positioned the Turing Test as both scientifically and practically important. The Turing-related STEP of surpassing the best intuitive practitioner for chess (Kasparov vs. "Deep Blue" in 1997) probably did not have major practical consequences, though I'm not in a position to judge its scientific value. I am not sure the Wright brothers' STEP had much scientific impact,[1] but it did contribute substantially to development that created an important component of the modern world.

I note that certain STEP goals (possibly including the Turing STEP) may not even make sense before hints of a relevant techno-scientific infrastructure are in place. Who knew, for example, that society could benefit from – or, at least be changed by – social media until late in the twentieth century? Mass literacy didn't make sense, nor do I think anyone anticipated it, until the technology of the printing press began to usher in widespread or universal literacies. In such a case, although the concept of STEP could still be insightful, we likely should adapt the idea to exclude experts, the professional class stipulated to be "already" aiming at (and perhaps to some extent achieving) the relevant goal: "hidden STEPs."

Some STEPs are difficult not just because the relevant science/technology is difficult to achieve, but because the relevant professional class is so good at its work. I put sword making in this category. I also happen to believe that the best teachers are a very difficult target to surpass, and also superior but intuitive curriculum designers and materials developers. I don't think the scientific community, for the most part, gives enough credit to "the best intuitive practitioners." See later comments on this.

I want to make one more general point about STEPs before application. It may often or always be true that STEPs have a *ragged edge*. That is, whether techno-science can surpass the best practitioners may depend on a lot of details one specifies in the relevant measuring stick. So, science may produce a better sword, but if one includes "economically viable" in the specification, that might be a different proposition. If one includes the potentially very important desire to pass the Turing Test with a device that everyone can afford and carry around in their pocket, it becomes a different kind of test. I should point out that the printing press's product, books, (eventually) passed the "everyone can have it and carry it around" criterion, and I personally think this was completely critical in instigating mass literacies. Similar considerations apply to the Wright brothers' STEP. It was a great accomplishment to achieve powered flight, but if that had never become economical, capable of carrying many (not just one or two) people, and even manageable as a complex infrastructure (hence the need for avionics or relevant social infrastructures), we would not be celebrating the narrower STEP at all.

So, here is my STEP framing of Danish et al.'s point. I think it is manifestly true that everyone knows a good deal, in a practical way, about knowledge. They can easily determine when people are ignorant of certain things and project consequences for that ignorance. They intuitively respect people who are expert in things they value. To take an example from this volume, parents are often skilled knowledge practitioners (Umphress, this volume). And yet, I think it is manifestly true that there are limits to the understanding of practitioners. It is not scientific. People, even expert practitioners, can be fooled, and sometimes this is highly consequential. I have claimed consistently for three decades that most people (including much of the research community) were fooled in their early characterization of "students' intuitive knowledge of science" as mere misconceptions.

The symmetrical formulation for interaction is equally cogent. Most people are plainly good at many facets of interaction, notably in everyday interaction with other people. Clinical interviewers are probably even more skilled in certain respects, in certain contexts, and more articulate than just plain folk (diSessa, Micro-Essays, this volume; diSessa, Greeno, Michaels, & O'Connor, this volume).

So, when will the science of human interaction reach a STEP against skilled practitioners who handle interaction intuitively in the analysis of knowledge? When will the science of knowledge allow those who study interaction to achieve a STEP in their own practice, where, currently, that community handles knowledge largely intuitively? Have we already reached such STEPs?

I don't intend to answer those questions because I think they stand beyond our current capacity to judge. My own inclination, however, is that we are clearly, at best, within some ragged edge, rather than having achieved either. Naturally, since I am (let's say, for argument) fairly characterized as primarily a knowledge-oriented person, I might more easily see the contributions that beyond-intuitive treatment of knowledge can confer on interactional analyses. Levin and diSessa (this volume) aim to provide at least a case study where we believe a KA-based theory can be seen clearly to augment an IA where knowledge is handled only intuitively. My perspective on the reverse STEP (interaction science's contribution to Knowledge Analysis) is probably equally prejudiced by my own expertise. In particular, while I appreciate things interaction analysts point out as potentially applying to my practice as an interviewer, on the whole, my practice remains unchanged. My "excuse" is that I feel (1) I know intuitively the things that have so far been pointed out to me about interaction (said differently, the relevant accomplishments are within the range of my techne); and (2) I suspect that the interaction community does not know a lot about important specifics concerning interaction that are involved in this particular context.[2] This mirrors my modest position about where we *all* are (IA and KA types) with respect to educational design and instruction. We can handle a few things better than the best intuitive practitioners, but the jury is still out on whether we can regularly surpass the best intuitive practitioners with the whole complex of things needed to be, for example, a good instructional designer or teacher. At the moment, I think our science is within the ragged edge, and we must respect and manage the parts of instruction and design that are outside our scientific understanding (see "managing the gap" in diSessa & Cobb, 2004).

I believe that charting where we are within the ragged edge concerning KA's helping capacity for IA purposes, and vice versa, would make a great follow-up to this volume.

## A Bridge Too Far? A Bridge Back to Where We Started?

Danish et al. began work on their KAIA project with the goal of producing a new and different theory of Coordination Classes, one oriented more toward interaction and less toward knowledge. In particular, they wanted to capture the idea of distributed knowing, where the effective knowledge that allows an accomplishment is spread across people (and, the common phrase goes, across external materials as well).

After a moment's consideration, I had a reaction that I think has stood the further scrutiny I've managed to afford it. It is a perfectly sensible goal to understand how knowledge and accomplishment may be spread across individuals, but Coordination Class (CC) theory, as it stands, already sustains that inquiry. No basic changes are needed to the theory in order to pursue the "distributed cognition" agenda from the perspective of CC theory. So, while distributed knowledge is an excellent inquiry, it likely won't instigate an interactionally motivated theoretical change. One *might* be able use the intellectual lever of social distribution of knowledge to revise some concepts from KA, but CC theory is not a likely place to start.[3]

The key insight is simple. CCs make no claim to be dealing purely with individual knowledge. The core chain,[4] from observation (extraction) through an inferential path (drawing from the inferential net) to readout, is not stipulated to exist in one person, nor is that in any way a hidden assumption of the theory. One individual may observe, and another may infer the relevant readout. Furthermore, to the extent that "observing" and "inferring" are not monolithic (they are almost always NOT monolithic in empirical studies using the CC model), it is easy to imagine these processes being spread out, possibly in complicated ways, across individuals.[5]

This reflects, in my view, an important observation concerning synthetic agendas, such as the KAIA one. Given presumed-to-be-distinct intellectual agendas, one tends to presume core ideas in one are antithetical – or at least orthogonal – to core ideas in the other point of view. I believe such presumptions are widespread and often unproductive. Cultures may (incorrectly) think that other cultures are different in all respects, especially near the core. Prejudice is often based on such assumptions.

My second reaction was to consider examples where social distribution is vivid and manifestly important. Professional science comes quickly to mind. To connect with CC theory, one can ask, "How does the scientific community 'observe' important things, such as the mass of the Higgs boson?" I think this is a brilliant question to ask, and I do wish someone had the energy and wherewithal to answer it. Here are some observations on the program.

Having come from physics, the cultural divisions between physicists of various sorts were vivid to me. I noticed that my colleagues in the Center for Theoretical Physics just thought about things differently from the experimentalists I worked with or had as instructors. I also noticed that the same mathematics was construed very differently between physicists and mathematicians, to the point that communication often just failed. And yet, physicists, together, could achieve a "readout," the mass of the Higgs boson, that I firmly believe – I'd be tempted to say "I know" – no individual had all the knowledge to achieve, even if said individual commanded the requisite resources. Even in my community of theoretical physicists, the know-how of lab technicians and equipment designers was legendary. As an undergraduate, I was told stories about important experimental landmarks of physics that were based on equipment that only one person in the world could manage: techne of a sublime and essential sort, which also challenges many essentialist views of science.

The big project that I have in mind is a socio-historical analysis of the whole chain involved in reading out (in the technical, CC sense) the mass of the Higgs boson. The headline from the CERN lab that "did" the "observing" had this occurring on July 4, 2012 (CERN, 2015). The compression of time and distributed expertise in this statement is nothing short of stunning.[6] So, my project would be to unpack this achievement. Can we track what "every physicist" knows, and how that plays into the readout? Can we track what various subcommunities know that other subcommunities don't know? What do theoretical physicists, who instigated the "readout," really know about the technology that achieved it? Can we track the influence of individuals or irreducible collaborative subgroups, subgroups that depend on each other in essential ways, so that they are *minimal* subgroups for any reasonable knowledge analysis?

A historical unfolding would be equally telling. Imagine a graphical space-time map of groups (including singletons) at various times and idea threads that wind their way through various groups and their accomplishments to converge in taking their place in a boson-mass readout. What individuals and subgroups originally developed links in the chain of observation at CERN and when did they do it? Who created the relevant "theory of observation" or particular technological innovations? Who supplied critical improvements in theory or practice along the way to that day in July of 2012 at CERN? What, if anything, was genuinely new in the theory or practice behind this observation, beyond a great allocation of resources to a particular STEP-like achievement?

There is actually a historical model of analysis that roughly approximates what I'm proposing. In the late 1970s, James Burke developed and narrated a television show called "Connections" that aimed to lay out the complex intellectual history of important achievements in technology. Burke was a historian of science with a great sensitivity to social aspects of change, including who controls the processes of change, and who gets to benefit from it.

Well, that's a grand program of study to consider. And, I've proposed the CC perspective as a way to frame it. I have no doubt that such an undertaking would make important contributions to both epistemology (what kind of knowledge do various groups and individuals have, with what degree of distinctiveness?) and social history (how do groups or individuals depend on each other, or gain the resources they need from others to effect their achievements?). The study would undoubtedly teach us a lot about the growth and fabric (modularity and interconnectedness) of knowledge, and its social distribution. But, with all that work, I don't see that any basic change would necessarily – or even plausibly – come about to CC theory. I don't foresee any particular pressure from what we would find out that would force a change in the top level of CC theory. The result would be much more like what Levin and diSessa (this volume) attempt to achieve, taking the framing assumptions of one perspective to see how they enhance an agenda that might be construed as belonging to another.

So, that's a bridge too far in the KAIA agenda: too much work (although manifestly important and interesting work), with too uncertain an outcome (I believe the reasons to think that CC theory is agnostic, at its core, about social distribution of knowledge are firm). And, the most likely positive outcome, viewed from the KAIA agenda, is to bring us back to things we are already doing, such as applying CC theory to augment analysis of situations that, on the surface, seem intrinsically to be about interaction and social matters.

In starting with a potentially impressive and obviously impactful hypothetical study, have I muddied the water by escalating the stakes too much, without considering more doable versions of the program? I don't think so. I don't think that considering the distributed nature of knowledge in Parnafes' original analyses at all gets to imposing new and distinctive constraints on the CC frame. The basic model "doesn't care" whether steps in the readout chain are accomplished in one or two heads. Similarly, the contributions of a partner to whatever does or does not wind up as individual knowledge have already appeared, unproblematically, in CC analyses.[7] In considering the illuminations rendered by explicit interactional analysis by Danish et al., I see extensions to Parnafes' original analysis. But she knew she was simplifying the analysis, and she did this advisedly after noting that the good coordination between these partners would make such a move "probably an acceptable simplification" rather than "an oversight." We know more about the communicative channels, too, how each person's knowledge affected the other's. But, I submit, we have not encountered anything that threatens the contribution of CC theory to the case, nor even anything that motivates consequential revision.

## Cumulative Notes

1. The best ground for debate on the scientific impact of the Wrights' contributions concerns their invention of the three-axis mode of controlling flight, arguably an intellectual achievement. In any case, the basis for their patent was *not* "a flying machine," but the means to control it.
2. These two cases in point: I did not realize the pervasiveness of my own use of the interactional form of revoicing before we looked (diSessa, Greeno, Michaels, & O'Connor, this volume). But I maintain that I showed implicit awareness of its value by using it extensively. In complementary manner, we learned in that work that revoicing takes different forms and serves different purposes in the clinical context compared to where it has been studied previously, in classrooms. So, I believe that previous documentation of revoicing was incapable of providing guidance up to the standards of its intuitive use in clinical interviews.
3. CC theory is largely a functional or performance-oriented theory. While more specific models of knowledge, like p-prims, have been valuable in empirical analyses, CC

theory itself is largely form-independent. That also makes it more immune to change under incursions of a variety of alternative views of knowledge.
4   The core of CC theory is an analysis of how one "sees" or "determines" theoretical things from observations. See diSessa, Sherin, & Levin (this volume).
5   I'll just suppress the "across external materials" aspect for simplicity. It's not a problem: just a complication.
6   See the discussion of punctualization in Hall, Nemirovsky, Ma, & Kelton (this volume).
7   Two examples of existing studies involving the distribution of knowledge across individuals in the construction of a CC: Levrini and I (Levrini & diSessa, 2008) looked at how a group of students collaborated – with self-conscious awareness that they wanted to instantiate a primary CC constraint (alignment) – to improve their understanding of the scientific concept of proper time. The analysis, however, did not explicitly break out the details of interaction, which Danish et al. do. The second and probably weaker example is Wagner (2006). Incidental to his analysis, he nonetheless clearly showed the impact of interventions he made (without initially realizing their effect) on the ability of a student to readout things like "expected value of a stochastic process." The effects of his interventions were easily framed in conventional CC terms (e.g., invoking a new basic inference in the inferential net).

## Cumulative References

Bamberger, J. (1990). The laboratory for making things: Developing multiple representations of knowledge. In D. A. Schön (Ed.), *The reflective turn* (pp. 37–62). New York: Teachers College Press.

CERN. (2015). The Higgs boson. Geneva, CH: CERN. Retrieved December 23, 2014, from http://home.web.cern.ch/topics/higgs-boson

Chinn, C. A., Buckland, L. A., & Samarapungavan, A. L. A. (2011). Expanding the dimensions of epistemic cognition: Arguments from philosophy and psychology. *Educational Psychologist*, 46(3), 141–167. doi: 10.1080/00461520.2011.587722

diSessa, A. A. (2002). Why "conceptual ecology" is a good idea. In M. Limón & L. Mason (Eds.), *Reconsidering conceptual change: Issues in theory and practice* (pp. 29–60). Dordrecht: Kluwer.

diSessa, A. A., & Cobb, P. (2004). Ontological innovation and the role of theory in design experiments. *Journal of the Learning Sciences*, 13(1), 77–103.

diSessa, A. A., & Sherin, B. L. (1998). What changes in conceptual change? *International Journal of Science Education*, 20(10), 1155–1191.

Erickson, F. (2004). *Talk and social theory: Ecologies of speaking and listening in everyday life*. Cambridge, UK: Polity Press.

Erickson, F. (2006). Definition and analysis of data from videotape: Some research procedures and their rationales. In J. Green, Camilli, G., & Elmore, P. (Eds.), *Handbook of complementary methods in educational research* (3rd ed., pp. 177–192). Washington, DC: American Educational Research Association.

Goodwin, C. (1994). Professional vision. *American Anthropologist*, 96(3), 606–633.

Goodwin, C. (2000). Action and embodiment within situated human interaction. *Journal of Pragmatics*, 32(1489–1522).

Goodwin, M. H., Goodwin, C., & Yaeger-Dor, M. (2002). Multi-modality in girls' game disputes. *Journal of Pragmatics*, 34, 1621–1649.

Greeno, J. G. (2011). A situative perspective on cognition and learning in interaction. In T. Koschmann (Ed.), *Theories of learning and studies of instructional practice* (pp. 41–71). New York: Springer.

Inhelder, B., & Piaget, J. (1958). *The growth of logical thinking from childhood to adolescence*. New York: Basic Books.
John-Steiner, V., & Mahn, H. (1996). Sociocultural approaches to learning and development: A Vygotskian framework. *Educational Psychologist*, 31(3–4), 191–206.
Jordan, B., & Henderson, A. (1995). Interaction analysis: Foundations and practice. *Journal of the Learning Sciences*, 4(1), 39–103.
Levin, I., & Gardosh, R. (1993). Everyday concepts and formal concepts: Do children distinguish between linear and rotational speed? In D. Tirosh (Ed.), *Implicit and explicit knowledge: an educational approach* (pp. 181–203). Norwood, NJ: Ablex.
Levrini, O., & diSessa, A. A. (2008). How students learn from multiple contexts and definitions: Proper time as a coordination class. *Physical Review Special Topics: Physics Education Research*, 4, 010107.
Parnafes, O. (2007). What does "fast" mean? Understanding the physical world through computational representations. *Journal of the Learning Sciences*, 16(3), 415–450.
Parnafes, O. (2014). A coordination class analysis of individuals in interaction. In J. L. Polman, E. A. Kyza, D. K. O'Neill, I. Tabak, W. R. Penuel, A. S. Jurow, K. O'Connor, T. Lee, & L. D'Amico (Ed.), *Learning and becoming in practice: Proceedings of the International Conference of the Learning Sciences (ICLS) Vol. 3*. Boulder, CO: International Society of the Learning Sciences.
Sacks, H. (1984). On doing "being ordinary". In J. M. Atkinson & J. Heritage (Eds.), *Structures of social action: Studies in conversation analysis* (pp. 413–429). Cambridge, UK: Cambridge University Press.
Schegloff, E. A. (2007). *Sequence organization in interaction: A primer in conversation analysis* (Vol. 1). New York: Cambridge University Press.
Stevens, R., & Hall, R. (1998). Disciplined perception: Learning to see in technoscience. In M. Lampert & M. L. Blunk (Eds.), *Talking mathematics in school: Studies of teaching and learning* (pp. 107–149). Cambridge, UK: Cambridge University Press.
Wagner, J. F. (2006). Transfer in pieces. *Cognition and Instruction*, 24(1), 1–71.
Wertsch, J. V. (1985). *Vygotsky and the social formation of mind*. Cambridge, MA: Harvard University Press.

# 7

# "SEEING" AS COMPLEX, COORDINATED PERFORMANCE

## A Coordination Class Theory Lens on Disciplined Perception

*Mariana Levin and Andrea A. diSessa*

> *There is more to seeing than meets the eyeball.*
>
> N. R. Hanson (1958)

Much work on expertise and its development builds upon the suggestive metaphor that expertise is a kind of "seeing," and developing expertise is a matter of honing or improving this seeing. Stevens and Hall (1998) introduced the term *disciplined perception* to capture the ability of experts to "quickly register features that are relevant to their particular practice, features that are invisible at a glance to non-experts" (p. 108). Disciplined perception (DP) is well cited in learning sciences research, especially within mathematics and science education (Abrahamson, Gutiérrez, Charoenying, Negrete, & Bumbacher, 2012; Arcavi, 2003; Enyedy, 2003; Lindwall & Lymer, 2008; Noble, Nemirovsky, Dimattia, & Wright, 2004). Research in literacy (Moje, 2008), engineering education (Gainsburg, 2006), architectural education (Lymer, 2009), teacher education (Grossman et al., 2009), and medical education (Gegenfurtner, 2009) has also cited the construct. However, few studies that cite the construct have tried to extend and develop the notion of DP beyond the initial usage of the term.

The premise of this chapter is that although "expertise as vision/perception" and "learning as tuning one's vision/disciplining perception through interaction" have face validity and wide appeal, a joint cognitive-interactional lens can move us forward toward a more robust understanding of what disciplined perception is and how it develops. We offer various extensions of the notion of DP, building upon a particular theory of conceptual change, coordination class (CC) theory (diSessa & Sherin, 1998; diSessa & Wagner, 2005). Bringing these two perspectives together obviously relates to the agenda of this volume, but it is also rooted in ongoing conversations between Stevens, diSessa, and others for the past 20 years. The idea of exploring the connection between disciplined perception and coordination class theory was even referenced, but not elaborated upon, in Stevens and Hall's original piece. We offer direction for this elaboration here.

## Theoretical Perspectives

### Disciplined Perception

Drawing upon Goodwin's influential work on *professional vision* (Goodwin, 1994), Stevens and Hall (1998) proposed that experts have specific visual practices that are characteristic of their disciplines. In addition to familiar manifestations of disciplined perception (doctors' ability to see tumors in x-rays, ornithologists' ability to identify birds, sociolinguists' ability to identify a dialect), they emphasize that DP is meant to entail "a broader set of actions that have extended duration in time and frequently stretch across people and things" (Stevens & Hall, 1998, p. 109). In particular, they focus on "active and embodied practices" by which individuals bring heterogeneous elements (e.g., various representational media) into coordination. In introducing DP, Stevens and Hall aim to "carefully describe *visual* [emphasis added] practices, both in relation to tasks, artifacts, and settings where they are deployed and in relation to other embodied practices (e.g., pointing and gesturing) that support them" (p. 108). In cases where participants share a DP, Stevens and Hall say the individuals have "developed a visual practice in which aspects across views can be coordinated to accomplish the tasks at hand" (p. 128).

Stevens and Hall focus not only on characterizing the nature of DP, but also on how it is learned through interactions between individuals who are differentially experienced. One of the results of their analysis is a first-order model based on communication between interlocutors for how "disciplining" perception occurs: Joint activity progresses until a breakdown of communication is noticed (usually by the more experienced participant). This breakdown in communication then leads to intervention and attempts at repair by the more experienced interlocutor. In this way, the perception of the less experienced participant is shaped and becomes more "disciplined" (Stevens & Hall, 1998, pp. 144–145).

We now turn to some of the general features of coordination class theory that we will use in our exploration of disciplined perception.

### Coordination Class Theory

As described in the introductory chapter on Knowledge Analysis (diSessa, Sherin, & Levin, this volume), coordination class theory is part of a broad perspective on knowledge and learning that views individual knowledge as a complex system (diSessa, 1993) that is composed of many diverse elements organized to accomplish "knowing." Within this perspective, a CC is a particular model of a concept, the function of which is to read out a concept-characteristic class of information across the many situations in which one encounters the concept in the world. CCs provide a way to understand knowing and learning in terms of perceptual and inferential processes, the management of which are at the heart of understanding complex scientific concepts (diSessa & Sherin, 1998). To exemplify, consider how an expert may "see" or determine the defining properties of an instance of a particular theoretical kind, say, "force," in the world (physical quantities constitute a broad class of prototypical CCs; diSessa, 1991). In different circumstances, one might just feel the amount of force (the weight of object held in the hand), one might calculate it (e.g., from other determinations, like the relevant mass and acceleration), or one might "just know" that the amount of force is stipulated by general principles (the universal law of gravitation). We call the collection of such methods of seeing/determining a *coordination class*. This represents a radically different approach to studying "what it means to know a concept" from other approaches within cognitive science (e.g., concepts as theories, concepts as categories; concept learning as theory change, or concept learning as categorization).

CCs are mental structures that have two components: (a) a perceptual component and (b) an inferential component. The perceptual component consists of *extractions*[1] – the various perceptually proximal means that individuals have for extracting information from the world in order to make determinations (e.g., what do you look at to determine the amount and direction of a force, the amount of slope or of volume?). The inferential component (the *inferential net*) involves all the reasoning capacities and strategies (inferences) that lead from the information that has been extracted to the relevant determination (e.g., after extracting "rise" and "run," one can infer slope by dividing). The net process of determining concept-characteristic information is called *readout*.

A full CC theory analysis of competence demands identifying the particular means (extractions and inferences) used in reading out the concept-characteristic information. It is this specificity that gives CC theory its "bite." Such details provide much of the basis for our extending the construct of disciplined perception.

To have a well-developed CC, one must have an appropriately broad collection of strategies for readout, across an appropriately large range of situations (providing *span* for the concept), but each strategy must lead to the same determination (providing *alignment*). In the case of force, one can measure a force or one might compute it from other quantities. But one must get the same amount of force from these different strategies. It is often true that different circumstances demand different determination strategies. One can feel (it's actually an inference) the force of gravity on an object in one's hand, but that option is not available for a planet in orbit.

Focal learning phenomena in CC theory include both extending span (the range of contexts for which one has workable readout strategies) and improving alignment (making sure that those strategies determine the same thing). Along with identifying the specific extractions and inferences that constitute a person's

CC, what changes about them in learning (say, a new inference is invoked, or new features of the world might be taken up in extractions) is equally important.

## Initial Points of Contact and Divergence Between Perspectives

Some general points of contact between DP and CC theory are apparent. In a fundamental way, Stevens and Hall's approach to DP and diSessa's CC theory both focus on the *role of perception* (suitably generalized) in expertise and its development. Both perspectives develop their theoretical accounts through the analysis of data of real-time processes of reasoning. For both, what individuals are attending to and noticing in real time is of critical importance. Further, the DP focus on individuals managing multiple representations, coordinating partial information in readouts, and adapting strategies to the exigencies of circumstances, possibly over extended periods of time, is quite amenable to study through a CC lens. These are all exactly the expert's readout strategies – with their accompanying extractions and inferences – and their dependence on particular circumstances.

An apparent initial point of divergence must also be noted. At its core, CC theory is a cognitive theory of knowledge that traces, at a moment-by-moment level, how individual knowledge systems are reorganized (perhaps via social and material interactions) to become more expert-like (e.g., Levrini & diSessa, 2008; Parnafes, 2007, 2012). The root conceptualization of knowing and learning in DP is not cognitivist but rather social-interactionist (individuals become more able to participate in communities of practice).

A superficial point of difference between perspectives involves the nature of the data that are taken as the starting point for theorizing. Stevens and Hall's DP account is developed within the methodological tradition of Interaction Analysis and ethnomethodology. Their account is built, in part, upon "naturalistic" data of professional practice in one case, and in the other, the data are of a relatively non-interventionist series of tutoring sessions. Much of the data collected with respect to CC theory have been either clinical interviews (e.g., diSessa & Sherin, 1998) or classroom-based (e.g., Levrini & diSessa, 2008; diSessa, 2014). However, we view this as a superficial difference in that both classroom and clinical interview data can be collected and analyzed from a "naturalistic" lens.

We ground our discussion with the two case studies presented in the Stevens and Hall 1998 paper in which (a) a pre-algebra student has an illumination and (b) an experienced engineer needs to innovate with respect to the use of available representations of terrain in order to support an argument. In both cases, we highlight foci of attention that are highly salient in a knowledge-oriented, CC theory view but which apparently play no role in Stevens and Hall's analysis. In particular, we discuss the need to account for individual differences in having and learning disciplined perception. We also discuss issues of both intention and variability with respect to "disciplining" perception across the cases. In the case of the pre-algebra student and tutor, we note the multiple and varied means, depending on the tutor's construal of the student's knowledge, for disciplining perception. In the case of the roadway engineers, we focus on understanding their higher strategic levels of competence, and understanding how to characterize longer-term trajectories of disciplining, even crossing disciplinary lines. We now turn to details of the two cases.

## Individual Differences: The Case of Adam and Bluma

Stevens and Hall (1998) analyze segments of an extended tutorial interchange between an experienced algebra teacher/tutor, Bluma, and a pre-algebra student, Adam. Adam has been working with graphing software to explore the connections between equations, the lines they correspond to, and various points and intervals on the graphing plane. Adam relies on a particular representational form in order to solve the problems posed to him, such as those that involve determining the relative locations of points and lines (e.g., whether a given point is on a line or not). The representational form in question is a conventional pair of crossed axes, but with dots added to mark grid points at integer x, y locations. Adam uses this framework exclusively, and when Bluma tries to provoke him to use alternative strategies, he persistently does not know how, and he also makes clear that he does not see the point of alternative strategies.

A focal case is the task of deciding whether a point is on a given line. To solve this problem, Adam draws a line by marking a few "representative" points on it, for example, $x = 1, 2, 3$, computing the corresponding $y$ values from the equation (of the form $y = mx + b$). Then he sketches the implied line and merely observes whether the point in question (also plotted on the graph) is on the line or not. Although Adam clearly knows how to identify points by their coordinates, and he can also determine coordinates given a plotted point, he systematically does not, and claims he cannot, use the equation directly to determine whether a point is on the line corresponding to a given equation. To Bluma (and probably any mathematically competent person), physical graphs are ancillary, and one can easily check whether a point is on a line by evaluating the $y$ corresponding to the relevant $x$, using the equation, verifying that the computed $y$ matches the $y$ from the point in question. Adam has knighted one particular strategy – one not near the inferential core of the ideas (as viewed by mathematicians) – as the exclusive means of determining relative position of lines and points.

Here is the transcript from the interchange where Adam finally realizes that he can use the equation of a line ($y = 2x + 5$) directly to check whether a given point (3, 8) is on it (Stevens & Hall, 1998, p. 125). This occurs after several attempts by Bluma to keep the grid view out of consideration, hoping Adam will then turn to the simpler and more epistemologically fundamental equation strategy by himself. She never suggests any details of how one does this; she only says that there is another way to determine whether a point is on a line that does not use drawing lines and plotting points. In the transcripts, an "=" denotes overlapping speech. Numbers denote gestures and actions and are described in detail following each turn.

> 4 **Adam:** Well, I'd draw, (inaudible) I'd draw two x plus five (1) one two three four five. I'd do that and see if three was on eight =
> 1 (draws two coordinate axes, marks points along the axes, and then draws in a line)
> 5 **Bluma:** = But you wouldn't know to =
> 6 **Adam:** = Oh, well, I could also go two times three plus five is eight. OH [emphatically]. That's what I should be doing. Ahh. Why didn't I do that? There we go.

Stevens and Hall (1998) say, in anticipation of their analysis of this episode, that (a) "the learner's understanding of linear functions on the Cartesian plane is eventually reorganized in response to both the alteration of the material environment and the tutor's acts of disciplining Adam's perception" (p. 114). At the point of analysis, they comment, (b) "As he begins to describe how he would use the drawing to 'see,' Bluma interrupts, and in what we take to be another major epistemic shift, Adam realizes that there is indeed a way to figure it out without the grid view (turn 6 ...)" (p. 125). Finally, in review, they say, (c) "The final, decisive challenge came when Adam was denied visual access to Cartesian space altogether (episode 8). As the case closes, Adam suddenly realizes ('OH. That's what I should be doing. Ahh,' at turn 6, above) that there is another way to 'figure it out' without relying on the grid calculus" (p. 126).

We note that in (a), Stevens and Hall emphasize Bluma's role in Adam's learning. They cite "acts of disciplining," and exemplify it by acts of altering the material environment. Neither Bluma's intentions nor anything about the reasoning she did to decide on those acts is discussed. Adam's thinking, what he knew before, and how he managed to make the final connection, are not elaborated. In (b), Stevens and Hall mark a "major epistemic shift," and they explain that Adam does the realizing. But, there is no analysis given of the specific reasoning processes leading to his realization. Finally, (c) again marks only that Adam is challenged materially ("decisive challenge," "denied visual access"), and from that, he "realizes...that there is another way to 'figure it out'..." What Adam knew and what role that played in his realization are unelaborated. In net, there are many, many vivid, knowledge-related questions that are not addressed from Stevens and Hall's perspective, which emphasizes physical actions, such as Bluma's denying visual access.

We now consider this episode as an example of CC phenomena. Mostly, we will identify slots where some kind of Knowledge Analysis clearly seems required. We will not be able to fill in a great deal of the specific analysis, owing to the sparsity of the data with which we must work.

## Using Coordination Class Theory to Account for an Individual Illumination

To begin, we name the relevant coordination class at play in the above episode of Adam and Bluma: It is the determination of *object location*. Here, we intend both "object" and "location" in an extended sense, including things like points and lines in Cartesian space with respect to one another. Stated another way, the competence at stake involves the kinds of strategies by which people "see" where things lie with respect to one another.

In this case, Adam observes the spatial relationship of a given point and a line. This involves only very slight complications beyond the everyday capacity to observe real-world spatial relationships just by looking at the relevant objects. First, he must instantiate the relevant point and line, as opposed to simply observing their relative location where they happen to lie. This is easy for Adam – and he knows it; he knows how to plot (position) points and lines given coordinates of a point and the equation of a line. Determining the relevant spatial relationship – the critical coordination class readout operation – is easier here than in many cases of determining relative position, since the only relevant determination is "point on line" or "not."

Assimilating the work Adam does in response to point-on-line questions to the "relative spatial location" CC does two pieces of work for us. First, it explains why the method he uses is so simple and obvious to him. "First, you put things where they belong, and then you observe their relationship." Second, it helps explain how natural Adam found this method and why he found the possibility of other strategies so foreign. How can you determine spatial relationships without observing? Why would you want to? Realizing a powerful continuity between everyday thinking and mathematics likely explains Adam's confidence in his methods (and probably something about generally easy components of learning, as well).

Let us unpack the process of discovery just a bit. Adam is prompted to explain how he would accomplish the relevant determining under the constraint that he not actually instantiate the relevant point and line. He explains that he would use a few representative points, at $x = 1, 2, 3$, draw the line, and then observe the relation to the point (3, 8). The point of Bluma's interruption ("But you wouldn't know to =") is unclear to us, but what follows is Adam's realization of what would happen if he accidentally used $x = 3$ as one of the points to determine the location of the line. He realizes that drawing the line is unnecessary because if the $y$ at $x = 3$ is 8, then (3, 8) is on the line (he would have to locate the line by making it run through this point). If the $y$ is not 8, (3, 8) is not on the line. The constraint that the line must go through any of his "sample" points means that his strategy reduces to computing $y$ and matching it against the point in question, $y = 8$.

There are two issues here. Adam noticed something. Bluma did not draw his attention to it, except in the general sense of putting him "in the vicinity" of the thing to notice. It was his choice (accidentally) to put himself in the position to notice, by selecting $x = 3$ as a line-grounding point. So, we conclude that we can only partially credit Bluma with "disciplining." The rest of the credit goes both to chance and to Adam's ability to notice this particular thing and see its generalization. Not every student will be able to generalize so easily, so we *must* have a way to talk about individual differences between Adam's knowledge and others' if we are to be able to predict (and foster) insight and learning.

This episode indicates the need to place the local illumination that Adam had along a longer trajectory of the development of disciplinary competence. We now turn to issues related to what the more experienced participant, Bluma, knew and how her knowledge (of mathematics, of typical student learning experiences, of Adam as a particular student, etc.) shaped her interactions with Adam.

## *Disciplining Perception: Diversity of Means in the Case of Adam and Bluma*

One of the reasons the case of Adam and Bluma was selected by Stevens and Hall was that the disciplinary expertise differential between the two participants was significant and therefore there would be opportunities to study the processes by which Bluma disciplined Adam's perception. However, Adam's illumination in the episode discussed above did not seem to result directly from some particular action on Bluma's part to shape his perception. The (nearly) independent nature of Adam's illumination indicates the need to have a way to discuss the cumulative creation of conditions that ultimately result in individuals' perception becoming more disciplined. For example, Adam's learning can be understood as a result of (a) Bluma and Adam's history of interactions, (b) Bluma's posing that particular problem in a certain way, (c) Adam's choosing a serendipitous point when imagining plotting points to construct the graph of the line, and (d) the knowledge necessary to recognize the implications of his choice, which it turns out Adam had. In addition to softening the determinism implied by the simple model of disciplining perception given in the original paper (which seems to us emphasized by not examining contextualities and ancillary conditions for disciplining), we wish to also point out the knowledge and intentionality on the part of the more experienced participant and the role that an account of these must play in a theory of how people learn through interaction.

Especially in explicitly instructional contexts like the tutorial sessions between Bluma and Adam, acts of disciplining perception are generally knowledge-intensive on the part of the more knowledgeable participant. Knowing when and how to discipline perception requires specific awareness of what the other person understands/doesn't understand and often a specific strategy for how to shape their perception.

Below, we give a brief sampling of the diversity of ways that Bluma's interactions with Adam disciplined his perception so as to expand his repertoire of strategies (increase span) for determining whether a point is on a line. Our sampling includes only the episodes that Stevens and Hall discussed in their paper, but even across those eight episodes, there is considerable diversity in the nature of these interactions.

In episode 1, Bluma asks Adam to "figure out exactly" where a graph crosses the $x$-axis. In response, Adam interprets her request in terms of precision of graphing as opposed to using equations to make the determination. In episodes 2 (Stevens & Hall, 1998, p. 117) and 6 (Stevens & Hall, 1998, p. 122), Bluma then tries a different approach in order to give Adam a rationale for having multiple means of determination, not just the graphical means (e.g., "What if it was sort of hard to make it from the line?"). In episode 3 (Stevens & Hall, 1998, pp. 119–120), Adam is reasoning about the graphical relationship between the two lines $y = x$ and $y = 3x$. Bluma notices that Adam seems to be relying upon the edges of the grid (a noticing based on her own knowledge of the domain and knowledge of why this would be problematic). She attempts to raise a conflict for Adam by physically blocking the edges of the graph. That is, she is attempting to show him that there is a problem of alignment (in the CC theory sense) with his means of determining the relationship between the graphs, because relying on the edges would produce a different determination when the graph is cut off. Her actions do not have the intended consequence because Adam concludes instead that the original graph and the graph with the edges blocked are just different graphs. Disciplinings must respond to the details of the "disciplinee's" thinking.

Later, in a task that explicitly directed Adam to use the equation and *not* the graph in order to determine the $x$-intercept, Bluma recalls a piece of knowledge that she knows has the potential to be generative for Adam by reminding him that he knows how to figure out the $y$-intercept (from the equation), hoping that this will prime him to think about the effect of substituting specific points in the equation of the line. Adam persists in declaring that one doesn't need to use equations since one can figure this out from the graph. However, this episode is the first time that Adam definitely realizes that there *is* another way to figure out information about the graph without graphing and that he just doesn't see how to do it (sighing and saying, "Well I wouldn't know [to do anything other than use the line]" and later, "I have no idea"). Overall, Bluma has gradually built a certain kind of readiness in Adam for his final illumination.

These are not incidental observations. If we want to understand Bluma's disciplining, perhaps to convey it to other teachers, recognizing this knowledge is central.

In addition to Bluma's in-the-moment knowledge and reading of what Adam understands, there is also knowledge embedded in the careful sequencing of tasks in the sessions. The tasks and their sequencing were part of a tutoring curriculum collaboratively planned by a research team. When Adam encounters tasks that require him to reason in blank view (no dots), this disrupts his usual graphical methods and created an undeniable need for him to come up with new means of determination.

We caution against giving the impression that we should ever expect *direct* links between tutor moves and student learning. One of the things we believe the case of Adam and Bluma shows is that although there are many interactions between Adam and Bluma that give him feedback and shape his perception, ultimately the illumination that resulted in expanding his repertoire of means of determination was *Adam's* illumination. Knowledge often (always?) mediates the learning effects of interaction. That is, although we can agree that perception is socially shaped through interactions, it is not always clear how to understand the effects of particular tutor moves unless one has a good account of the student's knowledge relevant to a possible insight and how tutor actions are responsive to the particulars of student knowledge.

## Understanding the Higher, Strategic Levels: The Case of Jake and Evan

We now turn to a contrasting case study given in Stevens and Hall (1998) involving two professional civil engineers, Jake and Evan, who are working together on a roadway design for a housing development. From the perspective of the objectives of this chapter, the case study affords the opportunity to explore different aspects of disciplined perception than were possible in the case of Adam and Bluma. For example, we will have the opportunity to view, through the perspective of CC theory, (a) how professional engineers make visible and resolve issues related to their practice that would be invisible and impenetrable at a glance to non-engineers, and (b) the expertise involved in improvising by coordinating across available representations when no single representation provided easy access to the information necessary to make determinations. One objective of viewing these episodes through the lens of CC theory is to try to characterize the qualitatively different nature of the disciplined perception described in these episodes from the disciplined perception in the case of Adam and Bluma. One of the upshots of the case analysis is that the problem-solving activity of the engineers is quite complex, relying upon multiple determinations (e.g., a coordinated strategy system), as well as specific professional knowledge (e.g., specific CCs) to accomplish the goal of providing a design rationale. Attempting to understand the engineers' activity in CC terms pushes us to consider some of the continuities (or discontinuities) between the DP Adam is developing and the professional expertise of the engineers.

We begin with some background given in Stevens and Hall on the case study from which this focal episode of DP is drawn. Jake is an experienced engineer who is leading the housing development project and Evan is a junior engineer working with Jake. Jake and Evan are revisiting the design of a particular roadway in the development. During the course of the discussion, they determine that the roadway is excessively steep according to city codes and they find themselves in the position of needing to create a rationale for the steep design. As they attempt to build the argument, they are primarily interested in "seeing" (that is, determining or reading out) quantities such as (a) the actual steepness or the *slope* of the roadway and (b) how much "cut" and "fill" would result from the roadway as designed (e.g., the *volume* of dirt that needs to be removed or added to particular sections of the terrain). Other knowledge that drives the design rationale is balancing, to the extent possible, the amount of cut and fill in a design (since moving dirt to and from the construction site is expensive). Another consideration the engineers must attend to is to avoid cutting too much into steep hillsides because this would require either an expensive retaining wall or to "chase grade" (e.g., level the hillside) in order to preserve the structural integrity of the terrain upon which the road is built.

To be more explicit about how Jake and Evan's activity can be reframed in terms of CC theory, we begin by explicitly noting that quantities like slope, cut, and fill (e.g., volume) are recognizable as prototypical CCs. That is, individuals have repertoires of strategies for "seeing" slope, cut, and fill; these strategies may differ across representational contexts (the issue of span); and the same determination of slope, cut, fill, and so on needs to be reached across different representations and different uses of them (the issue of alignment). Additionally, part of expertise involves knowing what information will be necessary in order to determine slope, cut, fill, and position in any of the representations available to the engineers and whether or not it is available in any particular representation. This knowledge guides the selection and use of appropriate representations.[2]

We now introduce the three primary representations of the roadway and terrain (generated by a CAD system) that Jake and Evan make use of in developing their rationale for the roadway design: plan view, profile view, and section view. Examples are shown in Figure 7.1, which is taken from Stevens and Hall (1998). The representations have a common quantitative scale (every 50 feet along the road, "stations" are marked) that assists in coordinating readouts across the three representations. Before continuing, we need at least a brief overview of the information that is accessible through each representation and strategies that could be employed in the context of each representation for determining relevant quantities like slope, cut, and fill.

*Plan view* shows a map of the proposed roadway (viewed from above) set against a topographic map of the terrain (marking planes of constant elevation every 10 feet above sea level). Plan view allows one to see the curvature and general shape of the roadway. One can quickly infer (from closer or farther spacing of lines) the relative slope of parts of the terrain, thus allowing engineers to easily locate potentially problematic steep regions. This has implications for areas where one may need to cut in order to create the road, but also areas where one should exercise caution in cutting because that could result in severely worsening the integrity of the hillside. To remark briefly on other relevant information related to slope that can be accessed in plan view, if one wanted to determine the (average) slope exactly (e.g., for compliance with code), one could use the fixed horizontal scale that is given on the representation and count the number of topographic (topo) lines between two points of interest on the terrain to determine the horizontal distance between the two points. This would allow one to read off the change in elevation (rise) by observing the topo lines at two points of interest and computing the change in elevation between them (the constant elevation that topo lines represent is written somewhere along each line). So, having read out (computed) the "rise" and "run," one can then determine the slope over the segment of interest (or similarly, over the entire segment of roadway).

*Profile view.* In profile view, we see a side view projection of both the proposed road and the existing terrain, both set against a grid. Both the vertical axis and the horizontal axis have gridlines every 50 feet. This works well to allow coordination with station numbers in the other representations. The elevations along the roadway can be read out from a chart that runs along the bottom of the representation that includes this information, both for the proposed roadway and the actual terrain at each side of the proposed roadway every 50 feet (corresponding to station numbers). In this view, the vertical discrepancy between proposed and actual terrain is shown (both at the centerline and sidelines of the proposed roadway). From this view, an engineer can determine locations where cut and fill will be necessary. However, since only the vertical distance between proposed and actual is recorded, one cannot see the *volume* of cut and fill that is necessary.

*Section view* gives a representation of "slices" of the roadway every 50 feet. The roadway is centered on a grid that extends horizontally and vertically. As in the profile view, the curvature of the road is not visible in section view. However, the cross-sectional area of cut and fill at particular points along the road is visible, which helps in making relative assessments of whether one roadway design would entail more cut/fill than another. The section view is not useful for determining slope because it only gives a "snapshot" of the road at one particular point along the terrain and hence does not give any information about how the terrain changes between two points along the road.

The above discussion of what is "visible" in these representations raises some interesting questions about the boundaries of disciplined perception. Certainly the representations of the terrain are very familiar to engineers who work with these particular kinds of representations in their daily practice. However, the representations themselves are not impenetrable to people who have some degree of familiarity with Cartesian coordinate systems and graphing. While it is likely that Jake and Evan first encountered these particular kinds of representations in their engineering coursework and later in their professional workplaces, there was already a good deal of knowledge infrastructure in place at that point that allowed them to easily appropriate and use the representations. For instance, in the particular case of creating representations of terrain, even children (Azevedo, 2000; Enyedy, 2005) can re-create the idea of topographic maps. This points to the importance of common aspects of the conceptual development of competences,

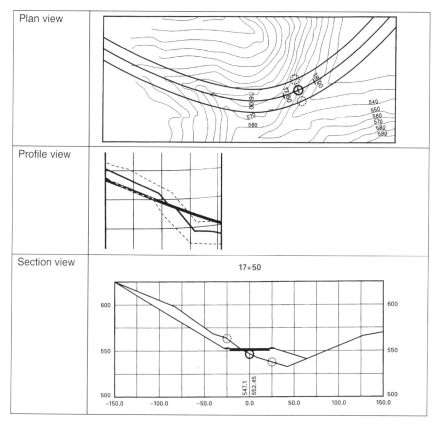

**FIGURE 7.1** The three representational forms available to the engineers, Jake and Evan, as they resolve issues related to the design of a roadway. Note: In the profile view, gridlines come every 50 feet. This is a segment of the entire profile view representation that would show the profile along the full length of the roadway.

Source: Reprinted from *Talking Mathematics in School: Studies of Teaching and Learning*, edited by Magdalene Lampert and Merrie L. Blunk. Copyright © 1998 Cambridge University Press. Reprinted with the permission of Cambridge University Press. Material excerpted from Figure 5.5 on pages 130–131 in the chapter, "Disciplined Perception: Learning to See in Technoscience," by Reed Stevens and Rogers Hall.

like constructing and interpreting graphs of terrain. The key point we are making is that the highly tailored practices of engineers have substantial and long developmental histories that feed in somewhat direct ways into their professional practice. And, attention to the specific knowledge they employ, and where they might have got it, is important in seeing exactly what is new in any particular instance of disciplining perception, and how the disciplining of perception was possible.[3]

## *Representational Improvisation as Knowledge-Intensive Activity*

We now turn to a discussion of the data involving a particularly interesting manifestation of disciplined perception (Stevens & Hall, 1998, pp. 128–139). We start at the beginning of the thread of the engineers' activity to give some context for the problem that emerges and how they go about resolving it over the course of an afternoon of work together. We will then zoom in only on a brief but illustrative moment of representational improvisation in order to ground our discussion of how CC theory and DP perspectives make contact in this case.

It comes up rather quickly in the engineers' discussion that the roadway in question is quite steep (nearly a 20% grade). Evan seems to remember that they went with the maximum slope allowed for this kind of roadway and Jake remembers that they went with more than max slope. They (Jake) decide to check this. Since they cannot just read slope directly from any of the representations of the roadway and terrain they are using, Jake engages in a relatively simple act of DP and uses the usual slope formula to "see" (or "determine") the slope, which he finds to be approximately 0.19 (or roughly a 20% grade). Such a determination is consequential in their practice, but relies upon methods for seeing slope that both Jake and Evan would have been familiar with since middle or high school – long before they entered an engineering firm.

Because of his familiarity with city planning codes, Jake knows that this choice results in making the road steeper than is usually allowed and will require specific justification. Following Jake's lead, the joint activity of the two engineers now orients towards creating a rationale for why the roadway has been designed to be excessively steep. Jake selectively draws upon information available to him across all three representations of the roadway and the terrain. He begins by orienting to a segment of road in the profile view (where he can see where cut/fill are required), then shifting to examining the road in plan view (where he can see the steepness of the terrain in that region). He tries to develop the argument that the reason they went with the excessively steep roadway was because they were trying to avoid a lot of cut in a steep section of the canyon. However once he looks at the roadway in that region relative to the topo lines in the plan view, he temporarily abandons this line of argument because it does not seem that avoiding excessive cut in that particular portion of the map would support his argument that they needed to go with greater than max slope for the roadway design.

Jake now orients to a different section of the terrain (around station 16+50). In creating and communicating the emerging argument, it would be convenient for Jake to have a plan view of the terrain that is also labeled with station numbers so that he could then use the station numbers to easily find the same location in profile and section views. However, Jake only has a plan view that includes topo lines and then another plan view that has station numbers (but no topo) available to him. Despite this less than optimal representational situation, in the segment below, we see how Jake purposefully "improvises" to use the two plan views, together with section and profile views, in order to orient to a section in which they will have to cut anyway. Below, the text on the left is the original transcript in Stevens and Hall (Stevens & Hall, 1998, p. 137) and the text on the right is our annotation accentuating the coordination of representations in the episode.

---

**21 Jake:** Yeah. See like right here *((overlaps and layers views with profile on top, plan and stations next, and then plan with topo))*. (5 seconds).

Like right at sixteen *((L finger points below "16+50" in profile))* fifty or so *((L finger moves to "16+50" on plan with stations and holds))*

Like right at this corner *((R pencil tip moves to corresponding spot on plan with topo))*, we're *((L hand moves back to profile at "16+50"))* actually gonna cut, we're gonna have to, we're gonna have to … take down

*((scribbles over the region above road in plan with topo))* the side of this anyways, you see that?

**22 Evan:** Yeah.

**23 Jake:** But um…That will be like… It's just this one area. *((R pencil draws dashed line in area next to road on plan with topo between stations "14+50" and "18+50"))*.

So it'll be somethin' like, you know, this. But then see here *((L finger moves back to road on profile around station "14+50"))*,

I think what was goin' on is, I think here. This is *((R pencil traces a circle around the area surrounding the road in plan with topo between stations "10+00" and "14+00"))* all trees, right?

*Jake arranges representations:*
**Profile** *(top)*
**Plan and stations** *(next)*
**Plan with topo** *(bottom)*

*Attends to* **profile** *to find region where cut is required. Finds location in* **plan with stations.**

*Finds corresponding location on* **plan with topo.** *Moves back to same location in* **profile.**

*Referring back to same region in* **plan with topo**

*Marks off this region where cut is required on* **plan with topo**.

*Moves back to* **profile** *and orients to beginning of the region just marked on plan with topo.*

*Moves back to* **plan with topo** *and orients to a nearby region that Jake notes is populated by trees.*

---

Let's now briefly recap what Jake was doing with the representations he had available to him in order to see what was going on with the roadway and the terrain. Jake first finds a region that they need to cut by looking at the profile view. He knows that profile view makes perceptually evident regions in which cut/fill are needed, so this is purposefully the first representation he goes to in constructing his argument (and this representation is placed on top). He then uses the common scale in order to find that same spot on the plan with station numbers. In the plan view, he can see the terrain around the place that they are going to need to cut. Now, he can make the move to transitioning to plan with topo (no stations). This is where, ideally, Jake would have had a plan view that included both topo and station numbers. Given that he cannot find such a representation, he locates the place of interest on plan with topo by orienting to the shape of the road (he finds a "corner"). He moves back to the profile view to "see" the region that he would need to cut anyway and then moves back to the plan with topo view to approximately mark out that region. Jake then moves back to the profile view and orients to a different station (14+50). He moves over to the plan with topo view and notes that the region around that station is all trees. According to Stevens and Hall, Jake will go on to explain that even a small amount of cut in that region would require them to "chase grade all the way up on both sides," which he then explains would violate an environmental constraint of the project: They are supposed to avoid, if possible, removing trees in order to grade the site. Hence, Jake and Evan's rationale for their design is now transformed: They had to go with the steeper roadway design since if they graded the side to bring the roadway into alignment with code with respect to steepness, it would then require they remove the trees in a large section of the development (and they have been directed to leave trees, if possible).

## Coordination Classes and Strategy Systems to Account for Representational Innovation in Argument Formation

Unlike the case of Adam and Bluma that involved reframing the learning events that occurred in terms of increasing the span and alignment of Adam's means of making relevant determinations, the case of Jake and Evan allows us to consider CC theory in order to understand interactions in which the participants largely share a sense of DP: that is, interactions in which professional engineers work together and selectively draw upon features of multiple representational forms in order to construct design rationales.

The example of Jake shows an impressive display of DP in which he coordinates the use of several representations simultaneously, precisely because any one representation of the terrain did not make easily visible the argument he is attempting to construct. From our perspective, Jake's representational innovation begs specification and highlights the role of personal invention. While we appreciate the tightly coordinated and purposeful display of DP that Stevens and Hall highlight in this example, we do not believe the richness of Jake's ability can be understood without a perspective that can illuminate the nature and variability of the individual knowledge involved. For example, there is significant knowledge involved in being able to make determinations of quantities like slope, cut, and fill across representational forms; in purposefully selecting the representational form that makes the information one needs in order to make a determination most visible; and in adapting and improvising with representations if the current representational forms at hand are insufficient on their own.

What we see Jake (in particular) doing is selecting foci of attention (e.g., closeness of topo lines, whether the line representing the road in the profile view is above or below the line representing the actual terrain, the location of trees within the housing development project and their relation to the proposed roadway via the plan view). Jake knows to focus in on these aspects, has strategies for reading out the information he requires (e.g., determining slope in plan with topo requires related, but different strategies than determining slope of a hillside in regular Cartesian coordinates). Furthermore, Jake can instrumentally use these determinations of slope, cut, fill, and location in order to pose and resolve issues with the design (e.g., Is the road as designed too steep with respect to code? Will the proposed roadway require more cut than the hillside can support without needing to be leveled? How much fill will the proposed roadway require? Is this amount within an acceptable bound?).

The perspective of a CC is a particularly apt one for characterizing and thinking about the ability to use multiple means to determine a single quantity like slope or to determine the relative position of objects. However, the more extended displays of DP that Stevens and Hall discuss, such as the description of "representational improvisation" on the part of the more experienced engineer in the service of refining and communicating a design rationale, do not fit neatly within the existing regime of CC theory as presented so far.[4]

In this particular case, the engineers' activity is a more ill-structured problem-solving activity than the local (and well-structured) task of making a particular determination of the slope of the hillside or the volume of cut/fill required in a particular section. There are certainly relationships between the two activities. For example, Jake and Evan are looking for inferential pathways, and, a bit at a time, those inferential pathways are pretty secure (e.g., in the service of the larger argument, they *do* need to make determinations of slope and of volume of cut/fill, etc.). Here, we propose that CCs are involved in judging the local inferential chains (e.g., determining slope or cut/fill) and also in judging the security of the total inferential chain. However, the search for an inferential chain is organized by meta-knowledge about the representations, what information they contain, what information they definitely *do not* contain, etc. That is, the meta-activity is trying to find a design rationale that will be acceptable by professional standards and constraints. Furthermore, as professionals, part of the disciplined knowledge that they have concerns what the professional standards and constraints even are. This knowledge, in and of itself, guides what the engineers know they need to determine.

So, while the individual determinations involved in the problem-solving activity *are* well handled by CC theory, the meta-activity involved in selecting what information one even needs to determine is indicative of the working of a more extensive knowledge system that draws upon multiple CCs simultaneously. Characterizing the knowledge systems that are involved in a problem-solving activity is a new endeavor within the general theory of CCs, initiated in Levin's (2012) dissertation work on *strategy systems*.[5] Thus, the very phenomenology pointed to within Stevens and Hall's analysis as an example of DP requires an extended version of CC theory, which is currently being developed. These are all positive signs for CC extensions of DP. The theory has enough bite so that we can see when it does not apply. And, still, the theory can provide a foundation for expanding it to deal – at a comparably fine level of detail – with a new class of phenomenology, a new kind of thinking.

## Discussion and Conclusions

A major theme of our exploration of disciplined perception through a coordination class theory lens was that both DP and how it is developed through social interactions (aka "disciplining" perception) are quite complex and broad in scope. According to Stevens and Hall, the ability to determine whether a point is on a particular graph and being able to navigate multiple representations of terrain in order to formulate a professionally grounded design rationale are both examples of having disciplined perception. This generality is a double-edged sword. On one hand, many different kinds of phenomena can be recognized as being related in how experts perceive the world. However, as we have argued, such diversity in the basic phenomenology may be better understood (and supported) if we distinguish between these different facets of DP and also between the diversity of ways that perception can be purposefully disciplined in interaction.

In the first example from the case of Bluma and Adam, we used CC theory to understand the process of developing a very specific but consequential competence. This case involved a relatively straightforward appropriation of CC theory in order to understand both the nature of key learning events (increasing span and improving alignment of means of determining relative position of points and lines in the plane), and why the need for or possibility of new methods seemed foreign initially to Adam. What could be more natural, and why would one need to go beyond: To determine if two things (set up in a specific way) coincide, set them up and look! In that episode, we also highlighted the individual thinking and agency involved in Adam's ultimate illumination. Without those details, it is all too easy to portray "external" interactions, mistakenly, as deterministic of learning. We also felt compelled to introduce more complexity into the account of the tutor. The tutor's actions are quite diverse and purposeful. Some of these connect with learning paths suggested by CC theory (e.g., in supporting an increase in span and improvement of alignment), but as the case of Adam demonstrates, there is a complex relationship between tutor actions and student learning moments. Tutors do not just discipline, they observe and interpret their student's actions, and they formulate specific disciplining strategies.

The two engineers, Jake and Evan, made evident the need to distinguish between the ability to make relatively simple determinations (e.g., the grade of a hillside or the volume of cut and fill needed at a particular place along the road) and using the ability to purposefully select information from multiple representational forms; improvising when necessary, in the service of creating a professional rationale; operating under many constraints of differing sorts for the design of a roadway. To be sure, the ability to make determinations and to check the chain of reasoning that supports the rationale involves CC-like competence, but the ability to purposefully select appropriate facets of knowledge in activity requires more complex knowledge systems than with a "simple" CC. The interplay between knowledge organization and problem solving is largely new ground (though not unexpected) from the perspective of development of CC theory.

Another major theme that ran throughout our reanalysis was to partition the development of DP into competences that we could see being developed in the local interactions from those competences that have quite long previous histories and perhaps even overlap with competences necessary for developing disciplined perception in other fields. For example, both Jake and Evan are able to see the terrain and use the given representations of their practice in ways that non-engineers would not be able to. However, the representations given (profile, section, and plan views) were not *so* unfamiliar that those who have some familiarity with graphing in the coordinate plane (and related mathematical representations) would not be able to understand them at all. So, we recognize that there must be a spectrum of DP from something that truly only experts in a specific domain would be able to perceive to aspects that have some intersection with the competences developed in other fields. This, naturally, will have significant consequences in organizing curricula in schools and universities.

The question of how experts develop a finely tuned and professional way of experiencing and perceiving the world is fascinating and a worthy, educationally relevant question. This chapter gives a dialectical reformulation and extension of Stevens and Hall's Interaction Analysis perspective on disciplined perception – a reformulation that includes analysis of what can be well rendered by coordination class theory. Reconsidering the data and analysis through a Knowledge Analysis lens (via coordination class theory) raised several issues for further elaboration. The small steps we have taken here suggest to us a very profitable future for the analysis of disciplined perception – augmented, when appropriate, by considerations of Knowledge Analysis – particularly in terms of exposing detail, diversity of forms of disciplining, individual differences, and tracking long trajectories of disciplinary competences.

## Notes

1. We use the revised terminology for elements of CC theory. See the appendix to diSessa, Sherin, & Levin (this volume).
2. We take this knowledge to be relatively unproblematic. One could probably just ask the engineers what they know about these issues. Very likely one could "see" this knowledge in the texts that the engineers used at school and also in their remembrance of the particulars of their own learning about these things.

3   This is the same point made by highlighting important continuities with Adam's prior knowledge that make some things easy (Adam's "look in order to see relative location" strategy and his ability to notice the generality of the new strategy he developed), and then, in disciplining perception, to focus on other things that are not so easy.
4   The core issue is lack of detail. Complex and strategic readouts are still readouts, but "classical" CC theory provides no detail on how such readouts are accomplished.
5   Briefly, a CC is a special case of a strategy system, one in which the problem to be solved is to determine a particular concept in a particular context. However, in general, solving problems relies upon multiple such determinations simultaneously and requires the solver to purposefully select knowledge resources and determinations in pursuit of a solution to the problem.

## References

Abrahamson, D., Gutiérrez, J. F., Charoenying, T., Negrete, A. G., & Bumbacher, E. (2012). Fostering hooks and shifts: Tutorial tactics for guided mathematical discovery. *Technology, Knowledge, and Learning*, 17, 61–86.

Arcavi, A. (2003). The role of visual representations in the learning of mathematics. *Educational Studies in Mathematics*, 52(3), 215–241.

Azevedo, F. (2000). Designing representations of terrain: A study in meta-representational competence. *Journal of Mathematical Behavior*, 19(4), 443–480.

diSessa, A. A. (1991). Epistemological micromodels: The case of coordination and quantities. In J. Montanegro & A. Tryphon (Eds.), *Psychologie génétique et sciences cognitives* (pp. 169–194). (Volume from the Eleventh Advanced Course.) Geneva, CH: Archives Jean Piaget.

diSessa, A. A. (1993). Toward an epistemology of physics. *Cognition and Instruction*, 10(2–3), 105–225.

diSessa, A. A. (2014). The construction of causal schemes: Learning mechanisms at the knowledge level. *Cognitive Science*, 38(5), 795–850.

diSessa, A. A., & Sherin, B. L. (1998). What changes in conceptual change? *International Journal of Science Education*, 20(10), 1155–1191.

diSessa, A. A., & Wagner, J. (2005). What coordination has to say about transfer. In J. Mestre (Ed.), *Transfer of learning from a modern multidisciplinary perspective* (pp. 121–154). Greenwich, CT: Information Age Publishing.

Enyedy, N. (2003). Knowledge construction and collective practice: At the intersection of learning, talk, and social configurations in a computer-mediated mathematics classroom. *Journal of the Learning Sciences*, 12(3), 361–407.

Enyedy, N. (2005). Inventing mapping: Creating cultural forms to solve collective problems. *Cognition and Instruction*, 23(4), 427–466.

Gainsburg, J. (2006). The mathematical modeling of structural engineers. *Mathematical Thinking and Learning*, 8(1), 3–36.

Gegenfurtner, A. (2009). What is seen on the screen? Exploring collaborative interpretation, representational tools, and disciplined perception in medicine. *Proceedings of the Ninth International Conference on Computer-Supported Collaborative Learning*. Volume 2, pp. 71–72.

Goodwin, C. (1994). Professional vision. *American Anthropologist*, 96, 606–633.

Grossman, P., Compton, C., Igra, D., Ronfeldt, M., Shahan, E., & Williams, P. (2009). Teaching practice: A cross-professional perspective. *Teachers College Record*, 111(9), 2055–2100.

Hanson, N. R. (1958). *Patterns of discovery: An inquiry into the conceptual foundations of science.* Cambridge, UK: Cambridge University Press.

Levin (Campbell), M. E. (2012). *Modeling the co-development of strategic and conceptual knowledge during mathematical problem solving.* (Unpublished doctoral dissertation). University of California, Berkeley.

Levrini, O., & diSessa, A. (2008). How students learn from multiple contexts and definitions: Proper time as a coordination class. *Physical Review Special Topics – Physics Education Research, 4,* 010107.

Lindwall, O., & Lymer, G. (2008). The dark matter of lab work: Illuminating the negotiation of disciplined perception in mechanics. *Journal of the Learning Sciences, 17*(2), 180–224.

Lymer, G. (2009). Demonstrating professional vision: The work of critique in architectural education. *Mind, Culture, and Activity, 16*(2), 145–171.

Moje, E. B. (2008). Foregrounding the disciplines in secondary literacy teaching and learning: A call for change. *Journal of Adolescent & Adult Literacy, 52*(2), 96–107.

Noble, T., Nemirovsky, R., Dimattia, C., & Wright, T. (2004). Learning to see: Making sense of the mathematics of change in middle school. *International Journal of Computers for Mathematics Learning, 9*(2), 109–167.

Parnafes, O. (2007). What does "fast" mean? Understanding the physical world through representations. *The Journal of the Learning Sciences, 16*(3), 415–450.

Parnafes, O. (2012). Developing explanations and developing understanding: Students explain the phases of the moon using visual representations. *Cognition and Instruction, 30*(4), 359–403.

Stevens, R., & Hall, R. (1998). Disciplined perception: Learning to see in technoscience. In M. Lampert & M. Blunk (Eds.), *Talking mathematics in school: Studies of teaching and learning* (pp. 107–149). Cambridge, UK: Cambridge University Press.

# 8

## WORKING OUT

### Mathematics Learning as Motor Problem Solving in Instrumented Fields of Promoted Action

*Dor Abrahamson and Dragan Trninic*

Educational researchers love "Eureka!" moments, when a student appears to transition from not-knowing to knowing. At laboratory meetings, during conference presentations, and in journal publications, we are wont to cherry-pick out of our terabytes of video data those very illustrative vignettes where things "click" for the student. That moment of clarity is at once the designer's vindication, the teacher's gratification, the student's triumph, and the audience's relief. As for the researcher, the student's dramatized epistemic metamorphosis offers a seductive epistemology: not-knowing, knowing. Unfortunately, this binary epistemology ignores and obfuscates the process of learning, which is longitudinal, idiosyncratic, desultory, and highly sensitive to contexts of origin, interaction, and application. By and large, the learning activity transpires modestly as "dark matter" (Lindwall & Lymer, 2008) outside of the "Aha!" moments graced by the researcher's rhetorical limelight.

And yet for the purposes of this chapter we also commit the sin of showcasing moments in which children, apparently, first figure something out – a new way of using available artifacts to operate on the environment – that we regard as vital to developing disciplinary conceptual notions. Such empirical vignettes create for us context in which to microanalyze learning as shifts in sensorimotor orientations to available affordances. We could even say "a person has learned" when we see that she has appropriated an artifact as a means of accomplishing a task which dialectically reconfigures how she engages the world (Vérillon & Rabardel, 1995).

To model these moments of reconfiguration, we have been drawing on perspectives and methodologies from the traditions of both Knowledge Analysis (KA) and Interaction Analysis (IA). Perhaps our chapter can be viewed as stoking and conciliating this productive dialectic (diSessa, 2008). We will be using our case studies to look very closely at what happens when a child who has already figured out an effective sensorimotor strategy for controlling the world (von Glasersfeld, 1987) is offered some cultural-historical form that, the tutor intimates, bears utility for operating even more effectively (Mariotti, 2009; Radford, 2000; Saxe, 2012; Sfard, 2002). Positioned primarily within phenomenological and enactivist views on being in the world, we will propose a skill-based epistemology of mathematical knowledge. Cultural forms play a hybrid role: even as they increase a child's grip on the world (Dreyfus & Dreyfus, 1999), they shift the child into representational intentionality (Young, 2011) and semiotic registers (Duval, 2006) for articulating the situated skill in line with common practice.

The thesis we present here hinges on a broad sociocultural perspective on human learning. We draw analogies between, on the one hand, a technologically enabled pedagogical activity for learning the concept of proportion and, on the other hand, various informal indigenous practices that cultures have developed to foster novices' motor skills. We see no essential difference between how we facilitate students' interactions in ways that promote the development of particular operational schemes and how sub-Saharan mothers move their infants' bodies in ways that promote the development of socially valued postures and skills (Reed & Bril, 1996).

We view these cross-cultural parallels in pedagogical activity as offering us an opportunity to broaden our theoretical scopes in ways that open our eyes to critical yet hitherto invisible dimensions of mathematical learning. In *explicitly* embodied domains of practice, such as dance, musical performance, and the martial arts, expert and novice interactions afford researchers transparency into practitioners' reasoning processes. However, in *implicitly* embodied domains of practice, such as mathematics, cognitive activity has historically remained opaque. By seeking to involve the physicality of mathematics teaching and learning through the design, implementation, and evaluation of embodied-interaction technologies, we strive both to improve mathematics education and to make it transparent to all stakeholders (Trninic & Abrahamson, 2013).

Granted, the learning of physical skill is often seen as drastically different from learning conceptual skills. We acknowledge that the reader may not feel comfortable with the connection we attempt to make here. Yet we ask the reader to keep an open mind, as looking to physical disciplines for inspiration may not be as radical as it appears at first glance. Over 30 years ago, in an address to the International Group for the Psychology of Mathematics Education, von Glasersfeld (1983) criticized research in mathematics education for having under-delivered. And yet, he added:

> this disappointment – I want to emphasize this – is not restricted to mathematics education but has come to involve teaching and the didactic methods in virtually all disciplines. To my knowledge, there is only one exception that forms a remarkable contrast: the teaching of physical and, especially, athletic skills. There is no cause for disappointment in that area.
>
> (p. 42)

He argues that we ought to look to those domains that have been exceptional, because:

> the primary goal of mathematics instruction has to be the students' conscious understanding of what he or she is doing and why it is being done ... [W]hat the mathematics teacher is striving to instill into the student is ultimately the awareness of a dynamic program and its execution – and that awareness is in principle similar to what the athlete is able to glean ... from his or her performance.
>
> *(pp. 51–52)*

We, too, believe that there are important parallels to explore, including the conscious awareness mentioned by von Glasersfeld (1983). Our program's intellectual gambit is thus to sidestep from mathematics to motor skill, learn over there what we can about practices and processes of teaching and learning, and then sidestep back to mathematics, where we search and design for useful parallels. Thus we hope to avail ourselves of humanity's ancient pedagogical traditions as we struggle to fashion contemporary mathematics pedagogy.

The next section steps back to open the theoretical scope by discussing generic mechanisms of guided motor learning and their relations to cognitive tasks. Then the following section explains our pedagogical design for the mathematics concept of proportion, and the one after that examines cases of motor learning in our video footage from implementing that design. The chapter will end with reflections on implications of this approach to the study of conceptual knowing and learning in interaction.

## Learning Emerges From the Situated Solution of Motor Problems: Scientific Antecedents

The thesis that mathematics learning sprouts from guided motor problem solving is inspired by a broad range of literature ranging from anthropology to neuroscience.

### *Scaffolding Motor Development: Edward Reed and Blandine Bril*

Edward Reed, an ecological psychologist, and Blandine Bril, a social anthropologist, describe indigenous practices that apparently foster infant development of culturally valued physical capabilities: Mothers in remote sub-Saharan villages were observed to enact shared routines of handling their infants so that they learn to move in new ways. Society thus intervenes in shaping infant development by creating circumstances – *fields of promoted action* – that encourage the building and exercising of particular motor capacities bearing utility for effective participation in valued cultural activities (Reed & Bril, 1996):

Specific motor problems are in many cases called to the infant's attention or even thrust upon the infant by one or more caretakers in what we call a field of promoted action. It is because human adults promote specific motor problems for infants – often before the child is capable of solving that problem – that human action development takes the course that is does.

*(p. 438)*

In fields of promoted action, the field is constituted and administered by experienced cultural agents, and the action is performed by novices. This global phenomenon, we submit, bears more than allegorical resemblance to mathematics education. Rather, it epitomizes pedagogical practice in general, or at least the pedagogical practice we envision, in which students are thrust into *motor* problem situations and begin learning to move in new ways before they signify these motor plans mathematically. Mathematics-education researchers, we therefore maintain, should benefit from closer scrutiny into fields of promoted motor action – their processes, contributing factors, and context sensitivities. In particular, researchers should closely examine the inception of solutions through rapid, reciprocal coupling between goal-oriented actions and the emerging affordances of objects, what Bamberger and Schön (1983) call the back-talk and feed-forward of "conversation with materials". In that spirit, we shall now consider empirical research on skill development.

## *Dynamical Systems Theory: Esther Thelen*

The work of developmental psychologist Esther Thelen and collaborators (Thelen & Smith, 1994; Vereijken & Thelen, 1997) lends insight into motor-action scheme epigenesis at the interface of organism and environment. Building on Gerald Edelman's *Theory of Neural Darwinism* (Edelman, 1987), Thelen's dynamical systems theory of infant motor learning "put the marginalized field of infants' motor development back on the scientific map as an important topic of study both in its own right and as a window into other, less accessible domains of development" (Savelsbergh, Vereijken, & Zaal, 2005, p. 97).

Thelen theorized cognitive and motor capacity as continuously co-emerging via resonance loops among overlapping neural groups that govern situated and goal-oriented multimodal perceptions and actions. The dynamical-systems view of neural development – as an alternative to the then-prevalent neuro-maturational view – was popularized through Thelen's demonstration that infants can develop walking motor schemes many months before their normative schedule, but only if their body mass is supported, such as in a water tub. Walking, Thelen posited, is not an innate capacity per se but, rather, emerges interactively *as the solution to a motor problem*: Where local goals interact dynamically with contingent circumstances, physical actions emerge that, if proven effective, are rehearsed and thus potentially reapplied upon other terrains.

Thelen's theory was dramatically validated by its proposed explanations for infant behavior on laboratory tasks that hitherto had been considered "purely cognitive" by appealing to the perseveration of perceptuomotor routines. One example of this is the "A-not-B error" task, in which an infant is first shown an attractive toy that is subsequently placed under box A. After the infant retrieves the toy a number of times from box A, the researcher places this same toy under box B. Infants younger than a year old look under box A despite seeing the toy placed under box B. One explanation for this behavior appeals to cognitive structure, such as mental models of object permanence. In contrast, Thelen and collaborators showed that particular bodily manipulation of infants, such as standing versus sitting, reduces or eliminates the error. As such, motor actions that agents perform in the service of gathering information (epistemic actions, see Kirsh & Maglio, 1994) can endure into prospective performance as much as the information these actions recover. Perhaps unsurprisingly, Clancey (2008) has implicated Edelman's legacy as one of several antecedents to "situated" views on learning (Greeno, 1998).

Further dynamical-systems research has demonstrated a rough dichotomy between "smooth" and "abrupt" transitions in the development of motor skill:

> Research initiated and conducted by Scott Kelso and Pier-Giorgio Zanone…has shown that learning can take on two main forms depending on the relationship between the new information to be learned and the learner's preexisting repertoire. In one, the "shift route," learning takes the form of a smooth and gradual shift in behavior toward the newly learned pattern. In the other, learning involves abrupt discontinuous changes, eureka-like phase transitions.
>
> *(Kelso & Engstrøm, 2006, p. 208)*

This distinction between smooth and abrupt transitions is reminiscent of Piaget's (1971) schema theory, and in particular his distinction between accommodation vs. differentiation of cognitive schemes in response to disequilibrating feedback. Furthermore, dynamical systems theory underscores neurophysiological transformations vis-à-vis emerging motor-action task demands – transformations that the theory interprets as attractions toward new dynamical stability. Later in this chapter, we too will be looking at both smooth and abrupt transitions. With respect to smooth transitions, we will consider the case of learning to control new phenomena that demand variations on existing schemes. With respect to abrupt transitions, we will consider the role of artifacts – auxiliary stimuli – as dramatically perturbing schemes previously established as effective for controlling phenomena, thus prompting individuals to establish new schemes still broadly within the task demands.

Esther Thelen was also a certified Feldenkrais practitioner, and her premature passing away curtailed her project to create a therapy clinic for treating infant abnormal motor development.

## *Motion Learning as Functional Integration: Moshe Feldenkrais*

The physicist, martial arts leader, and autodidact motor-action scientist Moshe Feldenkrais (1985) created a somatic awareness practice that is used by students interested in self-education and human development, kinesthetic artists looking to expand their skills, and individuals seeking to alleviate chronic muscle pains. With regard to the latter rehabilitation technique, empirical research has repeatedly demonstrated the effectiveness of this treatment, even indicating its superiority over conventional physiotherapy (e.g., Lundblad, Elert, & Gerdle, 1999). The rationale of the Feldenkrais somatic education methodology, its practitioners maintain, bears relevance to any pedagogical approach seeking to foster new action patterns.

An essential principle of motor learning in the Feldenkrais practice is to create guided opportunities for students to untangle their action complexes into simpler motor components, modify these components, and then foster their selective reintegration into more ergonomic complexes. Lessons vary, yet the student must always assume a degree of agency in achieving novel motion complexes.

Feldenkrais wrote in 1964 that:

> Without conscious attention to what one is feeling during an action and without applying the attention directly to the entire movement resulting from these actions, no development will occur – simple mechanical repetition will never make this come about.
>
> *(see in Beringer, 2010, p. 15)*

Ginsburg (2010) clarifies: "Learning itself is not conscious. The integration process itself is not conscious. Nevertheless the process depends on conscious processes in feeling and detecting changes. The consequence is felt as difference" (p. 185). This notion – that unconscious, subtle interactions drive adaptations to behavior, and that consciousness plays a *post facto* appraisal role in making sense of these changes – is important to our thesis of conceptual knowledge emerging from guided interactions. We will revisit this point in discussing our own study participants' interaction and learning.

In his more speculative essays, Feldenkrais viewed cognition as arising from such *post facto* reflection on the enactment of perceptuomotor schemes. In a passage reminiscent of Piaget's genetic epistemology, and in particular the ideas of a scheme and reflective abstraction, Feldenkrais (1985) wrote:

> [T]he use and experience of the body are necessary to form mental functions. After the formation of a sufficient number of paths and patterns, the somatic support becomes less and less essential; we can think – that is, re-excite the formed patterns, regrouping them into new ones.
>
> *(p. 79)*

Even closer to our focal content domain of mathematics, the veteran Feldenkrais practitioner Adam Cole (2004) introspects that mathematical concepts rely on a complex spatial-dynamical relationship that can be experienced only through embodied reasoning. It is such complex spatial-dynamical relationships that our pedagogical design attempts to foster through engaging students in activities within concept-oriented promoted fields of action. From Feldenkrais we learn further that it would be conceptually unproductive for a child to perform a sequence of locally effective operations unless that child eventually assumed conscious agency in initiating and monitoring an overall motor plan.

Just before we situate our design more broadly in the learning sciences, we now look more closely at what it means to learn a new motor action.

### *Learning as Motor Problem Solving: Nikolai Bernstein*

Independently of the work of Piaget, Feldenkrais, or, for that matter, Vygotsky, and half a century before Thelen's discoveries, the Soviet neurophysiologist Nikolai Bernstein (1896–1966) stated that motor-skill development is "repetition without repetition" (Bernstein, 1996). It is worth quoting Bernstein extensively, because his insights on cognitive processes underlying motor-skill development have implications for pedagogical investigations. In particular, Bernstein's work bears on the study of learning environments designed to foster conceptual development via engaging students initially in the solution of perceptuomotor coordination tasks (Abrahamson & Lindgren, 2014) – what Abrahamson (2013) calls the *action-based genre* of embodied design:

> The actual importance of repetitions is quite different [than what has formerly been believed]. *Repetitions* of a movement or action are necessary in order to *solve a motor problem* many times (better and better) and *to find the best ways of solving it*. Repetitive solutions of a problem are also necessary because, in natural conditions, external conditions never repeat themselves and the course of the movement is never ideally reproduced. Consequently, it is necessary *to gain experience relevant to all various modifications* of a task, primarily, to all the impressions that underlie the sensory corrections of a movement.
>
> *(Bernstein, 1996, p. 176, original italics here and below)*

Bernstein conceptualizes learning not as perfecting a particular motor-action sequence but, instead, as developing a perceptuomotor scheme – a process template that has the capacity to adjust to the vagaries of situated circumstances. Thus an athlete or musician who has perfected a physical skill in fact has become highly able to adjust her motor performance in real time on-line to the nuances of moment-to-moment emerging contingencies:

> During a correctly organized exercise, a student is repeating many times, *not the means for solving a given motor problem*, but *the process of its solution*, the changing and improving of the means.
>
> *(p. 205)*

Thus the mainstay of skill learning is not in performing an idealized motor routine but precisely in the repertory of agile fixes to emerging contingencies, which Bernstein called automatisms. These automatisms are traces from having engaged in regimented goal-oriented activity within a field of promoted action (see also Dreyfus, 2002; Masters, 2000; Schoenfeld, 1998). Bernstein (1996) draws an implication for instruction that is reminiscent of constructivist pedagogical philosophy:

> The fact that the "secrets" of swimming or cycling *are not in some special body movements but in special sensations and corrections* explains why these secrets are impossible to teach by demonstration.
>
> *(p. 187)*

Thus a master craftsperson may demonstrate an idealized enactment of a skill for the neophyte to emulate, but the neophyte learns only through attempting to imitate this enactment. Only when the rubber hits the road does the novice begin to respond to the road's variant properties and learn to negotiate all terrains. This principle has been repeatedly reported in ethnographic studies of craft training, such as carpentry (Ingold, 2011) or pottery (Churchill, unpublished manuscript). Indeed, you can show me how you apply saw to plank and you can guide my actions as I myself wield the tool, but I will have to learn how to perform this action on my own terms, and on a myriad of different types of wood. It is once again a field of promoted action, only the field includes an artifact that the novice learns to apply to an object – it is an *instrumented* field of promoted action.

## *Fostering Instrumented Fields of Promoted Action: A Design-Based Research Project*

We are interested in instrumented interaction, because it undergirds conceptual reasoning (Gallese & Lakoff, 2005; Hall & Nemirovsky, 2012; Hauk, Johnsrude, &

Pulvermüller, 2004; Lakoff & Núñez, 2000; Melser, 2004; Roth & Thom, 2009; Vygotsky, 1978). Yet just how instrumented interaction gives rise to conceptual reasoning, and what roles designers and instructors might play in staging and marshaling this process, is unclear.

In our design, which we detail below, students develop a new type of bimanual coordinated action. That new action turns out to be moving the hands while changing the spatial interval between them correlative to the hands' elevation above a datum line such as a floor or desk. This somatic phase shift, from a default naturalistic preservation of a *fixed* interval to the coordination parameters of a *changing* interval, is semi-inadvertent – initially it comprises nuanced local adjustments without a global motor-action plan. Yet these adjustments are consistent in the sense that the interval must grow with elevation and vice versa. Arguably, it is this consistency, as well the student's increasing dexterity in executing these automatisms, that eventually leads the student to notice a global interaction pattern. It is then, we propose, that actions become concepts through the learners' semi-spontaneous appropriation of available semiotic elements they perceive as bearing ad hoc enactive, discursive, and/or epistemic utility for accomplishing their objectives.

Our study participants' interactions occur within a carefully orchestrated context – a designed and monitored field of promoted instrumented action potentially formative of conceptual development. Left alone to solve the coordination problem, students are unlikely to derive its mathematical implications. They need framing and steering from the instructor so as to move from an "artifact-sign" to a "mathematical-sign" (Bartolini Bussi & Mariotti, 2008; Mariotti, 2009). By way of analogy, all bicycle riders regain balance by steering toward the direction of fall, and yet few will ever articulate this pervasive scheme as an analytical generalization. Rather, it is the socio-epistemic framing of the interaction as part of a larger cultural activity structure that may prompt an agent to reflect on an otherwise tacit inference and preserve this now explicit inference for future reference and elaboration.

## Somathics: Designing a Field of Promoted Mathematical Action

Our design project embarked from the following assertion: To the extent that mathematical knowledge is indeed grounded in motor-action schemes, constructivist instruction should attend to motor-action knowledge – its nature, construction, and interaction with enactive, semiotic, and epistemic means in the learning environment. One model for such instruction, embodied design (Abrahamson, 2009, 2012; Abrahamson & Lindgren, 2014), is to design fields of promoted action that elicit existing motor schemes yet challenge the learner to adjust these schemes, then to articulate the new schemes, and finally to signify them in accord with the discipline's semiotic system. Embodied design is a pedagogical framework that seeks to promote grounded learning by creating situations in which students can be guided to negotiate tacit and cultural perspectives on phenomena under inquiry. The Mathematical Imagery Trainer for Proportion (MIT-P, see below) is an example of the action-based design genre for achieving embodied mathematical learning – somatic mathematics or, in short, *somathics*.

## *A Design Problem and a Conjecture-Driven Research Project*

The MIT-P was developed in the context of design-based research methodology (Collins, 1992; Confrey, 2005; Edelson, 2002; Kelly, 2003; Sandoval & Bell, 2004). Our experimental design was driven by a conjecture drawing inspiration from the embodied/enactive approach (Barsalou, 1999; Lakoff & Núñez, 2000; Nemirovsky, 2003; Núñez, Edwards, & Matos, 1999; Varela, Thompson, & Rosch, 1991), yet seeking a distinct viewpoint. Namely, we conjecture that some mathematical concepts are difficult to learn due to a resource constraint of mundane life. Everyday being does not give students opportunities to embody and rehearse the particular dynamic schemes that would form the requisite cognitive substrate for meaningfully appropriating the target concepts' disciplinary analysis of situated phenomena. Specifically, we conjectured that students' canonically incorrect solutions for rational-number problems – "additive" solutions (e.g., "2/3 = (2+2)/(3+2) = 4/5"; cf. Behr, Harel, Post, & Lesh, 1993) – indicate a lack of multimodal kinesthetic-visual action images with which to model and solve situations bearing proportional relations (Goldin, 1987; Pirie & Kieren, 1994).

## *Design Solution: Materials and Tasks*

In response to the design problem articulated above, we engineered an embodied-interaction computer-supported inquiry activity for students to discover, rehearse, and thus embody presymbolic dynamics pertaining to the mathematics of proportional transformation. At the center of our instructional design is the *Mathematical Imagery Trainer for Proportion* device (MIT-P; see Figure 8.1).

The MIT device measures the heights of the user's hands above the desk. When these heights (e.g., 10″ and 20″) relate in accord with the unknown ratio set on the interviewer's console (e.g., 1:2), the screen is green. If the user then raises her hands in front of the display at an appropriate rate (e.g., raising her hands by 5″ and 10″, respectively, resulting in 15″ and 30″), the screen will remain green, otherwise, such as if she maintains a fixed distance between her hands while moving them up (e.g., raising both hands 5″, resulting in 15″ and 25″), the screen will turn red. Study participants were tasked first to make the screen green and then, once they had done so, to maintain a green screen even as they moved their hands. For technical details, see Howison, Trninic, Reinholz, and Abrahamson (2011).

**FIGURE 8.1** The Mathematical Imagery Trainer for Proportion (MIT-P) set at a 1:2 ratio, so that the favorable response (a green background) is activated only when the right hand is twice as high along the monitor as the left hand. This figure encapsulates the typical interaction sequence: (a) while exploring, the student first positions the hands incorrectly (red feedback); (b) stumbles on a correct position (green); (c) raises hands maintaining a fixed interval between them (red); and (d) corrects position (green). Compare 1b and 1d to note the different vertical intervals between the virtual objects.

We expected that once students found a first pair of hand locations resulting in a green screen, they would search for another bimanual configuration by moving both hands up or down *while maintaining a fixed distance between them* rather than changing the distance; consequently, the screen would turn red. We viewed such hypothesized behavior as marking legitimate interpretation of the interactive inquiry task (Borovcnik & Bentz, 1991; Smith, diSessa, & Roschelle, 1993). Namely, students initially have no empirical information or frames of reference to suggest that a fixed-distance expectation would prove "incorrect" – they thus default to their simplest available scheme for generating invariance, that is, a motor-action plan for maintaining identity (actual equivalence) rather than similarity (proportional equivalence).

We conceptualized this form of reasoning about a spatial-dynamical, non-numerical phenomenon to underlie and anticipate these students' prospective mathematical errors. That is, naively expecting to generate invariance by enacting absolute rather than proportional equivalence between spatial markers may be indicative of typical "additive errors" in solving rational-number problems, such as in reasoning that "1/2 = 2/3." Thus, we view fixed-interval physical actions as external manifestations anticipating inappropriate fixed-difference symbolic solutions. Again, our conjecture was that fixed-interval reasoning indicates a limited personal history of interacting with changing-interval situations of proportional covariation.

The initial phase of our project was explorative: we began collecting empirical data that would enable the emergence and development of viable models of student reasoning, even as we were working iteratively on improving both the instructional and experimental designs. We elected to organize this investigation in the form of generative case studies (Clement, 2000) that would enable us to identify and hone promising research foci. Specifically, we gathered empirical data for a set of case studies by devising and administering a task-based Piagetian semi-structured clinical interview (diSessa, 2007; diSessa & Cobb, 2004).

Mathematics Learning as Motor Problem Solving   **223**

 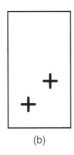 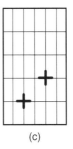 

(a)    (b)    (c)    (d)

**FIGURE 8.2** MIT-P display configuration schematics, beginning with (a) a blank screen, and then featuring a set of symbolical objects incrementally overlaid by the facilitator onto the display: (b) crosshairs, (c) a grid, and (d) numerals along the y-axis of the grid. These schematics are not drawn to scale, and the actual device enables flexible calibrations of the grid, numerals, and ratio.

The interview protocol included instructions for the researcher to incrementally layer onto the microworld supplementary mathematical instruments, such as a Cartesian grid. Our intent was that the participants could be guided to appropriate these symbolic artifacts as means of expressing their discovery of variant-interval equivalence and, so doing, would re-invent mathematical principles of proportional equivalence. We thus hoped to scaffold the development of proportional schemas as emerging yet gradually differentiating from additive schemas (see Fuson & Abrahamson, 2005).

At first, the condition for green was set as a 1:2 ratio, and no feedback other than the background color was given (see Figure 8.2a – this challenging condition was used only in the last six interviews). Then, crosshairs were introduced that "mirrored" the location of participants' hands (see Figure 8.2b). Next, a grid was overlaid on the display monitor to help students plan, execute, and interpret their manipulations and, so doing, begin to articulate quantitative verbal assertions (see Figure 8.2c). In time, the numerical labels "1, 2, 3,…" were overlaid on the grid's vertical axis on the left of the screen to help students construct further meanings by more readily recruiting arithmetic knowledge and skills and more efficiently distributing the problem-solving task (see Figure 8.2d). Not treated in this chapter is yet another structure layered onto the screen, namely a ratio table with interactive affordances (see in Reinholz, Trninic, Howison, & Abrahamson, 2010).

## *Participants and Procedure*

Participants included 22 students from a private K-8 suburban school in the greater San Francisco Bay Area (33% on financial aid; 10% minority students; one student participated twice). The school did not have an advanced mathematics curriculum, so the students' formal exposure to mathematical content was on par with that found in public schools. Students participated either individually (17 of the 20 interviews) or paired (the last three interviews) in a semi-structured interview (duration: mean 70 min.; SD 20 min.). All interviews were videotaped and transcribed.

## Data Analysis

Our chief methodological orientation toward empirical data is collaborative, intensive micro-ethnographic analyses of multimodal behaviors observed in videographed interactions among students and instructors (Nemirovsky, 2011; Schoenfeld, Smith, & Arcavi, 1991). Iterative, systematic analyses of the entire data corpus gradually give rise to the development of new constructs germane to the research questions. Typically, our investigative and expository efforts yield summative measures of student behaviors and converge on brief video excerpts that we agree upon as paradigmatically illuminating of the constructs.

The following section reports on learning as the co-accomplishment of students and teachers working together in a designed, instrumented field of promoted action.

## Findings: From Motor Problem Solving to Conceptual Learning

The findings presented below give rise to a conceptualization of grounded mathematical learning resulting from the emergence and articulation of motor-action schemes within a field of promoted action. In particular, we focus on the micro-processes by which our study participants changed their motor-action patterns. We will suggest that these changes occurred either:

a. to adjust to an unfamiliar phenomenon's interaction functions; or
b. to avail of an environment's familiar frames of reference.

We will thus discuss two types of behavior that are rarely addressed in educational research. We alluded to these in the second section, and view them as pivotal to grounded conceptual learning, in both formal and informal learning environments:

1. smooth transition from an ineffective motor-action scheme, via perceptuomotor coupling with a phenomenon, to enactment of a novel yet related scheme; and
2. abrupt transition from an effective motor scheme to a radically different scheme that incorporates features of the environment – specifically, symbolic artifacts – that the interviewer interpolates into the field of promoted action.

By "smooth" and "abrupt" we are referring not so much to the duration of the transition between operatory schemes as much as to the extent of reconfiguration inherent to this transition.

## Solving and Articulating a Motor Problem, or Arm-Waving for Proportion

Our first case analysis, Siena (all names are pseudonyms), is a 6th-grade student identified by her teachers as low achieving. Siena was interviewed by an apprentice researcher (DT, the second author), with the lead researcher (DA, the first author) occasionally intervening. Though initially shy and concerned about her ability to "do well," Siena quickly warmed up to the activity. We follow Siena's progression from actions that were initially exhibited by every student in our study, that is, from fixed-interval coordinated motions that proved ineffective in satisfying the task demand, to the changing-interval motions that satisfy the task demand.

This case followed the protocol undertaken with all the students in the study: With the interaction condition set at a 1:2 ratio, Siena was first tasked to "Make the screen green" and encouraged to explore the interactive space. Less than a minute into the activity, she generated a green screen and held her hands affixed at that posture. DA encouraged her to look for green somewhere else, and she continued the exploration. Like all 22 students in our study, Siena initially kept the distance between her hands fixed as she attempted to find another green, which resulted in a red screen. Two minutes later, DT asked Siena to explain her discoveries to a hypothetical student who had just walked into the room. She noted three green "places" on the screen, namely high, middle, and low arm postures that generate a green screen. Indeed, the interviewers had encouraged her to explore various areas beyond her initially timid attempts focused on the very bottom of the screen (e.g., "Maybe try up here?"). Siena noted, "You'd have to have the right hand higher up slightly... You'd have to be slow and careful."

Next, DT asked Siena to reproduce the "high" green. Once she had done so, DA attempted to steer Siena toward acknowledging and articulating the action theorem she was physically demonstrating, namely that the *higher* her hands moved, the *bigger* the distance between her hands became (keeping with the 1:2 ratio). We asked her to reproduce the low green, then the high, then the low again. She did so with relative precision. For us as observers, it was evident that the distance between her hands changed correlative to their elevation over the desk, and yet Sicna did not verbally acknowledge this change.

DA then asked Siena whether she could move from low green to high green keeping the screen "green all the time." Siena tried to accomplish this by moving fast, yet this resulted in the screen turning red as the distance between her hands remained fixed throughout most of the motion. She continued with this effort, moving slower, until a minute later she was able to keep the screen green continuously while raising and lowering her hands, making minor motor corrections as needed. At this point, both interviewers agreed (communicated via glances) that Siena apparently had determined a working theorem for "making green." And yet, the following exchange then ensued:

**DT:** <06:35> You seem to have figured something out. Can you share with us what it is?
**Siena:** [*shrugs, smiling*] Not really.
**DA:** So what have you learned so far?
**Siena:** [*pauses, looking for words*] It's really hard to keep steady, to go high up [*mimes smooth bimanual motion upward*] but it's possible.
**DA:** Is there any rule? How would you explain this to someone else?
**Siena:** Um, just try to keep focused on the screen... keep steady and try to keep like that at equal, and get to be sort of equal and like move your hands at the same time. Like, if it's like this [demonstrates by holding hands apart at a fixed distance], then you have to move them both up the same amount apart [moves hands up at a fixed distance].

Recall that just prior to the above exchange we had observed Siena skillfully "making the screen green" and so had assumed that she was entertaining the "higher-bigger" action theorem we were admittedly looking for. Yet it may be that Siena became proficient at the motor action in the absence of a conscious action theorem. That is, Siena's transition from fixed- to changing-interval action appears to have occurred outside of her conscious awareness: She articulated the fixed-interval strategy *despite manually demonstrating the appropriate changing-interval action*. As she was raising her hands, it appears that Siena performed a rapid succession of minute local corrections to green, yet the consistent pattern of these automatisms had not yet emerged as a global awareness. In other words, we offer that Siena's local corrections were so minute that they did not emerge as felt sensations in her awareness.

DA then guided Siena to evaluate her fixed-interval rule empirically, and Siena complied. She found green low down on the screen and then raised both hands, keeping a fixed interval, which resulted in a red screen. DT took over the right-hand device, and they worked together, moving up:

**Siena:** <12:48> Always the right hand should move up a little higher... this one [*right hand*] should move slightly faster than the other one. The right hand should be slightly faster than the left, but they should still keep at sort of the same pace.
**DA:** What do you mean by pace?
**Siena:** Like, if this one's [*right*] going like this [moves upward quickly] then this one [*left*] should be going slightly slower than the other one.

We thus witness a transition from the fixed-interval theorem to a different-pace theorem. Several minutes later, DA asked Siena to explain further what she meant by "pace." She offered that "[pace is] sort of a continuous speed. They should be at a different speed, but they're both at their own continuous speed." During this utterance, she gestured forward, in a series of away-from-body saccades. When asked, again, to summarize what she learned for the sake of the hypothetical student entering the room, she offered: "Make the right hand go a little bit faster, but let them both be at their own continuous pace."

Thus we see Siena's progress from: (a) performing fixed-interval action, to (b) performing changing-interval action yet articulating a fixed-interval strategy, to (c) reverting to fixed-interval performance when asked to demonstrate her verbal claims, to (d) both physically and verbally expressing a right-is-faster-than-left strategy. What we find striking in this process is that Siena had solved the motor-action problem before she could describe it. We see interesting parallels to Ginsburg's (2010) claim (see above) that the learning process depends on conscious processes in feeling and detecting bodily changes. As Ginsburg notes, what we experience as the Eureka! moment may "just" be the sensation of awareness arising from felt difference between our previous and current ways of interacting with the world.

Here we also witness how easily the learner may regress in the absence of such awareness. By mis-describing her effective motor-action skill and then actually operating on this mis-description, Siena regressed to her earlier ineffective motor action. By asking Siena to articulate verbally her effective motor action, the interviewers imposed on Siena what Bamberger and diSessa (2003) have termed "ontological imperialism," conventional semiotic systems that warp the perceptions of the uninitiated, perhaps by parsing dynamic phenomena into static forms that seem bereft of the felt sensations of those phenomena, as in the case of Siena. It is as though, being asked to explain where her arms are as she walks, a child asserted that the right arm swings forward when the right leg does and then actually walked that way!

## *Incorporating Mathematics: Mathematical Artifacts and Motor Solutions*

When the grid is overlaid on the screen (see Figure 8.2c), students tend to respond in a behavior pattern we have termed "snap-to-grid" – their hitherto simultaneous, continuous motions along the screen become parsed into sequential, discrete actions from one grid line to the next. Their utterances, too, transition from qualitative to quantitative language.

The case study here is that of Amalia, a 5th-grade student identified by her teacher as average achieving in class. Amalia was quick to locate her first green and even quicker at solving the motor problem of moving the hands upward while keeping the screen green. Interestingly, introducing the grid artifact onto the screen ostensibly impeded her green-making performance, even as it granted predictive and communicative power. Unlike Siena, who occasionally struggled with the manual dexterity, Amalia had no such issues. And this, we believe, makes Amalia's case particularly interesting, for she demonstrated a high degree of adroitness in effecting green yet forsook this adroitness in favor of a grid-based alternating right-left ratcheting up strategy, which we call a-per-b: in the case of the 1:2 ratio, "For every 1 I go up on the left, I go up 2 on the right." We suggest later that this shift can be illuminated by examining Amalia's experience with the underlying motor problem of making the screen green.

Similar to all other student participants, Amalia began by finding green and then attempting a fixed-interval action, which resulted in a red screen. Immediately subsequent to receiving this feedback, Amalia tuned in to the interactive phenomenon – she developed the skill of performing rapid local adjustments so as to maintain a green screen while moving both hands. The following conversation then ensues:

**DT:** <13:56> You're doing really well here. Do you have some sort of rule you're following?
**Ama:** [*continuing to move her hands up and down, creating a more-or-less continuously green screen with occasional flashes of red*] Um, I'm trying to keep them at a different distance.
**DT:** How so?
**Ama:** Well, I'm keeping this one [*right*] higher.
DT asks Amalia to say more on this "different distance" strategy:
**Ama:** Well, I'm keeping [*keeps left-hand at fixed height, moves right-hand up and down*]… I'm seeing if… which one… [*moves both left and right up and down*] how high I should keep them apart.

Amalia's utterance and actions suggested she was aware of the differences in the interval between her hands, even as she was repeatedly adjusting this interval in response to the color feedback:

**Ama:** <16:39> You have to keep this one [*right*] higher, and then you just have to try to see where it wants to be.

Soon after, we introduced the grid:

**DT:** <19:27> So, what does this look like?
**Ama:** A grid.
**DT:** So, maybe like something you do in… a math class?
**Ama:** [*nods*]
**DT:** Play around with it now, find some green places.

Amalia lifts the controllers from the desk, raises the left-hand virtual object on the screen to the first gridline, and the right-hand object to the second gridline. After a brief pause at those locations, she moves both objects upward, retaining some of the smoothness of her previous movement:

**DT:** <20:09> Can the grid help us in some way?
**Ama:** Yeah, because you can measure how high… how much farther one of them should be.

Immediately, Amalia snapped to grid. She utilized the measuring affordance of the grid, yet in so doing her hitherto continuous and simultaneous actions became saccadic and sequential – Amalia became grid-bound.

Ten minutes later in the interview, we removed the grid and asked Amalia if she could "keep it green now?" To our surprise, she did not revert to the pre-grid continuous actions but instead persevered with the gridded motor actions even though the grid lines themselves were no longer present on screen. To us, this indicated that the grid lines must have served an important purpose in her physical execution of the "keep it green" strategy. She explained her strategy as follows:

**Ama:** <39:09> I'm remembering where the… things were. I'm trying to do it in my head, remembering where they were.

We found this of interest, because Amalia had previously done well by merely "trying to see where it wants to be" – a sequence of micro-adjustments. Yet the abrupt and radical shift in her behavior instigated by the grid artifact was so substantial that it effectively replaced her previous motor scheme. We might wonder what led Amalia to jettison her earlier action strategy. A motor-skill analysis would note that the introduction of the grid transformed the underlying motor problem (see earlier discussion). Specifically, "find and keep green" with the grid is an easier motor problem than without because the grid acts as a constraint. In motor-skill parlance, a constraint of this sort reduces Amalia's degrees of freedom in this activity, making the motor problem easier. Indeed, Amalia finds the change so noticeable that she imagines the grid lines even once they are removed. In terms of the instrumental genesis theory of activity situations (Vérillon & Rabardel, 1995), by instrumentalizing the grid as a means of accomplishing the task objective, Amalia instrumented herself with a new utilization scheme.

## Conclusion

It has been argued that all cognition is embodied (Anderson, 2003; Wilson, 2002). Work in cognitive neuroscience points to the hypothesis that "rational thought is an exploitation of the normal operations of our bodies" (Gallese & Lakoff, 2005, p. 476). In other words, even when we reason "in our heads," or in the absence of apparent physical movement, still our reasoning is grounded in simulations of sensorimotor processes through the use of the same neural resources that are active in bodily perception and action. We find resonant views in the work of Vygotsky (1926/1997, pp. 161–163) and Piaget (1971, p. 6) and now more forcefully in philosophical essays on cognition (Chemero, 2009; Hutto & Myin, 2013; Melser, 2004). If we are to take seriously the thesis that mathematical reasoning is embodied, then research on motor-skill development may offer useful perspectives for research on mathematics learning. When instructors foster new schemes by creating interaction opportunities centered on manipulating pedagogical artifacts – "gifts," as Friedrich Froebel (2005) called his kindergarten resources – motor-action developmental research can help us understand the relation between task, context, action, and the effect of semiotic systems on perturbing and signifying the learners' budding schemes.

Inspired by the theoretical construct of a "field of promoted action" (Reed & Bril, 1996), we are interested in how culture's intervention in individuals' development results in the adjustment of an individual's behavior. These interventions may lead to conceptual development, and we reflect on the pedagogical ideology and design framework that may nurture new schemes into disciplinary practice. As designers of mathematics learning environments, our practice has been to create fields of promoted action that challenge and destabilize habitual coordination, stabilize these into new coordinated action structures, and support the learner in signifying these structures in the mathematics register. Accordingly, our analyses sought to monitor learning as emerging in the complex, dynamical synergy of individual goal-oriented problem solving and mediating, acculturating agents who construct and administer fields of promoted action.

The two episodes reported in this chapter were selected to demonstrate some aspects of smooth and abrupt transitions in motor-action skill development. The prime objective of these episodes was to contextualize and elaborate on the proposed two types of motor learning: (a) adjusting smoothly to control a natural (or naturalistic) phenomenon; and (b) transitioning abruptly to apply an artifact in the control of a phenomenon. Part of our aim was to demonstrate how these seemingly cognitive events may be illuminated by casting them as dependent on conscious processes involved in feeling and detecting embodied changes.

Similar to scholars of motor learning, we propose that students' idiosyncratic actions are more than relatively insignificant background noise that may provide, at best, a "helping hand" in learning – a perspective emerging at least as far back as Thorndike (1911) and casting a long shadow to present-day experimental psychology. Instead, we agree with Kostrubiec, Zanone, Fuchs, and Kelso (2012), who envision the learner's "spontaneous activities to be the initial backdrop upon which learning operates" (p. 1).

We find the role of conscious interpretation of transitions to novel motor solutions, both smooth and abrupt, to be particularly interesting. That is, for the students in our study, discovery came literally as that – a discovery – as they discovered in their own actions something they could not have predicted beforehand. What we call the Eureka! moment resulted from bringing conscious awareness to the felt difference of their action. As such, our findings on the emergence of mathematical reasoning through embodied interaction seem to support previous findings in therapeutic and academic studies of motor learning (Ginsburg, 2010).

Within education, motor learning and conceptual learning have long been seen as separate research programs, complete with their own theories and methodologies. Yet recent advances in studies of embodiment suggest that these disciplines share some – perhaps much – common ground. It may be enough to consider that motor learning is conceived of and studied *as solutions to motor problems*. After all, actions are not mere movement but involve goals and meaningful coping with circumstances. Motor learning, then, involves a degree of sense-making in the world, which is close to the heart of conceptual learning. Conversely, one might wonder, is the intellectual inactive because he merely sits and thinks, à la *Le Penseur*? Surely the thinker is engaged in some activity of his own, as suggested by Rodin's famous depiction. And indeed, neuroimaging evidence and embodied-cognition theory offer that this thinking activity involves abbreviated, or simulated, action. The two disciplines of motor and conceptual learning, in our view, stand to draw increasingly closer. In more than one sense, learning is moving in new ways.

## Acknowledgments

The intellectual positions elaborated in this chapter build on a succession of research studies conducted at the Embodied Design Research Laboratory (Abrahamson, Director), beginning with foundational statements in Abrahamson and Howison (2008). For their vital contributions to our most recent turns of mind, and for referring us to the *terra incognita* of motor-action research, we wish to thank Raúl Sánchez–García, a sociologist interested in skill learning, and Cliff Smyth, a Feldenkrais practitioner and scholar. A constant inspiration is Jeanne Bamberger, who views creativity as learning. We thank the editors of this volume for constructively stewarding this manuscript toward publication.

## References

Abrahamson, D. (2009). A student's synthesis of tacit and mathematical knowledge as a researcher's lens on bridging learning theory. In M. Borovcnik & R. Kapadia (Eds.), Research and developments in probability education [Special Issue]. *International Electronic Journal of Mathematics Education*, 4(3), 195–226.

Abrahamson, D. (2013). Toward a taxonomy of design genres: Fostering mathematical insight via perception-based and action-based experiences. In J. P. Hourcade, E. A. Miller, & A. Egeland (Eds.), *Proceedings of the 12th Annual Interaction Design and Children Conference (IDC 2013)* (Vol. "Full Papers", pp. 218–227). New York: The New School & Sesame Workshop.

Abrahamson, D., & Howison, M. (2008, December). *Kinemathics: Kinetically induced mathematical learning.* Paper presented at the UC Berkeley Gesture Study Group (E. Sweetser, Director), Berkeley, CA, December 5, 2008.

Abrahamson, D., & Lindgren, R. (2014). Embodiment and embodied design. In R. K. Sawyer (Ed.), *The Cambridge handbook of the learning sciences* (2nd ed., pp. 358–376). Cambridge, UK: Cambridge University Press.

Anderson, M. L. (2003). Embodied cognition: A field guide. *Artificial Intelligence*, 149, 91–130.

Bamberger, J., & diSessa, A. A. (2003). Music as embodied mathematics: A study of a mutually informing affinity. *International Journal of Computers for Mathematical Learning*, 8(2), 123–160.

Bamberger, J., & Schön, D. A. (1983). Learning as reflective conversation with materials: Notes from work in progress. *Art Education*, 36(2), 68–73.

Barsalou, L. W. (1999). Perceptual symbol systems. *Behavioral and Brain Sciences*, 22, 577–660.

Bartolini Bussi, M. G., & Mariotti, M. A. (2008). Semiotic mediation in the mathematics classroom: Artefacts and signs after a Vygotskian perspective. In L. D. English, M. G. Bartolini Bussi, G. A. Jones, R. Lesh, & D. Tirosh (Eds.), *Handbook of international research in mathematics education* (pp. 720–749). Mahwah, NJ: Lawrence Erlbaum Associates.

Behr, M. J., Harel, G., Post, T., & Lesh, R. (1993). Rational number, ratio, and proportion. In D. A. Grouws (Ed.), *Handbook of research on mathematics teaching and learning* (pp. 296–333). New York: Macmillan.

Beringer, E. (Ed.). (2010). *Embodied wisdom: The collected papers of Moshe Feldenkrais.* Berkeley, CA: North Atlantic Books.

Bernstein, N. A. (1996). On dexterity and its development. In M. L. Latash & M. T. Turvey (Eds.), *Dexterity and its development* (pp. 3–325). Mahwah, NJ: Lawrence Erlbaum Associates.

Borovcnik, M., & Bentz, H.-J. (1991). Empirical research in understanding probability. In R. Kapadia & M. Borovcnik (Eds.), *Chance encounters: Probability in education* (pp. 73–105). Dordrecht, NL: Kluwer.

Chemero, A. (2009). *Radical embodied cognitive science.* Cambridge, MA: MIT Press.

Clancey, W. J. (2008). Scientific antecedents of situated cognition. In P. Robbins & M. Aydede (Eds.), *Cambridge handbook of situated cognition* (pp. 11–34). New York: Cambridge University Press.

Clement, J. (2000). Analysis of clinical interviews: Foundations and model viability. In A. E. Kelly & R. A. Lesh (Eds.), *Handbook of research design in mathematics and science education* (pp. 547–589). Mahwah, NJ: Lawrence Erlbaum Associates.

Cole, A. (2004). Mathematics and the Feldenkrais method: Discovering the relationship. *The Feldenkrais Journal*, 17, 17–26.

Collins, A. (1992). Towards a design science of education. In E. Scanlon & T. O'Shea (Eds.), *New directions in educational technology* (pp. 15–22). Berlin: Springer.

Confrey, J. (2005). The evolution of design studies as methodology. In R. K. Sawyer (Ed.), *The Cambridge handbook of the learning sciences* (pp. 135–151). Cambridge, UK: Cambridge University Press.

diSessa, A. A. (2007). An interactional analysis of clinical interviewing. *Cognition and Instruction*, 25(4), 523–565.

diSessa, A. A. (2008). A note from the editor. *Cognition and Instruction*, 26(4), 427–429.

diSessa, A. A., & Cobb, P. (2004). Ontological innovation and the role of theory in design experiments. *The Journal of the Learning Sciences*, 13(1), 77–103.

Dreyfus, H. L. (2002). Intelligence without representation: Merleau-Ponty's critique of mental representation. *Phenomenology and the Cognitive Sciences*, 1(4), 367–383.

Dreyfus, H. L., & Dreyfus, S. E. (1999). The challenge of Merleau-Ponty's phenomenology of embodiment for cognitive science. In G. Weiss & H. F. Haber (Eds.), *Perspectives on embodiment: The intersections of nature and culture* (pp. 103–120). New York: Routledge.

Duval, R. (2006). A cognitive analysis of problems of comprehension in a learning of mathematics. *Educational Studies in Mathematics*, 61(1–2), 103–131.

Edelman, G. M. (1987). *Neural Darwinism: Theory of neuronal group selection*. New York: Basic Books.

Edelson, D. C. (2002). Design research: What we learn when we engage in design. *The Journal of the Learning Sciences*, 11(1), 105–121.

Feldenkrais, M. (1985). *The potent self: A guide to spontaneity*. San Francisco, CA: Harper & Row.

Froebel, F. (2005). *The education of man* (W. N. Hailmann, Trans.). New York: Dover Publications. (Original work published 1885).

Fuson, K. C., & Abrahamson, D. (2005). Understanding ratio and proportion as an example of the Apprehending Zone and Conceptual-Phase problem-solving models. In J. Campbell (Ed.), *Handbook of mathematical cognition* (pp. 213–234). New York: Psychology Press.

Gallese, V., & Lakoff, G. (2005). The brain's concepts: The role of the sensory-motor system in conceptual knowledge. *Cognitive Neuropsychology*, 22(3–4), 455–479.

Ginsburg, C. (2010). *The intelligence of moving bodies: A somatic view of life and its consequences*. Santa Fe, NM: AWAREing Press.

Goldin, G. A. (1987). Levels of language in mathematical problem solving. In C. Janvier (Ed.), *Problems of representation in the teaching and learning of mathematics* (pp. 59–65). Hillsdale, NJ: Lawrence Erlbaum Associates.

Greeno, J. G. (1998). The situativity of knowing, learning, and research. *American Psychologist*, 53(1), 5–26.

Hall, R., & Nemirovsky, R. (2012). Introduction to the special issue: Modalities of body engagement in mathematical activity and learning. *Journal of the Learning Sciences*, 21(2), 207–215.

Hauk, O., Johnsrude, I., & Pulvermüller, F. (2004). Somatotopic representation of action words in human motor and premotor cortex. *Neuron*, 41(2), 301–307.

Howison, M., Trninic, D., Reinholz, D., & Abrahamson, D. (2011). The Mathematical Imagery Trainer: From embodied interaction to conceptual learning. In G. Fitzpatrick, C. Gutwin, B. Begole, W. A. Kellogg, & D. Tan (Eds.), *Proceedings of the Association for Computer Machinery Special Interest Group on Computer Human Interaction* (CHI 2011) (pp. 1989–1998). New York: ACM Press.

Hutto, D. D., & Myin, E. (2013). *Radicalizing enactivism: Basic minds without content*. Cambridge, MA: MIT Press.

Ingold, T. (2011). *The perception of the environment: Essays on livelihood, dwelling, and skill* (2nd ed.). New York: Routledge.

Kelly, A. E. (2003). Research as design. In A. E. Kelly (Ed.), The role of design in educational research [Special issue]. *Educational Researcher*, 32, 3–4.

Kelso, J. A. S., & Engstrøm, D. A. (2006). *The complementary nature*. Cambridge, MA: MIT Press.

Kirsh, D., & Maglio, P. (1994). On distinguishing epistemic from pragmatic action. *Cognitive Science*, 18(4), 513–549.

Kostrubiec, V., Zanone, P.-G., Fuchs, A., & Kelso, J.A.S. (2012). Beyond the blank slate: Routes to learning new coordination patterns depend on the intrinsic dynamics of the learner – experimental evidence and theoretical model. *Frontiers in Human Neuroscience*, 6, 2012.

Lakoff, G., & Núñez, R. E. (2000). *Where mathematics comes from: How the embodied mind brings mathematics into being.* New York: Basic Books.

Lindwall, O., & Lymer, G. (2008). The dark matter of lab work: Illuminating the negotiation of disciplined perception in mechanics. *Journal of the Learning Sciences,* 17(2), 180–224.

Lundblad, I., Elert, J., & Gerdle, B. (1999). Randomized controlled trial of physiotherapy and Feldenkrais interventions in female workers with neck-shoulder complaints. *Journal of Occupational Rehabilitation,* 9(3), 179–194.

Mariotti, M. A. (2009). Artifacts and signs after a Vygotskian perspective: The role of the teacher. *ZDM–The international Journal on Mathematics Education,* 41, 427–440.

Masters, R. S. W. (2000). Theoretical aspects of implicit learning in sport. *International Journal of Sport Psychology,* 31, 530–541.

Melser, D. (2004). *The act of thinking.* Cambridge, MA: MIT Press.

Nemirovsky, R. (2003). Three conjectures concerning the relationship between body activity and understanding mathematics. In N. A. Pateman, B. J. Dougherty & J. T. Zilliox (Eds.), *Proceedings of the International Group for the Psychology of Mathematics Education* (Vol. 1, pp. 105–109). Honolulu, Hawaii: PME.

Nemirovsky, R. (2011). Episodic feelings and transfer of learning. *Journal of the Learning Sciences,* 20(2), 308–337.

Núñez, R. E., Edwards, L. D., & Matos, J. F. (1999). Embodied cognition as grounding for situatedness and context in mathematics education. *Educational Studies in Mathematics,* 39, 45–65.

Piaget, J. (1971). *Biology and knowledge: An essay on the relations between organic regulations and cognitive processes.* Chicago, IL: University of Chicago Press.

Pirie, S. E. B., & Kieren, T. E. (1994). Growth in mathematical understanding: How can we characterize it and how can we represent it? *Educational Studies in Mathematics,* 26, 165–190.

Radford, L. (2000). Signs and meanings in students' emergent algebraic thinking: A semiotic analysis. *Educational Studies in Mathematics,* 42(3), 237–268.

Reed, E. S., & Bril, B. (1996). The primacy of action in development. In M. L. Latash & M. T. Turvey (Eds.), *Dexterity and its development* (pp. 431–451). Mahwah, NJ: Lawrence Erlbaum Associates.

Reinholz, D., Trninic, D., Howison, M., & Abrahamson, D. (2010). It's not easy being green: Embodied artifacts and the guided emergence of mathematical meaning. In P. Brosnan, D. Erchick, & L. Flevares (Eds.), *Proceedings of the North American Group for the Psychology of Mathematics Education* (pp. 1488–1496). Columbus, OH: PME-NA.

Roth, W.-M., & Thom, J. S. (2009). Bodily experience and mathematical conceptions: From classical views to a phenomenological reconceptualization. In L. Radford, L. Edwards, & F. Arzarello (Eds.), *Gestures and multimodality in the construction of mathematical meaning* [Special issue]. *Educational Studies in Mathematics,* 70(2), 175–189.

Sandoval, W. A., & Bell, P. E. (2004). Special issue on design-based research methods for studying learning in context. *Educational Psychologist,* 39(4).

Savelsbergh, G. J. P., Vereijken, B., & Zaal, F. T. J. M. (2005). Putting the "motor" back into development: The legacy of Esther Thelen (1941–2004). *Infant Behavior and Development,* 28, 97–98.

Saxe, G. B. (2012). *Cultural development of mathematical ideas: Papua New Guinea studies.* Cambridge, UK: Cambridge University Press.

Schoenfeld, A. H. (1998). Making pasta and making mathematics: From cookbook procedures to really cooking. In J. G. Greeno & S. V. Goldman (Eds.), *Thinking practice in mathematics and science learning* (pp. 299–319). Mahwah, NJ: Lawrence Erlbaum Associates.

Schoenfeld, A. H., Smith, J. P., & Arcavi, A. (1991). Learning: The microgenetic analysis of one student's evolving understanding of a complex subject matter domain. In R. Glaser (Ed.), *Advances in instructional psychology* (pp. 55–175). Hillsdale, NJ: Erlbaum.

Sfard, A. (2002). The interplay of intimations and implementations: Generating new discourse with new symbolic tools. *Journal of the Learning Sciences*, 11(2&3), 319–357.

Smith, J. P., diSessa, A. A., & Roschelle, J. (1993). Misconceptions reconceived: A constructivist analysis of knowledge in transition. *Journal of the Learning Sciences*, 3(2), 115–163.

Thelen, E., & Smith, L. B. (1994). *A dynamic systems approach to the development of cognition and action.* Cambridge, MA: MIT Press.

Thorndike, E. L. (1911). *Animal intelligence: An experimental study of the associative processes in animals.* New York: Macmillan.

Trninic, D., & Abrahamson, D. (2013). Embodied interaction as designed mediation of conceptual performance. In D. Martinovic, V. Freiman, & Z. Karadag (Eds.), *Visual mathematics and cyberlearning* (Mathematics education in the digital era) (Vol. 1, pp. 119–139). New York: Springer.

Varela, F. J., Thompson, E., & Rosch, E. (1991). *The embodied mind: Cognitive science and human experience.* Cambridge, MA: MIT Press.

Vereijken, B., & Thelen, E. (1997). Training infant treadmill stepping: The role of individual pattern stability. *Developmental Psychobiology*, 30(2), 89–102.

Vérillon, P., & Rabardel, P. (1995). Cognition and artifacts: A contribution to the study of thought in relation to instrumented activity. *European Journal of Psychology of Education*, 10(1), 77–101.

von Glasersfeld, E. (1983). Learning as constructive activity. In J. C. Bergeron & N. Herscovics (Eds.), *Proceedings of the North American Group for the Psychology of Mathematics Education* (Vol. 1, pp. 41–69). Montreal: PME-NA.

von Glasersfeld, E. (1987). Learning as a constructive activity. In C. Janvier (Ed.), *Problems of representation in the teaching and learning of mathematics* (pp. 3–18). Hillsdale, NJ: Lawrence Erlbaum.

Vygotsky, L. S. (1926/1997). *Educational psychology.* (R. H. Silverman, Trans.). Boca Raton, FL: CRC Press.

Vygotsky, L. S. (1978). *Mind in society: The development of higher psychological processes.* Cambridge, MA: Harvard University Press. (Original published 1930.)

Wilson, M. (2002). Six views of embodied cognition. *Psychonomic Bulletin & Review*, 9(4), 625–636.

Young, K. G. (2011). Gestures, intercorporeity, and the fate of phenomenology in folklore. *Journal of American Folklore*, 124(492), 55–87.

# 9

# GESTURES, SPEECH, AND MANIPULATION OF OBJECTS AS A WINDOW AND INTERFACE TO INDIVIDUAL COGNITION

*Shulamit Kapon*

Knowledge and interaction are often considered complementary aspects of learning. A focus on knowledge often characterizes cognitive perspectives on learning, whereas a focus on interaction often characterizes situated and sociocultural perspectives. Jerome Bruner (1997) described the relations between these two perspectives as "fruitful incommensurability," stating that "the two approaches constitute two principled, incommensurate ways by which human beings make sense of the world" (p. 71). At its most extreme, the incommensurable but complementary nature of knowledge and interaction is described as analogous to the wave and particle duality of light (Givry & Roth, 2006). When one observes a phenomenon on which the particle nature of light comes to bear, the wave nature of light is not only invisible, but in principle cannot be observed (and vice versa). By extension, analyses in studies of learning tend to explicitly attend – for instance by their specific use of conceptual vocabulary – either to students' knowledge or to the interaction, but not to both simultaneously. Here, however, it is argued that the knowledge and interaction perspectives are not incommensurable *in principle* – that they can be employed together in an empirical analysis of learning and that by doing so we can better understand how learning takes place. The empirical analysis implements a combination of Knowledge Analysis (KA) and Interaction Analysis (IA) of an episode of learning in a clinical interview to illustrate how cognition and interaction are sequentially and temporally related.

## Rationale and Theoretical Grounding

One difficulty that students encounter when learning science is the need to build new ideas in the context of old ones. This broad, deep change in a learner's way of seeing and dealing with the world is known as "conceptual change." Modeling conceptual change and supporting students in achieving it has long been a primary goal of research and practice in science (Duit & Treagust, 2003). Conceptual change researchers concur that the dynamics of individual knowledge that is involved in learning science go beyond the simple accumulation of knowledge. However, they disagree on the form and nature of the cognitive change involved and the related implications for instruction (compare Chi, 1992; Smith, diSessa, & Roschelle, 1994; Vosniadou, 1994). Many studies of conceptual change can be placed on the extreme knowledge end of the spectrum between attention to knowledge-related and interactional aspects of learning, and tend to ignore the context in which learning takes place (e.g., Carey, 1991; Chi, 1992; Keil, Carter Smith, Simons, & Levin, 1998; Vosniadou & Brewer, 1992). Here, however, the dynamic development and use of knowledge is examined from a perspective that is inherently sensitive to contextual constraints and affordances; namely, the Knowledge in Pieces (KiP) epistemological perspective on conceptual change (diSessa, 1993; Kapon & diSessa, 2012; Parnafes, 2007; Sherin, 2001; Wagner, 2010).

The KiP epistemological perspective models the mind as a complex knowledge system comprised of knowledge elements that are diverse in terms of form, function, and complexity (diSessa, 2002). Knowledge elements manifested in episodes of learning are examined at a small enough grain size so that they are not perceived as intrinsically right or wrong, but as productive or not for a particular context. Analysis involves characterizing particular knowledge elements and conjecturing mechanisms that lead to recontextualization of those knowledge elements and reorganization of the system over a micro-timescale, as well as over longer periods of time.

This article draws on a study that examined differences between individual responses to an instructional analogical sequence (Kapon & diSessa, 2012). In 2010, I conducted a series of clinical interviews with high-school students before their first formal course in physics. The interviews were structured around an instructional sequence of bridging analogies (Brown & Clement, 1989) that aimed to help students make sense of the idea of the normal force in physics. Each interview took about 50 minutes and students could manipulate all the artifacts used in the analogies, such as springs, tables, flexible boards, ropes, books. All the interviews were videotaped, and three interviews were selected for a detailed knowledge analysis.

The results of the knowledge analysis (Kapon & diSessa, 2012) suggested that when reasoning through instructional analogies, students activate particular knowledge elements (termed explanatory primitives [e-prims]) which they implement to assess the plausibility of the analogical inference. E-prims are self-explanatory knowledge elements that, when activated, provide a sense of comfort and obviousness in reaction to certain phenomena, or surprise or rejection in reaction to others. A well-known, special subset of explanatory primitives are phenomenological primitives (p-prims) (diSessa, 1993) that have a very specific form of encoding and developmental history. P-prims are developed through direct interaction with the physical world, and they are non-verbally encoded in very simple unitary schemes. The findings revealed differences between the students with regard to the repertoire of explanatory primitives they each cued in particular contexts of reasoning, the explanatory power (intrinsic priority) and relevance to the particular context (contextual priority) attached to each knowledge element, and shifts in these priorities. Differences between individuals in the acceptance or rejection of the suggested analogical inferences were accounted for by differences in the students' repertoire of cued e-prims and their dynamic intrinsic and contextual priorities. Mechanisms for negotiating the relative priorities of activated e-prims with conflicting consequences were hypothesized.

Nevertheless, the actual physical manipulation of the artifacts involved in the analogy seemed to be an important feature in the students' dynamic reasoning. This observation coheres with findings from a study that replicated Vosniadou and Brewer's (1992) examination of students' intuitive models of the Earth, and showed that a slight change in the interviewing environment – the addition of a globe that was placed on a desk between the interviewer and interviewees – resulted in the generation of radically different intuitive models of the Earth (Schoultz, Säljö, & Wyndhamn, 2001). In addition, the interviews in my study were carefully planned and the interviewees' interactions with me (the interviewer) must have influenced the flow of their thoughts. Although the interviewees' interactions with the artifacts were documented in detail in the previous knowledge analysis, they were not analyzed frame by frame and the interviewer's speech and gestures were hardly examined at all.

Knowledge analysis is an attempt to infer representation of individual knowledge in use and in development from individual behavior. Arguing from situated and sociocultural perspectives, researchers might claim that attempting to assess what students "have in their heads" is presumptuous and misleading since such assessments cannot detach individual cognition from the larger system consisting of the teacher, test, available tools, curriculum, and any other conditions under which the assessment may take place (see, for instance, Givry & Roth, 2006; Lemke, Kelly, & Roth, 2006; Stevens & Hall, 1998). The centrality of context, however, is an underlying assumption in studies informed by the KiP epistemological perspective (diSessa, 1993; Sherin, 2001; Smith et al., 1994), although, to date, relatively little work has been done with process data to explicitly link transformational mechanisms with knowledge analysis.

The disparity between many of the situated and cognitive approaches may be ascribed to the conceptualization of communicating and thinking as identical activities, a central assumption of many situative and sociocultural theories (e.g., Lemke et al., 2006; Sfard, 2007). For instance, it was suggested that talk in interaction is not cognition's visible outer form but rather "the actual process itself, which is misnamed and misrecognized as 'cognition'" (Lemke et al., 2006, p. 89). Namely, the concept of "knowledge" is misleading since what we are witnessing as we follow students' learning is not a change in a permanently present feature in individuals, as described by the term "knowledge," but rather a dynamic construct that emerges on the fly through management and deployment of all available resources by all participants.

The episodes discussed in this chapter present instances in which a "dynamic construct that emerges on the fly" is interpreted as constructed in the individual's *mind* through interaction and responses to the environment (people and artifacts). I argue that the analysis demonstrates that the "dynamic construct" is influenced by the individual's prior knowledge, and can influence and change this knowledge in return. Thus, the knowledge and the interaction perspectives are considered here not as merely complementary, but as sequentially and temporally related. The analyzed instances aim to exemplify how features of situations that are perceived through various modes of interaction influence the activation of particular knowledge elements as well as the dynamic assessment of the relative salience of these elements. Students' reasoning is explored in fine grain from both perspectives in the particular context of reasoning through instructional analogies in physics.

The analysis of interaction examines both talk and gestures during the interview. The examination of gestures is inspired by two lines of thought. The first is Goodwin's (2000) notion that people attach meaning to gestures and words through their interaction with the semiotic resources in the environment, particularly environmentally coupled gestures, "gestures that cannot be understood by participants without taking into account structures in the environment to which they are tied" (Goodwin, 2007a, p. 196). The second is Goldin-Meadow's (2003) argument that gestures and talk are alternative modalities for expressing individual knowledge. Goldin-Meadow claims that people's gestures reveal knowledge which is often not encoded or cannot be accessed verbally, and that it is possible to empirically create a gesture lexicon of a particular individual.

Although not all gestures are communicative, an assumption underlying most studies of gestures is that they play a central role in communication (e.g., Goodwin, 2007a, 2007b; Hutchins, 2006; McNeill, 1992). The analysis of gestures discussed in this chapter employs David McNeill's classic taxonomy: *Beat gestures* are gestures that provide rhythm and emphasis to communication without any propositional content, *Deictic gestures* are pointing gestures, *Iconic gestures* are gestures that reference visual images and imitate perceptually similar concrete phenomena, and *Metaphoric gestures* are gestures that reference visual images that represent abstract entities. Deictic and iconic gestures reflect the grounding of cognition in the physical environment as they anchor and couple the information expressed verbally with the material world (Alibali & Nathan, 2012). Iconic and metaphoric gestures manifest simulations of action and perception (Alibali & Nathan, 2012). Whether a simulation is executed as a gesture depends on three factors: the strength of interaction with the world, the gesture threshold, and active engagement in speech (Hostetter & Alibali, 2008). I examine how the deictic, iconic, and metaphoric gestures used in the conversation during the interview reflect and acquire meaning through their relation with artifacts and structures in the environment (Goodwin, 2007a, 2007b; Hutchins, 2006).

The analysis of talk examines instances of recipient design. Sacks, Schegloff, and Jefferson (1974) use this term to describe components of talk in a conversation, such as the selection of words and topics or the ordering of a sequence in a conversation that is constructed by an interlocutor with an orientation and sensitivity to another interlocutor. Here this refers to the ways in which some of the interviewer's conversational moves were dynamically "tailored" to the interviewee's reaction in the moment.

The episodes chosen for the analysis presented in this chapter involve the activation of several p-prims (diSessa, 1993), one of which, *dynamic balance*, is central to the task. *Dynamic balance* explains situations of balance and rest when forces are recognized, i.e., when a pair of forces or directed influences are in conflict and happen to balance each other. This p-prim was chosen for the focal study since its activation was central to the students' evaluation of the instructional sequence, and because it is a phenomenological primitive (p-prim). P-prims are compelling candidates for additional gesture analysis since by definition they are not encoded verbally. Thus, a physical interaction may activate a p-prim through the focus of attention on an imagery similarity where an imagery gesture might reference the p-prim and thus have semiotic meaning. The analysis specifically attends to gestures as a means of communication as well as an expression of knowledge elements, and examines interactions with the artifacts (e.g., book, table) as semiotic actions as well as a stimulus for activation of knowledge elements.

## Analysis

The empirical goal in this reanalysis was twofold. The first goal was to connect a specific individual's gestures to particular knowledge elements that were cued and employed by this individual. The second goal was to establish a connection between the interviewee's cuing of a particular knowledge element or a shift in its relative priority and (1) the interviewee's specific manipulation of artifacts, and (2) the interviewer's conversational and gestural moves. I present an analysis of an episode drawn from a clinical interview with Jacob (pseudonym), who was at the time of the interview in the 11th grade and was planning to take his first physics course in school the coming year. The entire interview took 42 minutes and the episode in question took place between minutes 2:20 and 8:40. The interview took place after school hours in the school's chemistry/physics laboratory. Jacob appeared very engaged by the interview. He frequently paused to consider and evaluate ways of construing the situations, and he often examined and interacted with the artifacts.

The episode discussed here is divided into three sub-episodes referred to as Excerpts 1, 2, and 3. The transcripts are presented as figures since pictures of gestures are embedded in the text. Gestures and turns are numbered and are referred to in the text as Gesture # or turn #.

Gestures, Speech, & Manipulation of Objects   **241**

In the following analysis I refer to myself as "Shuly" when discussing my role as an interviewer and as "I" when discussing the considerations and interpretations employed during the analysis. The transcription conventions used are the following: (a) "//" for a break in speech, typically including a pause, then restart or new direction; (b) "/ ... /" for omission of part of the interviewee's or the interviewer's speech; (c) "[*Italic*]" for interpretive and informational commentary, including references to particular pictorial gestures; and (d) pictures of gestures are embedded in text.

## Excerpt 1

Excerpt 1 (Figures 9.1 and 9.2) starts when Shuly (the interviewer) reacts to Jacob's account of why the book she placed on the table did not fall to the floor. Jacob's explanation was that "the particles in the table /.../ are compacted too tightly for the book to get through." When explicitly asked, he claimed that it does not make sense that the table would exert a force while "preventing the book from moving through it." At this point, Shuly asked Jacob to hold out his hand and she placed a book on it.

| 1. | Shuly: | Okay. Can you hold the book? *[Jacob grasps the book between four fingers that are placed below the book and his thumb that is placed on it]*. Like that *[Shuly shows Jacob how to hold the book with the entire palm flat beneath the book]*. Does your hand exert a force on the book? |
|---|---|---|
| 2. | Jacob: | Hmm... *[silently thinking for about 15 seconds while examining the book and gently moving his hand - Gesture 1]*. |
| 3. | Shuly: | *[with a smile]* Let me put another book on you *[Jacob smiles too]* |
| 4. | Jacob: | *[As Shuly lets go of the book, Jacob's hand slightly, almost inconspicuously sinks and immediately returns to its original location - see Gesture 2.]* |
| 5. | Shuly: | *[Shuly is busy adding weight to Jacob's hand and is not looking at him - see Gesture 2]* and a fishing weight *[adds a fishing weight while laughing.]* |
| 6. | Jacob: | *[a slight gesture as in Gesture 2]* Hmm. *[Jacob stops for a second, as if starting to come up with an answer.]* |
| 7. | Shuly: | *[Shuly is still busy with the addition of weights and is not looking at Jacob]* and another fishing weight *[adds another]* |

**FIGURE 9.1**   Excerpt 1, Part I: turns 1–7, Gestures 1–2.

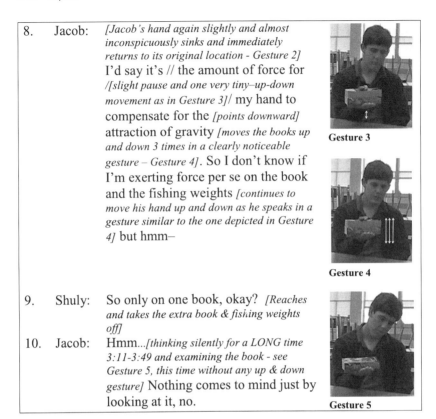

FIGURE 9.2 Excerpt 1, Part II: turns 8–10, Gestures 3–5.

As Shuly piled more weight on the Jacob's hand (turns 3, 5, 7), she focused his attention on the effort he felt in his muscles. Note the tiny movement depicted in Gesture 2 that Jacob made when each additional weight was placed on his hand (turns 4, 6, and the first movement in turn 8). This movement was inconspicuous (smaller than the arrow which represents it in Gesture 2) and was noticed only in the frame-by-frame examination. This movement appeared to be more like a balancing reflex rather than a gesture. However, Jacob sensed this movement, and in turn 8 he first recalled and relived it (additional tiny, almost inconspicuous, movement – see Gesture 3) just before he started to come up with an answer, and as he started to formulate it – "I'd say it's // the amount of force for" – he paused to simulate and sense it again (repeated the tiny motion in Gesture 3).

These two repeated movements of Jacob's hand cannot be interpreted as communicative gestures because they do not entail a communicative message. Instead, they served as semiotic anchors for Jacob which he used to develop his explanation: "I'd say it's // the amount of force for /[slight pause and one very tiny up-down movement as in Gesture 3]/ my hand to compensate for the [point downward] attraction of gravity [moves the books up and down 3 times in a clearly noticeable *gesture – Gesture 4]."* Gesture 4 is a clear and noticeable gesture. One possible interpretation is that the gesture in Gesture 4 is iconic and explicitly manifests a simulation of his recent perception. The word "compensate" is a verbal descriptor of the simulation, and Jacob's use of the word "force" may well stem from the fact that Shuly used it in previous turns.

This interpretation does not make use of the term knowledge. The question is whether it is sufficient and adequate to account for Jacob's reasoning. In the next paragraphs, I argue that it is not. Specifically, I present an alternative interpretation suggesting that: (a) Jacob activates elements of prior knowledge; (b) He dynamically evaluates the validity and relevance of each element with respect to the ongoing information he perceives (i.e., contextual priority); (c) The activation of a particular knowledge element and the dynamic assessment of its contextual priority is sequentially and temporally influenced by the nature of the interaction that Jacob is engaged in. Hence, the additional detailed focus on the interaction provides a means to account for the mechanism of change in the knowledge system; and (d) Some p-prims are simulated by metaphoric gestures. This suggests that a fine-grained analysis of gestures may serve as an additional means and provide additional triangulation in knowledge analysis.

The language used in turn 8 ("my hand compensates for…") as well as the accompanying gesture (Gesture 4) can be considered as evidence for the activation of the p-prim *dynamic balance*, for which the gesture depicted in Gesture 4 is a metaphoric simulation. The subtle, repeated, reflexive movement that Jacob experienced when each extra weight was placed on his hand (turns 4, 6, and the first movement in turn 8 – see Gesture 2) may have served as a stimulus for the activation of the p-prim (*dynamic balance*) for which the simulation in Gesture 4 was the executed.

*Dynamic balance* is relevant in situations where there are two conflicting forces acting on an object that is at rest. Jacob's words and gestures in turn 8 present an on-line evaluation of the contextual priority of this p-prim. The first time Jacob activated this p-prim he did not attribute high contextual priority to it. Jacob said, "I'd say it's // the amount of force for /*[slight pause and one very tiny up-down movement as in Gesture 3]/* my hand to compensate for the *[points downward]* attraction of gravity *[moves the books up and down 3 times in a clearly noticeable gesture – Gesture 4].*" If dynamic balance applies in this situation, there must be forces involved. Jacob accounts for one force by an explicit activation of prior knowledge – the attraction of gravity. Yet, according to his schema of dynamic balance, there must be an opposite force and he is uncertain whether indeed his hand is exerting this force ("So I don't know if I'm exerting force per se on the book and the fishing weights *[continues to move his hands up and down as he speaks in a gesture similar to the one depicted in Gesture 4]* but hmm…"). Jacob was clearly considering what he knew about forces and hands. Shuly misinterpreted Jacob's reaction and thought that he was wondering how the force "travels" from his hand through the books to the upper fishing weight. For this reason, in turn 9, she took off the extra weight from Jacob's hand, leaving only one book on his hand. As turn 10 shows, the withdrawal of the stimulus of the extra weight left Jacob confused, and after thinking for a while he said, "Nothing comes to mind just by <u>looking</u> at it, no." Note the use of the word "looking" and the absence of the up-and-down gesture (Gesture 5). Hence, by just *looking* at the book that was placed on his hand (unlike the previous experience of supporting extra weight), it did not make sense to Jacob that his hand was exerting a force on the book. Without the extra weight stimulus, the contextual priority of *dynamic balance* was low and Jacob dismissed it. The fact that Jacob could hold the book and feel its weight appears to have been very instrumental in his reasoning. I return to this observation later.

## Excerpt 2

Excerpt 2 (Figures 9.3 and 9.4) starts with Shuly's reaction to turn 10 in Excerpt 1.

The analysis of Excerpt 2 that will be discussed in the next paragraphs illustrates several points. The first is to provide further evidence that metaphoric gestures sometimes function as a simulation of p-prims. We saw evidence in Excerpt 1 for a metaphoric gesture that consistently simulated *dynamic balance*. In Except 2, this emerges again (turn 25, Gesture 10). The up-and-down metaphoric balancing (Gesture 10) is presented together with the words "keep it level" which are also consistent with the essence of *dynamic balance*.

Excerpt 2 also includes another example of a repeated metaphoric gesture that seems to act as a simulation of a p-prim. Notice that at some point Jacob describes the action that the book is exerting on his hand not as that of a force but as an attempt to "pass through" his hand (turn 14), while his hand is "preventing that from happening" (turn 16). The words "pass through" are associated with a gesture (see the spread-out palm facing downward while moving downward in Gesture 7). Moreover, the gesture reappears (turn 21, Gesture 9) when Jacob discusses again how his hand is "preventing" the book from "moving through" it. This may be interpreted as an instance of the activation of a different p-prim – *supporting* (diSessa, 1993). The *supporting* p-prim stipulates that a "strong" or stable underlying object merely keeps overlaying and touching objects from passing through without the necessity of applying a force but just simply by being there.

The metaphoric gesture for "pass through" (Gesture 7) is very different from the gesture accompanying the word "pulling" (Gesture 8) that was used when Jacob described in the same turn how the "*force* of gravity" exerted on the book pulls the book downward (turn 14). This gesture of the extended forefinger that pointed downwards iconically represented the direction of the force of gravity, and, interestingly enough, also appeared in Excerpt 1 (turn 8) when Jacob discussed the "attraction of gravity." Kapon and diSessa (2012) suggested that *gravity pulls things downward* is an explanatory primitive (but not a p-prim) activated in this context of thinking. Also note that Jacob activated the notion of gravity without any prompts from Shuly. As in the case of *dynamic balance* and *supporting*, a consistent representational gesture accompanied the related verbal statements, and actually assisted in their articulation.

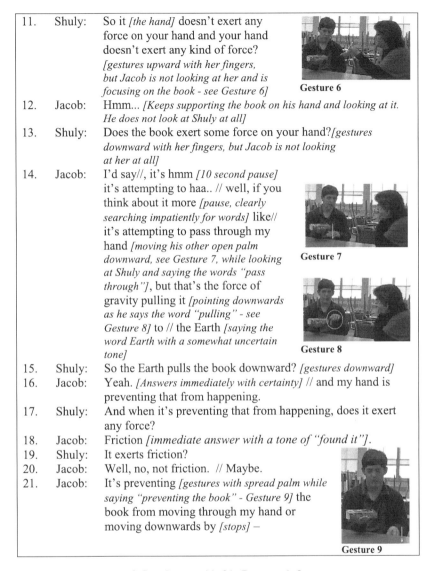

FIGURE 9.3   Excerpt 2, Part I: turns 11–21, Gestures 6–9.

Another interesting issue to explore is the interviewer's influence on Jacob's reasoning. Shuly revoiced (O'Connor & Michaels, 1993) Jacob's ideas three times (turns 11, 15, and 19) in a very similar way. In those turns, she rephrased an idea that Jacob discussed in a previous turn as a question that required reconsideration of what he had said and provision of an explicit articulated response (positive or negative). Following the revoicing in turn 11, Jacob elaborated and articulated his thoughts; following the revoicing in turn 15, he expressed a conviction in a

| 22. | Shuly: | By what? |
|---|---|---|
| 23. | Jacob: | Hmm..*[thinking silently for about 40 seconds - 5:10-5:53]*I'm not quite sure. |
| 24. | Shuly: | Do you feel that you have to /*[gestures up – Jacob is looking at the book not at her]*/exert some force or something like that? |
| 25. | Jacob: | Yeah *[in a certain tone].*// To maintain it at this level *[lifts the book a little higher]*, it requires a certain amount of force to // *[pause, and starts moving his hand up & down - see Gesture 10]*/ keep it level *[continues gesturing while saying "keep it""]*. |
| 26. | Shuly: | What direction does this force that you – |
| 27. | Jacob: | That I'm exerting? |
| 28. | Shuly: | Yes. |
| 29. | Jacob: | It's going upwards *[gestures "up" with his thumb]* while the book is exerting force downwards *[gestures "down" with his forefinger]*. |
| 30. | Shuly: | And huh // which one is– |
| 31. | Jacob: | Well, right now I'm winning that battle *[laughing tone]* of sorts because *[starts moving his hand up and down - Gesture 11]* I can change the elevation of it, so my muscles – |
| 32. | *Shuly:* | When this *[points to the book]* is still, who wins? |
| 33. | *Jacob:* | It's equal. |
| 34. | *Shuly:* | It's equal? |
| 35. | *Jacob:* | I mean because I'm shaking, the book is winning right now. |

**FIGURE 9.4** Excerpt 2, Part II: turns 22–35, Gestures 10–11.

specific idea that he had expressed in a previous turn (that Earth pulls down on things); and following the revoicing in turn 19, he rejected another idea that had popped out in a previous turn (the hand exerts friction).

Jacob's behavior clearly suggested that he attributed a high contextual priority to *gravity pulls things downward* (see, for example, his immediate approval in turn 16). However, the activation of this explanatory primitive did not mediate in itself the later reactivation of *dynamic balance* (turn 25). Jacob did not talk about his hand as exerting a force on the book but rather as preventing the book from moving through it, in conjunction with his words and related metaphoric gestures (Gestures 7, 9) representing the book as "attempting to move through" his hand (turns 14, 21), which was in line with his statement of the table preventing the book from moving through it at the beginning of the interview.

When Shuly asked Jacob how exactly his hand "prevented" the book from "passing through" it (turn 22), this conversational move forced Jacob to think about whether his intuitive notion of *supporting* was indeed self-explanatory or could be explained by other p-prims. It is clear that this was not an easy task for

Jacob (the 40-second pause that ended with "I'm not quite sure."). Shuly's particular use of the word "feel" (turn 23, "Do you *feel* that you have to exert some force?") seemed to direct Jacob's attention to the effort his muscles exerted, as did her previous embodied action in Excerpt 1 when she piled more and more weight on his hand. Jacob immediately approved and reactivated *dynamic balance* (words and metaphoric gesture – turn 25, Gesture 10).

Shuly's next conversational move, in which she asked Jacob to point to the directions of the forces he mentioned and discuss their relative magnitude, prompted Jacob to articulate his notion of *dynamic balance* in terms of the book on the hand scenario (turns 26–35), and thus strengthened the contextual priority of *dynamic balance*. Note that throughout the last exchange (turns 26–35), Jacob answered before Shuly had a chance to complete the questions she was trying to pose. In turn 29, he discussed the direction of two forces: the force that his hand exerted on the book and the force of gravity that the Earth exerts on the book. However, Shuly only asked him about one force – the force that his hand exerts on the book. Her next question was (turn 30), "And uh // which one is…". Jacob barged in before she ended her question, correctly understanding the question as referring to the relative strength of these forces. The fact that Jacob understood the "which one" as referring to the two forces is not surprising. What is really interesting is how Jacob immediately understood that Shuly was asking about their relative magnitude. It may have been the case that the schema of *dynamic balance* was highly active after turn 25, and Jacob was in fact articulating its components in relation to and in terms of the problem he was thinking about (book on the hand). An important feature of this p-prim is that there are *two* conflicting forces involved, and indeed, Jacob spontaneously referred to the direction of the two, not just the one he was asked about. The fact that these two forces *conflict* makes their relative magnitude an important feature, and Jacob correctly assumed that Shuly had asked him about the relative magnitude of the forces.

## Excerpt 3

Excerpt 3 (Figure 9.5) starts with Shuly's move to guide the discussion back to the original question about a book placed on a table.

In the first two excerpts, and Excerpt 1 (Figures 9.1 and 9.2) in particular, a significant part of Jacob's gestures and manipulation of the objects were not communicative but rather functioned as semiotic tools for Jacob's thought and exploration. In contrast, all the gestures that Jacob employed in Excerpt 3 were aimed at communicating his ideas to the interviewer (Shuly). Jacob used deictic and environmentally coupled gestures to anchor and couple the information he expressed verbally with the available material artifacts. He pointed at the table and later to his muscles (turn 39, Gesture 12) when he was talking about them. His metaphoric gestures were also aligned with the ideas he was expressing verbally. When reasoning with *dynamic balance*, claiming that the table is "doing the exact same thing /…/ creating the same // product" as the hand" (turn 39), Jacob made

**248** Kapon

| | | |
|---|---|---|
| 36. | Shuly: | Okay, but tell me, so you just said that your hand exerts a force *[holds the book in her hand]* and the table does not *[puts the book on the table]*. What's the difference between the table and the hand? |
| 37. | Jacob: | Nothing *[smiles]*. The table is doing the same thing. It's just //not using the same //, hmm – |
| 38. | Shuly: | The same what? |
| 39. | Jacob: | It's // The table *[place his hand on the table]* doesn't have muscles *[gestures with the same hand on his arm muscles - Gesture 12]* so I didn't assume that it exerted force, but it's doing the exact same thing *[gestures up and down - Gesture 13]*. It's doing// it's // creating the same // product, I guess *[continues to gesture up & down - Gesture 13]*, but it has // it's not fluctuating.// It doesn't have// The amount of force it exerts isn't fluctuating right now *[stress on "right now"]*. |
| 40. | Shuly: | How come a table can exert force *[gestures with her hand up]*? |
| 41. | Jacob: | Hm... I'd say...*[touches and examines the book quietly for a few seconds]* |
| 42. | Shuly: | I mean, some people would say a table; it's inanimate. You have a will. The table does not. So how come a table can exert a force on your hand? |
| 43. | Jacob: | Hmm // I guess I never really thought about it. I'm not quite sure. |
| 44. | Shuly: | Okay, so think now *[laughs]*. |
| 45. | Jacob: | Yeah *[laughs]*. Hmm... |
| 46. | Shuly: | Does it make sense? |
| 47. | Jacob: | Hmm... // Not just from a glance *[brushes the table with his hand]*, but I'm sure at a more *[stops for a few seconds and makes a gesture indicating "the essence" - see Gesture 14]* in-depth level it makes more sense. |

**FIGURE 9.5** Excerpt 3: turns 35–47, Gestures 12–14.

an environmentally coupled gesture that clearly referred to the book on the hand experience, similar to the metaphoric gesture he used when he reasoned with this p-prim in the case of the hand (turn 39, Gesture 13 – compare to Gestures 4 and 10). This further supports my contention that the activation of certain p-prims can be inferred from their simulation by metaphoric gestures.

Excerpt 3 (Figure 9.5) suggests that Jacob strongly believed that the table exerted a force on the book (turn 47: words "I'm sure," and the associated gesture – Gesture 14), although he completely dismissed this idea in the beginning of the episode. It is also clear that he was fully aware that he had changed his mind (turn 37). This final decision appears to have been based on shifts in the relative priority of the knowledge elements activated in the entire episode and cannot be explained merely by the interaction. Jacob's words, "the table doesn't have muscles" (turn 39), along with his deictic gesture indicating his arm (Gesture 12), suggest that he was not initially thinking of the table as capable of exerting a force because his focus of attention was on the inanimate nature of the table, and he assumed that inanimate things do not possess a mechanism for action. This conjecture was based on his prior knowledge. Note that even at the end of the episode, Jacob could not locate the mechanism for action in the table, and yet he was "sure" that it existed at an "in-depth level" (turn 47). Thus, the activation, and later the reactivation, of *dynamic balance* and the dramatic increase of its contextual priority facilitated this change, whereas the activation, reactivation, and dynamic priority shifts of knowledge elements were facilitated by the interaction with the interviewer and the available artifacts as demonstrated in the first two excerpts.

## Discussion

This section discusses whether the analysis of gestures and conversational moves that were presented in this chapter could or should be considered as an interaction analysis and how this analysis relates and contributes to the "classic" knowledge analysis (Kapon & diSessa, 2012) that was originally employed.

Many interaction analysts study gestures solely as a means to understand how participants respond to and make sense of social situations, whereas in the current study, the analysis of gestures was used to examine individual reasoning. Note that many social aspects of the conversation, such as participation stance and social construction (Goodwin, 2007a, 2007b; Sacks et al., 1974), that are examined in conversational analyses were not explicitly addressed in the current analysis.

Goodwin (2007b) describes five participation stances that shape the participation framework of an interaction:

1. The instrumental stance is the placement of entities in ways that are required for the exchanges necessary to the accomplishment of the activity in progress.
2. The epistemic stance is the positioning of the participants so that they can appropriately experience and grasp the relevant features of the events they are engaged in.
3. The cooperative stance is the visible display that one is orienting one's body toward others and a relevant environment to construct the activities in progress.
4. The moral stance describes how actors in the conversation are acting in a way that reveals to others that they can be trusted to sustain the actions in progress.
5. The affective stance is the emotions toward others that are generated.

The goal of the current analysis was to explain the change in Jacob's reasoning. Note that Jacob's and Shuly's mutual positioning were noted in the transcript. However, unlike the illustrative case study in Goodwin (2007b), Jacob was highly engaged *throughout* the interview – hands and mind. The level of engagement, involvement, and depth of his experience was stable along the five dimensions of the participation stance. This is why I did not elaborate on the microgenesis of the participation framework and the social construction of the interview (e.g., as in DeLiema, Lee, Danish, Enyedy, & Brown, this volume). Participation framework and social construction can certainly be used as evidence of Jacob's active engagement that facilitated a productive reasoning process, but they cannot account for the particular change in Jacob's reasoning since they were stable during this episode.

However, some social aspects of conversations were explicitly addressed in the analysis above, particularly the construct of recipient design (Sacks et al., 1974). The analysis was implicitly and often explicitly attentive to the interviewer's recipient design (i.e., how the specific selection of words and topics are constructed with a dynamic orientation towards the interviewee) – for instance, in the examination of how Shuly's specific conversational moves prompted a particular reaction from Jacob when relating to words and ideas that were presented in previous turns, and in the examination of instances of revoicing (diSessa, Greeno, Michaels, & O'Connor, this volume).

The original knowledge analysis (Kapon & diSessa, 2012) demonstrated how differences in the presence or absence of a particular e-prim in an individuals' cued set of explanatory primitives led to different reactions to an instructional analogy sequence, and that differences in the priorities attached to specific explanatory primitives resulted in different reactions to this sequence. Several instances were documented in which interviewees actively negotiated the priorities of competing explanatory primitives that entailed different trajectories of reasoning, a process that resulted in priority shifts. The analysis of the specific interaction here enriches this analysis as it highlights and explicates how such changes were prompted and influenced by the interviewer. The interview was not transcribed in the format used for conversation analysis. However, many aspects of the sequential organization of the conversation were documented, including points of overlap, intonational phenomena, pauses, and emphases. In fact, the interpretation of turns 26–35 as an instance in which the schema of dynamic balance was active, and in which Jacob articulated the components of this schema, is based on the sequential organization of the conversation between Shuly and Jacob at this time – the observation that Jacob answered before Shuly had a chance to complete the questions.

The most prominent addition to the original knowledge analysis is the fine-grained analysis of gestures. As stated in the introduction, the analysis was inspired by two lines of thought. One was the communicative role of gestures, particularly environmentally coupled gestures, which acquire their meaning through interaction with the semiotic resources in the environment (Goodwin, 2007a, 2007b; Hutchins, 2006). The other was the contention that gestures and speech are different alternative modalities for expressing individual knowledge (Goldin-Meadow, 2003). The noticeable environmentally coupled gestures in the third excerpt are indeed communicative, and in fact they were noted and considered in the original knowledge analysis (Kapon & diSessa, 2012).

In my view, the interesting story lies in the subtle gestures in Excerpts 1 and 2 that were only noticed in the new frame-by-frame analysis of gestures. Some of these gestures were so subtle that they were not picked up by the interviewer (Shuly) during the interview; thus I would not classify them as communicative gestures in the social sense of the word. However, they became visible to me during the frame-by-frame analysis. As an analyst, I could not have interpreted them without grounding them in the particular structures and artifacts in the environment or the accompanying speech. Hence, they are indeed environmentally coupled gestures, even though they did not function as communicative gestures during the conversation.

From the perspective of a knowledge analyst, the outcomes of the gesture analysis were highly informative. The discovery that I could systematically link a particular gesture to a specific activated p-prim supports Goldin-Meadow's contention that gestures are an alternative modality for expressing knowledge (Goldin-Meadow, 2003; Goldin-Meadow & Wagner, 2005), and suggest how a systematic analysis of gestures could be used as an additional way to identify particular p-prims. I am aware that truth is often in the eye of the beholder, and thus coming from a knowledge perspective, I explicitly look for evidence of knowledge in use and in development. Yet, for me, the explicit link between particular gestures and specific activated p-prims was a genuine discovery. Furthermore, p-prims are a model of knowledge elements that are abstracted from our experience in the physical world and are not verbally encoded. The gradual increase of the visibility of the gestures, from a very tacit inconspicuous movement to a noticeable clear communicative gesture (see Gestures 2, 3, 4, 10, and 11) demonstrates, in my view, how physical interactions that simulate an imagery schema of a p-prim can serve as a mechanism for its activation.

Interaction analysts tend to implicitly consider knowledge in their analysis, whereas knowledge analysts implicitly consider interaction (diSessa et al., 2014). I am aware that some interaction analysts may consider this analysis of gestures and conversational moves to be integration of a "third kind of analysis" rather than the addition of an interaction analysis. Nevertheless, I do not believe that integration is a mere combination of two methodologies but rather a conscious appropriation of one to the goals of the other. Hence, integration results in changes in the integrated methodology. The explicit gestures and conversation analysis that I added to the original knowledge analysis were inspired and guided by my readings about interaction analysis; they were not part of the original knowledge analysis. The insights from this analysis clearly enhanced the knowledge analysis. They show how the analysis of gestures can provide an additional means for identifying the activation of particular p-prims and highlight how physical experience can prompt the activation of a p-prim and how particular conversational moves can lead to priority shifts.

# Commentary

## "IA LITE": CAPTURING SOME OF THE EXPLANATORY POWER OF INTERACTION ANALYSIS WITHOUT COMMITTING TO ITS ONTOLOGY

*Andrew Elby*

In her well-argued reanalysis of an interview with Jacob about why a book on a table doesn't fall, Kapon uses tools from Interaction Analysis to show how Jacob's gestures support his sense-making. In explaining Jacob's transition from doubting to believing that the table exerts an upward force on the book, Kapon focuses on shifts in e-prim and p-prim activation and priorities. The reanalysis accounts for, among other things, how her moves as an interviewer brought about physical experiences and actions that helped cue and prioritize particular explanatory and phenomenological primitives such as *dynamic balance*.

In this commentary, I will use another tool from Interaction Analysis (IA), namely *framing analysis* (Goffman, 1974; Tannen, 1993), to offer a complementary explanation for why Jacob expresses certain ideas. In this "IA lite" treatment, I will not adopt the ontology of IA. First, I accept the existence and possible explanatory power of knowledge elements Kapon ascribes to Jacob. Second, instead of conceptualizing the framing of the interview as a property of the unfolding interaction, I analyze *Jacob's* framing, his implicit answer to the question "what is it that's going on here?"

Specifically, I argue that Jacob frames interview Excerpts 1–3 as *guided sense-making*, an activity in which an expert (Shuly) gently leads a novice (Jacob) toward productive ways of thinking and the novice engages in sense-making using those ways of thinking. This version of *guided sense-making* is not the stereotypical schoolish activity in which the teacher supplies answers and the student accepts them without further thought. For Jacob, this *guided sense-making* activity involves making sense of ideas for himself, informed by Shuly's productive guidance. So, by my account, the ideas Jacob expresses are not solely a product of interview dynamics. Instead, I am arguing that Jacob's framing of the interview contributes to the activation and stabilization of knowledge elements through a different interaction-based mechanism than the one Kapon discusses (in which the interviewer's moves lead to specific physical activities that cue specific p-prims and e-prims).

My analysis mostly complements but slightly disagrees with Kapon's. In her Discussion section, Kapon writes that interview dynamics can help explain Jacob's "active engagement" and "productive reasoning process" but "cannot help account for the particular change in Jacob's reasoning since they [the interview dynamics] were stable during this episode." I argue that Jacob's framing of the interview, partly *because* it was stable, helps to explain – but doesn't fully explain – some of the particular ideas he expresses. In doing so, I illustrate how knowledge analysts wishing to retain a cognitivist ontology of thinking and learning can use not only IA tools but also an interactionist lens – attention to social aspects of unfolding conversational dynamics that IA analysts often use to explain knowing-in-interaction within a different ontology of knowledge – to inform their analyses.

## Excerpt 1: Rethinking Why the Book Doesn't Fall

I start by briefly summarizing this excerpt and Kapon's analysis thereof. Following Kapon, I use "Shuly" to refer to Kapon in her role as interviewer.

Shuly has Jacob hold a book. She iteratively adds objects to the book. The book sinks a bit, and Jacob applies extra force to bring it back up. By Kapon's account, the added weight and associated extra effort Jacob exerts increases the cuing priority of *dynamic balance*, the idea that opposing influences of equal strength can balance, leading to no net effect. Jacob's prior knowledge leads him to think that the downward influence on the book is the "attraction of gravity." So, according to Kapon, the activation of *dynamic balance* leads him to think that "there must be an opposite force" although "he is uncertain whether indeed his hand is exerting this force." In short, Kapon offers an explanation based on Jacob's prior knowledge and the cuing of a p-prim – afforded by Shuly's adding weight to the book – for why Jacob affirms the existence of an upward force on the book and considers the possibility that he exerts this force.

I now revisit this episode, asking how Jacob frames the conversation. Immediately prior to Excerpt 1, Shuly had asked why a book on a table doesn't fall. Jacob said "the particles in the table [...] are compacted too tightly for the book to get through." Kapon writes, "When explicitly asked, he claimed that it does not make sense that the table would exert a force while 'preventing the book from moving through it.'" So, immediately before Excerpt 1, Jacob clarified that his explanation for why the book stays motionless does not involve the table exerting a force on the book. But now Shuly asks him to hold a book and asks "does your hand exert a force on the book?" (line 1). When he doesn't answer for 15 seconds (line 2), she does not draw him out or wait for him to finish thinking. Instead, she says "Let me put another book on you" (line 3), and then adds additional weight until Jacob finally says "I'd say it's [pause] the amount of force for...my hand to compensate for the attraction of gravity. So I don't know if I'm exerting force per se on the book and the fishing weights."

In everyday conversations, a participant rarely asks a question and then does a bunch of things to the other person until he answers. In school, by contrast, teachers regularly engage students in lab activities, and students expect those activities to inform their answers to the teacher's questions. Furthermore, Jacob is answering questions about science scenarios asked by an adult he presumably views as knowledgeable. I hypothesize that Jacob, taking up these schoolish cues, frames the interaction in these moments as *guided sense-making* in the sense I defined above. In such an interaction, changing the physical context slightly and re-asking the original question, as Shuly does in line 1, can signal that the guide wants the student to rethink his original answer (that no upward force acts on a book resting on a table). When Jacob does not affirm that an upward force could be acting, Shuly adds more weight to his hand, a move he could interpret as an effort to push his thinking. If Jacob frames these moments as *guided sense-making*, then it makes sense for him to interpret Shuly's actions as encouraging him to consider the possibility that the hand (and by extension the table) *does* exert a force on the book. And this could contribute to Jacob's response that his hand is counteracting gravity somehow, though he's not sure whether his hand is "exerting a force per se."

Although my framing-based interpretation is consistent with the data, there is no direct evidence that Jacob is indeed framing the interaction as I've suggested. Evidence for or against this interpretation could come from showing Jacob a video of Excerpt 1 and asking why he thinks Shuly kept piling books onto his hand. An answer such as, "she really wanted me to feel how I was compensating for the heaviness," would support both Shuly's attribution of *dynamic balance* and my claim that Jacob views Shuly as providing guidance, though of course it wouldn't prove that a *guided sense-making* frame was active during the interview itself.

My framing-based account does not contradict Kapon's. I accept Kapon's argument that *dynamic balancing* becomes central in Jacob's reasoning in line 8, and I agree that Jacob is thinking for himself, not telling Shuly what she wants to hear. My claim is that Jacob's framing of the interaction as *guided sense-making* contributed to his rethinking his earlier conclusion that no upward force acts on the book. In "shopping for ideas" (Hammer & Elby, 2003) that could help him make sense of such an upward force, Jacob finds *dynamic balancing* as a template into which to fit an upward influence to counteract gravity. By this account, Jacob finds and activates *dynamic balancing* partly because he interprets Shuly to be encouraging him to make sense of a possible upward force exerted by a hand or table. This reanalysis complements Kapon's account, by which the activation of *dynamic balance* emerges from Jacob's feeling and counteracting the greater weight and downward motion of his hand.

A disclaimer: I am not criticizing Shuly's moves as an interviewer. These moves elicited aspects of Jacob's cognitive ecology that likely would not have come out otherwise. My point is just that our explanation of Jacob's response in line 8 and elsewhere should consider the possible influence of Jacob's interpretation of "what is it that's going on here."

I now return to my reanalysis of Excerpt 1. Why is Jacob confused when Shuly removes some of the weight from his hand in line 9? Kapon explains the confusion in terms of p-prim cuing: "Without the extra weight stimulus the contextual priority of *dynamic balance* was low and Jacob dismissed it." My framing analysis offers a complementary explanation. By my account, Jacob interpreted Shuly's addition of extra weight as a cue to rethink his original ideas about the forces on the book and as a physical experience to help him do so. In line 8, he expresses that he has considered the existence of an upward force on the book. So, from Jacob's perspective, why would Shuly now *remove* some but not all of the weight? In this moment, he may be confused about what's going on in the interaction. This framing confusion may constitute part of the confusion Kapon observed in those moments and may help to explain why Jacob offers no new ideas in line 10 ("Nothing comes to mind just by looking at it.").

## Excerpt 2: Identifying the Upward Force

I now argue that Jacob's framing of the interaction as *guided sense-making* continues through Excerpt 2 and explains aspects of his behavior. In three of Shuly's four conversational turns between lines 11 and 18 (lines 11, 13, and 17), she asks whether there is a force acting between the book and Jacob's hand. The verbal act of reiterating a question multiple times fits into a *guided sense-making* frame, when the guide is leading the student to consider a certain answer. This could help explain why his answer of "friction" in line 18 is offered, according to Kapon, "with a tone of 'found it'"; he interprets Shuly's moves as focusing his attention on a possible force the hand might exert on the book, and he has indeed "found it" – a force the hand could plausibly exert on the book. Why does he quickly back off from this answer when Shuly says in line 19, "It exerts friction?" One possibility is that the pacing, intonation, and other features of Shuly's utterance were taken up by Jacob as an indication that "friction" is not an optimal answer. A full IA treatment of the utterance would be needed to test this hypothesis; a strong upward inflection in "It exerts friction," indicating doubt or challenge, would support my interpretation.

My analysis of the next segment of Excerpt 2 aligns with Kapon's discussion of the conversational dynamics:

> When Shuly asked Jacob how exactly his hand "prevented" the book from "passing through" it (turn 22), this conversational move forced Jacob to think whether his intuitive notion of *supporting* was indeed self-explanatory or could be explained by other p-prims.... Shuly's conversational move [a few turns later], in which she asked Jacob to point to the directions of

the forces he mentioned and discuss their relative magnitude, prompted Jacob to articulate his notion of *dynamic balance* in terms of the book on the hand scenario (turns 26–35), and thus strengthened the contextual priority of *dynamic balance*. Note that throughout the last exchange (turns 26–35), Jacob answered before Shuly had a chance to complete the questions she was trying to pose.

I agree that (1) Jacob took up Shuly's question in line 22 as an invitation to rethink his earlier answer, and (2) Jacob takes up Shuly's invitation to think in terms of forces and their relative magnitudes so completely that he can anticipate her questions in turns 26–35. I would add only that we can explain the smoothness of this uptake and his quick abandonment of a *supporting*-based explanation as reflecting his continued framing of the interaction as *guided sense-making*. Shuly's asking him to "point to the directions of the forces he mentioned and discuss their relative magnitude" signaled to Jacob that he should answer in terms of forces and consider their relative strengths. By my account, *dynamic balancing* is authentically Jacob's idea, as are his thoughts about the forces. But his framing the interaction as *guided sense-making* helps to explain why these particular ideas become central and stay central at the expense of his other ideas such as *supporting*. Again, evidence for or against my interpretation could come from inviting Jacob to comment on whether he thought Shuly was a physics expert, and whether he viewed her questions as leading somewhere vs. just trying to see what he thinks.

## Excerpt 3: Concluding That the Table Exerts Force

A *guided sense-making* framing can also help explain why Jacob, in Excerpt 3, "strongly believed that the table exerts a force on the book." Kapon writes that Jacob developed this belief "based on shifts in the relative priority of the knowledge elements activated in the entire episode and cannot be explained merely by the interactions." While I agree that interaction dynamics don't explain everything, I argue that they partly explain Jacob's behavior in this excerpt. Certainly, *dynamic balance*, cued and prioritized by Shuly's moves, gives Jacob a foothold to think about how the table exerts an upward force on the book. But by Jacob's own admission in response to Shuly's "Does it make sense?" (line 45), he has not yet fully made sense of the scenario:

> Hmm… // Not just from a glance [*"brushes" the table with his hand*], but I'm sure at a more [*stops for a few seconds and makes a gesture indicating "the essence"*…] in-depth level it makes more sense (*Jacob, line 46*)

So, as Kapon notes, Jacob does not develop a mechanistic explanation for how the table exerts a force on the book. Based solely on the ideas he has activated during the interview, it would be reasonable for him to treat the existence of an upward force exerted by the table on the book as a reasonable assumption, not as something he believes with full confidence. By contrast, if he frames the interview as *guided sense-making*, then it makes sense for him to assume the truth of the forces-based way of thinking Shuly has been encouraging him to adopt – not to please her, but because he trusts her expertise and therefore trusts the guidance she has been providing.

## Discussion and Conclusion

Pure interaction analysts do not attribute knowledge in the head and therefore do not view interviews as uncovering cognitive elements. For this reason, it is tempting for knowledge analysts to view an IA-style reanalysis of an interview – even a reanalysis such as mine, which does not deny the existence or importance of knowledge in the head – as an argument that the participant's ideas are all an "interview effect." My framing analysis, by contrast, does not challenge the authenticity of Jacob's ideas. My "IA lite" reanalysis, which focuses on the role played by framing and positioning in the interaction but does not adopt an interactionist ontology, nonetheless illustrates that analysis of social aspects of interactions can lead to different interpretations of and explanations for a subject's utterances than those resulting solely from analysis of conceptually driven e-prim and p-prim cuings/priorities. An ideal cognitivist microanalysis of an interview would include conceptual *and* social aspects (and epistemological and affective aspects), giving a priori primacy to none of these components.

## Acknowledgments

I thank Shuly Kapon and Andy diSessa for helpful feedback on this commentary, which led to crucial revisions.

## Cumulative References

Alibali, M. W., & Nathan, M. J. (2012). Embodiment in mathematics teaching and learning: Evidence from learners' and teachers' gestures. *Journal of the Learning Sciences*, 21(2), 247–286.
Brown, D. E., & Clement, J. (1989). Overcoming misconceptions via analogical reasoning: Abstract transfer versus explanatory model construction. *Instructional Science*, 18(4), 237–261.
Bruner, J. (1997). Celebrating divergence: Piaget and Vygotsky. *Human Development*, 40(2), 63–73.
Carey, S. (1991). Knowledge acquisition: Enrichment or conceptual change? In S. Carey & R. Gelman (Eds.), *The epigenesis of mind: Essays on biology and cognition* (pp. 257–291). Mahwah, NJ: Lawrence Erlbaum Associates.
Chi, M. T. H. (1992). Conceptual change within and across ontological categories: Examples from learning and discovery in science. In F. Giere (Ed.), *Cognitive models*

*of science; Minnesota studies in the philosophy of science* (Vol. 15, pp. 129–160). Minneapolis, MN: University of Minnesota Press.

diSessa, A. A. (1993). Toward an epistemology of physics. *Cognition and Instruction*, 10(2&3), 105–225.

diSessa, A. A. (2002). Why conceptual ecology is a good idea. In M. Limón & L. Mason (Eds.), *Reconsidering conceptual change: Issues in theory and practice* (pp. 29–60). Dordrecht, NL: Kluwer Academic.

diSessa, A. A., Levin, M., Stevens, R., Hall, R., Danish, J., Enyedy, N., & Parnafes, O. (2014). Is the sum greater than its parts? Reflections on the agenda of integrating analyses of cognition and learning. In J. L. Polman, E. A. Kyza, D. K. O'Neill, I. Tabak, W. R. Penuel, A. S. Jurow et al. (Eds.), *Learning and becoming in practice: The International Conference of the Learning Sciences (ICLS) 2014* (Vol. 3, pp. 1323–1331). Boulder, CO: International Society of the Learning Sciences.

Duit, R., & Treagust, D. F. (2003). Conceptual change: A powerful framework for improving science teaching and learning. *International Journal of Science Education*, 25(6), 671–688.

Givry, D., & Roth, W. M. (2006). Toward a new conception of conceptions: Interplay of talk, gestures, and structures in the setting. *Journal of Research in Science Teaching*, 43(10), 1086–1109.

Goffman, E. (1974). *Frame analysis*. Cambridge, MA: Harvard University Press.

Goldin-Meadow, S. (2003). *Hearing gesture: How our hands help us think*. Cambridge, MA: Belknap Press.

Goldin-Meadow, S., & Wagner, S. M. (2005). How our hands help us learn. *Trends in Cognitive Sciences*, 9, 34–241.

Goodwin, C. (2000). Action and embodiment within situated human interaction. *Journal of Pragmatics*, 32(10), 1489–1522.

Goodwin, C. (2007a). Environmentally coupled gestures. In S. Duncan, J. Cassell, & E. Levy (Eds.), *Gesture and the dynamic dimensions of language* (pp. 195–212). Amsterdam, NL/Philadelphia, PA: John Benjamins.

Goodwin, C. (2007b). Participation, stance and affect in the organization of activities. *Discourse & Society*, 18(1), 53–73.

Hammer, D., & Elby, A. (2003). Tapping epistemological resources for learning physics. *Journal of the Learning Sciences*, 12(1), 53–91.

Hostetter, A. B., & Alibali, M. W. (2008). Visible embodiment: Gestures as simulated action. *Psychonomic Bulletin & Review*, 15(3), 495–514.

Hutchins, E. (2006). The distributed cognition perspective on human interaction. In N. J. Enfield & S. C. Levinson (Eds.), *Roots of human sociality: Culture, cognition and interaction* (pp. 375–398). Oxford, UK: Berg.

Kapon, S., & diSessa, A. A. (2012). Reasoning through instructional analogies. *Cognition and Instruction*, 30(3), 261–310.

Keil, F. C., Carter Smith, W., Simons, D. J., & Levin, D. T. (1998). Two dogmas of conceptual empiricism: Implications for hybrid models of the structure of knowledge. *Cognition*, 65(2), 103–135.

Lemke, J., Kelly, G., & Roth, W. M. (2006). Lessons from the phenomenology of interviews. *Cultural Studies of Science Education*, 1(1), 83–90.

McNeill, D. (1992). *Hand and mind: What gestures reveal about thought*. Chicago, IL: University of Chicago Press.

O'Connor, M. C., & Michaels, S. (1993). Aligning academic task and participation status through revoicing: Analysis of a classroom discourse strategy. *Anthropology and Education Quarterly*, 24, 318–318.

Parnafes, O. (2007). What does "fast" mean? Understanding the physical world through computational representations. *The Journal of the Learning Sciences*, 16(3), 415–450.

Sacks, H., Schegloff, E. A., & Jefferson, G. (1974). A simplest systematics for the organization of turn-taking for conversation. *Language*, 50(4), 696–735.

Schoultz, J., Säljö, R., & Wyndhamn, J. (2001). Heavenly talk: Discourse, artifacts, and children's understanding of elementary astronomy. *Human Development*, 44(2–3), 103–118.

Sfard, A. (2007). When the rules of discourse change, but nobody tells you: Making sense of mathematics learning from a cognitive standpoint. *The Journal of the Learning Sciences*, 16(4), 565–613.

Sherin, B. L. (2001). A comparison of programming languages and algebraic notation as expressive languages for physics. *International Journal of Computers for Mathematical Learning*, 6(1), 1–61.

Smith, J. P., diSessa, A. A., & Roschelle, J. (1994). Misconceptions reconceived: A constructivist analysis of knowledge in transition. *The Journal of the Learning Sciences*, 3(2), 115–163.

Stevens, R., & Hall, R. (1998). Disciplined perception: Learning to see in technoscience. In M. Lampert & M. L. Blunk (Eds.), *Talking mathematics in school: Studies of teaching and learning* (pp. 107–149). New York: Cambridge University Press.

Tannen, D. (1993). *Framing in discourse*. New York: Oxford University Press.

Vosniadou, S. (1994). Capturing and modeling the process of conceptual change. *Learning and Instruction*, 4(1), 45–69.

Vosniadou, S., & Brewer, W. F. (1992). Mental models of the earth: A study of conceptual change in childhood. *Cognitive Psychology*, 24(4), 535–585.

Wagner, J. F. (2010). A transfer-in-pieces consideration of the perception of structure in the transfer of learning. *The Journal of the Learning Sciences*, 19(4), 443–479.

# 10
# BRIDGING KNOWLEDGE ANALYSIS AND INTERACTION ANALYSIS THROUGH UNDERSTANDING THE DYNAMICS OF KNOWLEDGE IN USE

*Ayush Gupta, Andrew Elby, and Vashti Sawtelle*

## Introduction

Theories of cognition and learning commonly deployed to analyze time spans ranging from seconds to minutes fall into two broad categories: cognitivist and interactionist. The cognitivist perspective emerging from the Artificial Intelligence tradition aims to uncover the structure and "flow" (dynamics) of knowledge, with "knowledge" typically modeled as information or cognitive elements to which an individual's mind has access. The interactionist perspective, by contrast, aims to understand human behavior as irreducibly connected to the communities and activities in which actors participate and the tools, artifacts, and resources they use. Within this perspective, researchers conceptualize *knowing* as a participatory act; accounts of cognition and knowledge elements "inside the head" are backgrounded or avoided.

These two perspectives are in tension with respect to the ontology and locus of knowledge/knowing and learning and the role and ontology of context (Hall, 1996; Jordan & Henderson, 1995). One perspective explores knowledge structures that contribute to particular behaviors while the other explores behaviors as emergent from interactions between human(s) and their cultural and socio-physical environment. Greeno (1997), for instance, calls these perspectives incommensurable, due to their different ontologies of learning. By this account, a Knowledge Analysis (KA) and an Interaction Analysis (IA) of a given event can be combined to provide multiple insights into the phenomena under investigation but cannot be truly integrated in the sense of providing a unified account based on a single coherent theoretical perspective. We, along with some other contributors to this volume, are exploring the possibility that KA and IA accounts can be integrated, not just combined. We can imagine that cognitive elements are activated in response to acting within the socio-material environment and that some (most?) of the stabilities in a person's behavior stem from emergent properties of the system that includes those knowledge elements and features of the socio-physical context, with that system constantly affecting and affected by the person's behavior.

Some researchers trying to combine and/or integrate the two perspectives have used the notion of *framing* – roughly speaking, a sense or co-construction of "what is the nature of the activity?" (Goffman, 1974) – to bridge cognitivist and interactionist views. Tannen and Wallat (1987), for example, analyze the interaction of knowledge schemas (drawn from a cognitivist perspective) and frames of interpretation (drawn from sociolinguistics and anthropology literature) to interpret shifts in a doctor's behavior as he talks to a child patient, the child's mother, or a recording device. Scherr and Hammer (2009), Frank and Scherr (2012), and Conlin, Gupta, Scherr, and Hammer (2007) build from Tannen (1993), using IA tools to explore participants' gestures, gaze, register, etc. to help make inferences about learner's cognitive elements. Similarly, Russ, Lee, and Sherin (2012) and Van de Sande and Greeno (2012) draw on framing to understand different participation structures and relative positioning of participants in interviews and group work. Much of this work, however, uses analytical *tools* from both perspectives to create accounts that are ontologically grounded in one perspective or the other.

Relying on the notion of framing, our new contribution to bridging cognitivist and interactionist perspectives is to draw not only on analytical tools but also on theoretical constructs grounded in the two different perspectives. Is the resulting account truly integrated? Not integrated but smoothly combined? Superficially integrated but actually ontologically incoherent? We are not sure. Our goal is to spark discussion of these issues grounded in our particular data, thereby contributing to the broader discussion of what it would mean to combine and/or integrate the cognitivist and interactionist perspectives.

Specifically, by analyzing an interview episode borrowing tools from both KA (diSessa, 1993) and IA (Jordan & Henderson, 1995), we aim to show how the dynamics of cognitive resources are in concert with the interactional dynamics of the interviewer, interviewee, and socio-material setting. Our analysis of cognitive dynamics differs from many previous analyses within the KA tradition by (a) attending to turn-by-turn conversational dynamics and (b) using interactional and cognitive dynamics to understand not just shifts but also *stabilities* in participants' knowledge activations, roughly analogous to how chemists understand chemical equilibrium as dynamic rather than static. However, as noted above, our overall explanation of stabilities and shifts in our subject Jim's behavior will take a gentle stab at integrating, not just overlaying, interactionist and cognitivist perspectives. Briefly, we will show how an epistemological stance connected to the framing of the activity – a stance that is an interactional achievement and does not "live" in either participant's head – is co-constructed and co-maintained by the participants. Later, however, the unfolding interaction leads to Jim's rationalization of a particular epistemological stance, which can be modeled in terms of the activation of epistemological and conceptual resources that differ in ontology from that of the earlier interactional achievement. So, this reanalysis does not merely layer onto our previously published KA-based analysis of Jim's epistemological shift. It *changes* our earlier analysis, by reconceptualizing an epistemological stance previously attributed *to Jim* as mutually constructed and sustained by the situated interaction between Jim and Ayush.

## Methods and Methodology

This chapter is an IA-based reanalysis of a clinical interview that the first two authors have discussed in previous work (Gupta & Elby, 2011). We now explain the methods of that original study and then describe how we conducted our reanalysis.

As part of a broader study of the ways in which engineering students use mathematics in physics and engineering courses, we videotaped one-on-one clinical interviews of Jim and six other engineering majors taking a first-semester physics course. Recruited from a lecture-based introductory physics class for engineers, participants were asked to imagine explaining both a familiar equation (discussed in that course) and an unfamiliar equation (not covered by the course) to themselves and to others, and to solve problems while thinking aloud. Additionally, subjects were asked direct questions about their personal epistemologies (Hofer & Pintrich, 2002; Hofer, 2001), such as "How do you know when you really understand a physics equation?" The interviews were transcribed with long pauses, indicators of strong emotions, and other "big" non-verbal cues captured, but without careful conversation-analytic notations such as lengths of pauses, rising/falling intonations, gaze, and so on.

In the episode that first caught our attention, Jim got stuck on a problem despite his fluency with mathematical manipulation and his understanding of the relevant physical ideas. Our analysis began with close scrutiny of when Jim gets stuck and later unstuck; we watched the episode in a video analysis session (Jordan & Henderson, 1995) and Gupta took insights from that session to continue close analysis on his own. We formed explanations for his behavior and looked for confirmatory or disconfirmatory evidence elsewhere in the interview (Miles & Huberman, 1984). Working from a knowledge-in-pieces perspective (diSessa, 1993), we did not attribute patterns of behavior to globally held robust (mis) conceptions and epistemological beliefs. Instead, we continually considered how contextual cues might trigger different local coherences in his thinking (Hammer, Elby, Scherr, & Redish, 2005; Rosenberg, Hammer, & Phelan, 2006). The result was a toy cognitive model consisting of cognitive elements ("resources") connected by excitatory and inhibitory links to each other and to the "physics-y context" of Jim's epistemological stance both before and after a shift. We also modeled the shift itself in terms of a cascade of resource activation and deactivation triggered by the introduction of a piece of conceptual knowledge into Jim's cognitive ecology. We did not unpack the "physics-y context." The results of this analysis were published in Gupta and Elby (2011).

We chose this episode for reanalysis for a mix of mundane and substantive reasons. Mundanely, the Jim data were fresh in our minds when we attended the KAIA conference described in the preface to this volume, and we were looking for a data set to (re)analyze from both a KA and IA perspective. More substantively, we knew that our original KA-based analysis had paid short shrift to the conversational dynamics (part of the "context" in which Jim's epistemological stances emerged). We suspected that analysis of those dynamics, for which IA is well suited, would lead to additional insights about Jim's behaviors.

More specifically, drawing on tools from conversation analysis (Goodwin & Heritage, 1990) and framing analysis (Goffman, 1974; Tannen, 1993), we began the reanalysis to help us understand the role that the interviewer (Ayush Gupta, referred to as "Ayush" in interviewer role) and conversational context – co-constructed by interviewer and interviewee – may have played in the emergence of the epistemological stances attributed to Jim in our earlier analysis. To understand this emergence, we attended to word choices, gestures, bodily postures, gaze, and voice characteristics (tone, prosody, pitch, and register), in addition to the flow and structure of the utterances and turn-taking (Jordan & Henderson, 1995; Stivers & Sidnell, 2005).

Motivated by Gupta's intuition that the first few (~10) minutes of the interview were consequential for setting the tone, we began by looking at the opening moments of the interview in a video analysis session. Colleagues of Gupta also contributed insights in later separate video analysis sessions. We reached a hypothesis about the framing co-constructed in those early portions of the interview. Gupta, working alone, then continued working through the interview chronologically, looking for evidence that the purported framing was or was not maintained. He concluded that the initial framing was reinforced in the unfolding interaction. Elby and Sawtelle agreed with him, upon checking later segments of the interview. Finally, we re-examined the focal episode from the original paper, where Jim gets stuck for a while but then resolves the confusion and undergoes what we called an epistemological shift. We asked ourselves to what extent Jim's behavior could be explained in terms of continued participation in the epistemological stance co-constructed by Jim and Ayush and whether additional explanatory power comes from attributing epistemological resources to Jim. For the interaction analysis, we retranscribed the relevant portions of the interview using notation typical of conversation analysis (Jefferson, 2004). The transcript conventions we used for this purpose are also stated in Appendix A.

## Analysis

In the first subsection of our analysis, we first briefly review the relevant parts of the earlier analysis (Gupta & Elby, 2011), which was conducted from a KA perspective. Then we reanalyze the interview from an interactionist perspective.

## Knowledge Analysis of the Focal Episode from Gupta & Elby (2011)

At the beginning of the focal episode, Ayush asks Jim whether the pressure 7 meters beneath the surface of a lake is greater than or less than the pressure 5 meters beneath the surface. Jim uses the hydrostatic pressure equation $p = p_0 + \varrho g h$, to which he had just been introduced ($p$ and $\varrho$, denote the pressure and density of water, and g denotes the acceleration due to gravity; $h$ denotes the distance beneath the surface; and $p_0$ is the pressure at the surface of the water). Jim thinks $h$ must be negative and hence he is comparing $h = -5$ m to $h = -7$ m. Substituting those negative $h$ into the pressure equation, he concludes that the pressure is greater at a depth of 5 meters.

The relevant knowledge element arising in this segment is *down is negative*, the idea that displacements (and other quantities) in the downward direction are assigned negative values. Over the next 10 minutes, this knowledge element appears to be stably activated for Jim and contributes to his erroneous conclusion that pressure decreases with increasing depth.

Gupta and Elby (2011) tried to analyze why Jim sticks with his equation-based answer. The reason, we argued, is that his perception of how difficult it would be to reconcile common sense and the formal result, especially while he's "on the spot" in the interview, stabilizes his epistemological stance that mathematical formalism and common-sense ideas need not speak to each other, and that mathematical formalism expresses confirmed truths. We also argued that this epistemological stance itself is fluid; at the end of the focal episode, a small conceptual clue provided by the interviewer helps Jim resolve the conflict and enthusiastically support the need for a reconciliation of mathematics with real-world perception. (For the purposes of this chapter, the analysis of that shift in epistemological stance is irrelevant, and we do not discuss it here.)

In what follows, we flesh out this argument by presenting evidence from the focal episode and elsewhere to show that *down is negative* is stable for Jim in this context and is coupled with the idea that pressure decreases with increasing depth. We also summarize evidence that, within the interview context, Jim has access to other knowledge resources that contradict these stances: He "knows" that downward can be considered positive, and he articulates his intuitive knowledge that pressure increases with increasing depth. In Gupta & Elby (2011), we used the existence of these contradictory knowledge resources to argue that the stability of *down is negative* and *pressure decreases with increasing depth* does not stem from lack of alternative knowledge resources; a more dynamic explanation is required. We argued in particular that these knowledge elements were stabilized in part by epistemological resources corresponding to Jim's epistemological stance that mathematical formalism expresses confirmed truths and that formalism need not connect directly to everyday experience. We now summarize pieces of that argument.

**Jim has access to common-sense knowledge about pressure that contradicts his mathematical conclusions**: Asked how a friend from his English class would answer the question about whether pressure is greater at 5 or 7 meters beneath the surface of the lake, Jim acknowledges that the friend might rely on experience being under water to argue for the pressure increasing with depth: "like, if they had gone snorkeling under water,...'it felt ((brings hands to his ears)) the pressure was higher when I was deeper.'" Here, Jim draws on intuitive knowledge that pressure under water increases with increasing depth. However, Jim soon rejects this knowledge resource, saying that the friend from English class would not be considering the sign of $h$ in the given equation. In brief, Jim sticks with *pressure decreases with increasing depth* and *down is negative* not because he lacks alternative ways of thinking about the scenario, but rather, because he privileges *down is negative*.

***Jim can use coordinate systems flexibly***: The stability of *down is negative* could arise from a static "misconception" about coordinate systems, that the positive direction is always upward. But earlier in the interview, solving a kinematics problem about balls falling under the influence of gravity, Jim spontaneously and unproblematically assumed that "down is positive" and solved the problem. Thus, the activation of *down is negative* in the focal episode is contextual.

***"Down is negative" is resistant to perturbation***: Some evidence of *down is negative*'s stability during the focal episode comes from Jim's reluctance to seriously consider the alternative that going down can correspond to positive $h$. Ayush tries to pose this alternative. Jim reluctantly entertains this possibility and maps out the consequences, but he does not buy into it. This becomes even more apparent in Jim's response a few minutes later when Ayush again prompts Jim to consider $h$ as positive:

> **Jim:** I mean ...what I keep thinking is that you are going *down* (gestures down) so seven cannot be greater than five and negative. that's why I keep coming back to that. meaning, if you do say it's positive then ... I guess it doesn't bother me. (sighs) seven is greater than five in positive-land.

Jim's utterance, "what I keep thinking is that you are going *down* (gestures down) so seven cannot be greater than five and negative," illustrates the "stickiness" of *down is negative*. While he seems to say that it does not bother him, the statement "seven is greater than five in positive-land" is delivered with a sense of sarcasm that signals his discomfort. Multiple times during the focal episode Ayush tries to prompt Jim to consider that $h$ is positive, and each time Jim reiterates that "down is negative."

***Jim considers math trustworthy***: Asked explicitly whether he would choose the perception-based answer or the equation-based one in an exam, Jim immediately chooses the equation-based answer and justifies his choice by saying that the mathematical answer is more trustworthy because it presumably follows from a confirmed physical law, while perceptions can be misleading:

**Jim:** For an equation to be given to you it has to be like theory and it has to be fact bearing. So, fact applies for everything. It is like a law. It applies to every single situation you could be in. But, like, your experience at times or perception is just different – or you don't have the knowledge of that course or anything. So, I will go with the people who have done the law and it has worked time after time after time.

*Jim thinks bridging the gap between formal and perceptual knowledge in this case is possible in principle, but difficult*: At one point during the interview, prompted by Ayush, Jim explicitly acknowledges that while it might be possible to reconcile the two positions, it wasn't "obvious" to him how to achieve that, saying, "probably somehow [the equation relates to perceptual experience] but not directly, like I think there is underlying in some way that just completely links the two together, but it's not obvious what that relation is."

## A KA Toy Model of Jim's Knowledge

Based on the analysis so far, we can form a "toy" cognitive model to describe Jim's stance towards pressure under water. The model includes conceptual and epistemological elements, some of which reinforce one another, forming a cognitive local coherence (Hammer et al., 2005) that helps explain why Jim sticks with his equation-based answer for so long. Gupta & Elby (2011) discussed these conceptual elements but included only the epistemological elements in their toy model. In order to make the toy model clearer in this brief recap, we include these conceptual elements in the model.

**Conceptual elements:**

(C1) *Down is negative*
(C2) *Pressure decreases with depth*
(C3) *Pressure increases with depth*

**Epistemological elements:**

(E1) *Knowledge from authority*
(E2) *Math is trustworthy*
(E3) *This is hard (affect+epistemology element)*
(E4) *Perceptual knowledge as relevant*
(E5) *Formal knowledge as distinct from perceptual knowledge* (modeled in Gupta & Elby, 2011 as emergent from the interaction of E1, E2, E3, and E4)

*Knowledge from authority* captures the sense that knowledge from authoritative sources, such as mathematical techniques learned in courses, should be prioritized.

*Math is trustworthy* captures the sense of greater reliability attributed by Jim to equations. *This is hard* captures Jim's emotionally charged sense that the task at hand (reconciling intuitive/perceptual knowledge with formal knowledge) would be prohibitively difficult. *Formal knowledge as distinct from perceptual knowledge* captures the epistemological distinction Jim draws between formalized, "proven" knowledge from authoritative sources versus other forms of knowledge such as ones based on perception.

Our toy model omits a variety of elements that are likely active for Jim in these moments, including the hydrostatic pressure equation and algebraic/arithmetical resources that Jim draws on to reach his conclusions. By design, the resources in our toy model are the ones that most help us understand why Jim sticks with his conclusion that the pressure under water is less at a depth of 7 meters than it is at a depth of 5 meters. Specifically, in our toy model, *knowledge from authority* and *math is trustworthy* strongly support the activation of *down is negative*, helping to stabilize *pressure decreases with depth*. In addition, *knowledge from authority*, *math is trustworthy*, and *this is hard* strongly support the activation of *formal knowledge as distinct from perceptual knowledge*, inhibit *perceptual knowledge as relevant*, and initially inhibit *pressure increases with depth* (which later pops up in the conversation). This combination of epistemological elements (activated and inhibited) stabilize *pressure decreases with depth* while making suspect *pressure increases with depth*, which helps explain why Jim sticks with his conclusion that the pressure is lower 7 meters beneath the surface – from a knowledge analysis perspective.

## *Reanalysis From an IA Perspective*

We now reanalyze parts of the interview from an IA perspective. Through the reanalysis, we support three claims:

1. *Throughout their interaction, Jim and Ayush generate and sustain a framing of the interview as an activity in which formal knowledge is relevant and foregrounded and in which Jim's role is to display his formal knowledge.* Gupta & Elby (2011) did not address these phenomena, instead making speculative assumptions about how Jim's history as a physics student might have led to a "default" stance of privileging *formal knowledge as relevant*. Our attribution of this co-constructed framing that "lives" in the interaction replaces our original attribution of *knowledge from authority* as an epistemological resource activated *in Jim's mind* during the focal episode.
2. *The knowledge element "down is negative" is stabilized through interaction.* We view this as adding onto rather than replacing our KA-based story, in which stabilization of *down is negative* results from a local coherence within Jim's cognitive ecology.
3. *The interaction between Jim and Ayush constructs and stabilizes the dichotomy between perceptual knowledge and formal knowledge, with the latter taking precedence.* This

interactional stabilization of the dichotomy replaces parts of the KA-based account, in which we attribute epistemological resources, *formal knowledge as distinct from perceptual knowledge* and *math is trustworthy*, to Jim during the whole focal episode. We are now confident in attributing such resources (or other resources that do the same cognitive work) *to Jim* only when he starts explicitly contrasting formal and perceptual knowledge and justifying his privileging of formal knowledge; we model his justification as arising in part from the activation of a locally coherent set of such resources. The Discussion section takes up this issue in detail.

### Early Stages: Co-Constructed Framing of the Interview as an Activity that Foregrounds Formal Knowledge

The interview starts with Ayush debriefing Jim on the consent form and the study's purpose. Ayush mentions that the researchers are interested in how Jim thinks about a problem, not whether he reaches the correct answer. As Ayush is finishing up this brief, Jim starts reading the first question on the sheet in front of him:

*Here's an equation you have probably seen in physics class: $v = v_0 + at$. How will you explain this equation to a friend from class?*

**Ayush:** so um: the other thing I wanted to uh:: tell you before we start is that,– ((Jim looks at interviewer)) <we> are really looking for how you think about the problems, right, so we're not interested in whether you get to an answer or not. just >you know< h-how are you thinking about it? so keep [talking you know,

**Jim:** °ok°

**Ayush:** tel-tell us about your thought process and – that's what is more important. okay?
((Ayush puts prompt in front of Jim, Jim looks at it))

**Jim:** ((reads the prompt from paper)) °probably an equation you have probably seen in your physics class. how would you explain this equation to a <friend from cla↑ss>?° ((gaze flicks between paper and interviewer))

Here, the content of Ayush's speech indicates that the interview is a space where Ayush attends to how Jim thinks, not to the correctness of his answers. However, the interview prompt on the sheet in front of Jim notes that the equation is from his physics class. Thus the sheet connects the interview to his physics class, a space suffused with expectations about "what kind of activity is this?" In what follows, we see how these potentially mixed messages are developed and negotiated through the interaction of Ayush and Jim. After a 2-second exchange establishing that Jim has seen the equation before, Jim asks Ayush what "class" the question refers to.

[00:01:50.10]
Ayush: so you've probably seen= ((chuckle))= -you've seen this [equation--=
Jim: yeah. from another class or fr↑om...]
Ayush: =umm] s-so suppose you had a friend fr::om uh::h >from an English class.<
Jim: ok.
Ayush: how would you explain that–equation?
Jim: ((looking at paper)) well, I guess velocity equals initial veloc::ity t-times acceleration times time. It's the equation for speed. and it comes fr::o::mm the <derivative of posit↑ion> or: the integral of acceleration. ((looks at interviewer))
(2 sec)
(that's what you see here) because >if you take the integral< of this thing you get the position–equation. so=
Ayush: ok.
Jim: wait) ((looks at paper))
(3 sec)
Jim: ((looks at interviewer)) I know the position ↑equ↑ation like >off the top of my head< so I could just write that down,–and then derive it and get this ag↓ain.
Ayush: OK. ok.

The tone of Jim's utterances here enacts a sense of confidence or at least avoids signaling a lack of confidence. "I know the position equation off the top of my head" contributes to the sense of confidence he is broadcasting. Jim seems at ease. His gaze is flicking back and forth between the paper and Ayush. The construction of Jim's utterances – "I know," "I could write that down" – suggests that he is mostly working out the question for Ayush, displaying his own skills rather than acting out how he would explain the equation to a friend from class. The pausing and looking at the interviewer also suggest that Jim is checking with Ayush whether this is what he should be doing. The tone of Ayush's "okay" suggests that Jim is doing what is expected. The approving tone supports Jim moving forward with the derivation he earlier suggested.

As early as 1–2 minutes in, the interview is coming to be a space where Jim displays his formal knowledge rather than just sharing how he thinks. The material setting reinforces this framing: In front of Jim is a blank page with a question written at the top, much like students see in an exam booklet. A couple of pens are on the table, and the camera facing Jim also indicates that he is "on display" in the interview.

The co-construction of this space as one in which formal knowledge is relevant and foregrounded continues over the next 6 minutes:

[00:02:40.21]
**Jim:** so. ((looks at paper, begins writing))
**Jim:** °so it's exx equ::als exx naught plus (3 sec) vee naught tee plus one half:: aay tee squa↑red? if you take the derivative of this you get– exx prime is that. this is constant, so this goes to zero::. this goes to vee plus tee as a function [and
**Ayush:** mhm.]
**Jim:** uh. you do the simple.= ((shakes head))
**Ayush:** mhm.
**Jim:** =>I don't know what it's called I just know it<
**Ayuh:** (hhh)
**Jim:** ((chuckle)) two go:es down. you get aay tee=
**Ayush:** ok.
**Jim:** =you get, and this goes to vee. which is (2 sec) dee exx dee tee. ((looks at interviewer))
(2 sec)
**Ayush:** ok. ((Jim looks back at paper))
(3 sec)
**Ayush:** o::ok.
**Jim:** or: >you could use< the acceleration, but– which (is just) taking the der:ivative which is– gee tee. ((gaze flicks back to interviewer))
**Ayush:** mhm.
**Jim:** °yeah.°
**Ayush:** Uh::h you said– you could use the acceleration. could you tel-[tell me more?
**Jim:** if you find the] <acceleration.> ((Jim's gaze goes back to the paper))
**Ayush:** uh huh.
**Jim:** then– in:tegrate the acceleration, and you'd get back to this. ((gaze flicks to interviewer then back to paper))
**Ayush:** ok.
**Jim:** so?
(3 sec)
**Ayush:** could you do th↑at?
**Jim:** ok:ay.
(2 sec)

Jim looks and acts comfortable as he works out this derivation. His speech is mostly at a lower volume, perhaps indicating that he is speaking mostly to himself. Ayush's short non-semantic utterances and *ok*s indicate that he is following what Jim is doing and perhaps encourages Jim to continue; these utterances do not seem to break Jim's flow in his derivation. So, the sequence of verbal and non-verbal messages signal that Jim is doing what's expected here – displaying fluency with formal physics knowledge – further establishing the foregrounded role of formal knowledge in this activity.

Over the next 2 minutes, the focus on displaying formal physics knowledge is further supported by Ayush's asking Jim to explain in more detail how acceleration can be integrated to get velocity:

**Jim:** uh::h aay equa::al::ss ((rolling hand in the air while looking up at the ceiling)) gee tee. –um - that's vee. aay equ::als (inaudible)

(7 sec)

((Jim smacks lips))

((Jim mutters through math for 10 sec))

((Jim leans back, touches hand to forehead, then leans forward to paper again))

((Jim mutters through math for 23 sec))

(inaudible) °if you integrate this: you get° (inaudible)

((Jim leans back, puts hand under chin, looks back at paper again))

**Ayush:** so what are you try↑ing to integrate?

**Jim:** >vee eff over tee< cause–that's–acceleration, ((Jim looks at interviewer)) >meters per second squared.< ((gaze back to paper)) °so if you integrate that…

(21 sec)

**Ayush:** YOU are ((Jim looks at interviewer)) essentially thinking that:: (.) if you integrate th::e=

**Jim:** (acceleration to get velocity)

**Ayush:** =accelera↓tion. you get::-you get the velocity.

**Jim:** ((nods head)) yeah.

**Ayush:** ok↑ay. so suppose th::e acceleration. so. SO. >where are you getting< snagged here? uh

**Jim:** uh I just can't >do the integral< of vee eff over tee.

Long periods of silence from Jim, along with his posture and gesture, indicate that this derivation (of acceleration from velocity) is harder for him to perform than was the previous derivation. His behaviors contrast with those in the earlier segment, where he worked out the derivation without long pauses and with a smoother flow to his vocalizations and writing. Jim's difficulty is made visible in the interview through Ayush's asking where Jim is getting "snagged" and the lack of Jim's refutation to that claim. Jim acknowledges that he "just can't do" the needed integral.

The activity of displaying formal knowledge can pose a threat to face. In the following segment, we see how the interview is a situation where Jim could become embarrassed at being unable to demonstrate proficiency:

| | |
|---|---|
| **Ayush:** | okay ↓okay ↓okay |
| **Ayush:** | >suppose I told you that< the acceleration is constant. |
| **Jim:** | <acceleration is constant?> |
| **Ayush:** | yeah: |
| **Jim:** | ok. |
| **Ayush:** | it is the sa:me acceleration. ((Jim nods)) |
| **Jim:** | okay. |
| **Ayush:** | can you integrate that? |
| **Jim:** | um:::::m °constant acceleration° ((Jim holds pen in the air and makes little dot motions in a straight line)) |
| **Jim:** | >I mean I< guess:: you d:o (4 sec) yeah you could. in-integrate that. cause the velocity's still changing= |
| **Ayush:** | ok. |
| **Jim:** | =it's increasing= |
| **Ayush:** | alright. |
| **Jim:** | =yeah↓ |
| **Ayush:** | ok↑ |
| **Jim:** | >if you have constant velocity then acceleration is zero< |
| **Ayush:** | right. |
| **Jim:** | yeah |
| **Ayush:** | ok↓. |

Ayush suggests that the acceleration is constant and asks whether Jim can carry out the integration under that assumption. Jim still seems unsure about how to do so, as indicated by pauses, "ummm," lower tone, and hedges such as "I guess." And he does not ultimately work out the derivation. The segment ends with Ayush accepting Jim's response, immediately followed by conversation-closing sequence of "right," "yeah," and "ok."

In analyzing these first 6 minutes of the interview, our point was to investigate how, through the actions and interactions of Ayush and Jim, the interview comes to be a space in which Jim displays his formal physics knowledge to Ayush. This sense of what is going on is layered with encouragement and high self-efficacy in some moments and a threat to the face in other moments; but throughout, formal knowledge is foregrounded. Ayush's and Jim's actions support and position each other to establish a shared framing of the interview as a place for Jim to display formal knowledge to Ayush. This framing is "shared" in that both Ayush and Jim consistently contribute actions aligned with this framing; we do not mean to imply that Ayush and Jim each have this framing in their heads or that either party intended for the interview space to unfold in this way.

Over the next 45 minutes, this framing is sustained across a range of conversational segments. This maintenance of the framing is unsurprising, given that its emergence early in the interview forms the context within which the conversation continues unfolding – though, of course, a discontinuity in the discourse could always lead to a renegotiation of the nature of the activity. But such a renegotiation did not occur.

## Focal Episode: An Interactional Account of Why Jim Chooses Formal Knowledge Over Perceptual Knowledge

We now fast-forward to minute ~20, when Ayush presents to Jim a blank sheet of paper with the following question written on top:

> Is the pressure at h=5 meters under water greater than, less than or equal to the pressure at h=7 meters under water?

Immediately before this prompt, Ayush had asked Jim to explain the equation for pressure at a given depth under the surface of a body of water, $p = p_0 + \varrho gh$, where $p_0$ is the pressure at the surface of water, $\varrho$ is the density of water, and $h$ is the distance below the surface. Jim analyzed the units on the left and right side of the equation and expressed satisfaction when they matched. While doing so, he displayed no hesitation in asking Ayush for help, specifically about the canonical units for pressure. While he displayed familiarity with the term "pressure," Jim stated that he had not encountered this hydrostatic pressure equation in his physics course so far.

Ayush then poses the question shown above:

[00:20:54.01]
(4)
**Ayush:** ↑so he:res=a::↓ (.) heres ↑a problem. u:m. with this:: equa:tion. so::=
**Ayush:** =suppose we asked you to compa:re the pressure at ai:ch equal to=
**Ayush:** =fi:ve and aich equal to (.)
**Jim:** °se[ven meters] under water°
**Ayush:** [se:ven]
**Ayush:** ((unclear word)) °↓do that.°
((Jim is bent on the table. flicking his gaze from one paper to the other. writing on one sheet. he squints his eyes repeatedly. he winces a couple of times. he is speaking under his breath. mostly the speech is un-hearable except for a few words such as "five" or "seven"))
(69)

During this 69-second silence, Jim is bent over the sheet of paper. His silence, hunched posture, and facial expressions (squinted eyes, wincing) indicate that the task is more difficult for him than was explaining the velocity equation, where he quickly offered an answer. Ayush's extended silence as Jim works signals that what Jim is doing is okay in this moment. After more than a minute has passed, however,

**Ayush:** °↓okay°
(3)
**Ayush:** >could you tell me what yo:u're ↓doing?<
**Jim:** uh i=just plugged=in se:ven for the he:ight.
**Ayush:** okay=
**Jim:** =and=then use:d the uni:ts (.)↓ to see how they ↑>cancel out.<
(2)
**Ayush:** °umhm°
**Jim:** °mmhm°
(2.5)
**Jim:** so this is ↑seve:↓n::::
(1.2)
**Jim:** pre:ssu:↓re u↓nits:?
(0.5)
**Jim:** >what are the uni:ts< of pre:ssu:↓re ↑pa:sca:::l?
(0.7)
**Ayush:** umm::
(1)
**Ayush:** un- yea:h whatever
**Jim:** ↓°okay°=
**Ayush:** =↓°you know°
(0.9)
**Ayush:** pasca::l i thi:nk.
(0.7)
**Jim:** so i:ts se:ven=to fi:::ve the:
(0.9)
**Jim:** °(va:ries=i:n) he:ight (fro:m) fi:↓ve to seven°
**Ayush:** °o↑ka:y°
(0.3)
**Jim:** °(eh)°
(1.4)
**Ayush:** so::: un::
(2.5)
**Ayush:** °>so which one ↓is< mo:::re?°
**Jim:** >whi:ch one is< ↑mo::re
**Ayush:** umhum.

Ayush's utterance in the previous segment ("here's a problem with [hydrostatic pressure] equation") and Jim's plugging numbers into that equation indicate that the participants consider the hydrostatic pressure equation to be relevant to addressing the problem, thereby sustaining the earlier framing of the interview as a space in which Jim displays his proficiency with formal knowledge such as equations. This contrasts with a hypothetical alternative framing that foregrounds everyday/intuitive knowledge and hence invites a common-sense comparison of the pressure at two different depths.

In response to Ayush's question about which pressure is "more" (greater), Jim expresses confusion or uncertainty by repeating the question in a tentative tone. We see multiple possible explanations for this. First, Ayush's new question is discontinuous with Jim's immediately preceding query about the units of pressure. In addition, asking which pressure is greater could be perceived as discontinuous with Ayush's earlier utterance that foregrounded *comparing* the pressures at 7m and 5m; to Jim, "compare" need not mean "decide which is greater." The written prompt includes "compare" and decide "which is greater" as two separate statements, which may contribute to Jim seeing these as two different tasks. And again, there is evidence in Jim's hesitation and extended pauses that this question is difficult for him.

After 40 seconds, Ayush breaks into Jim's quiet working by asking what Jim is thinking. In the conversation that follows, an emotional tone of frustration builds:

| | |
|---|---|
| **Ayush:** | ((inaudible syllable)) wha:t a̲re y̲ou thi:nki:ng |
| **Jim:** | ↑trying ↓to thi:nk=how=to plug in the nu:m↓be::rs to °use° in both = |
| **Jim:** | =case:s to ↓↓see °(whats bigger)° |
| **Ayush:** | whi::ch number do you ↓want to- °a̲re y̲ou wo:ndering abo̲ut° |
| **Jim:** | ↓huh |
| **Ayush:** | ↑whi:ch nu:mbe:r ↓<are you wondering about?< |
| (0.5) | |
| **Jim:** | >i=am ↑ju:st↓ trying to like< fo:rmulate=a pro:blem °to pl[ug in°.] |
| **Ayush:** | [↑o↓ kay.] |
| **Jim:** | °yeah.° |
| (1) | |
| **Jim:** | °i've never seen=a (.)° pre:ssure pro:blem ↓before so:: °I (inaudible)= |
| **Jim:** | =°think.° |
| (0.5) | |
| **Ayush:** | o↑ka::y |
| (3.1) | |
| **Jim:** | °the water° ((very low volume and pitch)) |
| (0.9) | |
| **Ayush:** | if=you- if=you ↑nee:d any qua:ntities i=ca:n ↓°give those° to you= |
| **Jim:** | =↑wait. it- do:es u:nder wa:ter ↓does it mean they're nega:ti:ve? |

The frustrated tone is evidenced through actions of both Ayush and Jim. Ayush opens this segment by exhorting Jim to explain his thinking, which may suggest a sense of impatience on Ayush's part. Additionally, the pace of turn-taking is faster than it was in the preceding utterances, perhaps suggesting agitation from both Ayush and Jim. Finally, Jim's utterance "just trying to formulate a problem" sounds frustrated/irritated; he conveys a sense of wanting to be left alone to think.

Jim's utterances ("trying to think about" …) combined with his trailing-off sentences suggest that he might be having difficulty and that this task is unfamiliar, requiring caution. As we noted earlier, a framing of the activity as a space in which Jim displays proficiency with formal knowledge could potentially be layered with a threat to face. Jim and Ayush's interaction could suggest that they are aware of this (fast pace, offer to help, hedging by Jim, etc.).

Ayush's proposal to provide needed quantities combined with Jim's "wait" and subsequent question in the last line of the snippet above indicate a start of a new line of conversation, with Jim drawing attention to something new:

**Ayush:** if=you- if=you ↑nee:d any qua:ntities i=ca:n ↓°give those° to you=
**Jim:** =↑wait. it- do:es u:nder wa:ter ↓does it mean they're nega:ti:ve?
(1.9)
**Ayush:** ↑↑SO: ↓↓°its° ↑↑SET UP ↓°so° ↑That
((Jim sits back))
(0.3)
**Jim:** °hmm°
(0.4)
**Ayush:** eI:ch I:S the ↓di:stance below the wa:ter.
(0.4)
(then which)
**Jim:** °(that would) mean it's nega:ti:ve°
((tone here is neither a full question nor a period ending. Sort of seeking confirmation. Jim's gaze is on Ayush as he utters this))
(1.8)
**Ayush:** ↑um::
(2.2)
**Jim:** depe:nds=on what=your a:xes ↓a:re
**Ayush:** rI::ght. so in thi:s- ↓in thi:s eq↑ua:tion we:
(0.3)
(inaudible)
(1)
**Ayush:** the way eich is mentioned
(0.5)
**Ayush:** is that eich is defined a:s, going down from the water surface.
((Jim is looking at Ayush and nodding))
(4)
**Jim:** so I'll say five is bi::gger and seven's smaller

Jim interrupts Ayush's offer to supply "quantities" by asking if $h$, the depth under water, is negative. Ayush has previously answered Jim's questions promptly, but here there is a pause of 2.6 seconds before Ayush responds that "$h$ is the distance below the water." Notice that Ayush's answer does not mirror Jim's query. A mirroring response would have taken a form such as "…is negative" or "…is positive." On the surface, Ayush's response restates the definition of $h$; and to a physicist, this answer hints that $h$ should be taken as positive. But the response in itself does not specify the sign of $h$. Jim's response indicates that he takes Ayush's statement as confirmation that $h$ is negative, though with hesitant tone suggesting he might be seeking further confirmation. Ayush again hesitates, uttering a non-committal "umm" that serves to hold his conversation turn. It could also signal that Ayush is unsure about or unwilling to provide a direct answer to Jim's query. In a student–teacher interaction, such an "ummm" following a student's response could also suggest that the student has made a mistake. Jim offers another choice to which Ayush promptly replies. Ayush says "right" – in a tone of agreeing with Jim. But Jim's preceding utterance ("depends on what your axes are") allows for flexibility in choosing the sign of $h$; confirming "depends on what the axes are" could support both $h$ as positive and $h$ as negative. After Ayush's statement on $h$ as going "down" (emphasis added), Jim is silent for 4 seconds and he looks back to the paper. Jim ends this silence by offering a conclusion that pressure at a depth of 5 meters is greater than the pressure at a depth of 7 meters. His utterance starting with "so" could indicate that his answer is contingent on what he takes Ayush to be confirming – in this case that $h$ is negative. Still, the tentativeness of his tone suggests a lack of confidence in this conclusion. As Jim finishes this utterance, he looks up at Ayush, marking his response as complete for now and opening it up for possible evaluation:

**Ayush:** why would you say that? [tell me
**Jim:** cause] if it's going down ((Jim points at the paper briefly)) then its negative.
**Ayush:** what is negative? ((this follows very closely to the previous utterance; not the usual space between turns))
**Jim:** eich is negative ((Jim points to the paper with his pen and looks up as he finishes this utterance))
**Ayush:** oka::y
**Jim:** a:nd this is a smaller number ((Jim momentarily gazes up at Ayush)) and five is the bigger number ((uncertain tone))
**Ayush:** because of the nega:tive
**Jim:** Yeah.
**Ayush:** okay.
(1.7)

Here Jim is committing to the idea – through reiteration – that the pressure is greater at a depth of 5 meters because of the sign of $h$. There's some frustration in Jim's tone as he reiterates his reasoning that $h$ is negative. Ayush's "okay" suggests that the segment of talk is closing. Ayush then makes a bid to introduce new information:

**Ayush:** suppo:se I told you that nega:tive is actually built insi:de of aich
**Jim:** so it's a::bsolute value?
**Ayush:** so yeah. suppose i told you that that's how it works.(1.7)
**Jim:** well (unclear speech)
**Ayush:** like don't take the negative.(4.3)
**Jim:** hunh(4)
**Ayush:** would that change your conclu:sion?(3.9)
**Jim:** i think it wi::ll. bu:t ((Jim is looking down at the paper nodding his head))
**Ayush:** okay
**Jim:** it will.
**Jim:** cause if (aich's) positive, then ((Jim shrugs his shoulders)) seven's bigger than fi:ve
**Ayush:** okay.

((Jim continues to look down; once in between he flicks his gaze up at the ceiling; but seems to be thinking, not a pose of waiting for Ayush to make the next utterance; his lips move a bit as if he was speaking to himself under his breath))
(7.2)

Ayush poses the hypothetical that $h$ is positive (indicated by "suppose"). Jim doesn't immediately respond; he halts, is silent or says something unclear in low tones that we could not hear on the video. Ayush then rephrases the question ("like don't take the negative"), to which Jim responds with silence and "hunh." Jim's actions and speech exhibit some discomfort, confusion, or difficulty – some form of hesitation – in considering this hypothetical. Alternatively, Jim may be responding to Ayush by imagining the hypothetical world where $h$ is positive, and considering the myriad of possibilities. Either way, in this segment, through the hypothetical, we see the emergence of two mutually exclusive choices: (a) $h$ is negative and pressure is greater at a depth of 5 meters, or (b) $h$ is positive and pressure is greater at a depth of 7 meters. But the choices are asymmetric. The "$h$ is positive" is marked by the several turns of clarification and taken up as a hypothetical when Ayush asks, "would that change your conclusion?" and Jim says, "if [h] is positive." As the conversation proceeds, this dichotomy gains more weight.

**Ayush:** could you figure out (.) which one of those should be::? could you (.) °like° reason through which should it be:?
**Jim:** which it should ((Jim raises eyebrows)) be::? ((Jim's gaze is at Ayush as he leans back))
**Ayush:** like should the seven be mo::re than five or should the five be more than seven. ((Jim leans forward again with gaze on paper))

| Jim: | I mean ((Jim shrugs his shoulders)) mathematically ((Jim has a smirk on his face as he makes a sweeping gesture moving his right hand from his left side to his right; he is holding the pen in the hand)) seven is bigger than fi::ve.= |
|---|---|
| Ayush: | umhum |
| Jim: | =but if you put in a ne:gative ((Jim raises eyebrows)) then five is bigger than seven negative five is bigger than negative seven. |
| Ayush: | okay. |
| (4.5) | |

Ayush asks Jim if he can make the choice between the two alternatives. Jim's gestures, facial expressions, and tone suggest a sense of disbelief toward the hypothetical choice (*h* is positive) and that he considers the other choice (*h* is negative) as a more serious answer.

Ayush then makes a bid to redirect the conversation.

| Ayush: | suppose um:: let me ask you another question. so suppo:se uh there was uh a friend of yours in English. right. not doing physics.= |
|---|---|
| Jim: | okay. ((Jim is looking down at the paper; flicks gaze to Ayush momentarily then back to paper)) |
| Ayush: | =so doesn't really know know physics (uuun) equations kind of thing. unh could they have a:nswered (.) um this question? ((Jim scratches his chin with his fingers)) |
| (2.8) | |
| Jim: | ((Jim purses his lips)) this question? ((Jim points to the paper)) |
| Ayush: | just the question that, you know, suppose uun you ha- you know under water is the pressure greater than, less than, or equal to (.) you know at a depth of seven meters versus a depth of five meters. ((Jim lowers his head to his hand and then looks back up and sits back)) (1.8) could they answer that without (.) without really knowing physics? |
| Jim: | ((Jim shakes his head in a no; purses lips)) not unless ((Jim shrugs shoulders)) they have experience being underwater themse:lves. |
| Ayush: | oka:y:: |
| Jim: | but [If= |
| Ayush: | um] |
| Jim: | =they haven't that then no they can't ((Jim nods head in negative)) |
| Ayush: | okay- so- what do you mean when you said, they have experienced |
| Jim: | like they have actually been ((Jim gestures downward with his left hand)) under wate::r= |
| Ayush: | umhum |
| Jim: | =felt the pressu::re then they might know like a little bit about pressure (.) under water. |

| | |
|---|---|
| **Ayush:** | what kind- uuu |
| **Jim:** | like if they have gone like snorkeli::ng or (snorkeling) under water |
| **Ayush:** | so do you know what- what would they know? |
| **Jim:** | huh? like a rough estimate, like i- it felt ((brings his hands to the sides of his ears)) the pressure was higher when I was deeper.= |
| **Ayush:** | oka:y |
| **Jim:** | =or the pressure was lower when I was higher. ((Jim stretched his neck upward)) to the surface. |
| **Ayush:** | °oka:y.° |
| **Jim:** | that's what. But like actually working an equation, I think- I don't think they'd be able to do that. |

In clarifying his initial question, Ayush describes the hypothetical English friend as someone unfamiliar with physics and equations, the kind of formal knowledge that has been foregrounded in the interview so far. This distinction between the kind of knowledge relevant in the interview (so far) and the kind of knowledge possessed by the hypothetical friend could have consequences for how Jim responds. He starts by clarifying which question Ayush is referring to and Ayush clarifies by rephrasing the question to be about deciding whether the pressure at 7 m is "greater than, less than, or equal to" the pressure at 5 m. Ayush's utterance further indicates that the answer should be accessible to someone who doesn't know physics; in other words, Jim is being asked to generate knowledge that Ayush's speech marks as distinct and discontinuous from physics knowledge. Jim's response maintains this distinction by noting that the hypothetical friend could not answer the question unless they had experiences under water.

Jim then engages with the scenario by highlighting that the friend can draw on perceptual knowledge leading to an answer that would align with the earlier "$h$ is positive" hypothetical (though we don't see evidence that Jim associates these two responses), a hypothetical toward which Jim was skeptical. Jim ends by saying that the friend still would not be able to work through the equation, again calling attention to the difference between using formal knowledge and relying on perceptual knowledge. Thus, in the unfolding conversation, the two hypotheticals – the supposition that $h$ is positive and the reasoning given by a friend who doesn't know the relevant equations – are placed in contrast to the relevant formal knowledge, the hydrostatic pressure equation. Given the continually reinforced framing of the interview as a space in which formal knowledge is foregrounded, it makes sense that Jim is skeptical of the conclusions following from the two hypotheticals, conclusions that contradict the one he reached using formal knowledge.

Furthermore, the manner in which the hypothetical scenarios are posed by Ayush and taken up by Jim place perceptual knowledge in contrast to formal knowledge from equations.

| | |
|---|---|
| **Ayush:** | so so uh gi:ven that informa:tion, gi:ven that expe:rience, could they have, argued which pressure would be mo:re? the seven meters or five meters? |
| **Jim:** | °i mean° |
| **Ayush:** | not from equations maybe, but |
| **Jim:** | just from tha::t? |
| **Ayush:** | umhmm. |
| **Jim:** | i mean (.) they (.) cou:ld've ar:gued it. but. |
| **Ayush:** | what would they argue then? |
| **Jim:** | they could've (.) argued about their personal experience. like. one time I was like scuba divi::ng and I was like thirty feet below the water and the pressure was- it felt like (1.7) pressure was very hi::gh. like- I was just swimming and I was like a couple feet below the water and if pressure wasn't that much like °they could have (argued that).°((Jim shrugs his shoulders as he looks up)) |
| **Ayush:** | so then they would say that the seven meters is= |
| **Jim:** | is greater. ((Jim nods his head)) |
| **Ayush:** | =is greater |
| **Jim:** | yeah. but they are not taking the factor of negative si:gn. |
| **Ayush:** | okay |
| **Jim:** | or aich. |
| (2.4) | |

In this segment, the dichotomy between equations and perceptual knowledge gets reinforced. Ayush poses the friend's argument as emphasizing personal experience and excluding equation-based reasoning. Jim's response begins by highlighting the reliance on personal experiences and ends by noting again that the friend's argument ignores the sign of $h$ in the relevant equation. So, this interaction continues highlighting the dichotomy between the formal-knowledge-based conclusion and the hypothetical scenarios, and Jim's utterance "but they are not" marks the foregrounding of the formal-knowledge-based conclusion.

The dichotomy becomes more formalized and is made visible as Ayush asks whether the mathematics is telling something different than the friend's answer based on perception.

| | |
|---|---|
| **Ayush:** | so:, do you think the mathematics here is telling you something different. |
| **Jim:** | yeah |
| **Ayush:** | °kay° |
| **Jim:** | I think it is |
| **Ayush:** | oka:y oka:y. |

We can see this as a "speech act" (Austin, 2013), objectifying and making available in the discourse the "difference" between two stances, with at least one labeled "mathematics". (Later the other stance is labeled, again by Ayush, as "experience.") Jim agrees, and Ayush does not challenge this rift. (For example, Ayush could have stated that equations and perceptions need to align; instead he says "okay," which, at the very least, is a lack of opposition to the rift.) So, at least functionally in the conversation, the dichotomy is created and accepted by both Ayush and Jim. The conversation calcifies these two opposing coherences ($h$-negative, 5 m-greater, knowledge from equation vs. $h$-positive, 7 m-greater, perceptual knowledge) and the dichotomy between these coherences becomes an object in the conversation.

**Ayush:** so suppose you have to a:nswer this question on an exa:m. which one would you pi:ck? the experience one, or uh
**Jim:** mathematics
**Ayush:** or mathematics one.
**Jim:** I would pick mathematics.
**Ayush:** you would pick the mathematics.
**Jim:** °yeah°

Ayush's posing the choice in a hypothetical high-stakes situation (the exam) also has parallels to a speech act. The stark choice, posed and answered, draws a deeper rift between the positions. Before Ayush finishes asking the question, Jim *chooses* the "mathematics" answer, borrowing the earlier labeling proposed by Ayush for $h$ being negative and pressure being greater at 5 meters. Posing, labeling, and making a choice between the two alternatives reifies the gulf between knowledge from perception/everyday experiences and formal knowledge from physics equations. Crucially, both Ayush and Jim contribute to the construction of this epistemological rift. And thus, our analysis from an IA perspective challenges the attribution *to Jim* of an epistemological stance in which formal knowledge is distinguished from perceptual knowledge and is considered more trustworthy, even within a dynamic Knowledge in Pieces (KiP) model of contextual activation. Our Discussion section clarifies and defends this conclusion.

A few moments later, by contrast, Jim's utterances are not as explainable in terms of co-constructed framing of the interview and associated co-constructed epistemological stances/rifts.

[28:39]
**Ayush:** >can you tell me why?<
**Jim:** U::mm ((Jim leans back, smiles, and leans forward again)) because mathematics like for equations to be gi:ven to you, it has to be like the:ory, and it has to be fact bearing. so. fact applies for e::verything. ((moves his hand sweepingly on table)) it's like a law. it applies for every single ((again sweeps hand on table as if counting items)) (3.2)

situation you can be in. but like, experience sometimes, your perception is just different ((Jim shrugs his shoulders)) or you don't have the knowledge of that (.) course or anything so, i'll go with the ((Jim cocks his head to the left)) people who have like done a la::w and it is has worked time after time after ti:me.

In this segment Jim justifies choosing the "math" answer. The ideas that equations apply to a wide range of situations and that they are trustworthy because they have been tested were *not* emergent stances in the earlier interaction. In addition, Jim here reifies for himself the rift between equation-based and perception-based reasoning. For these reasons, at this point in the interview, we see warrants for attributing *to Jim* a locally coherent activation of epistemological and conceptual resources, as in Gupta & Elby (2011).

## Discussion

In this section, we first clarify what we're *not* arguing in the service of clarifying what we *are* arguing. Then we reflect on how our analysis contributes to explorations of the relation between cognitivist and interactional perspectives.

### What We Are Arguing, and What We Are Not

*We are not arguing that Jim's knowledge plays no role in the interaction before the 28 min mark. Nor are we simply fleshing out the KA account presented above.*

To clarify this point, we distinguish between the *location* of a knowledge element and its *activation and stabilization*. The former refers to ontology – where does a knowledge element "live?" – while the latter refers to the dynamics by which a knowledge element "turns on" and stays on.

Even in light of our interaction analysis, we think it makes sense to attribute *to Jim* the idea that *down is negative* during the focal episode, and to assert that the persistent activation of this knowledge element contributes to the unfolding conversation. Our interaction analysis highlights, however, that the triggering and stability of *down is negative* emerges from interactional dynamics by which (a) the participants co-construct a framing of the activity as foregrounding formal knowledge, particularly equations, and (b) *down is negative* gets linked to equation-based reasoning and to the conclusion that pressure is greater at 5 m – a local coherence of reasoning that the interaction distinguishes from a hypothetical coherence of reasoning in which $h$ is positive, perceptual reasoning is foregrounded, and the pressure is greater at 7 m. By this account, *down is negative* "lives" in Jim's head but is stabilized by framings and dynamics that are a property of the interaction, not a property of Jim.

This differs from the KA-based account outlined above, in which *down is negative* stabilizes and is stabilized in large part by the activation of components of Jim's cognitive ecology, which we toy modeled as *formal knowledge as distinct from perceptual knowledge, knowledge from authority*, and *math is trustworthy*. In our IA-based account, the activation of these epistemological resources is not needed to explain the stability of *down is negative* during the focal episode. Instead, in the context of the unfolding conversational dynamics around the pressure problem, embedded within a co-constructed space where display and use of formal knowledge is foregrounded, the stabilization of *down is negative* is something closer to an interactional achievement.

In response, a cognitivist could wonder: How does Jim participate in this "interactional achievement" if the corresponding epistemological resources are not activated? We sympathize with this sentiment. Indeed, we assume that a host of Jim's intellectual resources are activated during this interview – their dynamics intertwined with the interactional dynamics – forming a complex system. So yes, Jim must possess intellectual resources, including epistemological resources, whose activation enables him to engage in his interaction with Ayush. Our claim is much narrower: Jim's epistemological resources do not necessarily need to be activated in order to explain Jim's participation in the framing and the associated epistemological stance towards formal knowledge co-constructed by Ayush and Jim during the interview. In other words, the foregrounding of formal knowledge (specifically equations) and the linking of equation-based reasoning to *down is negative* are constructed by both Ayush and Jim, as spelled out above, not by Jim's knowledge that formal knowledge is trustworthy and differs from other forms of knowledge.

Of course, a KA advocate could claim that those interaction dynamics serve to activate and stabilize *knowledge from authority, formal knowledge as distinct from perceptual knowledge*, and *math is trustworthy*, which then help to stabilize *down is negative* and the reasoning associated with it. That was precisely our argument in Gupta & Elby (2011). But since the stability of *down is negative* and associated behaviors/utterances can be explained well by the framing and conversational dynamics discussed above, without needing to assume the activation of specific epistemological resources, Occam's razor favors the IA-based explanation.

### The IA-Based Account Opens Questions into the Sociogenesis (Ontogenesis?) of Cognitive Coherences

Our original analysis of Jim focused on explaining why he chooses formal knowledge over perceptual knowledge. To do so, we modeled which of Jim's epistemological resources were at play in various moments. Our IA-based reanalysis, by contrast, suggests that the fact that Jim has to make a choice *at all* between these two kinds of knowledge is largely because of the interactional dynamics. Ayush and Jim together create a situation where the two explanations conflict and Jim must choose and rationalize his choice and where the rationalization aligns with the activation of *formal knowledge as distinct from perceptual knowledge* and *math is trustworthy*. By this account, the dichotomy and choice between formal and perceptual knowledge is constructed interactionally, with part of the construction happening before *formal knowledge as distinct from perceptual knowledge* and *math is trustworthy* are activated.

This is consequential because science education researchers usually attribute such dichotomies entirely to students (Hammer, 1994; Gupta & Elby, 2011; Mestre, 2002). Discourses in science and in science education communities also reinforce these dichotomies (as argued by Warren, Ogonowski, & Pothier, 2005). Our reanalysis makes us wonder how often these dichotomies are constructed through interactions similar to the one between Ayush and Jim. Indeed, some elements of the interview point to the other places where this dichotomy could have been constructed for/with Jim.

For example, we recruited Jim from a "traditional" physics class taught by a physics faculty. Such classes often invite or at least fail to discourage a distinction between formal/equation-type reasoning and reasoning that relies on intuition or common sense (Hammer, 1989; Hutchison & Hammer, 2010; Lemke, 1990). When Jim reads a prompt that explicitly labels an equation as one he has seen in class, what aspects of his past experiences are elicited? How would our analysis change if we knew that his personal history included many instances of seeing contradictions between formal reasoning and perceptual knowledge, or conversely, if he expressed a long history of integrating between these two ways of knowing?

Our reanalysis, and the questions that arise from it, highlight the need to understand how these types of dichotomies/contradictions are generated and sustained over the course of students' histories. Unfortunately, we lack the data to explore how Jim's personal history interacts with the unfolding interactional dynamics in the interview. Nonetheless, our IA-based account of how the contradiction between formal and perceptual knowledge arises compels us to re-examine the decisions we make about what data to collect and how to combine data sources to build up claims.

### Compared to the KA-Based Account, the IA-Based Account Changes not Only the Emphasis On but Also the Ontology of "Context"

One might argue that the KA perspective already takes context into account and that the contribution of IA is to document the role of context more carefully. For instance, context was a central feature of Gupta & Elby's (2011) KA-based account: We argued that the activation and stabilization of *down is negative* is not just a property of Jim but of Jim *in the interview context*. So, our IA reanalysis does not "bring in" context to our previous account or simply unpack the context more thoroughly. Instead, the interaction analysis redefines what context *is*.

Within the cognitivist tradition, context forms the background within which knowledge dynamics unfold. For example, Parnafes (2007) documents how students use the word "fast" with one meaning (more distance per time) in the *context* of non-periodic motion but with a different meaning (higher frequency) in the *context* of periodic motion. *Context* here indicates the physical scenario under consideration. Lising and Elby (2005) argue that changing the physical location of the interview venue from the Physics to the Education building, along with other cues, shifted a student's epistemological stances and associated problem-solving behaviors. *Context* here refers to the physical setting and purpose of the interview.

Within IA, however, context is understood as more fine grained and dynamic. Every action or utterance forms the context within which the next action/utterance gains (in part) its meaning and marks (in part) how the previous action/utterance is taken up. Thus, in IA, context is not the locally static crucible within which talk/activity take place. Rather, context and talk/activity are understood as intimately intertwined and co-evolving *at the same timescale*.

Ironically, this difference between the KA and IA meanings of "context" highlights both the necessity and the utility of the IA perspective in understanding the activation and stabilization dynamics of knowledge elements. A fine-grained, dynamic notion of "context" highlights how typical knowledge analysis can miss important features of knowledge activation/stabilization dynamics. For example, our original knowledge analysis, which took "context" to be the "physics-y" interview context, could not fully explain why *down is negative* was stable during the focal episode but not during the interview as a whole. We instead explained that stability by attributing to Jim active epistemological resources about formal knowledge, even though evidence of their activation was weak when *down is negative* first became prominent. In the IA-based reanalysis, by contrast, the dynamically evolving "context" of the unfolding interaction between Jim and Ayush before and during the focal episode enabled us to explain the stability of *down is negative*. In this way, the IA-based reanalysis challenges our KA-based conclusion that Jim sticks with *pressure decreases with depth* and *down is negative* because of *his* epistemological stance in those moments. Further, the reanalysis challenges the attribution of *knowledge from authority* and the distinction between formal and perceptual knowledge as cognitive elements attributable solely to Jim. Our point is that the IA-based notion of "context" provides more explanatory power *about knowledge dynamics* than does a traditional KA-based treatment of "context." An IA moment-by-moment unpacking of a phenomenon such as an interview-based conversation helps us better understand the functioning of the cognitive machinery underlying the phenomenon. This shared emphasis on fine-timescale unpacking of such phenomena is, we feel, a pathway through which IA and KA can find common ground and reach higher peaks.

## *Have We "Integrated" KA and IA?*

We don't think there is a clean answer. However, our "IA-based" explanation of Jim's persistence in asserting that down is negative and that pressure is greater at shallower depths provides a concrete example in which to ground discussion of what would count as a KA–IA integrated explanation.

At the level of analytical tools, our explanation is integrated. Our new analysis incorporates the activation of *down is negative* in Jim's head as part of an explanation of his behavior, an attribution supported by KA-based tools. Our new analysis also incorporates analytical tools and explanatory constructs from IA, most notably close attention to the dynamic "context" constituted by the unfolding interaction, notions of framing as "living" in the interaction (not in participants' heads), and close attention to tone, gesture, pauses, turn-taking, and other conversation-analytic indicators. In this particular case, our explanation gives fairly equal weight to KA and IA constructs, with neither perspective acting as the foundation on which the other is layered. However, we do not think that "integrated" explanations need to be equally weighted. In some cases, IA may provide more explanatory power, with KA constructs providing additional insights that can be layered onto a foundation built from IA. In other cases, KA may provide more explanatory power, with IA constructs layered onto a foundation built from KA. What makes an explanation "integrated," in our view, is that (1) both knowledge analysis and interaction analysis are conducted; (2) the final explanation includes insights arising from both perspectives; and (3) the relative weighting of the two perspectives arises from considerations of simplicity and explanatory power, NOT from a priori preferences.

Philosophically inclined readers will notice that we are coming dangerously close to saying "let the data determine which explanation is best," which seems to rest on the philosophically untenable notion of a theory-unladen evaluation of competing explanations. We acknowledge that a researcher's theoretical inclinations will influence which mix of IA and KA tools/constructs she deems best suited for explaining a given phenomenon. Our point is more nuanced. We want the main theoretical inclinations on which the decision rests to arise, as much as possible, from the researcher's beliefs and intuitions about explanatory power and simplicity, beliefs and intuitions that are undoubtedly entangled with but not simply deduced from the researcher's commitments to KA vs. IA. In this way, researchers' decisions about how much weight to give IA and KA in a given explanation are not "objective" but nonetheless arise from more than just the researcher's preference for IA or KA. This chapter illustrates how researchers can indeed make these judgments. The first two authors are steeped in KA, but considerations of explanatory power and simplicity contributed to their sense of joy with an explanation that relies substantially on IA constructs and even overturns aspects of their initial knowledge analysis.

Still, in a sense, our explanation of the focal episode is not integrated. At the level of ontology, our explanation is at best "mixed" and at worst incoherent. "Mixed," because it combines elements derived from incommensurable (Greeno, 1997) theoretical perspectives grounded in different worldviews about the ontology and genesis of knowing. At least for now, explanations drawing on both IA and KA constructs cannot be ontologically integrated; they are at best ontologically mixed. So, the issue becomes, is "mixed" productive, or is it just a kinder word for "incoherent?"

To explore this issue, we make an analogy with the field of cosmology, which employs tools and constructs from both general relativity theory and quantum theory. General relativity and quantum theory are at least as incommensurable as the IA and KA perspectives; the fundamental fields posed by the two theories are ontologically distinct kinds of things, and the two theories have not been successfully reconciled into a grand unified theory. Yet, cosmologists forge ahead in using both theories to create new models and analytical tools leading to explanations of the development and current behavior of the universe. These explanations are ontologically mixed, not ontologically integrated. But these explanations provide insight; no one argues that cosmologists should put their work on hold until general relativity and quantum theory have been unified. We think the same should go for learning scientists creating ontologically mixed explanations drawing on KA and IA. In creating such explanations, both KA and IA advocates must relax some of their ontological commitments. If cosmologists can do it, then so can we.

## Acknowledgments

We thank "Jim" for volunteering for the interview that provided data for this paper. We thank the editors for reviewing the paper and providing feedback. We also thank Shulamit Kapon and Reed Stevens for discussions and for providing feedback on the analysis presented in the paper. This manuscript is based on work supported by the National Science Foundation grant EEC-0835880.

## Appendix A

Below we provide a glossary of symbols used for transcription in the interaction analysis portion of the paper.

|  |  |
|---|---|
| (( )) | Text within the double parentheses refers to facial expressions, gestures, body posture, etc. as noticed by the transcriber in the video data |
| : | Colon indicates a prolonged syllable with the number of colons indicating roughly the extent of prolongation |
| > < | This use of brackets indicates that the bracketed text is uttered faster than the surrounding speech |
| < > | This use of brackets indicates that the bracketed text is uttered slower than the surrounding speech |
| ° ° | Speech within two degree signs was uttered softer than surrounding talk |
| ↑ | Up arrows indicate a sharp rise in pitch (more than one arrow indicates a sharper rise) |
| ↓ | Down arrows indicate a sharp fall in pitch (more than one arrow indicates a sharper fall) |
| = | Equals sign indicates no break or pause in speech. This is used to indicate continuation of speech across multiple lines (e.g., when lines are broken on the page because of fixed page width, or in case of overlapping speech where one speaker's utterance was continuous) |
| Underline | Syllables that are stressed are underlined |
| Vertical alignment | Used to show overlapping speech from two speakers |
| Capitalization | Used to indicate stress in the speech |
| Punctuation | Used to indicate intonation, so a period at the end of a word would indicate an intonation signaling the end of a sentence or utterance. Not all utterances end with a period intonation |
| (.) | A period inside parentheses marks a short untimed pause |
| – | A long dash indicates an long untimed pause |
| (2.5) | A number in parentheses indicates a timed pause, with the number representing the number of seconds (resolution of a tenth of a second) of silence. |
| [ | left-box parenthesis indicates the onset of overlapping speech |
| ] | right-box parenthesis indicates the end of overlapping speech |
| - | short dash indicates cut-off of speech |

## References

Austin, J. L. (2013). Performative utterances. In M. Ezcurdia & R. J. Stainton (Eds.), *The semantics–pragmatics boundary in philosophy* (pp. 21–31). Peterborough, ON: Broadview Press.

Conlin, L. D., Gupta, A., Scherr, R. E., & Hammer, D. (2007). The dynamics of students' behaviors and reasoning during collaborative physics tutorial sessions. *AIP Conference Proceedings*, 951(1), 69–72.

diSessa, A. A. (1993). Toward an epistemology of physics. *Cognition and Instruction*, 10(2/3), 105–225.

Frank, B. W., & Scherr, R. E. (2012). Interactional processes for stabilizing conceptual coherences in physics. *Physical Review Special Topics-Physics Education Research*, 8(2), 020101.

Goffman, E. (1974). *Frame analysis: An essay on the organization of experience.* Cambridge, MA: Harvard University Press.

Goodwin, C., & Heritage, J. (1990). Conversation analysis. *Annual Review of Anthropology*, 19, 283–307.

Greeno, J. G. (1997). On claims that answer the wrong questions. *Educational Researcher*, 26(1), 5–17.

Gupta, A., & Elby, A. (2011). Beyond epistemological deficits: Dynamic explanations of engineering students' difficulties with mathematical sense-making. *International Journal of Science Education*, 33(18), 2463–2488.

Hall, R. (1996). Representation as shared activity: Situated cognition and Dewey's cartography of experience. *Journal of the Learning Sciences*, 5(3), 209–238.

Hammer, D. (1989). Two approaches to learning physics. *The Physics Teacher*, 27(9), 664–670.

Hammer, D. (1994). Epistemological beliefs in introductory physics. *Cognition and Instruction*, 12(2), 151–183.

Hammer, D., Elby, A., Scherr, R. E., & Redish, E. F. (2005). Resources, framing, and transfer. In J. P. Mestre (Ed.), *Transfer of learning from a modern multidisciplinary perspective* (pp. 89–120). Greenwich, CT: Information Age Publishing.

Hofer, B. K. (2001). Personal epistemology research: Implications for learning and teaching. *Educational Psychology Review*, 13(4), 353–383.

Hofer, B. K., & Pintrich, P. R. (2002). *Personal epistemology: The psychology of beliefs about knowledge and knowing.* Mahwah, NJ: Lawrence Erlbaum.

Hutchison, P., & Hammer, D. (2010). Attending to student epistemological framing in a science classroom. *Science Education*, 94(3), 506–524. doi:10.1002/sce.20373.

Jefferson, G. (2004). Glossary of transcript symbols with an introduction. *Pragmatics and Beyond: New Series*, 125, 13–34.

Jordan, B., & Henderson, A. (1995). Interaction analysis: Foundations and practice. *The Journal of the Learning Sciences*, 4(1), 39–103.

Lemke, J. L. (1990). *Talking science: Language, learning, and values* (Vol. 1). Norwood, NJ: Ablex.

Lising, L., & Elby, A. (2005). The impact of epistemology on learning: A case study from introductory physics. *American Journal of Physics*, 73, 372–382.

Mestre, J. P. (2002). Probing adults' conceptual understanding and transfer of learning via problem posing. *Journal of Applied Developmental Psychology*, 23(1), 9–50. doi:10.1016/S0193-3973(01)00101-0.

Miles, M. B., & Huberman, A. M. (1984). *Qualitative data analysis: A sourcebook of new methods.* Beverly Hills, CA: Sage.

Parnafes, O. (2007). What does "fast" mean? Understanding the physical world through computational representations. *Journal of the Learning Sciences*, 16(3), 415–450.

Rosenberg, S., Hammer, D., & Phelan, J. (2006). Multiple epistemological coherences in an eighth-grade discussion of the rock cycle. *Journal of the Learning Sciences*, 15(2), 261–292.

Russ, R. S., Lee, V. R., & Sherin, B. L. (2012). Framing in cognitive clinical interviews about intuitive science knowledge: Dynamic student understandings of the discourse interaction. *Science Education*, 96(4), 573–599.

Scherr, R. E., & Hammer, D. (2009). Student behavior and epistemological framing: Examples from collaborative active-learning activities in physics. *Cognition and Instruction*, 27(2), 147–174.

Stivers, T., & Sidnell, J. (2005). Introduction: Multimodal interaction. *Semiotica*, 156, 1–20.
Tannen, D. (1993). *Framing in discourse*. New York: Oxford University Press.
Tannen, D., & Wallat, C. (1987). Interactive frames and knowledge schemas in interaction: Examples from a medical examination/interview. *Social Psychology Quarterly*, 50(2), 205–216. doi:10.2307/2786752.
Van de Sande, C. C., & Greeno, J. G. (2012). Achieving alignment of perspectival framings in problem-solving discourse. *Journal of the Learning Sciences*, 21(1), 1–44.
Warren, B., Ogonowski, M., & Pothier, S. (2005). "Everyday" and "scientific": Re-thinking dichotomies in modes of thinking in science learning. In R. Nemirovsky, A. Rosebery, J. Solomon, & B. Warren (Eds.), *Everyday matters in science and mathematics: Studies of complex classroom events* (pp. 119–148). Mahwah, NJ: Lawrence Erlbaum Associates.

# 11
# ENSEMBLE LEARNING AND KNOWING

Developing a Walking Scale Geometry Dilation Strategy

*Jasmine Y. Ma*

While typical formal schooling is generally more concerned with the learning of individuals, much of human activity takes place in groups, and little research focuses on ensemble learning, where activity and learning *necessarily* occurs in groups and is treated as a property of groups. For this reason, an analysis of the knowledge developed in the course of ensemble learning should focus, at least in part, on the learning of the group. A common theoretical assumption of Interaction Analysis is that "knowledge and action are fundamentally social in origin, organization, and use, and are situated in particular social and material ecologies" (Jordan & Henderson, 1995, p. 41); an Interaction Analysis takes as given that knowledge under development in a setting is inextricably tied to the exchanges between members of the group, as well as to the social, cultural, and material resources available to and recruited by them. In the spirit of exploring the possibilities of treating knowledge and learning as an ensemble property, I offer the analysis of the learning of a group of students solving a geometry task designed to be completed by multiple individuals together. As an extreme example of ensemble learning, one where the task was designed to be difficult or impossible to complete individually, I hope to provide a useful comparative case as fodder for discussion regarding the knowledge and learning of multiple individuals in interaction. I present a multimodal Interaction Analysis of an episode of a group's problem-solving activity. In their insightful commentary to this chapter, Conlin and Hammer extend the exploration by viewing the case through the lens of Knowledge Analysis.

The analysis of the learning of the ensemble activity presented in this chapter follows the work of others who have very deliberately expanded their units of analysis from individuals to groups and other resources in the setting. Specifically, I draw from Cobb, Stephan, McClain, and Gravemeijer (2001) in their thinking about emergent classroom mathematical practices, and Hutchins' (1995a) distributed cognition approach to more explicitly account for representations and material resources.

Cobb and his group (2001) felt that, given their design orientations for classroom mathematics learning, it was important to be able to characterize the collective learning of a classroom community in order to make design conjectures or claims about individual student learning, necessarily situated in the activity of the classroom community. Rather than focus on the historically developed ways of joining or being in an established community or discipline, they adapted the sociocultural idea of "cultural practice" to account for the local, emergent activity of teachers and students in a particular classroom. They analyzed the collective learning of a classroom community by attending to "normative taken-as-shared ways of talking and reasoning" (p. 119) at three levels: classroom norms (participation structure; they cite Erickson, 1986), socio-mathematical norms (related to mathematics in particular), and classroom mathematical practices (related to a specific topic of mathematics).

Hutchins' (e.g., 1995a, 2010) distributed cognition approach is a different, though related, treatment of a social analysis of knowledge. Cobb and his colleagues (2001) acknowledged the contribution of theories of distributed cognition to their work. However, Hutchins (1995a) resisted attributing particular forms of knowledge, memory, or cognition to individuals based on observations of activity. Instead, he argued that the whole setting (for example, the cockpit of a commercial airplane or the bridge of an aircraft carrier) should be taken as the cognitive system. Analysis, in alignment with the cognitive science view of cognition as computation, followed "the creation, transformation, and propagation of representational states" (p. 49). Hutchins (2010) argued that "cognitive science made a fundamental category error when it mistook the properties of a person in interaction with a social and material world for the cognitive properties of whatever is inside the person" (p. 91). Larger systems may have cognitive properties that are irreducible to individuals within the system. Additionally, an advantage of this expanded unit of analysis is that many of the representations and actions of the cognitive process are directly observable in activity.

Following Cobb and colleagues, I track the emergent mathematical practices of the group as they solve problems together. However, like Hutchins, I make claims only about the cognition and learning of the group as a whole, rather than as individuals. This is not to claim that there is not individual knowledge or mental activity in the heads of individuals. Instead, the focus on the activity of the group highlights the problem-solving accomplishments and learning of the three students in interaction; the developing representational tools; and the contributions of the material resources, including students' bodies, available in the setting. Over the course of the analysis, it is inevitable that the contributions of particular individuals and materials are highlighted. However, overall, the analysis provides insight only into the ensemble as a unit of analysis. Additionally, I argue that the accomplishments and learning of the ensemble would not be possible given solely the knowledge of any given individual (or the properties of any material resources) in the episode. The problem-solving strategy carried out in the episode below is a collective accomplishment. The analysis will show how it came about.

I focus on questions of whether or not the group is learning, what they are learning, and how. Individuals within the group see, know, and learn very different things, but by the end of the task, the group has the capacity to perform the dilation of a geometric figure, which it did not have at the start. I take a sociocultural, interactional, and embodied stance on learning and knowledge. From a sociocultural and interactional perspective, learning is a trajectory of participation in activities within communities of practice, and knowing is the ability to perform tasks and solve problems in ways valued by that community, aligned with the goals of the group, in coordination with its tools, technologies, and representational systems, and in ways distributed across people and practices (Greeno & Middle School Mathematics through Applications Project Group, 1998; Hall, 1996; Lave, 1988). Following the traditions of conversation and interaction analysis, the analysis foregrounds how participants are making sense of ongoing activity (and therefore their learning) in moment-to-moment, unfolding interactions (Goffman, 1964; Sacks, Schegloff, & Jefferson, 1974; Schegloff, 1991; Stevens, 2010). I pay deliberate attention not just to talk in interaction but to bodies, materials, and spatial relations as well, in an attempt to represent a richly multimodal theory of interaction, learning, and knowledge. From an embodied stance, whole bodies are actors in and resources for learning and knowing, not just for doing (Hall, Stevens, & Torralba, 2002; Nemirovsky & Ferrara, 2009; Núñez, Edwards, & Filipe Matos, 1999). The analysis in this chapter combines these views to present an example of multimodal interaction analysis that takes seriously the role of multiple actors, whole bodies, and other material resources as constituent parts of learning and knowledge.

## Setting

The focal episode of the chapter follows a group of three high-school students completing a large-scale geometry task outdoors on a university campus lawn using everyday materials such as ropes, lawn flags, and flagging tape. I call this type of task *Walking Scale Geometry* (WSG), to emphasize the engagement of students' whole bodies in motion during problem solving, using the ground as a "drawing" surface. Participants are not allowed to engage in problem solving using paper and pencil; instead, they use their bodies and other everyday materials as representational tools.

I draw from part of a design experiment (Brown, 1992; Cobb, Confrey, diSessa, Lehrer, & Schauble, 2003) that introduced a geometry task setting for secondary students that deliberately disrupted targeted aspects of typical classroom activity (Ma, 2012, 2014). The geometry task setting was designed to drastically alter the setting of problem solving so as to support more diverse opportunities to learn by inviting students to engage in geometry activity in novel, sensible (to them) ways.

The WSG setting was designed to support conceptual agency. Because of the scale and available materials of WSG, students needed to adopt new tools for drawing, representing, and completing mathematical procedures. They no longer had paper, pencils, rulers, protractors, or compasses, and could no longer engage by filling out solutions to problems on, for example, worksheets. Instead, students were asked to reason with and about everyday material objects and their bodies, and find ways to mathematize them. Additionally, individual students' perspectives on the same geometric objects were radically different. Not only were students much smaller in comparison to the objects, they had to view them from within, rather than from a birds-eye view as they did when working at paper-and-pencil scale. As a consequence, judging whether constructed lines were straight or parallel, or whether angles had familiar degree measures (e.g., 90 degrees) became problematic, inviting or requiring new techniques for making or judging these mathematical properties.

WSG was also designed to support access to participation for all students. Students were no longer able to draw and manipulate the geometric representations individually because of the scale of the figures and the students' perspectives. The large size of the figures made the materials difficult to manipulate and fix as inscriptions. Students standing within or alongside the figures did not generally have the same view as others. This meant a figure looked significantly different to each individual, and they needed to coordinate and assemble varying perspectives in order to reach agreement.

At walking scale, the division of labor of geometry problem solving was distributed so that individual solutions to tasks were difficult, if not impossible. Students had to work together and communicate effectively to develop, negotiate, and accomplish their goals. WSG was designed to support ensemble learning (Hall & Ma, 2011), where learning must be done together. Students were held accountable to each other to participate and to coordinate access to participation for others in their group in order to complete tasks.

The episode below took place in a summer enrichment course (SEC) held on a university campus, centered on the theme of spatial reasoning and analysis. The 12 students in the course had known each other for only one day before engaging in this task, and had spent just a half-hour prior working on similar tasks together. While general norms of school mathematics were clearly in play, the SEC setting of the episode produced a complex dynamic of informal learning and exploration, untethered to the regimes of discipline and assessments typically found in school. The students, coming from different schools and grade levels, actively negotiated participation norms in ways apparent to the research team, who served as instructors for the course.

**FIGURE 11.1** Tahir, Natalie, and Lauryn stand by their original WSG quadrilateral, made of flagging tape. Lawn flags mark the four vertices.

The three students in the episode, Lauryn, Natalie, and Tahir (pictured in Figure 11.1), all had successful histories of participation in school mathematics, and demonstrated positive mathematics identities. Natalie was a rising 10th-grader and had already completed a year of high-school-level geometry before SEC. Lauryn and Tahir were rising 9th-graders, and had not. Over the course of the episode, various researchers dropped by to check on the group's progress. Nate carried the video camera and was present throughout. Other researchers who appear in the transcript include Rogers, Jasmine, and Jillian.

## Dilating a WSG Quadrilateral

Before the start of the episode, the group had made a large quadrilateral out of flagging tape (Figure 11.1). The three had wanted to make a trapezoid, but Natalie pointed out that it was only "trapezoid-like" and "trapezoid-ish" because, as Lauryn explained, "we didn't measure it exactly." Now they were at the beginning of solving a problem involving scaling their quadrilateral 1.5 times. Natalie quickly proposed a dilation strategy that she vaguely remembered learning in school. It involved choosing, at random, a point to be the center of dilation, then stretching pieces of tape from that point out through each vertex of the quadrilateral. The length of each of these "spokes" (Tahir's term, later when describing their inscription) would be 1.5 times the distance from the center of dilation to the relevant vertex. The endpoints of the spokes would be the vertices of the new quadrilateral (Figure 11.2).

Natalie's explanations of her dilation strategy were not sufficient to convince Lauryn and Tahir, even though she attempted to describe her idea many times.

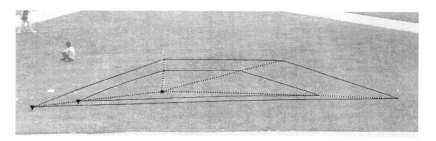

**FIGURE 11.2** The group's final drawing, highlighted to clarify the dilation strategy. Flagging tape has been retraced for visibility. Original and dilated quadrilaterals are traced with solid line segments, while "spokes" are dotted. The center of dilation is labeled with a star. The vertices (new and old) the group worked with during the episode here are labeled with triangles.

Lauryn and Tahir wanted to scale each side of the quadrilateral 1.5 times, and the group initially began this process by producing one new side. Natalie was dissatisfied with this strategy, since simply scaling each side of the quadrilateral would not guide the group in arranging them so as to produce angles congruent to those in the original. Lauryn and Tahir had not considered this aspect of their plan, and Natalie had some trouble explaining her concern to the other two. After some disagreement, and the prompting of a researcher (Nate), Lauryn and Tahir agreed to try Natalie's strategy, although they were still reluctant. Lauryn and Tahir not only did not know how their mathematical goal (scaling their quadrilateral 1.5 times) and envisioned plan (making each side longer by a factor of 1.5) related to what Natalie wanted to do, but they also did not have a sense of Natalie's plan with respect to material manipulations. It is worth noting that Natalie had not fully formulated her plan yet either. She was explicit that she was not sure how much to dilate the distance from the center of dilation to the original vertex in order to find the new vertices. As the group worked, it also became apparent that the details of implementing the dilation of each spoke were still under development.

The episode is divided into three excerpts below. Each excerpt begins with a brief summary of what to expect, then the transcript. Following the transcript, I describe the progress of the group, focusing on talk, bodily engagements, and material manipulations, along with the meanings they take on in the unfolding interaction. This will provide a moment-to-moment accounting for how this part of the dilation strategy was accomplished. Following the three excerpts, I make some general comments about the contributions of components of the system to the group's learning.

## Excerpt 1

As the episode opens, the group was beginning to try Natalie's dilation strategy. They already had a strip of green tape that had been measured to be 1.5 times the length of one side of the quadrilateral. Natalie had already placed a flag inside the quadrilateral as their center of dilation, but not near what might be considered to be the center of the figure. In this first excerpt,[1] Lauryn and Tahir tried to engage in implementing the strategy and make sense of it at the same time. Natalie alternated between responding to their questions and statements that did not align with her plan, and trying to direct their actions to carry out her plan.

[254] Natalie: Ok. Let's just try it. Ok(h)ay.
[255] Lauryn: [Are we gonna use the same length? ((holding the green tape that was just measured to be 1.5 times the length of the side, and handing one end to Natalie))
[256] Natalie: [Guess we can use this to measure.
[257] Lauryn: Cause this is [the one] and a half,=
[258] Natalie: [Well,
[259] Tahir: =That's not the center point though.
[260] Natalie: It doesn't need to be. You can dilate from any point. Just as long as you go out the same distance from ea- ((kneels down at the flag at the center of dilation with her end of the green tape in her hand)) So like make this line go out from ((points to the vertex between her and Lauryn)) that point?
[261] Lauryn: What?
[262] Natalie: Like(h),
[263] Tahir: Cross this ((points to green tape)) over here ((points to flag marking the vertex)) (on) the flag- [(front)] flag
[264] Natalie: [Yeah. Okay.=
[265] Lauryn: =Like that?=
[266] Natalie: =Put it to the ground? And hold it there? And then- ((addressing Tahir)) could you like, ((points to vertex)) hold it- [°there?]
[267] Tahir: [(Yeah. Like here?) ((<Figure 11.3, Panel A> kneels down and holds green tape down at vertex with right hand))
[268] Natalie: Yes. ((stands up with her end of the tape and walks toward vertex)) Okay. Okay ((backs up and kneels down again near center of dilation)) sorry. ((microphone transmitter falls off)) Yikes! Okay. And then like, here. Loosen up just a tad? Just so it can like, pull out here ((Tahir lifts his fingers a little))? Okay. Yah. And then like, ((walks with her end of the tape to the vertex, puts it down by Tahir's hand)) find whatever half of this, is? Like hold that tight ((Tahir puts his hand on the tape)) there too? ((steps back, pulling the doubled tape through her hand until it is taut <Figure 11.3, Panel B>)) Okay. ((puts down green tape)) So we're probably gonna have to keep ((picks up yellow rope that's nearby on the ground, and takes the end of it to the center of dilation flag)), like this just to make sure we're on the same line. So put- ((points at yellow rope)) the- yellow rope ((Tahir picks up yellow rope with left hand)) like ((points at the vertex)) over there ((Tahir starts moving the yellow rope toward the vertex)) too? But like make sure it can still reach- ((pulls back on the yellow rope)) eheh(hhh) it's mostly,
[269] Tahir: Yeah, the rope is kinda tied [(together)]
[270] Natalie: [It's okay, jus::s- I think it's better now ((Tahir stands up and walks over to where the rest of the yellow rope lies in a tangled ball)), cause-

Ensemble Learning and Knowing  299

**FIGURE 11.3** Still frames from Excerpt 1. Panel A: Tahir kneels down to hold the green tape at the vertex. Panel B: Natalie pulls the doubled green tape taut.

As Lauryn handed Natalie the end of the green tape that they had just measured to be 1.5 times the length of the side, the two spoke at the same time, at cross-purposes. Lauryn, handing Natalie one end of the green tape, asked, "Are we gonna use the same length? Cause this is the one and a half" [255, 257]. The green tape was the new side that they had produced earlier in the first, aborted, strategy. To Lauryn, it was still the side of the new quadrilateral, measured to be 1.5 times the length of the corresponding side on the original. She was asking if they would use it, since it had already been measured. Meanwhile, Natalie no longer thought of it as a part of their new quadrilateral, but just a long piece of tape that they could "use … to measure" [256] where a new vertex of the quadrilateral would go.

Tahir, still unsure that this plan would work, pointed out that the flag (their center of dilation) was not at the center of the quadrilateral. Natalie claimed that it did not have to be, but did not explain why, mathematically. She only answered him in terms of the rules of the procedure she remembered, and did not even complete her thought [260]. She knelt down with her end of the green tape at the flag, interrupting herself to tell Lauryn to pull it taut so it would stretch through a nearby vertex ("make this line go out from that point?" [260]). Lauryn asked, "What?" leading Tahir to translate, telling her to "Cross this over here (on) the flag- (front) flag" [263], pointing to the green tape ("this"), then to the vertex of the quadrilateral that was between Lauryn and Natalie ("over here on the flag"). Once Lauryn did this, Natalie asked her to put the tape to the ground and hold it there, and asked Tahir to hold the tape at the front flag. They had now produced a line segment between the center of dilation and the vertex. In order to find the new vertex, they needed to extend this line segment by half its own length. Another way to say this is that they had traced, with the green tape, the distance from the center of dilation to the first vertex. The new vertex would be half this distance beyond the old vertex, in the same direction.

In her instructions to Lauryn, Natalie used some mathematical language to refer to parts of the materials they were using ("So like make this line go out from that point?" [260]). Lauryn did not know what Natalie wanted her to do, and Tahir revoiced the instruction for her. Tahir's version of the instructions substituted gestures and language referring to the materials ("Cross *this* over here (on) the flag" [263]) for the mathematical entities that Natalie referred to ("this line," and "that point"). Natalie approved of Tahir's revision of her direction, and Lauryn completed the action.

This is not to say that Lauryn does not know what a point or line is, or that she was not familiar with the group's now established practice of representing points with flags and lines with tape. However, it was not clear to Lauryn which tape-as-line and which flag-as-point Natalie was talking about. Additionally, with her still-developing understanding of Natalie's strategy, and her lingering interpretation of the green tape as one of the sides of the new quadrilateral, it would not make sense to place it where Natalie was asking her to place it. However, Tahir's translation allowed Lauryn to engage with everyday language and objects in order to execute the direction, even if she had not yet made mathematical sense of it. In this way, both Lauryn and Tahir had access to participating in the task even as they were still making sense of the solution strategy. The everyday materials and manipulations became resources for the two to engage, and therefore to have access to the mathematics that Natalie was proposing. At the same time, Natalie was able to obtain Lauryn and Tahir's help to try out her strategy, even if she did not yet have a clear plan for how to carry it out.

Natalie began to find half the distance from the center of dilation to the vertex by bringing her end of the green tape over to Tahir and asking him to hold it. She then backed up a few steps, holding the now doubled-over green tape. In backing up she was able to pull this until it was taut. Then she placed it down on the ground. At this point Natalie decided that they should use the yellow rope that was lying on the ground "just to make sure we're on the same line" [268]. While Natalie had a general plan about both how they would dilate the quadrilateral and how they would find the new corresponding vertices, the exact actions they would execute were still under development for her. In particular, she was still figuring out how to find 1.5 times the distance from the center of dilation to the original quadrilateral vertex. She wanted to use the yellow rope as a visible trace of this distance, and they continued to use it throughout the task, even though it was mathematically unnecessary. The yellow rope was mostly in a tangled ball, and Tahir stood up to untangle it.

## *Excerpt 2*

As Tahir abandoned his post at the vertex to deal with the yellow rope, Natalie took the opportunity to check in with Nate for reassurance. Lauryn and Tahir took the opportunity to express their confusion and resistance to this strategy further. In this excerpt, Natalie repeatedly asked Nate if her idea was "stupid," while Lauryn and Tahir struggled to make sense of Natalie's plan. Other researchers also join the group to check in on their progress.

| [271] | | *((Natalie looks back at Nate.))* |
|---|---|---|
| [272] | Natalie: | I feel like I'm like, doing something really stupid. |
| [273] | Tahir: | I don't think either of us really understand what you're doing. |
| [274] | Lauryn: | Yeah I'm not really, |
| [275] | Natalie: | You know like dilating on a, grid? Like when you get like a triangle and you pick a point in the center and you go out with your ruler? To like make it bigger? Like |
| [276] | | *((Lauryn shrugs.))* |
| [277] | Natalie: | Like I don't know how to like describe it if, *((looks back at Nate again.))* |
| [278] | Nate: | Just keep trying it, see what happens. |
| [279] | Natalie: | Ok. |
| [280] | Tahir: | I thought we were gonna like add onto this *((sweeps arm along the side of the quadrilateral that they had originally already scaled))* and make it a bigger trapezoid. |
| [281] | Natalie: | Well it's like easier cause now we don't have to like mess with, angles. So just like, *((laughs))*. |
| [282] | | *((Rogers walks over with a microphone for Lauryn.))* |
| [283] | Natalie: | I feel like I'm, being stupid. Ok. So just like, |
| [284] | Tahir: | (This is a) very tangled rope. |
| [285] | Natalie: | (hh)Yeah(hh). I don't even know if this is like, half. *((Picks up the green and unfolds it, pulling it back to the center flag.))* Could you loosen up on it a little, like, step closer just a tiny bit. Ok there. That's good. |
| [286] | Tahir: | (I don't see how to untangle this rope.) |
| [287] | Natalie: | Yeah(h) |

| | | |
|---|---|---|
| [288] | Tahir: | I don't even think it's tangled I think it's just really like, [()]. |
| [289] | Lauryn: | [So how is this gonna, (1s) like, |
| [290] | Natalie: | ((sighs, looks back at Nate)) Well I don't know yet. |
| [291] | Lauryn: | Yeah. |
| [292] | Natalie: | Well I mean like, I don't know what like the, [growth] factor is supposed to be. |
| [293] | Lauryn: | [Wow, from this angle, our sides are really off. |
| [294] | Tahir: | (yeah) |
| [295] | Natalie: | Yeah they are. |
| [296] | Lauryn: | I didn't notice that before. |
| [297] | Natalie: | ((Looks back at Nate again.)) Am I just, |
| [298] | Nate: | They're not o- They're not off, right? Because you just were supposed to make a quadrilateral. |
| [299] | Natalie: | Yeah, yeah. |
| [300] | Lauryn: | Yeah that's true but |
| [301] | Natalie: | Am I just doing something really stupid? |
| [302] | Nate: | Just try it, it's fine! There's no right answer, just give it a shot, see what happens. |
| [303] | ((Jasmine comes over asking Lauryn why she thinks it looks off. This cuts in and out (mostly out) in the audio stream.)) |
| [304] | (2s) |
| [305] | Lauryn: | So, we're gonna go <Figure 11.4, Panel A>, this way? ((She uses her forearm to trace a quadrilateral rotated from the original, treating the green length as a side.)) |
| [306] | Natalie: | Like, we're going a<Figure 11.4, Panel B>round<Figure 11.4, Panel C> it<Figure 11.4, Panel D>. Like the <Figure 11.4, Panel E> same growth factor. |
| [307] | Lauryn: | O:::::OH! |
| [308] | Natalie: | Yeah. |
| [309] | Lauryn: | [Okay I get it now. |
| [310] | Jillian: | [So what is that stake in the middle (doing)? |
| [311] | Natalie: | Well this is just like the point of dilation. Like where we're taking it out from. |
| [312] | Jasmine: | Is that a specific point or is that- you just picked it randomly? |
| [313] | Natalie: | Just wherever. |
| [314] | Jasmine: | So you're dilating from that point, one point five times. |
| [315] | Natalie: | Yeah. |
| [316] | Jasmine: | Ok. |
| [317] | Natalie: | Is that gonna work? Ca- |
| [318] | Tahir: | I think it might need to be the center. |
| [319] | Jasmine: | I don't know. I think it's a cool idea. |
| [320] | Natalie: | I doesn't- It shouldn't need to be a center, it'll just be li- |
| [321] | Lauryn: | I think we should have (did) a square. |
| [322] | ((Lauryn and Jasmine laugh.)) |
| [323] | Jasmine: | So- how did you decide on this green thing? |
| [324] | Natalie: | Well, we're just waiting- |
| [325] | Tahir: | Well the green thing is actually one point five times the length of that. |
| [326] | Lauryn: | Yeah. |
| [327] | Natalie: | Yeah. |

| [328] | Jasmine: | Ok. |
|---|---|---|
| [329] | Natalie: | So we we- we were gonna do something else but then we realized like the angles would be hard to like, copy, so, now we're just getting this untangled, so we can li- |
| [330] | Jasmine: | Oh, so you're avoiding copying angles. I see. |

**FIGURE 11.4** Still frames from Excerpt 2. Panel A: Lauryn traces the first side of her imagined new quadrilateral with her arm, starting with the green tape as a new side. Panels B–E: Natalie traces her imagined new quadrilateral with both of her arms, with her body inside of it.

Natalie, knowing that the others were not in agreement with her about the strategy, looked at Nate and said that she felt like she was "doing something really stupid" [272]. Tahir responded, "I don't think either of us really understand what you're doing" [273] and Lauryn agreed. Natalie tried to explain again, this time appealing directly to the paper-and-pencil version of the procedure: "You know, like dilating on a, grid? Like when you get like a triangle and you pick a point in the center and you go out with your ruler? To like make it bigger?" [275]. Lauryn just shrugged in response. She and Tahir did not know about this, because they had not yet learned it in school. Natalie's description was of a procedure rather than the mathematical relationships they needed to manipulate in order to produce a scaled figure. Talk alone was not enough to communicate the plan to her group mates.

Although Nate encouraged them to "Just keep trying it, see what happens" [278], Tahir and Lauryn remained unhappy with the plan. Tahir reminded them of their original plan by saying "I thought we were gonna…" [280], implying that their current course of action was a surprise to him, not what he thought they had agreed to do. Soon after, Lauryn asked, "So how is this gonna, like" [289]. She did not finish her question, but her quick affirmative response to Natalie's "Well I don't know yet" [290] revealed her lingering skepticism. If even Natalie did not know what was going to happen, there was clearly a problem. However, Natalie was not willing to give in, clarifying that what she did not know was "what like the, growth factor is supposed to be" [292].

At this point, Lauryn interrupted Natalie to notice that, "from this angle, our sides are really off" [293]. Lauryn, standing in her position from outside and some distance from the quadrilateral, was attending to their representation as a whole and assessing it. Nate reminded her that they had agreed they made a quadrilateral, not specifically a trapezoid [298]. After I walked over to ask Lauryn what she meant by saying that their sides were off [303], two seconds passed, and Lauryn, still looking out over the whole quadrilateral, asked, "So, we're gonna go <Figure 11.4, Panel A>, this way?" [305]. Using her forearm to represent sides of the quadrilateral, Lauryn traced a quadrilateral in a way that began with the green tape lying on the ground as one of the new sides. Natalie responded, "Like, we're going a<Figure 11.4, Panel B>round <Figure 11.4, Panel C> it <Figure 11.4, Panel D>. Like the <Figure 11.4, Panel E> same growth factor" [306]. Kneeling inside the original quadrilateral, at the center of dilation, Natalie used both arms to trace a quadrilateral around her. In response to this, Lauryn exclaimed, "O:::::OH! Okay I get it now" [307, 309]. It is unclear what sense Lauryn made of Natalie's response, but the contrast highlighted in this exchange at least served to specify the planned orientation of the new quadrilateral and its spatial relationship to the original one.

At this point, Jillian and I (Jasmine) began asking the group some clarifying questions about the center of dilation and the green length of tape [310–330]. This gave Natalie more opportunities to describe her strategy, and given the specificity of the questions, she was positioned to articulate, in interaction with her group mates, the materials, and us, some of the particulars of the process. Natalie named the flag inside the quadrilateral ("the point of dilation" [311]), reiterated that it was set "Just wherever" [313], and I summarized the plan ("So you're dilating from that point, one point five times"), articulating it as a procedure that was familiar to me [314]. Natalie again requested confirmation that it would "work"

[317], and her uncertainty provided Tahir another opportunity to voice his concern about the center of dilation being in the center of the quadrilateral [318].

When I asked the group about how they "decide[d] on this green thing," [323] Natalie began to explain that it hadn't been "decide[d]" on yet, but Tahir cut her off, letting me know that it had "actually" been measured to be "one point five times the length of that" [325], the side of the quadrilateral. Both Lauryn and Natalie agreed with this; the green tape did not yet have a new mathematical identity, although Natalie had new plans for it.

## Excerpt 3

Once Tahir finishes untangling the yellow rope, the group resumes creating the first spoke of their dilation. Tahir and Lauryn continued to participate both physically and in talk, at times trying to anticipate Natalie's unfolding plan, but also following her directions and asking questions. As Natalie folded the green piece of tape into three pieces, each half the distance between the center of dilation and the vertex, both Tahir and Lauryn continued to demonstrate confusion and some resistance.

| [331] | Tahir: | Okay I think this is [probably] (about) |
| --- | --- | --- |
| [332] | Natalie: | [Okay. Okay. Do you wanna just like, pull it over to that corner? Just so we have like a straight [line as comparison |
| [333] | Lauryn: | [O:I get it <u>now</u>= |
| [334] | Natalie: | =Yeah. I felt really stupid like- I- like= |
| [335] | Lauryn: | =I- I just didn't really understand what you were saying for a minute, 'til we actually started doin' it. |
| [336] | Natalie: | Okay. *((To Tahir))* Yah. And just like leave it there? |
| [337] | Lauryn: | And is he going to this one? *((points at vertex to her left))* |
| [338] | Natalie: | Uh, no. Not yet. *((She folds the portion of green tape inside the quadrilateral, bringing the end to the vertex, to represent half the distance between the center of dilation and the vertex. To Tahir))* And then just, could you hold that there *((the end of the green tape at the vertex))*? With that. Okay. *((She holds the now folded end of the green tape to the ground. Then, to Lauryn))* And then, fold? *((pointing down the length of the green tape))* hnn, the green, the other green back over? |
| [339] | Lauryn: | [This one? |
| [340] | Natalie: | [Just so it's the same length at this *((points to the folded segment she and Tahir are holding))*? *((To Tahir))* But keep- holding that there *((points to vertex))*. So we like measure off, *((Lauryn brings her end of the tape over to the vertex and bends down))* NO like,= |
| [341] | Lauryn: | =Okay now I'm confused. |
| [342] | Natalie: | Like bring this (hh) over (hh)here. *((Lauryn hands Natalie the tape end))* [And then like, *((puts Lauryn's end at the end of her folded half))* |
| [343] | Lauryn: | [So it's the same length as that. |

| [344] | Natalie: | Yah. And so, wait. We need to, *((pulls the end behind her until the tape is folded at the vertex))* pull it until, it's right, there, and hold it there. (Like,). |
| [345] | Jasmine: | So you're re-measuring now? What's happening? |
| [346] | Tahir: | [(I don't know.) |
| [347] | Natalie: | [Now we're= |
| [348] | Lauryn: | =I'm not sure.= |
| [349] | Natalie: | =going- out the- point- *((tears the excess off the green tape))* five. So we [already have the one that's within? |
| [350] | Tahir: | [I get it! |
| [351] | Natalie: | [And then if we, continue, so, |
| [352] | Lauryn: | [Oh I get it. |
| [353] | Tahir: | [It's, yeah I get it I get how that's, [one point five |
| [354] | Natalie: |                                       [If someone wants to- [carry THAT back, out? |
| [355] | Lauryn: |                                                                                    [Yeah. |
| [356] | Lauryn: | This way? |
| [357] | Natalie: | [Yeah. To there. |
| [358] | Jasmine: | [So that's one *((points with her hands at the center of dilation and vertex))*, and then that's point five *((points with her hands at vertex and other end of green tape))*? [And so that's how you know your dilation? |
| [359] | Natalie: |                                 [Yeah. |
| [360] | Natalie: | Yeah. And then, just ended up with that, and then we need, this is our vertex corresponding to THAT one. |

Natalie asked Tahir to bring over the yellow rope to act as a straight line, for reference. Lauryn declared again that "I get it <u>now</u>," that "I just didn't really understand what you were saying for a minute, 'til we actually started doin' it" [333, 335]. But then she tried to anticipate Tahir's next move, "And is he going to this one?" [337] pointing to the vertex to her left. That vertex would not come into play until after this spoke was finished; Lauryn's anticipated next move was not aligned with Natalie's strategy.

Natalie walked her end of the green tape over to the vertex and asked Tahir, squatting there, to hold it down. She backed up to the folded halfway point, telling Lauryn to "fold? hnn, the green, the other green back over? Just so it's the same length at this?" [338, 340]. She wanted Lauryn to bring her end of the green tape to her so they could fold that part of the tape at Tahir's vertex and lay it over the already folded "half" between Natalie and Tahir. Lauryn's part of the green tape would determine where they tore Lauryn's section of tape to produce a length 1.5 times the distance from the center of dilation to the vertex. Lauryn walked to the vertex, and began to put the end of tape down. In the green tape's previous role as a side of the new quadrilateral, both of the ends had meaning as the endpoints of that particular measured line segment. However, for the dilation strategy, the procedure that they were in the midst of implementing would determine the new endpoint of that green tape (which would also tell them where the new vertex should be). As a length of tape with an as yet undetermined length, the end of the tape that Lauryn was holding did not have any mathematical meaning. Lauryn attributed some meaning to it by bringing it to the vertex.

Natalie stopped her ("NO like"), prompting Lauryn to quickly respond, "Okay now I'm confused" [341]. Lauryn's visible, whole-body motion made it clear that they still did not share an understanding of the plan. Natalie then gestured for Lauryn to bring the green tape end over, and Lauryn handed it to her. Natalie herself then struggled to complete the measurement. Her action was similar to Lauryn's, in that she momentarily gave mathematical meaning to the end of the green tape, putting it at the fold that she was holding (which demarcated the half-way point between the vertex and the center of dilation). She then hesitated and stumbled in her talk ([342]). Finally Natalie pulled the green tape end back past her body (and also the center of dilation) until it was folded at the vertex that Tahir held fixed.

Here, Lauryn's manipulation of the green tape was not what Natalie expected or wanted, and Natalie took over and did it herself. Unlike earlier, when Tahir revoiced Natalie's instruction for Lauryn [263], the spatial configuration of this sub-task (finding the final "half" to create 1.5 times the distance between the center of dilation and the vertex) was such that it was not difficult for Natalie to take it over once Lauryn handed her the tape end. Although Natalie denied the opportunity for Lauryn to engage in the task, by doing so she provided feedback to Lauryn about her current understandings. She was able to do so because of the visual availability of Lauryn's actions. The large-scale physical space, whole-body engagements, and distributed perspective of WSG gave students add-itional resources for assessing each other in the midst of problem solving, and the division of labor made it necessary to give each other feedback in order for the activity to progress.

At this point I came over to see what they were doing. Both Tahir and Lauryn were quick to say that they did not know. Natalie reported, "Now we're going- out the- point- *((Tears the excess off the green tape.))* five. So we already have the one that's within?" [347, 349]. As soon as Natalie tore the green tape at the point it overlapped with her halfway fold, in conjunction with her utterance that this is "point- five," Tahir exclaimed that he understood how the newly ripped tape is 1.5 [350, 353], even though two turns at talk before he had just told me that he did not know what was happening. Lauryn agreed that she understood as well [352]. Tearing off the excess destroyed the previous mathematical measure (and corresponding physical properties) of the green tape, allowing it to take on the properties of the new scaled measure of the distance between vertex and center of dilation.

I responded by stating my understanding of the 1.5 ("[So that's one *((Pointing at the center of dilation and vertex))*, and then that's point five *((Pointing at vertex and other end of green tape))*? [And so that's how you know your dilation?" [358]) and Natalie agreed. She then narrated the end of the procedure, "and then we need, this is our vertex corresponding to that one" [360]. This was the first time that anyone had stated explicitly that what they were doing was finding a new vertex (rather than a new side, or something else entirely). Up until now, Natalie had pointed outward past vertices and referred to the vertices (old and new) as "that" and "over there."

As the students completed the rest of the quadrilateral dilation, while the process was not completely smooth, it was clear that their understandings of what they were going to do were aligned. Rather than challenging and questioning each other, they successfully completed each other's sentences or left sentences unfinished rather than overlapping and interrupting. They anticipated each other's actions and material manipulations. They swapped roles (e.g., for the next spoke, Lauryn stood in the middle, Natalie held the tape down at the original vertex, and Tahir handled the end of the tape that would become the new vertex). By the time they were working on the fourth vertex, much of their talk was topically unrelated to coordinating their actions, including chitchat with the researchers about their school geometry course experiences, and the dilation activity was completed with little explicit negotiation. Lauryn and Tahir took the lead, and in the end it was they who initiated and completed producing the sides of the new quadrilateral, excited to find out if the group's strategy worked.

## Discussion

The multimodal interactional analysis above demonstrated how talk, bodies, materials, and other representational resources combined to constitute the group's learning and knowledge of this dilation strategy. There were three primary obstacles to, or goals for, the successful implementation of the quadrilateral dilation strategy. First, Lauryn and Tahir had to be recruited to participate. Natalie could not implement her idea on her own. Second, they needed a way to participate, to know what to do. Natalie was having trouble articulating, through talk, what the general plan was and the specific actions she wanted them to take. Finally, new vertices needed to be placed for the new quadrilateral, based on the original. For the purposes of this chapter, the episode focused on just the first new vertex, a sub-goal of the solution in its entirety.

Because of the large-scale, distributed division of labor of the WSG setting, it was crucial for all students to participate in order for the strategy to develop. The dynamic of this group was also such that they always tried to come to agreement and work together. Therefore, Lauryn and Tahir's ongoing skepticism and reluctance was a visible source of trouble for the group and specifically for Natalie, who repeatedly made appeals to the researchers for validation that the strategy would work. Lauryn and Tahir consistently made bids for further explanation or feedback while the group worked together. They did this by anticipating next moves ("Are we gonna use the same length?" [255]) or by challenging Natalie

("That's not the center point though" [259]; "I don't think either of us really understand what you're doing" [273]). Lauryn and Tahir's physical actions and engagements with the materials also served as openings for, and at times requests for, further explanation or feedback from Natalie (e.g., [340–342]). While Lauryn and Tahir's reluctance and confusion may be taken as obstacles to the development of the strategy, these exchanges provided a resource in the form of opportunities for the group to articulate, rehearse, and revise the strategy, and to assess their ongoing work together. As Lauryn and Tahir became convinced the strategy was a good idea, the mood of the group shifted (as they produced the final three vertices, talk mainly turned to banter and small talk), and the two moved around more (and more quickly), taking ownership of different aspects of the dilation.

Additionally, the many researchers who came and went over the course of the episode played a role in the recruitment of Lauryn and Tahir (and in Natalie's persistence). Knowing that this was a solution no other group had tried in our work with WSG tasks, we were all eager to see how it might play out. Nate had let us know earlier that Natalie had proposed something interesting, and Jillian and I were spending a lot of time observing the group. Rogers had also heard about the dilation effort, and brought over the extra microphone to try to capture as much of their activity as possible [282]. These were all additional resources available for the group to implement this strategy. Natalie actively recruited Nate's reassurance and validation in the face of her classmates' skepticism. He voiced strong support, and helped her idea maintain its status as something to try. Jillian and I tried not to "give away" that the strategy would work, but we helped to name some parts of Natalie's plan (e.g., "you're dilating from that point" [314]). In the end, I also validated Natalie's concern about copying angles by explicitly understanding ("I see" [330]) why they switched from scaling the sides to this new strategy.

In the end, Lauryn and Tahir's conversion to enthusiastic dilators (Lauryn later announced, "This is a <u>really</u> good idea now") was the demonstration of a successful placement of a new vertex. I call it a demonstration because Lauryn and Tahir could see and experience the actions necessary for the vertex to be located, and the 1.5 relationship was also made visible to them through the manipulations of the green tape, and through talk and gesture, and they played a crucial role in the production of this demonstration.

The three students, with differing initial (and final) understandings of the mathematics, all participated in solving the task, and as they did so, they had more opportunities to participate more centrally in mathematically significant ways. Lauryn attended intently to what Natalie was saying and doing, and followed Natalie's instructions carefully. In the beginning, Natalie gave her instructions using mathematical language to refer to parts of the materials they were using ("So like make this line go out from that point?" [260]). Tahir's revoicing used gestures and terms related to the materials to help Lauryn comply with Natalie's request. As they progressed, the group continued to use gestures and language rooted in the everyday uses of the materials rather than the mathematical referents while negotiating and coordinating their actions. The three group members all had access to participation due to the everyday materials and whole-bodied, readily visible actions required to manipulate them. This led to increased and more mathematically engaged levels of participation as the activity progressed.

As for the placement of that first new vertex, the negotiation of meanings for and mathematical relationships between the WSG "drawing" materials was crucial. The everyday materials of WSG were constantly mathematical tools-in-the-making, as determined by the activity of the group. As the students shared a local history of engaging in the tasks together, the materials' mathematical meanings or uses became more stabilized and tacit. This at times served as an impediment to developing new understandings (e.g., the end of the green tape), and at times allowed the continuing co-construction of the mathematical strategy (e.g., a shared routine of doubling tape over, one person holding the ends together and another holding the fold, developed in the construction of the green tape length the first time). However, as the students negotiated meanings and uses for the materials, they all could – and because of the division of labor, had to – still manipulate their bodies and the materials in the context of the mathematical activity.

The large-scale spatial configurations, interconnected whole-body and material manipulations, and distributed perspective in this setting allowed the students visual and physical access to each other's actions, making possible ongoing assessment and providing opportunities for feedback. When these actions were counter to the mathematical meaning or relationship one student attributed to materials, or prevented a student from completing his or her own action, there was a clear indicator of divergent understandings. Natalie could see and physically feel Lauryn and Tahir's actions, easily identifying when they were misaligned with her dilation plan. Because of the need for multiple bodies to complete the WSG tasks, it was in the best interest of the students to give each other feedback and continue to negotiate their understandings.

This analysis provided an example of a form of multimodal interaction analysis that accounts for a larger set of resources for meaning making and the accomplishment of a mathematics task. The analysis attended to whole bodies, available material resources, developing representational infrastructure, and spatial relations, as well as talk and gestures. The analysis took a sociocultural perspective on learning and knowledge, inviting questions of what counts as evidence of learning and knowledge, taking all of these resources into account. The development of the strategy emerged though the interaction of the group, and the capacity for dilating quadrilaterals was a property of the ensemble, not of any one individual.

# Commentary

# FROM THE INDIVIDUAL TO THE ENSEMBLE AND BACK AGAIN

*Luke D. Conlin and David Hammer*

Jasmine Ma presents an analysis of three students' interactions during an episode of a mathematical activity, Walking Scale Geometry, which she designed to support "ensemble learning." In this case, the challenge was to dilate a quadrilateral, laid out on the lawn with flagging tape, by a factor of 1.5. Her analysis of the students' interactions with each other and the physical materials shows that it was the ensemble – Natalie, Tahir, and Lauryn as a group – that learned to complete the task. Thus Ma has offered a rich and compelling example of Interaction Analysis (IA).

The aim of KAIA and this volume being to bridge IA with KA, Knowledge Analysis, we see ourselves charged with adding a KA take on the data. Our interest more broadly is to offer a view on coordinating IA and KA, which we believe is not only possible but necessary for progress. Like Cobb (1994), we argue for coordinating IA and KA based on the evidence at hand.

Most of the literature in both IA and KA makes assumptions about the unit of analysis based on a priori theoretical commitments and interests. Ma is explicit about that here. Following Hutchins (1995a, 1995b), Ma attributes cognition and learning to the ensemble, and resists making claims about individuals, although "this is not to claim that there is not individual knowledge or mental activity." To be sure, she makes numerous individual attributions in the course of her analysis, nested within her compelling case for ensemble learning. From our perspective, this is not only appropriate but necessary: The dynamics of cognition and learning take place at a range of scales, in Ma's data as in general, from within individual minds to across multiple minds and materials. Understanding ensemble learning involves attention to its members. Of course, we argue the reverse as well: Any sensible account of individual knowledge and mental activity must attend to the larger situation. Ideally, an approach that bridges KA and IA would include strategies to guide researchers' selection of the unit of analysis, perhaps analogous in some ways to strategies researchers use to guide their development of theory from qualitative data (Glaser & Strauss, 1967) or synthesizing coding categories (Chi, 1997).

Elsewhere (Conlin, Gupta, & Hammer, 2010a, 2010b), we have posited empirical heuristics for keeping track of evidence of the scale of cognitive dynamics, allowing for decisions regarding the unit of analysis based on the data. In what follows, we review that previous work, present the heuristics, and apply them to Ma's data. Our analysis agrees with Ma's central claim that the ensemble learns a strategy for how to dilate the quadrilateral. However, by allowing our attention to shift to individuals, guided by our heuristics, we can say more about how those individuals' roles may contribute to ensemble learning.

## Heuristics for Tracking the Unit of Framing

Our focus in earlier work was on students' *epistemological framing*, a construct Redish (2004) proposed, connecting resource-based accounts of intuitive epistemologies (Hammer & Elby, 2002; Rosenberg, Hammer, & Phelan, 2006) with accounts of framing in cognitive science (Minsky, 1988) as well as sociology and anthropology (Bateson, 1955; Goffman, 1974; Tannen, 1993). The former consider learners' intellectual resources for understanding knowledge and knowledge-related activities. The latter consider people's sense of "what is it that's going on here?" (Goffman, 1974, p. 8). "Epistemological framing" considers learners' sense of what is going on with respect to knowledge. Most examples of epistemological framing in the literature focus on individuals (Bing & Redish, 2009; Lising & Elby, 2005), but a number attribute framing to a group or class (Louca, Elby, Hammer, & Kagey, 2004; Scherr & Hammer, 2009). Scherr & Hammer (2009) argued:

> The question of which system to consider, or what scale of system to treat as the cognitive unit, should not be decided *a priori*, and it does not have a general answer. Rather, it should be decided by the case at hand, by the evidence of what resources (cognitive, physical, material, representational, etc.) participate in the dynamics of reasoning.
>
> *(p. 173)*

Our group at the University of Maryland conducted a variety of studies of collaborative groups working on tutorials in introductory physics (Elby et al., 2007). As a collection, these studies reveal a range of dynamics, at various scales. We drew on this work to extract a set of heuristics to identify the relevant unit of analysis, specifically with respect to epistemological framing (Conlin et al., 2010a, 2010b).

Scherr and Hammer (2009), for example, presented evidence of framing for a group as a whole. Scherr had noticed collective shifts in behaviors at the group level. For instance, groups transitioned from what Scherr labeled the "blue" cluster – students hunching over the table, eyes on their papers, and speaking in soft tones with hands gesturing discreetly – to what Scherr labeled "green" – sitting up, making eye contact, speaking in full voice and gesturing conspicuously. Analysis of the discourse in these distinct clusters of behavior revealed that they corresponded to different epistemological frames, "completing the worksheet" vs.

"having a discussion." The locus of stability of these frames tends to reside with the group, as evidenced in moments in which a group would be completing the worksheet and one student would pop up in a "bid" to have a discussion, only to hunch back over and return to their worksheet when nobody else followed suit.

In another analysis of students in physics tutorials (Conlin et al., 2010a, 2010b), we presented evidence of two students' (Veronica and Jan) contrasting frames, drawing on analyses from Lising and Elby (2005). Working on a tutorial in optics, Veronica and Jan clashed over how to describe the path taken by light from a bulb to a screen. Veronica gave an intuitive answer of how the light moves, while Jan was trying to make things more "physics-oriented" by using official vocabulary ("rays" and "vectors" that are "polarized"). Veronica resisted Jan's use of these phrases, saying that she was "making it too complicated." A disagreement over which way the light moves revealed that Jan and Veronica had different stable framings of what it means to be "physics-oriented."

Frank (2009) showed multiple scales of dynamics in his analyses of tutorial groups. Across various groups, he showed evidence of ensemble thinking, the group as a whole making a particular inference about the speed of an object and shifting, as a group, to a different inference. Interestingly, groups' shifting in conceptualization co-occurred with their shifting in epistemology, from reporting something they found obvious to reasoning carefully based on mechanism. Looking moment to moment at one group, however, Frank showed evidence of contrasting dynamics for one student, who was doing something different from the others. Her thinking, at first distinct from the group's both conceptually and epistemology, led the group to shift as a whole. This analysis demonstrates the dynamics of how the locus of stability of a framing can shift levels, from the individual to the group (and back again).

Looking across this collection of analyses, we posited a set of four heuristics that highlight distinct forms of evidence for deciding the relevant unit of cognition. While they are influenced by a complex-systems view of cognition, the heuristics are largely consistent with forms of evidence detailed in Interaction Analysis (McDermott, Gospodinoff, & Aron, 1978; Schegloff, 1991). We describe them here, and then we apply them to Ma's data.

## Clustering

Clustering refers to the patterns of co-occurrence in multiple aspects of what researchers observe, such as Scherr (Scherr & Hammer, 2009) recognized in students' posture, gestures, and speech. McDermott et al. (1978) have also noted that mutually interacting participants tend to organize their postures in coherent patterns that signal their mutual sense of what is going on. We take these behavioral clusters as evidence of the unit of framing which resides across whatever actors and materials are involved in the pattern. We have described how distinct clusters of speech and behaviors can at times signal a shared epistemological frame (Conlin et al., 2010a, 2010b; Scherr & Hammer, 2009). At other times, the clustering is at the level of the individual, as was the case for Jan and Veronica (Lising & Elby, 2005), who each had a distinct way of framing what it means to be "physics-oriented."

## Transitions

We see evidence of the unit of framing in transitions between clusters of speech and behavior across the set of actors and materials that participate in the transition. This is consistent with the observation in McDermott et al. (1978) that transitions between group members' positionings can reveal shared aspects of their sense of what they are doing together. Scherr and Hammer (2009) describe how tutorial groups would often transition from one group activity (having a discussion) to another (completing their worksheets) abruptly and without any explicit bid to shift activities. This transition thereby provides evidence that they shared a sense of these alternative ways of framing their activity together.

Transitions can reveal individual differences in framing as well, as was the case when a new tutorial group member asked "Can we discuss our answers now?", thereby challenging and ultimately shifting the established norms of the group, which had been dismissive of discussions up to that point (Conlin, 2012). Frank's (2009) analysis of tutorial groups also detailed a case in which one student's thinking led to a shift in the group's thinking. These transitions provide evidence of both the individual-level framing before the shift and the new group-level framing after the shift.

## Persistence

Persistence refers simply to duration in a set of observables. Again, we take it as evidence of the unit of cognition, i.e., the set of actors or materials participating in a pattern over time. Regarding the tutorial groups, it was typical to observe the group in a particular behavioral cluster, e.g., hunched over in the blue-worksheet cluster, for minutes at a time. For most of the groups, their time in tutorial could be generally described as long periods of shared behavioral clusters, punctuated by brief transitions between clusters. But at times, and for some groups more than others, we found evidence of individual students' distinct epistemological frames that persisted over time, as was the case for Jan and Veronica.

## Resistance

Resistance refers to persistence in the face of a challenge. In the physics tutorials, the group-level patterns of behavior and reasoning would often show resistance to "bids" from individual students for a shift in activity, say, from completing the worksheet to having a discussion. These bids could be implicit, as when a group is hunched over their worksheet and one student sits up for a moment, puts her pen down and looks to talk, but finds the group unresponsive and so returns her attention to the worksheet. In other instances, the student would sit up and stay up, start speaking and trying to engage others in the group more directly, as in, "Can we discuss our answers now?" (Conlin, 2012). Persistence of the group in the face of individuals' bids for a shift in activity would be evidence that the locus of stability of the framing of their activity resides with the group.

Further examples of resistance can be evident in repairs of understanding (Schegloff, 1991) and explicit disagreements. Conversational repairs offer resistance against whatever is being repaired, be it a conceptual understanding of a phenomenon or an epistemological understanding of what's going on in a situation. Veronica's resistance to Jan's use of physics vocabulary signaled that each of them had their own framing of what it means to be "physics-oriented."

Of course, there are always many scales and layers of framing. A group framing their activity as "having a discussion" is typically comprised of individuals framing their participation in different but coordinated ways. While one member momentarily frames their participation as articulating an idea, the others may be framing it as trying to understand the idea. The group's framing may be stable even if individuals momentarily diverge: the stability in one respect does not imply stability in another. For example, consider a group that remains stable in having a discussion even after realizing at some point that individuals have been making different assumptions – "I thought we were talking about dinner tonight, and you've been thinking of sometime next week." Thus the heuristics apply to an aspect of what is taking place ("having a discussion" vs. understanding of the details of that discussion), and they guide analysis of the scale involved in that aspect.

We have suggested these heuristics can support researchers in selecting the unit of analysis with respect to framing, and perhaps regarding other aspects of cognition as well – such as a "concept" or an affective state. Importantly, they allow for the possibility of identifying shifts in the evident unit of cognition, moment to moment. These shifts can proceed from the individual to the group, and vice versa, as Frank's (2009) analysis showed. We believe this is evident in Ma's data as well.

We turn to her data now, using these heuristics. We agree with Ma that the ensemble learns a strategy to dilate a quadrilateral that they did not know before; her analysis allows us to see the moments that constitute ensemble learning. However, we argue that when we apply these heuristics, the unit of understanding the strategy evidently begins with the individual and shifts to the ensemble. And, we hope, perhaps it shifts back again to the individuals.

## Tracking the Unit of Learning

In tracking the unit of analysis, it is important to be clear on just what aspect of cognition we are referring to when we say cognition is shared, situated, and/or embodied. Hutchins (1995b) referred specifically to the act of *remembering*, while Hall (1996) described *representation* as a situated action rather than a mental object. In our previous work, we have focused on the epistemological framing of physics students at the individual and group levels.

Ma focuses on *learning* as distributed across an ensemble of students and materials. While we have not used our approach to address the dynamics of *learning* per se, we expect the heuristics will apply. If we think of understanding as the current state of a cognitive ecology, i.e., the set of resources activated in the moment, then learning would be a persistent change in the cognitive ecology, whether that ecology resides within an individual, within a group, or both. Learning could be evident, for example, as a shift in the cluster of resources the individual or group cues in a context, or as a shift in such a pattern's resistance to change.

### *How an Ensemble Learns to Dilate a Quadrilateral*

Ma recounts a group of three students solving a math problem laid out on a lawn: The task is to make a copy of a quadrilateral, laid out in flagging tape, 1.5 times as large as the original. "Natalie quickly proposed a dilation strategy that she vaguely remembered learning," but "Lauryn and Tahir wanted to scale each side of the quadrilateral 1.5 times." Natalie resisted, noting that their strategy presented them with the challenge of copying the angles precisely. "After some disagreement and the prompting of a researcher (Nate), Lauryn and Tahir agreed to try Natalie's strategy," which was to pick a center point and extend a line from it through each vertex. By scaling those lines by 1.5, they could "avoid copying the angles." Natalie was just unsure whether dilating out by 1.5 meant the sides would also be 1.5 bigger. As they carried out Natalie's strategy, Lauryn and Tahir initially "did not have a sense" of her plan, and she directed their participation, asking them to hold things down so she could measure out a new vertex. But as they moved on to make subsequent vertices, Ma's analysis of their interaction reveals gradual shifts in the group's understanding of the plan and willingness to pursue it, as manifest in their increased anticipation of each step, and their shared investment in its unknown outcome. When they ultimately find out that the strategy was successful, Ma argues, it is the ensemble that has learned how to dilate a quadrilateral.

The physical scale of the task that Ma set out for the students prohibits any one individual from seeing the entire shape they are dilating, since the shape is so large. With different perspectives on the shape depending on where they stand, the students need to coordinate with each other to determine whether lengths and angles are really equivalent. Based on these factors, Ma takes this task to be set up for ensemble learning – no one can easily do it on their own. By taking an explicitly sociocultural, interactional, and embodied account of knowing and learning, Ma's analysis seems to presume that students in the group will take up the task in a way that is inherently distributed at all times. The evidence we find, however, shows a dynamic shift from an individual, Natalie, to the ensemble, with respect to understanding the dilation strategy. We detail each phase of this shift in what follows.

## *Phase 1: From the Individual…*

In her analysis, Ma attributed several things to Natalie as an individual, including dissatisfaction, the start of an alternative strategy, as well as a more rigorous standard for what counts as scaling up the quadrilateral. This is an observable cluster in Natalie's speech and behavior, and the data show its persistence and resistance to Lauryn's and Tahir's reasoning. Lauryn and Tahir, for their part, showed a different pattern of evidence, also persistent and resistant – it took a researcher's prompting, presumably an authority figure for them, to persuade them to try Natalie's approach.

Even before they began to try her approach, Natalie showed higher standards of precision in measurement. To extend a side by 1.5, Tahir asked Natalie to hold down the tape at one vertex, while Lauryn and Tahir rolled out the tape along the full length of a side of the quadrilateral. Tahir held the tape at the other vertex, then with the excess tape Lauryn doubled back until the tape made it about halfway back to Natalie's vertex. Lauryn and Tahir were all set to rip the tape off where they had eyeballed it to be about halfway (Tahir: "Okay, rip it off there, I guess…"), when Natalie stopped them to insist that they "make it exact." She told Tahir to hold down his vertex as she folded the tape in half. Handing him her vertex, she pulled the halves taut, and then asked Lauryn to rip off the excess in line with the halved tape. This ensured the tape was 1.5 times the original side. Thus, in resisting Lauryn and Tahir's strategy for extending a side, Natalie constructed her own strategy for extending the side by 1.5, a strategy situated in the materials at hand.

Lauryn and Tahir then walked this new extended side out away from the quadrilateral to eyeball where it would sit for the new quadrilateral. Again, Natalie resisted by questioning how they would make sure the angles were congruent, to insure that the new side was precisely parallel. With Tahir and Lauryn showing no signs of sharing her concern, Natalie reached out to the researchers/facilitators. She asked them what they considered to be a loaded question: "What would be like, how much would we dilate it if we wanted it to be like one and a half?" Nate, the researcher, encouraged her to try it. She then walked to what she selected as the "point of dilation" in the quadrilateral and called the others over.

In Excerpts 1 and 2, Natalie, Tahir, and Lauryn were trying to construct the first vertex. Tahir and Lauryn showed resistance, apparently because they did not understand Natalie's strategy. Natalie directed them around, telling Tahir to hold down the tape at the old vertex, to put the yellow rope down, which involved untangling it, etc. When Tahir noted that the point Natalie was using to dilate from was not the center of the quadrilateral, Natalie asserted that it did not have to be, without offering justification, and Tahir did not press further. Perhaps as a result of their passive direction-following without sign of agreement, Natalie shared that she felt like she was "doing something really stupid." This allowed Tahir and Lauryn to say they didn't understand her strategy. Natalie tried to explain, but she had a hard time putting it into words.

Throughout, the evidence shows Natalie's individual persistence and resistance to Tahir's and Lauryn's suggestions and behavior, and theirs, as a pair, to hers. While there are certainly aspects of the group's work that reflect ensemble thinking – they are out on the lawn, they are taking turns speaking and listening, etc. – applying our heuristics to the data allows us to attribute distinct understandings of the dilation strategy to Natalie, as an individual,[2] and to Lauryn and Tahir as a pair. Natalie's shows greater persistence, perhaps in part due to the adults' support. Lauryn and Tahir transition from pressing their idea to implementing Natalie's.

## Phase 2: To the Ensemble…

As the group was finishing the first vertex (~9:30), there is evidence of a group-level transition. Natalie was applying her folding strategy for extending the side by 1.5, using the same tape, only now she was using it to find the location of the new vertex. Tahir was observing Natalie folding the tape, at first confused by the extra tape left over from the side they had already extended, but suddenly realizing what Natalie was doing: "I know how it's 1.5 now." It also became apparent that Lauryn had thought they were creating a side to the new quadrilateral, which was not what Natalie had in mind. When Natalie explained they weren't creating a new side at all but a new vertex, Lauryn also expressed a sudden realization, saying "Ohhh, I get it now."

Tahir spoke to express ongoing doubt, but signaled his willingness to follow through, and Lauryn offered support (lines 356–359 of Ma's transcript):

[356] Tahir: Are you sure it's gonna be proportionate to the other, ah, angles? I guess we can just try it and see what happens.
[357] Jasmine: Yeah let's find out.
[358] Natalie: Yeah. Ok, so now,
[359] Lauryn: Yeah cause if we go that way ((points right hand to where the next new vertex will be)) and then connect them here ((points left hand to the new vertex they just made)), or wherever the flag is over there, then it should be.

Lauryn's gestures helped clarify her meaning: She pointed to the new vertex with her right hand while pointing to the dilated vertex they just constructed with her left, indicating she was sizing up the new side to see that it "should be" about 1.5 times as large. In this way, the evidence shows Tahir's and Lauryn's shift from resistance to acquiescence, as a pair, a transition that signals a shift toward a shared understanding[3] of the dilation strategy, and a shared willingness to try it.

From this moment forward, Tahir and Lauryn supported the dilation strategy, and the evidence increasingly suggests the ensemble is now the unit that understands the strategy. As they worked on the second vertex, Lauryn and Tahir started to anticipate Natalie's instructions, a shift from their earlier stances of resistance and then passive obedience. Thus Lauryn walked to the center of dilation and asked, "do you want me to hold this here?" Tahir corrected Natalie on not ripping the tape at the old vertex, suggested she tie it back together, and Natalie followed his suggestion. Tahir anticipated the next step, which was to have Lauryn fold over her end of the tape from the center, finding half the distance to the vertex "and now she [Lauryn] has to bring it over, like." Lauryn finished his sentence with "half."

At this scale of analysis, the clustering was evident at the level of the group, to the point of the students' finishing of each other's sentences, and this continued. As they started to construct the third vertex, Tahir anticipated the results of their strategy:

[399] Tahir: It's gonna look like a, wheel or something like a, four-sided wheel.
[400] Natalie: Yeah. With the spindles coming out. Ok.
[401] Tahir: It's gonna have spokes.

Once Natalie had stretched the pink tape out to the vertex, Lauryn started to walk the pink tape in from the center to fold it in half so they could rip the excess off at 1.5. As Lauryn walked, Natalie acknowledged what she was doing: "bring it in, yeah."

A researcher (Rogers) started asking questions, and Lauryn was answering first, before Natalie had a chance to answer. Although she attributed the strategy to Natalie, Lauryn's responses showed it was no longer just Natalie's. Working on vertex 4 (~14min) the group showed more evidence of ensemble thinking: Natalie was no longer giving directions, and in fact it seemed they no longer needed to talk to each other to coordinate. The facilitator noted they were "much more efficient," and the evidence shows all three students involved in these patterns of activity and (lack of) speech that persist over time.

When they had all four vertices dilated, the ensemble transitioned seamlessly to making a new side, both to finish the construction and to test that the strategy worked. Together, they constructed a new side to test whether their dilating of the vertices by 1.5 would mean that the sides were also scaled by 1.5. Using the side they had originally extended, they repeated the folding procedure to again measure out a new side that was 1.5 times bigger. The same measurement now meant something very different: they were checking for coherence between the new strategy and the original strategy. When they stretched out the new side and found it perfectly connected the new vertices, they exulted. Satisfied, they completed the other three sides of the new quadrilateral without much suspense.

Throughout this, Natalie, Tahir, and Lauryn all participated in the cluster of activity of construction as well as the transition to the new cluster of testing and celebration, and finally the falling action of completing the dilated quadrilateral.

Even though Natalie was originally directing the activity, they succeeded as a team. The episode reminds us of team-building exercises; for example, the challenge of getting a group over a wall that is too tall and smooth for any individual to climb. Even if the team uses one person's strategy, it is still the team that succeeds or fails in making it over the wall. In the end, we agree with Ma that it is the ensemble that succeeded in dilating the quadrilateral.

## Conclusion

Our analysis supports Ma's claim that the ensemble learns to dilate a quadrilateral. It also supports her analysis, including her attributions to members within the ensemble: What the ensemble learned started with Natalie, with Lauryn and Tahir first in opposition, then in acquiescence, and finally in support, invested, and participating.

If we differ with Ma, it is in our view that attention to this finer grain size – to individuals within the group – is important. For one, it contributes to understanding the ensemble, as evident in Ma's analysis and ours. For another, we argue in the next section, education research must ultimately care about individual students.

### *From the Individual to the Ensemble*

Ma's and our analyses of the group involve looking within it, recognizing and describing individuals within it as epistemic agents. Viewing the ensemble as the unit of analysis in this way is continuous with analyses of individuals, from "society of mind" (Minsky, 1988) perspectives of "individuals" as ensembles themselves, ensembles of various perceptual, affective, cognitive, meta-cognitive "agents." There are various models of that ensemble in the literature, with various theoretical commitments and foci of attention, such as of modules (Fodor, 1983) and p-prims (diSessa, 1993) and schemata (Rumelhart, 1980). We have used the generic term "resources."

Many of these accounts, including Minsky's of agents and Rumelhart's and many others' of schemas, conceptualize resources as manifold themselves, comprised of resources interacting in generally stable patterns. Knowledge Analysis and many other methodologies identify evidence of these resources and the dynamics of their interactions, including how they may coordinate into larger patterns and the "soft assembly" of existing resources in local time, sometimes coming to stabilize into new resources (Thelen & Smith, 1994).

All of which is to say that Ma's "Interaction Analysis" of the ensemble is itself a kind of "Knowledge Analysis," of an "individual mind" at a larger scale. It is analysis of an "individual" made up of multiple agents, which are themselves made up of multiple agents.

Whether considered at the individual or ensemble level, these agents can be at odds with each other, and this is part of what drives learning. There are times when an individual person may be "of two minds" – having multiple conflicting ways of understanding something. Learning occurs when these conflicts are somehow resolved, or at least coordinated. The same holds true for an ensemble. The ensemble of Lauryn, Tahir, and Natalie progressed from having individual, conflicting understandings of the dilation strategy to having a shared understanding. The conflicts serve as evidence of individual understandings, but also of ensemble learning: It was only through resolving and repairing these conflicting understandings that the ensemble learned the strategy.

## ...And Back Again

But what *about* the individual students? Would Natalie or Tahir or Lauryn have been able to carry out this task on her or his own, or lead another group in the strategy? How about on a paper-and-pencil task? It is difficult to make claims about the individual students' learning with the data given, partly due to the decision to take data (and even set up the activity) in ways that were attuned to the theoretical commitment to take the ensemble as the unit of analysis. This is an example of how video data are theory-laden (Hall, 2000), which motivates our seeking a broader theoretical perspective.

Still, from what we see in the data, we believe Natalie would be able to dilate a given shape on a paper-and-pencil task. She had introduced the strategy, and over the course of the episode she came to articulate her reasoning clearly. We are not as sure about Lauryn and Tahir, but there is some evidence to suggest they had progressed as well, each as individuals: By the fourth vertex, they each seemed to know how to carry out the procedure, without direction. Even so, the extent to which the stability of their understanding was bound up in their interactions with this ensemble and these materials remains an open question.

But these questions prompt a bigger one: *Should we care* whether these students individually learn how to dilate a quadrilateral, out in a field or on a piece of paper? For us, the answer is emphatically yes, we should care. This particular ensemble will not work together very often, if ever again, but the "individual" ensembles that we think of as Natalie, Tahir, and Lauryn will go on to other things.

It is important to question whether their experience of working together to dilate a quadrilateral will find any relevance in their future learning and experiences. We hope and suspect that it will. We would hope, for instance, they learned that by working together they can accomplish something none of them could do alone, rather than, say, learning how to follow instructions from someone who knows the answer. The choice to focus solely on the ensemble makes this sort of question more difficult to answer.

Hall (1996) described IA as focused less on transferring content knowledge from task to task and more on engaging students in authentic practices of the discipline, and we share this preference. Cognitivist accounts, Hall pointed out, have generally focused on what individual students might learn and be able to bring to new situations, with pedagogical activities often explicitly focusing on these content goals. Situative accounts, on the other hand, tend to want to create opportunities for communities of learners to take part in the disciplinary practices of a larger community, e.g., scientists or mathematicians.

We want both, and for both individual learners and the ensembles they comprise. Pedagogical activities such as Ma's provide wonderful opportunities for both conceptual learning and participation in disciplinary practices, for the ensemble of students as well as for its members. The dynamics of what takes place are important at both scales.

## Cumulative Notes

1. Transcripts follow a modified version of Jefferson's transcription convention (Atkinson & Heritage, 2006). Turns at talk and new lines, determined by topic of talk or activity, are labeled with [Line#], in accordance with the original transcript in the data corpus. Non-talk activity is enclosed in *((italicized, double parentheses))*. Overlapping talk across turns is signified by vertically aligned [left open brackets. Emphasis is underline, louder utterances are CAPITALIZED, and drawn-out speech with co::olons. Transcriber uncertainty is indicated with (parentheses). Duration of pauses in speech is indicated in seconds by (#s). When frame-by-frame images are provided, they are labeled <Figure#>.

2. Aspects of Natalie's understanding of the dilation strategy are bound up in her use of the materials; for instance, folding the tape and ripping off excess to extend the side by 1.5. Still, the overall approach of dilating the quadrilateral from a point through each vertex is a strategy she learned in geometry class, and with different materials.

3. There are many possible senses in which an understanding could be thought of as "shared," which may or may not include multiple individuals' "having the same thing in mind." For instance, it may be that each individual understands only their piece of the strategy, but an ensemble-level understanding emerges when these pieces are woven together in coordinated action. Whether the individuals have anything like a shared mental representation that could guide future action apart from the other ensemble members is a different but important question. The data here are insufficient to make any strong claims on this matter. For present purposes, we take the ensemble's understanding to be "shared" in the sense that the locus of stability of the students' carrying out of the strategy resides at the group level, as suggested by the heuristics.

# Cumulative References

Atkinson, J. M., & Heritage, J. (2006). Jefferson's transcript notation. In A. Jaworski & N. Coupland (Eds.), *The discourse reader* (pp. 158–165). London: Routledge. (Original work published 1984).

Bateson, G. (1955). A theory of play and fantasy. *Psychiatric Research Reports*, 2(39), 39–51.

Bing, T. J., & Redish, E. F. (2009). Analyzing problem solving using math in physics: Epistemological framing via warrants. *Physical Review Special Topics-Physics Education Research*, 5(2). doi: 02010810.1103/PhysRevSTPER.5.020108.

Brown, A. L. (1992). Design experiments: Theoretical and methodological challenges in creating complex interventions in classroom settings. *Journal of the Learning Sciences*, 2(2), 141–178.

Chi, M. T. H. (1997). Quantifying qualitative analyses of verbal data: A practical guide. *Journal of the Learning Sciences*, 6(3), 271–315.

Cobb, P. (1994). Where is the mind? Constructivist and sociocultural perspectives on mathematical development. *Educational Researcher*, 23(7), 13–20.

Cobb, P., Confrey, J., diSessa, A., Lehrer, R., & Schauble, L. (2003). Design experiments in educational research. *Educational Researcher*, 32(1), 9–13.

Cobb, P., Stephan, M., McClain, K., & Gravemeijer, K. (2001). Participating in classroom mathematical practices. *Journal of the Learning Sciences*, 10(1–2), 113–163.

Conlin, L. D. (2012). *Building shared understandings in introductory physics tutorials through risk, repair, conflict, & comedy*. (Doctoral dissertation). Retrieved from ProQuest Dissertations and Theses (UMI 3517523).

Conlin, L. D., Gupta, A., & Hammer, D. (2010a). Framing and resource activation: Bridging the cognitive–situative divide using a dynamic unit of cognitive analysis. In S. Ohlsson & R. Catrambone (Eds.), *Proceedings of the 32nd Annual Meeting of the Cognitive Science Society* (pp. 19–24). Austin, TX: Cognitive Science Society.

Conlin, L. D., Gupta, A., & Hammer, D. (2010b). Where to find the mind: Identifying the scale of cognitive dynamics. In K. Gomez, L. Lyons, & J. Radinsky (Eds.), *Learning in the disciplines: Proceedings of the 9th International Conference of the Learning Sciences* (Vol. 1, pp. 277–284). Chicago, IL: International Society of the Learning Sciences.

diSessa, A. A. (1993). Toward an epistemology of physics. *Cognition and Instruction*, 10(2–3), 105–225.

Elby, A., Scherr, R. E., McCaskey, T. L., Hodges, R., Redish, E. F., Hammer, D. M., & Bing, T. (2007). *Maryland tutorials in physics sense-making* [DVD]. United States: Open Source Tutorials.

Erickson, F. (1986). Qualitative methods in research on teaching. In M. C. Wittrock (Ed.), *Handbook of research on teaching* (pp. 119–161). New York: Macmillan.

Fodor, J. A. (1983). *The modularity of the mind: An essay on faculty psychology*. Cambridge, MA: MIT Press.

Frank, B. W. (2009). *The dynamics of variability in physics students' thinking: Examples from kinematics*. (Doctoral Thesis), University of Maryland, College Park.

Glaser, B. G., & Strauss, A. L. (1967). *The discovery of grounded theory: Strategies for qualitative research*. Chicago, IL: Aldine.

Goffman, E. (1964). The neglected situation. *American Anthropologist*, 66(6), Part 2, 133–136.

Goffman, E. (1974). *Frame analysis: An essay on the organization of experience*. Cambridge, MA: Harvard University Press.

Greeno, J. G., & Middle School Mathematics through Applications Project Group. (1998). The situativity of knowing, learning, and research. *American Psychologist*, 53, 5–26.

Hall, R. (1996). Representation as shared activity: Situated cognition and Dewey's cartography of experience. *The Journal of the Learning Sciences*, 5(3), 209–238.

Hall, R. (2000). Video recording as theory. In D. Lesh & A. Kelley (Eds.) *Handbook of research design in mathematics and science education* (pp. 647–664). Mahwah, NJ: Lawrence Erlbaum.

Hall, R., & Ma, J. Y. (2011). Learning a part together: Participant trajectories with ensemble spatial forms in a high school marching band. In R. Hall (Ed.), *Difference, culture, and distribution in mathematics and science learning*. Berkeley, CA: Symposium conducted at the 41st Annual Meeting of the Jean Piaget Society.

Hall, R., Stevens, R., & Torralba, T. (2002). Disrupting representational infrastructure in conversations across disciplines. *Mind, Culture, and Activity*, 9(3), 179–210.

Hammer, D., & Elby, A. (2002). On the form of a personal epistemology. In B. K. Hofer & P. R. Pintrich (Eds.), *Personal epistemology: The psychology of beliefs about knowledge and knowing* (pp. 169–190). New York: Lawrence Erlbaum Associates.

Hutchins, E. (1995a). *Cognition in the wild*. Cambridge, MA: MIT Press.

Hutchins, E. (1995b). How a cockpit remembers its speeds. *Cognitive Science*, 17(1), 49–59.

Hutchins, E. (2010). Imagining the cognitive life of things. In L. Malafouris & C. Renfrew (Eds.), *The cognitive life of things: Recasting the boundaries of mind* (pp. 91–101). Cambridge, UK: McDonald Institute for Archaeological Research.

Jordan, B., & Henderson, A. (1995). Interaction analysis: Foundations and practice. *Journal of the Learning Sciences*, 4(1), 39–103.

Lave, J. (1988). *Cognition in practice: Mind, mathematics and culture in everyday life*. Cambridge, UK: Cambridge University Press.

Lising, L., & Elby, A. (2005). The impact of epistemology on learning: A case study from introductory physics. *American Journal of Physics*, 73(4), 372–382.

Louca, L., Elby, A., Hammer, D., & Kagey, T. (2004). Epistemological resources: Applying a new epistemological framework to science instruction. *Educational Psychologist*, 39(1), 57–68.

Ma, J. Y. (2012). *Changing local practice for good: Walking scale geometry as designed disruptions for productive hybridity*. Unpublished doctoral dissertation. Vanderbilt University, Nashville, TN.

Ma, J. Y. (2014, June). Disruptive scales in 7th grade geometry: Designing for productive hybridity. In J. Y. Ma (Chair), *Disrupting learning: Changing local practice for good*. Symposium conducted at the International Conference of the Learning Sciences, Boulder, CO.

McDermott, R., Gospodinoff, K., & Aron, J. (1978). Criteria for an ethnographically adequate description of concerted activities and their contexts. *Semiotica*, 24(3–4), 245–276.

Minsky, M. L. (1988). *The society of mind*. New York: Simon & Schuster.

Nemirovsky, R., & Ferrara, F. (2009). Mathematical imagination and embodied cognition. *Educational Studies in Mathematics*, 70(2), 159–174.

Núñez, R. E., Edwards, L. D., & Filipe Matos, J. (1999). Embodied cognition as grounding for situatedness and context in mathematics education. *Educational Studies in Mathematics*, 39(1), 45–65.

Redish, E. F. (2004). A theoretical framework for physics education research: Modeling student thinking. In E. F. Redish & M. Vicentini (Eds.), *Proceedings of the International School of Physics Enrico Fermi: Course CLVI Research in Physics Education* (pp. 1–60). Amsterdam, NL: IOS Press.

Rosenberg, S. A., Hammer, D., & Phelan, J. (2006). Multiple epistemological coherences in an eighth-grade discussion of the rock cycle. *Journal of the Learning Sciences*, 15(2), 261–292.

Rumelhart, D. E. (1980). On evaluating story grammars. *Cognitive Science*, 4, 313–316.

Sacks, H., Schegloff, E. A., & Jefferson, G. (1974). A simplest systematics for the organization of turn-taking for conversation. *Language*, 50(4), 696–735.

Schegloff, E. A. (1991). Conversation analysis and socially shared cognition. In L. B. Resnick, J. M. Levine, & S. D. Teasley (Eds.), *Perspectives on socially shared cognition* (pp. 150–171). Washington, DC: American Psychological Association.

Scherr, R. E., & Hammer, D. (2009). Student behavior and epistemological framing: Examples from collaborative active-learning activities in physics. *Cognition and Instruction*, 27(2), 147–174.

Stevens, R. (2010). Learning as a members' phenomenon: Toward an ethnographically adequate science of learning. In W. Penuel, K. O'Connor, & National Society for the Study of Education (Eds.), *Yearbook of the national society for the study of education* (Vol. 109, pp. 82–97). New York: Teachers College, Columbia University.

Tannen, D. (1993). *Framing in discourse*. New York: Oxford University Press.

Thelen, E., & Smith, L. B. (1994). *A dynamic systems approach to the development of cognition and action*. Cambridge, MA: MIT Press.

# 12

# PARENTS AS SKILLED KNOWLEDGE PRACTITIONERS

*Jessica F. Umphress*

*A mother and her 9-year-old daughter in their garden:*
**Mother:** Ok. Should we pick one corn?[1]
**Daughter:** Um, ok. I'll choose what one, though. *((walks into the sweet corn patch of the garden))* (4.2) We could pick that one, or – I think we should [pick this one. *((places her hand on an ear of corn))*
**Mother:**                [This one's pretty big. *((gestures to a different ear of corn))*
**Mother:** Which one? Do you think that one?
**Daughter:** Ok.
**Mother:** I don't know how to tell. (·) Do you?
**Daughter:** Mm hmm. This all- this has to be brown. *((runs her fingers along the silk at the top of the ear of corn))*
**Mother:** Oh really? (1.1) And then it's ripe? <u>How do you know?</u>
**Daughter:** I don't know. I just know. That one is the brownest.
**Mother:** Should we pick it then take it in and see what it's like?
**Daughter:** Yeah. *((twists the ear of corn off of the stalk))*

*The same mother/daughter dyad, a little later in the garden:*
**Daughter:** Mom, is dill another word for sour? *((sitting on the ground, idly plucking at stalks of mint))*
**Mother:** Um…. *((walks around to position herself facing her daughter from a few feet away, standing above her))* I don't think so. But maybe. Maybe it is.
**Daughter:** It's so dill. (2.7)
**Mother:** I guess you could say that. (2.3) <u>What do you think?</u>
**Daughter:** Yeah. We could make up our own language. It's gonna be called the Garden Language.

**Mother:** *((laughs and bends forward to weed out crabgrass from among cucumber vines))* The Garden Language?
**Daughter:** Dill means sour.
**Mother:** OK. What are some other words in our language?

In these brief episodes, we see a mother posing two important questions to her daughter: "How do you know?" and "What do you think?" As researchers of knowledge and interaction, talk about *knowing* and *thinking* flag for us that something interesting might be happening. We might ask: What is going on during these little moments with respect to knowledge? Is there any significance to the mother asking these epistemically laden questions at these particular points in the activity with her daughter? How does the daughter respond to them?

In the course of everyday family conversation, these questions (i.e., "How do you know?" and "What do you think?") appear to be quite casual, but they also sound like what we might expect other types of adults to ask children less casually – adults whom I will call *skilled knowledge practitioners* (SKPs). Teachers, for example, may be the most visible type of SKPs in children's lives. They are professionally invested in the development and manipulation of children's knowledge, and ideally they also have some training in pedagogy and pedagogic content knowledge (e.g., Shulman, 1986) to assist in their work. Clinical interviewers are another kind of SKP who spend their careers assembling professional toolkits of best practices to coax children's knowledge into view and use it to test understandings (e.g., Ginsburg, 1997). It would be expected for clinical interviewers and teachers to ask children epistemic questions like "How do you know?" and "What do you think?", and in the environment of a classroom or clinical interview, these questions can be extremely important in the interactions between teacher/student and interviewer/interviewee. For example, they can preface assessment or be markers of genuine curiosity. They can also signal a challenge or disagreement or bring into focus that a child's thinking is relevant and valued. Much depends on their placement and usage in interaction.

While it is not the work of this chapter to fully describe the work of either teachers or clinical interviewers, let us consider *skilled knowledge practitioners* for a moment through the lens of this volume. Each of the two paradigms at hand here, *Knowledge Analysis* (KA) and *Interaction Analysis* (IA), has a range of commitments as to how knowledge is treated in research. KA, for example, wants to understand what people know and how they think. Traditionally that has led to a mix of static and dynamic descriptions – models of conceptual knowledge alongside theories of knowledge use (e.g., conceptual ecologies, coordination classes). IA, being concerned with how people move forward in interaction with one another, explores how people monitor knowledge in conversations. Analyses focus on how we position our own epistemic rights and authority to know in relation to others. The idea of a *skilled knowledge practitioner* suggests, to me, a person who sits at the intersection of these KA and IA interests. In their work with children, such a person would, almost by definition, need to be engaged in *both* arenas – critically reflecting on knowledge/knowing *and* the interaction around the knowledge/knowing.

While parents' training has been more that of laymen than professionals, they would certainly have ample opportunity to develop skills in the manipulation and exploration of their children's knowledge while navigating the demands of everyday life. Simply consider that some middle-class preschool children have been found to ask around 100 questions per hour in conversation with their parents, and that parents answer around 75 percent of those questions (Chouinard, 2007). At a rate of more than one question per minute, ranging from the mundane "Can I have a snack?" to more complex causal and teleological questions (e.g., Callanan & Oakes, 1992; Kelemen, Callanan, Casler, & Perez-Granados, 2005), a parent – willingly or not – could quickly develop some skills in handling their child's emerging and developing knowledge, as well as ideas about what their children know and think. Certainly, as we shall see by further exploring the larger episode featuring the mother and daughter shown at the start of this chapter, parents can make epistemic interactional moves that appear every bit as skilled as those made by other SKPs.

This chapter will claim that parents are SKPs, while thinking of SKPs as positioned at the intersection of KA and IA interests. To do that, the chapter will explore a case of everyday family activity that displays particularly clear interactional moves around *knowing* that might allow some comparison to other kinds of SKPs (clinical interviewers in particular). First, though, I present a few reflections about the work of clinical interviewers as SKPs that will be relevant to the case-study analysis, followed by some brief background on previous studies of family knowing, and introduce some useful analytic ideas from IA. Because understanding parents as a possible kind of SKP is the goal in this chapter, the analytic focus will be on the work of a mother in interaction with her child. That is, while I view SKPs as having feet in both KA and IA, in the interests of space I will only do an *Interaction Analysis* of this case study (that incorporates the knowledge that is in play) and leave a more rigorous *Knowledge Analysis* for another time. Ultimately, I want to address the questions: What benefit (if any) do we get in studies of families' everyday knowing by thinking of parents as a possible kind of SKP? And, in return, how does thinking of parents as a possible kind of SKP help in our understanding of other kinds of SKPs?

## The Epistemic Work of Clinical Interviewers as SKPs

While I have cited schoolteachers and clinical interviewers as two types of SKPs, the case study to be presented here really bears more resemblance to a kind of work done by the latter. This is particularly true because the mother in this study enacts what I refer to as the epistemic practice, *manipulating epistemic authority*, which is precisely what good clinical interviewers do, too. IA theorists might point out that this sort of manipulation can be done on the micro-scale, as people position themselves epistemically turn by turn in conversations. However, what happens in a successful clinical interview – while it does happen turn by turn – has a more cumulative, macro effect.

The interviewer's goal in an interaction is to have children describe their thinking without constraint in response to the interviewer's questions, as in a comfortable conversation. diSessa (2007) describes a good clinical interview as one "that is developmentally derivative of naturally occurring individual and mutual inquiry" (p. 531), which he describes as having a "flow of give and take, of suggestions and counter-suggestions, of judgments offered, and so on." The key is to alter the child's perceived sense of epistemic authority enough so that their conversation with a strange adult (a presumed authority, both epistemically and practically speaking) feels similar to naturally occurring inquiry. diSessa proposes that this is done in essentially two ways. First, the relevance of the child's ideas is raised compared to the relevance of the interviewer's ideas. This is accomplished partially by the social conventions of an interview setting (i.e., the interviewer is assumed to be interested in the thoughts of the interviewee) and also by the interviewer withholding their own ideas. Second, the interviewer offers no judgment of the child's ideas, instead leaving it entirely to the interviewee to judge the "reasonableness of a description or explanation" (diSessa, 2007, p. 534). The application of these two strategies is one version of a practice I call *manipulation of epistemic authority*.

Of course, the clinical interviewer has other tools to use in enacting this practice, too. Russ, Sherin, and Lee (this volume; Russ, Lee, & Sherin, 2012) have also written about how different interviewer moves can shift students' framing of what is happening in a clinical interview. The technique of revoicing, for example, can be used to signal either judgment or clarification (e.g., see diSessa, Greeno, Michaels, & O'Connor, this volume). However, the important thing to note for the comparison of parents and clinical interviewers as SKPs is that *manipulation of epistemic authority* is a critical part of the interviewer's work.

## Studies of *Knowing* in Families

Before discussing studies of *knowing* in families, I would like to note that I chose the term *knowing* here quite deliberately. In observing parents and children in action together, it would be strange to describe them as "doing knowledge," but it feels right to say that we often see them "doing knowing" – where *knowing* encompasses all of the ways that *knowledge* is used, developed, problematized, manipulated, contested, explored, encouraged, and so forth. This does not mean that it is unreasonable to talk about *knowledge* in family activities (I, myself, will do so). I simply want to tweak our idea of what it means to look for and see it in data of family activities by emphasizing the perspective that *knowledge* is a dynamic and reactive piece of parent/child interactions – perhaps more a verb than a noun.

That having been said, there is a growing body of work on everyday parent/child interactions that feature *knowing* in some respect.[2] The UCLA Sloan

Center on the Everyday Lives of Families (CELF) has, in particular, drawn on and expanded interactional studies of parents and children in and around their own homes (e.g., Fasulo, Loyd, & Padiglione, 2007; Paugh & Izquierdo, 2009; Sirota, 2006; Tulbert & Goodwin, 2011; Wingard, 2006; Wingard & Forsberg, 2009).[3] Elinor Ochs and Marjorie Goodwin, both also involved with the genesis and evolution of the CELF project, each have lines of research describing family activities that are uniquely *knowing* in substance.

For example, Ochs and her colleagues, in a series of articles on family dinnertime conversations, have attended to the careful ways in which children and parents collaboratively construct narrative stories about events from their days (e.g., Ochs, 1992; Ochs, Smith, & Taylor, 1989). The participation framework surrounding the construction of these narratives – which takes place inside the participation framework of having dinner together – is one of sharing and establishing a mutually agreed-upon family record of events. However, the process of eventually *knowing* these narratives, both individually and collectively, involves family members initially both supporting one another's contributions and challenging them on a variety of levels, including the veracity of their "facts." Family members can even engage in redrafting events for one another, suggesting foundational shifts of interpretation in the narratives being recounted by a sibling, parent, or spouse. Ochs and her colleagues lay bare this complex collaborative narrative construction process, which is rich in contests about *knowing*, and compare it to how scientists build theories.

In one particular study, Goodwin draws from a wider array of family activities (e.g., walking around the neighborhood, reading bedtime stories) to cull examples of what she refers to as "occasioned knowledge exploration" (M. H. Goodwin, 2007). She describes how parents offer their children opportunities to explore and engage in *knowledge/knowing* by doing things like offering up idioms or conceptual glosses for unpacking, inviting word play, and signaling where there are options for more assessment of an idea. These moments are marked by warmth and positive affect and distinguished by the restraint shown by the parent in offering subtle invitations instead of didactic lessons, followed by the children's willing uptake of joint knowledge exploration with their parent. The father featured in most of Goodwin's examples engages in a fairly subtle (perhaps even unconscious) baiting and seeding of knowing opportunities with his children.

Neither Ochs nor Goodwin goes so far as to say that the parents in their research are deliberately or consciously strategic about how they approach *knowledge* or *knowing* in their daily lives, as we would expect from professional SKPs in the course of their work (see diSessa et al., this volume, for a description of the explicitness of some SKP strategizing). However, by closely attending to the interactional moves these parents (and children) are making, we can see that they are adeptly engaged in complex *knowledge practices* with their children. *Collaborative narrative construction* and *occasioned knowledge exploration* are both rich kinds of everyday epistemic practices.

The data to be explored in this chapter offer another lens into family knowing by showing how a mother strategically uses *knowing* as a way to engage and reorient her daughter from being an unwilling participant to being playfully engaged. We will see how the mother makes managerial moves to direct the activity and set the affective tone of the interaction while also making crucial epistemic moves to diminish the relevance of her own epistemic authority and elevate the relevance of her daughter as a *knower* – moves which ultimately drive the interaction forward in a case of *manipulating epistemic authority* similar to the description of how it is practiced by clinical interviewers.

Tracking *knowing* between parents and children in this data set required dipping into the IA toolkit of ideas about how *knowing* gets done during conversation and interaction. For example, *epistemic authority* is a term important to this work (and to SKPs in general). Here and elsewhere, epistemic authority operates on two levels. On a macro level, it refers to the social judgments being made about the most authoritative source of knowledge on a given matter in or outside of a social arena (e.g., Kruglanski, Dechesne, Orehek, & Pierro, 2009; Kruglanski et al., 2005). For example, in a classroom, students generally cede epistemic authority to their teacher, who may in turn cede that authority to scientists or historians outside of the classroom (e.g., Raviv, Bar-Tal, Raviv, Biran, & Sela, 2003). On a more micro level, epistemic authority refers to a closely monitored aspect of conversation wherein participants continually (and largely subconsciously) monitor who is most entitled to *know* or make assessments about something, and subsequently do interactional/conversational work to assert that authority (e.g., Heritage, 2012a, 2012b; Heritage & Raymond, 2005; Kärkkäinen, 2003; Stivers, 2005). In any given conversational turn in a classroom, a student may assert their epistemic authority and rights over a teacher when, for example, recounting their own personal experience of the kind of fish they caught using a specific lure over the weekend. In that case, the student has claimed both the right to know and some level of authority over what kinds of bait different kinds of fish like to bite.

One other important IA concept that has already been mentioned is participation frameworks (e.g., Goodwin & Goodwin, 2004), which are the physical and dialogic ways in which participants arrange themselves with respect to one another and the activity they are doing together. In everyday family life, participation frameworks are instantiated through parents' and children's positioning of their participation in things like homework (C. Goodwin, 2007) and personal grooming activities (Tulbert & Goodwin, 2011). Parents and children can have aligning or conflicting participation frameworks during any given activity. In the case of conflicting frameworks, it can be very difficult for the activities of daily life to proceed smoothly and without conflict or struggle. In the episode of parent/child interaction that will be examined here, a mother and daughter begin a session of their gardening practice with misaligned participation frameworks, which makes the situation unpleasant for both of them.

This background about previous studies of family knowing and the IA ideas of participation frameworks, epistemic authority, and epistemic rights provide us with some footing to examine how events unfolded in the following case study. I will use them as a lens through which to view the interaction of mother and daughter gardening together from what will largely be an IA perspective. The goals are to understand (a) how *knowing* is being manipulated here between mother and daughter, and (b) if the mother is, in fact, a SKP.

## Research Design and Analysis

The data in this chapter come from a larger study of everyday family practices. Families with at least one child between the ages of 7 and 10 years old participated in recording themselves doing a variety of their everyday practices together, generally in and around their homes. No researcher was present during the recording sessions, which each lasted for about an hour. All families recorded themselves gardening together in their yards, and had been vegetable gardening for a minimum of three years prior to participating in the study. Participants were recruited largely through fliers and postings in online parenting and gardening message boards, and were told that the study was about how family members talked with one another in their daily lives, including when they were in nature, as they were while gardening. The data corpus consists of first-person-perspective videos taken with small, point-of-view shoulder-mounted cameras (V.I.O. Inc., 2009) worn by the focal parents, synchronized with additional audio streams generated by the focal children who were wearing individual digital voice recorders (Umphress & Sherin, 2015). The recording equipment was generally considered to be unobtrusive by all of the participants. However, the voice recorders needed to be placed in a pocket or worn in a shoulder bag or fanny pack, which caused – as we shall see – occasional wardrobe troubles for some of the children in the study.

In this chapter, I will be looking at the gardening session from a middle-class family of four as an instrumental case study of the epistemic practice *manipulating epistemic authority*. As an instrumental case study, the purpose of analysis is to assist in theory generation and the exploration of new concepts and ideas (Stake, 2003). By closely scrutinizing one example of how *knowing* can function in an everyday family activity we may be able to better understand both how a parent could be a SKP and how including parents in the category of SKPs helps shape that category. I will be drawing largely on IA methods, tracking how epistemic work gets done in the conversational turns and physical movements of the participants in this setting, and looking at how epistemic authority and rights are conferred or privileged by attending to the use of epistemic stance markers (e.g., Kärkkäinen, 2003) and responses to knowledge claims.

On the morning of this recording, Anna[4] (the mother) is gardening with her participating daughter, Joy (age 9 years old), and her younger daughter, Bailey (age 5 years old). Bailey wanders in and out of the scene as a semi-participating gardener (as does the family cat, Tonto). The father is not present. The family has recently returned home from a summer vacation and Anna has asked Joy to help clear away weeds and other plants that have become overgrown during their absence.

In the excerpts from this morning that are included here, it is important to keep in mind Anna's expertise in the garden – she is not a novice gardener. Entrance into the study was predicated on having a minimum of three years of vegetable gardening experience. While gardening was chosen as a focal practice partially because it is a constant process of trial, error, experimentation, and learning (and we would therefore genuinely expect Anna to continually make discoveries and sometimes express legitimate uncertainty), it is unlikely (though not impossible) that she really lacked the knowledge underpinning the decisions that we will see her hand over to Joy.

## Manipulating Epistemic Authority

This case study unfolds in three parts. At the beginning of the video recording, and described in Excerpt 1, Joy expresses explicit displeasure at her mother's instructions to prepare for their joint activity. She is hard to please while Anna tries to make her comfortable and engage her. The first part of their interaction that displays *knowing*, described here in *Part I: Becoming a knower in the garden*, is actually a series of interactions where Anna increasingly elevates Joy's epistemic rights while dropping her own into the background, starting with Excerpt 2. She transitions Joy from laborer to knower. The second part of *knowing* is described in *Part II: Knowing in the garden*, which shows the kind of knowledge sharing and exploration that happen once Anna's epistemic manipulation has taken place. Finally, *Part III: Working to maintain knowing rights*, shows that Anna makes an effort to continue to support Joy's epistemic standing in the garden in relation to her own, even after Joy has become cheerfully engaged in the gardening.

When the recording begins, Joy is lounging on the living room sofa, reluctant to get up and get ready to go outside. Excerpt 1, the first two minutes of the recording, establishes Joy's grumpy reluctance to transition into the gardening activity at that moment as her mother wishes. It is launched with a string of imperatives from Anna, who stands above Joy, already wearing her own recording gear and holding out the voice recorder to her daughter. The moment culminates in a severe expression of displeasure with Joy declaring, as she departs the scene, "I hate you."

Excerpt 1. (00:00.4–02:15.7)[5]
1    A:   Here, put this on. *((J sits up. A holds out the voice recorder to J, who takes it. A clips the lapel mic onto J's shirt))* (8.0) Okay.
2    J:   (whispers something)

3   A:  Do you have pockets? You need to have a pocket, so that this *((the recoding unit))* can go somewhere. Or like a little bag or something. *((A leaves the room, surveys pocketbooks, canvas bags, and jackets in the hallway. J slowly follows and stands in the doorway of living room, holding the voice recorder))* (18.0)
4   J:  Why do you want me to have pockets? *((J goes back into living room, A walks to hall closet and opens the door))* (0.4)
5   A:  Hey, Joy, can you please be a little bit more cheerful? *((A pulls out a shoulder bag from the closet and lengthens the strap))* (12.0)
6   J:  Really, I'm going to be videotaped wearing that?
7   A:  Well, you don't have pockets, so… *((A takes the voice recorder from J, pushes buttons until it's recording, then puts the recorder in the shoulder bag))* (19.2) Okay. (4.0) What's the matter?
8   J:  Nothing. (yawning) It's just that's the biggest thing you can get.
9   A:  What?
10  J:  I don't know why, but I just don't want to be videotaped wearing something so big like that. I feel so weird!
11  A:  Well, let's put it in the back of you, or don't you-
12  J:  Unh-unh.
13  A:  Well, then go change your pants and put on some with pockets. You need both of your hands to help me, and you can't have both your hands if you're holding this. (7.0)
14  J:  I hate you. *((J goes to her room and changes her clothes))*

Contrary to the tone of Excerpt 1, I should note that Anna and Joy have a very loving and mutually respectful relationship. Also, Joy was an enthusiastic participant in the research study and eager to wear the recording equipment at other times during her family's participation. However, Excerpt 1 clearly shows that Anna is having difficulty getting Joy outside to the garden and oriented toward the work she wants them to accomplish together. In this opening directive sequence (M. H. Goodwin, 2006), Anna is attempting to establish a frame for their participation together by using a physical *facing formation* (Kendon, 1990), suggesting an expectation of precipitate action and a *participation framework* in which she will be issuing the directions. Joy does not attempt to establish her own competing framework, but she clearly resists giving her mother her full participation.

When they do make it outside a few minutes later, Joy continues arguing with her mother over wearing shoes, petulantly agrees to a pair of gardening gloves from Anna's offered choices, complains about being cold and uncomfortable, and when she finally physically engages in the gardening she declares, "Eeewwww, I hate weeding," and directs her mother to deal with weeding out the crabgrass, "Because I hate crabgrass." Joy may be present and participating in the garden at this point, but she is not jointly oriented toward her mother's desired framing of the activity (and she is not "more cheerful"). Anna is solicitous, offers Joy choices, tries to rearrange materials and tools so that Joy is more comfortable, and repeatedly gently reminds Joy of why their work that day is necessary after the family's vacation.

## Part I: Becoming a *Knower* in the Garden

At around 11 minutes into the recording, only a few minutes after they have entered the garden, Joy asks, "When are we going to be done?" Anna evades directly answering by giving a transformative (Stivers & Hayashi, 2010), describing instead the list of things they will do together in the garden. She then makes her first epistemically interesting move. As Anna lists the chores, she mentions the peppermint plants, which badly need to be trimmed. Joy responds with an arching question (Mishler, 1975) regarding the name of the plant, which momentarily hijacks the conversation by requesting a repair (e.g., Schegloff, Jefferson, & Sacks, 1977). Anna, in response, hedges her initial answer and concedes to Joy's challenge of nomenclature. Excerpt 2 contains the exchange.

Excerpt 2. (11:26.2–12:01.7)
1   J:   When are we going to be done? *((J sits on the ground, hacking at weeds))*
2   A:   *((standing above and facing J))* Well, let's weed for a while, and then we can do something fun, like go and check on the cucumbers, and then maybe we'll make pickles. (2.9) And you know what else we have to do? *((bends over and resumes plucking weeds))*
3   J:   What?
4   A:   You know how the, um, peppermint is getting all crazy?
5   J:   You mean the mint?
6   A:   What?
7   J:   You mean the mint? Or is that peppermint? (1.3)
8   A:   I don't know. I think-I thought it was peppermint; I guess it's mint.
9   J:   Well, whatever it is.
10  A:   Yeah, it's getting crazy. And it's taking over.

Anna's pre-announcement in Line 4, introducing the topic of the overgrown peppermint, is met with an arching question from Joy that redirects the exchange away from the chore list. Anna appears unsure of how to respond in Line 6 (Joy's question could be received as either making a correction or asking for clarification), and signals that a repair is needed on Joy's question (i.e., "What?"). Joy repeats her question in Line 7, adding an additional question that locates the plant's name as the site of her requested repair. In Line 8, Anna prefaces her response with the epistemic stance marker, "I don't know" (Kärkkäinen, 2003). When used in the first part of a conversational turn, "I don't know" usually serves to soften a dispreferred response – often a disagreement – and not to signal an actual lack of knowledge (Pomerantz, 1984; Tsui, 1991). Therefore, Anna begins her turn in Line 8 by taking steps to disagree with Joy's possibly implied correction, doubling down with another hedging epistemic stance marker, "I think." In everyday conversation, both "I don't know" and "I think" are moves most often used to initiate future disagreement without striking direct challenge or confrontation. However, after laying the groundwork for a face-saving disagreement, Anna changes course and speculatively agrees with Joy that the plant *could* be called just "mint." By using the hedging stance marker, "I guess," Anna has not fully conceded the point about the plant's name, but she has conceded that Joy's question has epistemic standing (Kärkkäinen, 2010). In response, Joy signals in Line 9 that she is willing to let the conversation move forward, although, perhaps still grumpy, she withholds agreement or approval of her mother's answer.

Anna's course change in Line 8 of Excerpt 2, where she deliberately downplays her own epistemic authority while elevating Joy's, turns out to be pivotal. About 20 seconds later, Joy offers her first hint of willing participation by announcing that she thinks one of the carrot plants might be ready to harvest. Anna seizes the moment and comes over to Joy's position in the garden to inspect the indicated carrot. She brings herself physically into alignment with Joy, establishing a new facing formation wherein both of their bodies are physically oriented toward the same task and not in opposition to one another for the first time in the recording. Looking at the carrot fronds standing above the soil, Anna responds (around Bailey's loud and enthusiastic competing cries for attention in the tomato patch), "It might be (ready). You could pull it." Joy unearths the carrot, which turns out to be quite small, and holds it up for inspection, remarking, "We could have let it go longer, though." Anna agrees, "We could have let it go longer. But it would be good to have for lunch." Joy's first harvesting judgment of the day has been proven miscalculated, but Anna slides past it and puts a positive face on it.

This exchange over the carrot marks Anna's second epistemic maneuver. Joy proposes a bit of knowing – she believes that a carrot might be ripe – and Anna explicitly agrees and confers her permission to act on that knowing, further indicating that Joy's epistemic rights are valid and actionable in this scenario. Anna underscores that Joy's knowing is legitimate, even if her judgment of the carrot's ripeness was faulty, by saying, "We could have let it go longer." A full repeat from the second position in sequential conversational turns offers confirmation of the first speaker's assessment (Stivers, 2005). Thus *Joy's* assessment stands confirmed, and the daughter has shifted from reluctantly weeding to joining in as another active *knower* in the garden. In just two minutes of interaction and over the added chaos of an attention-seeking younger sibling, Anna has started to reorient Joy's participation framework for gardening that morning.

A few turns later, after Bailey has also inspected the small carrot and heard Joy's assessment that they need to wait longer before pulling any more of them, Anna extends an invitation for Joy to harvest a different vegetable (cucumbers) which they will need to make pickles later that afternoon. Joy (who has not made pickles before) immediately signals her willingness to participate by asking for some guidance, and is met with enthusiasm by Anna. Over the course of the cucumber harvest, shown in Excerpt 3, Bailey again enters the scene and tries to negotiate the right to participate by seeking permission first from her big sister and then from her mother. Joy denies Bailey entrance into the harvest, and Anna echoes that denial by citing Joy's authority – further explicitly naming Joy as a collaborator and joint knower.

Excerpt 3. (14:01.7–16:07.7)
1   A:   Are you going to pick those cucumbers? (2.0)
2   J:   What ones? There's a lot.
3   A:   Really?
4   J:   Yeah. There's that one, and that one, and that one
5   A:   Let me see. ((steps closer to J, who is sitting on the ground with her back to A))
6   A:   I think that's-
7   J:   ((gestures to a bigger cucumber hidden under plant leaves)) And we could make a bigger gherkin.
8   A:   Yeah? Okay. Well, let me come over and check it out, and see. ((walks over to directly behind J))
9   J:   This is the bigger gherkin. ((discovers a smaller cucumber)) (3.2) Oh, yeah, we could make- This is a little tiny gherkin.
10  A:   Oh, well- Well let's pick the big ones.
11  J:   Like this?=
12  A:   =And maybe one little one. Oh, my gosh, look how big that one is!
13  B:   Let me see how big that one- Whoa!
14  A:   Did it grow like that while we were on vacation?
15  J:   Yeah.
(Conversation continues with comments on how big the cucumber is, covering 16.2 seconds)
16  J:   That one sure is ready.
17  A:   Yeah.
18  B:   Well, the bigger one is this one. ((picks up a cucumber still attached to a vine near her feet))
19  J:   But don't pull it, though. Bailey, that one is almost ready, but don't pull it. ↓Don't pull it. Check the other. Let's check the other plant. Ooo, Bailey, get out of the way. ((J stands up and brushes past B to reach another plant, her back turned to B and A))
20  A:   Well, do you want to pick any more cucumbers?
21  B:   (says something unclear)
22  J:   Well, there might be some on this plant.
23  A:   True. (5.6)
24  J:   Oh, weeds!
25  A:   Pull the weeds. If you see weeds, just pull them out. ((reaches down to pull weeds from around her feet)) (10.2)
26  B:   Can I pick this one? Can I pick these- this pickle?
27  J:   No, Bailey, don't pick any pickles.
28  B:   Can I pick this one, mama?
29  A:   Um, (·) well=
30  J:   =Leave it a little longer.
31  A:   No. Joy said that she didn't want me to pick it.
32  B:   Okay.
33  A:   She wants it to grow a little more
34  J:   So that we'll have big pickles.

Unlike her negative responses to Anna's previous requests or suggestions for activity, this time Joy meets Anna's question in Line 1 with acceptance. In the ensuing turns of talk, Lines 3 through 9, Anna matches Joy's rising enthusiasm and comes again to physically meet her. In Line 10, following Joy's allusion to making pickles, Anna extends her guidance on which cucumbers they should harvest for the pickles. Her advice could be interpreted as reclaiming authority over the activity, but in Lines 12–15 Joy receives Anna's amazement and surprise at the growth of the cucumbers as a literal question and invitation for response. This suggests that Joy does not read Anna's guidance as sublimating her own role or rights as a co-knower, which peak in Line 19 when she hands down instruction/guidance to Bailey about a particular cucumber: "don't pull it." Seconds later, Bailey takes her request to harvest the cucumber to their mother, who makes another key epistemic move in Line 31 by answering her younger daughter, "No. Joy said that she didn't want me to pick it." This response accomplishes two things. First, it explicitly signals that in this arena at this moment Joy's judgments count equally with her mother's *and* can publicly determine her mother's actions. Second, it establishes Bailey as a subordinate knower to Joy, implicitly producing an epistemic hierarchy and two tiers of knowing.

A third harvesting event (part of which is featured in the opening to this chapter) follows on the heels of the cucumber harvest, wherein Anna asks if they should pick an ear of their sweet corn. Joy, now fully engaged as a joint knower with the freedom to act on her ideas, responds by saying, "Um, ok. I'll choose what one, though." Anna gives Joy full rein, saying, "I don't know how to tell (if it's ready). Do you?" Joy asserts with confidence that she does know how to tell, and proceeds to use her criterion (the silk on the ear will be brown) to choose an ear of corn. Upon opening the husks, the ear turns out to be underdeveloped. As with the puny carrot that Joy chose a few minutes earlier, they agree that the corn was, in fact, not yet ripe, and Anna instructs her daughters (Bailey has rejoined them again), "Don't pick anymore. Now we know we have to wait." This is as close as Anna comes to establishing a limit on Joy's position as a knower in the garden, but she does it with epistemic inclusivity by using the plural "we know."

These three harvesting events, which last for about 10 minutes, display Anna's manipulation of *knowing* as one tool for engaging her daughter.[6] In a few quick conversational moves, beginning with her concession to Joy's challenge about the name of the peppermint plant and capped with her declaration that she does not know how to tell if corn is ripe, she shifts Joy from a *laborer* pressed into service to a *knower* whose decision making is as important as her wielding of a garden hoe. Furthermore, Anna works physically to establish facing formations that align with Joy as a co-knower in the garden by repeatedly abandoning her own weeding activities to join Joy and see what is engaging *her*. Interrupting her own work – which is carrying out the primary goal of the morning by weeding the garden – in order to join her daughter is a further kind of epistemic move (in addition to often being immensely practical).

This sequence of epistemic moves by Anna, while situated in the activity context and participation framework of gardening, are highly reminiscent of moves made by a good clinical interviewer. The interviewer works to establish an implicit contract with the interviewee that *their* ideas and knowledge are more relevant in the interaction than the interviewer's own ideas and knowledge. Anna has begun her *manipulation of epistemic authority*.

## Part II: *Knowing* in the Garden

After these events, the gardening moves into an easier, lighter tone. Joy stops using negatively valenced language like "hate" and helps Anna cut back the overgrown mint and do more weeding for another 20 minutes before drifting over to the patio to lay down and play with Tonto, the family cat, for the final 20 minutes of the recording session. She spends this time pleasantly talking with Anna (who remains weeding in the garden) and sometimes Bailey. Interestingly, now that Joy's participation has been epistemically shifted, those last 40 minutes are punctuated by a series of episodes that closely resemble what Marjorie Goodwin (2007) calls *occasioned knowledge exploration*, "when children and parents extemporaneously connect new knowledge to existing knowledge in collaborative endeavors … they thus differ from didactic 'lessons' in which parents lecture children about science … without a child's inviting them to do so" (p. 97). However, Joy and Anna's moments of knowledge exploration have a pattern that differs significantly from that described by Goodwin, in which the parent initiates these opportunities and waits for uptake by the children. In a reverse of Goodwin's pattern, Joy volunteers ideas or bits of knowledge and opens them up for discussion. She then waits for Anna to acknowledge and respond to them.

While there are several cases of this in the recording (including the light-hearted stretch of word play featured in the opening of this chapter), Excerpt 4 provides a nice example. In Excerpt 4, mother and daughter are identifying and trimming overgrown mint runners. Joy makes a connection between mint and the medicinal herbs used in a series of fictional fantasy books she is reading (*Warriors*, published by HarperCollins). The book series details the adventures of clans of wild cats, including cat warriors trained in medicinal arts. Joy is an avid reader of the *Warriors* series and often talks about the family cat in terms paralleling the *Warriors* fictional realm. Anna's response to Joy's connection between their garden and the book series again walks a fine line between challenging/disagreeing and agreeing with her daughter.

Excerpt 4 (32:42.9–33:27.7)

1  A:  There we go. That's much better. *((J and A are squatting together on the ground, facing one another and collaboratively cutting back mint runners))*
2  J:  But my flowers?
3  A:  I know your flowers are getting invaded, too. That's why I'm trying to save everything from this crazy mint. *(A holds a stalk of mint while J clips it at its base))* (2.2)
4  J:  Cat mint. (5.8) You know what? You know what's a- a healing herb?
5  A:  What?
6  J:  From Medicine Cats? [Catnip.
7  A:                      [What?
8  A:  Catnip? Really?
9  J:  Yeah from Medicine Cats. *((J clips a large mint stem and hands it to A))*
10 A:  Oh, but they go crazy when they eat catnip.
11 J:  And stinging nettle.
12 A:  Oh, I don't like stinging nettle.
13 J:  They only use- they- they use the leaves.
14 A:  Oh, really?
15 J:  Yeah.
16 A:  Hmm. (2.2)
17 A:  Let's see. *((stands up and turns to the side))* Alright.

The knowledge exploration begins with Joy's pre-announcement in Line 4 signaling to Anna that she has something interesting to share. Anna expresses surprise and uses a direct repeat in Line 8 ("Catnip? Really?") to register a bit of a challenge by requesting a repair. She reiterates her challenge in Line 10 by referencing what happens in real life when cats eat catnip. Anna ultimately closes the exchange with a non-committal, "Hmmm" and then redirects their attention back to trimming the peppermint.

Anna's subtle challenges to Joy's connection between the novels and real life (her repair request in Line 8 and confirmation request in Line 14) indicate that she might have the urge to disagree or want Joy to reconsider her assertions. However, staying true to her course of downplaying her own epistemic rights (or at least signaling that she is not fully asserting those rights now), she closes this exchange, as with many others, on a note of accord, using the retrospective 'carry-on' signal, "Alright" (Gardner, 2007; Stenström, 1987). Her epistemic stance of encouragement without judgment, exemplified in Excerpt 4, continues Anna's positioning of Joy as a legitimate knower and buttresses Joy's freedom to express her knowing. It is also, again, parallel to another core clinical interviewer move in *manipulating epistemic authority* – the withholding of judgment.

## Part III: Working to Maintain *Knowing* Rights

In Excerpt 2, where Joy questioned the name of the mint plant, a single turn of talk had Anna veer from initiating a disagreement to acknowledging Joy's possible epistemic standing. This midstream course correction by Anna was not an isolated incident and occurs repeatedly throughout the morning, showing how Anna works to maintain the elevated sense of Joy's epistemic rights. Excerpt 5 shows one additional example – the moment from the chapter opening that turns into wordplay and the creation of "the garden language." In this case, while talking about what kind of pickles they will make that afternoon, Joy asks Anna for a confirmation of her understanding of the word "dill." Anna begins her response once again with an epistemic stance marker signaling disagreement ("I don't think so"), but then shifts to allow that Joy could be correct.

Excerpt 5 (38:46.7–39:09.4)
1  J:  Mom, is dill another word for sour? *((sitting on the ground, idly plucking at stalks of mint))*
2  A:  Um… *((walks around to position herself facing J from a few feet away, standing above her))* I don't think so, but maybe. Maybe it is.
3  J:  It's so dill. (2.7)
4  A:  I guess you could say that. (2.3) What do you think?
5  J:  Yeah. We can make up our own language. It's gonna be called the Garden Language.
6  A:  *((laughs and bends forward to weed out crabgrass from among cucumber vines))* The Garden Language?
7  J:  Dill means sour.
8  A:  OK. What are some other words in our language?

In all of the cases where Anna changes her response to preserve Joy's epistemic standing, (e.g., Excerpts 2 and 5), she consistently hedges her responses with "maybe" and "I guess so." Importantly, these midstream conversions – where she sets up a disagreement but then acquiesces to Joy's ideas – make Anna's efforts to do this epistemic positioning of Joy (and herself) visible to us. Like a clinical interviewer, we see her making improvisational moves as the interaction progresses, moving her own epistemic rights into the background and putting Joy's in the spotlight in order to achieve her goal of bringing Joy into the desired participation framework. Although, since Joy is now cooperatively engaged in gardening, we can perhaps assume that Anna's motivations for continuing this interactional work may have also shifted. Possibly she just enjoys hearing what her daughter is thinking, or maybe – as is often the case in everyday life – being "right" is just not that important when balanced with getting along.

## Discussion

### Is Anna a SKP?

The data used in this chapter show a mother and daughter negotiating their way through an interaction – one that begins with friction but closes with everyone at ease. Anna, strategically or not, finds a way to reorient her daughter using epistemic maneuvering after a failed string of attempts to ease Joy into the activity through other means. Those moves parallel ones used by clinical interviewers in *manipulating epistemic authority*. Anna (a) gives Joy fairly wide latitude in expressing her own epistemic rights by making decisions about what to harvest, and also (b) persistently tries to maintain a state of epistemic agreeableness by refraining from negative judgment, even when she might disagree with Joy's knowledge claims. We see her do this by marking her utterances as though she is about to disagree but then stopping and giving sway to *Joy's* epistemic rights, and also by closing knowledge exploration exchanges before they reach serious disagreement.

While in a clinical interview the goal of these moves within the activity is to cultivate the child's unconstrained expression of their knowledge, here Anna's recognition of Joy's epistemic rights and elevation of her as a co-knower work to soften Joy's initial annoyance and ease her into full participation. Consequently, once Joy is engaged as a *knower* and not just a *laborer*, she also becomes available for other forms of knowledge sharing and exploration with her mother on non-combative terms. This seems not unreasonably like the desired outcome of the epistemic manipulation in a clinical interview. Within the garden, we may assume that Anna's goals do not necessarily parallel (at least at a primary level) those of other SKPs in their activity settings, but her interactional moves and their outcome do. Unfortunately, we only have access to Anna in the gardening video, as I was unable to interview her later about that morning, so we cannot know if she would have had thoughtful reasoning about why we did not see her push further on Joy's ideas about ripeness.

As education and learning researchers, or folks interested in KA, we might ask why Anna, if she is a SKP, did not engage Joy in more pointed reflection on her ideas about ripeness, as she was given latitude to pursue them to their unfortunate conclusions. That would be a familiar move of some other SKPs. Consider classroom teachers, who often rely heavily on the initiate-respond-evaluate discourse pattern (e.g., Mehan, 1982) to solicit and assess children's ideas. A clinical interviewer might have also wanted to understand more about Joy's concept of "ripe" and probed further with additional (non-judgmental) questions. Instead, Anna consummately refrains from deeper exploration of Joy's knowledge (in this recording). Can she be a SKP without expression of KA interests?

I would argue that Anna has, in this setting, an option for exploring Joy's knowledge that is not often afforded to other SKPs in their professional settings. Anna could argue/evaluate/probe Joy's ideas explicitly like other SKPs, or she could let Joy test them as they arise, ask her own questions, and learn. In fact, in giving support to Joy's pursuit of her knowledge claims by allowing her to test them out in the garden, Anna also accumulates interactional capital that opens up further possibilities for mutual inquiry. For example, later in the session as they are clearing away the trimmed mint foliage, mother and daughter pause and dangle mint leaves in front of the cat, Tonto, gauging his reaction to the herb as a follow-up to Joy's report on the characters in her book series. It is a warm, playful exchange and simple idea-check that Anna has perhaps purchased both by earlier turning away from her skepticism of Joy's attempted knowledge connection between the book and real life and also by giving Joy the freedom to check her ideas using plants and objects in the garden.

Each SKP engages in exploration of children's knowledge according to the constraints of their activity setting. Teachers can trade on a socially accepted activity structure that includes questioning and assessment. Clinical interviewers trade on the socially accepted structure of an interview wherein one person asks another a list of questions. Parents, including the most skilled SKPs amongst them, must find opportunities for knowledge exploration within their own activity settings – which they do. For example, in the data corpus from which this case study is drawn, there are also cases of parents doing direct instruction, simple experiments, and extended sense-making/problem-solving with their children in their gardens. If we accept that the interaction analysis presented here makes the argument for Anna's skillfulness in dealing with *knowing* interactions with her child, and that she may also be doing some exploration and development of Joy's knowledge along the way *in this setting*, then I believe that we can call Anna a SKP.

## Conclusion

### *Does Thinking of Anna as a SKP Help the Study of Family Knowing or the Category of SKPs?*

If we consider parents as SKPs, how does that help anyone? At the very least, framing this kind of parental work, or these kinds of everyday epistemic practices (e.g., *manipulating epistemic authority*) in such a way that they have a relationship with how children are treated in other learning environments (I consider the home/family to be the first and possibly most important learning environment) is really useful. Children do interact with other SKPs when they are students and research participants. It seems very important to understand those interactions in relation to one another both for the sake of SKPs being reflective practitioners and for enhancing the probability of creating learning environments that mutually help children to learn. What if teachers, instead of leaning on conventions of epistemic and managerial authority, could facilitate the kind of epistemic transition with their students that Anna did here with Joy? Would it help them more productively frame their classroom learning endeavors? How would students respond if their epistemic rights were acknowledged more often and their teachers' downplayed? Clinical interviewers could also perhaps benefit from understanding the range of epistemic games played between parents and children in everyday mutual inquiry – it might add more tools to their toolbox.

Studies of family knowing also benefit from seeing parents as potential SKPs. This perspective gives increased legitimacy to the hard epistemic work that parents and children do together all the time. It also helps to further empirically ground the intuition that home/families are important sites of children's knowing and learning. Everyone stands to benefit from seeing parents in this more three-dimensional way.

Thinking about parents as SKPs also provides a framework for understanding what they do from both the KA and IA perspectives together. As described earlier, SKPs operate at the intersection of KA and IA interests. Their work is equally about understanding what and how people think *and* how to move interactions forward when knowing is a critical part of the scenario. In this way, they embody the spirit of collaboration between the two. This chapter is a step toward the integration of ideas from these perspectives for understanding the role of knowledge in adult/child interactions – specifically in everyday parent/child interactions

## Acknowledgments

This work was partly funded by a grant from the Spencer Foundation and made possible by the participating families who opened their homes and recorded parts of their daily lives for the sake of research. In writing this chapter, the author would like to thank the scholars who participated in the KA/IA discussions and especially the editorial team of this volume for their support and feedback. Credit for the term "skilled knowledge practitioners" belongs to Andy diSessa.

## Notes

1  Transcription conventions for conversation analysis come from Jefferson (2004). Non-talk activity is enclosed in *((italicized, double parentheses))*. Overlapping talk across turns is signified by vertically aligned [. Interruptions are indicated with single dashes -, rising and falling intonation with arrows ↑↓, and connected speech with no break or gap with =. Brief pauses are represented by (·). Longer pauses are measured to tenths of seconds in parentheses (0.2).
2  To be clear, "everyday" in the sense used both in this chapter and in the IA work discussed here means *truly* everyday activity and not family activities that might be considered epistemologically special, such as trips to museums. There is a strong and growing body of research on parent/child interactions in museums which can make many contributions to our overall understandings of the variety of roles that knowing plays in adult/child interactions. However, museums have a complex epistemic hybridity due to their nature as constructed environments designed by "experts" for public education and learning. When visiting them, each family experiences a unique set of pressures and/or expectations to play the part of teachers and students, to locate knowledge authorities inside or outside of their group, and to "learn" (in addition to other goals such as having fun together). While there may also be complex epistemic factors at play in everyday family activities such as playing board games, I would argue that their effect displayed through family interactions is more attributable to the individual culture of a family.

3   In addition to CELF, the Learning in Informal and Formal Environments (LIFE) National Science Foundation Science of Learning Center and Center for Informal Learning and Schools (CILS) have also done excellent work exploring aspects of children's everyday lives.
4   Pseudonyms are used throughout this chapter.
5   Time stamps are given with each transcript excerpt to allow an accurate sense of the passage of time in the recording.
6   Anna's epistemic manipulation is undoubtedly only one of several pieces of her overall management of the situation. Almost certainly, practical concerns like preserving vegetables for future harvests and keeping her younger, more inexperienced daughter from doing damage in the garden by limiting her activities also play a role here.

## References

Callanan, M. A., & Oakes, L. M. (1992). Preschoolers' questions and parents' explanations: Causal thinking in everyday activity. *Cognitive Development*, 7(2), 213–233.

Chouinard, M. (2007). Children's questions: A mechanism for cognitive development. *Monographs of the Society for Research in Child Development*, 72(1), 1–129.

diSessa, A. (2007). An interactional analysis of clinical interviewing. *Cognition and Instruction*, 25(4), 1–43.

Fasulo, A., Loyd, H., & Padiglione, V. (2007). Children's socialization into cleaning practices: A cross-cultural perspective. *Discourse & Society*, 18(1), 11–33.

Gardner, R. (2007). The *right* connections: Acknowledging epistemic progression in talk. *Language in Society*, 36(3), 319–341.

Ginsburg, H. P. (1997). *Entering the child's mind: The clinical interview in psychological research and practice*. Cambridge, UK: Cambridge University Press.

Goodwin, C. (2007). Participation, stance and affect in the organization of activities. *Discourse & Society*, 18(1), 53–73.

Goodwin, C., & Goodwin, M. H. (2004). Participation. In A. Duranti (Ed.), *A companion to Linguistic Anthropology* (pp. 221–244). Malden, MA: Blackwell.

Goodwin, M. H. (2006). Participation, affect, and trajectory in family directive/response sequences. *Text & Talk*, 26(4–5), 515–543.

Goodwin, M. H. (2007). Occasioned knowledge exploration in family interaction. *Discourse & Society*, 18(1), 93–110. doi: 10.1177/0957926507069459.

Heritage, J. (2012a). The epistemic engine: Sequence organization and territories of knowledge. *Research on Language and Social Interaction*, 45(1), 30–52.

Heritage, J. (2012b). Epistemics in action: Action formation and territories of knowledge. *Research on Language and Social Interaction*, 45(1), 1–29.

Heritage, J., & Raymond, G. (2005). The terms of agreement: Indexing epistemic authority and subordination in talk-in-interaction. *Social Psychology Quarterly*, 68(1), 15–38.

Jefferson, G. (2004). Glossary of transcript symbols with an introduction. In G. H. Lerner (Ed.), *Conversation Analysis: Studies from the first generation* (pp. 13–23). Philadelphia, PA: John Benjamins.

Kärkkäinen, E. (2003). *Epistemic stance in English conversation: A description of its interactional functions with a focus on I think*. Philadelphia, PA: John Benjamins.

Kärkkäinen, E. (2010). Position and scope of epistemic phrases in planned and unplanned American English. In G. Kaltenböck, W. Mihatsch, & S. Schneider (Eds.), *New approaches to hedging* (pp. 203–236). Amsterdam, NL: Elsevier.

Kelemen, D., Callanan, M. A., Casler, K., & Perez-Granados, D. R. (2005). Why things happen: Teleological explanation in parent-child conversations. *Developmental Psychology*, 41(1), 251–264.

Kendon, A. (1990). Spatial organization in social encounters: The F-formation system. In A. Kendon (Ed.), *Conducting interaction: Patterns of behavior in focused encounters* (pp. 209–238). Cambridge, UK: Cambridge University Press.

Kruglanski, A. W., Dechesne, M., Orehek, E., & Pierro, A. (2009). Three decades of lay epistemics: The why, how, and who of knowledge formation. *European Review of Social Psychology*, 20(1), 146–191.

Kruglanski, A. W., Raviv, A., Bar-Tal, D., Raviv, A., Sharvit, K., Ellis, S., … Mannetti, L. (2005). Says who? Epistemic authority effects in social judgement. *Advances in Experimental Social Psychology*, 37, 345–392.

Mehan, H. (1982). The structure of classroom events and their consequences for student performance. In P. Gilmore & A. Glatthorn (Eds.), *Children in and out of school* (pp. 59–87). Washington, DC: Center for Applied Linguistics.

Mishler, E. (1975). Studies in dialogue and discourse: II. Types of discourse initiated by and sustained through questioning. *Journal of Psycholinguistic Research*, 4(2), 99–121.

Ochs, E. (1992). Storytelling as a theory-building activity. *Discourse Processes*, 15(1), 37–72.

Ochs, E., Smith, R., & Taylor, C. (1989). Detective stories at dinnertime: Problem-solving through co-narration. *Cultural Dynamics*, 2(2), 238–257.

Paugh, A., & Izquierdo, C. (2009). Why is this a battle every night? Negotiating food and eating in American dinnertime interaction. *Journal of Linguistic Anthropology*, 19(2), 185–204.

Pomerantz, A. (1984). Agreeing and disagreeing with assessments: Some features of preferred/dispreferred turn shapes. In J. M. Atkinson & J. Heritage (Eds.), *Structures of social action: Studies in conversation analysis* (pp. 57–100). Cambridge, UK: Cambridge University Press.

Raviv, A., Bar-Tal, D., Raviv, A., Biran, B., & Sela, Z. (2003). Teachers' epistemic authority: Perceptions of students and teachers. *Social Psychology of Education*, 6, 17–42.

Russ, R. S., Lee, V. R., & Sherin, B. L. (2012). Framing in cognitive clinical interviews about intuitive science knowledge: Dynamic student understandings of the discourse interaction. *Science Education*, 96(4), 573–599.

Schegloff, E., Jefferson, G., & Sacks, H. (1977). The preference for self-correction in the organization of repair in conversation. *Language*, 53(2), 361–382.

Shulman, L. E. (1986). Those who understand: Knowledge growth in teaching. *Education Researcher*, 15(2), 4–14.

Sirota, K. G. (2006). Habits of the hearth: Children's bedtime routines as relational work. *Text & Talk*, 4/5, 493–514.

Stake, R. E. (2003). Case studies. In N. Denzin & Y. Lincoln (Eds.), *Strategies of qualitative inquiry* (2nd ed., pp. 134–164). Thousand Oaks, CA: Sage.

Stenström, A.-B. (1987). *Carry-on signals in English conversation*. Paper presented at the Seventh International Conference on English Language Research on Computerized Corpora, Amsterdam, NL.

Stivers, T. (2005). Modified repeats: One method for asserting primary rights from second position. *Research on Language and Social Interaction*, 38(2), 131–158.

Stivers, T., & Hayashi, M. (2010). Transformative answers: One way to resist a question's constraints. *Language in Society*, 39(1), 1–25.

Tsui, A. B. M. (1991). The pragmatic functions of "I don't know." *Text*, 11(4), 607–622.

Tulbert, E., & Goodwin, M. H. (2011). Choreographies of attention: Multimodality in a routine family activity. In J. Streeck, C. Goodwin, & C. LeBaron (Eds.), *Embodied interaction: Language and body in the material world* (pp. 79–92). New York: Cambridge University Press.

Umphress, J., & Sherin, B. (2015). The body as viewfinder: Using wearable cameras in learning research. In V. Lee (Ed.), *Learning technologies and the body: Integration and implementation in formal and informal learning environments* (pp. 220–237). New York: Routledge.

V.I.O. Inc. (2009, Retrieved September 21, 2009 from www.vio-pov.com). POV. 1.5.

Wingard, L. (2006). Parents' inquiries about homework: The first mention. *Text & Talk*, 4/5, 573–598.

Wingard, L., & Forsberg, L. (2009). Parent involvement in children's homework in American and Swedish dual-earner families. *Journal of Pragmatics*, 41(8), 1576–1595.

# 13
# KNOWLEDGE AND INTERACTION IN CLINICAL INTERVIEWING

Revoicing

*Andrea A. diSessa, James G. Greeno, Sarah Michaels, and Catherine O'Connor*

Clinical interviewing has a long history as a method to study subjects' ways of understanding and coming to understand (Gruber & Voneche, 1977). It remains commonly used by learning researchers (Clement, 2000; diSessa, 2007; Ginsberg, 1997).

Clinical interviewing is provocative and potentially fertile as a subject of study from the complementary perspectives of knowledge and interaction. It is provocative because it has been criticized as a research method from interactional and sociocultural points of view (Bannon & Bødker, 1991; see also Talmy, 2011). Criticisms include that it is ecologically invalid; that clinical interaction is very likely to introduce interactional artifacts that obscure analysis of the subject's "knowledge"; and even a skepticism concerning the validity of knowledge itself as stable and transportable to new contexts. On a broader front, some influential researchers of interaction (particularly conversation analysts and ethnomethodologists) sometimes at least give the appearance of denying the relevance of knowledge to understanding interaction. For example, consider:

> EM [ethnomethodology] argues that one can observe the meaning-making processes at work by carefully studying the discourse between people; one does not have to make inferences about hidden changes in mental models or invisible social structures [or, presumably, other "invisible" mental entities, like knowledge].
>
> *(Stahl, 2012, p. 2)*

As a topic for study, clinical interviewing is fertile because, although the methodology is mainly of interest to Knowledge Analysis (KA) researchers, clinical interviewing must have significant interactional properties that Interaction

Analysis (IA) researchers are likely in the best position to understand. While the *focus* of clinical interviewing and subsequent analysis is knowledge, the *means* of the method transparently involves (primarily) linguistically mediated interaction, which it behooves us to understand (see also Russ, Sherin, & Lee, this volume, which also intersects many of the particulars developed here).

Although it is only tangentially relevant to the work here, the perspective on knowledge applied here is not generic. Within this perspective, the conventional category of "knowledge" is deliberately extended to include things that are inarticulate, driven unconsciously by context, and possibly encoded in sensory-specific modalities to the extent that they would not count as knowledge under many interpretations. We use the term *knowledge\** to emphasize this expansive and open attitude toward what counts as knowledge and how it works. diSessa, Sherin, and Levin (this volume) elaborate these points.

We report on an exploratory study of the interactional properties of clinical interviewing aimed at determining the ways in which IA and KA problematics, methods, and empirical strategies may be (a) deeply synergistic, (b) complementary, or (c) contradictory. We are not, here, interested in defending clinical interviewing as a methodology, but only in investigating how it works.

## Revoicing

Our analysis focuses on one particular strategy of orchestrating interactive discourse called *revoicing* (O'Connor & Michaels, 1993, 1996). Revoicing was identified first as a strategy used by exceptional classroom teachers to promote academically productive interactions among students. Revoicing occurs when a teacher picks up the ideas and words of a student and then repeats or restates them in her own way. Students are granted authority over their ideas by accepting, declining, or modifying teachers' attributions. When a teacher revoices a student's comments, she simultaneously can accomplish a number of important purposes, including clarifying a student's ideas, setting them in a larger scientific or social context, adding technical vocabulary, eliciting elaboration from the student, and so on.

### Two Key Linguistic Issues

Two core linguistic issues help frame our investigation. The first is *participant frameworks* (Goffman, 1974, 1981), on which O'Connor and Michaels drew in studying revoicing. Participant frameworks specify basic assumptions about roles, relationships, rights, and obligations of participants in linguistic exchange. In "school as usual," teachers are seen as authorities on normative knowledge and bringers of that knowledge to students. Students, in complementary fashion, are treated as ignorant (not necessarily in a deprecative sense) to start, and are meant to be brought to "having knowledge" by the actions of the teacher. Pervasive interactional forms in schools can be seen to follow from this framing (e.g., the teacher initiates questions, the student responds, the teacher evaluates: Cazden, 2001; Mehan, 1979).

Revoicing entails a shift in participation framework (a "shift in footing"), where students are not conceived of as ignorant to start, and "givers of right answers" at the end. Instead, they are viewed as legitimate thinkers and possessors of understanding that is worthy of being engaged and considered. Revoicing marks and may even help instantiate potentially dramatic shifts in instructional forms and attitudes. To anticipate, clinical interviewing, while different from schooling, is more aligned with practices implicated by systematic use of revoicing in school than with linguistic patterns typically associated with "school as usual." The whole point of a clinical interview is to comprehend the subject's ideas, so their value and worthiness for pursuit go without question. We should immediately expect that revoicing would be common in clinical interviews.

The second core linguistic issue, which is deeply engaged here, concerns the form and function of utterances. A classic example of form/function considerations is the function of "directives" (Austin, 1962; Searle, 1969), utterances that are intended to get someone to do something. Imperatives like "Open the window!" merge form with function in "wearing on their sleeve" (in their very form) the imperative function. However, an utterance like, "It's really hot in here" may have the same function, even though, "formally," it is merely an assertion. The details of form/function mapping are intricate, and depend on many features of context, including social conventions, pragmatics, previous utterances, and readings of speaker intentions.

Form and function are core to our analysis of revoicing in clinical interviewing, so we elaborate directly below.

## Forms and Functions for Revoicing in Classrooms

The definitive function of revoicing in classrooms is evoking and marking for continued consideration something that the student has said (O'Connor & Michaels, 1996). At nearly the same level of importance, classroom revoicing typically also invokes the student's right to judge the teacher's rendition of the original utterance, thus at least temporarily positioning the student and teacher as having equal status as meaning makers.

As with any powerful linguistic tool, revoicing can simultaneously serve multiple functions at multiple levels beyond its core function. For example, a teacher can use her inherent visibility to draw a particular student, or a particularly useful student idea, into the common ground of public discussion. By selection and framing, she can create intellectual landmarks of particular ideas. "I think I hear an important idea in what you say, Johnny. Are you saying …?" The teacher may clarify students' tentative and unclear renderings or introduce technical vocabulary.

At higher levels, we noted that the general footing for discussion in classrooms (established mainly by the teacher) might be affected by – or, at least marked by – revoicing, where student ideas approach the center of discussion rather than being marginalized as "just wrong" or "insufficiently clear." More particularly, the teacher can sketch and invoke models of collaborative scientific inquiry via revoicing. A student claim that the teacher hears as contradicting another may be marked: "So, are you *disagreeing with* Sue? I heard her saying … But you said …." An unmarked contribution can be labeled as a "hypothesis," or an informal justification can be characterized as "data." Later, we will undertake a somewhat systematic comparison of functions of revoicing found in classrooms compared to those found in clinical interviews.

To expose formal structure in revoicing, let us look at a prototypical example: "So, you're saying that in the southern hemisphere it's summer right now? Did I get that right?"

We identify four components:

1. ***So* marker** – Revoicing in classrooms often starts with the distinctive marker "so," which communicates a warranted inference (Schiffrin, 1987). Typically, it marks the fact that the teacher is positioning her own revoicing as inferred from the original utterance – it says something like, "based on what you said, I take your contribution to be X." As Schiffrin notes, the use of "so" as a marker of a warranted inference automatically opens up a next slot for the person being interpreted to agree or disagree, even if only implicitly.
2. **Attribution** – This component attributes an idea to the student, typically using a verb of saying or thinking. In our example, just above, the teacher says, "you are saying …."
3. **Reformulation** – The core of the revoicing is a (re)formulation of what the student said or was assumed to have thought. The reformulation may range from literally identical to a student's contribution to substantially reformulated or characterized in order to serve ancillary functions.
4. **Validation request** – "Did I get that right?" explicitly calls for the student's validation. A student might respond minimally by nodding, or may decline or offer extensive qualifications or revisions.

Typical of many compound linguistic forms, various parts may be elided. It is easy to imagine the teacher omitting the *so* marker: "You're saying that in the southern hemisphere it's summer right now. Did I get that right?" One can also easily imagine that a questioning tone (rising intonation at the end) could allow dropping the explicit request for confirmation. Finally, a (possibly skeptical) questioning tone might reduce the revoicing to the reformulation alone, which in this case is close to, but rather different in function from, a bare restatement of the student's idea. "In the southern hemisphere it's *summer* right now?" The elided forms generally still serve to signal a warranted inference and credit the interlocutor as being the originator of the idea.

In addition to accepting elision, it is likely best to consider each formal component to be one way of instantiating some more general function. "So" marks an inference that may be obvious, if implicit, or the inference might be highlighted in other ways. Asking for confirmation might not be necessary if the student has taken an authoritative attitude toward his/her contributions and expects to (and is expected to) make sure they are taken up properly.

## The Study

The core of our study involves analysis of a one-hour interview conducted by one of us (diSessa), which was part of a seven-hour corpus of interviews of the same student over the course of a term. The student was then taking a freshman course on physics, and the point of the interviews was to understand her understanding of physics. The topic of this interview was a common one in science education study: Why is it colder in the winter and warmer in the summer? That is, what causes the seasons?

The entire seven-hour corpus has been analyzed in several ways for different purposes. The main output has been an analysis of the student's intuitive ideas about physics, per se (e.g., diSessa, 1996). A second analysis involved studying her "intuitive epistemology," that is, what she took to be the nature of physics knowledge, and how she, therefore, strategized to understand and learn it (diSessa, Elby, & Hammer, 2002). A third analysis involved understanding the interactional ground rules embedded in clinical interviewing of this sort in order to warrant reasonable inferences about student knowledge from such an interview and to protect against unreasonable ones (diSessa, 2007). Starting with a well-studied corpus, we hypothesized, would provide a relatively firm grounding for this new work.

Our analysis involved developing a grounded coding scheme through iterative study of the corpus. We started by identifying segments of revoicing (where the interviewer made reference to the interviewee's ideas or words, and then turned initiative back to the student for commentary), and then we gradually built a set of codes (Appendix A) that characterized formal and functional features of each example. In order to save space, examples of revoicing will be somewhat spare, and distributed over the analysis. For that reason, readers might find it convenient to get a sense of revoicing in this corpus by skimming the examples quoted in Appendix B.

Consistent with a grounded approach, we did not start with any codes representing either the formal or functional characterizations of revoicing, described above. The following lists the top-level categories of our coding scheme and examples of the lower-level codes. The full set of codes appears as Appendix A.

1. **Goal** – What was the intended function of the revoicing, the goal the interviewer had for doing the revoicing? In cases where the interviewer could recall his intention or could construct a plausible retrospective intention, we

used that information. In the absence of such recollection or in combination with it, we did the best we could at identifying the purpose of the revoicing. For both methodological reasons and analytic clarity, "goal" is a natural target for improvement for subsequent study. For present purposes, we do not believe these issues threaten the basic results here. Twelve goals were identified, one of which had two subtypes. See Appendix A for details.

2. **Formulation** – How was the revoicing presented? This entailed two main subcategories.
    a. Focus – Focus classifies how the revoiced item was identified in the revoicing. This included the canonical case where the revoiced item is identified specifically as something the interviewee said or thought, something like a proposition such as "you said…," "you decided…," or "you thought …." A different case is where the target of concern was an inference that the interviewer (or interviewee) made, or might have made (see later comments). In another case, the interviewer made clear that his focus was a chain of reasoning by explicitly saying so.
    b. Anticipation Frame (a-frame, for short) – The interviewer partially specifies or suggests the form of response in which he is interested, for example, suggesting a yes-or-no response, or providing other help in terms of what kind of response is hoped for or expected. A special category, "bare," was used when no visible work was done to focus or anticipate the form of response.

3. **Interviewee response** – What was the form of the interviewee's response? Possible responses included:
    a. Bare yes or no. Example:
    Interviewer: So, you don't think that's sensible.
    Interviewee: No.
    (The interviewee is implicitly accepting the interviewer's rendering in these cases.)
    b. Yes or no, plus elaboration.
    c. Various versions of rethinking the target of the revoicing, including eventual rejection, ratification, or elaboration of what was previously expressed and revoiced.
    d. Reject attribution – The interviewee rejected the interviewer's attribution.

A fair number of these response types seem closely related to goals the interviewer had or they could function in specific ways that would be of value to him. A simple example is that the student might provide exactly the information requested, for example whether the interviewee viewed the interviewer's reformulation to be an adequate rendition of what she said or thought. In other cases, other potential functions became evident in the interviewee response (which is not to say that they were necessarily not already in the intentions of the interviewer). For example, in rethinking the idea that the interviewer had revoiced, the interviewee could show the interviewer other ways in which she could construe the problematic situation, which, in fact, might also be a goal of the interviewer to uncover.

Altogether, there were nine categories classifying the interviewee's response, one of which had two subcategories (see Appendix A).

4. **Interviewer follow-up** – The interviewer's response to the interviewee's commentary was classified into six categories, which included various forms of closure, or iterative refining of the focus or anticipation frame. This last category will be of no concern here.

Most of the work of developing and applying the coding scheme was done from transcripts. However, the video was rechecked a number of times to identify prosody, intonation, length of pauses, gestures, and gaze, which might disambiguate interpretations. Quotations from the transcript, codes, and commentary were entered into a database, which allowed easy searching, counting, and other analysis operations.

## Results

### Analysis of Formal Elements

Nearly 30 percent of interviewer turns were coded as revoicings.[1] This proportion would be significantly higher if we removed: (a) questions that the interviewer used to initiate discussions and (b) procedural statements and other commentary. Clearly, revoicing plays a central role in interviewing, if this interview is at all representative. As anticipated, this should not be particularly surprising. The very purpose of a clinical interview is to expose interviewee thinking, and it makes sense that the interviewer would spend a lot of time picking up elements of that thinking to propose further consideration. Such a high proportion of revoicings also suggests that the interviewer took few interviewee responses as definitive and clear.

We next consider each of the formal elements of revoicing: "so" marker, attribution, reformulation, and validation request. Not all of these elements show directly in our coding scheme. On the other hand, the ground-up categories allowed us to do simple searches on the code database to answer questions about each of these elements.

### So *marker*

About half the revoicings (14/30) included the "so" marker. Many of these were relatively simple and perfunctory revoicings in the early part of the interview, for example, "so, your high school course you found interesting?" (in response to: "I had a really, really good physics professor, ... [he] had the most incredible demonstrations."). This "so" serves the canonical function of marking that the interviewer had inferred the point from what the interviewee had said. Some of the "so" markers, however, had a different function. They marked inferences that the student *might have made*, usually ones that the interviewer believed the interviewee would easily agree to. Even when the interviewee agreed quickly with the proposed inference, this type of revoicing sometimes constituted a very strong intervention.

Here is a case in point. The interviewee was reviewing the fact that (she knew that) orbits are ellipses, and therefore planets are at different distances from the sun at different times. She was in the process of explaining how this could account for the seasons (closer is warmer). However, she had previously also made clear that she knew that winter in the northern hemisphere implies summer in the southern hemisphere. [Transcription notes: Italic text in brackets is commentary; ellipses denote omission of speech; // denotes a break or interruption; "I:" denotes interviewer; and "J:" denotes the interviewee, consistent with prior papers on this data.]

I: So that means it's got to be summer at the same time all over the world?
J: No, it shouldn't be *[recognizing the contradiction to what she knew, that seasons are different in different hemispheres]*. Oh, you're right. That does mean it's got to be summer all over at the same time. *[J reviews the logic and concludes:]* It doesn't make sense. So something's wrong.

One might object that anticipating something that a student might say or think ("that means it's got to be summer at the same time all over the world?") is not technically a revoicing at all. However, O'Connor and Michaels (1993) mention teacher moves of this sort (inferences from what a student said) and classify them as revoicings.[2] In addition, if not narrowly revoicings, almost all of these inferences were quickly accepted, so it seems sensible to count them as pulling out for consideration aspects of the student's thinking, even if those aspects were not voiced or otherwise already in the conversation.

Even at this preliminary level of analysis, one can see a theme emerging. Revoicings are exceedingly diverse. Those tagged with "so" involve at least two possible types of inference: The interviewer infers something inherent in the interviewee's talk, or the interviewer proposes to consider an inference from what he takes to be the interviewee's position. Although we will turn to goals or functions systematically later, we note that, with respect to the example here, some revoicings are quite innocuous in appearance: They ask for more information or even just put an interviewee's idea out for reaction. In contrast, sometimes a revoicing may be intended to have more substantial effect. In the case of the inference that led to a contradiction, and therefore a rejection of a point of view (the example above), the interviewer, from long experience, expected precisely that reaction and was using the conversational move to shift the topic of conversation to other ways of thinking about the situation.

## Attribution

Only about one-third of revoicings (11/30) included clear attribution in terms of expressions like *you think*, *you said*, *you decided*, and so on. Some were more indirect, such as, "It sounds to me like there are two ideas here." The implication of that statement, however, seems clear. It references ideas that the interviewer is hearing, which can only be those of the interviewee. In other cases, especially when the interviewer uses literally the words of the interviewee, there is no ambiguity concerning whose ideas or words the interviewer is invoking; explicit attribution can be dispensed with. This is a particular case of the generalization made earlier, that formal elements of a revoicing may be present in function (e.g., knowing whose ideas are being referenced), but not shown in the form of the revoicing. Instead, the function might be carried only in the pragmatics of the situation (e.g., only the interviewee is present, in contrast to a classroom; the topic of conversation in an interview is almost always precisely the ways that the interviewee has of construing the problematic situation).

## Reformulation

All revoicings made reference to something that the interviewee was assumed to have thought, said, or might have thought (per the above). However, in a reasonable number of cases, there was literally no reformulation in this aspect of the revoicing; the interviewer repeated exactly what the interviewee said. Literal repetition can function in just the same way as other revoicings, for example, to turn the interviewee's attention to the "revoiced" thought, with the intention of promoting continued consideration.

## Validation request

Few revoicings in the interview contained literal requests for validation: only 4 out of 30. However, 4 others implicated a request for validation. One such revoicing was preceded by an explicit statement of ignorance on the interviewer's part about what was said, thus setting up a situation where the interviewee could literally repeat her initial assertion with authority (which she did in this case). Another revoicing was prefaced by an explicit declaration of intention, "I want to understand your question. Your question was …?" Yet another revoicing was a simple statement (implicitly attributed to the interviewee), which ended with a rising tone to convert it to a yes-or-no question.[3]

And yet, a significant majority of revoicings (22/30) did not seem to have any request for validation in any form. There appear to be a number of reasons for this. In the first instance, it is reasonable to assume that there may be pragmatic substitutes for validation requests. One such implicit source of validation request could well be the general orientation of the interview, which made clear to the interviewee that the interviewer's understanding of the interviewee's ideas was the central purpose of the interview. Beyond constant reminding (see diSessa, 2007), implicitly or explicitly, that a main goal for the interviewee should be to help the interviewer understand her thinking, the interviewee probably needed very little local reminding that affirming, denying, or correcting an interviewer's attributions was part of her job.

Another reason for few solicitations of validation is that the purpose of the revoicing was often not mere validation that the interviewer understood, in some superficial way, what the interviewee had said or thought, per se. The interviewer may not have understood *to the level of precision he needed for his ongoing research* what the interviewee said. "I know you said X, but what I don't understand about that is Y." Such revoicings may function merely to establish a locus within which more particular questions about the interviewee's thinking might be put. More generally, many instances of revoicing merely function to focus on a particular issue for continued consideration, whether a particular direction of consideration is specified or not. This simply does not anticipate validation or invalidation, all the more clearly so if what was revoiced was something that previously had been unambiguously established as within the common ground.

So far, we have the following alternative functions that do not seem to entail validation or invalidation: (1) provoking elaboration, perhaps assuming what the interviewee said was clear enough, but expecting more details might be forthcoming; (2) provoking continued consideration to see if anything more may turn up. It is even possible that an interviewer might revoice (3) merely because he is on the spot and has nothing more valuable than "rehashing" to fill in a turn. Yet another purpose might be (4) to propose another way of thinking, specifically with reference to something the interviewee said ("You said X. Another student said Y."). The interviewer might similarly provoke by (5) noting and then characterizing the interviewee's response as, for example, strange, puzzling, or, on the contrary, obvious, to see how she reacts (an example of this is given later: "… it seems obvious to you"). Although all of these functions focus on something the interviewee said or might have thought, none necessarily call for validation and thus they may legitimately be barren of that component of revoicing.

The present coding scheme is not optimal for exploring details. However, we note that a reasonable number of revoicings (5/30) resulted in the interviewee apparently reconsidering her prior contention, which resulted in a fairly even spread across affirming (2/30), modifying (2/30) or rejecting (1/30) her prior contentions that the interviewer had marked in his revoicing. Some related considerations appear directly below.

## Goals

Let us first look at goals that emerged from grounded development of this category. Afterwards, we compare the goals thus determined to those of revoicing in the context of classroom discussion. We look at goals roughly in order of most to least frequent.

Check inference: Ten revoicings were coded as checking an inference. Inferences were of various types: (a) one that the student made, (b) one that the interviewer made from what (in his judgment) the student was thinking, or (c) an inference that the student *might have* made. As mentioned, most inferences in the last category were, in fact, quickly accepted by the student, probably indicating that the interviewer had a good sense of what inferences the interviewee might make. He thus, apparently, used that version of "revoicing" mostly to anticipate something the student might well have said or thought but had not done, so far.

A goodly number of inferences about what the student said seemed unimportant and innocuous. Many occurred early in the interview. For example: "So your high school course you found interesting?"; "And was he [*the teacher*] pretty clear in explaining things?"

In contrast, a few of the "check inference" revoicings were at critical points in the interview, where the interviewer was trying to untangle central, complex, and ill-understood issues concerning the interviewee's thinking. Here are two examples that are closely spaced in the interview, concerning the same topic. (1) "So the problem that you are having now is that you are thinking that this part of the world is just going to get cooked? Is that // [*interrupted by interviewee*]" (2) "I just want to get straight on this, the logic of this cooking thing, how is it you // You are telling me that if things are just like this, then it's going to get real hot down there. I'm trying to understand why, then, it's going to get real hot down there, and I'm trying to understand why, why that's // I mean, it seems obvious to you."

The first revoicing just checked the conclusion of an inference the interviewee was apparently making, that something would be getting "cooked." It also checked the status of that inference in the interviewee's mind, that it was a "problem." The second revoicing focused specifically on the linkage to the conclusion, the underlying causal mechanism that the interviewee seemed to be imputing, but which was not named or described. This pair of examples also illustrates that the interviewer sometimes worked to focus the interviewee's attention not just on an inference, but specifically on the conclusion or, alternatively, on the inference link itself. That implies a highly refined focus of attention on the part of the interviewer concerning what the interviewee has said or thought. The interviewer, naturally, tries to make the interviewee aware of that focus. Overall, four "check inference" revoicings focused on the conclusion, and two on the link, itself. Others were too ambiguous to code.

The second most popular function seems innocuous, but is perhaps telling. There were nine revoicings that were coded as "confirm/continuer." This is a familiar interactional device, where speakers mark merely that they are tracking what is being said (Schegloff, 1982). Other confirm/continuers might involve nodding or parallel "uh huhs." Once again, formally identical – or nearly identical – contributions may serve very different functions. Something that might look like a typical revoicing might be intended only as a confirm/continuer. The distinction is both in the intention (the interviewer probably does not anticipate any response or obvious recognition at all from a revoicing-like confirm/continuer), and in reception (the interviewee marks the "revoicing," if it is registered at all, as a mere sign that the interviewer is tracking). Both the interviewee and interviewer are implicitly or explicitly taking the reformulation as direct and unproblematic. Hence it may be better to consider this to be a different move altogether. Or, perhaps, it could be viewed as a confirm/continuer in the form of an innocuous revoicing. In any case, it seems the functions of confirm/continuer revoicings are recognizably different from prototypical revoicings, even if things that function as revoicings appear in identical form, say, a repetition literally of what the student said. They are different specifically in that they do not or are not intended to open up space for commentary on a point.

The next most frequent goal (6/30) for revoicing was to provoke the interviewee to provide more detail about a conceptual point. This seems in line with the overall goals of clinical interviews, so it should not be in any way surprising. Indeed, if we remove confirm/continuers, and remove apparently perfunctory inference checks, "more detail" has the greatest frequency of coded goals.

The next most frequent goal codes, tied at 5/30, are those that established a common, public ground, and those that tracked an extended line of reasoning. The former is easy to understand as orchestrating the interaction by creating landmarks for future discussion, just as happens with classroom revoicing. In one case, the interviewer was thoroughly confused by what the interviewee was saying and wanted to pick out a few things that seemed most evident, partly for his own purpose of tracking the conversation while, at the same time, confirming some elements of what he thought he had heard. On another occasion, the interviewer was convinced that the interviewee had transiently invoked ideas of her own without marking them for memorial purposes. His intention was to get her to agree, publicly and on the spot, that she had maintained particular points so that the conversation could return to them at some later time as points that she had, indeed, put forward. It happened that, in this particular instance, the referenced points did not ever seem useful to bring up again.

The second tied-in-frequency goal for revoicing at 5/30 was "tracking an extended line of reasoning." That is, the revoicing focused on one part of a "logical line" from a long sequence of the interviewee's thinking, probably both for purposes of checking with the interviewee that she tracked the line similarly, but also for the interviewer's own purpose of marking trod territory for his own memory. All five of these instances came from the same line of reasoning. Each might also have been coded as inference checks (although they were not coded in that way), enlarging that category with substantial (not perfunctory) inference checks. The importance of separately coding this kind of sequence is to mark that revoicing can sometimes span long periods of interviewee thinking, and not just react locally to particular things the interviewee says or appears to think.

For reference, we transcribe the revoicings in this extended sequence. Note that the interviewer started by explicitly marking his intention as following a train of reasoning, "follow your reasoning."[4] Each lettered utterance below was coded as a revoicing that tracked an extended line of inferences.

a. So you decided // Let me try to follow your reasoning. You decided that // It sounded like in the beginning you weren't quite sure if it was cold in Australia when it was hot here or not. *[Confirmed: "Right."]*
b. Then you decided you did know that it's wintertime there, it's cold season there when it is warm here. Did I // *[interrupted with confirmation: "Yeah."]*
c. So you decided that you knew that. That was pretty certain. *[Confirmation: "Right, definitely."]*
d. OK. Definitely.
e. Now that's a problem because your little theory says that if it's closer *[uncertain transcription: to the sun, then it is hotter.]* *[This revoices J's "So something's wrong," with reference to her "little theory."]* *[Confirmation: "Right."]*

One of the more interesting, although infrequent (1 example), revoicing types was coded as providing a synthesis or summary of the conclusion to which the interviewee had come, similar in function to the above long sequence. One revoicing was coded as an attempt to provide the interviewee time and space to rethink a particular point. Having only one such coding seems slightly anomalous because a goodly number of interviewee reactions (5/30) were coded as involving rethinking or reconsidering. It is possible that, as suggested by these numbers, rethinking happened more frequently than was intended by the interviewer. The numbers are too small and coding of intended goals is uncertain enough that we will not pursue the point.

Interestingly, only one revoicing was coded with the goal to supply language to the conversation. Teachers also supply language, but are more likely to supply normative language, unlike here. The interviewer proposed an informal description ("cooking thing") for an idea that the interviewee had been considering. He wanted more detail on a (to him) mysterious causal mechanism by which part of the earth was imputed to get exceptionally warm. The language was adopted by the interviewee.

## Reflection on Forms and Functions in Revoicing

This section aims to synthesize observations made above, comparing clinical revoicing with classroom revoicing, and bringing out suggestions for revisions to the idea of revoicing that might derive from this work. We will refrain from arguing for particular recharacterizations or redrawing the boundary between what is and what is not a revoicing. Instead we observe some considerations that might motivate such actions and some consequences.

## *Core Functions*

We start at the "top" by observing that the defining goals of interviewing and teaching in classrooms differ. Teaching in classrooms aims to move students along, bringing them to a better, or more normative, view of content, and often to improve their understanding of and participation in scientific inquiry processes. Clinical interviews aim to "make data appear." They very seldom teach, they abstain from making judgments about the quality of ideas, and they may even, for example, hide any authority that might be associated with particular ideas (an example is to come). Depending on these top-level construals of the point of activity in the relevant context, interactional strategies and purposes will often differ in small or larger ways.

We began this inquiry with the idea that the core purpose of revoicing is to draw out something said or thought by a student/interviewee, presenting it for further consideration. At this level, there does not appear to be much difference between clinical revoicing and the classroom variety. Typical of bottom-up studies, however, our data give some reason to pause and reflect on generalities. Interviewer moves that anticipate something that a student might easily admit to (they *might* have said it, and they might also acknowledge the idea as something they "own") seem not very far removed, functionally, from revoicing in the classic sense. Drawing an inference from what an interviewee has said does not literally repeat what a student has said, nor even give voice to a revised/reframed version of the idea. Yet it is not clear that it is useful to refuse to call these by the same name for "technical" reasons (the student/interviewer did not actually give voice to the idea that is "revoiced"). Similarly, marking epistemic attitudes ("that seemed obvious to you"), perhaps drawing on prosody and tone rather than the content of something said, again does not literally request comment on an idea so much as an attitude toward it. At least from the standpoint of "making data appear" about an interviewee's thinking, however, there seems little difference.

Let us proceed to considering the functional niches induced from the four formal characteristics typical of classroom revoicing. Here, a critical observation is that the same function might be served in different ways, and, indeed, systematic differences in the goals and pragmatics of teaching and interviewing might give rise to systematic differences in the importance of the functions and the ways they might be accomplished.

The *so* marker functions, typically, to help make the point that the teacher/interviewer is drawing on what the student/interviewee made present in the conversation. In the clinical context, with a single conversational partner and unrelenting focus on the interviewee's ideas, not much explicit help should be expected to be required. Correspondingly, we found relatively few revoicings with *so* markers. Similarly, attribution – typically a verb of saying or thinking – seems less important to instantiate explicitly. Most ideas present in the conversation will be those of the interviewee. The different pragmatics of clinical interviews can lead to fewer attributions, at least, as expressed in this way.

But, consider the range of attributions that we found to appear in clinical interaction: *said, thought, inferred, felt* (epistemic attitude), *might have said* (an idea was owned, but not voiced, perhaps only because of accidents of sequencing), and so on. These all attribute, but they also *focus* in the technical sense of our coding scheme; they give details as to what part, exactly, of the interviewee's thinking is of interest. Schematically, the interviewer might be interested in: (1) literally the words used; (2) the thought expressed by it; (2a) particular details of that thought; or (2b) just a rough gist of it; (3) a conclusion; (4) the inference link that drew the conclusion; or (5) what an interviewee might think if she happened to evoke a particular idea in her repertoire, but not yet instantiated in the conversation.

This functional niche is complicated and may rely on extended constructions, rather than verbs of attribution. Consider the preface ("I just want to get straight on this, the logic of this cooking thing," transcribed fully above) produced by the interviewer to focus the interviewee's attention on, not a conclusion, but an undescribed causal link in the "cooking thing" phenomenon. At some point, an interviewer will run out of easily understood descriptions of the focused knowledge, and likely would have to use other techniques than revoicing to make data appear. "So, you attended to the agentive framing of this version of the conceptual task and thus changed your answer" will not work.[5]

One would expect this level of detailed interest might be much more common in the clinical context, where the interviewer might have very specific questions about the interviewee's thinking and virtually an unbounded amount of time (after the interview) to consider the data that arises concerning what the interviewee says about her thinking. Highly refined focus should be rarer in classroom revoicing.

Similar considerations apply to the request for confirmation or disconfirmation. The interviewer, having very refined foci of investigation, might well suggest what he thinks would be the most efficient way an interviewee could respond. This is the idea of an a-frame, anticipating/suggesting a form of response. Confirmation that the interviewee/student thinks the interviewer/teacher has given a decent description of her idea might be a simple, helpful response in a classroom (hence an appropriate a-frame), whereas the real-time constraint of keeping up with a full class and a lesson plan might make refinement minimally helpful. On the other hand, in a clinical context, where data need only appear and are not necessarily assimilated in real time, a varied set of a-frames might be much more valuable. As for the attribution function (generalized to focus), the inquiry in this chapter suggests that the call for validation by the teacher might profitably be generalized (to "posting an a-frame") in order to put variations seen in the clinical context on the same footing as those that occur most frequently in classrooms.

## Ancillary Functions

Consider the following list of functions for revoicing in classrooms, largely drawn from O'Connor and Michaels (1993):

1. Valuing – Validating students as sources of ideas worth pursuing, and engaging them as authorities on their own understanding.
2. Normative "bending" – Teachers will often edit students' contributions so as to move them closer to normative understanding. Proper terminology may be introduced, or a teacher may select only the most important or most productive parts of a student contribution for revoicing.
3. Reframing – The teacher may explicitly connect students to their roles in the scientific enterprise. The reframing may be with respect to normative scientific categories – a guess (of a certain sort) is called a "hypothesis" – or it may position students with respect to each other in scientific roles: The observations of one student might be framed as "producing data" "disputing" "the claims" of another student.
4. Clarification – Students' contributions may be muddled in their language, and a teacher can "fix" those features.
5. To bring to the floor or emphasize – Students' contributions may warrant repeating for pragmatic reasons, such as to compensate for the quiet voice of a student, or for the use of non-standard English (ESL), which might not be understood by classmates. But a teacher can also be strategic in emphasizing or returning to an idea that she believes to be particularly important to the discussion. "A little while ago, Johnny said he thought energy is just energy, whether in physics or chemistry." She might even add her own weight to the claim. "I think Johnny had an idea that we should think about when he said…"

Making no pretense that such a list is complete or definitive, we use it to identify some loci of similarities and differences between clinical and classroom revoicing.

As far as valuing and validating student ideas, revoicing in clinical interviewing may have a similar function, but it is not nearly as important or difficult to achieve in that context. First, the avowed and explicit purpose of the interview is for the interviewer to come to understand the interviewee's ideas. Indeed, almost every action on the part of the interviewer validates the fact that he is interested in the interviewee's ideas, pursuing them doggedly, all the while insisting that the interviewee is the one to make the judgment on whether the ideas are viable or not (see diSessa, 2007). The interviewer almost always withholds his personal judgment concerning validity, and rarely, if ever, pronounces that any ideas are good or scientific. Unlike students, interviewees (in this genre of interviewing, in contrast to "clinical teaching experiments") are not expected to learn anything while participating in a practice where their ideas are valued just as much as in the classroom case. On the whole, then, interviewees surely learn fairly quickly that their own ideas are of high value for the purposes of the interviewer. Perhaps the clinical context even emphasizes this more than the classroom, since in classrooms, normative ideas compete with students' own ideas more visibly.

Other functions in the list seem more rare in clinical interviewing. The interviewer has no particular interest in "normative bending," in pressing the interviewee toward normative understanding. This goal did not appear at all in any codes of revoicings in this interview. The same goes for introducing standard terminology to overlay on good student ideas when they are expressed in idiosyncratic language. Only one instance was coded as introducing terminology, and it was idiosyncratic and not normative – "cooking thing" – as mentioned and illustrated above.

The interviewer's bringing up normative ideas generally happens in two different ways, for two different purposes. First, an interviewer might supply particular information for the purposes of heightening focus on other aspects of the situation. In this interview, the interviewer at one point informed the interviewee of the fact that the orbit of the earth is only very slightly elliptical, only a few percent. This allowed the student to consider, and, it turns out, to reject certain of her ideas (there is no way to rescue the "closer is warmer" idea with respect to elliptical orbits with this information), thus focusing on other possibilities. A second mode and purpose for introducing normative ideas is to do so just as one might a non-normative idea "from another student" – to see how the student responds to such a possibility, rather than as part of convincing the interviewee to think in that way. Indeed, one important goal for the interviewer is not to reveal these normative ideas as normative-by-assertion (e.g., "Newton said …"), but to let the interviewee make an independent judgment on her own initiative. Freed of obvious normative framing, interviewees may, and, in fact, do often reject such ideas out of hand. We call the strategy of proposing other ideas, normative or non-normative, a "feint," and, again, its purpose is to bring up for consideration ideas that the interviewee might have, or be willing to pursue, without sanctioning them positively or negatively. No instances of feints with normative ideas were observed in this interview, although they did appear in other interviews with this interviewee.

Consider the function of reframing the conversation or contribution of the student so that she might see herself in legitimate scientific roles in the larger exchange within the classroom. This, like teaching content, is missing from the general motivation for clinical interviews. It is not surprising that scant evidence appears in the codes for this use of revoicing. The only "close miss" was an occasion where the interviewer framed a proposed discussion of two different ideas as a competition between two theories. However, that was not done in order for the interviewee to see herself as scientific, but only to prepare for an orderly discussion (for example, of pros and cons of each "theory") of two of the interviewee's own proposals.

Clarifying language happens in clinical interviews, just as it does in classrooms. However, the purpose cannot (for one-on-one interviews) be to make things clear to "other members" of the discussion (the class). These are solely so that the interviewer and interviewee understand each other better.

The final function, bringing ideas to the floor, putting them in common ground, also does make sense in clinical interviewing, and it appeared as a code. But, obviously, common ground applies only to the pair, interviewee and interviewer, and the function of highlighting productive points on the way to normative understanding is irrelevant in the clinical case.

To summarize, while there are important similarities between clinical and classroom revoicing, there are also differences. These are complex, situated practices with similarly complicated sets of commonalities and differences. Many of the differences flow from differences in top-level goals: teaching versus making data appear. Other differences flow from the particular pragmatics and working principles of the two different activity structures: There are usually only two people present at a clinical interview, and clinical interviewing has a relentless and genuine focus on the details of the interviewee's personal ways of construing the world, as opposed, for example, to a dual focus on student ideas and their possible futures in instruction. Finally, the interviewer may have years to devote to understanding the data unearthed in an interview, while a teacher must, generally, make use of what appears from a revoicing on fairly short order.

## The Role of Knowledge in Interaction: Lessons Learned

The overarching aim of this study was to explore possible relations of KA to IA. Are the views opposed? Are they complementary perspectives, each talking about different phenomenology? Or, are they actually tightly interconnected? In a sentence, our conclusion is that, at least in this case, the two "perspectives" are so tightly interrelated that one does not really make sense without the other.

To pursue this agenda, we started with an interactional perspective on some things that happen in clinical interviews. We took up the task of studying the phenomenon of revoicing, which seems, on the face of it, both linguistic and characteristically IA. However, by looking at this phenomenon in a context, clinical interviewing, that *does* KA, we might expect to see interesting connections between knowledge and interaction, with the special case of revoicing as interaction's proxy. In this conclusion, we review where we find the relevance of knowledge to the phenomenon of revoicing. We organize the discussion into four related lines of argument.

## Revoicing as a Complex, Varied, and Adapted Strategy

Revoicing appears to be a complex, highly varied, and adapted practice. The easiest explanation for this is to assume that it is, in fact, strategized. Teachers/interviewers may know what their goals are (with qualifications), and have perhaps conscious access to multiple resources out of which they can fashion particular well-adapted moves. (See the next subsection for relevant "data.")

Consciousness of the process of strategizing is not necessary. The program of knowledge★ deliberately enfolds inarticulate forms of knowledge. If revoicing is not articulately strategized, we still have the problem of explaining how it is that the particular forms of revoicing that we see seem so well adapted to the local and global interests of the interviewer/teacher. Teachers teach with it; interviewers make data appear, sometimes with apparent pinpoint accuracy on what it seems they are interested in, and with due respect to details of the interactional context. This coordination simply needs explanation.

Consider an example, already introduced, that seems to bespeak intricate strategizing and adapting:

I: I just want to get straight on this, on the logic of this cooking thing. How is it you // You are telling me that if things are just like this *[gestures to model setup]*, then it's going to get real hot down there. I'm trying to understand why then it's going to get real hot down there, and I'm trying to understand why, why that's // I mean, it seems obvious to you.

The interviewer had a problem of which he seems perfectly aware, and he even named it: "this cooking thing." The interviewee knew that "cooking" was her idea (she responded in line with this presumption), if not her word for it, so the interviewer did not revoice at this stage: He did not need to say "you thought" or "you said" just yet. In some cases, if not here, the interviewer undoubtedly knew (thought) that the interviewee might not identify a particular idea as her own, so he deliberately framed the idea as such.

After naming the issue, "this cooking thing," the interviewer starts down one line ("How is it that you //" – perhaps anticipating "inferred ..." as a continuation), but then appears to believe he needs a more vivid approach, invoking more detail from the interviewee's own voicing of the locus of the problem on which he is focusing "You are telling me that if things are just like this ...."

The interviewer was aware (well, he presumes he was aware) of the precise focus of the issue. The issue, in this particular revoicing, was not in the *fact* of cooking, but in the *inference* that implicated cooking. And, the interviewer worked hard to make clear what particular focus he wanted the interviewee to take: a focus on an inference, not on a fact.

Of course, the details of this sketchy analysis may be contested. But some analysis like it seems a foregone conclusion. Although it may be difficult to study, the on-line reasoning of interviewers is an important and provocative target of study, especially from a knowledge★ point of view. The interactive knowledge of everyday communicative actions is almost certainly deeper into the murky depths of knowledge★ compared to that of professionals, whose livelihood depends on understanding and even being able to say, at least in part, what they are doing. Professional "reflective practitioners" are perhaps ideal subjects to study at this stage of understanding the knowledge★ behind interaction. Unlike participants in everyday conversations, they may have a lot to say about how they think about and strategize interaction.

Saying that interviewers (or teachers) know a lot about interaction does not mean to say that their knowledge of interaction is valid or "true." Certainly it is not well articulated or well grounded enough to count as a scientific theory of interaction. So, "true," in this context, as for most intuitive knowledge, is a category error (diSessa, 2014). It might not even be productive, at least in every case. The reactions of interviewees are often other than what is projected by the interviewer. An a-frame may be ignored or misunderstood. But, like much intuitively developed knowledge, what an interviewer (or teacher) believes (at least sometimes) guides the interviewer's (or teacher's) actions. We propose that knowledge★ guides the formulation, enactment, and retrospective judgment of the results of a revoicing.

## Interviewers/Teachers Are Often Articulate About Their Knowledge About Interaction

O'Connor and Michaels (1993) made an important observation concerning the teachers from whom they originally abstracted the idea of revoicing. They marked that at least one of the teachers was quite articulate about the practice. She knew that she did things like revoicing, and she had many explicit goals in using it (e.g., concerning developing a scientific community in the classroom). More generally, the teacher was explicit and strategic with respect to her own discourse practices in the classroom.

The equivalent remark is that the clinical interviewer involved in our data analysis here (diSessa) believes that his interviewing practice is rich with explicit strategizing with respect to interactional properties of the interview. He claims to remember particular strategizing and can easily (retrospectively) reconstruct plausible goals and means, including the histories of specific issues that get invoked in particular interactions.

We noted some of this in our data analysis. As professional researchers, general goals and the current state of the research project are topics of everyday conversation. They give every indication of being knowledge in any reasonable sense of the word. The project of constructing and evaluating local goals in a data-collecting enterprise with those articulate long-term goals as targets is just as likely to be explicitly cognized and considered. The enterprise, from stem to stern, is knowledge-intensive and at least to some extent articulate.

Once again, this does not mean we can trust everything an interviewer or teacher says about their practice (Cohen, 1990). In addition, there are without doubt things about the practice that are not consciously cognized (as most everyday interactional strategies are unlikely to have very much of a conscious or rational trace). Such things need scientific treatment significantly beyond what practitioners can articulate about them. And yet, (1) professionals, who depend strongly on particular actions they might take, are very likely to have thought and articulated something about that practice to themselves; and (2) as researchers of the knowledge★ that interviewers and teachers possess about interaction, what they say about it certainly makes an accessible starting point.

## Undermining the Contrary Case

It is very difficult for those committed to Knowledge Analysis not to see knowledge or knowledge-focused issues everywhere. But how would the above considerations look to those committed to marginalizing or eliminating the concept of knowledge from analysis, the more extreme conversation analysis or ethnomethodology proponents cited earlier, who are dedicated to barring analysis of things that are not visible in the interactions between participants?

In the first instance, much of what seems sensible to put into the category of "knowledge about interaction" does, indeed, seem to be more or less directly visible in the interaction itself. Attribution is there, and an interviewee/student responding to – or, more particularly, refusing that attribution – seems unquestionably visible. Perhaps more subtly, a-frames and focus show also in the interaction. An interviewee might show us that by saying, "I don't know what you are getting at," referencing a failed attempt at establishing focus. Whenever her continuing turn is responsive to the a-frame or focus, we also have evidence (albeit indirect) that those are present in the interaction.

Understanding the sense in which focus and a-frames are knowledge is certainly a worthy goal. Even if they might be explicitly cognized and strategized by the interviewer/teacher, it is unlikely that, while responding to them, those "ideas" have a similar status for the interviewee/student. But, again, this kind of inarticulate, reactive knowledge is just exactly the kind of thing that KA researchers study. The case that these are present in the interaction studied in this chapter already seems reasonably firm to us, and we see no basis for denying, a priori, that a better scientific theory of these types of knowledge★ might be forthcoming.

There is a common-sense but powerful argument against methodologically dismissing knowledge of interaction from analysis because it cannot be directly seen in the interaction. Influential, knowledge-like things might not show directly in an interaction for completely comprehensible reasons. For example, there is little point for an articulately strategizing interviewer to show that strategizing to the interviewee. It is simply off-topic and a distraction from the interviewee's doing her job, thinking about the situation at hand. The result of the strategizing, the enacted strategy (say, a particular focus), is much more likely to be visible since it is intended to be visible. An enacted plan to make focus clear in a particular way is supposed to make focus clear to the interviewee, and it therefore, incidentally, may do so for an analyst.

More obviously, the theoretical or empirical point of a particular focus might be essentially impossible to convey to the interviewee, even if it were relevant. The whole theoretical and epistemological basis of his inquiry would probably take months to convey to an interviewee, even if she were interested enough to want to learn about it. And yet, these things are responsible for some of the most basic facts about the interview, such as what things are brought into focus at all. See continuing discussion below.

We transiently made the point earlier that some of the interviewer's motivations may not show in the interaction itself for different, but still entirely understandable, reasons. Revoicing so as to bring an idea into common ground in anticipation of its returning later might never be realized. The move toward common ground might in some sense be observed, but the knowledge behind it (e.g., experience suggesting that the point might return, and then would be better handled if the interviewee registered it more or less consciously) and the construals that motivated it (the knowledge-based judgment that the interviewee had not consciously registered the point) would not show.

How should we handle such issues? We could start by asking the interviewer, or use other more indirect, but possibly less error-prone, ways of inferring what he knows. This is precisely the rationale for clinical interviewing in the first place. Students, for entirely understandable reasons, are unlikely to show much about what they really know and believe in the normal course of everyday interaction in school. So, we bring them into an environment where we can set up conditions that make much more explicit how they might think. We arrange a more optimal setting to "make data appear."

Of course, we have not tried to optimize conditions to show interviewer knowledge about interaction here. Still, a good slice of that knowledge seems to show in the interaction, and suggestions of more and deeper things (like strategizing) are pervasive.

## *Two Opportunities to Further the Inquiry into "Knowledge of Interaction"*

This subsection briefly elaborates two opportunities for studying knowledge of interaction that were mentioned in passing previously. Both concern the coordination of interactional strategies with other aspects of an interviewer's knowledge and activity.

Interviewers with rich and articulate views of knowledge afford a special opportunity to investigate coordination between knowledge of one sort (knowledge about students' knowledge) and interactional adaptation. Simply put, one should see good coordination between theories of student knowledge and the strategic repertoire and particular adaptations that are used to make data appear within a clinical interaction. For example, one sees in the present case: (1) near total absence of orientation toward the list of normative concepts (which might, for some interviewers, constitute precisely the target: to determine which normative ideas a student knows and which she does not know); (2) great attention to diversity of ways of thinking (constantly asking for rethinking, with major or minor perturbations); and (3) occasional management of modality, asking a student to feel a force and describe it, turning attention deliberately to models and spatial representations, and so on.

Such an inquiry concerning the coordination of knowledge about knowledge and interaction may be productive in several ways. It should illuminate perhaps invisible reasons for particular interactional forms. But it might also illuminate contradictions and discoordinations. For example, strategies of interaction imported reflexively from everyday life might have counterproductive consequences. We suspect that most or all educational interviewers are aware that, for example, standard classroom routines have consequences that may be counterproductive in an interview. An interviewer who asks the same question twice might provoke the interviewee to change her answer for pragmatic reasons rather than because she genuinely feels a different answer is better.[6] So, an inquiry into coordination between avowed knowledge principles and perhaps implicit interactional principles might well improve clinical practice, or at least render it more articulate.

The second apparently productive avenue of study of knowledge about interaction is to take a learning approach to it. When do professional interviewers learn their craft, and can we see sensible ideas about interaction developing during that process? While we know of no studies of this, we posit that such processes of learning are, in at least some respects, generic strategies that professionals use to capitalize on their ongoing work in order to learn – that is, to acquire helpful knowledge and coordinated (in this case, interactional) practices. Such learning processes are, in part, the reflections of a reflective practitioner (Schön, 1983).[7] Because this learning might not be externalized (talked or written about), and because the knowledge that arises from it is not empirical or theoretical exactly in the sense that science is theoretical and empirical, studying the development of interactional knowledge, such as that which implements revoicing, is an excellent and prototypical knowledge* pursuit.

## Acknowledgments

We wish to acknowledge contributions by Janet Koster van Groos, Ayush Gupta, Mari Levin, Bruce Sherin, and Reed Stevens in the beginning conversations that led to this chapter. The first author thanks the Spencer Foundation for supporting the original and subsequent interviewing studies, which provided the data involved in this work.

## Appendix A – Codes

("Interviewer" and "interviewee" are abbreviated as "IER" and "IEE," respectively.)

**GOAL**: What is the reason for focus on the revoiced item, or the intended function of this revoicing from the interviewer's perspective?

- Confirm-continuer – Simple confirmation of hearing, to move the conversation along. May be a "desperation" move, e.g., when the IER is confused.
- Words – Query about the literal words said.
- Ground-establishing – Putting/securing an item into public space.
- Contradiction/other-relation – Intended to establish general or particular relation to another item, e.g., "You said X, but earlier you said Y."
- Refined-view – Attempt to get more detail on the item.
- Non-refining "about" – Query about referenced item, not elaborating its meaning.
- Check-inference – The referenced item is an intended inference, or the (judged-to-be, by the interviewer) conclusion of "in play" items. Another version would be check HOW interviewee got to a stated conclusion, most likely checking the core reason for the conclusion.
    - Conclusion
    - Inference-link.
- Supply-language.
- Exogenous-interest – Item is elaborated for non-local reasons (e.g., interview "required" items that have come up, or nearly come up).
- Chance-to-rethink – Intent to have the interviewee rethink a contribution.
- Extended-reasoning-tracking – One item in an account of an extended line of reasoning. Often seemingly in expectation of confirmations on each item.
- Synthesis/summary – Synthesis or summary as check or as ground for continuing work.

**FORMULATION**: How is the revoicing presented?

- Bare – Just a bare assertion, often literally repeating a contribution.
- Focus – How is the revoiced item identified?
    - IDed-as-revoice – Identified as a revoicing, e.g., "you said…", "you think…", "you decided…" …
    - IDed-as-inference
        - So – Literally, "so…." Note that there would be a wide range of these: testing "obvious" inference, or "so maybe that might mean…"
        - And – Literally, "And <therefore>…"; or "and" meaning, e.g., adding to a list.
    - IDed-as-reasoning – e.g., "I'm just trying to follow your reasoning."
    - Other-f-scaffolding: Help was given.

- A-Frame: What "anticipation frame" was provided (sketch or hint as to proper or expected response).
  - Yes-or-no – Yes or no response is foreshadowed (simple question)
  - Other-a-scaffolding
    - Trying-to-understand (explicit explanation).

**IEE-RESPONSE**: Form of interviewee response.

- Yes-or-no – Response to yes or no question.
  - Bare-yes-or-no
  - Elaborated-yes-or-no – Elaborated (as if to explain, no evident rethinking, per below).
- Confirm – Usually "right," or "uh huh."
- Continue – Interviewee merely continues her line of reasoning.
- Rethink-reject – Rethinking leading to rejection of original voiced claim.
- Rethink-refine – Change or refinement of the voiced claim.
- Rethink-affirm – Consideration leading to reaffirming the claim.
- Ask-for-clarification – Clarification on topic, focus, or a-frame.
- Null.
- Reject-attribution.

**IER-FOLLOWUP:** Interviewer's reception and possible extension of revoicing turn.

- Closure – e.g., "OK."
- New-topic – Interviewer proceeds directly to a new topic.
- Content-iteration – Iteration on content of revoicing question.
  - Rethink – Push to rethink
  - Alternative – Providing another alternative to consider
  - Sub-focus – Moving to yet more detail.
- Confirm-continuer.
- Adj-Focus – Adjust focus (new, or correction of improperly received revoicing).
- Adj-a-Frame – Adjust anticipation frame, e.g., "No, I meant…."

## Appendix B: More Examples

Because our primary mode of analysis was to use our grounded coding scheme, pre-processing revoicings into categories, we present additional examples of revoicing here. "I:" denotes the interviewer and "J:" is the interviewee. Rather than being prototypic, several were chosen for their unusual characteristics.

The following revoicing is the only one in the interview that was rejected outright by the interviewee. Notice that the interviewee is rejecting the very fact of deciding something, not the particulars of what was decided. So it is declining, specifically, the interviewer's attribution, "you've decided...." In addition, the interviewer immediately accedes to her judgment, one of numerous examples that show the interviewee that she retains full rights concerning judging her own thinking:

I: So you've decided now that probably //
J: *[interrupting]* I haven't decided anything yet. I'm just thinking; see if it makes more sense.
I: I understand. That's great.

The following aborted revoicing emphasizes the functional equivalence of at least some revoicings with other ways of getting the student to reveal more ("make data appear") concerning her ideas. The interviewer starts with a revoicing, but then reconsiders and appears to believe that drawing would be a more efficient way for the interviewee to show how she is thinking about the situation. This is eminently sensible, given the focus of attention; portraying complex geometric relations in words is difficult.

I: So you've got // *[self-correction, aborting a verbal description of what the interviewee "had," and restart]* Want to draw me a picture of how this is working?

The next revoicing shows different-than-prototypic structures that serve core functions we've identified for revoicing:

I: I'm trying to understand what you said a little bit. You said like it's a question of being in the shadow behind the earth. Is that the idea?

"I'm trying to understand what you said a little bit," explicitly notes the intended function of the revoicing, to understand more ("a little bit") about what the interviewee said. What follows seems more standard ("you said"), but the "reformulation" itself selects and synthesizes a specific aspect of what was said – hardly all of it – for consideration. In particular, the interviewer names the key causal features apparently at issue in the interviewee's mind ("being in the shadow behind the earth"). The final tag provides (or confirms) an a-frame, suggesting that the relevant precision is just "the idea," rather than some precise and technical issue of meaning.

The interviewee's response to this revoicing was:

J: Well [pause] Actually, the more I think about it, the more I think that's actually very wrong. Because it doesn't move fast enough for you to be in the shadow.

The revoicing evidently fostered a rethinking and rejection of a contention, even though the interviewer made no move toward a negative judgment. She does not explicitly respond to the interviewer's question, "Is that the idea?" Rather, it seems that providing another opportunity or time to reflect led to the rejection of the idea (not the attribution). Whether or not the interviewer intends it, a revoicing can provide an opportunity to rethink. (diSessa, 2007, brings data to show that interviewees, after coming to understand the clinical genre, do not regard repeated questions or requests for additional information systematically as implicitly critical.)

The following is an unusual version of revoicing, where the interviewer says what he believes the interviewee is thinking, even though she does not articulate that particular thing at all. The interviewee seems to validate the "revoicing," with a minor correction ("would" becomes "might"). By structural standards, this is not a revoicing. It has literally no characteristics listed in the formal decomposition of revoicing. However, the interviewer's move serves to clarify for him what the interviewee is thinking, which is the main function of revoicing. One might call this version of revoicing "pre-voicing." Notice the interviewee's subtle correction of the pre-voicing:

J: I have no idea. *[Pause]* But I think if you told me //
I: It would ring a bell.
J: It *might* ring a bell.

The next example of a revoicing and the response to it by the interviewee show, again, in a perspicuous and remarkably compact form, the way that revoicing works sometimes to promote rethinking. In this case, J appears to just confirm the interviewer's gloss of what she has just told him. But, then, she seems to have second thoughts, "well...." Then she returns to her affirmation, "yeah," confirms that take with a stronger (emphatically pronounced, as to emphasize more confidence, now) "*Yeah*," and proceeds to elaborate why she believes the contention.

I: So the problem that you are having now is that you are thinking that this part of the world is just going to get cooked? Is that // *[The interviewer is interrupted.]*
J: Right *[pausing as if to think]*, well *[pauses and turns to model earth and pauses again as if to reconsider]*, yeah. Yeah *[strong emphasis, as if to definitively confirm]*, because *[J continues with a confirming analysis]*.

## Notes

1  See roughly comparable counts in Russ et al. (this volume), Table 1.
2  See contribution 4b on p. 322 of O'Connor and Michaels (1993), which is the first-mentioned revoicing in that paper.

3   The more ambiguous of these potential requests for validation might have been mere requests for more information. Space prohibits pursuing the issue, but it is worth noting a potential theoretical limit: Multiple goals may be in play at the same time, or the intent of an interviewer action might be ambiguous at its heart, perhaps being construed only as "an action taken because it often leads to useful consequences."
4   The interviewer might have started with the intention only of checking the conclusion – "So you decided" – but then restarted with a check of the full chain of inferences.
5   In this sense, interviewing is a slave to common and even, to some extent, lexicalized conceptions of knowledge available to the interviewee. While knowledge* transcends this, interactional constraints limit the use of revoicing for making data about unfamiliar kinds of knowledge* appear.
6   See diSessa (2007) for documentation that the interviewer/informant here was aware of these issues, and engaged a number of strategies to forestall them.
7   The issue of where interactional strategies, like a refined use of revoicing, might develop is particularly salient in the case of our interviewer/informant. He had not read about clinical interviewing, nor did he apprentice with or even watch more expert interviewers before the interview we studied here was done. Learning as a reflective practitioner was likely to be particularly strong in this case, whereas other clinical interviewers might well learn their craft at least partially in other ways.

## References

Austin, J. L. (1962). *How to do things with words*. Cambridge, MA: Harvard University Press.

Bannon, L., & Bødker, S. (1991). Beyond the interface: Encountering artifacts in use. In J. M. Carroll (Ed.), *Designing interaction: Psychology and the human–computer interface* (pp. 227–253). New York: Cambridge University Press.

Cazden, C. B. (2001). *Classroom discourse: The language of learning and teaching* (2nd ed.). Portsmouth, NH: Heinemann.

Clement, J. (2000). Analysis of clinical interviews: Foundations and model viability. In A. Kelly & R. Lesh (Eds.), *Handbook of research design in mathematics and science education* (pp. 547–589). Mahwah, NJ: Lawrence Erlbaum Associates.

Cohen, D. K. (1990). A revolution in one classroom: The case of Mrs. Oublier. *Educational Evaluation and Policy Analysis*, 12(3), 311–329.

diSessa, A. A. (1996). What do "just plain folk" know about physics? In D. R. Olson & N. Torrance (Eds.), *The handbook of education and human development: New models of learning, teaching, and schooling* (pp. 709–730). Oxford, UK: Blackwell.

diSessa, A. A. (2007). An interactional analysis of clinical interviewing. *Cognition and Instruction*, 25(4), 523–565.

diSessa, A. A. (2014). An epistemological perspective on misinformation. In D. N. Rapp & J. L. G. Braasch (Eds.), *Processing inaccurate information: Theoretical and applied perspectives from cognitive science and the educational sciences* (pp. 279–296). Cambridge, MA: MIT Press.

diSessa, A. A., Elby, A., & Hammer, D. (2002). J's epistemological stance and strategies. In G. Sinatra & P. Pintrich (Eds.), *Intentional conceptual change* (pp. 237–290). Mahwah, NJ: Lawrence Erlbaum Associates.

Ginsburg, H. (1997). *Entering the child's mind: The clinical interview in psychological research and practice*. Cambridge, UK: Cambridge University Press.

Goffman, E. (1974). *Frame analysis*. Cambridge, MA: Harvard University Press.

Goffman, E. (1981). *Forms of talk*. Philadelphia, PA: University of Pennsylvania Press.

Gruber, H. E., & Voneche, J. J. (1977). *The essential Piaget*. New York: Basic Books.

Mehan, H. (1979). *Learning lessons*. Cambridge, MA: Harvard University Press.

O'Connor, M. C., & Michaels, S. (1993). Aligning academic task and participation status through revoicing: Analysis of a classroom discourse strategy. *Anthropology and Education Quarterly*, 24(4), 318–335.

O'Connor, M. C., & Michaels, S. (1996). Shifting participant frameworks: Orchestrating thinking practices in group discussion. In D. Hicks (Ed.), *Discourse, learning, and schooling* (pp. 63–103). Cambridge, UK: Cambridge University Press.

Schön, D. (1983). *The reflective practitioner: How professionals think in action*. New York: Basic Books.

Searle, J. (1969). *Speech acts: An essay in the philosophy of language*. Cambridge, UK: Cambridge University Press.

Stahl, G. (2012). Ethnomethodologically informed. *Computer-Supported Collaborative Learning*, 7, 1–10.

Schegloff, E. A. (1982). Discourse as an interactional achievement: Some uses of "uh huh" and other things that come between sentences. In D. Tannen (Ed.), *Georgetown University Roundtable on Languages and Linguistics* (pp. 71–93). Washington, DC: Georgetown University Press.

Schiffrin, D. (1987). *Discourse markers*. Cambridge, UK: Cambridge University Press.

Talmy, S. (2011). The interview as collaborative achievement: Interaction, identity, and ideology in a speech event. *Applied Linguistics*, 32(1), 25–42.

# 14

# THE INTERSECTION OF KNOWLEDGE AND INTERACTION

## Challenges of Clinical Interviewing

*Rosemary S. Russ, Bruce L. Sherin, and Victor R. Lee*

Much of science education research is concerned with understanding children's prior knowledge of the natural world (Pfundt & Duit, 2009). This work is motivated by the assumption that students possess intuitive knowledge of science – knowledge gained outside of formal instruction – that impacts how they learn formal science (e.g., NRC, 2007). It is hoped then that finding out more about the intuitive knowledge itself will help make classroom instruction more effective and meaningful. As Clement (2000) claims, "Mapping this 'hidden world' of indigenous thinking is crucial for the success of instructional design" (p. 547).

One methodology, the cognitive clinical interview, has dominated the field's study of the "hidden world" of students' intuitive knowledge (Ginsberg, 1997; Piaget, 1929). These one-on-one, semi-structured interviews are both planned in advance and responsive to the in-the-moment thinking of the interviewee. Research interviewers typically design a set of questions to probe student thinking about a particular scientific phenomenon or mathematical topic. However, it is assumed "that subjects' ways of thinking are delicate and complex, and skill is necessary to surface them" (diSessa, 2007, p. 525). In clinical interviews, that skill takes the form of improvisation; interviewers have the freedom to diagnose and follow up on student ideas as they arise.

These interviews have the potential to provide very rich access to student ideas (e.g., Carraher & Schliemann, 2002; Ellis, 2007; Goldstone & Wilensky, 2008; Gottlieb, 2007; Hmelo-Silver, Marathe, & Liu, 2007; Izsák, 2005; Taber & García-Franco, 2010), and, like other authors in this volume (Brown, this volume; diSessa, Greeno, Michaels, & O'Connor, this volume), we are interested in the data they produce. However, the fact that clinical interviews have the potential to provide such rich access to student thinking does not mean they always do so. Researchers who use clinical interviews know that sometimes the interviews reveal a lot about the nuance of a student's understanding and sometimes they do not. Two short examples are sufficient to illustrate this point.

Consider the following moment from an interview about chemical and physical changes with a middle-school student. After a brief introduction about the purpose and logistics of the interview, the interviewer asks what happens when sugar is mixed with water. In response, the student, Aaron, answers as follows (speaker gestures are indicated with <>):

| | |
|---|---|
| **Interviewer:** | Imagine that we have two beakers like these here <points to beakers on table>, all right. And one is full of water and one is full of sugar. Okay, so what do you think happens if I pour the sugar into the water. |
| **Aaron:** | It'll dissolve. |
| **Interviewer:** | What does that mean? |
| **Aaron:** | It means that it will spread out even through, like, the water molecules. Like – <spreads open his hands on the table in front of him> |
| **Interviewer:** | So the sugar, the sugar will spread out evenly through the water molecules in the beaker? |
| **Aaron:** | Mm-hmm. |
| … | |
| **Aaron:** | It's like the sugar molecules are, uh, littler than the water molecules. So then they're in between the li-, the water molecules. |

Here the interviewer learns that Aaron is familiar with dissolution and has had some formal instruction in chemistry since he references molecules. The interviewer also learns that Aaron can use everyday language (i.e., littler) to describe the relative sizes of the molecules.

In contrast to Aaron's interview excerpt, there are times when clinical interviews fail to produce meaningful or useful data about student thinking. Consider another interview, with Cassie, whose interviewer tries to understand her thinking about dissolution:

| | |
|---|---|
| **Interviewer:** | Okay. Um, what does, where did it [sugar] go [when it gets dissolved in water]? |
| **Cassie:** | Just like gets like mixed in with the water. |
| **Interviewer:** | Okay. What do you, what do you mean exactly? |
| **Cassie:** | I don't really know. I mean like um, like gets, I don't know. |
| **Interviewer:** | Well is it still sugar? |
| **Cassie:** | Yeah. |
| **Interviewer:** | Does it turn into something else? |
| **Cassie:** | I don't think so. I don't really know. |
| **Interviewer:** | Well what do you think? |

| | |
|---|---|
| **Cassie:** | I'm not really sure. |
| **Interviewer:** | Well that's okay. |

In this second excerpt, we get very little data about Cassie's understanding of dissolution. Other than her statement that the sugar gets mixed with the water, most of her answers are short statements suggesting lack of immediately accessible knowledge of the topic. However, our past experience with this interview prompt and our intuitions about children's everyday experiences suggest that Cassie likely has the capability to reason more deeply about the phenomenon. She likely has dissolved sugar (or Kool-Aid or lemonade) in water, or seen someone mixing spices into hot liquid while cooking. Unfortunately though, this interview has failed to give us evidence of what the nature of that knowledge or experience might be.

With these two interview excerpts arranged consecutively, the following point is clear: sometimes clinical interviews provide substantial evidence about a student's understanding (as in the case with Aaron) and sometimes they do not (as in the case of Cassie). In this chapter we explore the question "Why might this be so?" We ask, "What has 'gone wrong' in the interview with Cassie?" and "What 'went right' in the case of Aaron?"

To answer these questions, we frame our argument around two major challenges that we have identified for clinical interviews. We believe that speaking to these challenges can account, at least in part, for differing levels of "success" in clinical interviews. We refer to these as the *challenge of restriction* and the *challenge of interpretation*. The first challenge can best be understood by applying a *knowledge analytic* lens to clinical interviewing, and the second by applying an *interaction analytic* lens.

In what follows, we first describe clinical interviews from each perspective – Knowledge Analysis and Interaction Analyses – and use those perspectives to elaborate on the aforementioned challenges that clinical interviewers face in eliciting and probing student thinking. We then document the ways that interviewers navigate those challenges. To do so, we describe two dimensions of that navigation and present several categories of interviewer turns in each dimension. We then provide short examples of these turns to give the reader a sense of how these turns play out in interviews. Within these examples, we speculate on how those turns are interpreted, either productively or unproductively, by the interviewees. We present frequency and case analyses of the types of turns interviewers use to jointly navigate these challenges of restriction and interpretation. Finally, we describe the implications of this joint Knowledge and Interaction Analysis for future work involving clinical interviews.

## "Good" Cognitive Clinical Interviews: Knowledge and Interaction

While their open-endedness and flexibility make clinical interviews powerful instruments, those features also create challenges for judging their quality. Given that a key feature of the interview is non-standardization, we cannot measure its success in terms of fidelity to a protocol. How then should we assess it?

We suggest that the quality of a clinical interview should be characterized by the richness of the data it provides. That is, good interviews provide rich and generative data on student thinking. But what does "good data" look like? Characterizing good data requires precision about the purposes of employing the clinical interview. We now consider two perspectives on employing clinical interviews in research – the knowledge perspective and the interactional perspective.

### Knowledge Analysis Perspective: Success and Challenges

In much of our own work, we adopt a perspective on scientific cognition that has been described by such terms as *conceptual ecology* (diSessa, 2002; Strike & Posner, 1992), *knowledge in pieces*, (diSessa, 1993) and a *systems perspective* (Smith, diSessa, & Roschelle, 1993). In this perspective, knowledge about the natural world is seen as consisting of a large number of elements of knowledge, each with relatively limited sub-structure. From this perspective, the goal of a clinical interview is generally seen as mapping some portion of this conceptual ecology.

Although no brief interview can map a substantial fraction of a conceptual ecology in a particular territory, in this perspective an interview is successful when it allows researchers to make a maximal trek through a desired portion of a student's conceptual ecology. It is important to note that this definition characterizes the success of an interview in terms of the amount of student knowledge it allows us to infer. This approach is highly cognitively oriented; it represents a traditional *Knowledge Analysis* style of work (see diSessa, Sherin, & Levin, this volume).

From this perspective, there are many ways in which interviews can fail. First, if we are only seeing a small number of isolated elements, then the interview is likely not providing much of an empirical foundation for a knowledge analyst. For example, a student who only parrots back nuggets of formal knowledge acquired in school gives only a limited picture of his or her broader, underlying ecology. diSessa (2007) also describes how interview problems that are too difficult or complex for the interviewee to engage with fail to tap into a student's conceptual ecology and thus do not provide interviewers or analysts with access to that ecology.

Second, in this perspective, the words that students use cannot be taken as a direct reflection of underlying knowledge (diSessa, 2014); we must rely on inferences. It is possible, then, for an interviewer to participate in a way that obscures – or limits our ability to make inferences about – student knowledge. For example, if the interviewer introduces many new ideas into the conversation, it may become unclear which knowledge elements are attributable to the student and which to the interviewer. Furthermore, when seeking to map a portion of students' conceptual ecologies, we care not just about what elements are there; we also want to know the relevant prominence of elements and how they are connected. These latter attributes of the conceptual ecology can be obscured if interviewers introduce, in a strong manner, their own judgments about the centrality of ideas or their relationships in a way that is "coercive" or "seductive" (diSessa, 2007). We refer to this issue as *the challenge of knowledge restriction*; a student's conceptual ecology is inevitably obscured – and thus our inferences about that conceptual ecology restricted – by the knowledge and judgments the interviewer introduces in the interview.

## *Interaction Analysis Perspective: Success and Challenges*

Recently, this highly knowledge-centric approach to understanding clinical interviews has been brought into question. For example, Roth and Middleton (2006) have called for "researchers to acknowledge that the interview is not an unbiased tool for eliciting information but a collaboratively constituted, irreducibly social event" (p. 15). Researchers both within and outside of the community who use them have highlighted the interactional nature of clinical interviews (Brown, this volume; diSessa, 2007; Grossen & Orvig, 1998; Roth, 2008). For example, in his work, Brown (this volume) adopts this perspective and demonstrates the ways that – even when interviewers are silent – they still contribute substantially to the interaction and to the explanations interviewees construct.

Beyond these calls from the literature, a simple word-count analysis of the interviews in our corpus (see description in subsequent sections) suggests the importance of attending to the role of both participants in the interaction. Counting the total number of words uttered by each participant reveals that they each speak in approximately equivalent amounts during the interview (49.7% students, 50.3% interviewers). Thus, at least in terms of quantity, interviewers and students share the discourse floor evenly during these interviews, as opposed to what might happen in a more one-sided interview context (e.g., Clayman, 1988; Tannen, 1993).

Essentially, this approach moves away from thinking of interviews as elicitations of a single participant's ideas toward thinking of interviews as inherently discourse interactions (Goodwin & Heritage, 1990; Sacks, Schegloff, & Jefferson, 1974; Schegloff, 1987) between two participants in which the talk of one influences and constrains the talk of the other. Using this *Interactional Analysis* lens, interviews are successful to the extent that each participant can engage in them in a way that is ecologically valid (diSessa, 2007). That is, both participants – the interviewer and the interviewee – must view the interaction as "normal" from their own perspective.

From the interactional perspective, interviews can provide only limited evidence of students' thinking when interviewers and students have different interpretations of the purpose and goals of the interaction. For example, in other work, we have described how we get very limited data on students' intuitions when students frame the interview as a test of their school-based science knowledge (Russ, Lee, & Sherin, 2012). In these cases, the student may interpret the interviewer's repeated requests for clarity and elaboration as a push for and evaluation of correctness. diSessa (2007) also describes what we might term interactional-type challenges in his case-study analysis of an interview about intuitive physics with a college student. These include times when an interviewer (unintentionally) conveys that he has a correct response in mind, or when he fails to pose a task that makes sense to the student. We refer to this phenomenon as *the challenge of interactional interpretation*, because the interviewer's probing can make the nature of the interaction – exploration of the student's own thinking – unclear and non-negotiable for students.

## *Refinement of Research Goals: Understanding "Good" Interviews*

This discussion of the challenges of "good" interviewing allows us to refine our focus. Here we focus on the successful and unsuccessful dynamics of cognitive clinical interviewing with an eye toward both *knowledge* and *interaction*. Specifically, we seek to answer the following questions:

1. How do interviewers manage the challenge of knowledge restriction?
2. How do interviewers manage the challenge of interactional interpretation?

Our focus here begins on the interviewer's discourse turns and then moves to cases of how student participants take up what interviewers do and say. This approach contrasts with that taken by Brown (this volume), who begins by identifying what he calls "feedback-relevant places" in student discourse and then analyzes the interviewer talk in relation to it. Our reason for beginning with the interviewer is twofold. First, since we are the interviewers in our data corpus, we have a firsthand knowledge of the intention and goals of the researcher. That insight makes it easier to make inferences about the challenges interviewers face (and in some sense reduces the amount of inference needed). Second, it is only through the actions of the interviewers that we as researchers have control over the quality of an interview. Knowing how interviewers attempt to navigate the challenges they face allows us to systematize some of the craft-like knowledge that successful interviewers possess, with the hopes that we can train future interviewers in the craft.

## Research Methods

### *Data Corpus: An Existing Set of Clinical Interviews*

In this research, we expand prior exploratory work (Lee, Russ, & Sherin, 2008) by systematically exploring a large data corpus and by centrally examining interactional effects. Our analysis focuses on a set of clinical interviews originally designed to explore the ways in which students' science knowledge changed as a result of different types of instruction. Students were interviewed both before and after instruction in a content area, with some students receiving traditional instruction and others receiving reformed, project-based instruction. We collected interviews with middle-school students (grades 6–8) on a range of physical, chemical, and biological topics. A total of 13 interviewers with varying levels of experience conducted approximately 150 interviews across these topics. All interviews were videotaped and transcribed and students' written artifacts were collected.

Although not initially collected for the analysis conducted in this work, the relatively large number of interviews conducted by an experientially diverse group of interviewers sharing a common philosophy of interviewing provided an opportunity to see both the range of challenges interviewers face and the range of potential responses to those challenges. As such, we found the corpus to be rich with the phenomena we hoped to explore in this study.

## Data Analysis

### Phase 1: Description of Common Interviewer Turns

In Phase 1, we defined interviewer turns-at-talk as a complete conversational turn of the interviewer regardless of its length or any pauses during its completion. A turn may be only one word (e.g., Okay) or it may be a lengthy elaboration. A change in speaker from the interviewer to the student marks the end of a turn-at-talk by the interviewer.

In the first phase, we randomly selected portions of student interviews of approximately one to five minutes in length, and watched short segments of the video while simultaneously examining the transcript. For each turn-at-talk, we attempted to characterize its *function* in the discourse. In particular, we were interested in characterizing how, from the point of view of the interviewer, a particular utterance could help in achieving the goal of drawing out and better understanding the thinking of the student.

To assist this identification of turn function, we examined discourse analyses of other forms of conversation centered on explaining knowledge, such as tutoring dialogue (e.g., Graesser & Person, 1994; Graesser, Person, & Magliano, 1995; Person, Kreuz, Zwaan, & Graesser, 1995) or classroom discussion (e.g., Hogan, Nastasi, & Pressley, 2000; Louca, Tzialli, & Zacharia, 2008). After reviewing several video episodes, we examined the identified list of functions, grouped similar ones together, and looked for instances of those functions in the entire interview corpus. The result was a description of nine types of utterances that interviewers in our sample commonly used to navigate the challenges inherent in conducting and managing clinical interviews (Lee et al., 2008).

## Phase 2: Defining Dimensions of Interviewer Turns

Since our goal in this work is to understand how interviewers specifically navigate the challenges of knowledge restriction and interactional interpretation, in Phase 2 we split the overall functions identified in Phase 1 into two different dimensions.

First, from the knowledge perspective, the main goal of interviewing is to construct a map of a student's conceptual ecology of a topic. Constructing that map requires that interviewers elicit knowledge elements and infer the relationship between them. To do so, interviewers may draw attention to particular elements of knowledge and in doing so prompt students to talk about both that knowledge and related knowledge. We refer to this dimension of the interviewer turn as the knowledge-restriction dimension.

To explore how interviewers navigate the challenge of restriction, we compared the interviewer's turn-at-talk to the student's previous turn-at-talk to understand whether and how interviewers explicitly cued particular elements of students' conceptual ecology. We then identified the origin of the knowledge elements that interviewers used in their turns. Specifically, we asked: Does the interviewer reference – either explicitly or implicitly – knowledge previously put into the common ground (Clark & Schaefer, 1989) by the student? Or does the interviewer introduce new information into the common ground? In identifying the source of the knowledge elements, we began with existing literature on *revoicing* (diSessa, Greeno, Michaels, & O'Connor, this volume; O'Connor & Michaels, 1993) – moments in which conversational partners restate portions of their partner's speech – and expanded as needed to fit our data corpus. Similar origins were clustered into larger categories (Coffey & Atkinson, 1996). The final set of discourse turns in the knowledge dimension – ten turns clustered into three categories – serves as a way to answer the first research question: How do interviewers manage the challenge of knowledge restriction? This analysis allows us to explore the ways interviewers may restrict (either by introducing or cuing) the knowledge elements discussed in the interview.

Second, from the interaction perspective, the interviewer's goal is for students to interpret the interview as a time for substantively and authentically engaging with the tasks at hand (diSessa, 2007; Ginsberg, 1997; Piaget, 1929). We refer to this dimension of the interviewer turn as the interactional-interpretation dimension.

One way in which interviewers convey to students this understanding of the interaction is by asking students questions (making requests) that engage them in constructing and exploring ideas about the science topic. We operationalized this dimension of interviewer turns-at-talk by comparing the interviewer's turn to the student's subsequent turn. We then asked, "What does the interviewer's utterance explicitly or implicitly ask the student to do in the student's following turn?" For example, interviewers may ask students to clarify an existing idea or explore the implications of an idea. We identified some potential request types in the literature (Graesser et al., 1995; Hogan et al., 2000; Louca et al., 2008), while others were generated from the data in an emergent fashion. Again, similar requests were clustered into larger categories (Coffey & Atkinson, 1996). The final set of discourse turns in the interaction dimension – 11 turns clustered into 5 categories – serves as a way to answer the second research question: How do interviewers manage the challenge of interactional interpretation? This analysis allows us to explore how interviewers potentially impact students' interpretation of the purpose of the interview interaction.

### Phase 3: Examining Cases of Student Responses to Interviewer Turns

Once we identified common interviewer turns, we conducted qualitative, microgenetic analyses (Chinn & Sherin, in press) to explore how students take up these turns. First, we examined individual extended cases of several types of interviewer turns and explored the ways in which students responded to those turns. Using intensity sampling, we chose information-rich cases that were clear but non-exceptional demonstrations of interviewer turns (Creswell, 2012). Second, we conducted contrasting cross-case analyses (Lichtman, 2011; Maxwell, 2012) of successful and unsuccessful interviews along the two dimensions (knowledge and interaction).

### Phase 4: Coding and Quantifying Interviewer Turns

The turns-at-talk identified in Phase 2 were applied to 25 interviews in which students were asked to explain the causes of the seasons and the temperature variation between Alaska and Florida (Sherin, 2013; Sherin, Krakowski, & Lee, 2012). In total, approximately 825 interviewer turns-at-talk were coded, each with multiple codes per dimension. The first author served as the primary coder and trained the third author as the secondary coder. After this training, the researchers independently coded 3 of the 25 transcripts, or 87 of the 825 interviewer turns-at-talk, along each of the two dimensions. Turns-at-talk that were multiply coded within a dimension were considered agreed upon if at least one code matched across researchers. Inter-rater reliability was calculated for each dimension independently using Cohen's kappa, and indicated high agreement among coders (0.905 and 0.829 for knowledge and interaction dimensions respectively). Disagreements were discussed and resolved. The quantitative analysis presented in this work deals only with the primary code assigned to each dimension for each turn-at-talk.

## Navigating Interviewing Challenges

In what follows, we first describe interviewer turns in each of the two dimensions separately and provide qualitative examples of their instantiations in the data corpus. Second, we analyze the dimensions jointly by examining the frequency of different combinations of turns, and explore an extended case of an interviewer drawing on various combinations of turns to navigate both challenges in the interview.

## Knowledge Analysis Perspective

From the perspective of Knowledge Analysis, interviewer turns-at-talk activate, or highlight, particular elements in a students' conceptual ecology. Throughout the interviews, we see interviewers drawing attention to a range of knowledge elements from a range of different sources. Table 14.1 shows the three categories of interviewer turns along with specific codes within each.

TABLE 14.1 Interviewer turns for navigating knowledge restriction

| Knowledge cluster | Source of knowledge | Brief description | Percentage of total interviewer turns | Sub-codes |
|---|---|---|---|---|
| New knowledge | Researcher: either individual interviewer or protocol | Interviewer references some new information not previously discussed in the interview | 22% | New factual information<br>New features of the scenario<br>New task criteria |
| Selective restatement | Student prior turn-at-talk | Interviewer references part of the student's previous statement either verbatim, rephrased, or summarized | 46% | Partial verbatim repeat<br>Terminology reference<br>Representation reference<br>Prune and rephrase<br>Summarize<br>Substituting words for intended meaning<br>Imposing coherence |
| Generic prompt | None | Interviewer does not reference any content relevant to the task | 32% | Generic |

Intersection of Knowledge and Interaction    **387**

These clusters, along with the specific types of interview turns (the sub-codes), constitute a first-order answer to our first research question. That is, interviewers navigate the challenge of restricting (or not restricting) access to a students' conceptual ecology by introducing new knowledge only 22 percent of the time, restating part of the student's knowledge nearly half of the time (46 percent), or not specifically referencing any knowledge 32 percent of the time. The relatively high occurrence of interviewers restating student knowledge in our interviews is consistent with diSessa, Greeno, Michaels, and O'Connor's (this volume) findings and their claim that revoicing is central to the interviewer's toolkit.

Consider the two following contrasting examples, one in which the interviewer turn highlights new knowledge and one in which it highlights student knowledge. These examples allow us to explore the different ways in which the types of turns described in Table 14.1 provide access to students' conceptual ecologies. In the transcripts throughout the chapter, italics are used to highlight portions of interviewer turns that exemplify the different coding categories.

### Example of Interviewer Turn that Highlights New Knowledge

In the first example, interviewee Diedra explains the seasons using an explanation she asserts she learned from her teacher the previous week. Her explanation involves several parts, including attention both to the earth spinning on an axis and to it sometimes being closer to or farther from the sun. She initially draws the picture in Figure 14.1.

**FIGURE 14.1**   Diedra's drawing of the seasons.

When asked about the fact that it is summer in Australia when it is winter here, she admits that she had thought of that but had not included it in her explanation. The interviewer presses her to consider that knowledge explicitly:

I: So is that a problem for your picture?
D: I don't know. Where's Australia at? I don't know my geography. That's one thing I don't know.
I: *Well, we're sort of in the north part of the Earth.* And Australia is-
D: Down south.
I: Yeah, way down south.
D: Australia is also on the opposite side of the Earth though.

…

D: Okay, so Australia will be over here <adds to drawing>. So during our summer they'll be having winter… And then over here, they'd be over here so they'd be having summer.

Here, the interviewer introduces new knowledge about the location of Australia and specifically highlights its north/south location. The interviewer presumably provided Diedra with geographical information because without it, he could trek no farther through her conceptual ecology. Introducing new knowledge created the potential for him to see whether and how she connected that knowledge with the knowledge used in her first explanation.

What we see in this moment, though, is that despite the interviewer's attempt to highlight knowledge about Northern and Southern hemispheres, his turn instead activated her knowledge element of opposites (diSessa, 1993). This element, when connected with her knowledge about the Earth spinning on its axis, reinforced her explanation that the seasons are caused by different parts of the Earth either facing or not facing the sun. In this case, the interviewer added his own knowledge into the conversation to navigate the challenge of restriction, but that turn did not significantly expand the elements of Diedra's conceptual ecology that were visible. Instead, it mirrored existing relationships between existing knowledge.

### *Example of Interviewer Turn that Highlights Student Knowledge*

In contrast to the previous example, consider the case of a student, Edgar, in which the interviewer highlights the student's own knowledge. Edgar first discusses the seasons in relation to the earth's rotation around a tilted axis but then changes his explanation:

E: Actually, I don't think [the axis] moves, [the Earth] turns and it moves [orbits] like that and it turns and it's further away once it orbits around the sun.

I: *It's further away?*
E: Yeah, and somehow like that goes further off and the sunrays wouldn't reach as much to the Earth.

Here the interviewer does not introduce any new knowledge into the conversation that Edgar has not already used but instead reintroduces the student's knowledge. Specifically, in his turn, the interviewer *selectively restates* part of Edgar's previous turn verbatim. Edgar has just finished talking about both the rotation ("turn") and orbit ("moves") of the Earth in relation to the sun but the interviewer only repeats Edgar's comments about the location of the Earth in its orbit. In doing so, the interviewer restricts Edgar's attention to only the newest knowledge element that has been introduced into the conversation. This restriction allows the interviewer to explore whether and how this knowledge is connected to other aspects of Edgar's conceptual ecology previously discussed. In response, Edgar explains the connection, providing evidence of additional knowledge elements; he describes the importance of distance and the sun's rays.

## *Interaction Analysis Perspective*

From the perspective of Interaction Analysis, interviewer turns-at-talk send meta-messages (Bateson, 1972; Tannen, 2001) to students about the nature of the interview interaction and appropriate ways to engage in it. Specifically, the interviewer's requests convey judgments about whether the student's thinking to that point is sufficient and/or clear. Table 14.2 shows five categories of such messages along with specific codes within each.

These clusters, along with the specific types of interview turns (the sub-codes), provide a preliminary answer to our second research question. That is, interviewers navigate the challenge of interpreting (or reinterpreting) the purpose of the interaction by asking students a pre-defined question from the protocol (new protocol request or other protocol request) only 17 percent of the time. All other turns are improvisational – either seeking clarification or elaboration or vaguely asking them to continue – and occur with approximately the same frequency. We provide examples of two of the five categories – elaboration and clarification requests – of interviewer turns for navigating the challenge of interpretation because we suspect these turns are familiar to readers.

For each of these turns, we infer particular meta-messages from our own use of these turns in interviews; they are the messages we suspect interviewers *intend* to convey. However, the descriptions in Table 14.2 are not necessarily how students understand these interviewer turns. To make sense of how students understand these turns, in the examples that follow we will highlight evidence of student interpretations.

**TABLE 14.2** Interviewer turns for navigating interactional interpretation

| Interactional cluster | Meta-message about the interaction | Brief description | Percentage of total interviewer turns | Sub-codes |
|---|---|---|---|---|
| New baseline request | Previous idea sufficient and clear | Interviewer asks the student a question about a new topic | 6% | Answer new question |
| Clarification request | Previous idea sufficient but unclear | Interviewer asks the student to confirm or clarify an idea | 27% | Confirm<br>Clarify<br>Decide among given alternatives |
| Elaboration request | Previous idea insufficient | Interviewer asks the student to talk more in depth about an existing idea | 27% | Zoom in<br>Provide a mechanism<br>Follow implications |
| Minimal request | Student can decide about the sufficiency or clarity of the previous idea | Interviewer does not explicitly ask the student to do anything or provides little information about how to proceed | 29% | Null<br>Minimal guidance |
| Other protocol request | Interviewer has decided about the sufficiency or clarity of the previous idea | Interviewer asks the student to perform an activity such as drawing a picture or describing where an idea came from | 11% | Perform an activity<br>Describe knowledge origin |

## *Example of Interviewer Turns that Suggest Insufficiency and Need for Elaboration*

In this first example, student Ovadya talks with the interviewer about why it is generally warmer in Florida than in Alaska. Ovadya's first response is that it is warmer because it is near the equator, which is in "the middle" of the earth. The interviewer probes this idea further using an elaboration prompt:

> **I:** *I guess I'm sort of wondering what does, so how does being in the middle make it warm?*
> **O:** Cause you're not close to the poles.

**I:** *And the poles are just cold?*
**O:** Yeah.
**I:** *What makes the poles cold then?*
**O:** The sun doesn't reach over there, that much.
**I:** *I see. I see. Umm, and why doesn't the sun reach the poles as much?*
**O:** Cause the sun stays in the same spot and the Earth stays the same way it is and it spins around and doesn't reach the poles that much.

Ovadya's initial explanation for differences in temperature is entirely geographical and it is not clear whether or how his understanding of climate is connected to his larger conceptual ecology involving the Earth/sun system. The interviewer asks Ovadya "how" and "why" this explanation works. In doing so, he attempts to convey to Ovadya that his ideas make sense but need further explanation.

With each request for elaboration from the interviewer, Ovadya provides the interviewer with further evidence of knowledge elements in his conceptual ecology and the relationship between them. For example, we learn Ovadya sees the poles and the equator in some sense as opposites, that the sun does not move but in some way "reaches" the earth, and that the earth spins but maintains its general orientation. The fact that we see him drawing on this knowledge is evidence that he is treating the interaction as an opportunity for sense-making about the scenario.

### Example of Interviewer Turns that Suggest Imprecision and Need for Clarification

Now consider a different example in which an interviewer repeatedly requests clarification, rather than elaboration, from a student. Kimberly says that it is warmer in the summer and colder in the winter because the earth "goes around" and the sun "hits more during the summer" when it is not "facing further away." The interviewer then asks her to draw a picture (Figure 14.2) to clarify her thinking.

**K:** Well, okay…<smiling> Well, okay…okay, well, here's Earth and here's where we live. And the sun is up over here. <draws it> And during summer, it faces and hits it directly so it's hotter <draws lines>
**I:** *I see. And how is the Earth moving?*
**K:** It's revolving around the sun.
**I:** *It's moving like this?* <does circular arm gesture>
**K:** Yeah.
**I:** *Is it also spinning?*
**K:** Yeah. It's… 'cause each circle is a day and it revolves all around.

In this excerpt, the interviewer first asks Kimberly to clarify how the Earth is moving. This is an idea Kimberly had brought up in her verbal statement but

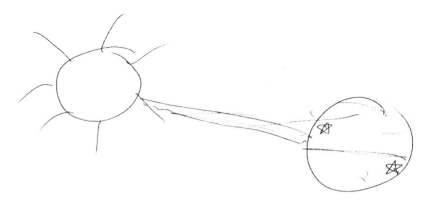

**FIGURE 14.2** Kimberly's drawing of the seasons.

is not represented in the picture. He then asks her to confirm his understanding of the word "revolution" with an arm gesture. The interviewer then seeks to clarify if revolution is the only movement of the Earth by asking about spinning.

The interviewer's requests for clarification highlight for Kimberly that specificity and precision are important in this context as he tries to understand her thinking. In asking these questions, the interviewer is not attempting to push Kimberly to draw on new knowledge (as was the case in the elaboration example). Instead he is pushing her to clarify what appears, up to that point in the interview, to have been tacit knowledge wrapped up in her explanation and drawing (e.g., the Earth rotates and revolves; rotation is associated with a daily cycle). For her part, Kimberly appears to take his requests for clarification as genuine interest and curiosity. She does not express hesitation in her response, nor does she change her thinking. She treats the interview as an opportunity to clarify her own thinking for the interviewer and perhaps also for herself.

## Knowledge Analysis/Interaction Analysis (KA/IA) Joint Perspective

The previous distinction between the knowledge and interactional perspectives is a convenient one for analysts because it reduces complexity. It takes a multifaceted challenge and breaks it apart by focusing on how single turns-at-talk address single challenges. However, in the moment of the interview, interviewers do not encounter knowledge and interaction challenges independently. In fact, from the perspective of the interviewer, the challenges may not even be separable. As such, it is important for us to look at the interviewer turns from both perspectives simultaneously.

**TABLE 14.3** Frequency of interviewer turns by dimension and cluster

|  | Minimal request | New baseline request | Clarification request | Elaboration request | Other protocol request | Totals |
|---|---|---|---|---|---|---|
| Generic prompt | 165 | 3 | 11 | 27 | 60 | 266 |
| New knowledge | 17 | 46 | 36 | 72 | 11 | 182 |
| Selective restatement | 63 | 1 | 174 | 129 | 17 | 384 |
| Totals | 245 | 50 | 221 | 228 | 88 | 832 |

## Frequency Analysis

To do so, we first explore the overall trends of interviewer turns along both dimensions, treating the entire corpus as a single unit; all transcript segments related to the seasons from interviews across all participants were combined. Table 14.3 shows the counts of the number of interviewer turns in each cluster organized by knowledge dimension in the rows and interaction dimension in the columns.

Three types of interviewer turns occur more than twice as often as each of the other types of turns. First, the most commonly used knowledge/interaction combination is the selective restatement/clarification turn, of which there were 174 instances (or 20.9%) in our data corpus. This turn involves an interviewer repeating part of the student's thinking and then asking the student to clarify that thinking. How does this combination help interviewers navigate the challenges of restriction and interpretation? First, the interviewer/analyst maintains the ability to make claims that the student "knows" or "possesses" that particular knowledge element. Second, the interviewer tacitly conveys that the student is engaging appropriately in the task in bringing that type of knowledge to bear. And finally, the interviewer conveys that he or she believes the particular knowledge being discussed is productive and worthy of further inquiry.

The next most common interviewer turn is the content-free/minimal request combination, which occurs 165 times, or 19.8% of the time. A closer look at these turns reveals that they are mostly (11% of the 19.8%) back-channel feedback (Duncan, 1972) such as "Hmm" or "Uh-huh." Sacks et al.'s (1974) model of turn-taking in everyday conversation suggests that these turns serve the vital function of granting the student speaker additional allotments of conversational turns (see Brown, this volume, for further discussion related to this point).

How does this turn help interviewers navigate the challenges of restriction and interpretation? First, this turn grants the student more space to talk (Matarazzo & Wiens, 1972), thereby providing the opportunity for the student to express additional elements in his or her conceptual ecology. Second, Clark and Schaefer

(1989) suggest that this type of turn confirms "common ground"; the interviewer conveys to the student both that he is listening and that he has understood what the student is saying. Third, back-channel feedback is an implicit affirmation that the student is engaging in the interview in the appropriate way and should continue to do so. Finally, this turn – perhaps more than any other – allows students to make their own inferences about the nature of the interaction and the nature of the knowledge they should use in it.

Finally, we found the selective restatement/elaboration turn, in which the interviewer repeats part of what the student says and asks him to elaborate on that thinking, in 129 (15.5%) interviewer turns-at-talk. This turn helps navigate the challenges in much the same way as the previous two. It both allows interviewers to attribute particular knowledge to students (because no new knowledge elements are introduced) and provides space for further knowledge elements to become visible. Additionally, by highlighting and probing a particular piece of thinking, the interviewer opens up the conversation to explore other knowledge elements that are closely related to it in the student's conceptual ecology. As with the other turns, it conveys to students that they are engaging in the interview in a way that is appropriate, and also suggests that their current line of thinking is worthy of intellectual pursuit.

Our purpose in describing these three common turns is to highlight that each of them serves multiple overlapping "functions" for the interviewer (akin to what diSessa, Greeno, Michaels, and O'Connor [this volume] observed with regard to revoicing). Some of these functions are related to navigating knowledge challenges and others to interactional challenges. Every interviewer turn simultaneously opens or obscures access to a student's conceptual ecology and reinforces or disrupts the student's interpretation of the interaction.

## *Case Analysis*

The frequency analysis provides a sense of how often these turns occur and also the functions they *may* serve in interviews. However, it gives us very little information about how these turns play out in actual interviews. Do interviews actually get data on students' conceptual ecologies in the way we describe? Do students actually interpret the turns as we suggest? To answer these questions, we now turn to an extended example concerning a student, Angela.

Angela initially articulates a closer-farther explanation for the seasons and draws a picture (Figure 14.3, reproduced from the video capture) to describe her thinking.

> **A:** See, that's what winter would be like, the Earth orbits around the sun (she motions over the oval shaped orbit she has drawn). Like summer is the closest to the sun. Spring is kind of a little further away, and then like

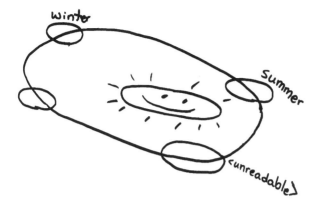

**FIGURE 14.3** Angela's initial drawing of the seasons.

> fall is further away than spring but not as far as winter, and then winter is the furthest.
>
> ...
>
> **I:** Mm hmm, okay. So that makes a lot of sense. *One thing I wanted to ask you though about was, one thing that you might have heard is that at the same time, and you can tell me if you've heard this, when it's summer here, it's actually winter in Australia.* Have you heard that before?
> **A:** Mm hmm.
> **I:** *So I was wondering if your picture the way you drew it can explain that or if that's a problem for your picture.*
> **A:** Umm, I need another picture.

Here the interviewer introduces new knowledge about there being different seasons on different parts of the Earth at the same time that Angela had not explicitly voiced prior to this turn. In doing so, this interviewer turn may restrict analysts from making claims about whether that knowledge element existed independent of the interviewer, but it allows us to see whether and in what ways that knowledge element is related and connected to other elements in her conceptual ecology.

Interactionally, the interviewer's elaboration request suggests to Angela that he wants more than just an acknowledgment of the new knowledge; he also wants her to do something with that knowledge. He conveys that her previous response was clear, but was insufficient from the perspective of the interviewer. Angela seems to take up his request in this way and as she starts to draw a new picture:

> **I:** So is that a problem for your picture?
> **A:** Yeah, that is. Um, okay. There is the sun. <drawing> Yeah, I remember that now cause um it's like as the Earth is rotating, as it's orbiting, it's rotating too. I guess I don't understand it.

I: *You're saying as the Earth is going around here,* it's doing what?
A: It's like spinning, cause it's going like <spinning gesture>, that's how it's day and night too
I: *Spinning like a top.*
A: Yeah.
I: Okay.
A: So, yeah, I guess I really don't understand it that much…
I: So you're thinking that somehow the spinning, that somehow if you take into account the fact that the Earth is also spinning, that might help to explain why it's summer and winter at different times?

…

I: *Just to be clear, what was the problem with this picture for the-*
A: Because, yeah I rethought that and it looks really stupid because summer is really close but how could you winter on the other side, how could it be winter on the other side if it's really close here, and how could it be really warm if this [winter earth] is really far away.

At the start of this second excerpt, the interviewer asks for clarification about whether that new knowledge about Australia is a problem. Angela interprets that request as a sign that she should continue her explanation (the "Mm hmm") and she goes on to use her picture to provide a specific description of the challenge the new knowledge poses for her explanation. The interviewer's request for clarification is successful; he gains further evidence of her knowledge and also maintains her productive stance toward the interview.

Throughout the rest of the excerpt, the interviewer gains further access to Angela's conceptual ecology solely by highlighting knowledge that she herself introduced into the conversation and then asking for clarification. Each of his turns involves some form of selective restatement with a clarification or minimal guidance request; he points to the Earth's movement in her drawing and he pulls out her use of the word spinning. With these turns, he first learns about additional knowledge elements (that the Earth spins). He also learns about additional relationships between the knowledge; she connects spinning to the day/night cycle, and highlights a problematic connection in her previous explanation (the existence of spinning means that the distance explanation cannot work). In each case, Angela maintains an interpretation of the interview as an opportunity to explain and work out her thinking.

Near the end of the excerpt, the interviewer again asks Angela to clarify her thinking. In fact, he begins his turn with, "Just to be clear." Angela takes up this request by precisely identifying which aspects of her conceptual ecology she had inappropriately activated – distance and "sidedness." Notice that her reasoning for rejecting her original explanation is not directly related to the knowledge the interviewer introduced in the previous section. Instead, his question about Australia led to a new explanation that highlighted her knowledge of spinning. This final picture of Angela's conceptual ecology (one in which she rejects the common misconception about distance from the sun causing the seasons) includes far more knowledge elements and connections than the interviewer (and analyst) had access to prior to his introduction of new knowledge or his probes for clarification.

## Discussion

Thus far, our focus has been on examples in which interviewers successfully navigate the challenges of restriction and interpretation. We now return to one of the excerpts from the introduction to examine a moment of failure in the interview. Recall the interview with Cassie about what happens when sugar is dissolved in water:

| | |
|---|---|
| **Interviewer:** | Okay. Um, what does, where did it [sugar] go [when it gets dissolved in water]? |
| **Cassie:** | Just like gets like mixed in with the water. |
| **Interviewer:** | Okay. What do you, what do you mean exactly? |
| **Cassie:** | I don't really know. I mean like um, like gets, I don't know. |
| **Interviewer:** | Well is it still sugar? |
| **Cassie:** | Yeah. |
| **Interviewer:** | Does it turn into something else? |
| **Cassie:** | I don't think so. I don't really know. |
| **Interviewer:** | Well what do you think? |
| **Cassie:** | I'm not really sure. |
| **Interviewer:** | Well that's okay. |

We see this portion of the interview as a failure both because the interviewer gains very little (if any) access to Cassie's conceptual ecology and also because Cassie and the interviewer seem to grow more and more uncomfortable with one another as the interaction continues. How did this failure occur?

In response to the interviewer's first question, Cassie provides a sensible answer – the sugar gets mixed into the water. The interviewer follows up by asking Cassie to clarify "exactly" what she means. In doing so, the interviewer conveys that Cassie's idea is insufficiently precise from the perspective of the interviewer but does so without providing guidance in which aspect of the idea needs clarification and/or explaining why it might need clarification in the first place. Cassie responds to this request from the interviewer by saying that she doesn't know. She makes an attempt to clarify her idea but stops in the middle and again states that she doesn't know. From this attempt, we infer that Cassie sees the interaction as one in which she is supposed to know an answer and provide it for the interviewer. This moment is an interactional failure that limits access to Cassie's conceptual ecology.

The interviewer, perhaps because she sees Cassie's discomfort with the original question, changes tactics and introduces some new knowledge into the conversation by asking Cassie if the sugar is still sugar. Cassie treats this request for elaboration as a request for clarification; she sees the question as an obvious statement that she is merely meant to confirm with a one-word response. Cassie's response is consistent with an interpretation of the interview that involves answering rhetorical questions as though she were in school (e.g., Does everybody understand?) or talking with adults (e.g., Do you like the present I got you?). The interviewer then introduces further new knowledge – the idea that the sugar has the ability to transform/change, though it may or may not do so in this case. Here the interviewer restricts the knowledge Cassie has to draw on by asking her to explore a space that is unfamiliar and possibly unconnected with her conceptual ecology for "mixing." Additionally, by asking about sugar changing into something else when Cassie has already confirmed that she believes it is still sugar, the interviewer may confuse Cassie's interpretation of the previous question as a rhetorical one, almost turning it into a "trick" question. The introduction of new knowledge leads to both a knowledge-based and interaction-based failure.

In her final question, the interviewer seems to recognize the challenges she and Cassie are facing. Specifically, she recognizes that Cassie is treating the interview as one in which she needs to provide a precise and correct answer. To counteract that interpretation, the interviewer asks Cassie to say what she thinks. However, after the inertia of the previous turns, this move is insufficient to access any part of Cassie's conceptual ecology; Cassie is no longer drawing on her own knowledge elements related to sugar "mixing" with water. Cassie states that she is not even "really sure" what she thinks. In this excerpt, both knowledge and interaction perspectives are essential for understanding how and why this interview provides so little evidence for Cassie's understanding of dissolution.

## Conclusion

Throughout the chapter, we have highlighted how interviewers navigate the challenges of both restriction and interpretation. We have described the various types of turns that interviews use to traverse students' conceptual ecologies by defining those turns in relation to the students' previous and subsequent utterances. Some of those turns are successful while others are not successful. The short and extended excerpts are intended to flesh out our argument about the nature of the challenges and responses in specific cases, and the analysis of the frequency of these turns is intended to provide a sense of how often interviewers engage in "knowledge" work and "interaction" work.

Stepping back from these specifics, though, our work in this chapter is intended to highlight that we cannot disentangle Knowledge Analysis from Interaction Analysis. They are both part and parcel of the success and navigation of cognitive clinical interviews used for research purposes. In fact, we can even go so far as to say that there can be no meaningful Knowledge Analysis without understanding the dynamics of the interaction (Russ et al., 2012), and that there can be no substantive analysis of the interaction without also considering how it impacts and draws on knowledge. As such, as researchers we must conduct analyses that, at the very least, are sensitive to both aspects of interviews, and, at the most, are intentional about exploring cases in which these various challenges surface and take precedence.

If knowledge and interaction are inherently intertwined in cognitive clinical interviews, then interviewers must (a) be prepared to recognize different types of failures, (b) maintain constant awareness of both knowledge and interactional cues from students, and (c) develop a set of strategies – or turns – that they can flexibly use to navigate failures. Those of us who conduct these interviews in order to map students' conceptual ecologies spend a great deal of time training interviewers in the art of developing appropriate diagnostic and follow-up questions. Additionally, those who critique our interview practice often focus heavily on whether and how we have "biased" the knowledge that students draw on when answering the question. That is, the focus is heavily weighted toward the challenge of restriction.

In contrast, many of us may tacitly assume that our interviewers already know how to navigate interactions. After all, interviewers are people who presumably regularly engage in conversations with others. However, the analysis of Cassie's interview suggests that we cannot always trust that assumption. Navigating the interactional challenge of interpretation must be part of our training for cognitive clinical interviewers. To do so, we might take suggestions from those who engage in and study other types of qualitative interviews (e.g., Kvale & Brinkmann, 2009; Rubin & Rubin, 2012). For example, we might draw on approaches Mishler (1986) uses in his narrative interviews to make space for interviewees to talk about aspects of the problem that are interesting to them, or on the methods Briggs (1986) uses in his ethnographic interviews to set up conversations that make sense from the interviewee's perspective. These other types of qualitative interviews centered on the authenticity of the interviewer–interviewee interaction may provide cognitive clinical interviewers with some sense of how to navigate the challenge of interpretation. Those of us in a Knowledge Analysis tradition cannot assume that training for interviewers and analysts should focus largely on identifying and probing knowledge elements. We must also impress on them the importance of attending to features of the interaction. The success of interviews from a knowledge perspective necessitates that the interview is first successful in the interactional perspective.

# References

Bateson, G. (1972). A theory of play and fantasy. In G. Bateson (Ed.), *Steps to an ecology of mind: Collected essays in anthropology, psychiatry, evolution, and epistemology* (pp. 177–193). New York: Ballantine.

Briggs, C. L. (1986). *Learning how to ask: A sociolinguistic appraisal of the role of the interview in social science research*. New York: Cambridge University Press.

Carraher, D., & Schliemann, A. (2002). The transfer dilemma. *Journal of the Learning Sciences*, 11(1), 1–24.

Chinn, C., & Sherin, B. L. (in press). Microgenetic methods. In R. K. Sawyer (Ed.), *The Cambridge handbook of the learning sciences* (2nd ed.). New York: Cambridge University Press.

Clark, H. H., & Schaefer, E. F. (1989). Contributing to discourse. *Cognitive Science*, 13, 259–294.

Clayman, S. E. (1988). Displaying neutrality in television news interviews. *Social Problems*, 35(4), 474–492.

Clement, J. (2000). Analysis of clinical interviews. In A. E. Kelly & R. E. Lesh (Eds.), *Handbook of research design in mathematics and science education* (pp. 547–590). Mahwah, NJ: Erlbaum.

Coffey, A., & Atkinson, P. (1996). *Making sense of qualitative data*. Thousand Oaks, CA: Sage.

Creswell, J. W. (2012). *Qualitative inquiry and research design: Choosing among five traditions*. Thousand Oaks, CA: Sage.

diSessa, A. A. (1993). Toward an epistemology of physics. *Cognition and Instruction*, 10(2&3), 105–225.

diSessa, A. A. (2002). Why "conceptual ecology" is a good idea. In M. Limón & L. Mason (Eds.), *Reconsidering conceptual change: Issues in theory and practice* (pp. 29–60). Dordrecht, NL: Kluwer.

diSessa, A. A. (2007). An interactional analysis of clinical interviewing. *Cognition and Instruction*, 25(4), 523–565.

diSessa, A. A. (2014). The construction of causal schemes: Learning mechanisms at the knowledge level. *Cognitive Science*, 38(5), 795–850.

Duncan Jr., S. (1972). Some signals and rules for taking speaking turns in conversations. *Journal of Personality and Social Psychology*, 23(2), 283–292.

Ellis, A. B. (2007). The influence of reasoning with emergent quantities on students' generalizations. *Cognition and Instruction*, 25(4), 439–478.

Ginsberg, H. P. (1997). *Entering the child's mind: The clinical interview in psychological research and practice*. New York: Cambridge University Press.

Goldstone, R. L., & Wilensky, U. (2008). Promoting transfer by grounding complex systems principles. *Journal of the Learning Sciences*, 17(4), 465–516.

Goodwin, C., & Heritage, J. (1990). Conversation analysis. *Annual Review of Anthropology*, 19, 283–307.

Gottlieb, E. (2007). Learning how to believe: Epistemic development in cultural context. *Journal of the Learning Sciences*, 16(1), 5–35.

Graesser, A. C., & Person, N. K. (1994). Question asking during tutoring. *American Educational Research Journal*, 31(1), 104–137.

Graesser, A. C., Person, N. K., & Magliano, J. P. (1995). Collaborative dialogue patterns in naturalistic one-to-one tutoring. *Applied Cognitive Psychology*, 9, 495–522.

Grossen, M., & Orvig, A. S. (1998). Clinical interviews as verbal interactions: A multidisciplinary outlook. *Pragmatics*, 8(2), 149–154.

Hmelo-Silver, C. E., Marathe, S., & Liu, L. (2007). Fish swim, rocks sit, and lungs breathe: Expert–novice understanding of complex systems. *Journal of the Learning Sciences*, 16(3), 307–331.

Hogan, K., Nastasi, B. K., & Pressley, M. (2000). Discourse patterns and collaborative scientific reasoning in peer and teacher-guided discussions. *Cognition and Instruction*, 17(4), 379–432.

Izsák, A. (2005). "You have to count the squares": Applying knowledge in pieces to learning rectangular area. *The Journal of the Learning Sciences*, 14(3), 361–403.

Kvale, S., & Brinkmann, S. (2009). *Interviews: Learning the craft of qualitative research interviewing*. London: Sage.

Lee, V. R., Russ, R. S., & Sherin, B. (2008). A functional taxonomy of discourse moves for conversation management during cognitive clinical interviews about scientific phenomena. In V. Sloutsky, B. Love, & K. McRae (Eds.), *Proceedings of the 30th Annual Meeting of the Cognitive Science Society* (pp. 1723–1728). Austin, TX: Cognitive Science Society.

Lichtman, M. (2011). *Understanding and evaluating qualitative educational research*. Thousand Oaks, CA: Sage.

Louca, L. T., Tzialli, D., & Zacharia, Z. C. (2008, June). Identification-interpretation/evaluation-response: A framework for analyzing classroom-based teacher discourse in science. In *Cre8ting a learning world: Proceedings of the Eighth International Conference of the Learning Sciences (ICLS)*, Utrecht, NL.

Matarazzo, J. D., & Wiens, A. N. (1972). *The interview: Research on its anatomy and structure*. New Brunswick, NJ: Aldine Transaction.

Maxwell, J. (2012). *Qualitative research design: An interactive approach*. Thousand Oaks, CA: Sage.

Mishler, E. G. (1986). *Research interviewing: Context and narrative*. Cambridge, MA: Harvard University Press.

NRC (National Research Council). (2007). Committee on science learning, Kindergarten through eighth grade. *Taking science to school: Learning and teaching science in grades K-8*. Washington, DC: The National Academies Press.

O'Connor, M. C., & Michaels, S. (1993). Aligning academic task and participation status through revoicing: Analysis of a classroom discourse strategy. *Anthropology and Education Quarterly*, 24, 318–318.

Person, N. K., Kreuz, R. J., Zwaan, R. A., & Graesser, A. C. (1995). Pragmatics and pedagogy: Conversational rules and politeness strategies may inhibit effective tutoring. *Cognition and Instruction*, 13(2), 161–188.

Pfundt, H., & Duit, R. (2009). *Bibliography: Students' alternative frameworks and science education*. Kiel, DE: Institute for Science Education.

Piaget, J. (1929). *The child's conception of the world*. New York: Routledge.

Roth, W.-M. (2008). The nature of scientific conceptions: A discursive psychological perspective. *Educational Research Review*, 3, 30–50.

Roth, W.-M., & Middleton, D. (2006). Knowing what you tell, telling what you know: Uncertainty and asymmetries of meaning in interpreting graphical data. *Cultural Studies of Science Education*, 1(1), 11–81.

Rubin, H. J., & Rubin, I. S. (2012). *Qualitative interviewing: The art of hearing data*. Washington, DC: Sage.

Russ, R. S., Lee, V. R., & Sherin, B. L. (2012). Framing in cognitive clinical interviews about intuitive science knowledge: Dynamic student understandings of the discourse interaction. *Science Education*, 96(4), 573–599.

Sacks, H., Schegloff, E. A., & Jefferson, G. (1974). A simplest systematics for the organization of turn-taking for conversation. *Language*, 50, 696–735.

Schegloff, E. A. (1987). Analyzing single episodes of interaction: An exercise in conversation analysis. *Social Psychology Quarterly*, 50(2), 101–114.

Sherin, B. L. (2013). A computational study of commonsense science: An exploration in the automated analysis of clinical interview data. *Journal of the Learning Sciences*, 22(4), 600–638.

Sherin, B. L., Krakowski, M., & Lee, V. R. (2012). Some assembly required: How scientific explanations are constructed during clinical interviews. *Journal of Research in Science Teaching*, 49(2), 166–198.

Smith, J. P., diSessa, A. A., & Roschelle, J. (1993). Misconceptions reconceived: A constructivist analysis of knowledge in transition. *Journal of the Learning Sciences*, 3(2), 115–163.

Strike, K. A., & Posner, G. J. (1992). A revisionist theory of conceptual change. In R. A. Duschl & R. J. Hamilton (Eds.), *Philosophy of science, cognitive psychology, and educational theory and practice* (pp. 147–176). New York: State University of New York Press.

Taber, K. S., & García-Franco, A. (2010). Learning processes in chemistry: Drawing upon cognitive resources to learn about the particulate structure of matter. *Journal of the Learning Sciences*, 19(1), 99–142.

Tannen, D. (1993). *Framing in discourse*. New York: Oxford University Press.

Tannen, D. (2001). *I only say this because I love you*. New York: Random House.

# 15

# FEEDBACK-RELEVANT PLACES

Interpreting Shifts in Explanatory Narratives

*Nathaniel J. S. Brown*

In conceptual change research dating back to Piaget (2007; Piaget & Inhelder, 2000), explaining observed or hypothetical phenomena of everyday and/or scientific relevance has been the prototypical cognitive activity in which participants engage. Related activities are common, such as predicting which phenomenon will occur in a given situation (in the context of chemistry, see Mulford & Robinson, 2002) or identifying whether a phenomenon is of a particular class (in the context of physics, see Ioannides & Vosniadou, 2002). However, investigating participants' explanatory narratives of various phenomena remains a primary focus in the field.

One of the major findings of this work is that interviewees often revise and rework their explanations on a moment-by-moment basis, giving conflicting accounts at different times. This observation has sometimes prompted the question of how researchers can know what people "really" believe. Does a shift indicate that an interviewee has changed their mind in response to new information or a new focus of attention? Or does a shift indicate that an interviewee has interpreted follow-up questions as evidence they must be wrong, and is changing their explanation to say something they hope will be correct? For example, Southerland, Abrams, Cummins, and Anzelmo (2001), in a study of students' conceptions of biological adaptation, reported that 40 percent of students gave different explanations for the same phenomenon in response to follow-up questions from the interviewer. Ultimately, however, they were unable to decide whether to attribute these shifts to aspects of the students' knowledge systems or to aspects of the interaction between the interviewer and interviewee.

The concern that unaccounted-for aspects of interaction may lead to misinterpretation of knowledge systems is not without precedent. Indeed, in the broader literature from which the learning sciences draw, careful attention to interactional detail has produced many alternative accounts of the nature of knowledge systems involved in cognitive activity. For example, studies have debunked mythologies of logical reasoning and sudden insight in scientific discovery (Latour & Woolgar, 1979), revealed the tactical utility of ignorance as a means of achieving social ends (Goodwin, 1987), exposed teacher and classmate collusion in the performance of learning disability (McDermott, 1993; McDermott, Goldman, & Varenne, 2006), relocated cognitive achievements such as solving geometry problems outside the individual mind (Hutchins, 1995), belied the feasibility of interpreting responses to standardized questions (Antaki & Rapley, 1996; Suchman & Jordan, 1990), and unmasked the co-construction of knowledge during semi-structured interviews (Button, 1987; Macbeth, 2000).

This work has established that interaction contributes to the organization and content of cognitive activity in deep and complex ways, and that researchers who make inferences about knowledge systems must be wary of how interaction affects their data. However, caution is not enough. This work has also demonstrated that the particular mechanisms by which interaction structures and influences cognitive activity are varied and non-obvious. Interaction is not a monolithic procedure but a vast collection of unwritten rules and expectations that change in different contexts. In order to disentangle the relationship between knowledge and interaction in a particular cognitive activity, researchers need to understand the particular mechanisms involved.

To help researchers interpret shifts in explanation, this chapter describes a particular mechanism of interaction that speakers and listeners use during explanatory narratives. This mechanism allows the speaker to gather feedback from the listener at specific moments, in order to monitor the success of the explanation as it unfolds. These moments are called *feedback-relevant places* (FRPs), and are designed by the speaker to check on either comprehension or agreement. In response, the listener may supply or withhold different kinds of feedback, prompting the speaker to continue or repair the explanation.

As described and illustrated later in this chapter, attention to the FRP mechanism provides important evidence to the analyst of why a shift in explanation occurs at a particular moment, and what that implies about the cuing and reliability priority of certain knowledge elements. To cast this in terms of the agenda of this volume, careful attention to the details of interaction allows for a more complete and more precise interpretation of the qualities of a student's knowledge system. Interaction Analysis can directly enhance a core practice of Knowledge Analysis.

## Data and Methods

Feedback-relevant places were first described in the author's doctoral dissertation (Brown, 2009), in which the goal was to characterize the sequential organization of explanatory narratives. The use of FRPs in disentangling and analyzing systems of knowledge and interaction, as described in this chapter, was a method developed using data collected as part of that study. Consequently, relevant details of the data and methods of that study are given below; a more complete discussion is given in Brown (2009).

Eight undergraduate students, enrolled in the introductory general chemistry course for non-majors at the University of California, Berkeley, were recruited to participate in a series of four interviews, approximately two per week, during the last month of the semester. During each interview, the participant was asked to explain why four hypothetical chemical phenomena would occur. As a goal of the study was to understand how explanatory narratives depend on framing and interaction, the students were asked to explain the same four phenomena in each of the four interviews, but to different people for different purposes.

## Phenomena

Each phenomenon involved alcohol evaporating or condensing in a closed, air-filled container. In each case, a stimulus (e.g., an increase in temperature) would cause some of the alcohol to partially evaporate or condense, eventually stopping before the process reached completion. These phenomena illustrate important chemistry concepts, including phase equilibrium, the Law of Mass Action, and Le Chatelier's Principle, but they were not identified as such to the participants.

Each phenomenon was described to the participants and illustrated in a printed diagram in which before and after states were depicted. Figure 15.1 illustrates the first phenomenon, in which liquid methanol partially evaporates after being placed in a closed container. Figure 15.2 illustrates the second phenomenon, in which liquid ethanol – consisting of larger and more massive molecules – partially evaporates to a lesser extent than methanol after being placed in a similar container. Figure 15.3 illustrates the third phenomenon, in which an increase in temperature causes additional liquid ethanol to evaporate. Figure 15.4 illustrates the fourth phenomenon, in which shrinking the size of the container causes some of the ethanol vapor to condense back into liquid.

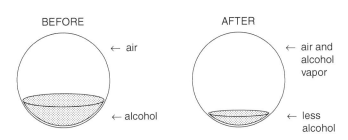

**FIGURE 15.1** Liquid methanol partially evaporating in a closed, air-filled container.

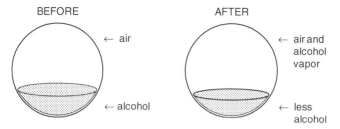

**FIGURE 15.2** Liquid ethanol partially evaporating in a closed, air-filled container, to a lesser extent than methanol.

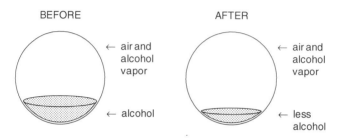

**FIGURE 15.3** Additional liquid ethanol evaporating in response to an increase in temperature.

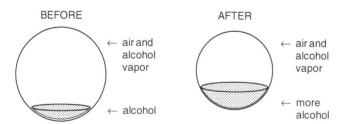

**FIGURE 15.4** Some ethanol vapor condensing back into liquid in response to a decrease in the size of the container.

## Interview Types

Although the phenomena were the same during each interview, the framing of each interview was varied by having the participant explain the phenomena to different people for different purposes: (1) answering questions during a typical semi-structured interview, in which the interviewer is a stranger probing their understanding; (2) discussing with a friend until the friend is satisfied they understand; (3) teaching a stranger until the stranger is satisfied they understand; and (4) being tutored by an expert. By varying the relative expertise and familiarity of the student and their interlocutor, these situations were chosen to engender interesting differences in interaction, with the goal of inducing variations in the students' explanatory narratives in which framing and interaction were factors.

## Semi-Structured Interviews

The first interview was framed as a semi-structured interview, one of the principal methodologies in research on conceptual change. (I call these semi-structured interviews rather than clinical interviews because the latter generally involve extended time spent with participants in which the range of topics is less constrained; see, for example, those conducted by diSessa [1993, 2007], Ginsburg [1997], Piaget [2007], and Piaget & Inhelder [2000].) The interviewer, the present author, introduced himself as an educational researcher interested in how people explain things in chemistry using their own words rather than relying on the chemical terminology they have learned. The students knew that the interviewer had taught past sections of the chemistry course from which they were recruited. That he possessed knowledge of the material was also made salient by the fact that the final interview was described as a tutoring opportunity for the student. While the specifics of the interviewer's expertise were not discussed openly, each student, usually at the conclusion of the interview, positioned the interviewer as being in possession of the "right answers" by asking to know what those answers were.

During the interview, after asking the student to explain each phenomenon, a series of follow-up questions were asked in order to further probe or clarify their understanding. These follow-up questions were tailored to the particular student and often invented on the spot in response to what had just been said. Throughout, the interviewer emphasized that he was not interested in accuracy but instead in whatever way the student happened to think about the phenomena. Follow-up questions often asked the student to explain any chemical terminology they had used and to rephrase their explanation in their own words. The semi-structured interviews lasted, on average, 45 minutes to one hour.

## Peer Discussions

The second interview was framed as a peer discussion, and the student was asked to bring a friend with them. The interviewer described the phenomenon and set the goal of having the student explain the phenomenon convincingly to their friend. The interviewer then limited his direct involvement to interjecting when a long pause would develop and asking the friend whether they were convinced yet by the explanation. Unlike the semi-structured interview, the interviewer did not ask the students follow-up questions, though the friends were encouraged to do this if they did not understand or were not convinced by the explanation. Despite this encouragement, the friends did not ask many follow-up questions. Consequently, the peer discussions were the shortest, ranging from 15 to 30 minutes.

## Teaching Sessions

The third interview was framed as a teaching session, with the student teaching a stranger lacking any substantial chemistry knowledge. The author recruited eight colleagues who were also graduate students in education. In each case, the invited graduate student had not taken a chemistry course in about ten years and was not particularly knowledgeable about chemistry. As during the peer discussion, the interviewer described the phenomena, set the goal of getting the stranger to understand why the phenomena occurred, and interjected during pauses to ask the stranger whether they were satisfied yet with their understanding. Like the peer discussions, the interviewer refrained from asking follow-up questions, but unlike the peer discussions, each stranger did so freely. Indeed, the strangers requested so much discussion of the phenomena that the teaching sessions were by far the longest interviews, with each lasting over an hour and with some lasting nearly two hours.

## Tutoring Sessions

The final interview was framed as a tutoring session, in which the interviewer asked the student to attempt to answer the questions correctly, using scientific terminology as needed. As would a chemistry tutor, the interviewer asked leading questions, corrected mistakes, critiqued each explanation, and suggested better explanations. The tutoring interview was held last in order to postpone a discussion of the "right answers" as long as possible. Tutoring interviews ranged from one hour to 75 minutes, with the bulk of the time spent reviewing and critiquing the students' prior explanations and developing a normative molecular kinetic model of equilibrium. Once this model had been taught in the context of the first phenomenon, each student successfully applied it to explain the remaining three phenomena in rapid succession.

## Data Collection

The study of interaction demands the use of video data in order to capture the moment-by-moment detail of the participants' interactions and the multiple semiotic fields (Goodwin, 2000) they use to transmit information, including talk, intonation, gaze, gesture, body position, and external representation. In the present study, the provided diagrams (Figures 15.1–15.4) were one source of representation and a small whiteboard with colored markers was an available means of creating additional representations as needed by the participants.

Each interview was video-recorded using two cameras, one capturing a wide-angle view of all the participants and another capturing a close-up view of the provided diagrams and the whiteboard. As described next, camera angles were chosen to reflect the theoretical assumptions of the researcher (Hall, 2000).

The wide-angle view was broad enough to keep all participants in frame at all times, including the interviewer, who was nearly silent during the second and third interviews. This reflects the assumption that, even when participants do not appear to be actively involved in the discussion, their presence and non-verbal body language have the potential to structure the interaction in ways that would be difficult to reconstruct without keeping them in frame. At the same time, the wide-angle view was kept close enough to make out gaze direction.

The close-up view was directed down onto the table surface between the principal discussants. This area, centered on the whiteboard and including the diagrams, was assumed to form a shared representational space. That this was the case is supported by three observations. First, the gazes of all participants were directed downward to this space by default, even when nothing was written on the whiteboard; gaze shifts to people's faces were temporary excursions. Second, when talk referred to one of the provided diagrams, the speaker moved the diagram from the outskirts of this space to the center. Third, the majority of gestures made by the speaker were made in this space, above the surface of the whiteboard. These observations identify this area as a shared representational space used by the participants to coordinate focus.

## Analysis

Using the methods of Video Analysis (Engle, Conant, & Greeno, 2007; Erickson, 2006; Goldman & McDermott, 2007), Conversation Analysis (Goodwin & Heritage, 1990), and Interaction Analysis (Jordan & Henderson, 1995), the larger study from which this chapter draws had the goal of characterizing the sequential organization of constructing explanatory narratives in speech.

Sequential organization is a description of the structure of interaction on a moment-by-moment basis and an explanation of this structure in terms of the unwritten rules and expectations of human interaction. As a substantial body of work in sociolinguistics, linguistic anthropology, ethnomethodology, and conversation analysis has demonstrated, human interactions are facilitated and constrained by a multitude of unwritten rules and expectations (Garfinkel, 1967; Goffman, 1967; Goodwin & Duranti, 1992; Goodwin & Heritage, 1990; Schegloff, 2007). These govern, for example, the proper sequencing of conversational turns (Sacks, Schegloff, & Jefferson, 1974), how understanding is monitored and repaired (Schegloff, 1992; Schegloff, Jefferson, & Sacks, 1977), how talk is designed with the recipient in mind (Schegloff, 1972), how relationships between participants are displayed and managed (Goffman, 1955; Goodwin, 1981), and how competence is performed with respect to the multiple communities in which participants are members (Goodwin, 1994; Hall, 1999).

The phrase "sequential organization" refers to the observation that human social interaction consists of a sequence of moves or acts or turns, and that these units have a recognizable organization to both participants and researchers. Thus, answers follow questions and, importantly, if something follows a question that is not an answer, it is recognizably "not an answer." That is, those involved recognize that the person who was expected to provide an answer has not done something random, but has specifically avoided or postponed providing an answer to the question (Schegloff, 1968, 1972, 2007). Through a close analysis of the ways that participants interact on a moment-by-moment basis, researchers can develop a model for how a particular type of interaction is organized into expected sequences.

The sequential organization of explanatory narratives, as described in Brown (2009), reveals that spoken explanations that appear to be monologues are in fact joint constructions between speakers and listeners. Participants rely on several interactive mechanisms to monitor for trouble in the unfolding narrative and provide opportunities for repair. This chapter focuses on one such mechanism: the design of moments by the speaker to elicit specific types of feedback, how such moments are taken up or ignored by the listener, and the consequences this has for how the speaker continues the narrative.

## Feedback-Relevant Places

In everyday conversation, an important aspect of sequential organization is the mechanism of turn-taking (Sacks et al., 1974). According to this model, conversation consists of a sequence of turn-constructional units, which can vary in length and serve a range of grammatical functions (i.e., sentential, clausal, phrasal, or lexical). At the end of each unit, a moment, called a transition-relevant place (TRP), occurs where speaker change is expected (but not required) to happen. Participants' understanding, perhaps unconsciously, of this expected mechanism allows them to interpret deviations meaningfully. For example, if the current speaker continues after a TRP, this may be interpreted as the speaker "not letting someone else speak," whereas if speaker change occurs before a TRP, this may be interpreted as the listener "interrupting the speaker."

One of the things that set explanatory narratives apart from ordinary conversation is the preference for who should speak after a turn-constructional unit. In ordinary conversation, another interlocutor is expected to take the floor (Sacks et al., 1974); this is why these moments are called transition-relevant places. In explanatory narratives, the speaker is expected to continue the story (Brown, 2009). Consequently, the role of the listener between steps in the explanatory narrative is restricted to providing or withholding feedback on the just-completed step. These moments, in which feedback is expected but not required, are called feedback-relevant places (Brown, 2009).

## Types of Feedback-Relevant Place

During an explanatory narrative, there are two forms of feedback about the unfolding explanation that a speaker may need: whether the listener comprehends and whether the listener agrees. The speaker requests such feedback at the end of each step in the explanation, designing these feedback-relevant places to project which form of feedback is expected. Although the design of an FRP is sometimes accomplished through explicit talk (e.g., "does that make sense?" or "is that right?"), in the majority of cases, the design is accomplished through the use of intonation, pacing, and gaze. The two types of FRP — agreement checks and comprehension checks — have different characteristic designs.

## Agreement Checks

Agreement checks project the speaker as needing feedback about whether the listener agrees with the current step in the explanation. This type of FRP is characterized by a gaze shift to the other interlocutor and a pause until feedback is received. If feedback is not received, this is interpreted as a potential disagreement. In some cases, the FRP includes a rise in intonation evocative of a question, but this is not universally true, and many agreement checks have no change in intonation or there is a drop in intonation evocative of a period. Like all FRPs, agreement checks are usually non-verbal; explicit verbal requests for confirmation are generally reserved for cases when expected feedback is not forthcoming.

Transcript 1 illustrates a series of FRPs designed as agreement checks. (Transcript conventions are summarized in Table 15.1 and explained in more detail in the Appendix.) In this excerpt, which took place during the teaching session, the speaker is the stranger and the listener is the student. The stranger is asking the student whether they are correct in thinking about the alcohol molecules as having different energies, with molecules needing a certain amount of energy to be in the gas phase.

In this excerpt, at each FRP, the speaker shifts their gaze to the listener as they approach the end of the current step (Lines 3, 4, 9, and 14), and ends the step with lower intonation and a pause (Lines 3, 5, 10, and 14). The speaker then waits for the listener to provide feedback before moving on. At the first three FRPs, the listener does, in fact, provide feedback through a combination of a gaze shift to the speaker, nodding, and the non-lexical sound "mm hm." At the fourth FRP, however, the listener does not nod or say "mm hm." This is apparently interpreted by the speaker as a lack of feedback, because rather than move on, they strengthen the design of the FRP by pairing an explicit verbal request for confirmation with

**TABLE 15.1** Transcription conventions

| Convention | Meaning |
|---|---|
| ↓ | The speaker's utterance on this line coincides with the listener's actions on the line below |
| ↑ | The listener's actions on this line coincide with the speaker's utterance on the line above |
| ( ) | Boundary marker containing one or more pauses or pause-fillers before the next utterance continues |
| . | Up to one-half-second of silence |
| : | Up to one-half-second of lengthening of the previous word |
| = | No pause or pause-filler before the next utterance continues |
| tex- | Word is cut off before its natural end |
| /text/ | Pitch is higher than surrounding speech |
| \text\ | Pitch is lower than surrounding speech |
| text | Speech is softer than surrounding speech |
| text> | Speech is faster than surrounding speech |
| <text | Speech is slower than surrounding speech |
| [text] | Content is conveyed by a gesture or inscription |
| ^ | Nodding |
| ^text | Nodding while speaking |
| ▼ | Gaze shifts down to the shared representational space |
| ▶ | Speaker gaze shifts to the listener |
| ◀ | Listener gaze shifts to the speaker |
| ▲ | Gaze shifts away from both the shared representational space and the other interlocutor |

a rise in intonation (Line 15). Note that this question is asked softly and quickly, using a register associated with information that has already been established or is assumed to be unproblematic. In this case, the speaker is projecting that they have already asked for feedback but have failed to receive it. The listener ratifies this interpretation by vigorously nodding and saying "mm hm."

Transcript 1
```
1    Speaker    ↓    ▲so (.)
     Listener   ↑    ◀
2    Speaker         is it /right/ so ▼if I> /think/ of it as (: .)
3               ↓    there's going to be this /range/ of ▶e\nergies
                     in [the molecules]\ (.)
     Listener   ↑                                  ▼        ◀ ^ ^ ^
                     ^mm ^hm (^.)
4    Speaker    ↓    ▼and they either have /enough/ energy to be
                     in gas (▶.)
     Listener   ↑         ▼
5    Speaker         or \not\ (.)
6    Listener        ^mm ^/hm/ (^◀.)
```

```
7   Speaker    ↓    ▼and the ones (:)
    Listener   ↑         ▼
8   Speaker         that (.)
9              ↓    /aren't/ (.▶. .)
    Listener   ↑         ◀
10  Speaker    ↓    plomp down here in li\quid\ (.)
    Listener   ↑    ^ ^ ^ ^ ^ ^ ^ ^
11  Listener   ↓    ^mm ^hm (^▼.^◀.)
    Speaker    ↑         ▲
12                  \okay\ (. .)
13             ↓    ▼which would suggest that how many are in /
                    gas/ depends on (.)
    Listener   ↑              ◀              ▼
14  Speaker         ▶tem\perature\ (. .)
15             ↓    /is that right/> (.)
    Listener   ↑    ^ ^ ^ ^ ^ ^ ^ ^ ^ ^
16             ↓    ^mm ^/hm/ (^.^. .)
    Speaker    ↑         ▼
17                  okay (.)
18             ↓    I guess that makes sense (. . . . .)
    Listener   ↑              ^ ^ ^ ^ ^ ^ ^ ^ ^ ^
```

## Comprehension Checks

Comprehension checks project the speaker as needing feedback about whether the listener is following along and comprehends the current step in the explanation. This type of FRP is characterized by a rise in intonation and a short pause, without a shift in gaze to the listener. The listener's response to a comprehension check is expected to be more minimal than their response to an agreement check, and may even be withheld on occasion without indicating a problem of comprehension. Like all FRPs, comprehension checks are usually non-verbal; explicit verbal requests for confirmation are generally reserved for cases when expected feedback is not forthcoming.

Transcript 2 illustrates a series of FRPs designed as comprehension checks. In this excerpt, which took place during the teaching session, the speaker is the student and the listener is the stranger. The student is explaining to the stranger that they think ethanol molecules have less velocity than methanol molecules at the same temperature, because temperature is related to kinetic energy and ethanol molecules have greater mass.

In this excerpt, at each FRP, the speaker ends with a rise in intonation and a short pause, but does not shift their gaze to the listener (Lines 3, 6, and 8). After the first FRP, the listener gives a minimal piece of positive feedback ("mm hm" with no nodding), but then withholds all feedback for the next FRPs. The speaker initially presses on, not yet interpreting the absence of feedback as negative. Unlike agreement checks, comprehension checks do not require feedback after each FRP. However, when feedback continues to be withheld, the speaker strengthens the design of the FRP, shifting their gaze to the listener (Line 9) and adding an explicit request for confirmation (Line 10). Note that, as in Transcript 1, this question is asked softly and quickly, projecting that the speaker has already asked for feedback but has failed to receive it. In this case, however, the listener continues to withhold feedback. The speaker interprets this as a potential failure of comprehension, prompting them to try a new tack (Line 11). But the listener then indicates that the explanation should be continued, vigorously nodding (Line 12), giving verbal encouragement (Line 13), and demonstrating that they can complete the speaker's sentence (Line 15). The listener does not necessarily concede that the explanation is correct ("that makes some sense yes"), but they confirm that it is being comprehended and can continue.

```
Transcript 2
1    Speaker     ↓     ▼so kinetic energy is [KE = ½ m v²] (. .)
     Listener    ↑     ▼
2    Speaker           is a function of mass (.)
3                      and velo/city/ (.)
4    Listener          mm /hm/ (.)
5    Speaker           so (.)
6                      be/cause/ kinetic energy is going to /stay/
                          the /same/ (.)
7                      yet (.)
8                      /mass/ is now a great deal /high/er (. .)
9                      ve/lo/city is going to be a great deal
                          /low/er (▶.)
10                     does /that make sense/> (. .)
11                     ▼I mean (.)
12                 ↓   to make this (. um)
     Listener    ↑     ^ ^ ^ ^ ^ ^ ^ ^ ^ ^
13                     ^that ^makes ^some ^sense ^yes> =
14   Speaker           to make this the same> =
15   Listener          at the same kinetic energy> =
16   Speaker           ^right (. .)
```

## Complex Designs

The previous excerpts should not be taken to imply that a single type of FRP is used throughout an explanatory narrative. Speakers use agreement checks and comprehension checks as needed, switching between them depending on the type of feedback needed on a moment-by-moment basis. Moreover, because the nature of an upcoming FRP is projected in advance (i.e., by gaze shifts and the intonation contour of the utterance), different types of FRP may even overlap.

Transcript 3 illustrates an explanatory narrative that contains both agreement checks and comprehension checks, including several that overlap. In this excerpt, which took place during the tutoring session, the speaker is the interviewer and the listener is the student. The interviewer is explaining to the student how a dynamic equilibrium is reached between the rate of evaporation (alcohol molecules escaping from the surface of the liquid) and condensation (alcohol molecules in the gas phase striking the surface and being captured by the liquid). The rate of condensation (capture) starts low, but increases as the amount of alcohol in the gas phase increases. Eventually, the rate of condensation catches up with the rate of evaporation (escape) and the alcohol appears to stop evaporating.

In this excerpt, the FRPs on Lines 6 and 8 are designed as agreement checks. The speaker shifts their gaze to the listener (Lines 3 and 8), doesn't raise their intonation at the end of the step, and pauses until the listener gives verbal confirmation of agreement, either by saying "yeah" (Line 7) or by completing the speaker's sentence (Line 9). However, after the speaker has already begun projecting the first upcoming agreement check (by the gaze shift in Line 3), the speaker initiates and completes two comprehension checks (Lines 4 and 5) before the agreement check is completed (Line 6). Both comprehension checks involve a rise in intonation and a pause, and both are acknowledged and responded to by the listener with nodding.

Transcript 3

```
1    Speaker    ↓    ▼and (: .)
     Listener   ↑    ▼
2    Speaker         as (: .)
3                    as /long/ as the rate of escape is /great/er
                       than the rate ▶of /cap/ture (.)
4               ↓    there's going to be this /net/ (. .)
     Listener   ↑                              ^ ^
5    Speaker    ↓    /flow/ (.)
     Listener   ↑    ^ ^ ^ ^ ^
6    Speaker    ↓    of molecules out (.)
     Listener   ↑    ◀ ^ ^ ^ ^ ^ ^ ^ ^ ^
7               ↓    ▼^yeah (. .)
     Speaker    ↑              ▼
8               ↓    but /once/ the rate of /cap/ture ▶gets /
                       fast/ enough (. .)
     Listener   ↑              ▼          ◀
9                    they'll be equal =
10   Speaker         they'll be equal =
11   Listener        you won't be able to tell (.)
```

## *Feedback Requests and Speaker Confidence*

Both Transcript 1 and Transcript 3 contained agreement checks, yet the two speakers had very different levels of confidence in their explanations. The first speaker was using agreement checks to ask a more knowledgeable other whether their explanation was correct. There are indications at the beginning of their explanation ("So is it right? So if I think of it as…") and at the end ("Okay, I guess that makes sense.") that they were not confident in their understanding. In contrast, the second speaker was using agreement checks to confirm that a less knowledgeable other was learning a normative explanation. The speaker in this case was a tutor teaching the listener. This illustrates an important distinction: in general, speaker confidence in their explanation is orthogonal to the type of feedback being requested. Designing an FRP as an agreement check does not, by itself, indicate confidence or a lack thereof.

This can also be seen for comprehension checks. In Transcript 2, there are indications that the speaker was reasonably confident in their explanation. The pace of speech is steady and there are few pauses within phrases. In contrast, consider the speaker in Transcript 4. In this excerpt, which took place during the semi-structured interview, the speaker is the student and the listener is the interviewer. The student is trying to explain to the interviewer why the alcohol molecules in the gas phase would return to the liquid phase when the container shrinks. In this excerpt, there are indications that the speaker is relatively uncertain. They hedge the steps in their explanation ("I'm guessing," "I suppose," "I don't know") and take many pauses within each phrase. Despite this uncertainty, the speaker designs FRPs to check for comprehension rather than agreement. Intonation rises at the end of each step (Lines 6, 9, 10, 11, and 13) while gaze remains down at the shared representational space through most of the FRP. The one exception is on Line 11, when the speaker strengthens the design of the FRP by shifting their gaze to the listener. This happens after the listener has stopped providing feedback in the form of nodding. Once the listener resumes their minimal feedback (Line 12), the speaker returns their gaze downward.

```
Transcript 4
1     Speaker     ↓     ▼and (: .)
      Listener    ↑     ▼
2                       then (:)
3                       they (. .)
4                       like (.)
5                       I'm guessing that they ran into more (. .)
6                       molecules or they lost /energy/ through too
                          many col/lisions/ (:)
7                 ↓     and then (. . .)
      Listener    ↑     ^ ^ ^ ^ ^ ◄
8     Speaker           they (.)
9                       like s- m- /less/ molecules /had/ (.)
10                      the available ener/gy/ (. .)
11                      to ►re/main in the gas phase/ (:)
12                ↓     ▼so they became (.)
      Listener    ↑     ^ ^ ^ ^ ^ ^ ^ ^ ^
13    Speaker     ↓     went back to the li/quid phase I suppose/
```

```
                         ( . . . . .)
         Listener    ↑   ^ ^ ^ ^ ^ ^ ^  ^ ^ ^ ^ ^ ^ ^ ^ ^ ^ ^ ^ ^ ^ ^
                         ^ ^ ^ ^
14       Speaker     ↓   I don't \know\> =
         Listener    ↑   ^ ^ ^ ^ ^ ^ ^ ^ ^
```

The four previous excerpts illustrate that the type of feedback requested by a speaker is not constrained by the speaker's confidence in their explanatory narrative. However, the particular combination of FRP and confidence level does depend on the framing of the interaction. In particular, the combination of comprehension checks and a relative lack of confidence was especially prevalent during the semi-structured interviews and relatively rare in the other types of interview. This reflects the unique character of the semi-structured interview in which the listener (interviewer) is expected to resist agreeing or disagreeing with the speaker (student) even when the speaker constructs an uncertain explanatory narrative.

## Using Feedback-Relevant Places in Knowledge Analysis

The previous discussion has described a mechanism that allows a speaker to monitor the extent to which a listener comprehends and agrees with the speaker's unfolding explanatory narrative. This mechanism, involving the design of feedback-relevant places and how they are taken up or ignored by the participants, is an example of the unwritten rules and expectations that characterize systems of human social interaction. The following discussion explains how an understanding of this mechanism can help researchers better characterize the knowledge systems of students.

While knowledge analysts collect and analyze video data, the transcripts they produce to report and support their analyses predominantly record the content of speech and gesture but not the additional semiotic fields that participants use to communicate information about systems of interaction. With respect to FRPs, these include paralinguistics – particularly intonation, volume, and pace – and kinesics – particularly nodding and gaze.

To show the effect of excluding this information, the same excerpt is presented twice in Transcripts 5 and 6, first without and then with the interactional detail required to identify and characterize FRPs. In this excerpt, which occurred during the peer discussion, the speaker is the student and the listener is their friend. The student is explaining to their friend why ethanol, which has larger molecules, evaporates less than methanol in the same-sized container.

Transcript 5
Speaker:    Because [the ethanol molecules] are bigger, they take up more room. So there's… With the, with the same space, there can be less

gas molecules in the air. And so there's more of them in the liquid state, because they take up less space that way. Yes.

Listener: Mm hm.

Transcript 5 supports several inferences about the student's knowledge system. For example, the idea that bigger things take up more room, implying that fewer of them will fit into a container, appears to have high cuing priority in this context. It appears to be the first (and so far only) knowledge element expressed. There is evidence, however, that the reliability priority of this knowledge element may be somewhat low. There is a long pause during the narrative ("So there's…"), some stumbling over words ("with the, with the"), several additional phrases that sound like the speaker is working through the implications of their initial idea as a double-check, and a concluding word ("yes") that gives the impression that they eventually succeeded in convincing themselves. The overall impression an analyst might get from this transcript is that the student is quick to initiate this explanation, perhaps because the size of the molecules is particularly salient, but that they then seem somewhat unsure that what they are saying makes sense. Other analysts may disagree with this interpretation of the evidence and draw different impressions of the speaker's knowledge system. However, it is precisely this ambiguity that describing and interpreting FRPs is designed to address. Understanding how the FRP mechanism is playing out in this excerpt is meant to clarify how knowledge and interaction are contributing to the speaker's explanatory narrative, ultimately providing stronger evidence to support an interpretation of the student's knowledge system.

Transcript 6

```
1    Speaker    ↓    ▼<be/cause [the ethanol molecules] are
                          big/ger (: .)
     Listener   ↑    ▼              ◀
2    Speaker    ↓    <they take up /more/ room (: .)
     Listener   ↑                              ▼
3    Speaker         so (:)
4    ↓               there's (. . . . . . . .)
     Listener   ↑                    ◀  ▼
5    Speaker         with the with the> /same/ space (: .)
6                    there can be (.)
7                    /less/ (: . .)
8                    gas mole/cules/ (.)
9                    in the \air\ (.)
10                   and so (.)
11                   there's more /of them/ in the li/quid state/
                          because they take up \less space\> (:)
12                   that way> (. . .)
13                   ▶yes (^.^.^. . .)
14   Listener   ↓    \mm hm\ (.◀.▼. . . . .)
     Speaker    ↑                ^ ^ ^ ^ ^ ^
```

Transcript 6 contains the same text as Transcript 5, but it also includes the necessary interactional detail to identify and characterize FRPs. The first FRP doesn't appear until Line 7, when the rise in intonation, the pause, and the downturned gaze indicate a confirmation check. Before Line 7, the intonation contours of the utterances are rising and falling, consistent with an expected continuation on the part of the speaker, and there is no shift in gaze to the listener. The speaker is not designing places for the listener to provide feedback, even though the listener indicates they are engaged by shifting their gaze twice to the speaker before returning it downward. This suggests that the speaker is engaged primarily with their own knowledge system.

They also appear to be having difficulty during this time. The four-second pause is an indication of this, but the speech before the pause is also slowed down and drawn out. The large size of the ethanol molecules does appear to have high cuing priority for this student, but the important implication of this seems to be missing. They can't make a connection between the molecules taking up more room and the molecules evaporating less. Then, at Line 5, there is evidence that an "aha" moment has occurred: the rapid pace – so fast as to lead to stumbling over the beginning of the utterance – leading to the emphasis on "**same** space" suggests that focusing on the containers rather than the molecules, and imagining different-sized molecules fitting inside, has provided the necessary breakthrough.

Starting at Line 5, the speaker appears to be confident in this explanation. Confirmation checks appear on Lines 7, 8, and 11, but even though the listener withholds feedback, the speaker pushes on. Halfway through Line 11, the speech becomes softer and quicker, positioning this information as already established or otherwise unproblematic. The end of the explanation, on Line 12, is not initially designed for feedback. After a 1.5 second pause, the speaker eventually designs an agreement check by shifting their gaze to the listener, saying "yes," and starting to nod. Initially, the listener withholds feedback, eventually saying "mm hm" after 2.5 seconds. Despite evidence that the listener is reluctant to fully agree with the speaker (e.g., further silence, no nodding, gaze briefly meeting the speaker's before returning downward), the speaker presses on with the agreement check, aggressively nodding for four more seconds.

The overall impression an analyst might get from this transcript is that the speaker has initial trouble making a connection between two knowledge elements, but that once the connection is made, the speaker is very confident in their explanatory narrative. In terms of the student's knowledge system, the idea that ethanol molecules are bigger has both high cuing and reliability priority in this context. In contrast, the idea that fewer big things can fit into a container has low cuing priority in this context but, when it eventually is activated, has high reliability priority. Indeed, the reliability priority is so high that the speaker initially can't articulate it fast enough, isn't deterred by the lack of feedback on the part of the listener, and aggressively positions the listener as needing to agree with them.

Transcripts 5 and 6 give different impressions of the speaker. They also support different interpretations of the student's knowledge system. Whereas Transcript 5 suggested a single knowledge element with moderate reliability priority, Transcript 6 provided evidence of two distinct knowledge elements, both with high reliability priority, but the second with low cuing priority in this context.

## Discussion

The important difference in the interpretations supported by Transcripts 5 and 6 is not in the content of the student's knowledge system. This is not surprising, given that both transcripts record the content of speech and gesture. Instead, the additional interactional detail and an understanding of the FRP mechanism support a more precise analysis: Transcript 6 provides additional evidence of when knowledge elements are activated and their relative cuing and reliability priority. Describing these aspects of a student's knowledge system is not a trivial concern, but is instead a valued practice of Knowledge Analysis.

To speak to the larger agenda of this volume, Interaction Analysis in this case is not merely supplying a different account of cognitive activity, nor is it supplementing Knowledge Analysis by explaining additional but different features of cognitive activity. Instead, Interaction Analysis, by characterizing the unwritten rules and expectations of human social interaction, is allowing the analyst to clarify how moments of cognitive activity are responsive to and dependent upon both knowledge and interaction. In this case, understanding the FRP mechanism allows the analyst to characterize when and how speakers are requesting and responding to subtle feedback, which in turn allows the analyst to more precisely characterize the cuing and reliability priority of the speaker's knowledge elements. To state matters more bluntly, Interaction Analysis is allowing the analyst to conduct a better Knowledge Analysis.

A knowledge analyst playing devil's advocate might attest that an experienced analyst working directly from the video could arrive at the same conclusions regarding the nature of a student's knowledge system, regardless of whether or not they conducted an Interaction Analysis. For example, they might attest that careful observation of the original video recording would have led to the same conclusions supported by the analysis of Transcript 6, without the need to attend to the FRP mechanism. This was not the case for the author, for whom the analysis of Transcript 6 provided a more thorough and more precise interpretation than did repeated viewings of the video recording, but a more experienced analyst might have fared better. In any event, this argument is impossible to refute in the abstract.

However, interpretation is only half the job of an analyst. The other half is supporting that interpretation with convincing, objective evidence, and it is here where even the most experienced knowledge analyst would benefit from the

Interaction Analysis toolkit. Impressions, however accurate they may be, are difficult to articulate and difficult to challenge. Interaction Analysis, in contrast, allows an analyst to document how patterns of interaction are affecting cognitive activity, using specific evidence that can be reported and independently checked by others.

In analyzing Transcript 6, the author relied on the FRP mechanism to more precisely interpret the speaker's knowledge system. He then relied on it again to justify his interpretation by citing specific, detailed paralinguistic and kinesic evidence. In presenting this evidence, the reader is empowered to reach their own conclusion, perhaps challenging the author's interpretation in the process. None of this would have been possible without Interaction Analysis. In short, being an interaction analyst has made the author a better knowledge analyst.

## Appendix: Transcript Conventions

Transcript conventions are a mixture of some standard conversation-analytic conventions and some new elements. When a symbol used in the Jeffersonian transcription system (Jefferson, 1978) appears in a transcript, it retains its meaning from that prior convention. The meaning of all conventions are described in detail below and summarized in Table 15.1.

### Utterances and Boundary Markers

Each explanatory narrative is broken down into utterances, segments of speech demarcated by pauses. Each utterance appears on a separate line. When the listener is doing something while the speaker is talking (e.g., nodding, shifting their gaze), these actions appear on a separate line below the speaker's utterance. In these instances of co-occurrence, the speaker's utterance is preceded by a downward-pointing arrow and the listener's actions are preceded by an upward-pointing arrow.

At the end of each utterance, a *boundary marker* appears: a set of parentheses containing one or more symbols. Within a boundary marker, silence is represented by one or more periods, with each period representing silence of up to one-half-second. Place-holding sounds like "um" are also contained within the boundary marker. A word that is drawn out (e.g., "sooooo") covers what would otherwise be a pause; the lengthening of such words is represented by one or more colons, with each colon representing extension of up to one-half-second. All of these symbols may be combined within a single boundary marker. In the following example, the word "so" is extended by an additional second, there is a pause of one half-second or less, the sound "um" is uttered, and this is followed by a further pause of 1.5 seconds. Altogether, this boundary marker indicates a break between utterances of approximately 3.5 seconds.

```
so (: : . um . . .)
```

On some occasions, there is evidence that two utterances have been run together without an intervening pause. The full justification for deciding whether a contiguous segment of speech is one utterance or two is given in Brown (2009), but these breaks generally coincide with a linking word (e.g., a conjunction) and a change in intonation contour (e.g., a return to a baseline pitch). Speaker changes also indicate breaks between utterances. When two utterances are run together without a pause, the boundary marker is replaced by an equals sign.

## *Semantics*

Both lexical (e.g., "molecule," "the") and non-lexical ("mm hm," "um") speech is transcribed. Although it is common practice in conversation analysis to attempt to capture aspects of pronunciation in the transcript ("cuz," "gonna"), Bucholtz (2000) has noted that particular pronunciations that pass without notice in everyday speech become marked as deficient when represented in written form. For example, while the natural pronunciation of the word "the" may be either "thuh" or "thee," either inscription stands out misleadingly in text and therefore could be construed as deficient. Because unusual pronunciations or differences in dialect do not appear to be relevant in this data, no attempt has been made to represent the phonetic aspect of speech. Instead, all speech is represented using written forms that evoke competently produced mainstream American talk.

## *Paralinguistics*

Paralinguistic information, including pitch, intonation, speed, and laughter, is represented in the following ways. Marked changes in pitch from baseline are indicated with slashes: forward slashes surround speech of higher pitch while backward slashes surround speech of lower pitch. High pitch at the beginning or middle of an utterance often indicates emphasis. High pitch at the end of an utterance often indicates uncertainty and is sometimes represented by a question mark in other transcription systems. Low pitch just before the end of an utterance often indicates an expected continuation, and is usually represented by a comma in other systems. Low pitch at the very end of an utterance often indicates the completion of an idea, and is usually represented by a period in other systems.

Speech that is consistently softer than surrounding speech is italicized. Speech that is produced at a consistently different rate than surrounding speech is underlined; slower speech is preceded by a left triangle bracket to suggest a backward-pointing arrow, while faster speech is followed by a right triangle bracket to suggest a forward-pointing arrow.

## Representation

Representational information, including gestures and inscriptions, is indicated in the following ways. Gestures used for emphasis or other non-semantic purposes are not transcribed, nor are indexical gestures that provide redundant information to the content of the speech. When an indexical gesture is used in combination with a pronoun for which the referent would be otherwise difficult to discern, the pronoun is replaced by the referent indicated by the gesture. This has the effect of looking like the speaker is saying the content represented by the gesture; this "gesture-speak" is contained within square brackets. To minimize putting words into people's mouths, the language in square brackets is borrowed from nearby speech when possible. Inscriptions on the whiteboard in front of the participants are also contained in square brackets, as if the speaker had spoken what they had written.

## Kinesics

Kinesic information, including nodding and gaze, is represented in the following ways. Nodding is represented by carets. When a speaker nods while talking, each word is preceded by a caret. Gaze is indicated by triangles. When a participant looks down at the shared representational space on the table surface, this is represented by a downward-pointing triangle. When a speaker shifts their gaze to the listener, this is represented by a right-facing triangle. When a listener shifts their gaze to the speaker, this is represented by a left-facing triangle. When a participant shifts their gaze away from either the table surface or the other interlocutor, as might be interpreted as looking out into space, this is represented by an upward-pointing triangle. At the beginning of a transcript, triangles indicate where gaze is currently focused. In the middle of a transcript, triangles are placed as close to gaze shifts as possible, without breaking apart a word.

## References

Antaki, C., & Rapley, M. (1996). "Quality of life" talk: The liberal paradox of psychological testing. *Discourse & Society*, 7, 293–316.

Brown, N. J. S. (2009). *Information performances and illative sequences: Sequential organization of explanations of chemical phase equilibrium* (Doctoral dissertation). Retrieved from https://escholarship.org/uc/item/9zw1p1ps.

Bucholtz, M. (2000). The politics of transcription. *Journal of Pragmatics*, 32, 1439–1465.

Button, G. (1987). Answers as interactional products: Two sequential practices used in interviews. *Social Psychology Quarterly*, 50, 160–171.

diSessa, A. A. (1993). Toward an epistemology of physics. *Cognition and Instruction*, 10, 105–225.

diSessa, A. A. (2007). An interactional analysis of clinical interviewing. *Cognition and Instruction*, 25, 523–565.

Engle, R. A., Conant, F. R., & Greeno, J. G. (2007). Progressive refinement of hypotheses in video-supported research. In R. Goldman, R. Pea, B. Barron, & S. J. Derry (Eds.), *Video research in the learning sciences* (pp. 239–254). Mahwah, NJ: Lawrence Erlbaum.

Erickson, F. (2006). Definition and analysis of data from videotape: Some research procedures and their rationales. In J. L. Green, G. Camilli, & P. B. Elmore (Eds.), *Handbook of complementary methods in education research* (pp. 177–191). Mahwah, NJ: Lawrence Erlbaum.

Garfinkel, H. (1967). *Studies in ethnomethodology.* Englewood Cliffs, NJ: Prentice Hall.

Ginsburg, H. (1997). *Entering the child's mind: The clinical interview in psychological research and practice.* Cambridge, UK: Cambridge University Press.

Goffman, E. (1955). On face-work: An analysis of ritual elements in social interaction. *Psychiatry,* 18, 213–231.

Goffman, E. (1967). *Interaction ritual: Essays in face to face behavior.* Garden City, NY: Doubleday.

Goldman, S., & McDermott, R. (2007). Staying the course with video analysis. In R. Goldman, R. Pea, B. Barron, & S. J. Derry (Eds.), *Video research in the learning sciences* (pp. 101–113). Mahwah, NJ: Lawrence Erlbaum.

Goodwin, C. (1981). *Conversational organization: Interaction between speakers and hearers.* New York: Academic Press.

Goodwin, C. (1987). Forgetfulness as an interactive resource. *Social Psychology Quarterly,* 50, 115–130.

Goodwin, C. (1994). Professional vision. *American Anthropologist,* 96, 606–633.

Goodwin, C. (2000). Action and embodiment within situated human interaction. *Journal of Pragmatics,* 32, 1489–1522.

Goodwin, C., & Duranti, A. (1992). Rethinking context: An introduction. In A. Duranti & C. Goodwin (Eds.), *Rethinking context: Language as an interactive phenomenon* (pp. 1–42). Cambridge, UK: Cambridge University Press.

Goodwin, C., & Heritage, J. (1990). Conversation analysis. *Annual Reviews of Anthropology,* 19, 283–307.

Hall, R. (1999). The organization and development of discursive practices for "having a theory." *Discourse Processes,* 27, 187–218.

Hall, R. (2000). Videorecording as theory. In A. E. Kelly & R. Lesh (Eds.), *Handbook of research design in mathematics and science* (pp. 647–664). Mahwah, NJ: Lawrence Erlbaum.

Hutchins, E. (1995). *Cognition in the wild.* Cambridge, MA: MIT Press.

Ioannides, C., & Vosniadou, S. (2002). The changing meanings of force. *Cognitive Science Quarterly,* 2, 5–61.

Jefferson, G. (1978). Sequential aspects of storytelling in conversation. In J. Schenkein (Ed.), *Studies in the organization of conversational interaction* (pp. 219–248). New York: Academic Press.

Jordan, B., & Henderson, A. (1995). Interaction Analysis: Foundations and practice. *The Journal of the Learning Sciences,* 4, 39–103.

Latour, B., & Woolgar, S. (1979). *Laboratory life: The social construction of scientific facts.* London: Sage.

Macbeth, D. (2000). On an actual apparatus for conceptual change. *Science Education,* 84, 228–264.

McDermott, R. P. (1993). The acquisition of a child by a learning disorder. In S. Chaiklin & J. Lave (Eds.), *Understanding practice: Perspectives on activity and context* (pp. 269–305). Cambridge, UK: Cambridge University Press.

McDermott, R. P., Goldman, S., & Varenne, H. (2006). The cultural work of learning disabilities. *Educational Researcher*, 35, 12–17.

Mulford, D. R., & Robinson, W. R. (2002). An inventory for alternate conceptions among first-semester general chemistry students. *Journal of Chemical Education*, 79, 739–744.

Piaget, J. (2007). *The child's conception of the world* (J. Tomlinson & A. Tomlinson, Trans.). Lanham, MD: Rowman & Littlefield.

Piaget, J., & Inhelder, B. (2000). *The psychology of the child* (H. Weaver, Trans.). New York: Basic Books.

Sacks, H., Schegloff, E. A., & Jefferson, G. (1974). A simplest systematics for the organization of turn-taking for conversation. *Language*, 50, 696–735.

Schegloff, E. A. (1968). Sequencing in conversational openings. *American Anthropologist*, 70, 1075–1095.

Schegloff, E. A. (1972). Notes on a conversational practice: Formulating place. In D. Sudnow (Ed.), *Studies in social interaction* (pp. 75–119). New York: Free Press.

Schegloff, E. A. (1992). On talk and its institutional occasions. In P. Drew & J. Heritage (Eds.), *Talk at work: Interaction in institutional settings* (pp. 101–134). Cambridge, UK: Cambridge University Press.

Schegloff, E. A. (2007). *Sequence organization in interaction: A primer in conversation analysis* (Vol. 1). Cambridge, UK: Cambridge University Press.

Schegloff, E. A., Jefferson, G., & Sacks, H. (1977). The preference for self-correction in the organization of repair in conversation. *Language*, 53, 361–382.

Southerland, S. A., Abrams, E., Cummins, C. L., & Anzelmo, J. (2001). Understanding students' explanations of biological phenomena: Conceptual frameworks or p-prims? *Science Education*, 85, 328–348.

Suchman, L., & Jordan, B. (1990). Interactional troubles in face-to-face survey interviews. *Journal of the American Statistical Association*, 85, 232–241.

# PART III
# Theoretical, Methodological, and Meta-scientific Issues

# 16

# COMPUTATIONAL ANALYSIS AND THE IMPORTANCE OF INTERACTIONAL DETAIL

*Bruce L. Sherin*

Although Interaction Analysis (IA) and Knowledge Analysis (KA) differ in important respects, they nonetheless face a common nexus of questions relating to theory and method. Researchers in both traditions must, for example, select instances of human behavior for study. In this regard, we can ask: Is it necessary to observe behavior only in naturally occurring contexts? Similarly, both sets of researchers must make decisions about what is attended to in the observations that are collected, and with what precision. Here, for example, we might ask: Under what conditions is it important that we give careful attention to minute detail in gesture?

The latter set of issues – what we attend to in our observations – is the focus of this chapter. Here, there are perhaps some important differences between IA and KA. The two traditions differ in the amount and kind of attention focused on what might be called *interactional detail*. Research in IA is often characterized by a very explicit and focused attention to such things as gesture and eye gaze (Goodwin, 2000). Practitioners of KA do not *ignore* interactional detail of this sort; however, their attention to interactional detail is usually not systematic or theoretically grounded.

The question to be addressed by this chapter is this: For researchers interested in thinking and learning, what types of research questions can be addressed, and what types of analysis are possible, without systematic attention to various types of interactional detail?

It is manifestly the case that some research questions require systematic attention to interactional detail. If our research questions are explicitly about aspects of interactional detail, then clearly we must attend to that detail; if we want to answer questions about gesture and learning, then attention to gesture is required.

More fundamentally, many of the core questions that are explored by researchers in IA necessitate a focus on interactional detail. For example, if we care about how specific artifacts "set up a social field within which certain activities become very likely," (Jordan & Henderson, 1995, p. 75), then careful attention to interactions with the environment will be required.

But what about questions at the heart of the KA enterprise? Suppose that we accept the basic premises of KA and that our goal is to identify the knowledge that is drawn upon as an individual engages in some task. How much, and what type, of attention to interactional detail is required?

To begin to answer these questions, this chapter draws on a corpus of 54 one-on-one interviews in which middle-school students were asked to explain the seasons. The original goal of these interviews, and the analysis we performed, was to identify the knowledge resources possessed by the students we interviewed (Sherin, Krakowski, & Lee, 2012). However, we did not treat the interviews as an unproblematic means of "reading out" the students' knowledge. Instead, we viewed the interviews as interactions. Furthermore, we saw quite clearly that the explanations constructed by students, and the knowledge drawn on, changed as an interview unfolded.

The question to be investigated here is how much of this analysis can be replicated with an extreme version of a logocentric analysis (Goodwin, 2007), one in which we attend only to talk. In this chapter, I address this question in a very specific manner. Recently, techniques have been developed by computational linguists that have found increasing usage across the social sciences. Some techniques, such as Latent Semantic Analysis, have been employed across a wide range of applications (Landauer, Foltz, & Laham, 1998). One feature that is shared across many of these methods is their use of what has been called a *bag-of-words* model. Computational text analyses that employ a bag-of-words model have the striking feature of ignoring all information about word order; they look only at what words appear, not the order in which they appear.

I have had some success in applying these bag-of-words computational techniques in my own research (Sherin, 2013). Like much KA research (diSessa, 1993; Parnafes & diSessa, 2013; Sherin, 2001), my own work is concerned with the study of intuitive science knowledge. For data, I make use of clinical interviews with participants in a variety of areas, and my analyses are attentive to unfolding processes in these interviews. My application of computational techniques to these data has seen some substantial success; the computational techniques capture what I take to be deep characteristics of the knowledge of interviewees, and capture the dynamic processes of the unfolding interview.

Looking closely at the successes of these methods – and examining their limits – has the potential to answer the questions raised by this chapter. The relative success of these methods can help us gain an understanding of what an attention to interactional detail contributes to an analysis of this type of interview. Because so much information is brutally stripped away, and because the analysis is done in such a mechanical manner, we can draw conclusions about the contribution of different types of information to the analysis.

Despite my earlier successes, there are many reasons to think that an analysis of this sort is unlikely to be successful. Intuitively, attention to the order in which words are spoken seems to be essential to understanding what a speaker intends to convey. Furthermore, interaction analysts have argued convincingly that the content of an utterance is conveyed by much more than the words spoken. Goodwin (2007), for example, argues that utterances in general are multi-party and multimodal. According to Goodwin, even an apparently passive listener can be seen to contribute, in important ways, to the construction of an utterance. Given these observations, one might be led to assume that attending to only one speaker, and to only their words, might provide too limited a window for a meaningful Knowledge Analysis.

However, even if we accept (as I do) the observations of IA researchers such as Goodwin, there are reasons that my extreme logocentric analysis might nonetheless be successful:

*Separability and redundancy.* Even if utterances are multi-party and multimodal, the communicated information might be distributed over parties and modes in a manner that allows logocentric analyses to produce certain types of useful insights. First, it might be the case that information is divided up among channels of communication in a manner that allows for a sensible analysis focused on just one information channel. This I refer to as *separability*. For example, conceptual content might be conveyed primarily in the spoken words, and confidence might be conveyed by prosody. If that is the case, it might be possible to perform a meaningful Knowledge Analysis focusing on just the words. Second, if utterances are multi-party and multimodal, there may be a great deal of redundancy across information channels. This *redundancy* might be essential for reliable human communication. But a computer-based logocentric analysis might be able to make do without it.

*Unique features of the particular interaction under study.* Even if separability and redundancy do not hold in general for human interaction, they might hold in certain specific types of circumstances. For example, when people converse over a telephone, more of the burden of communication is necessarily carried by the words. The clinical interviews under study here are highly constrained, very particular types of interactions, and they might thus have unique properties that support certain types of logocentric analysis.

*A different task.* The task faced by my computational analysis is in many ways different than that faced by participants in an ongoing communication. For example, participants in a conversation sometimes need to *anticipate* what will be required of them in the interaction. Some of the additional information conveyed by such things as body position might help them perform this function. In contrast, an after-the-fact computer analysis doesn't need to anticipate what will be required so that it can participate in a conversation; it can look retrospectively at complete interactions. Furthermore, the interviews are highly engineered interactions, partly designed to facilitate after-the-fact interpretation. So the task of interpreting them is different than the general task of understanding utterances.

*Sleight of hand.* Finally, the logocentric analysis might succeed only because it is not truly logocentric. As we will see, there are several ways in which other types of information might leak into the analysis.

The remainder of this chapter will be structured as follows. I will begin with a summary of the data to be employed here. Next, I will explain how the computational analysis works. Then I will present the results of the automated analysis, and I will examine what the computational analysis captures and what it fails to capture. Finally, I will return to the questions posed at the start of the chapter and I will draw conclusions about what we learn by paying attention to interactional detail.

## Background and Prior Work

### The Data Corpus

As stated above, the analyses presented in this chapter are based on a corpus of 54 one-on-one interviews in which middle-school students were asked to explain the seasons. Our interviews about the seasons always began with the interviewer asking "Why is it warmer in the summer and colder in the winter?" After this initial question, the interviewer asked the student to draw a picture to illustrate their explanation. The interviewer was also prepared with challenge questions as responses to certain explanations. In addition, the interviewer was free to ask follow-up questions throughout the interview, in order to better understand the student's explanation.

The explanations given by students were quite varied. However, we have found it helpful to have in mind three prototype explanations. We call the first of these prototypes *closer-farther* explanations. In closer-farther explanations, the earth moves so that the entire earth is at some times closer and at other times farther from the sun. When the earth is closer to the sun, all locations on the earth experience summer. In contrast, in *side-based* explanations, the seasons are caused by motion (usually the rotation) of the earth, which causes one side of the earth or the other to face the sun. At a given point in time, the side facing the sun experiences summer, and the side facing away experiences winter. Finally, *tilt-based* explanations depend on the observation that the earth's axis is tilted relative to its plane of orbit. The part of the earth tilted toward the sun experiences summer, and the part tilted away experiences winter. The correct explanation of the seasons is a type of tilt-based explanation. In the correct explanation, the part of the earth tilted toward the sun experiences summer because it receives more direct sunlight.

## Example Interviews

For concreteness, I briefly describe three interviews from the larger corpus. These same interviews will be used later to illustrate the automated analysis. The first interview is with a student named Angela, who started by giving a typical closer-farther explanation. In this explanation, the earth orbits so that it is sometimes closer and sometimes farther from the sun. ("I" is the interviewer and "A" is Angela.)

> **I:** I want to know why it's warmer in the summer and colder in the winter.
> **A:** That's because like the sun is in the center and the earth moves around the sun and the earth is at one point, like in the winter, it's on- it's like farther away from the sun and towards the summer it's closer, it's near, towards the sun.

When prompted, Angela illustrated her explanation with a drawing, which was consistent with this explanation. After Angela finished and explained her drawing, the interviewer introduced one of our standard challenges. In cases in which a student offered a closer-farther explanation, our interviewers would ask if the student had heard that different locations on the earth can be experiencing different seasons at the same time. Based on Angela's response to this challenge, and her demeanor, it was clear that she recognized the problem posed by this challenge, and that she realized that it posed a serious difficulty for her explanation. She asked for a new sheet of paper to begin a new drawing.

> **I:** One thing I wanted to ask you though about though was, um, one thing that you might have heard is that at the same time – tell me, you can tell me if you've heard this – when it's summer here, it's actually winter in Australia.
> **A:** Mm hmm <laughs nervously>
> **I:** Have you heard that before?
> **A:** Yeah.
> **I:** So I was wondering if your picture the way you drew it can explain that or if that's a problem for your picture.
> **A:** Uh::::. I need another picture.

At this point Angela tried to draw a new diagram, and construct a new explanation. But from this point on she floundered. She first tried briefly to construct a new explanation incorporating the fact that the earth rotates. She quickly abandoned this effort, however. In the end, she commented, rather sheepishly, that she was planning a trip to Australia, and was well aware of the fact that their seasons are reversed relative to those of North America.

> I: So is that a problem for your picture? <hands new paper to her>
> A: Yeah, that is. Cause, okay, um. There's like the sun. <starts making a new diagram> And, okay, yeah, I remember that now cause um it's like [pause] I guess as the world is rotating, or is go- orbiting, it's rotating too, so – [pause] I don't really I guess I don't understand it. Um.
> I: Were you saying as the earth is going around here, <gestures a circle following the orbit path drawn on the original diagram> it's doing what?
> A: It's like spinning <gestures spinning motion>, because that's how it's day and night too.
> I: Spinning like a top?
> A: Yeah.
> I: Okay.
> A: So, yeah, I guess I really don't understand it that much … Yeah, I have heard that, cause I was supposed to go to Australia this summer but it was going to be winter when I was going, but there, winters are really warm.

Angela's initial model fit neatly within one of the categories of models mentioned above. The model was also clearly expressed right from the first moment of the interview, and remained stable up until the moment that it was challenged by the interviewer. This was not always the case. As described in Sherin et al. (2012), the students often assembled and revised their models on the spot, out of bits and pieces of knowledge, as the interview unfolded. This was the case for the second student I will discuss, Alex. Alex began with an explanation that depended on the fact that the earth's axis is tilted. In this initial explanation, the part of the earth tilted toward the sun experiences summer because it is closer to the sun:

> A: Well it's warmer in the summer because of how the earth is on its axis, it's, when it's rotating it's closer to the sun and then it's tilted a little. And in the summer it's, your, our part of the, where we are is tilted closer to the sun, so it's warmer, and then in the winter we're tilted like away from the sun.

As the interview unfolded, Alex's explanation evolved in multiple ways. For example, he later maintained that the earth's non-circular orbit is also partly responsible for the seasons.

> A: It's not, but it's not in like a perfect circle. It's, I don't know, it'll be farther away here and then maybe a little closer depending on what time of year it is.
> I: So how close it is, does that affect-
> A: Yeah, how close it is, and then how it's on its axis.
> I: Okay. So both those things affect summer or winter.

Computational Analysis & Interactional Detail **435**

The last interview I will discuss is with a student named Holly. It turns out that the vast majority of the students interviewed had a basic understanding of the relative positions and motions of the sun, earth, moon, and other planets in the solar system. However, Holly was an exception. In her initial explanation, she stated that the sun moves around the earth, and that the side of the earth facing the sun is warmer because it's closer to the sun. She also mentioned that this might have something to do with day and night:

> H: Because of the way the sun rotates around the earth. When it's on our side, it's warmer, and then when it's on the other side, it's colder. Although that might be day and night, but yeah, it has something to do with how the sun and the earth rotate.

Though there is some ambiguity in this initial explanation, follow-up questioning seemed to confirm that Holly believed the sun moves around the earth. For example, she produced the diagram in Figure 16.1 when pressed to clarify her explanation.

The brief descriptions of interviews above are intended to give a sense for some of the core aspects of a Knowledge Analysis of these interviews about student understanding of the seasons. The question in the remainder of this chapter is the extent to which key features of these analyses can be captured by an automated analysis, one that adopts an extreme logocentric perspective. We want to see, for example, if the analysis can capture Angela's initial explanation, as well as the fact that she abandoned that explanation partway through the interview. We also want to see if it can capture how Alex assembled an explanation out of a few elements of knowledge, and that his explanation changed over the course of the interview. Finally, we want to see if the analysis can capture the unusual motion described by Holly.

## The Automated Analysis

Education research, and research on human behavior more generally, has seen a recent upsurge in interest in novel, computer-based analysis methods (Martin & Sherin, 2013). These new methods draw on techniques from fields such as

FIGURE 16.1   Holly's drawing of the sun orbiting the earth.

machine learning and computational linguistics to automate the analysis of data that frequently were only previously tractable with qualitative methods.

In prior work, I reported success in using automated techniques to analyze interviews from the seasons corpus (Sherin, 2013). However, the analysis techniques employed in that work were, in an important sense, ad hoc. I described a recipe for discovering patterns in the interview data; but the major justification given for that recipe was simply that it worked – it produced patterns that could be interpreted in a way that aligned with qualitative analyses of the data. In contrast, the automated analysis described in this chapter is based on a simple generative cognitive model. The automated analysis works by fitting this simple generative cognitive model to the transcript data. This has a number of important advantages. First, it means that, at least in broad outlines, each step in the analysis is determined by the model. Second, it means that the interpretation of the results is much clearer than in the case of my ad hoc analysis. However, as I will point out below, this model-based analysis introduces its own new challenges.

## *The Generative Cognitive Model*

My explanation of the automated analysis begins with a description of the generative cognitive model. The model assumes there is a common set of cognitive elements, shared by all of the students who were interviewed. Within a given interview, a student might draw on some of these elements, and not others. But the elements themselves, when employed, are the same for each student.

An "element" is defined by a set of probabilities of producing individual words. Figure 16.2 gives an idea of what these elements might look like. There are five elements,[1] each of which tends to produce somewhat different words. For example, Element 4, when activated, has a 7 percent chance of producing the word "farther" and a 6.5 percent chance of producing the word "away." (It also is assumed to produce other words with lesser probabilities, which aren't shown.) Similarly, Element 5 produces the word "tilted" 5.7 percent of the time and the word "hemisphere" 4.4 percent of the time. In addition, each element has parameters that govern how likely, overall, it is to be activated.

During any segment of a given interview, each of the elements will have a level of activation that governs how likely it is that it will be given the opportunity to produce a word during that segment. We then imagine an interview unfolding as follows: At the start of a segment, each of the five elements is assigned an activation level. Then within the segment, the model iterates: it randomly selects one

| Element 1 || Element 2 || Element 3 || Element 4 || Element 5 ||
|---|---|---|---|---|---|---|---|---|---|
| night | 0.067 | side | 0.054 | light | 0.032 | farther | 0.07 | tilted | 0.057 |
| day | 0.066 | spring | 0.03 | rays | 0.031 | away | 0.065 | hemisphere | 0.044 |

**FIGURE 16.2** Cognitive elements.

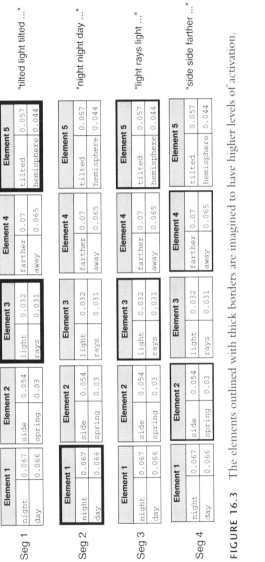

FIGURE 16.3 The elements outlined with thick borders are imagined to have higher levels of activation.

of the elements, based on the current activation levels. The selected element then, in turn, produces a word, based on its probability distribution over words. This iterates, filling up the segment with words. This whole process then is imagined to repeat for each segment of the interview. This is illustrated in Figure 16.3. In the figure, the elements that have a high level of activation are surrounded by boxes of varying thicknesses.

## Fitting the Model to the Data

The above section describes a simple, hypothetical cognitive model. In order to perform our analysis, we must work backward from the data we are given (i.e., the transcripts) to a model that is consistent with that data; in short, we must *fit* this model to the data. This means adjusting the parameters that govern the model to best fit the data. As I have laid it out here, the cognitive model is characterized by a large number of parameters. These include:

- the number of elements
- the probability distribution over words for each element
- the base-level probability associated with each element
- the activation level of each element during every segment of every interview in the corpus.

In selecting values for these parameters, we seek to find values such that our probability of observing the corpus that we do observe is maximized. Although this is a very difficult problem, it is a problem that has already been solved (with some caveats to be mentioned shortly). In particular, a technique called latent Dirichlet allocation (LDA) is designed to fit a model of precisely this form to textual data (Blei, Ng, & Jordan, 2003). Using this technique requires that we select the number of elements in advance. This technique has, to date, generally been used in quite different applications, and is usually conceptualized in a different manner. However, it has precisely the form desired for this application.

The inputs to the analysis are transcripts of the 54 interviews, created by human transcribers, working from videos of the interviews. As a first step in the analysis process, everything is removed from each transcript except for the words spoken by the student. This includes all words spoken by the interviewer, as well as any other annotations made by transcribers. Next, the analysis removes words that appear on a so-called *stop-list* of highly common words, such as "the" and "or." The stop-list used for this analysis consisted of 776 words. When this is done, I find that 645 unique words are used across the 54 transcripts. This set of 645 will henceforth be called the *vocabulary*.

The next step is to segment the transcripts so that it is possible to capture change over time in an interview. To accomplish this, each of the transcripts is broken into 50-word segments with a moving window that steps forward 10 words at a time. This means that the first segment contains words 1–50 of the transcript, the next segment contains words 10–60, and so on. The use of overlapping segments of a fixed size allows me to segment transcripts in a very simple way, while minimizing the possibility that any results are due only to accidents in how a transcript was segmented. When this is done, I obtain a total of 2,132 segments across all of the transcripts. These 2,132 segments are then passed as input to LDA.

For this analysis, I used an algorithm called Gibbs sampling (Heinrich, 2005; Porteous et al., 2008) to perform the LDA analysis. Although there are several published algorithms and publicly available libraries for performing LDA, these algorithms can be difficult to apply in specific contexts. Fitting the model described above to the data is a difficult computational task. There is a very large number of parameters to fit, and all computational approaches, including the Gibbs sampling approach I employed, are non-deterministic. They all randomly select a starting shape for the analysis and then gradually move parameters in the direction of a better fit. There is no guarantee that the result will even approximate the model that is the best fit; indeed, every time these analyses are run, results are obtained that are at least slightly different. For some applications, such as document searches, this indeterminacy might be acceptable. However, for scientific applications, such as the one here, indeterminacy is undesirable; at the least, it makes it difficult to know how to interpret the results.

Applying the Gibbs sampling method to my data, I found that when I restricted the model to five elements, I got results that were virtually the same across runs. If I ran the model with more elements, I obtained different results across runs. If I employed seven elements, for example, three or four of those elements would be the same as elements from a five-element run. The other three or four elements from the seven-element run would divide up the remaining space in inconsistent ways. At present, I am not certain how to interpret this limitation. It is possible, for example, that a larger data set would allow for more conceptual resolution in the knowledge elements. However, for the purposes of this chapter, I report results using a single five-element run.

This is not entirely ideal. In my prior computational studies of the seasons data, using ad hoc methods, I got good results using the equivalent of seven elements (Sherin, 2013). Our human-based qualitative analyses generally assumed a much larger number of elements (Sherin et al., 2012). Using only five elements means that the possibility for conceptual resolution is greatly reduced.

## Results of the Automated Analysis

### The Knowledge Elements

Running the analysis as described above produced a set of five knowledge elements, each of which is characterized by a probability distribution over the 645 words in the vocabulary. Figure 16.4 shows the 15 highest probability words for each of the five discovered knowledge elements. Looking at these most common words can give us a sense of the meaning of each of the elements.

Element 1 seems to be concerned with day and night, as well as the rotation of the earth. It makes intuitive sense that these ideas would be seen in combination; the rotation of the earth is responsible for the day–night cycle, and students often did discuss these things in conjunction with each other. Element 2 seems to be about the side (of the earth) facing the sun, and also includes mentions of specific seasons. (It's unclear why these should be together in an element.) The word "united" comes from mentions of "United States."

Element 4 seems to contain words we'd expect to see in closer-farther explanations. In addition to the words "closer" and "farther," we see the words "orbit" and "circle." In closer-farther explanations, students did often talk about the shape of the earth's orbit, and how it affected the proximity of the earth to the sun. Finally, the last two elements have words we would expect to see in tilt-based explanations. Element 5 is about the tilting of the earth, and mentions words associated with discussion of the earth's hemispheres. Element 3 is about light rays. It has the words "light" and "rays" as well as "directly" and "angle." Recall that in the correct explanation of the seasons, the tilting of the earth causes parts of the earth to receive more direct sunlight. The parts of the earth receiving more direct sunlight experience summer.

In the above paragraphs, I associated each of the elements with one of the three prototype explanations. However, my intent is to interpret the elements as capturing knowledge at a finer grain size. Thus, within given interviews, we should expect to see the elements combined in different ways. For example, as we

| Element 1 | | Element 2 | | Element 3 | | Element 4 | | Element 5 | |
|---|---|---|---|---|---|---|---|---|---|
| night | 0.067 | side | 0.054 | light | 0.032 | farther | 0.07 | tilted | 0.057 |
| day | 0.066 | spring | 0.03 | rays | 0.031 | away | 0.065 | hemisphere | 0.044 |
| moon | 0.059 | fall | 0.03 | heat | 0.028 | closer | 0.063 | away | 0.036 |
| rotates | 0.051 | united | 0.03 | side | 0.026 | point | 0.035 | north | 0.031 |
| spins | 0.028 | spinning | 0.029 | hitting | 0.023 | colder | 0.029 | sunlight | 0.031 |
| axis | 0.028 | facing | 0.024 | chicago | 0.023 | time | 0.028 | towards | 0.028 |
| time | 0.027 | draw | 0.024 | directly | 0.023 | warmer | 0.024 | northern | 0.028 |
| rotating | 0.02 | day | 0.024 | colder | 0.022 | guess | 0.021 | facing | 0.024 |
| spinning | 0.02 | axis | 0.024 | angle | 0.022 | axis | 0.019 | farther | 0.022 |
| make | 0.017 | time | 0.02 | takes | 0.02 | circle | 0.017 | part | 0.022 |
| side | 0.015 | spins | 0.019 | cold | 0.018 | moves | 0.017 | southern | 0.022 |
| chicago | 0.013 | explain | 0.019 | time | 0.018 | cold | 0.017 | closer | 0.018 |
| seasons | 0.013 | seasons | 0.018 | australia | 0.018 | hot | 0.016 | south | 0.017 |
| moves | 0.012 | sort | 0.016 | hit | 0.017 | rotates | 0.015 | toward | 0.016 |
| daytime | 0.012 | year | 0.013 | axis | 0.017 | far | 0.015 | tilt | 0.015 |

**FIGURE 16.4** The five knowledge elements. For each element, the 15 most probable words are listed along with their probabilities.

have seen, a student might state that the tilt of the earth (Element 5) affects the directness of rays (Element 3) or causes parts of the earth to be closer or farther (Element 4) from the sun. We would also expect to see Elements 1 and 2 together in side-based explanations.

## Results for Individual Transcripts

Next, I examine the results for specific interviews. As explained above, the automated analysis outputs the activation level of each of the elements for every segment of every interview. For illustration, I will present the analyses produced for the three interviews presented earlier. To begin, recall that Angela initially produced a clear and consistent closer-farther explanation. Then, when challenged, she floundered, and attempted briefly to produce an explanation that introduced the rotation of the earth.

The result of the automated analysis of the interview with Angela is shown in Figure 16.5. In this plot, the interview has been broken into 35 segments, and time progresses in the interview from left to right. Each row corresponds to one of the five knowledge elements, and a darker color in a row means that there was a higher probability for the element in the given interview segment.

As expected, the first part of the interview is dominated by the element we would expect to be most associated with closer-farther explanation (Element 4: farther-away). Then, following the challenge, there is a new portion of the interview dominated by the element associated with day, night, and the rotation of the earth (Element 1: night-day). Starting around Segment 27, the interviewer asks Angela to clarify the problem with her original explanation, and she discusses her trip to Australia.

Thus, in some important respects, the automated analysis aligns with the qualitative analysis of the interview. It captures the initial focus on proximity of the earth to the sun, and it captures transitions that occurred as the interview unfolds. There is, of course, much that it misses that is critical to the story. For example, it doesn't in any way capture her initial apparent confidence in her closer-farther explanation, nor her later embarrassment in the same explanation.

Figure 16.6 displays the analogous chart for the interview with Alex. When I discussed Alex's interview earlier, I focused only on the first part of our interview. Recall that, initially, Alex gave an explanation in which the tilt of the earth causes parts of the earth to be either closer or farther from the sun. Then, he introduced the idea that the earth's orbit is non-circular, and that received increasing focus. This seems to be well captured by Figure 16.6. At the very start of the interview, the automated analysis seems to show a combination of Element 4 (farther-away) and Element 5 (tilted-hemisphere) for the earliest part of the interview. Then there is a long stretch with a heavier emphasis on Element 4, beginning around Segment 10. Segment 10 corresponds to the moment in the interview when Alex introduced the non-circular orbit of the earth.

**FIGURE 16.5** Analysis of interview with Angela. Each row corresponds to a knowledge element. The time of the interview proceeds from left to right.

Although I did not discuss the remainder of Alex's interview earlier, the other major transitions in Figure 16.6 do correspond with those identified by human analysts.

Finally, recall that Holly gave an explanation in which the sun "rotates" around the earth, and this causes the seasons because the parts of the earth closer to the sun are warmer. The analysis for the interview with Holly is shown in Figure 16.7. It is possible to see how the analysis reflects important features of the interview. The rotation of the sun around the earth is captured by the day-night element, and the focus on proximity to the sun in the early parts of the interview is captured by the farther-away elements, starting especially in segment 7.

However, there is no obvious way in which the automated analysis captures the fact that Holly had the sun orbiting the earth, rather than the reverse. Beginning around Segment 14, the interviewer worked hard to get Holly to clarify how the earth, sun, and planets move. This resulted in a long digression which focused solely on this movement. This shows up, in the automated analysis, only as strong emphasis on the day-night element.

## Reflection

I now return to the main question posed in the introduction to this chapter: What types of research questions can be addressed through an extreme logocentric analysis, one that attends only to the words spoken? There are clearly many types of questions that could not be addressed, including many – perhaps most – of the questions that are of concern to IA research. But what about questions at the core of KA?

The results described here, as well as in other published accounts (Sherin, 2013), suggest that it might well be possible to address some questions in KA with an analysis of this sort. The automated analysis seems to capture at least some of the core conceptual action. It is also particularly noteworthy, I believe, that the automated analysis seems to have an easy time of recognizing transitions between sections of an interview. The places in Figures 16.5, 16.6, and 16.7 that appear to involve major transitions are the same places that, in our qualitative analyses, were treated to be transitions. IA researchers have pointed out that human interactions are always segmented, and that participants do work to make this segmenting structure visible for each other (Jordan & Henderson, 1995). Furthermore, participants can be seen to use subtle changes in the spatial orientation of their bodies

**FIGURE 16.6** Analysis of interview with Alex.

**FIGURE 16.7** Analysis of interview with Holly.

to signal and negotiate these transitions. In contrast, the logocentric, automated analysis seems to capture much of the segmenting structure looking solely at the word stream.

There are still, however, several ways in which the program suggested could fail. First, at present, the conceptual granularity is perhaps not as fine as a Knowledge Analysis would like. The analysis presented here only discovered five elements. Given the results obtained so far, it seems likely that the granularity could be made finer when more data become available. Nonetheless, it might never be possible to achieve the sort of granularity necessary for full alignment with a serious Knowledge Analysis of these sorts of data.

There is a more profound way in which this program could fail. Methods such as LDA have generally been developed with very different uses in mind. LDA in particular was developed as a means of extracting the latent *topics* in text documents, as a way to support retrieval of documents from large text corpora. It would be quite reasonable to worry that discovering latent topics might not be the same as discovering tacit *knowledge*. Thus, the analyses presented here might capture the ebb and flow of topics in an interview discussion, without discovering (as I have assumed) the knowledge underlying the generation of contributions to that discussion. If that were the case, the type of analysis presented here might still be useful, but it would need to be interpreted quite differently.

There are potentially deeper questions here, questions that go beyond the potential usefulness of automated analysis for various research aims, and even beyond the question of whether this type of automated analysis captures knowledge. Does the relative success of these automated analyses say anything deep and general about the nature of human interaction? Or is the success a result of idiosyncratic features of the particular research context examined here? To examine these questions, I return to the list of possible reasons for success presented in the introduction.

## Separability and Redundancy

In the introduction, I pointed out that, even if utterances are always multi-party and multimodal, communicated information might still be distributed over various modalities in such a way that an analysis of just the words spoken could produce sensible results. I believe that the results described here give us reason to believe that separability and redundancy, while certainly not universal, might be quite common and prominent features of the type of communicative interaction studied here.

We saw, for example, that just focusing on the words spoken was enough to recognize major transitions in the dialogue. Before conducting this work, it was far from obvious that this should have been the case. It seems plausible, for example, that different sections of an interview would be marked only by the way that words were combined, which words were stressed by a speaker, or by other more subtle features of the interaction. Apparently, however, enough information resides in the raw word stream to detect transitions – at least the sort of transitions relevant to a knowledge analyst.

## Unique Features of This Interaction

However, the interactions studied here have characteristic features that might be associated with more separability and redundancy. The conversations in our interviews are strongly guided by the interviewers. Thus, for example, interviewees did not have the freedom – or did not feel they had the freedom – to transition from one topic to another at their own whim. Segues between topics were often clearly marked by interviewers, and frequently involved the introduction of new ideas to consider.

The interviewees were constrained in other ways. For example, they had to sit in the chair offered to them, in the position suggested, and they did not have the freedom to get up out of their chairs. This restricted their ability to employ other means of conveying information. Thus, in some ways, the interaction in these interviews might be more like a phone call than an in-person conversation.

At the same time, however, there are characteristic features of the interactions studied here that might pose additional difficulties for an extreme logocentric analysis. For example, there are features that might tend to minimize separability and redundancy. Gestures and drawings frequently played a central role in how students expressed themselves, and spoken words often referred to features of gestures and drawings. Thus these were densely multimodal utterances.

## A Different Task

There are many ways in which the task faced by the automated analysis is different than the task faced by an individual who is actively participating, in real time, in an interaction. As noted in the introduction, for example, a participant must anticipate what will be required of them. In contrast, the automated analysis can look at the entirety of the interaction retrospectively.

Furthermore, our clinical interviews are highly engineered interactions, and they have been engineered partly to simplify the task of interpretation. They were designed, for example, with an idea of the types of knowledge that students would bring to bear when explaining the seasons. Assuming we were correct, an analysis needed only to distinguish which parts of this space of knowledge students were employing. This is a simpler task than the one of understanding any possible discourse.

## Sleight of Hand

Finally, my discussion above was predicated on the assumption that the analysis does not have access to any information beyond the words spoken by a student.

But there are some respects in which this claim is not quite true. The automated analysis doesn't look only at an individual interview to interpret that interview; it looks across the whole corpus first, and learns something about the space of ideas that are raised. In the act of assembling the corpus, we have thus provided extra information that can be brought to bear in understanding individual interviews.

More importantly, human researchers (and readers of this chapter) played an important role as interpreters of the results produced by the automated analyses. The automated analyses produced only lists of words along with probabilities and activation levels for interviews. It is up to us to give meaning to that output, and we, in producing our explanation, draw on much more than the words spoken by students, regardless of their order. We know, for example, the subject matter and purpose of the interviews. We know that the interviews were focused on the earth's seasons, and that they were intended to investigate some particular features of students' explanations of the seasons. We are aware of typical explanations of the seasons given by students. Finally, we might know more about the specific interviews themselves. Researchers on my team had viewed video of the interviews in their entirety, and they read portions of the interviews represented in transcripts.

Where does this leave us on the importance of interaction detail for Knowledge Analysis? In truth, we are not all that far from where we began this chapter. We knew at the start of this chapter that, when people talk face-to-face, they use gestures, facial expressions, and the like to communicate. We knew that these gestures and facial expression *matter* for communication. However, we also knew that it's possible to figure out quite a lot about what people are talking about, just from hearing their words. The question, thus, is really one of degree: how far can we, as knowledge analysts, get with just words? The results described above cannot answer this question in any definitive way. But they do, I believe, tip the scales a bit in one direction; they suggest that much of the important content in a discussion is reflected in the words alone.

# Commentary

# THE NEED FOR THE PARTICIPANT'S PERSPECTIVE IN A KA|IA JOINT ENTERPRISE

*Noel Enyedy and Joshua A. Danish*

Given the theme of this volume, Sherin begins his chapter by establishing a rather provocative goal: identifying the research questions and analytic approaches that might explore thinking and learning *without attention to interactional detail*. As researchers who are passionate about the centrality of interaction in accounts of thinking and learning, and who are deeply committed to an agenda of integrating ideas from KA and IA, it would be an understatement to say that we initially found this proposal to be quite puzzling. However, upon further reflection, we believe that this kind of discussion is in fact central to the project of reconciling ideas from disparate approaches such as KA and IA. The power of a question such as this is that it challenges us to make our assumptions visible, and to question them in an effort to move forward with an increasingly robust analytic toolkit. It is in this spirit that we therefore respond to Sherin's provocative proposal in an effort to highlight and discuss what we see as some key tensions in his proposal, and with a goal of promoting discussion and debate. We believe that this kind of debate can strengthen all of our collective research efforts as we move forward. The thrust of our response is that to frame the question as Sherin has (i.e., when can we safely ignore interaction when analyzing knowledge?), closes off, from the beginning, inquiry into what knowing "is." If what counts as knowing is an open object of inquiry, *and* we intend to pursue this line of inquiry from both a KA and an IA perspective, then the goals of the analyst – and how these goals affect the selection and omission of data – need to be balanced by attention to the goals and perspectives of the participants and how the participants attend to selective aspects of their experience. It is the latter focus that is central to the IA approach and is missing from Sherin's proposal.

## On the Relationship Between Knowledge and Interaction

From the outset, Sherin frames the methodological issues in a manner that highlights his commitments regarding the relationship between knowledge and interaction: "If our research questions are explicitly about aspects of interactional detail, then clearly we must attend to that detail" (Sherin, this volume, p. 429). From this initial framing, knowledge and interaction are separable, in the sense that an analyst may not need to attend to interaction to answer some questions about knowledge – a framing that we believe contradicts the core tenets of IA. Sherin certainly acknowledges that interaction and knowledge may interact at some level, but at the same time, he is arguing that the "heart of the KA enterprise" is to "identify knowledge that is drawn upon as an individual engages in some task" (Sherin, this volume, p. 430), and that interaction is not at the heart of this lens on knowing and learning.

In the quote above, Sherin reminds us that the methods we choose need to be linked to the questions we ask. An admittedly simplified characterization of Sherin's position is that, if your question has to do explicitly with interaction then, yes, you need to attend to interaction; but if your question is about knowledge then, no, you can omit Interaction Analysis. However, we view this framing as in opposition to the exploration of a joint KAIA enterprise which necessitates engaging with the IA premise that knowing is inseparable from the interaction. Saying that knowledge and interaction are inseparable is not to necessarily say that they are one and the same, but it starts with the close examination of the relationship between the two. One might infer a simplistic linear relationship wherein interaction is the context that cues up certain cognitive resources and the goal for the interaction provides the context that may steer cognition in one direction or another. However, this is problematic from an IA standpoint, which not only recognizes the interrelationship between knowledge and interaction but also treats knowledge as distributed amongst participants and assumes that interaction is non-linear in the sense that participants are continually monitoring their interlocutor and adapting their communication on the fly. Sherin's framing highlights the fact that the field as a whole continues to recognize multiple definitions of knowledge – those that are inherently distributed, and those that are not. Our goal in responding from an IA perspective is to foreground the ways that some treatments of knowledge do not address questions that are raised by IA.

An alternative read of Sherin's framing is that at some point, it is useful to consider the organization and structure of knowledge first, before revisiting how interaction plays a role in it. This relationship would still leave knowing "at the heart" of the enterprise, and interaction as the context that surrounds the text we are really interested in – an individual's knowledge. It would, however, be a possible path to integration if one took seriously the need to revisit what one had learned about knowing once it was reanalyzed with an eye towards interaction (and vice versa).

However, one could go a step further and frame the relationship between the knowing and interacting as fundamentally simultaneous and co-constituting. Conversational Analysis (the tradition that in many ways gave rise to IA as presented here) provides numerous examples of where the interaction is shaped simultaneously by both the speaker and the listener. For example, Goodwin (2006) analyzed the communicative abilities of a man who had had a stroke and whose speech had been reduced to three words: "yes," "no," and "and." Despite the fact that the words that he could say had no semantic content of their own, this man was still able to communicate and even tell stories. He accomplished this by working with his conversational partners to produce meaning, using his limited vocabulary and his prosody to steer the contributions of his partners. The narratives were co-produced from the simultaneous contributions of multiple parties, specifying a very different relationship between knowing and interacting than the accounts outlined above. They also helped to reveal that the man who could only communicate with simple phrases had knowledge of many complex prior experiences that simply could not be articulated individually, nor analyzed individually as a result. This may seem to be an extreme case, but it may also be that the co-construction of knowledge in interaction is the norm rather than the exception.

Our point is that to advance discussions of what knowledge is, we need to specify a hypothetical relationship between IA and KA and then choose methods and frames that attempt to honor and investigate that relationship. Such an explicit articulation would allow us to read Sherin's proposal within the context of his strong assumption that knowledge and interaction can be separated and that the broad contours of what constitutes knowledge are already known. Further, it would allow us to interpret Sherin's analytic moves in this light, even if we value a more nuanced articulation of the relationship between knowing and interacting.

## On Letting the Data Decide

Conlin and Hammer in their response to Ma (this volume) suggest that one approach to clarifying the relationship between knowledge and interaction is to let the data decide rather than choosing a priori based on theoretical commitments. Sherin's chapter provides a compelling context in which to vet this approach. We believe that Sherin would argue that is exactly what he is doing; he is stripping off interaction and letting the data decide whether or not this omission affects the quality of his analysis.

However, the trouble with "letting the data decide," is that the data cannot decide. Data is made through the analysis, and the analysis is theory-laden at every step (Hall, 2000; Ochs, 1979). In this case, we believe that Sherin has begun with a theoretical assumption that there are meaningful patterns in knowledge that can be viewed outside of their interactional context, which justifies the initial step of removing that context. We suggest instead that if we are to integrate these two perspectives and traditions, we need to start with a priori theoretical commitments that seem reasonable to both.

That being said, we agree that the data should also play a role in shaping the analysis, but this brings us again to tension that needs to be worked out. Sherin opens by saying that regardless of one's theoretical commitments, "researchers must make decisions about what is attended to in the observations that are collected, and with what precision" (Sherin, this volume, p. 429). This is true, but stating it this way hides what guides the choice the analysts make. For example, Sherin makes particular note of the ways in which the interviews he analyzes are "engineered partly to simplify the task of interpretation," such that "an analysis needs only to distinguish which of this space of ideas students were employing" (Sherin, thin volume, p. 445). The point here is that analysts choose what to include and what to focus on based on the analysts' goals, interests, and commitments (theoretical and otherwise). Interaction analysts also make choices about what to look at and what to focus on; however, these choices are guided by the goal of recovering the participants' perspectives. What is important and consequential to the interviewer *and* interviewee during a conversation about what one knows about the seasons is what the interaction analyst strives to understand and cannot be fully determined ahead of time. Ultimately, an analysis that does not shed light on the participants' perspectives on their own activities is not fertile ground for the integration of KA with IA because it ignores this central commitment of IA. We are not assuming a priori that knowing has to be too complex to be usefully analyzed by a machine. But we are suggesting that the details and assumptions of what is erased and deemed as erasable in the process of automation are not a good fit with a tradition that seeks to understand the participants' perspectives on their own activities.

## On Separability and Redundancy of Information

Sherin proposes that:

> Even if utterances are multi-party and multimodal, the communicated information might be distributed over parties and modes in a manner that allows … for a sensible analysis focused on just one information channel.… If that is the case, it might be possible to perform a meaningful Knowledge Analysis focusing on just the words. Second, if utterances are multi-party and multimodal, there may be a great deal of redundancy across information channels. This *redundancy* might be essential for reliable human communication. But a computer-based logocentric analysis might be able to make do without it. (p.444)

We do not contest the idea that information can be conveyed by different modalities, and that in some sense, information in one channel may overlap with information in another. However, we believe it is equally true that the sense and meaning of an exchange is often (if not always) more than the sum of its parts. The meaning participants construct integrates different aspects of experience, including information presented in different modalities. Aspects of the interaction co-evolve with one another in ways that may go beyond any simple treatment of the information. Saying "pass me the ball," and saying it while jumping up and down waving one's arms may mean the same semantically, but they have different emotional valences.

At first glance, it seems completely reasonable to ask, "Do I need this interactional detail *all the time*? How far can I get by just attending to the content of talk? When does attending to the content of what was said fall short?" However, as mentioned above, these questions only make sense if "knowing" has already been equated with the semantics of talk and interaction is seen as something that modifies the core of what was "really" meant.

We believe that, for an integrated KAIA set of methods, the selection and potential omission of modalities and other aspects of the experience should be responsive both to the goals of the analysis *and* the participants' perspectives. We should be conservative in omitting aspects of the lived experience from our accounts of that experience, and for an integrated KAIA approach, one criterion should be: Do the participants' interactions hinge on that element in any way? We also see a crucial difference between examining some of the interactional details in a context and then determining that they need not be considered in detail versus determining a priori that they can and should be ignored at the beginning of an analysis.

This commitment could be rephrased as a suggestion that one could productively look to the commitments of both KA and IA as a method for vetting key analytic decisions. For example, an analyst interested in analyzing knowledge in the manner proposed by Sherin might find value in noting how this would fundamentally violate the assumptions of IA regarding the need to look towards how the participants experienced the situation as a yardstick for whether or not any given information can be productively omitted from analysis.

Note that we are not suggesting that all analysts interested in KA must therefore always integrate IA. Rather, we believe that acknowledging these alternative commitments might make for a stronger analytic approach. For example, an alternative approach to the one Sherin proposes might be to analyze the interaction, and then look to see whether the interactional moves are in fact "significant" for the final analysis or not. In Sherin's analysis, he ultimately points to some fluctuations in how students' knowledge is made visible. We suspect that an effort to code the interactions around those moments of fluctuation would in fact reveal that the interviewer played a significant role in those moments and in making those elements of knowledge visible. Only a reanalysis would answer this question for sure, but our hope is that in future efforts of this kind, we will see more work to systematically demonstrate the utility (or lack thereof) of analyzing some aspects of interaction through conducting those analyses rather than removing them a priori.

## On the Unique Features of the Particular Interaction Under Study

Sherin next highlights the distinctive nature of the clinical interviews he is examining and suggests that:

> Even if separability and redundancy do not hold in general for human interaction, they might hold in certain specific types of circumstances.... The

clinical interviews under study here are highly constrained, very particular types of interactions, and they might thus have unique properties that support certain types of logocentric analysis. (p. 431)

It seems reasonable to assume that particular methodological shortcuts can be made under certain circumstances. Further, special cases such as interviews may, in fact, be revealing about some aspect of the phenomenon even if the special case does not generalize. However, Sherin goes beyond identifying the interviews as a unique and yet valuable context to suggest that these interviews can further be analyzed without examining the role of the interviewer. This is a move that has been questioned and debated extensively elsewhere (diSessa, Greeno, Michaels, & O'Connor, this volume; Hall, 2000; Halldén, Haglund, & Strömdahl, 2007; Russ, Sherin, & Lee, this volume). To be fair, it is clear that Sherin is completely aware that the arc of the interview is dependent on the contributions of the interviewer. What he is proposing is that, even so, the interactional detail can be dropped from the analysis of knowing *in some cases*.

To examine this part of Sherin's proposal, we need to look more closely at his data. Below we present an excerpt from an interview from Russ, Sherin, and Lee (this volume) of a student named Angela, but with the interviewer's turns removed.

1. A: See, that's what winter would be like, the Earth orbits around the sun (she motions over the oval shaped orbit she has drawn). Like summer is the closest to the sun. Spring is kind of a little further away, and then like fall is further away than spring but not as far as winter, and then winter is the furthest.
2. A: Mm hmm.
3. A: Umm, I need another picture.
4. A: Yeah, that is. Um, ok. There is the sun [drawing]. Yeah, I remember that now cause um it's like as the Earth is rotating, as it's orbiting, it's rotating too. I guess I don't understand it.
5. A: It's like spinning, cause it's going like [spinning gesture], that's how it's day and night too
6. A: Yeah.
7. A: So, yeah, I guess I really don't understand it that much…
8. A: Because, yeah I rethought that and it looks really stupid because summer is really close but how could you winter on the other side, how could it be winter on the other side if it's really close here, and how could it be really warm if this [winter earth] is really far away.

Looking at this interaction without the interviewer raises a few questions about how to interpret what the interview reveals about what the interviewee "knows" about the seasons. It starts off in line 1 with a fairly coherent narrative. However, the statement in line 3 seems curious, why does she need a new picture? What is motivating her attempts to include rotation into her new drawing?

The need for a new drawing and the elements that are included make much more sense in light of the question she was asked by the interviewer:

> Mm hmm, okay. So that makes a lot of sense. *One thing I wanted to ask you though about was, one thing that you might have heard is that at the same time, and you can tell me if you've heard this, when it's summer here, it's actually winter in Australia.* Have you heard that before? (p. 395)

One might argue that understanding the motivation for the elaboration of her model is beside the point; what the analysis is trying to recover is the network of understandings. However, this cuts off many potentially important ways to understand knowing. For example, one might propose that one's confidence in one's knowledge is part of knowing. And in this case, it is unclear that the interviewee's meta-cognitive insight in line 7 would occur or make sense if not for the interviewer's probing between lines 7 and 8:

> So you're thinking that somehow the spinning, that somehow if you take into account the fact that the Earth is also spinning, that might help to explain why it's summer and winter at different times? … *Just to be clear, what was the problem with this picture for the* – (p. 396)

Likewise, one might propose that an important part of knowing is understanding the conditions and purposes of how knowledge should be used. Removing the interviewer from the analysis prevents the analyst from understanding what the interviewee is attempting to do with their knowledge. Some of these purposes may be practical, like packing for a trip, and other purposes may be social, like saving face in front of a professor. Thus, removing the interviewer from the analysis is problematic not only from an interactional perspective but also if one wants to expand the definition of knowledge to include more than just a semantic network of understandings. If we believe that what people "know" is in direct relation to what they are doing, then the interactional detail is necessary to the analysis. The interactional detail is what helps us recover the participants' perspectives on their own activities. In this case, it helps us see that the interviewees are demonstrating a particular kind of school-like knowledge – they are being asked "known-answer questions" and then having their answers challenged.

## On the "Different Task" of Computational Analysis

Sherin also notes that there is value in distinguishing between the task of a computational analyst and that of an interlocutor in interaction:

> The task faced by my computational analysis is in many ways different than that faced by participants in an ongoing communication. For example, participants in a conversation sometimes need to *anticipate* what will be required of them in the interaction. Some of the additional information conveyed by such things as body position might help them perform this function. In contrast, an after-the-fact computer analysis doesn't need to anticipate what will be required, so that it can participate in a conversation; it can look retrospectively at complete interactions. (p. 431)

We certainly agree that a post hoc analysis has the added power of hindsight. In fact, Interaction Analysis has long proceeded from this standpoint as well, given that analysts can look at an entire transcript rather than needing to analyze it line-by-line in a manner mirroring how it was produced. Additionally, Interaction Analysis pays close attention to the participation framework of an interaction – cues that the participants use prospectively to set their expectations for what will happen – who can say what, and how certain events or words should be interpreted.

These analyses attend closely to what participants are in fact anticipating at any given moment, and how they both reveal and confirm that anticipation. Participants who appear to anticipate a specific response will often adjust and adapt their talk when that response is not received, further validating the analysts' assumption that such anticipation existed. For example, when a participant is explaining something, they look to their interlocutor for confirmation that they are making sense. When the interlocutor does not nod their head, say "uh huh" or otherwise indicate understanding, the speaker will often continue and elaborate their idea (Brown, this volume; DeLiema et al., this volume).

How might this apply to Sherin's analysis? We believe that a valuable next step for this kind of analysis would be to explicitly examine issues such as the role of the interviewer, the motivation that students might have, and the participants' recognition of the participation frameworks that are present. If our assumptions are correct, then these elements, which are motivated by IA, will shed additional light on Sherin's results, and provide both greater nuance and greater coverage of the data. Either way, explicitly examining these issues within the current framework will allow us to ground our discussions in results which explicitly acknowledge, and thus examine, the assumptions of IA. If, in some cases, those interactional details appear not to change the analysis in a dramatic way, as Sherin appears to suggest, then we would view that as an important point of discussion for refining and revisiting the assumptions of the role of interaction in knowledge.

## Implicit Bleed-over Between KA and IA

In his final point, Sherin admits that:

> human researchers (and readers of this chapter) played an important role as interpreters of the results produced by the automated analyses. The

automated analyses produced only lists of words along with probabilities, and activation levels for interviews. It is up to us to give meaning to that output, and we, in producing our explanation, draw on much more than the words spoken by students.... Researchers on my team had viewed video of the interviews in their entirety, and they read portions of the interviews represented in transcripts. (p. 446)

We'd like to further note that Sherin's analytic approach also drew quite productively upon taxonomies of student reasoning which he developed in prior studies that relied upon at least implicit acknowledgment of the interactional cues that played a role in the interviews under study. That is to say, there is quite a bit of interaction considered within Sherin's analysis, even if it is then stripped out once the computational model is applied. We view this as a key point that might be further explored in future interactions because it points to an approach similar to the one suggested above which uses ideas from IA to help determine when IA might be conducted in a more limited manner rather than simply rejecting the assumptions of IA out of hand. In our view, Sherin has done this, and even acknowledges aspects of it. By highlighting this, our goal is to provide a starting point for future work that can further explore how analyses such as those that Sherin implemented might draw even more explicitly upon these interactional elements.

## Conclusion

Knowledge Analyses have a long tradition of making visible the recurrent patterns in how both novice and expert knowledge of the world is structured. Sherin's extension via computational analysis is no exception, and we see real value in being able to use the power of computers to find these patterns in increasingly reliable, nuanced, and efficient ways. However, we also believe that acknowledging the importance of interaction for knowing and learning can play an important role in extending this enterprise, and in both complementing and continuing the work that Sherin has begun in his chapter. In particular, we see several points of convergence between the IA and KA approaches that might be further explored to strengthen both. We propose this first set of convergence points in the hopes that others will extend and refine the list over time.

First, integrated KAIA methods and the selection of data need to be responsive to both the goals of the analysis and the goals of the participants. Just as analysts make choices about what is included, omitted, and highlighted in an analysis, the participants in interaction make similar choices to highlight, background, or ignore aspects of their shared experience. Integrated analyses need to stay true to both. Second, knowing can be looked at retrospectively as a whole, prospectively in terms of the participation framework (O'Connor & Michaels, 1996) that sets the expectations of the participants, or in the moment-by-moment unfolding of knowing as it happens. Participants as well as analysts take all three perspectives, and for the integrated KAIA enterprise, these views should be coordinated and used to inform one another. Sherin's provocative proposal to adopt an analytic method that infers what knowing looks like without attending to the interactional detail is informative in that it has highlighted for us some concrete ways that we might move forward in a way that coordinates the choices analysts make with the same type of choices that the participants themselves make in an interaction. While we believe strongly that these ideas, grounded in IA, will provide richer analyses, we agree with Sherin that results speak louder than theories, and would like to see future computational analyses which explicitly incorporate them as a way of then exploring what role they play, and for which analyses, in more explicit detail.

## Cumulative Note

1  These five elements are presented here as hypothetical elements that the analysis might discover. However, I chose to use some values that align with what was ultimately discovered, as will be revealed later in the chapter.

## Cumulative References

Blei, D. M., Ng, A. Y., & Jordan, M. I. (2003). Latent Dirichlet allocation. *Journal of Machine Learning Research*, 3, 993–1022.

diSessa, A. A. (1993). Toward an epistemology of physics. *Cognition and Instruction*, 10, 165–255.

Goodwin, C. (2000). Action and embodiment within situated human interaction. *Journal of Pragmatics*, 32, 1489–1522.

Goodwin, C. (2006). Human sociality as mutual orientation in a rich interactive environment: Multimodal utterances and pointing in aphasia. In N. Enfield & S. C. Levinson (Eds.), *Roots of human sociality* (pp. 96–12). London: Berg Press.

Goodwin, C. (2007). Interactive footing. In E. Hole & R. Clift (Eds.), *Reporting talk*. Cambridge, UK: Cambridge University Press.

Hall, R. (2000). Video recording as theory. In R. A. Lesh & A. E. Kelly (Eds.), *Handbook of research design in mathematics and science education* (pp. 647–664). Mahwah, NJ: Lawrence Erlbaum.

Halldén, O., Haglund, L., & Strömdahl, H. (2007). Conceptions and contexts: On the interpretation of interview and observational data. *Educational Psychologist*, 42(1), 25–40.

Heinrich, G. (2005). *Parameter estimation for text analysis* (Technical Report). Retrieved from www.arbylon.net/publications/text-est.pdf.

Jordan, B., & Henderson, A. (1995). Interaction analysis: Foundations and practice. *Journal of the Learning Sciences*, 4(1), 39–103.

Landauer, T., Foltz, P. W., & Laham, D. (1998). An introduction to latent semantic analysis. *Discourse Processes*, 25, 259–284.

Martin, T., & Sherin, B. L. (2013). Learning analytics and computational techniques for detecting and evaluating patterns in learning: An introduction to the Special Issue. *Journal of the Learning Sciences*, 22(4), 511–520. doi:10.1080/10508406.2013.840466.

Ochs, E. (1979). Transcription as theory. In E. Ochs & B. B. Schieffelin, (Eds.), *Developmental pragmatics* (pp. 43–72). New York: Academic Press.

O'Connor, M. C., & Michaels, S. (1996). Shifting participant frameworks: Orchestrating thinking practices in group discussion. In D. Hicks (Ed.), *Discourse, learning, and schooling* (pp. 63–103). New York: Cambridge University Press.

Parnafes, O., & diSessa, A. A. (2013). Microgenetic learning analysis: A methodology for studying knowledge in transition. *Human Development*, 56(1), 5–37.

Porteous, I., Newman, D., Ihler, A., Asuncion, A., Smyth, P., & Welling, M. (2008). Fast collapsed Gibbs sampling for latent Dirichlet allocation (pp. 569–577). Presented at the 14th ACM SIGKDD international conference, ACM, Association for Computing Machinery, New York. doi:10.1145/1401890.1401960.

Sherin, B. L. (2001). How students understand physics equations. *Cognition and Instruction*, 19(4), 479–541.

Sherin, B. L. (2013). A computational study of commonsense science: An exploration in the automated analysis of clinical interview data. *Journal of the Learning Sciences*, 22(4), 600–635. doi:10.1080/10508406.2013.836654.

Sherin, B. L., Krakowski, M., & Lee, V. R. (2012). Some assembly required: How scientific explanations are constructed during clinical interviews. *Journal of Research in Science Teaching*, 49, 166–198.

# 17
# NAVIGATING TURBULENT WATERS
Objectivity, Interpretation, and Experience in the Analysis of Interaction

*Ricardo Nemirovsky and Molly L. Kelton*

This chapter reflects on a central tension characterizing different traditions and practices for studying interaction. In particular, we explore the rich – if sometimes turbulent – array of methodological approaches arising from two different analytic desiderata: (a) to develop empirical accounts of endogenous meanings while avoiding the imposition of external theoretical frameworks, on the one hand, and (b) to analyze interaction in ways that speak to broader psychological, social, political, and ethical concerns while acknowledging the perspectives the analyst inevitably brings to bear on the data, on the other hand. We trace some of the scholarly debates that have tended to cast these analytic goals in relatively purist and oppositional terms. We then explore the complex and variegated methodological possibilities opened up by the productive tension between them. Through a reflective account of our own analytic approach to a video case study, we raise questions about the roles and possibilities for the evaluation of evidence and participant experience within contemporary practices for analyzing interaction.

## Methodological Tensions in Interaction Analysis

The main roots of Interaction Analysis can be located in the empirical studies of talk in interaction (Hall & Stevens, this volume). Initially, the studies on spoken language as it occurs focused on the analysis of naturalistic audio recordings. Notational technologies were developed, in the form of transcription codes, to transliterate aural details of talk into textual formats. The use of these techniques led to Ochs' well-known thesis of transcription as theory, based on the notion that "transcription is a selective process reflecting theoretical goals and definitions" (Ochs, 1979, p. 44). With the advent of video-recording technologies, many other aspects, such as gesture, gaze, and facial expression, became as analytically relevant as speech. This latter trend expanded dramatically with the spread of digital technologies, which brought a radical facilitation of the selection, streaming, and editing of video over "microscopic" time periods. Video proved to be much more complex and data-dense than audio for textual transcription. Furthermore, Hall (2000) discussed how video recording is itself theory-informed. While audio recording can be open to whatever is being said in the proximity of a microphone, video recording involves a much more active and selective role for the camera's lenses and angle of view.

The different approaches to the study of talk in interaction have always been entangled in debates about the nature of research and diverse theoretical perspectives. We believe that it is possible and productive to describe these tensions as spanning across two poles: (1) Conversation Analysis-Ethnomethodology and (2) Studies of talk incorporating psychological and cultural categories. These two poles do not form a duality (i.e., researchers are not at either one or the other), but open up a wide expanse of ideas traversed by practitioners in different directions and in-between perspectives.

The core of the Conversation Analysis-Ethnomethodology "side" can be rendered by this quotation:

> For ethnomethodology the objective reality of social facts, in that, and just how, it is every society's locally, endogenously produced, naturally organised, reflexively accountable, ongoing, practical achievement, being everywhere, always, only, exactly and entirely, members' work, with no time out, and with no possibility of evasion, hiding out, passing, postponement, or buyouts, is thereby sociology's fundamental phenomenon.
>
> *(Garfinkel, 1991, p. 11)*

Garfinkel's vision of sociology was one founded on the study of how actors' natural and spontaneous talk reveals their own accountability with respect to mutual norms of interaction, as they objectively display their methods to accomplish interactive goals and repair violations of those norms. As taken up by Conversation Analysis, these principles of sociological research amounted to microanalysis of talk and the search for regularities and patterns by which means actors organize their talk and generate conversational methods to accomplish their aims. In pursuing this research agenda, a conversation analyst stresses the endogenous nature of these methods. As members spontaneously articulate their methods, they also make explicit their views of what counts as relevant in the local interactive circumstances. Of paramount importance in identifying the members' criteria of relevance is the analyst refraining from imposing her own criteria onto the data, otherwise:

> However well-intentioned and well-disposed towards the participants ... there is a kind of theoretical imperialism involved here, a kind of hegemony of the intellectuals, of the literati, of the academics, of the critics whose theoretical apparatus gets to stipulate the terms by reference to which the world is to be understood.
>
> *(Schegloff, 1997, p. 167)*

Wetherell (2007) articulated this principle clearly: "the task of the analyst is not to interpret the world but to study how the world has already been interpreted by participants" (p. 670).

On the other hand, those who pursue studies of talk in interaction for the sake of illuminating how psychological and social concepts and categories, such as identity, emotion, gender, ethnicity, social class, and so on, shape talk and interaction, find this type of principle overly restrictive: "Psychological assumptions and presuppositions are unavoidable when language production is studied in its contexts of use" (Wetherell, 2007, p. 661). In order to avoid limiting constraints and to be consequential on social issues faced by our communities at large:

> We usually take discursive practices, rather than the individual, as our unit of analysis. And, because we are psychologists, we are interested in studying how people do psychological things – emotions, memory, gender, identity, knowledge – in talk and texts, as discourse.
>
> *(Wetherell, 2007, p. 665)*

In addition, Billig (1999) argued that the search for endogenous worldviews without "contamination" from those of the analyst is illusory and prone to be deceptive. Others often stress this point:

> I want to reiterate a point made by feminist philosophers of science for a long time – the impossibility of impartiality in any analytical approach. Values and biases get into the most rigorous of empirical approaches by, for example, the types of questions asked and the kind of interpretations made. Thus what becomes desirable, or "more objective" for any analysis is a conscious reflexivity about the position one brings to a piece of research and a consideration of what is hidden by taking that perspective.
>
> *(Weatherall, 2000, p. 287)*

These tensions arise from concerns that are common throughout the social sciences, such as: How to accomplish objective accounts of social events? What are the issues that need to be theorized? How do these relate to matters pertaining to political and ethical struggles? How to give voice to the marginal and the oppressed? They also arise from existing disciplinary traditions caring about distinct problems, such as psychologists invested in the nature of subjective lives, or sociologists striving to challenge racism and misogyny.

Far from seeing these tensions as superfluous or needing to be "resolved," we think that they stir the vitality of the social sciences and generate, always anew, some of the most significant problems social scientists face. Consequently, we think that it matters for social scientists to reflect on these questions and to grapple with the social, historical, and political issues that they raise. The reflections we have in mind do not get addressed by listing a series of beliefs or by naming schools of thought one follows; instead, we see value in reflections that stimulate new perspectives or bring established practices into productive question. In this chapter we attempt to contribute this kind of reflection with a focus on issues that have been raised by Streeck (2013).

Streeck pointed out that the expansion of the phenomena of interest beyond speech tended to emphasize and preserve visual attention to human interaction:

> Naturalistic research on human interaction has primarily conceived the human body and its movements in visual terms. After the initial concentration on verbal interaction, conversation analysts who investigated an ever-expanding range of embodied phenomena of interaction primarily conceived of these as visual conduct.
> *(Streeck, 2013, p. 69)*

Like analyses based on transcriptions of audio records, visual analyses can maintain a certain distance to the subjects in the recorded scenes, as if the analysts were scrutinizing them from afar and paying attention exclusively to aspects that can be unambiguously traced in terms of visible, physical events, which in many research traditions seems necessary to satisfy conditions of scientific rigor:

> How we can study the moment-by-moment production of intersubjective understanding and concerted action in a fashion that accounts for phenomena presumed to be "internal" such as kinesthesia (the subject's perception of his or her own movements) while maintaining *rigorous standards of observability*, is a question that is beyond the scope of this paper and will have to be answered by future research.
> *(Streeck, 2013, p. 70)*

This chapter is an effort to address Streeck's question on the basis of our ongoing research practices. The question is related not only to matters of empirical validation but also to the determination of what research questions are deemed acceptable. In his analysis of an interaction between Hussein, a car dealer, and Richie, a customer and friend, Streeck writes:

> Richie's tactile gesture in this sequence conveys a certain intimacy and affirms a long-standing bond between them (they have known each other for years), but in combination with her positioning, locking Hussein between herself and the car, she also "corners" him and thereby frames the structure of the dialogue as a forced interrogation. In other words, the participation framework is reinforced by the way her position constrains his movements. We may also explain Hussein's turning away from her and his pained facial expression as indicators of the physical and emotional discomfort that Richie causes him.
> *(Streeck, 2013, p. 78)*

Are we allowed to describe a certain gesture as manifesting intimacy? What is the role of our familiarity with the actors? Is the parenthetical remark ("they have known each other for years") necessary or an accessory to seeing "bonding" in Richie's gesture? Is cornering someone something that we can identify independently of the content of this exchange (i.e., asking for information that a client is not entitled to, although a friend might be)? Is a pained facial expression an "indicator"? If so, what does it indicate? Are face expressions objective data? Streeck strives to address them by describing a minimal ground of agreement:

> Of course, these are only interpretive glosses of the behavioral dynamics of the interaction, *betraying the difficulty of giving precise and verifiable accounts of embodied meaning*. And yet, this methodological problem notwithstanding, *there can be no doubt* that intercorporeal maneuvers and defenses such as Richie's and Hussein's induce bodily sensations and affective responses and constrain how social meaning in interaction is physically experienced.
> (Streeck, 2013, p. 78, italics added)

To what extent are bodily sensations, affective responses, and physical experiences legitimate subjects of research on interaction? How might we push analyses like Streeck's to move beyond the mere *fact* of physical-affective experiences in social interaction by working to explore, unravel, and interpret their *nature*? To explore this and other questions we cited above, we examine an interaction from video data on a school field trip to a science museum.

## Tessellations and Shamanism at the Hmong House

The video corpus from which we selected this case study consists of naturalistic recordings of a 5th-grade summer school field trip to the Science Museum of Minnesota. Upon entering the museum, the children divided into groups and they were given worksheets to define and guide their activities. Museum educators were pilot-testing various kits for school groups that aimed to integrate mathematical ideas and modes of inquiry into the museum's existing galleries. The participants in this study were engaging in worksheet activities around the theme of tessellations, developed particularly for a region of the collections galleries that included real and replicated art and artifacts from Hmong culture. The tessellations worksheet consisted of four pages, shown in Figures 17.1–17.4.

Two Hmong girls, Evelyn and Sylvia, are the participants in the group that we follow. Evelyn, Sylvia, and their teacher, Ruth, have been sitting on the floor. Ruth has been helping them read the worksheet, as English is not their first language. After reading the worksheet, the group prepares to follow the worksheet prompt to search for and record tessellations within the collections galleries. Evelyn points to a region of the collections gallery where she sees "a lot of patterns": the *Hmong House*, a life-size replica of a traditional Hmong home.

Objectivity, Interpretation, & Experience in IA   463

> **Archeologists** are scientists and historians who discover things about past cultures through the materials they leave behind, for example, pottery, clothes, buildings, tools. They study people of the past, not dinosaurs or fossils.
>
> Things often have patterns or designs on them, and the patterns can be repeated over and over on the object. Patterns may have special meanings to the people who made them, so there is a lot that an archeologist can learn from studying patterns.
>
>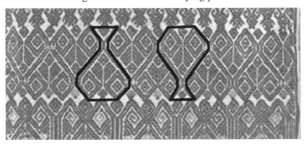

**FIGURE 17.1**   Tessellations Worksheet, Page 1.

> A special kind of repeated pattern is a tessellation.
>
> Tessellation is a math term. It is a pattern of closed shapes that completely covers a surface.
>
> **Examples of Tessellation:**
>
>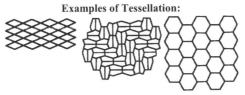
>
> There are no overlaps or gaps in a tessellation.
>
> Overlaps          Gaps
>
>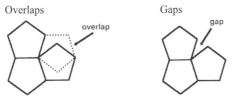

**FIGURE 17.2**   Tessellations Worksheet, Page 2.

When Evelyn, Sylvia, and Ruth enter the Hmong House, Evelyn quickly breaks away from the group, boisterously darting toward a replica of a Hmong altar. Ruth and Sylvia attempt to regain Evelyn's attention, beckoning her to come see a tessellation they have found on another a quilt hanging on a wall next to the entrance of the Hmong House. But Evelyn's interest in the altar proves too magnetic, and Ruth and Sylvia are ultimately drawn towards the altar as well.

> Like the examples on side 1, tessellation patterns use the same shape to cover the whole space. If the shapes are colored or have smaller patterns within, the overall pattern can be very complicated and beautiful.
>
> African Cloth
>
>
>
> In this example the tessellation shape is a rectangle (outlined in black). Each rectangle is colored differently creating a beautiful pattern.
>
> Maya Cloth
>
>
>
> In this example the tessellation shape is the fish-like shape (outlined in black). It is flipped upside down every other step to fill the space completely.
>
> This pattern only goes across a single row. The other rows are other shapes.
>
> **Mandan/Hidatsa Burden Basket**
>
>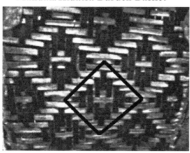
>
> In this example the tessellation shape is a rhombus (outlined in black). The pattern is made from two different colors of reeds woven together.
>
> **Hmong Collar**
>
>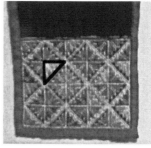
>
> In this example the tessellation shape is a triangle (outlined in black). The triangle is reflected in many directions covering the entire space.

**FIGURE 17.3**  Tessellations Worksheet, Page 3.

When they arrive, Evelyn is energetically bouncing up and down on a bench positioned in front of the altar, chanting in a singsong voice syllables that we do not recognize. Ruth laughs a little, and then asks Evelyn if she sees any examples of tessellations on the Hmong altar. Evelyn readily replies yes, tracing over tessellated patterns on the altar with a finger atop the exhibit's protective glass. When Ruth asks her if she would like to draw those tessellations on her worksheet, Evelyn happily sets to work with pencil and worksheet, drawing the shapes of the tessellation she has just traced with her finger.

As Evelyn draws tessellations, she is interrupted twice. First, a classmate comes by and asks Evelyn what the altar is. Evelyn stops writing on her worksheet and gives an elaborate, whole-body response. She describes "Hmong people" who

> **TO DO**
>
> (1) Read the plastic covered sheet.
>
> (2) Find an object that has a tessellation pattern on it in the *Collections* gallery.
>
> (3) Draw a section of the pattern with the colored pencils in the box below.
>
> (4) OUTLINE the tessellation shape with a black line, like the examples on the plastic covered sheet.
>
> (5) Take a close look at your object, what shapes do you see? (circle ones you see)
> **Circle**           **Rectangle**                    **Square**
>
> **Pentagon** (five sides)          **Hexagon** (six sides)
>
> **Parallelogram** (2 pairs of parallel sides) **Rhombus** (4 equal sides)
>
> **Trapezoid** (1 pair of parallel sides)   **Kite** (2 pairs of equal sides)

**FIGURE 17.4**  Tessellations Worksheet, Page 4.

light candles at the altar and "say a little prayer so the ghosts don't come back and haunt them forever." She points out the candles on the altar that the Hmong would light and bounces her body up and down on the bench rhythmically with the words "say a little prayer." The classmate, perhaps unsure how to respond, walks away without comment and Evelyn returns to drawing tessellations.

Shortly after, Ruth sits down next to Evelyn on the bench. Although Evelyn now appears fully engrossed in her tessellations worksheet, Ruth asks her if she has been to a shaman's house before. This time Evelyn replies that her grandpa and grandma are shamans. Setting pencil and worksheet fully aside now, Evelyn engages in an even more elaborate description and enactment of the shamanic ritual, explaining how people like her grandpa move, chant, and arrange objects on the altar in order to help others who might be troubled by ghosts.

As Evelyn answers several follow-up questions from Ruth about her grandparents and the people who come to seek their assistance, another Hmong boy from the class arrives on the scene. He announces, "I know how to do this," and Evelyn responds, "I know how to do it too," bouncing up and down again on the bench in demonstration. Evelyn and the boy now take turns showing Ruth and a growing group of student onlookers what they know how to do. They each enact the role of the shaman again, now with exaggerated volume and increasingly dramatic physical performance.

Sylvia, who has left for other regions of the gallery for a few minutes, returns and sits on the bench in front of the altar as well. She gently taps a bouncing, chanting Evelyn on the shoulder as if to remind her of the mathematical task at hand, and Evelyn returns to drawing tessellations on her worksheet. In what follows, we explore several of the issues we raised in the introduction through a series of selected microanalytic episodes from this interaction. We present some interpretations of these episodes as a way of reflecting on our own analytic process in relation to the theoretical and methodological issues raised in the introduction.

## Episode 1: "now and you were anxious to go in here so let's see" (54 seconds)[1]

1   R: girls what we're looking for are examples of tessellations
2   (0.6)
3   So patterns
4   E: [ooh! Yeah I see a lot of patterns (see Figure 17.5)

**FIGURE 17.5** Evelyn follows up on Ruth's uttering of "patterns" by pointing towards the Hmong House with her right hand, holding a pen, as she starts walking towards that Hmong House.

5   R: now (see Figure 17.6) and you were anxious to go in here so let's see (see Figure 17.7)

**FIGURE 17.6**  Ruth and Sylvia turn toward the Hmong House following Evelyn's movement.

**FIGURE 17.7**  Ruth points to the Hmong House.

6 (7.3) ((*They walk inside the Hmong House*)) (see Figure 17.8)

**FIGURE 17.8** Upon entering into the Hmong House, Evelyn walks towards the altar.

7 R: Do you see the tessellations here? (see Figure 17.9)

**FIGURE 17.9** Ruth points to a tessellation bordering a quilt, which hangs on a wall. Then Sylvia calls Evelyn to look at it.

8 S: Evelyn? Evelyn?
9 R: Evelyn? Oh! (0.2) wel- ((*E ignores their calls, she stays sitting in front of the*
10 *altar*)) okay ((*R and S start walking towards E*)) let's take a quick look
11 (0.3)
12 E: nyung yang nee nee ((*singsong chanting*)) he hee hee ((*laughing*)) (see Figure 17.10)

Objectivity, Interpretation, & Experience in IA    **469**

**FIGURE 17.10** Ruth and Sylvia walk toward Evelyn as she looks back to them while singsong chanting and moving up and down on the bench she sits on.

13  R: ahhh ((*laughing exhale*))
14  (0.6)
15  R: so (0.9) d'you see? [um
16  E:                    [yeah
17  (0.6)
18  R: do you see some tessellations [here (see Figure 17.11)
19  E:                               [yeah
20  (0.2)

**FIGURE 17.11** The three of them look at the altar. Evelyn smiles and continues to bounce up and down slightly.

21  R: where
22  (0.3)
23  E: um right here (see Figure 17.12) (0.6) some (0.2) like right here?
24  (1.2)

**FIGURE 17.12**  Evelyn touches the acrylic panel in front of the altar, pointing at patterns cut on paper. The paper is hanging from the edge of the shelf. She circles her finger several times.

25  R: Do you want to draw that, on your clipboard?
26  ((*Evelyn sits with crossed legs and starts drawing*)) (see Figure 17.13)

**FIGURE 17.13**  Evelyn draws a pattern on her worksheet.

## Interpreting Episode 1: Reflections on Our Process

Some of the issues we were moved to grapple with as we watched Episode 1 arose from Evelyn being anxious to go into the Hmong House and, once inside, to sit in front of the altar. As soon as Ruth sets them out to look for patterns, Evelyn points at the Hmong House and says: "I see a lot of patterns" (Line 4) – even though all she could see at that point were the outside walls of the house, somehow she knew a little treasure of patterns was inside and was eager to show it to Ruth and Sylvia. We wondered about the nature of caring about something, as Evelyn does about the Hmong House. We further pondered how something such as the Hmong House becomes present not just by virtue of physically occupying space, as an inert material thing, but, most prominently, by how it matters to those who notice it. In our watching, it was as if the Hmong House was whimsically clamoring to Evelyn "Come in, I have what you are looking for!" Ruth expressed diverse aspects of what she cared for. A conspicuous one was making sure that the girls find and copy tessellations (Lines 1, 7, 19, and 26), but also being responsive and attentive to what seemed to matter to the girls. The latter is manifest in her turning bodily towards the Hmong House (Line 5, Figures 17.6 and 17.7) as if anticipating the overall intent of Evelyn, or in leaving behind the tessellation around the quilt and walking, with Sylvia, near the altar (Lines 9–11, Figure 17.10). We sensed that in the same way that Evelyn managed to shift what mattered to Ruth, she also gave direction to what came to matter to us, as researchers. At some point, we connected our impressions about caring with the idea of a non-countable multiplicity, of the kind that has been so important for Bergson (1910) and Deleuze (2013). Their notion was of a multiplicity that cannot be accounted for or explained by listing separate items or factors. It does not make sense to list what one cares about as a discrete array of things. The foci of caring *drift* in tune with the circumstances, or rather, with the present and past circumstances of life. There is such drift in Ruth's turn toward the Hmong House and in our own questions.

The initial question at the forefront of our work had been how children approached mathematical ideas – tessellation in this case – in the course of their field trips to the museum. We weren't even aware that there was a Hmong House exhibition at the museum, nor did we anticipate a focus on cultural contributions of Hmong communities in diaspora, of which the one in St. Paul is a large one. It is not as if we just forgot the question about children's grasp of tessellation. But it got transformed into questions such as: What is the significance of Evelyn's tracing with her finger a tessellation *on the altar*? We do not know whether Evelyn saw a pattern that was, in fact, a tessellation (i.e., covering a plane without gaps and overlaps), but such not-knowing did not preclude, in us, a surge of seemingly new questions about tessellation and learning about it. After all, like all visual patterns, tessellations can be profoundly expressive. Could tessellations express some of the emotional or spiritual tones of an altar? And if this is what someone grasps from it, does she learn anything about tessellation? What makes something mathematical? How does emotional engagement play in mathematics learning? Could it be that what was going to be memorable for Evelyn about tessellations was that they were to be found in the Hmong House? Aside from the ability to articulate its definition, what is the significance of tessellation being memorable?

In Line 13 and Figure 17.10, Evelyn is joyously seeing that Ruth and Sylvia are nearing her in front of the altar. She not only smiles to them but also chants and waves her body up and down. Does our attribution of a feeling, such as joyousness, cross a boundary between objective description and subjective interpretation? It is straightforward to note that Evelyn turns toward Ruth and Sylvia (see Figure 17.10), but joyously? Analytic traditions sometimes make a tacit distinction akin to the philosophical difference between primary and secondary properties. The size of an apricot is a primary quality, its taste a secondary one. Everyone would coincide regarding its size, but not its taste; perhaps similarly to how Evelyn's turning toward Ruth and Sylvia in Figure 17.10 would count as an objective fact, but her joy would not. Furthermore, perhaps we tend to use transcription notations as records of primary properties, filtering out feelings and preserving the facts of body motion and sound patterns. Unless supplemented, this filtering results in an irretrievable loss, because no matter how much detail gets documented about, say, the physical traits of a facial expression or the pitch of an utterance, it will never make up for the value of a simple description such as "she looks sad."

Such filtering creates complicated puzzles, like the one Streeck has articulated so well in relation to the "physical and emotional discomfort" that Richie causes Hussein, a matter that betrays "*the difficulty of giving precise and verifiable accounts of embodied meaning*" (Streeck, 2013, p. 78, italics added). Is felt joy accountable in a precise and verifiable manner? In everyday life we are all constantly ascertaining our and others' feelings, and the need to verify feelings, even to oneself, often arises. Habitually, we verify feelings by reviewing life circumstances in an effort to make certain feelings more or less reasonable to be had. Do these methods satisfy precise and verifiable standards? What are these standards? We can guess that the standards in question are those of authoritative quantitative measurements. It is possible that some aspects of intense emotions (e.g., intense fear) could be ascertained as primary properties by means of brain images or physiological signals, but this is not the case of feelings in general; and we suspect that the issue preventing feelings from such treatment is not a matter of methods but of their nature. Like the aesthetic value of a piece of music or the pictorial quality of a painting, which are unsuitable for authoritative quantitative measurements, feelings are not reducible to isolatable physical and physiological processes because they fully mesh with the present, past, and anticipated circumstances of life. One not uncommon response to the difficulty of giving "precise and verifiable accounts" of feelings is to exclude them from research inquiries. The consequence is a kind of tunnel vision, as if literary criticism, for instance, were to be exclusively constrained to number of pages, word frequencies, chronologies, and the like. Under these tunnel visions, one is likely to find and validate regularities (e.g., rhythmic patterns in a type of music or turn sequences in conversations), which is a worthwhile endeavor per se, but not one conducive to grasping their psychological-social-historical significance or to opening up new ways of thinking.

Based on everyday practices to ascertain feelings, we do not hesitate to claim that, in all likelihood, Evelyn feels joyous in Line 13. Sometimes we are unable to ascertain feelings because of the insufficiency of the recorded videos, other times because we are unknowing of the circumstances, or because the participants belong to communities and cultures exceedingly foreign to us. More often than not, a range of possible feelings rather than a single one appears more or less likely. But this diversity does not imply an essential relativism or the sense that anything can be the case upon our arbitrary choices. Many other descriptions, other than joy, could be chosen for Evelyn's feelings in Line 13, but claiming, for instance, that Evelyn was disappointed at Ruth and Sylvia joining her next to the altar would be practically untenable.

The contingent but consequential choices that we make are not those about the attribution of feelings but those dealing with the research matters we grapple with. We could choose, say, to examine methods that participants put into practice in the course of their interactions. Through Lines 8–10, we could specify a method that Evelyn uses to bring the altar to the attention of Ruth and Sylvia: *repeatedly ignore their calls* to examine the quilt; or, through Lines 20–25, to specify to others the presence of certain patterns: *touch and trace* them with a pointing finger. Instead, we choose to grapple with whatever is new and surprising, in one way or another, for us, such as, in this case, the intermingling of a mathematical idea with Hmong Shamanism (Lines 16–27). Hmong Shamanism will come to the forefront in Episode 2.

## *Episode 2: "That's my grandpa" (47 seconds)*

28  ((*R sits next to Evelyn while she draws on her worksheet*)) (7.0)
29  R: so have you been – have you been to a shaman's (.) house (.) where you
30  E: that's my grandpa (0.3)
31  R: is a shaman? (0.8) ((*Evelyn assents with her head*)) awesome!
32  E: u:m (1.0) my grandma's a shaman too they u::m like (.) if you (.) like say (.)
33  they're not s'posed to – people are not (see Figure 17.14) s'posed to sit by 'em
34  (0.2) and they say a little prayer and they say that (.) like (see Figure 17.15) help them (.)

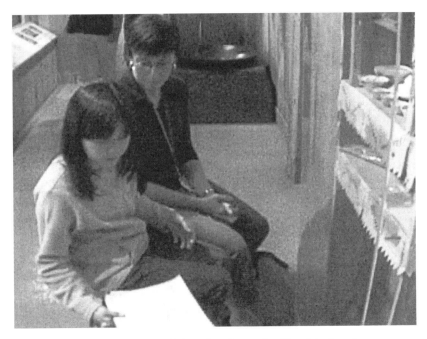

**FIGURE 17.14** Evelyn puts the clipboard on her right side of the bench.

**FIGURE 17.15** Evelyn bounces up and down while keeping her hands towards the altar.

Objectivity, Interpretation, & Experience in IA **475**

35  E: like they light that (see Figure 17.16) (.) they u:m (.) they put (see Figure 17.17)
    (.) um (.) all this right here (.)
36  and they go ((*Evelyn briefly enacts the "little prayer" body motion*))

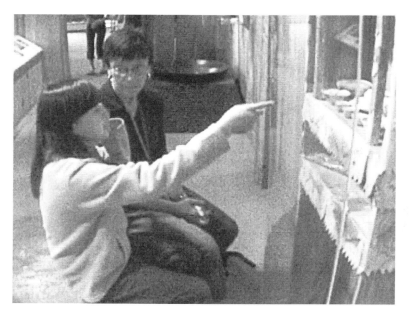

**FIGURE 17.16**  Evelyn points at some element in the altar, possibly a candle.

**FIGURE 17.17**  Evelyn sweeps her arm along the elements on the shelf of the altar.

37  R: so it looks a lot like this? (1.7) ((*R sweeps her hand on the altar*))
38  E: (then) (See Figure 17.15) they um (.) ((*Evelyn grabs the clipboard and puts it on her lap*))
39  they pray so the (.) ghosts don't come back to them? (.) so they don't get haunted
40  (0.9)
41  R: so people will come to the:m [to
42  E: [it's like – like gho:sts? They come to 'em?
43  And like haunt them forever? (0.2) because they did something to them

## *Interpreting Episode 2: Reflections on Our Process*

Evelyn's explanations of what shamans do to help people not to get haunted were striking to us in many ways. She literally animates the altar, so that what at first might have seemed to us a piece of furniture holding an unusual collection of things becomes an essential part of a ritual with social and metaphysical ramifications. Her chanting and rhythmic motion is fully placed in relation to the altar: having put aside her clipboard, she positions herself to face it in a characteristic body posture with her arms lifted. Evelyn made clear that people should not sit next to the shaman (Line 33), granting Ruth the right to stay next to her but with the caveat that she is not supposed to. Now we can make sense of the slight up and down motion Evelyn had enacted in Figure 17.10: Evelyn's ritual motion is a manner of making the altar an altar, for her and for others. Often we call for something by means of a body enactment, such as when one asks for a key by gesturing the action of turning a key in the air, or for a comb by mimicking combing one's hair. Far from a passing curiosity, this type of bodily enactment might be crucial to imagining. There is a vast difference between just being told, say, "this is an altar used for…" and being shown bodily what you do in front of it. Thinking about these differences led us to pursue questions about imagination and body enactment and about the collective nature of imagining, the latter having to do with our sense that we have become able to vividly imagine what Evelyn's grandparents do when working as shamans.

Evelyn's explanations to Ruth prompted us to wonder about Hmong Shamanism and how it had evolved in the Hmong diaspora; seeking ways to learn about this, we partnered with an anthropologist, Don Duprez, who is completing his dissertation on Hmong communities in the Western United States. We are just beginning to grasp the cultural origins of Evelyn's "little prayer" and her account of haunting ghosts. We have learned, for instance, that her body motion evokes riding a horse towards mythical locations. The location of the altar inside the Hmong House and each of the elements on it convey stories and visions that were unknown to us. Perhaps many of them were unknown to Evelyn as well, but this does not make them less relevant, because cultural practices and historical trajectories circulate through her and her actions independently of her theorizing about them.

## Discussion

In trying to characterize our ways of navigating research practices, as illustrated by the ongoing analysis of the Hmong House episodes, it may be important to start by making salient that we work to avoid the "kind of theoretical imperialism … of the critics whose theoretical apparatus gets to stipulate the terms by reference to which the world is to be understood" (Schegloff, 1997, p. 167). We neither attempt to fit the interactions among Evelyn, Ruth, Sylvia, and the Hmong House's components along some coding scheme that we design, nor do we try to make them address questions emanating from our own pre-set worldviews, such as ascertaining, say, whether Evelyn understands the concept of tessellation based on what we know tessellations to be. Instead, we strive to open ourselves into questioning what we think tessellations are and how they relate to all other cultural expressions. In other words, rather than imposing our own categories, our practice is to bracket them, to allow our ideas and ourselves to be destabilized or transformed by our interpretive engagement with the events caught on video.

During a couple of professional development events for science museum staff – educators, exhibit designers, and evaluators – we showed the videos of the Hmong House episode. In subsequent discussions, participants argued that the field trip design appeared unsuccessful because, rather than learning about tessellations, Evelyn ended up performing for others how the altar is used. From this viewpoint, the didactic goal of the activity had not been achieved. We think that this response is exactly a way of assessing the recorded interactions in terms of pre-set worldviews, the kind of "theoretical imperialism" that, for us, is important to resist. In contrast, the episode raised for us the possibility that, due to the life experiences of Evelyn and other Hmong children, participants might have gained a memorable sense of the presence of tessellations in enthralling ritual performances, and that there may be other ways of thinking about tessellations, hitherto unknown to us, connected to healing and cosmic events. This is our attempt to elucidate a line of flight towards opening up new vistas on tessellations in particular, and mathematics learning in general.

On the other hand, we experience a complex relationship to the principle that "the task of the analyst is not to interpret the world but to study how the world has already been interpreted by participants" (Wetherell, 2007, p. 670). We *could* claim, for example, that Evelyn, as a member of certain community, holds a definite interpretation of the Hmong House and what it contains, and that our task is to figure it out. It does seem to be a straightforward and innocent claim. Some of the snags associated with it begin to be suggested by our impulse to partner with an anthropologist with expertise in the history, politics, and sociology of Evelyn's community. A worldview is not owned by individuals, and much of what it consists of is buried in a history, mythology, and geography that members of a community may not only be unaware of, but that are graspable just through organic differentiation with other worldviews, such as ones we, the analysts, live in. In other words, it seems to us that the task is not to display Evelyn's worldview as something that exists out there, like a completed whole open to inspection, but to transform our worldviews, and hopefully the worldviews of our readers (which might include members of Evelyn's community), led by the thought-provoking disruption that Evelyn performed at the Hmong House.

In any case, it is clear to us that we do not possess capabilities allowing us to inspect members' methods *as such*, as if we were a "tabula rasa" on which they get written. We cannot grasp a member's perspective other than in how it alters our perspective, which implies that the actual "data" is an encounter of perspectives and their mutual, interdependent drifts. This, of course, goes back to the point that what interests us is not to diagnose whether Evelyn "gets" tessellations or not, but to allow her to provoke us into rethinking what tessellations are. It also reflects that we aim not to identify regularities, techniques, or ethno-methods on their own, but to adumbrate new ways of thinking about learning, teaching, exhibit design, diversity, and all that pertains to the growth of living interactions. The practices that are emerging from our ongoing work should perhaps be named not so much "interaction-conversation analysis," but "interaction-conversation synthesis," because the whole effort is to study interactions very closely (i.e., with nuance and detail) for the sake of complicating all of our life experiences in playful and creative ways.

## Note

1  Numbers in parentheses indicate pause duration in seconds. Brackets mark overlapping speech. Italicized remarks enclosed in square brackets include descriptive commentary of prosodic features and non-verbal participation. (.) indicates noticeable pause. Words in parentheses are guessed ones.

## References

Bergson, H. (1910). *Time and free will: An essay on the immediate data of consciousness*. London: George Allen & Unwin.

Billig, M. (1999). Whose terms? Whose ordinariness? Rhetoric and ideology in conversation analysis. *Discourse & Society*, 10(4), 543–558.

Deleuze, G. (2013). *Theory of multiplicities in Bergson*. Retrieved from http://deleuzelectures.blogspot.co.uk/2007/02/theory-of-multiplicities-in-bergson.html.

Garfinkel, H. (1991). Respecification: Evidence for logically produced, naturally accountable phenomena of order, logic, reason, meaning, method, etc. in and as of the essential haecceity of immortal ordinary society (I) – an announcement of studies. In G. Button (Ed.), *Ethnomethodology and the human sciences* (pp. 10–19). Cambridge, UK: Cambridge University Press.

Hall, R. (2000). Video recording as theory. In D. Lesh & A. Kelley (Eds.), *Handbook of research design in mathematics and science education* (pp. 647–664). Mahwah, NJ: Lawrence Erlbaum.

Ochs, E. (1979). Transcription as theory. In E. Ochs & B. Schieffelin (Eds.) *Developmental pragmatics* (pp. 43–72). New York: Academic Press.
Schegloff, E. A. (1997). Whose text? Whose context? *Discourse & Society*, 8(2), 165–187.
Streeck, J. (2013). Interaction and the living body. *Journal of Pragmatics*, 46, 69–90.
Weatherall, A. (2000). Gender relevance in talk-in-interaction and discourse. *Discourse & Society*, 11(2), 286–288.
Wetherell, M. (2007). A step too far: Discursive psychology, linguistic ethnography and questions of identity. *Journal of Sociolinguistics*, 11(5), 661–681.

# 18

# THREE META-SCIENTIFIC MICRO-ESSAYS

*Andrea A. diSessa*

This chapter is a sequence of three turn★s, micro-essays about the KAIA project. A *turn*★ is a written edit/extension of a turn in a conversation. The problem with conversations is you often don't get a chance to say all that pops into your head before your partner just walks away in boredom (or in shock – such long turns are not allowed in polite conversation). Nor do you get to "edit" what you said a few turns before, even if a much better formulation occurs to you.

On the other hand, a turn★ is unlike an essay, which is aimed at a more general audience (although the point of a turn★ is that others are intended to listen in), and about which one is supposed to have thought more carefully and covered some reasonable span of bases in terms of breadth of consideration and careful argumentation. But, a turn★ is certainly a turn (an "utterance") in Bakhtin's sense (Bakhtin, 1986).

Compared to a turn in a conversation, a turn★ is most certainly in the direction of an essay, but there is a good reason to resist making turn★s into essays. One point of a turn★ is to display heuristic, transient, and generative strategies of thinking that may never appear explicitly in an essay, but which may insightfully characterize community ways of thinking. They often bring to light influential considerations and ways of thinking that, for various reasons, just don't appear explicitly in the written scholarly record. For example, people don't often talk about their meta-scientific commitments.

Nobody expects turns in conversation to be complete and "correct" in anyone's careful estimation. Turn★s have that property too. Most nitpicking and searching for fatal flaws is probably a waste of time: "Don't bite my finger; look where I'm pointing."

## A Turn* on Intact: Approximate Modularity in Science

**Setting**: At one of the many face-to-face meetings during which contributors to this volume worked on our common agenda, I believe I heard the idea that studying fully intact human systems (such as the complex of situations that a professional encounters "at work," or studying a classroom or school culture) gives a kind of relevance, reality, and credibility that other, more "artificial" modes of study do not. Whether or not my interpretation was what was intended, I think this is an attractive idea, and it deserves consideration.

**Turn★**: On the one hand, almost all educational researchers want their results to apply to the real world of "intact" human systems, where we hope to find learning happening with large consequences for our civilization. On the other hand, "intact" sounds to me, at least in part, like a proxy for "natural," and the distinction between natural and artificial can be a slippery, even dangerous one.

"Natural food is best for you." Good heuristic, maybe. But a fair number of naturally occurring things – from mushrooms to minerals – can kill you. And, Nature is not so benevolent as to have made all the very best things for us, in just the right proportions.

Comparable questions about natural contexts in education research can be raised: Is any contemporary culture or interactive context really natural in any reasonable sense – or is it merely familiar? In complementary manner, does unfamiliar or unusual automatically mean unnatural? Educationally, aren't we aiming precisely to design new (hence "artificial") cultures and interactive patterns that have better properties for learning than the ones that have evolved "naturally"? Many familiar everyday (intact) contexts are toxic to learning. They don't have a lot of face value for instantiating, for study, the kind of learning we want. Isn't adaptation to the not-everyday a hallmark of human capacities? Isn't the adaptation process, per se, and not just its result, an important study?

Let me start a slightly more systematic inquiry: What does "intact" mean, and why and in what ways should it have force in directing our research?

Analytically, one might well ask, "What are the *boundaries* of an intact situation?" Every situation has important larger embeddings (and parallel-level connections, too, such as home-to-school connections), so studying only intact systems seems to me to be unworkable if understood literally. It would mean that we must study the whole history of human civilization in order to comprehend, say, a classroom. I'm actually happy to concede the fact that everything is connected to everything, at least heuristically. A case of particular interest to me is the fact that a lot of our present civilization – and certainly schooling – is embedded in powerful, historically and socially constituted frames called "literacies." As researchers, our own scientific work is similarly framed both by literacies but also by other historically constituted framing practices and assumptions. But can't we get along reasonably (I think we do!), if not optimally, without fully understanding those?

What exactly are we doing, then, when we study "intact" systems? When might systems be regarded as not intact, and with what consequences?

I don't think there is a deep mystery here, really. We are always studying some slice of full reality that we have some reason to believe is, in some respects at least, loosely coupled with its larger or neighboring system components. We have a sense of the local dynamic[1] that allows us to see important things, even if we simply must admit the influence of a larger scale that we suppress, in some respects, "for present purposes." AND, I think we also believe that we can "proxy" for some of those broader nestings and connections, without fully studying them just in this moment. So, for example, as much as it is a valid insight to say that one cannot really understand a classroom without understanding the larger societal embeddings and assumptions, I do not reject the research of people who think they can see interesting things going on in a classroom that are not (fully) determined by those structures, but instead can be causally connected to locally observable things. We can follow the quasi-independent "causal threads" of the local context. Perhaps we should even select a different context to study in order to emphasize the causal thread of interest, and minimize the influence of other such threads.

Science is about approximately independent systems, or about approximately taking into account the effects of embeddings and neighboring systems of our focus. We know roughly what "schooling" is in a large-scale and historically constituted sense, and we are not tempted to try to explain, locally, how those conditions were created. Neither the teacher nor anyone else in the school is responsible for the *fact* of classrooms.

This is certainly not to say no one should study a field as a whole, perhaps specifically in order to frame what happens in more local settings. It is not to say that we can *always* separate effectively. It's just that we simply cannot study all nestings, all threads, and all wider connections at once. We need to find a niche, and manage it, as best we can, with respect to contingencies that are just impossible to focus on all at once. We need to hypothesize quasi-independent causal threads and pursue them as we can. And we certainly need to accept that our assumptions of rough independence and proxying are subject to contest.

Perhaps the most interesting – and possibly trickiest – quasi-independent subsystems are those that exist in the same phenomenological focus, "causal threads," as characterized above. Intuitively, we divide lines of influence in everyday flow – and I don't think this is initially problematic. While I strongly believe that affect can sometimes importantly influence learning, I also believe that some aspects of learning are *sometimes* "independently causal." A confident individual (a judgment we do need to make) can solve a problem or not usually because of his knowledge, not because of his overt affect. Failure to solve a problem in general relativity can usually (but not always!) be convincingly "blamed" on missing knowledge, not interfering affect.[2]

Allow me to get some distance and perspective by taking a look at intact and non-intact in another domain, where intact has a strong and sensible meaning: studying biology, the science of life.

Studying intact life is certainly a good thing to do. But does that rule out dissecting deceased creatures, where the processes of life are definitively not intact? Isn't "I wonder what that thing does?" a good starter for humans trying to understand how bodies work? I believe this is just how some early biology (anatomy) worked.

Similarly, one does chemistry experiments as part of the enterprise of understanding life. It turns out that chemistry is "the machinery" of life. It is really important to understand the Krebs Cycle, and biologists did not figure that out entirely by studying intact life. That study involved some really "bizarre" contexts (e.g., chemistry laboratories) far away from the relevant intact (live) things. The researchers involved might not even have thought they were doing "life"! Yet, they made powerful contributions. Taking this as a rough analogy, I, as a KA type, may appear more like a chemist and the IA types are more like the biologists in the conventional sense. (Perhaps… although this is certainly not a good mapping in all or even many respects; I hope it's good enough for present purposes.) A relevant observation is, however, that biologists and chemists get along fine. Neither trouble to deny the other's methods, or even assert that their heuristics and techniques are apt for the other. Both enterprises have their own sensibility, and, in fact, both the people and their enterprises collaborate wonderfully. There are even biochemists!

Let's think a bit more about almost-separable subsystems, causal threads, proxying, and related tactics in the service of biology. We remove from the body and culture tissue, or bacteria, that are part of the bodily process of disease. Clearly we do not learn *all* the things about the intact system, such as the etiology of the disease. But, we have learned not to expect that. Instead, we use *some* of the things we learn from the separated study to implicate *some* of the characteristics of the intact system.

Ecology is another example domain. Surely we want to look at intact systems. But, as far as I know, ecologists do not carp that a non-ecologist would want to study certain animals out of the wild, for example, to understand their metabolisms. A nice example is coming to understand hyenas' processing of the calcium they ingest from grinding bones of prey. It turns out that hyenas and their processing of calcium play an important role in the giraffe's life cycle. So, why do you often find giraffes and hyenas together? Do you think it is more likely that giraffe populations follow hyenas, or vice versa? The thread of calcium metabolism, collection, and distribution becomes highly relevant to certain particulars of the intact ecological system.

Should we close off experiments on cognitive capacities of animals (e.g., consider the experiments synthesized in Call & Tomasello, 2008) because the studies do not take place in the wild? Of course, there is plenty to worry about in these tentative separations, and it is good to look through the literature for a litany of things to be concerned about. But we are all more or less involved in the same problematic of "relevant things we have somehow accidentally excluded," as much as we might want to be exempted from it.

To synthesize, no one knows with any certainty the absolute and non-violable separations that we cannot make for the purposes of research, the connections that *cannot* be severed for productive independent study. The history of science in developing quasi-independent threads that can be productively studied without "naturally" co-present threads is compelling.

My turn★ on clinical interviewing follows up on these ideas in a bit more detail in that particular context. I talk about some important causal threads that are unlikely to be well handled without separating them from everyday, intact circumstances.

## A Turn* on Modeling and Reality: The Question of "Punctual" Knowledge Elements

**Setting and Preface**: Throughout history, debates have arisen about the ultimate nature of thinking and what we can say about that. In recent history, for example, debates arose concerning whether symbolic artificial intelligence had any cogency at all. Newell and Simon (1976) said that intelligence was, with minor caveats, precisely symbolic computation, which takes place, usually, in the head, but which could easily be situated in computers. On the other hand, others (e.g., Dreyfus & Dreyfus, 1986) maintained that rules, the infrastructure of much of AI, were external things – things one read or was taught about – and real expertise could never be represented in that way. Searle (1980) seems to want to do away with the mind altogether and replace it with an understanding of brain (neural) processes. Generally, I find most assertions about the essential nature of thinking unconvincing. I feel we should look carefully to see what different levels and types of description have to contribute to the larger program, and in what way.

At one KAIA meeting, I perceived some claims about the core nature of thinking (or possibly just intuitive thinking) that make the idea of p-prims (for example) implausible. They reminded me of historical discussions, and I wanted to write a brief meta-theoretical statement of my position.

**Turn★**: How do we square the idea of discrete, *punctual* ("point-like" in duration and in effect) knowledge elements, such as p-prims, with the fuzzy, meandering impressions we have concerning our own intuitive ideas? Those impressions are never sharp and precise, so how can the underlying knowledge have those characteristics?

Here are some thoughts:

### *Why can't we imagine that there are some more or less punctual elements of thought?*

The KiP paradigm that nurtured and was nurtured by the study of p-prims assumes a great variety of kinds of knowledge. P-prims are a very particular class, and they were always explicitly marked as *not* defining extended flow, but momentary-but-critical judgments. How and why would one want to rule out that such things exist, even if they are not the dominant thing going on in extended thinking?

## P-prims are explicitly a model, which, as I frequently say,[3] will definitively break down at some point.

The good thing about the model is that it has had a considerable number of successes over two or three decades: explaining episodes of reasoning of many students; explaining more precisely than most accounts how people learn from reuse of prior knowledge; constituting a critical focal point in the argument against assumptions of narrowness, inflexibility, and unreasonable coherence in student intuitive thinking; mapping consequential differences among students, which are very often completely ignored; …

## Even if p-prims are put forward as punctual entities, this is a benign and very familiar modeling fiction.

Talking about p-prims as punctual is very much like narrative forms of exposition where an evidently continuous plenum of activity is represented as discrete, distinct "events." He went to the store; THEN he bought a soda; THEN he came home. Obviously, stages or events blend into one another and the narrative is (Rashomon-like) only one way of parsing.

Consider, in a bit more detail, the following example: "The earthquake caused the book to fall off the shelf." This is an example of what I call "elliptical causality" because the bare causality is extremely schematic: Punctual event $A$ (earthquake) caused punctual event $B$ (book falling). But, everybody can and often does imagine the earthquake slowly building over seconds, the shelf simultaneously rattling more and more, and the book very gradually bumping along toward the edge. Even the final fall can easily be re-imagined as a "slow and continuous" event. To say "the earthquake caused the book to fall off the shelf" does not deny more continuous views. It's a perspective, used for convenience and parsimony, and it does not in any way rule out non-punctual interpretations.

If p-prims are viewed as elliptical descriptions of more continuous occurrences – for easy discussion – what could be the problem? We do this every day, and refine at need. Two conditions play in. First, at the level of consideration that has led to p-prims' success, we have not been *forced* to the continuous level. Second, the continuous level is *very difficult* to elaborate, and I do not think we are ready to take on modeling that seriously. I avoid moves I think are probably proper if I think they are premature, given the state of the art. I believe one takes science where one can get it and should not refuse to do anything before one can do it all perfectly.

*I never believed p-prims were really punctual (even if talking about them in this way is innocuous, or a convenient modeling fiction).*

First, the submodeling language that I used in 1993 (connectionist systems) has a continuous dynamic. Again, I don't think trying to unpack the continuity in detail at this point is worth the trouble.

Second, many of the phenomena I discuss as "recognized" by p-prims quite evidently are "recognitions" across time; for example, patterns of amplitude (violent vs. gradually building bursts), and successions of events (push, move, …). To "recognize" these seems obviously to incur directed attention managed over time. This is *not* a punctual event (except in the elliptical approximation).

I don't think I have ever written (at least I have not published) about the fact that I believe people can and do manage their attention so as to better promote and sense p-prims. (For a case, consider Jacob's attending to his own bodily motions in Kapon [this volume].) These activities spread the "event" out further in time and implicate nearly simultaneous, enabling processes.

For the record, there is a similar issue with respect to p-prims' nature as "primitive explanations." That is, people (students) treat them as bedrock, atoms, as "all there is to say." This is another kind of "punctual" property to which critics of p-prims react. As a matter of fact, p-prims are only locally primitive in this sense. People learn by reconsidering, unpacking their bedrock, or shifting it. So, this punctual primitiveness is only local in time, "for present purposes." This non-punctual aspect is actually built explicitly into the theory in virtue of the fact that learning happens; primitives become non-primitive, for example.

My modeling attitude is that one should "correct rather than reject." If you think the modeling language is too poor, for example, in this punctual way, please correct and extend. You can thus build on existing insights (which I will defend) in directions I have no a priori reason to exclude. In fact, recent work of mine has brought clarity to me concerning certain aspects of the p-prim model that definitively need extension to deal with specific and empirically tractable phenomena.[4] I am, in fact, proud that cycles of extension and improvement have been a core part of my own research program (see diSessa, Sherin, & Levin, this volume).

I do suspect that people sometimes look too exclusively for categorical ways to dismiss other points of view rather than to build on their insights. That is probably not a good thing, although I am sure I do this myself on occasion. If people think I believe p-prims are flatly punctual and that property is essential to the model, they are not making a good assumption.

## Tarred with a Clean Brush: An Update in the Continuing Discussion on the Viability of Clinical Interviewing in Studies of Learning

**Setting**: One of my IA colleagues recently commented that we (some of us in particular, but also, by extension, the IA and KA communities) have been participating in a 20-year-long conversation about the relationship between IA and KA. During that time, a leitmotif has been a persistent critical attitude in the IA community toward clinical interviewing as a research methodology. This turn★ is a response to a few particular criticisms that continue to show up during the KAIA project, both in somewhat formal settings (conference presentations) and more informal discussion. I also broach here the topic of how I think we can make the best progress going forward.

Before turning to particulars, I'd like briefly to recount features of my own history of use of clinical interviews. This will set a general context but also constitute a platform that will concretize and prepare for some issues I take on later in this turn★.

**A Thumbnail History:** When I began studying student knowledge using clinical interviewing, the general focus was already clear to a fairly large community of researchers: Students' "prior conceptions" have a dramatic effect on student learning. A range of methodologies had already been used. Paper-and-pencil tests were common, but many researchers also used clinical interviews. A notable mode of both discovery and pedagogical use can be illustrated in the work of high-school teacher and researcher Jim Minstrell (e.g., Minstrell, 1982). In his own instruction, Minstrell had noticed many particulars of the phenomenon of prior conceptions and had simultaneously built various classroom practices to engage them productively (e.g., in "benchmark lessons," diSessa & Minstrell, 1998). As early as the mid to late 1980s, there were hundreds of articles on students' prior conceptions (Pfundt & Duit, 1988).

The phenomenon was also clear to me in my own experience as an instructor of high-school and beginning university physics. As a practitioner, I had some of my own ways of integrating a respect for the phenomenon with what I hoped was good instruction.

In order to explore the phenomenon carefully, I undertook clinical study of students' thinking, which is described in process and outcome in the KA introduction to this book (diSessa, Sherin, & Levin, this volume). In short, this work rejected the most common framing of prior conceptions – as definitively wrong and interfering with instruction – and it gave a more focused view of the generally positive "spin" on "misconceptions" that Minstrell had pursued in his instructional work.

Fast-forward more than two decades: What was uncovered in that early work is still proving productive. In diSessa (2014), I produced a high-resolution analysis of a remarkable learning event where a classroom of students, without any direct instruction, invented and agreed on a model of thermal equilibration that is essentially indistinguishable from the normative model originally proposed by Isaac Newton. Readers can examine for themselves, but I think it is completely evident that the 2014 study simply could not have been performed without the clinical study, done over 20 years earlier. It turns out that a surprising number of knowledge elements and their detailed properties that were documented in that early work played an absolutely central role in the learning of that class. So, clinical work can set the ground (and has done so consistently) for understanding real-world, classroom-based learning.

I want to be clear on two facts. First, the overall arc is from naturalistic observation of potentially important phenomena to focused study under conditions that can expose more and better data, and back to the classroom. Second, I chose a contemporary example, long after the original clinical study, to emphasize how careful study can lead to long-term scientific capacities beyond what can be accomplished if we stay always in "natural" contexts that are suboptimal for scientific study of particular phenomena. The time gap between the original work and the present does not mean to imply that anyone waited 20 years to look at real-world learning. Indeed, even the original clinical paper referenced implicitly here (diSessa, 1993) contained a good deal of information about expected long-term progressions ("development," one of four top-level foci) in student learning.

Most of my current work is rooted in designing, implementing, and studying classroom interventions. Yet, clinical work still has strong affordances as a complementary method to careful analysis of classroom video, finding out things that one can almost never find in classroom data. What did a student really mean by some possibly confused and seemingly off-hand remark? How do individuals benefit, or not, from particular events in the classroom instruction?

A second recent piece of more "real-world" work (Kapon, this volume; Kapon & diSessa, 2012) involves one-on-one tutoring, which is often considered the "gold standard" of general instructional methods. (There is a huge body of literature on "tutoring as gold standard." Bloom, 1984, is an early and influential reference.) This work also builds on both the theory and particulars of my early work. It aims to track the learning trajectories of several students at a level of detail similar to my 2014 work, described above. Students were brought through an experiential curriculum designed by Brown and Clement (1989) by a one-on-one tutor/researcher who could also probe the students' level of confidence and other details of their thinking beyond what had been visible in the many more "distanced" studies Brown and Clement carried out. One of the main results of the study was to identify particulars in each student's "conceptual ecology" that made huge differences in (a) their trajectories of both belief and understanding during the instruction, and also in (b) the success or failure of the instruction as a whole. Accounting in detail for individual differences such as this, particularly in real-time data, is between rare and non-existent in other conceptual change research.

**The Big Picture:** The overall view that continues to be presented in critiques of clinical interviewing is that it is very likely ecologically invalid, full of interactional artifacts, and most certainly not "of the same fabric" as what goes on in real-world, intact environments: Clinical interviewers, since they do not understand interaction, do not understand the basic nature of what is happening in producing the displays of knowledge that they take to be "knowledge of the interviewee."

Before presenting some thoughts on how we can best make progress in this apparently stark difference of opinions between KA and IA practitioners, let me address some smaller issues that came up in KAIA discussions. The particulars mentioned here, quotes and paraphrases, were selected from comments by Reed Stevens and Rogers Hall at ICLS 2014 in a symposium concerning the KAIA project (Stevens & Hall, June 2014).

## Some Particulars

*"You can't make this stuff up."* Implicitly, one must look at real-world contexts to discover what is actually working in them. You will always be surprised.

It is an excellent thing to do to examine everyday (I suppose that is the operational criterion for "real-world") professional and other environments. Certainly, what one finds in "artificial" contexts like clinical interviewing does not come, automatically, with a pedigree for direct application to everyday instructional contexts.[5] But, real-world relevance of the phenomenon of misconceptions was already established in the minds of a very large community before my clinical studies got started. Students in classroom discussion, in homework problems, and in examinations (not to mention paper-and-pencil tasks and interviews designed to chart and further clarify the phenomenon) showed the same kinds of ideas. Any science instructor could, if they doubted the phenomenon, pull a few students aside and ask simple questions to expose surprising student thinking. This "easy access" was one of the important facts that brought prior conceptions to the attention of the instructional world. As I pointed out above, as a physics instructor, I had already taken (crude) note of the phenomenon and made (ad hoc) accommodations in my instructional practices. Minstrell (1982) had already integrated his similar take on prior conceptions with both their discovery in classrooms and some uses in everyday instruction.

So, the historical function of clinical interviewing, here, was not discovery of the basic phenomenon, but theoretical and empirical elaboration. That elaboration was a discovery of a different order, "discovering" an elaborated theory that could then be brought back to "real-world" contexts, as exemplified in my historical narrative above. In particular, I believe that naturalistic data is flatly unworkable in studying the details of students' prior conceptions, the details that allowed the discovery of p-prims. There is simply not enough density of data around particular conceptions, and everyday contexts don't provide sufficient and systematic variability of the context of use of those conceptions to get a good characterization of them.

P-prim analyses, like the two mentioned in my historical narrative, have also inspired instruction. Our standard mode of instruction of the topic involved in that surprising spontaneous construction of thermal equilibration by high-school students is really a more elaborated and scaffolded reconstruction of what those students originally did, essentially by themselves. And, as I mentioned, clinical "side-car" interviews are helping us to discover things that are happening in classrooms that are not clear or evident in those data alone.

The larger issue is simple but overwhelmingly important. One cannot examine a single methodology to deduce what researchers can or cannot get from it. Instead, one should examine the larger program of studies in which it is embedded, and its history and motivation. Clinical and naturalistic methods, and even instructional design, are combined in our work in multiple ways. A critique of clinical methods (only) as a proxy critique of the larger program does violence to the everyday and long-term practices of practitioners in a program of scientific research.

I want to push a little harder on the usefulness of the clinical context for raw discovery. I feel, for example, that I have learned a lot about the meaning of students' "epistemological beliefs" (e.g., diSessa, Elby, & Hammer, 2002) in ways other than observing learning in context. One interesting hypothesis that arose in the clinical context is that meta-linguistic knowledge also affects learning: Some students seem not to know the general nature of technical terms.

I think it is an interesting issue, without a foregone conclusion, to consider how the clinical context might discover things about professional practice that naturalistic study has failed to discover. In this agenda, one problem to overcome is that it is easy to present relevant phenomena in physics in the clinical context. It is less so, but hardly impossible (video of professionals at work?), with manifestly human interactional phenomena. In addition, professional practice involves self-conscious orientation and persistent effort toward very long-term and life-defining goals, which is not so salient in learning, say, freshman physics. But I do not consider this to be a sufficient reason to give up before trying. In fact, my overall attitude is that one doesn't know which methods and contexts might prove fruitful in which scientific pursuit before trying. Similarly, I believe the real-world application of ideas discovered in one context to other contexts just cannot be known in advance. Consider the critical practical value of number theory (cracking codes, creating secure ones) or group theory (understanding crystallography and the spectral structure of molecules), which were once proudly put forward as definitively useless (Hardy, 1940). I think those who seem to want to exclude, up front, the relevance of clinical contexts to the "real world" are swimming upstream in the larger scientific experience.

One more related comment before moving on: One should not confuse the data collection context with the methodology of analysis. What KA has to contribute to the study of real-world professional practice in the context of professional practice, for example, is not a foregone conclusion. In the chapter I co-authored with Levin (Levin & diSessa, this volume), we apply KA to the same real-world data that Stevens and Hall use for their Interaction Analysis. And our and their analyses most definitely intersect; they are not orthogonal or "merely" complementary.

"*Power asymmetry in the clinical context is a serious problem.*" (paraphrase) This has long been a refrain of critics of clinical interviewing. The problem with the critique is that it presumes things about clinical interviewing that are false. In particular, critics seem to assume that clinical interviews are about determining which of the normative concepts of the discipline a subject holds and, possibly, how well they understand those ideas. But that is, in my view, a bankrupt point of view of how one studies "prior conceptions," and I have written extensively against it. Without elaborating here, the point is, instead, to discover how subjects, students, make sense of things and to characterize that. Whether or not those ideas are normative barely ever enters into my clinical studies.

In a paper about the clinical method from a few years ago (diSessa, 2007), I wrote, "Interference from authority-dominated activity types can be expected to constitute a primary block to establishing [a sensible context in which to pursue clinical analysis of knowledge]." I then described the alternative power structure one seeks to create in a clinical context (the interviewee is and feels that they are the main or sole judge of the sensibility of their own ideas), described generally how one does that, and validated the process of one particular interviewee coming to take this position in response to my efforts to establish it.

Judgments of correct or incorrect, and the authority of normative conceptions, continue to be a topic in the following concern:

> If a research subject is monitoring an interviewer for when they have something right or wrong, or accurate enough or they are too vague, no matter how restrained or careful or skilled the interviewer may be, the possibility must be considered in all interaction that the knowledge on display has been influenced by that social interaction.

I don't mean to be flippant, but my instant and genuine reaction to that comment was, "Who doesn't know that?"[6] I am, in fact, not interested in how students read "what is proper physics" in the subtle reactions of interviewers or teachers, nor very much in how they reconstruct their own ideas based on evaluative inputs of any sort concerning normative understanding.[7] I have found some subjects (just a few) are initially attentive to my (they suppose) judgment about the correctness of their ideas – although many simply don't know that I know much physics at all. But the fact is I am pretty much *not* interested in normativity in any respect, and I believe that I provide massive support, explicitly and implicitly, to convince interviewees that that is so. Again, see diSessa (2007) for details and empirical test.

The chapter I wrote with Greeno, Michaels, and O'Connor (diSessa, Greeno, Michaels, & O'Connor, this volume) provides a similar analysis. Power to define what is right and proper in many school interactions is exercised by teachers in the "third turn" in typical exchanges. The grammar of this form is, to a first approximation: (1) teacher asks a question; (2) student responds; (3) third turn: teacher evaluates.[8] But what does the third turn look like in clinical interaction? The chapter shows that the third turn in a clinical interview is overwhelmingly not evaluation, but, instead, picks out an interviewee's idea and puts it forward for continued consideration.

Presumptions about the power structure and the role of normativity in clinical interviews need to be tested. In my experience, caricatures of the actual power structure seem to me to be far off-base. We need to look more and harder to see if such characterizations have a basis in the real practice.

The larger point behind the critical remark above stands, but loses force as a criticism: Clinical interviewing does not abrogate the effects of social context; that is impossible. Instead, it can seek to instigate a social "agreement" that is maximally helpful in uncovering what ideas students have and how they, themselves, judge them.

## *The Way Forward*

I do not think we have made much progress concerning the status of clinical interviewing. The charges against interviewing do not seem to have changed much, despite the duration of the discussion and the attempts by me (e.g., diSessa, 2007; diSessa, Greeno, Michaels, & O'Connor, this volume) and others (e.g., Russ, Sherin, & Lee, this volume) to reveal and clarify the interactional and epistemological properties of the clinical context. So far, I feel that good clinical practice works pretty well in achieving the goals we have for it, and much criticism of it seems to be "tarring with a clean brush." I do think it is an intrinsically interesting form of professional practice that bears much more study for scientific and practical purposes, including separating substance from rhetoric concerning its scientific status.

Here is my "wish list" for the involvement of IA experts in the program of understanding clinical interviewing and its consequences.

1. Please join in the serious study of clinical practice. Presumption needs to be replaced by study. Is it not a little ironic that a perspective that is committed to the actual practice of professions – that takes the position that "you can't make this stuff up" – has not taken on a critical boundary professional practice that has played out strongly in the history of KA/IA relations? Serious IA study should help a lot in externalizing what are now intuitive professional practices, making them both better and easier to teach. I am particularly interested in the dynamics of change in participant frameworks and their social/epistemological/conceptual consequences (e.g., how both interviewers and interviewees learn the clinical "game," but the same issues apply to "teacher/student discussion in school"). As far as I have been able to uncover, there is minimal literature on the dynamics of change in participant structures.

2. For your own purposes, as well as for KA purposes and for KA/IA rapprochement, one would like to have something to say about how articulation of multiple perspectives (or methodologies) works in researchers' professional practice. I pointed out how the articulation of clinical methods with other methods and perspectives (e.g., instruction) appears to have been ignored in IA criticisms. My impression is that study of professional practice treats it, as yet, in a relatively homogeneous way, and does not seriously attend to multiple complementing, competing, or even conflicting, threads within any community's practices.

3. I am anxiously awaiting major new perspectives on the phenomenology of most enduring interest to me over my career as an education researcher – that related to what I've here stylized as "prior conceptions." As I pointed out in my turn* on modeling and reality, I am resolutely not a naive realist with respect to how science progresses, and it would be excellent for my own interests if serious alternatives to currently visible and viable points of view came to exist. There have been some nascent attempts, such as Greeno and van de Sande's (2007) moves toward a deeply discursive approach to conceptual change, and, more recently, some "encroachment" on conceptual change territory from, for example, cognitive linguistics (e.g., Amin, 2009). But I also have unsatisfied reservations (diSessa, 2009) concerning which a critical mass of alternative work could force reconsideration.

## Notes

1 There's bootstrapping here. A "sense of connections" or of "lack of connection" should develop into a stronger, more particular, and more scientific take on these issues.
2 I believe that educational research is full of intuitive and, occasionally, more explicit consideration of proxying strategies and judgments of when related things have been disconnected well enough "for present purposes." That would be a wonderful general topic of research out of which we certainly would learn things of practical value. It also might turn out that, at present, about all we can accomplish is to get better with respect to particular instances of concern to us, rather than understanding the issues in the most general sense.
3 I keep saying it because it continues to surprise people that I think of myself more as a model builder than a "discoverer of reality."
4 In diSessa (2014) [e.g., Section 7.4.4: Status of learning mechanisms] I remark that plasticity of activation and other phenomena that are important to understand in learning using p-prims would seem to require us to further develop continuous extensions of the "punctual" p-prim model, including possibly relying more heavily on continuous representations, such as neural/connectionist models.
5 It probably should *not* relate to real-world instruction if the aim is to build practices that surpass the state of the art.
6 Here's where Interaction Analysis could make an important contribution. I feel I have known about the liabilities of a focus on normative ideas and inappropriate power relations in the clinical context for years. But I could be missing something. Pointing

out what I'm missing and the bad consequences it might have would be compelling. I could also just be wrong that most or all clinical interviewers know about these issues, too, even though I have much less investment in what others do. Establishing that would also require studies that have not been done. These are scientific issues, but they remain merely rhetorical ones.
7   This strikes me, in the abstract, as an interesting set of issues. But one that I consider of marginal importance to good instruction, and certainly not one for which I have had any deep concern.
8   There is a huge literature on this interactive form and its properties. See, for example, Cazden (2001).

# References

Amin, T. G. (2009). Conceptual metaphor meets conceptual change. *Human Development*, 52(3), 165–197.

Bakhtin, M. M. (1986). *Speech genres and other late essays* (C. Emerson & M. Holquist, Eds.). Austin, TX: University of Texas Press.

Bloom, B. S. (1984). The 2 sigma problem: The search for methods of group instruction as effective as one-to-one tutoring. *Educational Researcher*, 13(6), 4–16.

Brown, D. E., & Clement, J. (1989). Overcoming misconceptions via analogical reasoning: Abstract transfer versus explanatory model construction. *Instructional Science*, 18(4), 237–261.

Call, J., & Tomasello, M. (2008). Does the chimpanzee have a theory of mind? 30 years later. *Trends in Cognitive Sciences*, 12(5), 187–192, doi:10.1016/j.tics.2008.02.010.

Cazden, C. B. (2001). *Classroom discourse: The language of learning and teaching* (2nd ed.). Portsmouth, NH: Heinemann.

diSessa, A. A. (1993). Toward an epistemology of physics. *Cognition and Instruction*, 10(2–3), 105–225.

diSessa, A. A. (2007). An interactional analysis of clinical interviewing. *Cognition and Instruction*, 25(4), 523–565.

diSessa, A. A. (2009). A new approach to conceptual change? ... Maybe: A comment on Amin. *Human Development* (Letter to the Editor; July 1, 2009), 1–6.

diSessa, A. A. (2014). The construction of causal schemes: Learning mechanisms at the knowledge level. *Cognitive Science*, 38(5), 795–850.

diSessa, A. A., Elby, A., & Hammer, D. (2002). J's epistemological stance and strategies. In G. Sinatra & P. Pintrich (Eds.), *Intentional conceptual change* (pp. 237–290). Mahwah, NJ: Lawrence Erlbaum Associates.

diSessa, A. A., & Minstrell, J. (1998). Cultivating conceptual change with benchmark lessons. In J. G. Greeno & S. V. Goldman (Eds.), *Thinking practices in mathematics and science learning* (pp. 155–187). Mahwah, NJ: Lawrence Erlbaum Associates.

Dreyfus, H., & Dreyfus, S. (1986). *Mind over machine: The power of human intuition and expertise in the era of the computer*. Oxford, UK: Blackwell.

Greeno, J. G., & van de Sande, C. (2007). Perspectival understanding of conceptions and conceptual growth in interaction. *Educational Psychologist*, 42, 9–23.

Hardy, G. H. (1940). *A mathematician's apology*. Cambridge, UK: Cambridge University Press.

Kapon, S., & diSessa, A. A. (2012). Reasoning through instructional analogies. *Cognition and Instruction*, 30(3), 261–310.

Minstrell, J. (1982). Explaining the "at rest" condition of an object. *The Physics Teacher*, 20, 10–14.

Newell, A., & Simon, H. A. (1976). Computer science as empirical inquiry: Symbols and search. *Communications of the ACM*, 19(3), 113–126, doi:10.1145/360018.360022.

Pfundt, H., & Duit, R. (1988). *Bibliography: Students' alternative frameworks and science education* (2nd ed.). Kiel, DE: IPN.

Searle, J. (1980). Minds, brains and programs, *Behavioral and Brain Sciences*, 3(3), 417–457, doi: 10.1017/S0140525X00005756.

Stevens, R., & Hall, R. (2014, June). Yipee KAIA and other cowboy expressions of joy. In M. Levin & O. Parnafes (co-chairs), *Is the sum greater than its parts? Reflections on the agenda of integrating analyses of cognition and learning.* Symposium conducted at the biennial International Conference of the Learning Sciences, Boulder, CO.

# 19
# TOWARDS A GENEROUS* DISCUSSION OF INTERPLAY BETWEEN NATURAL DESCRIPTIVE AND HIDDEN MACHINERY APPROACHES IN KNOWLEDGE AND INTERACTION ANALYSIS

*Rogers Hall, Ricardo Nemirovsky, Jasmine Y. Ma, and Molly L. Kelton*

This chapter explores different orientations to research practices that are present in both Knowledge and Interaction Analysis. Rather than rehearsing the familiar controversy between individual and sociocultural theories of knowing and learning, we analyze differences associated with what we call "natural descriptive" (ND) and "hidden machineries" (HM) orientations. The writing was undertaken as a conversation among the authors, following a series of lively (and sometimes difficult) conversations with others in the KAIA community. The text came in pieces, with many gaps and alternate paths taken that are not reflected here. We have tried to smooth the remaining pieces together in a way that reflects some of our discoveries along the way, starting by characterizing the work of hidden machineries and natural description in scientific practices, and then illustrating the latter in two historical cases. Next, we pose a series of generous*[1] questions for exploring differences and possible interplay between these two orientations, using cases from previous studies in the learning sciences. We end with an invitation to think differently – in generous* ways – about these differences, in efforts to integrate Knowledge and Interaction Analysis in studies of learning and teaching.

Hidden machineries approaches postulate a domain operating either above the phenomena of interest – such as cultural scripts in anthropology, generative rules of universal grammar in linguistics, or relations of production in Marxist history, or beneath the phenomena of interest – such as interactions between atoms and light producing color patterns or mental structures in cognitive psychology. The main goal of HM approaches is to identify structures and processes in these hidden domains that have predictive and causal powers over the phenomena of interest. Natural descriptive approaches, on the other hand, focus on close examination of the phenomena of interest, noticing unexpected relationships and documenting previously unnoticed cases and circumstances. It is key to note that we are not mapping HM approaches to "theory" and ND approaches to "observation." Theorizing and observing are germane to both. Theories in HM tend to be models of postulated mechanisms, whereas theories in ND are means to highlight phenomena and relations that had previously remained unnoticed or without broad significance.

We argue that: (1) natural description and hidden machineries are both legitimate enterprises with their own traditions, methods, and diverse professional communities; (2) rather than a hierarchical (i.e., one being "better") or developmental (i.e., description comes first, explanation later) relationship, they are parallel strands of work that benefit from interplay with one another; and (3) in order to enable this interplay it is crucial to acknowledge and grasp the cultural and historical roots of natural description and hidden machineries perspectives.

## Interplay Between Natural Descriptive and Hidden Machineries Orientations

> Method? What we're dealing with here is not, of course, just method. It is not just a set of techniques. It is not just a philosophy of method, a methodology. It is not even simply about the kinds of realities that we want to recognise or the kinds of worlds we might hope to make. It is also, and most fundamentally, about a way of being. It is about what kinds of social science we want to practise. And then, and as a part of this, it is about the kinds of people that we want to be, and about how we should live (Addelson 1994). Method goes with work, and ways of working, and ways of being. I would like us to work as happily, creatively and generously as possible in social science. And to reflect on what it is to work well.
>
> *(Law, 2004, p. 10)*

We intend to be generous*, but we set out in this exploration with an extensive background of writing about what science properly consists of and what it is for. Normative or idealized accounts of scientific practice, as we have learned from the social studies of science, may not adequately describe what scientists know, do, or learn. As Law (2004) points out, scientists inhabit their own cultures, with different personal commitments and broader, public values. In this section, we consider historical cases of the interplay between ND and HM orientations. Our purpose is to explore a more open relation between these orientations, in order to further a discussion about how these differences can be leveraged in new ways.

Our paper is a reflection on the philosophy of sciences, which we hope will enrich the ongoing exchanges in the KAIA community. This reflection arose as we wondered how differences between practitioners of Knowledge Analysis and Interaction Analysis could be productively grasped and described. On the face of the KA and IA labels, their corresponding differences seem to make little sense. How would it be possible to examine knowledge if not through the interactions among knowing people and their materials? Conversely, can there be a way of making sense of interactions regardless of what participants know, as evidenced by their talk and skilled actions? Another difference commonly discussed in our field is between individual and social; is that the one that applies here? We think that the prevalent discourse about individual/social distinctions has become stereotyped or fossilized. For instance, the same cognitive structures proposed by a learning researcher can, in principle, be ascribed to each of the tested individual minds, or to the individuals' internalization of structures historically established by their society or their professional communities. In this paper, we attempt to articulate another distinction that seems to offer, in our opinion, a language for a generous* and inclusive treatment of differences – the one between what we call "hidden machineries" and "natural description" approaches.

Before we characterize these approaches, let us be clear that we are not trying to establish a foundational or a priori dichotomy. The distinction we propose is provisional and open to refinement. In fact, it is easy to find cases that do not fit, that fit both sides of the distinction, that seem indifferent to it, and so forth; the value of this distinction is that it may open up fresh questions and provoke a generative and respectful exchange.

In drawing these distinctions, we intend to describe scientific worldviews that can be different and equally productive. We do not believe, for example, that what we call a hidden machineries orientation is deeper or more fundamental as a guide to scientific knowing than are natural description approaches. While these approaches may lead investigators to different epistemic stances, we believe they can be mutually informative, and we will give historical examples of this. The sense we want to invoke with the term "hidden" is not so much that the layer of reality causing the phenomena of interest is out of sight, but that it is "behind" or "above" observable phenomena, on another relatively autonomous stratum. For instance, cells, which are nowadays directly visible with proper instruments, have their own dynamics and are regulated by specific biological rules and principles – which is what "machinery" alludes to. The latter can causally explain, say, symptoms reported by a person construed as a supra-cellular phenomenon.

In natural description approaches, on the other hand, practitioners strive to discover phenomena that had previously remained unnoticed or without broad significance. Goodall's studies of a community of chimpanzees at the Gombe Stream Park in Tanzania are a popular example of natural description research. The term "natural" indicates that practitioners struggle to verify that observed phenomena are not merely artifacts of their own choices, methods, and instruments. For example, Goodall's observations about chimpanzees' aggression have been criticized as a result of feeding stations used at the Gombe Stream Park, suggesting that war-like behaviors observed by Goodall were not "natural" among chimpanzees. This controversy was explored further by other studies using natural description. Note that this use of "natural" is different from the one invoked by the phrase "natural science" which is often taken as a synonym for "non-social science." The quality of natural description studies we want to foreground is that they do not posit layers of causal explanation hidden behind the realm of observed phenomena. Avoiding this kind of explanatory stratification could be said to make natural description approaches "ontologically flat" (i.e., explanations remain meshed with the observable ontology).

To illustrate diverse and complex relationships between natural description and hidden machineries approaches, we chose two examples from the work of highly accomplished scientists: Charles Darwin and Santiago Ramón y Cajal. The broad pattern of discovery that we find in these two cases is consistent with the ideas that: (1) natural description and hidden machineries co-exist, and (2) they are not related by developmental sequence.

## *Darwin: The Mockingbirds*

On September 15, 1835, the research sailing vessel, HMS *Beagle* reached the Galapagos island chain. It visited several islands over a period of five weeks. Darwin, who was then 26 years old, worked to gather specimens and observations on the geology and biology of the archipelago. His servant hunted 65 birds, Darwin dissected the specimens and wrote notes, and in most cases only their skins were brought back to England. At the time Darwin did not have in mind the geographical distribution of species as a major focus of study. Looking back, Darwin remarked how he came to notice:

> [T]he most remarkable feature in the natural history of this archipelago … the different islands to a considerable extent are inhabited by a different set of beings. My attention was first called to this fact by the Vice-Governor, Mr. Lawson, declaring that the tortoises differed from the different islands, and that he could with certainty tell from which island any one was brought. I did not for some time pay sufficient attention to this statement, and I had already partially mingled together the collections from two of the islands. I never dreamed that islands, about 50 or 60 miles apart, and most of them in sight of each other, formed of precisely the same rocks, placed under a quite similar climate, rising to a nearly equal height, would have been differently tenanted.
>
> *(Darwin, 2011, p. 162)*

Even though Darwin had "mingled" the birds from different islands, there were four of the "mockingbird" type, for which he had recorded their island of origin. Three of these four birds were very similar in appearance, and Darwin was unsure whether they represented different species (Sulloway, 1982, p. 349). In 1837 Darwin delivered his collection of birds and mammals to the Zoological Society of London. The birds were subsequently studied by an expert ornithologist, John Gould, who found that most of the Galapagos land birds were "forms new to science and confined exclusively to the archipelago" (p. 359). In particular, he described the "distinct insular form" (p. 379) of the mockingbirds.

Although no unique event or insight during the voyage of the *Beagle*, or its aftermath, can be said to have prompted Darwin to develop the theory of evolution, he wrote in his autobiography how he was struck by:

> the manner in which they [species] differ slightly on each island of the [Galapagos] group; none of these islands appearing to be very ancient in a geological sense. It was evident that such facts as these, as well as many others, could be explained on the supposition that species gradually become modified; and the subject haunted me.
>
> *(Darwin, 2006, pp. 71–72)*

The *Origin of Species*, published 22 years later, includes Darwin's (2009) remark that in the Galapagos archipelago:

> almost every product of the land and of the water bears the unmistakable stamp of the American continent. There are twenty-six land-birds; of these, twenty-one, or perhaps twenty-three are ranked as distinct species, and would commonly be assumed to have been here created; yet the close affinity of most of these birds to American species is manifest in every character, in their habits, gestures, and tones of voice.
>
> *(pp. 384–385)*

Darwin compared these observations with the Cape Verde archipelago, which bears resemblance to the Galapagos in terms of latitude, climate, size of the islands, etc., but in which the inhabitants are closely related to African species. Species differences could be explained by assuming that the fauna and flora of the two archipelagos were descendent "with modifications" from American and African ancestors. Darwin proposed descent with modification, coupled with the geographic isolation of the islands, as the origin of new species in these archipelagos.

While his explanation can be understood to involve a "mechanism," it is important to realize that it does not invoke a subjacent domain, or a distinct ontological layer, causing new species to appear. In other words, Darwin's account of evolution did not depart from his natural description of geological and biological phenomena. Only much later were hidden machineries of evolution proposed, in the disciplines of molecular biology and genetics, emerging from the work of new communities with expertise in technologies and laboratory settings that flourished during the second half of the twentieth century. In this historical case, hidden machineries approaches followed the discovery of an integrative theory of evolution using a natural description approach.

### *Ramón y Cajal: The Neuron Doctrine*

The case of Ramón y Cajal and the neuron doctrine illustrates how technical developments, in many cases generated by theories embedded in hidden machineries approaches, allow for the opening of new realms to natural descriptive work. Based on extraordinary developments in optics and histology, Ramón y Cajal pursued tantalizing natural descriptive explorations of the nervous tissue.

In 1673 Antonie van Leeuwenhoek mailed his first letter to the Royal Society's Philosophical Transactions describing observations with his self-made microscopes. Over the next 50 years, he kept reporting to the Royal Society, becoming famous all over Europe and gaining recognition as a leading scientist. But his microscopes were difficult to use – they required steady hands holding them at a correct angle with respect to a light source and great visual acuity. Van Leeuwenhoek kept secret the specifics of microscope fabrication and "following his death in 1723, there was little scientific use of the microscope until Joseph Jackson Lister (1786–1869) developed the achromatic objective during the 1820s" (Reeves & Taylor, 2004, p. 1103). Different colors refracted differently in microscopes, creating blurry images with optical artifacts. Achromatic lenses were constructed by joining halves made of two different materials such that they neutralized, to a large extent, differences in refractive deviation. Initially used successfully in telescopes, achromatic lenses in microscopes took much longer to develop because of difficulties posed by their small size.

The dismissal of microscopy among anatomists and medical professors was not only rooted in technical hindrances, but also in prevalent cultural traditions. Ramón y Cajal described how, as a student of medicine in 1877,

> I was completely surprised by the almost total absence of any curiosity on the part of our professors, who spent their time talking to us at great length about healthy and diseased cells without making the slightest effort to become acquainted visually with those transcendental and mysterious protagonists of life and suffering. What am I saying! – Many, perhaps the majority of professors in those days, despised the microscope, even considering it prejudicial to the progress of biology! In the opinion of these academic reactionaries, the marvelous published descriptions of cells and of invisible parasites were pure fantasy.
> 
> *(Ramón y Cajal, 1937/1989, p. 252)*

As a newcomer to the field – open to different and emerging research practices – Ramón y Cajal described his fascination with the new worlds he discovered:

> There was presented to me a marvelous field for exploration, full of the most delightful surprises. With the attitude of a fascinated spectator I examined the blood corpuscles, the epithelial cells, the muscle fiber, nerve fiber, etc., pausing here and there to draw or photograph the most captivating scenes in the life of the infinitely small.
> *(Ramón y Cajal, 1937/1989, p. 252)*

While microscopic studies of plant and animal tissues had led to wide acceptance of the theory that all living organisms were primarily made of cells, "there was plenty of room for exceptions to the rule. Foremost among these appeared to be the nervous system" (Shepherd, 1991, p. 25). The main reason was that "gray matter is formed by something like a very dense felt of excessively fine threads; and for following these filaments thin sections or completely stained preparations are worthless" (Ramón y Cajal, 1937/1989, p. 310). Camillo Golgi's discovery of silver nitrate staining in 1873 provided Ramón y Cajal with a tool for close descriptive exploration of what had previously appeared to be a uniform fabric of felt-like tissue. A surprising benefit of the Golgi stain was that it impregnated only a few (1 to 5%) of the nerve cells:

> To follow the entire course of a long nervous process, it is necessary to prepare very thick sections. If the technique had impregnated all the nerve cells present in such a section, it would have been impossible to follow individual nerve processes among the inextricable tangle of all the others.
> *(Pannese, 1999, p. 133)*

As Ramón y Cajal set to work with silver nitrate stains, he favored the view that nervous tissue was composed of fully formed and self-contained cells, rather than a network of continuous protoplasmic connections, which was a competing theory favored by Golgi. Working with less dense, embryonic nervous tissue in microscopic studies over a period of about four years, Ramón y Cajal published a collection of papers describing cellular structures that were visible using the new stain:

> The continuity of substance between cell and cell being excluded, the view that the nerve impulse is transmitted by contact, as in the junctions of electric conductors, or by an induction effect, as in induction coils, becomes inescapable.... If the method is applied before the appearance of the myelin sheaths upon the axons (these forming an almost insuperable obstacle to the [Golgi] reaction), the nerve cells, which are still relatively small, stand out complete in each section; the terminal ramifications of the axis cylinder are depicted with the utmost clearness and perfectly free.
> *(Ramón y Cajal, 1937/1989, pp. 322–344)*

Santiago Ramón y Cajal's papers included careful illustrations of the visible structure of nerve cells and their physical connections, but his efforts of natural description were finally cemented when he traveled to meetings of the German Anatomical Society at the University of Berlin. He did not present a paper, but instead offered demonstrations using several microscopes set up to explore tissues using the Golgi stain. Despite his halting mastery of French, Ramón y Cajal managed to demonstrate the fine, cellular structure of nervous tissue to leading professors who attended the meeting. Despite their initial skepticism, "when there had been paraded before their eyes in a procession of irreproachable images of the utmost clearness ... the prejudice against the humble Spanish anatomist vanished and warm and sincere congratulations burst forth" (Ramón y Cajal, 1937/1989, p. 356–7). Ramón y Cajal's success with a natural description approach eventually resulted in a Nobel prize, which he shared with Golgi (controversially) for work on the fine structure of the nervous system.

The two cases, Darwin and the theory of evolution and Ramón y Cajal and the neuron doctrine, illustrate the diversity of natural descriptive approaches across disciplinary fields in the natural sciences, and their interplay with hidden machinery types of work. At the same time, and while the distinctions we discuss are fluid – there are surely boundary cases and counter-examples – it also seems reasonable to recognize that there may be differences in how the two approaches mesh with diverse scientific practices. One apparent difference is that hidden machineries in the social sciences – examples include Piaget's schema, Lakoff's conceptual metaphors, diSessa's p-prims, Chomsky's rules of generative grammar, or Fauconnier's blends – remain a concern of relatively small scientific communities, and in this way are distinct from ideas which originated in the natural sciences that have become "normalized" by society at large, such as the various kinds of forces, bacteria, or molecules that are commonly invoked in public discourse. Another difference is that hidden machineries in the natural sciences have often become examinable, through various tools, in multiple and mutually independent ways (e.g., viruses, DNA). It is difficult to find clear precedents in the social sciences for hidden machineries that could be examined apart from the social behavior that expresses them.

One of the great hopes of the cognitive revolution initiated in the 1950s, based on the premise of a foundational similarity between brains and computers, was that the hidden machineries of cognition were to be found in the form of programmable codes (Gardner, 1986). In similar fashion, a recurring hope is that progress in cognitive neuroscience will allow for the discovery of the hidden machineries of psychology, education, and culture in the expressive capacity of neuronal populations and their connections. Neuroscience findings, particularly in the form of brain imaging, are increasingly positioned in our society as precursors to a causal explanatory framework for why humans and animals behave the way they do.

It is possible, of course, that future hidden machineries emerging from the social sciences will be scrutinized apart from social behavior in multiple independent ways and that they will be widely accepted as explanatory, but the question of why this has not been the case so far remains open and relevant. Certainly it is not because of the lack of effort on the part of many practitioners of the social sciences. In order to open up discussions about this asymmetry, we will reflect on three explanations that have been offered: (1) the human sciences are younger, (2) the mathematics needed for the articulation of hidden machineries in the human sciences have not yet been developed, and (3) culture is inherently holistic and does not allow for an analytic stratification in which one layer causally explains another.

## Youth

A frequent argument is that the human sciences are newer, which explains why they are still unprepared for work in hidden machineries. This argument assumes that there is a developmental sequence culminating in the articulation of hidden machineries that has to be traversed by scientific disciplines. This thesis contradicts the simple historical fact that the social and natural sciences emerged around the same historical period (Cohen, 1994). We have tried to dismantle this developmental model through some of the preceding examples.

## Mathematical Support

This argument is based on the observation that formalism in general and mathematics in particular are often crucial for the articulation of hidden machineries. Sometimes a branch of mathematics has been developed for the sake of a hidden machinery approach (e.g., Newton's invention of calculus); at other times a corpus of mathematical ideas has been found already in place for this purpose (e.g., Einstein's use of non-Euclidean geometries in relativity theory). The inference is that the mathematics needed for the articulation of hidden machineries in some of the human sciences is still to be invented (or discovered, depending on one's philosophy of mathematics). Perhaps stemming from this perspective, the explosive growth of non-linear dynamics – a relatively new branch of mathematics over the last 60 years – prompted some psychologists to develop new lines of research to explain psychological development. Similarly, the "social networks" approach to studying the dynamics of social organization has been fed by mathematical and computational advances in graph theory.

Economics is a fascinating case for the relationship between mathematics and hidden machineries. For many of its practitioners, economics is an exact science. This conclusion is sometimes supported by the observation that quite a few mathematicians work for companies operating in financial and investment domains, or by noticing that a crucial target of work in economics is the mathematics of decision making (e.g., game theory). But on the other hand, many economists see their subject as shaped by cultural and historical forces that do not appear amenable to formal laws, such as Weber's well-known thesis linking the rise of European capitalism to the work ethics of Protestantism.

## Cultural Holism

We group in this category those views according to which culture is inherently holistic in the sense that it does not allow for a stratification of layers, some operating as causally explanatory of others. The associated conjecture is that hidden machineries approaches necessitate such stratification in order to be workable. For example, according to this holistic view, postulated principles regulating the economy could not causally determine cultural dynamics, because culture and history themselves shape economic phenomena. Or, given the extraordinary plasticity of the nervous system, it seems impossible to discern whether animals' behavior is dictated by their neuronal networks or whether these networks emerge from life in certain environments and communities, or whether they co-emerge in non-striated ways, which amounts to posing again the age-old nature/nurture debate. It is consistent with the thesis of cultural holism that the social sciences could be the "advanced" ones, in the sense that the natural sciences might encounter, at some point in the future, holistic edges undermining the consensus about stratified hidden machineries.

What we have called the interplay between natural descriptive and hidden machineries approaches to scientific work has historically been both more diverse and more productive than adherents to either Knowledge or Interaction Analysis might typically acknowledge. As our conversations around this chapter have continued, we have tried to remain open to what we perceive as a driving or motivational force for researchers involved in this attempt at integration, particularly around what typically counts as an explanation in the research that we do. In the remainder of this paper, we take up a series of generous* questions that we hope will make this space of possibilities for interplay easier to appreciate and inhabit as forms of research practice.

## Generous* Questions About Interplay Between Natural Descriptive and Hidden Machinery Approaches

There are many productive discussions possible in the space we are trying to open. In this section, we pose four questions that have emerged in our work and sketch our progress thus far. Our approach has been to consider concepts developed in research in the learning sciences that have been widely influential, asking how forms of interplay between ND and HM orientations are present (or not) in each. These include concepts of socio-mathematical norms (Yackel & Cobb, 1996), inscription devices as material for constructing knowledge in Actor-Network Theory (Latour & Woolgar, 1979), meta-representational competence as an explanation for productive diversity when inventing representations (diSessa, 2004), and legitimate peripheral participation as a theory of situated learning developed in studies of apprenticeship (Lave & Wenger, 1991). Each of these cases can be used to think about the generous* questions we pose, though in what follows we locate each case within a particular question. For each, we summarize these concepts and focus on interplay and problems of method that have been important in our continuing conversation.

## *(1) Whichever approach we take (ND, HM, or deliberate interplay between them), how can we best remain open to what the actual details of human activity can show us?*

As Charles Goodwin put it at the Marconi meetings, "You could not make this stuff up, sitting in your office."

> We start from a particular interview on a particular day between two identified persons in the presence of a child, a camera and a cameraman. Our primary data are the multitudinous details of vocal and bodily action recorded on this film. We call our treatment of such data a "natural history" because a minimum of theory guided the collection of the data.
> 
> *(Bateson, 1971, p. 6)*

> First, go to the site where the event being studied normally occurs. Second, show up on the occasions at which it would happen anyway. Third, view experienced participants who know each other. Fourth, take all possible measures to avoid changing the situation. And fifth, observe rather than participate directly in the event under study.
> 
> *(Scheflen, 1973, pp. 313–314)*

These quotes from Bateson (1971) and Scheflen (1973) draw from what many consider to be the origin of the field of communications studies (within which methods of Interaction Analysis developed) – the Natural History of an Interview (NHI) project, started as the Center for Advanced Study in the Behavioral Sciences was opening its doors (1955 and 1956), but never published in wide circulation. The recording analyzed most closely in the NHI project features one of the analysts (Gregory Bateson) lighting a mother's cigarette, in an interview about her son, in the context of ongoing family therapy.

That something consequential might be found in activity convened and conducted by people other than the analyst remains as a central commitment of Interaction Analysis (Jordan & Henderson, 1995). But we are also committed to the possibility of discovery in studies of designed environments in which investigators deliberately intervene to change things, something that is not entirely alien to IA traditions – e.g., consider the elaborate series of breaching experiments reported in the second chapter of Garfinkel (1967). Learning unexpected things in design studies is a hallmark of research in the learning sciences. So again, how to remain open to discovery?

> Discovery of new foci of attention is actually quite common in design experiments, if it is not absolutely necessary. Failures or surprising successes not infrequently push toward, and sometimes enable, new lines of inquiry, possibly involving new ontologies. In some other cases, typically in initial failures, we manage the gap by patching enough to get by, without pulling the surprising occurrence into the core scientific program.
>
> *(diSessa & Cobb, 2004, p. 86)*

In discussing this question, the concept of "socio-mathematical norms" (SMNs) developed by Paul Cobb and his colleagues (Cobb, Stephan, McClain, & Gravemeijer, 2011) seemed particularly interesting. As Cobb notes (above), their team did not set out to study this concept or to create it in classrooms. Rather, recurring patterns of talk in classrooms led them to pay careful attention to how a teacher talked about the content of valued mathematics with her students and how these conversations developed over time. We give a brief description of SMNs and then make some comments related to how investigators might remain open to discovery.

## Socio-Mathematical Norms

SMNs occupy a middle region of specificity in what we now understand as a trio of related concepts developed by Cobb and his colleagues to describe the development of micro-cultures in mathematics classrooms. The first, social norms, "refer to obligations and expectations regarding classroom participation" (Bowers, Cobb, & McClain, 1999, p. 27). Examples of social norms include justifying solutions and listening to others' explanations, and they may be established in classrooms for any subject area. SMNs are similar, but specifically relate to mathematical activity. Typical examples include what counts as an acceptable justification or explanation, and what counts as mathematically different. The third concept, classroom mathematical practices, "focus on the taken-as-shared ways of reasoning, arguing, and symbolizing established while discussing particular mathematical ideas" (Cobb et al., 2011, p. 126). Our conversations have focused on SMNs, which we treat as interactive structures of knowledge-in-use that shape expectations about what counts as knowing or doing mathematics in particular classrooms.

SMNs were discovered[2] in the work of a particular teacher, as she pushed for mathematical content under investigation by Cobb and his colleagues. Talking with students about how to talk about mathematics later became a research design goal, in an effort to further understand how processes of interaction supported the development of particular (highly valued) versions of knowing and doing mathematics. Now, years (and many publications) later, the field (as we read the literature) has realized that something like SMNs exist in any mathematics classroom, in that what will count as mathematical knowledge (and who has agency for working on and with that knowledge) can vary dramatically across classrooms, teachers, and schools. The relation between individual activity and SMNs is reflexive, in that individuals contribute to the ongoing negotiation of SMNs, while at the same time SMNs shape, support, and constrain their learning. As a consequence, SMNs can (and often do) develop in ways that lead away from what many (not all) in the education research community value as mathematical knowledge-in-use. As an object of design, SMNs that support making and arguing about mathematical conjectures in ways that are preferred by educational reformers may be very difficult to achieve, depending on the institutional contexts of teachers' work.

Analyses of SMNs used interactions in the classroom community as a unit of analysis rather than individuals or individual learning. The notion of "taken as shared" was interesting in this regard, since participants in the classroom did not "tell" the researchers what they took to be normative. Analysts identified SMNs by noticing when students committed violations of what was expected and were held accountable by others in the classroom community. Given a provisional description of an SMN, if actions the analysts expected to be violations were treated as legitimate in the classroom (going unremarked or accepted after negotiation), their description of the SMN was revised. Making SMNs visible, then, required making inferences about what was hidden or explicit for participants in the classroom.

Cobb described SMNs as part of "the hidden curriculum of mathematics classrooms," part of "what students had to know" and do to be successful in the classroom (diSessa & Cobb, 2004, p. 94). This hidden layer of mathematics classrooms was treated both as a phenomenon to be investigated (the work of analysts) and as having mechanistic properties that drove the development of students' dispositions and learning about mathematics (the work of classroom participants). SMNs that treated computational results as a sufficient justification, for example, promoted a computational view of mathematics. Contributions by students and the teacher shaped, reproduced, and changed SMNs, either explicitly (e.g., through discussion or other forms of instruction) or implicitly (e.g., through holding each other accountable). In this sense, SMNs arose within the phenomena under investigation, and their consequence as a concept (and object of design) did not depend on a form of machinery that was hidden inside people or in some other way that was different, in kind, from the phenomena in which they were originally discovered.

As research using this concept has continued, our field now sees SMNs as a range of agreements, built through interactional work between students and teachers, that specifies how to engage with particular kinds of mathematical activity. The concept of SMNs has shifted from a discovery (something found, ongoing within the relevancies of people being studied), to an object of design (something made, brought forward as an intervention to reorganize classroom talk and action), to something that is (arguably) always already there, though of varied quality, depending on what one values.

> The case of sociomathematical norms seems particularly analogous to that of germ theory. Just as germs are tiny, invisible biological elements, so we no more observe sociomathematical norms directly than we can directly perceive students' conceptual processes. Instead, we have to infer the norms established in a classroom by identifying patterns and regularities in teachers' and students' classroom interactions.... Further, just as germ theory is an interpretive perspective that enables us to make sense of certain biological phenomena, so sociomathematical norms are constituents of an interpretive framework that enables us to make sense of certain social phenomena. In both cases, the primary motive was to understand while remaining vigilant that proposed theoretical constructs do useful work.
>
> *(diSessa & Cobb, 2004, p. 98)*

## (2) How can an explanation or a theory be consequential, most importantly in ways that reduce suffering and provide for more humane and equitable forms of pedagogy?

> If the question *what to do* no longer depends on *what is real*, then what else might it be linked up with? I suggest that if we can no longer find assurance by asking "is this knowledge true to its object?" it becomes all the more worthwhile to ask, "is this practice good for the subjects (human or otherwise) involved in it?" If faithful representations no longer hold the power to ground us, we may still seek positive interventions. Thus, instead of truth, goodness comes to the center of the stage. Or rather, not *goodness*, as if there were only one version of it, but *goodnesses*. Once we accept that ontology is multiple and reality leaves us in doubt, it becomes all the more urgent to attend to modes and modalities of seeking, neglecting, celebrating, fighting, and otherwise living *the good* in this, that, or the other of its many guises.
>
> *(Mol, 2002, pp. 165–166)*

Our second question concerns the kinds of explanations or theories we might hope to develop in an integration of Knowledge and Interaction Analysis. In particular, what would we like the consequences of these to be as explanations are taken up and used by other researchers, in other settings? As the quote from Mol (2002) suggests, this process of uptake both changes the concept and creates new arrangements that may serve very different interests. In our brief description and analysis of the developmental trajectory of SMNs, for example, further study and design using that concept has revealed a variety of structural relations, enacted in talk and activity over time in classrooms, concerning what would count as valued mathematical knowledge. If many versions of mathematical knowledge are possible in classrooms (we believe this is possible; others may not), then how do explanatory or theoretical concepts help to produce versions that are (perhaps multiply) "good" for learners and for teachers?

To help think about this question of how more humane or productive forms of pedagogy might be possible, we have discussed how "inscription devices" (IDs), a particular concept describing how representational technologies are used to fix evidence or technique in scientific practice, have been taken up and used in learning sciences research. One aspect of our discussion has been to see IDs as constructive media both for building up knowledge claims and as critical resources for dissent or building alternative claims about what counts as (or is valuable about) particular versions of knowledge. In choosing IDs as a case, we intend to highlight that the reflexive nature of the concept – creating IDs to do research that is useful – could lead to interplay between ND and HM approaches that serve different meanings (held vigilantly) of "useful."

## Inscription Devices in Actor-Network Theory

Actor-Network Theory (ANT) is rooted in the discipline of science and technology studies, particularly as it has been developed by Michel Callon (e.g., 1986, 1991), Bruno Latour (e.g., 2005), and John Law (e.g., Law & Hassard, 1999). While the decades of work in this tradition are diverse, ANT can be characterized broadly by the conviction that socio-technical objects, actors, and institutions are the relational outcomes or effects of heterogeneous assemblages. In other words, ANT treats scientific knowledge as contingent and assembled, not as an outcome of an already present, singular, and transcendent Nature. Some knowledge claims are more stable than others (more realistic) because the network assembly that makes them stable holds up to dissent.

Latour and Woolgar's (1979) notion of *inscription devices* provides an early example of the kind of socio-technical assemblages posited within the ANT tradition. An ID is an arrangement of materials, humans, technologies, and practices that transforms some material object or observation into a usable inscription, where inscription is construed broadly to include diagrams, traces, text, or drawings that might figure in a scientific publication. An ID in a neuroendocrinology laboratory, for example, could be a bioassay composed of recording technologies and human practices that convert animals or their cells into drawn curves whose peaks and valleys can be inspected by members of the lab and used as figures in their papers. IDs as a concept were discovered in ethnographic observations of human and machine activity that was neglected or actively suppressed in scientists' accounts of their own work (deletion of human modality makes some scientific claims stronger or "harder"). In this sense, IDs grounded in ethnographic description had the (still) somewhat radical effect of making scientific fact-making visible as a process of assembly.

Taking IDs in ANT as our exemplar, how can we understand the discovery of this concept (and its later use by others) as the possible interplay of ND and HM approaches to life in laboratories and the knowledge used and produced there? Prima facie, certain aspects of the ANT framework lend themselves to a HM approach. Images of complex arrangements producing socio-material objects, analytic choices that radically decenter human agency, materialist leanings that foreground laboratory apparatus, methodological restrictions on "cognitive explanations" until after the network has been exhausted (Latour's "Rule 7," 1987, p. 268), and injunctions to study the "*mechanics* of organization" (Law, 1992, p. 389, emphasis in original) abound in the ANT literature and certainly evoke a machinic imaginary. Indeed, an introductory text on science and technology studies defines (albeit crudely) IDs as "*machines* that … allow the scientist to deal with nature on pieces of paper" (Sismondo, 2004, p. 67, emphasis added).

Considering the extent to which actor-networks are hidden complicates the initial temptation to classify ANT as a hidden machineries approach. On the one hand, there is a sense in which assemblages can be hidden, forgotten, or elided in practice. In Latour and Woolgar's (1979) neuroendocrinology lab, the processes by which IDs produced their effects were quickly bracketed once scientists had the inscription in hand. Instead of acknowledging the complex arrangements required to make diagrams, spectra, and numerical tabulations, the scientists treated inscriptions as transparent pointers to their objects of investigation. It is for this reason that scholars working with ANT varyingly refer to socio-material processes that are "forgotten or taken for granted" (Latour & Woolgar, 1979, p.63), to black-boxed or *punctualized* (Callon, 1991) actor-networks, to *hinterlands* (Law, 2004) of pre-established practices and assumptions, or to "invisible work [that] lies below the waterline" (Law & Singleton, 2005, p. 337). On the other hand, a critical feature of ANT's assemblages is that their practical elision is forever tenuous; "punctualization is always precarious" (Law, 1992, p. 385). The neuroendocrinologists may un-bracket the socio-material conditions of scientific literary production, for example, when IDs don't perform as expected or when a scientific claim is in doubt. So the heterogeneous assemblages of ANT perennially flirt with the boundary between hidden and unhidden: their endless complexity may be in full view or neatly punctualized; they may be elided or center-staged; they may recede into the hinterland or come charging back out of it. In this sense, IDs are useful for both building up and dissenting from knowledge claims, providing a leverage point for creating alternative versions of knowledge.

Understanding ANT as a hidden machineries project becomes even more doubtful in light of its commitment to a radically *flat* ontology (Latour, 2005). That is, ANT resists the a priori deployment of social science's usual arrangement of scales – for example, in micro–macro debates about bottom-up agency versus top-down social determinism. In the present volume and KAIA project, this might take the form of locating individual cognition within social interaction (e.g., as "context") without exploring generative relations between the two. ANT's flatness invites us to wonder how dialogues in educational research might be transformed if we jettison ontologies that nest psychological states, individuals, and social groups like matryoshka dolls. At any rate, if we take the hallmark of hidden machineries approaches to be the appeal to a sub- or supra-personal stratum of invisible, causally potent structures, then IDs and the associated ANT framework are not consistent with the use of hierarchical strata as explanation.

But if theoretical and empirical work in ANT seems imperfectly captured by the language of hidden machineries, it is not for want of structure. Latour and Woolgar (1979) are quite explicit, in fact, that the notion of IDs provides crucial theoretical leverage by which the non-scientist ethnographer can organize and make sense of the apparent chaos of laboratory practice: "At this point, the observer felt that the laboratory was by no means quite as confusing as he had first thought … the laboratory began to take on the appearance of a system of literary inscription" (pp. 51–52). Moreover, ethnographic work informed by ANT uses extended participant observation in order to identify principles and regularities that characterize actor-networks and their processes of formation or dissolution. In this way, although ANT does not appeal to hidden, sub- or supra-individual causal layers, the theoretical framework can be seen as a search for structure by meticulously tracing connections as they appear through close empirical analysis of ethnographic data.

## *(3) What is the appeal of mechanism in theories or explanations for human activity?*

If by mechanism we mean structural regularities that influence patterned, human activity, what sorts of mechanisms, at what levels of aggregation or scale are consequential (see Question 2)? Are there advantages to an explanatory approach that is "ontologically flat" (i.e., without using super- or sub-ordinate entities and relations to explain the observed phenomena)?

> The major result of our retrospective analysis was the "discovery" of meta-representational competence or simply MRC. MRC, as an ontological innovation, implicates a specific body of knowledge that students

have, and which can be developed, lying behind students' abilities to create, critique, and adapt a very wide range of effective scientific representations.
(diSessa & Cobb, 2004, p. 88–89)

All we can observe is interaction, and we can only see one interaction at a time. An interaction is an example of process, which is always visible. The guidelines underlying the choices made at the level of process are what can be called structure, but structure remains invisible. We know of its existence only because of the regularities we find in interaction. This means finding logical sets of behaviors to study, and paying attention to the regularities found to exist in these sets. This is why researchers study conversational openings or closings, or service encounters, or civil inattention – the goal is to find a type of communication behavior, and then examine many different examples in an effort to begin to understand how that type works.
(Leeds-Hurwitz, 2005, pp. 143–144)

In any of the studies explored in our paper, and in our own work as well, it is never possible to see processes of learning and teaching as things that are just "lying around" in the moment. These processes always involve multiple perspectives on (and in) activity, they extend over durations of time that are difficult to capture and organize effectively for close analysis, and there are many details that have uncertain relevance to participants and could hide structural regularities of interest to analysts (what is relevant to members and analysts may diverge, we understand). The discovery and subsequent pursuit of "meta-representational competence" has been a productive case for our conversations.

## Meta-Representational Competence

Meta-representational competence (MRC) is a concept diSessa and colleagues (diSessa, Hammer, Sherin, & Kolpakowski, 1991) developed to describe the capacity of children (or anyone) to notice that some representations work better than do others, to be critical of different representations proposed for use in the same task, and to tinker with representational systems to make them more effective. They conjecture that these capacities are grounded in underlying knowledge structures that support inventing or designing new representations, comparing and critiquing the adequacy of representations, understanding how representations work, explaining these things to others, and learning new representations quickly. These underlying knowledge structures are said to be a form of "native competence" (diSessa, 2004, in the title, "Metarepresentation: Native competence and targets for instruction," and throughout the paper), and this might reasonably invite a view of MRC as part of the innate endowment of the human cognitive architecture. Instead, this competence is "gradually developed through cultural practices in and out of school" (p. 294) and, since it is not taught (again, not to be confused with an impoverished stimulus, understood as input to a mental faculty), MRC is a "free resource." It may be available in formal learning environments and could be a resource for learning in a broad array of conceptual domains (e.g., kinematics, mathematics, or computation), depending on how settings are organized (or designed).

MRC was developed at a time (late 1990s, early 2000s) when there were a number of studies discovering flexible use of "informal" or everyday representational media to manage (or to solve) problems associated with use of "formal" or schooled representational forms. These included Sylvia Scribner's (1986) studies of "thinking in action" among workers in a dairy, comparative analysis of "oral" versus "written" arithmetic in the informal economy of street sellers in Brazil (Carraher, Carraher, & Schliemann, 1987; Saxe, 1991), gap-closing practices of quantity use in shopping and cooking (Lave, Murtaugh, & de la Rocha, 1984), and use of informal representations and strategies to solve school algebra problems among engineering and computer science undergraduates (Hall, Kibler, Wenger, & Truxaw, 1989). Three lines of research developed out of this work: (1) studies of the organization and development of representational practices, (2) studies of the "representation effect" from different affordances of representational forms, and (3) the discovery that learners invent representational forms that, with direction, come to resemble conventional (and powerful) historical conventions. The first focuses on the social organization of technical practice (hewing closely to science studies), the second on task and instructional design for purposes of school instruction, and the third on trajectories or pathways for conceptual domains in particular disciplines (e.g., the statistical concept of variability, the concept of speed or velocity in kinematics).

After some discussion, we remain interested in what an account of native competence that lies hidden beneath the conventions of formal instruction can tell us about representational practices, and we certainly would not argue that these practices are (instead) lying around "in plain sight" for straightforward study by means of Interaction Analysis. The discovery of MRC was made possible (diSessa et al., 1991) by iterative analyses of records of classroom talk over time, as learners were encouraged by their teacher and diSessa's team to explore alternative representational displays for describing motion. As with his provocative use of "native" in the later summary article (diSessa, 2004), diSessa places "inventing graphing" in the title of the original report, but he (and co-authors) quickly replace this with a more familiar description of schooling – students settled on a preference for conventional Cartesian graphing in conversations orchestrated by their teacher. MRC may consist of previously hidden knowledge structures, but the analysis that discovers them as a form of invention is conducted primarily (as far as we can tell) from a natural description perspective. The results of that analysis are attributed to structures that are doubly hidden, first by the politics of conventional schooling (we agree and value this meaning) and second by a causal explanation from hidden mechanisms (knowledge structures, in pieces or otherwise).

The claim to "invention" (later, "native competence") foregrounds the agency of learners, while putting into the background (not really hiding,[3] we think) the agency of teachers, researchers, and their suitcases full of tools, tasks, video cameras, and assessments. What is hidden in MRC is a kind of subversive learning, done in private or in activities that are either unsanctioned or actively eliminated in conventional practices. In approaching this subversive learning (i.e., not school; see Sefton-Green, 2013), and similar to the account of discovery we gave for SMNs, we see researchers looking for structures of interaction that drive particular values in what counts as knowledge (i.e., Cartesian graphing rules over local inventions). We would expect that comparative talk about representations, reaching a critical consensus concerning adequacy, and the very idea that students could "invent" forms in a typical classroom would *also* require concerted efforts on the part of students, teachers, parents, and school administrators to keep practices of invention going in typical schools. A similar set of arguments can be found in focal analysis chapters and commentaries from a recent, multiple analysis project in which students were described as "inventing representations" of statistical concepts in classrooms studied (and designed) by Rich Lehrer and Leona Schauble (Koschmann, 2011).

We could be wrong about what will be a consequential explanation or theory of these kinds of representational fluency. Our desire to continue asking what these activities mean for their participants, or how relations between people and material at different levels of organization enable (or dissolve) these activities, may just delay new cycles of design and refinement along a developmental path that makes invention a commonplace occurrence in classrooms (Hall, 2011). Positing mental structures as an ontological layer behind these more complex, but primary (we think), phenomena reflects a desire for a particular kind of theory and explanation.

## *(4) What kinds of comparative analysis are productive and ethical, and what kinds should we avoid?*

> With schooling as the template, questions about apprenticeship were framed mostly in negative terms. True, the binary distinctions between "formal" and "informal" education posited some definite characteristics for formal education. Mainly, however, things present and important for carrying out schooling were presumed absent in apprenticeship – teaching as the central prerequisite for school learning, for example, and with its absence, a lack of effective organization to the learning aspects of apprenticeship. This tenacious perspective clearly directed the questions I asked in Happy

Corner [tailoring enclave in Monrovia, Liberia] to begin with and defined my expectations about what should be happening if the apprentices were going to learn. It explains the difficulties I had in coming to see that other things that were happening were crucial matters of learning.
*(Lave, 2011, p. 59)*

Most research in the learning sciences treats a particular site (e.g., a physics classroom, an after-school club, a museum exhibit) as a type of setting for studying learning or teaching. Whatever develops in the particular site is described and explained as the kind of thing that happens (or might happen) in this type of setting. In framing the role of comparison in this way, we do not mean to invite more careful forms of inference from sample to population (evaluation studies and education sciences are doing a bang-up job with that argument). Rather, we mean to ask how to draw comparisons across studies, or to conduct comparative analysis as part of a single study, in ways that may be enhanced by the interplay between ND and HM orientations. This is a form of inference from case to theory (Yin, 2011) rather than from sample to population. In our conversations, Jean Lave's development (with Etienne Wenger; Lave & Wenger, 1991) of the concept of "legitimate peripheral participation" has been very helpful in thinking about productive and ethical comparative analysis. The introduction of this concept, of course, came on the heels of a thorough critique of information-processing psychology as a hidden mechanism theory of cognition, learning, and meaningful human activity.

## *Legitimate Peripheral Participation*

The concept of legitimate peripheral participation (LPP) provides a structural, explanatory framework for a theory of "situated learning" (Lave & Wenger, 1991) that is made up of changing social relations to ongoing practice. These changing relations shape practice-linked identities – who one is understood by others to be – as much as they change what one knows or is able (or allowed) to do in practical activity. The unit of analysis is the relation between person and setting, understood as part of ongoing (perhaps changing) cultural activity. This theory and explanation for learning, often without explicit forms of teaching, is based on comparative analysis of apprenticeship relations across a wide variety of cultural practices. But the concept (LPP) has probably been most influential for critical and design-oriented studies of schooling, extending more recently into research on the relation between learning in schools and in other valued cultural practices. Even in settings where individual instruction and testing are dominant activities, and even if these are understood by participants to involve expert knowledge transmission to individual learners, these activities (and interpretations of learning) also can be understood as structured in social relations, with a history and the potential for both reproduction and for change.

LPP as a concept describes regularities that may not be lying around "in plain sight" for participants in the cultural practices being studied, or for analysts who visit the practice to study learning. In this sense, there is a structural account that could be read as a "mechanism" or "machinery" (Lave does not use these terms), which is not immediately visible or even sensible to the observer (particularly an alumnus of Western schooling) but must be revealed through comparative analysis of naturally occurring human activity. It is possible but not particularly responsible, Lave suggests, to study these things without becoming involved in their politics. These structural regularities, once adequately described, might serve as models for designing activities in or around schools, and many have attempted to do this (Gutiérrez & Vossoughi, 2010; Taylor & Hall, 2013).

The theoretical pathway here, as we argued at the outset in this paper, is not from natural description to hidden machineries. Instead, there is careful analysis and description of phenomena in historically specific, cultural situations, and a persistent effort to understand the activity from the social actor's point of view. The structural regularities that are developed as a theoretical concept (LPP) hold up to comparative case analysis, by suggesting which cases to study next (in terms of developing grounded theory, "theoretical sampling") and providing for structural refinement and a better understanding of conditions under which the concept operates. Through a form of interplay between ND and HM (describing structural influences), comparative analysis of ethnographic cases can be quite rigorous but still open to discovery.

Looking back on her initial fieldwork with Liberian tailors, Lave (2011, quote above) describes a series of misadventures in trying to understand learning in apprenticeship, treated as a "negative space" formed by comparing tailoring activities to seemingly more deliberate (or formal) practices of Western schooling. By trying to understand the historically particular setting of tailoring shops as a type of some other, idealized cultural form (Western schooling), her fieldwork produced a series of absences that neither satisfied Lave nor made much sense to her study participants (i.e., masters could perform didactic instruction, when asked in interview, but they never did so on their own). Eventually, by attending instead to the organization of tailoring work, the path of learners through this work, and to forms of assessment concerning apprentices' capacity for sewing garments in the service of producing sellable clothes, Lave arrived at a positive, structural description of apprenticeship learning in its own terms. In this sense, she struggled to remain open to what the particular practice under study could tell her, as an intact activity system with its own logics of production and learning.

If a comparison with idealized models of formal instruction (whether to valorize or critique apprenticeship) was not initially productive, the subsequent analysis leading to the concept of LPP did involve productive forms of comparative analysis. The monograph with Wenger (Lave & Wenger, 1991) describes structural regularities across a deliberately diverse collection of ethnographic cases. We will not rehearse that history here, but it is worth noting that the dimensional terms of LPP provide for structural descriptions of settings that both support and inhibit learning.

Participation, as a basic mode of engagement in cultural life, varies in ways that are influenced by two other dimensions. The learner can be seen and treated – with dramatic consequences for access to practice – as being a legitimate or illegitimate participant. Similarly, participation can range in centrality from peripheral to full. The particular configuration of legitimate, peripheral participation describes a pathway towards full participation. This configuration (LPP) tends to be used as if it were the theory, and in a romantic genre (i.e., Learning in this place is LPP, and therefore it is good!), to the exclusion of other possibilities available in the theory. We sometimes joke that freeloading contemporaries in difficult teamwork are legitimate, central, non-participants, for example. The single, negative case reviewed in the monograph concerns butchers in large-volume, middle-class supermarkets, who can spend years wrapping routine cuts of meat in plastic, without gaining access to the broader array of butchering activities available to their peers working in smaller, working-class stores (Marshall, 1972). There are very few studies of how LPP accounts for a failure to learn in the extant literature, but as this concept is extended to new cases, whether in or out of schools, we expect there will be further discoveries and refinements to the theory.

We end this discussion of a generous★ question with a comment on three forms of comparative analysis. In the first, one form of cultural activity about which relatively little is known (e.g., craft tailoring apprenticeships) is analyzed using comparative terms drawn from a theoretical account of some other activity, sometimes a normative or idealized explanation for how a universe of activities of a general type work (or more normatively, *should* work). This describes, we think, the initial misadventures Lave described in Liberia, and so raises the question of when and how to avoid these problems of creating "negative (comparative) space." In the second, multiple particular cases of cultural activity are studied and compared in hopes of identifying what they have in common, usually to outline a new type of cultural activity that will be of general interest (e.g., adolescent and professional use of location-aware communication devices; see Hall & Leander, 2010) or that could be used for some other purpose (e.g., designing learning activities in which adolescents learn new things about STEM concepts enabling these devices; see Taylor & Hall, 2013; Ma, this volume). In the third, comparative analysis focuses on transitions experienced by study participants as they move between cultural activities, or even as they assemble interstitial spaces that support new forms of learning (e.g., children's ways of talking around the dinner table by comparison with their structural access to conversation in classrooms as they begin formal schooling; see Erickson, 2004). Differences between these forms of comparative analysis (and others) run in parallel with King Beach's (1999) theoretical account of different types of "consequential transitions" in studies of learning and transfer. As he pointed out, not only are sites of study and participation juxtaposed, but each involves differently inflected values about the future of changing practices, as well.

## A Concluding Note on Doing Being Generous*

If Latour and subsequent ANT explorers have captured an important aspect of using/creating scientific knowledge-in-use, the stability of what in retrospect we might call a scientific contribution based on a ND (or a HM, or their combination) approach is tenuous until the dust (and network making) has settled. Some of the concepts, treated as cases in an as yet unwritten history of the learning sciences, have not been settled. We intend the conversation about generous* questions to be a conversation about methods, and about what we desire to make as researchers engaged in research on learning and teaching in conceptual domains that we care deeply about.

We have at this point had a lot to say. In the spirit of the events bringing the KAIA community together in the first place, we invite readers to take up these questions, and we look forward to further conversation and comparative analysis of cases as themselves generous* activities in an effort to develop more productive methods and concepts.

# Commentary

## "OPENNESS" AS A SHARED RESEARCH AESTHETIC BETWEEN KNOWLEDGE ANALYSIS AND INTERACTION ANALYSIS

*Mariana Levin*

Thinking about the four generous★ questions that Hall, Nemirovsky, Ma, and Kelton pose provided a convenient impetus for focusing and sharing some of my ongoing reflections on our agenda. Their piece covered a lot of terrain, and in this reflection I'm only going to try to follow up on one thread from it – that of what it means to have an "open" perspective on research. I hope this brief reflection is only the beginning of a longer conversation, both within the KAIA community and more broadly.

One of the key moves made by Hall, Nemirovsky, Ma, and Kelton was to suggest a reformulation of the discussion in terms of commonalities and differences across research practices and aesthetics as opposed to the surface differences in attributed topic of theorizing (e.g., knowledge or interaction). I found this move intriguing, productive, and "integrative" in spirit. In the piece, the authors propose a distinction between "natural descriptive" (ND) and "hidden machineries" (HM) approaches to theoretical work in science, and they point to several cases that they feel are illustrative of these two approaches. While I think it would be good at some point to return to a broader discussion of the sensibility of ND and HM as categories, in this essay I wanted to focus instead on the second part of the paper, in which the authors pose four generous★ questions to provoke discussion.

I found all four of the questions Hall et al. posed interesting and, each in their own way, provocative (in a good way – as in generative and stimulating). The first question, "Whichever approach we take (natural descriptive or hidden mechanism), how can we best remain open to what the actual details of human activity can show us?" in particular spoke to me. It seemed to point to something I feel is a shared value across our (KAIA) community. I wanted to take the opportunity in this turn★ to begin to explore the theme of openness in our research, especially in relation to work done in this community.

## Explorations Under Rocks and in Outer Space

In his plenary lecture at the KAIA conference in Marin, Chuck Goodwin talked about the importance of being open to what the world can show you – and then looking systematically to characterize what might be going on. The line "You couldn't make this up, sitting in your office" was taken as emblematic of the kind of open aesthetic we should have to our research. This line was quoted in the statement of the four questions in Hall et al., as well as referenced in our later discussions in Vancouver.

At a follow-up meeting in Vancouver, Rogers Hall reiterated this idea of openness in the search for the unexpected aspects of activity to notice in a story he told about how as a kid growing up in Texas he used to turn over rocks and find "really weird stuff." He likened the experience of doing research and finding unexpected things about how people think and learn as they engage in activities to being sort of like turning over those rocks in Texas. I was struck by Rogers' description of the personal joy that he felt in discovering the "really quite beautiful things that you can find in human interaction." I was struck not because openness to seeing new things was a foreign idea, but rather because it was an idea that at least in some ways deeply resonated with me. As I listened to this story of Rogers in Vancouver and the general discussion concerning maintaining an open stance in research, it reminded me of a story, the allegory of the Jungle on Mars, that Andy diSessa sometimes tells when he is introducing Knowledge in Pieces and Knowledge Analysis.

The story is this: Two scientists journey to a new planet ("Mars") for the purpose of studying the flora and fauna of the new planet. The first scientist comes ready to use the wealth of analytic methods and measurements he has developed for categorizing the vegetation on Earth. He immediately embarks on matching what he is observing on "Mars" into these existing categories, using the methods that he knows from his experience on Earth. In contrast, the other scientist also comes with a breadth of knowledge about plant life and methods of studying it on Earth, but the very first thing that she does is take a good look around the planet and just observe what is there before attempting to categorize. Even as new categories of classification emerge, this scientist retains a skeptical stance towards applying the categories – checking to make sure they really apply or whether a different category system entirely might be more apt and need to be developed.

Andy used the allegory to make the point that we as learning scientists need to appreciate the complexity and beauty of human knowledge. He argued that a basic part of research should involve questioning the very ontological categories we use to describe knowing. Characterizing the nature and form of knowledge is an empirical endeavor that involves observing both knowledge-in-use and knowledge-in-development. While we *do* build upon categories that have been created in previous analyses in our ongoing empirical studies, we must retain a skeptical stance toward those categories and we must always remain open to what the data can reveal about how knowledge (knowledgeability? knowing?) can be seen to function in activity. From a methodological perspective, the allegory can be understood as encouraging an open and evolving perspective in research. Not all studies can be perfectly designed a priori to shed light on an already conceptualized phenomenon. Not only is it not possible, but such a perspective is not always the most illuminating. In line with Goodwin's exhortation, it isn't possible to just make this stuff up sitting in our offices.

## *A Personal Turn Toward a Version of Openness*

Indeed, I first heard this parable of the scientists and the jungle on Mars at the very first AERA symposium I co-organized (on Knowledge in Pieces perspectives on the role of representations in mathematical cognition). This was the first substantive opportunity I had to interact personally with Andy and others using KiP in their work. For context, leading up to that conference, based on my own reading and work, a goal I had for an analysis was to use coordination class theory to trace the development of a student's understanding in an unexpected learning event that I had happened to capture as part of a study I was doing for a completely different project. Despite a lot of struggle, my initial analysis wasn't really getting off the ground because I didn't really have the right idea of what a coordination class was, much less how to recognize one or use the theory to guide my analysis. But more germane to this discussion on openness, before that AERA, it hadn't occurred to me that perhaps coordination classes were not even what I *should* expect to see in my data and that in order to determine that, I should work from the other direction: to look with fresh eyes at the data and see them for what they were instead of trying to see them in terms of some particular construct.

This personal turn toward a more "open" research attitude was sparked both by Andy's telling of the parable of the jungle on Mars in his discussant remarks at our symposium and also by a conversation before the symposium with some of the other participants. Given my struggles with the analysis I was trying to do, I was especially eager to get to talk to Andy and the others about coordination classes. After letting me explain the data and discussing them for a little bit, Andy said what at the time I thought was a most surprising thing: (something like) "You know, I actually tire quickly of this game – people always asking me 'Is THIS a coordination class or is THAT a coordination class?' Whether or not coordination class theory applies is actually what you might discover in the course of the analysis of your data. Is it about coordination classes? I don't know. Is it? Or is there something else going on?" In the moment, I was a bit taken back by how unhelpful Andy seemed to be in my quest to "see" coordination classes in my data! I turned at that point to Joe Wagner, another one of the symposium participants, who continued the discussion with me for a bit and helped me to understand a bit more what the function of coordination classes as a model of a particular kind of concept was.

Eventually it turned out that coordination class theory did serve a useful role as a kind of reference model in the later analysis that emerged. However, the way it was involved in the analysis was in a much more organic and generative way than a typical top-down, "identify and apply" model of the relationship between constructs and data. Of course, actually figuring out how to develop an interpretation of the data that is both grounded in open, "naturalistic" observation, and also guided by a heuristic epistemological frame (that includes an evolving "toolkit" of precise, yet malleable and extendable constructs like coordination classes) is a learned art in and of itself (and could be a topic for further discussion…). An important aspect for our ongoing work that I haven't tried to unpack here concerns the importance of naming the underlying epistemological assumptions and guiding metaphors for knowledge and learning that would even make the "negotiation" between data and a particular theory (e.g., coordination class theory in this case) sensible. I do think we need to articulate those assumptions and be aware of those metaphors because they can be both an asset in pushing our theoretical work forward and also a constraint in "blinding" us to other ways of seeing.

## Concluding Remarks

Returning to the original question of how we can remain open to the details of human activity – there seems to me to be (at least on the surface) a tension between on the one hand remaining open and "neutral" in noticing surprising, unexpected, and unexplored aspects of knowledge/knowing of learning interactions in data, and, on the other hand, recognizing previously explored conceptual categories when we see them in data. One heuristic for remaining open is to be sure that our theories are actually "doing real work" in their application to particular data. Painting the data with different theoretical perspectives and constructs can almost always be done. We need to make sure that theoretical categories not only apply but are insightful. Another heuristic for openness is assuming that we simply don't know much about cognition and how it functions in activity.

As Rogers pointed out in Marin – one thing that unites us as researchers working on the KAIA agenda is that we are a community of learning theory *builders*. As such, we have to learn to expect the unexpected, notice it when it presents itself, try to understand it, and then build on those insights in further studies. If we only went out and saw what we expected to see, we would never generate fundamentally new insights, as our job would be more concerned with assessing and measuring empirical data against our a priori theoretical expectations (like the first scientist in the allegory of the jungle on Mars).

I think we do need both an open and a skeptical attitude to the interface between previous theoretical categories and new data – we must always be prepared to see something new in the data. However, I think that we can (and do) practice more of a form of "disciplined openness." Obviously, given our differences in intellectual histories and research aesthetics, we have some differences in where we are looking in the data and what we're attentive and prepared to be open to. I think this is a point of potential strength in the agenda of bringing KA and IA together. At the follow-up meeting in Vancouver, we talked a little bit about stewardship of our ways of doing research and what kinds of researchers we want to be. On a personal note, one of the things I hope to get out of the interactions with researchers in this broader KAIA collaborative effort is a collection of new ways of seeing and interpreting data and new ways to being open to what it can show us.

# Commentary
# HOW SCIENCE IS DONE

*Andrea A. diSessa*

As one of the initiators of the Knowledge Analysis/Interaction Analysis (KAIA) agenda, I was gratified to find a chapter such as this one, offered by Hall, Nemirovsky, Ma, and Kelton.[4] The chapter is, indeed, generous – in the everyday sense, and also in the narrower generous* sense – in its treatment of some knotty issues. I find it to be without partisanship, and the intention to be neutral and balanced is everywhere visible. The reviews of histories of accomplishments, both within the KA and IA communities and outside them (Charles Darwin, Santiago Ramón y Cajal, Jane Goodall), are, in themselves, interesting, revealing, and good fodder for discussion. But, I'm most grateful that the chapter explicitly raises a meta-scientific perspective. It is more than possible (but I would not take it for granted) that what has separated IA and KA – or what might unite them – is as much meta-scientific as it is scientific. Predilections for ways to do science are almost certainly consequential, and the case of connections or disconnections between IA and KA really ought to be examined from that perspective.

Let me start with a sketch of what I think Hall et al. accomplished and then proceed with a sketch of my commentary. The generous* chapter centers on two modes of doing science: the hidden machineries mode (HM) and the natural descriptive mode (ND). HM seeks to find and defer explanation to things that are "behind" (below) the phenomenology of our investigations on an ontologically distinct level. It also projects a nature to this initially (but not ultimately) invisible level: It is, in some sense, like a machine (hence the term "machineries").

A workable and historically pregnant metaphor is that the HM level is something like "how a clock works": assembled of elements that interact in a kind of lock-step mechanism that produces the behavior that we see. However, the behavior – hands that go around and tell time – constitutes a distinct ontology from gears and springs. Indeed, we can know this because there are clocks that have hands that go around that have nothing like gears and springs in them. We can even dispense with hands and going around completely with a digital clock. The attitude that Hall et al. project on the HM mode is that, ultimately, scientific explanation is in discovering the gears and springs and how they work, and then there is nothing more to clocks.

The ND mode, in contrast, aspires to, or actually enacts, an *ontologically flat science*. One sits firmly within the level of the "phenomena of interest," and employs extensive and careful observation. Instead of seeking hidden machineries, the ND mode seeks such things as "noticings" that have not been previously taken into account, or whose wide import has been neglected. In complementary manner, one also seeks to prune accounts of the phenomena of interest of spurious observations through careful and rigorous attention to the details of the relevant phenomena, or by taking into account the accumulated body of work, specifically using the breadth of occurrences of the phenomena of interest.

It seems evident to me that the HM and ND modes might be abstracted from prominent strains in the KA and IA agenda, respectively. Indeed, my own construct of p-prims (presumably representative of the KA approach) is cited along with historical examples like Piagetian schemata and information-processing structures as prototypical HM science. On the other side, prominent contributors to IA, such as Charles Goodwin ("you could not make this stuff up," as cited by the authors) motivate and ground the ND perspective.

It's just at this point that generosity enters the argument prominently. Rather than pursuing the HM and ND modes as "KA vs. IA," Hall et al. recognize the legitimacy of each mode, and inquire as to when and how each can be valuable, often in concert with the other. In particular, in addition to rejecting any absolute primacy, they reject simple versions of articulating HM and ND, such as stage theories that contend that, for example, extensive ND exploration is always necessary as a precursor to HM modes of inquiry.

I've used the unassuming description of "mode" for HM and ND, although I believe that Hall et al. have inclinations of a particular scale both in time and in terms of community distribution in mind for these perspectives. They have "their own traditions, methods, and diverse professional communities." So, traditions and methods, and even whole professional communities, accumulate separately around HM and ND. In other places in Hall et al.'s chapter, HM and ND are referred to as "worldviews" and "ways of being." It seems that one can go a long time working within one or the other perspective: As described in the chapter, Darwin's ND work is followed years later by the HM of DNA; Ramón y Cajal's extended ND work followed the completion of HM work that elaborated optics and matter–light interactions. Similarly, the authors' "professional communities" comment (just above) suggests that one might not even meet adherents of the contrary perspective on an everyday basis, as one does within one's immediate professional cohort.

After this meta-scientific set-up, Hall et al. continue by asking an important and interesting set of questions, which I will not review (see the explanation offered, just below). We are invited to consider these questions in the light of recognizing both the HM and ND modes, while continuing to seek to understand their sensible relationships.

My comments on Hall et al. center on the HM and ND modes as constructs. In particular, I have to admit that I had a rather large set of quick reactions that problematize these as cogent categories. There is a lot to explore before I, at least, feel I can use these ideas productively as analytical tools. In addition, exploring the ideas of HM and ND in some detail will give priority to some important and potentially impactful meta-scientific issues that may otherwise not have a voice here.

I recognize that this choice is not exactly polite, deferring an offered avenue of continued consideration. However, such are many conversations where offered continuations are deferred or reformulated in succeeding turns, or even within turns. And, in giving even partial due to the constructs of HM and ND, a lot is in play, to which I don't believe I can do any justice while simultaneously continuing with the generous* questions.

## A Pithy Account of My Meta-Science

The following is a set of reflections on my own experience as a scientist, and also reflections on the nature of science more broadly, supported by cases in the history of science with which I have some acquaintance (just as Hall et al. did). The points were stimulated in their contrast to (or at least in relation to) many distributed points in the generous* chapter. However, I present them together, in the order of my own choice, and only occasionally and minimally with reference to the context of the related points made in the chapter. I do this in order to help show systematicities among the elements. I have chosen a personal approach in part because I don't want to project these ideas on the whole of the KA community, much less pretend that they have some authority over how everyone must view science. I don't want to go too far in the direction of "how things are." "How things seem to me" is good enough for present purposes.

While I believe that many elements I put forward are commonplace, a few are more idiosyncratic, and I expect it's safer just to put forward this little system of ideas as mine, rather than trying to be scholarly about the nature of science, which space here would not allow in any case. Even then, my exposition will be elliptical in various degrees, depending on the predilections of the reader. What I believe will become most clear, however, is that these elements contrast vividly with those that support and justify the HM and ND analytic.

### 1. Diversity and generativity in our toolkit for doing science: Kicking and screaming.

I think that all scientists, especially those in the learning sciences, have or should have a wide variety of tools to try out in any given inquiry. Speaking more carefully, I should call these *tool sketches*, because I believe any "tools" we use are always subject to further invention and refinement for the cases that we pursue. So, we schematize what we've found successful in the past, but our schematizations are always open to reinterpretation and development.

Empirical methods constitute such tools (tool sketches), but there are also sketches of bits and pieces of theories. Collins and Ferguson (1993) suggest "epistemic forms and games" to describe the final forms of scientific inquiry and related practices for developing them. I'll adopt their terminology, if not everything in their theory. An element of Collins and Ferguson's point of view that I do strongly support, and which will become important here, is that there are a lot of such forms and games. Looking at science from the standpoint of only two "games" (say, HM and ND), and even "doing" only one of those for extended periods of time, seems a rather severe simplification. The essential diversity of the category of "theory" (here represented by various forms) becomes a main element in my continuing discussion. Incidentally, the Collins and Ferguson form-and-game type that best matches my p-prims theory is called "primitive elements," as in the periodic table of elements.

With a bevy of epistemic forms and games at our disposal, what determines which to use? The easy, but simplistic, answer is "the ones that best fit present circumstances." The first bit of complexity is that it is likely or certain that individuals or groups have preferences and expertise for some games over others. But, also, the open nature of the set of forms and games is, for me, essential. And above many other things, I believe that science, done well, will inevitably drag us – kicking and screaming if necessary – toward non-preferred, but more apt forms and games. That process is not much like free choice, nor is it like being able to know in advance how things will work out, nor even like having on the table the particular form or game that will work best. Scientists should be aware of the kicking and screaming phenomenon, and they should cultivate a sensitivity to the ways that science should be allowed to drag us, including both sensitivities to problems and limitations in our current understanding and also sensitivities to possibilities that are not just trotting out things that have worked in the past.

The next two items in my list implicate a lot that is familiar, even conventional, concerning the nature of science, starting from the top-level categories: theory and observation. That fact certainly does not mean that these concepts are not in need of refinement and development. But they are serviceable as a starting place, and they constitute a benchmark that improved views of the nature of science should surpass.

## 2. Theory is never on the surface of things.

Pretty much everyone I know subscribes to the fact that theory is important. In my prior life as a physicist, this was not even slightly contentious. Even the most ND of physics researchers, experimentalists, recognized theory's central importance. Interestingly, the importance of theory is sometimes contested in the learning sciences, or it is even characterized as harmful. But I don't think very many in the KA or IA circles contest the importance of theory. What gets more complicated is the *nature* of theories.

It may be more controversial to say that theory cannot be found on the surface of things. What support this belief, for me, are endless examples of theories – and only questionable counter-examples – where theory does not look much like the world that it purports to explain. The world does not look like quantum mechanics. For example, impenetrability of solid matter is only a statistical fact in quantum mechanics, not a basic principle; there is a chance that a book on a table will fall right through it without breaking it. Similarly, space does not look curved. In fact, for many people, this is literally an unimaginable possibility. Yet, Einstein says it is curved, and he also says that the curvature of space replaces the notion of gravity as any kind of force, such as what is immediately salient in holding a heavy object in our hand. Gravitational force, per se, is literally gone in general relativity. Touching on a point to be developed later, Darwin transformed species from categories of similarity among animals and plants to categories of *essentially* diverse products (each individual) of very long-term processes that are beyond any sensible version of "observable."

The reasons that I support the non-superficial nature of theory in science also include theoretical ones, such as the basic fact that science is, after all, a human construction, made up to help us do things like explain and predict. My basic epistemological convictions also include the counterintuitive fact that, while the science we create will cleanly surpass our naive ways of thinking, it will always bear some earmarks of those ways of thinking. "The whole of science is nothing more than a refinement of everyday thinking," Einstein said. Although he did not in this quote mention the remaining earmarks of everyday thinking, he did so in other parts of his commentary on the nature of his science.[5]

## 3. Observation is never theory-free.

Auguste Comte (1855) said:

> If it is true that every theory must be based upon observed facts, it is equally true that facts cannot be observed without the guidance of some theory. Without such guidance, our facts would be desultory and fruitless; we could not retain them: for the most part we could not even perceive them.
>
> *(p. 27)*

While I don't endorse much of Comte's positivistic philosophy, this quotation contains, for me, the nub of a highly consequential truth. I think allegiance to this idea is widely shared. My guess is that the spirit of this idea is broadly shared in KA circles, and probably a little less so in IA circles. But see, for example, the interesting spin on this point in Hall (2000).

Now, I need to make a few modifications and extensions of this observation to make it maximally helpful. "Theory" in this quote is problematic in a number of respects. I do not think everyday observation implicates scientific theories, per se.

We need to extend the meaning of "theory" for these purposes to make contact with the inarticulate and non-scientific frameworks that lie behind observations of all sorts.[6] Being able to see everyday things imputes conceptions of objects and space that are certainly not articulately formulated nor explicitly tested. I would say they are just not of the same fabric as scientific theories.

It is also relatively common and convenient to separate the *observation theory*[7] from the focal ("substantial") theory, that which is in development. Optics might constitute an observation theory for Galileo's telescopic investigations of the celestial sphere; then, one might inquire about the substantial theory, what are the markings on the moon's surface: mountains, craters? Optics, per se, doesn't tell you what's on the moon, but it allows you to interpret what you see through a telescope. Consistent with my felt need to extend the meaning of theory to make sense of the idea that observation is always theory-based, another rendering of "theory" is as the *vocabulary of observation*: a collection of ontologies of things we believe we can just "see" in the world (even if we often don't recognize the theoretical/conceptual infrastructure of "seeing").

## 4. Science "rethreads" the universe.

Science consistently, if not always, rearranges the things we take as "going together" in the world. Here's a homely example. Let's say we are interested in the phenomenon of flames, such as a candle flame. As a matter of fact, one needs at least two perspectives, theories let's call them, to understand flames. First, a flame is an example of an exothermic (it gives off energy) chemical reaction. Now, naively, flames are not much like the things that are joined under the rubric of exothermic chemical reaction, such as rusting or explosions. It is easy to imagine (if it is not inescapable) that the pre-scientific construction of "the phenomena of interest" would leave out both rusting and explosions, since their qualitative features are so distinctive (violence rather than steady state; absence rather than presence of discernable heat and light).

The second theory of relevance to flames is fluid dynamics: in this case, steady state or chaotic flow of "fluids" such as air and vaporous hydrocarbons. From this perspective, flames go together with laminar (seen as layered symmetry in the flame) or chaotic flow (flicker), which create friction against a moving car. And flames go together with things that saliently display viscosity, such as considering certain properties of honey versus water, which properties are hardly perceptible as consequential, naively, in flames. Science "rethreads" flames from "a phenomenon of interest" to something with at least two major interwoven threads that each connect to bizarrely different things, at least as perceived by the pre-theoretical mind. In my micro-essay on approximate modularity (diSessa, this volume), I used the term "causal threads" to describe the general class of things exemplified here by exothermic chemical reactions and fluid mechanics within the phenomenon of flames. I believe that, in the learning sciences, nearly every phenomenon of interest will turn out to be multi-threaded in ways we mostly do not have a good grasp on right now, or in ways that are often construed as alternative accounts, like culture and individual cognition, rather than contributing threads.

I have not been able to think of any counter-examples to the rethreading principle.[8] Some of the phenomena and theories mentioned under "theories are not on the surface," naturally and for understandable reasons, also count as rethreadings – from initial or surface-based threadings to alternative ones.

## 5. Levels are legitimate, if complexly and diversely related.

The best and easiest starter example of levels that I know concerns digital computers. First, one has the surface phenomenology of interacting with a modern computer. Then, below that, there's the level of programming. Below that lies the level of device circuitry. And finally, below that, there's the level of the physics of the devices (often, quantum mechanics, which is necessary to understand transistors and larger-scaled devices built out of them). Now, one striking fact about these levels is their apparent independence. One doesn't have to know about programming to operate a computer (although whether one should is a different matter). Programmers, in turn, don't need to know anything about circuits. I believe that circuit designers don't, in general, know much quantum mechanics.

Part of the specialness of these particular levels is that they are designed, and they are designed, in part, so that people acting at one level do not need to understand the lower levels (or much about the higher ones). Levels that are not designed might not often have such clean modularity relations; that's just a fact of life.

In general, the phenomenon of levels gives me essentially no pause in physics and even less in the learning sciences. We certainly don't know everything about levels as a general phenomenon in science, but the rough landscape seems clear and unproblematic. Here are some representative observations, mostly having to do with relations between levels.

- *Homomorphic levels* – One of my favorite levels examples comes from physics, and I think it is scientifically unassailable. It turns out that there is an axiomatic formulation of thermodynamics. My first graduate textbook on thermodynamics took this approach (ter Haar & Wergeland, 1966). Shockingly (especially to many educators), one does not need to know anything about little randomly moving particles to develop axiomatic thermodynamics. In fact, that version of thermodynamics "doesn't care" whether the world is Newtonian or quantum mechanical. The world turns out to be quantum mechanical, but one doesn't have to know that to learn axiomatic thermodynamics. It doesn't in any obvious way do a learner good even to know quantum mechanics before learning axiomatic thermodynamics.

So, the basic phenomenon is that one can know a lot about thermal phenomena (not all that is possible, just a lot) without the details of the lower level. This reminds me of homomorphism in mathematics, where a slice of the structure of a system happens to be a perfectly understandable and complete "theory" all by itself, even maintaining a lot (or all!) of the vocabulary and structural relations of the "lower," more complex level. Hence, I'll appropriate "homomorphic" for this kind of levels relationship.

A different kind of homomorphic-level relationship involves approximate or rough models. Bohr's atom is one such example. It came before the full machinery of quantum mechanics, but got the essence of what quantum mechanics could explain that classical treatments could not: discrete spectra. At the same time, I believe everyone knew from the very beginning it was "wrong," at least in its details. Then, after quantum mechanics was more developed, Bohr's model was discarded, although it had played a critical role in the process that led physicists "kicking and screaming" into the quantum mechanical world.

Approximate but theoretically productive models are frequent in physics, and I think they may be more frequent in the learning sciences – except that I seldom find the equivalent epistemic attitude in the learning sciences. Learning scientists seem to me to be fixated on right or wrong, using the things a theory cannot do just to reject it (and thus not learning from the things it can do), rather than as opportunities to advance understanding.

I regard popularizations of scientific theories, also, sometimes as honorary homomorphic levels. They may use the same words as professional scientific discourse, but may not be sufficiently precise or detailed to constitute science proper. However, they are a proxy for the more subtle and often inaccessible theories in the highly consequential crucible of, let's say, educational application of theories of cognition.

- *Implementation relation* – The original computer example of multiple levels displays canonical implementation relations. For example, one doesn't need to know anything about circuitry to program a computer. Yet, if we could not realize the abstract structure of the programming level in physical devices – that is, if we could not implement it – we would have no computers. In some cases, we are in a good position to know that there must be some implementation relations to an underlying level, even if we do not even understand that level much at all. So, realizing the detail of the implementation will always remain a good scientific project, no matter how good the *implemented* level is for our practical purposes. I think we can create good theories of knowledge★ (good, modern theories of knowledge; see diSessa, Sherin, & Levin, this volume), yet I recognize that it would be good to know how those get implemented in biological mechanisms (as mysterious as the mechanisms of the brain still are). It might be useless to understand the implementation if our theories at the knowledge level are good enough. But it still stands as an important scientific thing to do.

- On the other hand, I think the right default assumption is that understanding implementation will probably add useful detail, at least.[9] To take a perhaps controversial example, we might propose that culture (or interactional structure) is implemented within a cognitive level; then I would strongly suspect that the cognitive level would be quite illuminating of the higher level. Said differently, I would guess that culture is not as independent of cognition as one finds, for example, between programming and circuits. This contrasts with my guess that, at this stage, we do not have a lot to gain by reducing cognition (knowledge★) to brain processes.

- *Function/structure relation* – This is a special kind of implementation relation. Any act of design generally has a functional "top" level. That does not mean the top level has no structure[10] in the sense of an articulation of entities, relations, and even processes (consider, again, programming). Anticipating later discussion, one might say that the functional level may also have "machinery," even if one is more tempted to use the term for the underlying level, the one that implements the upper level.

  I believe that it is fair to say that whatever ontology function belongs to, it is immaterial. One "sees" things like the function of tiger claws in their ability to catch and hold prey only metaphorically.

I close this section with a negative tone. Since I believe in levels and the value of understanding their complex and diverse relationships, I personally find the idea of eliminative materialism abhorrent. In cognitive science, *eliminative materialism* comes down to the claim that since the mind is a biological machine (neural mechanisms, let's say), all explanation must, ultimately, be at this material level. Within the eliminative perspective, we must categorically throw out all the "folk" beliefs that we have inherited (such as belief in "concepts," or even "mind," as separate from brain), both because folk ideas are just wrong (which is easy to show; consult the huge literature on "misconceptions") and because they are of the wrong type, wrong ontology: They are not brain processes. John Searle (1980) and various neural scientists such as Paul and Patricia Churchland (e.g., Churchland, 1981) have argued for versions of this position. I believe that there is no basis to rule out important homomorphic levels before trying to find or create them. Ruling them out might greatly stall worthy and practical advances that could even provide hints and constraints in aid of understanding the implementation level. If statistical thermal physics had occurred first in the history of science, would the axiomatic version have been ruled out? Should we have refused the more phenomenological roots of thermodynamics because they were independent of quantum mechanics? For a congenial critical view of reductionism (a more general form of eliminative materialism), see Midgley (2011).

## Illumination and Critique of HM and ND

Most of the real work for this commentary is done. The astute reader has noticed anticipations and probably filled in a lot of what is to follow, which is a set of observations concerning, on the one hand, the meta-scientific point of view laid out by Hall et al. in their concepts of HM and ND, and, on the other hand, the comparable view laid out here. Mostly I find misalignment and difficulties assimilating the HM/ND view into mine. In what follows, I use the principles announced above singly or in combination, developing them a bit when the need arises, in order to consider the nature of HM and ND as cogent and helpful in construing cases of scientific inquiry.

## *General Considerations: HM and ND Versus Theory and Observation (First Pass)*

I put forward the constructs of theory and observation, augmented by the concept of levels, as a kind of competitor to the HM/ND dichotomy. It's not exactly a replacement, but it deals with similar phenomena.[11] Indeed, I think it deals better with some phenomena explored in the Hall et al. paper than the HM/ND frame does. After unveiling relevant considerations at this level, I will turn specifically to what I find difficult to assimilate individually about HM and ND.

Let me rehearse more of what I take to be useful lore concerning theory and observation. First, "everyone knows" that theory and observation are both necessary and important in science, even if, at various times, one may be highlighted more than the other. After a strong, well-formulated theory is put forward, one seeks to test it via observations. Theory also can emerge from extended, careful consideration of a large body of observations. This is a mode with which I have a particularly strong connection (e.g., Parnafes & diSessa, 2013). Examples of diverse short-term and long-term interactions between theory and observation and examples of different sequential relationships are easy to generate. This is the same epistemic game that Hall et al. propose to play concerning HM and ND. I mention a few more useful such relations below.

Theory and observation are taken by many to be intimate, reflecting Comte's formulation. So, extended phases of working on one without also working on the other should be relatively rare. Phases of doing one without the *presence* of the other should be rarer, or possibly non-existent. I don't see any sensibility in theory and observation being alternative world views (as HM and ND are put forward) nor for professional communities to settle around one or the other, exclusively (though, perhaps, mathematics, which is so important to the infrastructure of certain theories and to the "processing" of some classes of observations, might be an exceptional case). I don't perceive any of my immediate colleagues, including the authors of the generous★ paper, to be markedly unbalanced with regard to theory and observation. Perhaps that is a great unrecognized resonance between KA and modern IA.

Observation theories, per se, offer another model of the relation between theory and observation. Some theories are necessary for our very observations, but they often or always are unconcerned about the key theoretical elements of emerging new theories – the theories for which observation theories produce observations. Recall that optics, as a kind of observation theory, can justify interpretations of what Galileo saw in his telescope; then one can go on and investigate matters concerning what is observed. Optics, per se, has nothing to say about the structure of the moon. Being relatively independent of the theories on which their observations bear is, in fact, one of the main epistemological points of observation theories. The theories of light and interactions with matter (the case of Ramón y Cajal in Hall et al.'s chapter) are precisely of this form – they serve as observation theories – a point not noted by Hall et al. So, relatively (or extremely) independent trajectories of development for, on the one hand, theories of particular domains and, on the other hand, observation theories, are not at all surprising. Darwin's case is decidedly different. DNA, identified as a HM phase in Hall et al., most definitely intersected the theory of natural selection. It filled in details of inheritance and also of the causes and kinds of variation that Darwin knew he needed but could not resolve. It seems this particular relation could be rendered well by saying that DNA constituted an implementation level for some aspects of natural selection that were inaccessible to Darwin.

Observation theories are sometimes applied over extended periods of time and in composition with other theories to produce workable *technologies of observation*. Hall et al. make a similar point in the second half of their paper. This form of development in science seems to me very insightful concerning what Ramón y Cajal was doing with microscopy and tissue staining. More generally, the degree of interaction and time overlap between technology development and observation theory development are generic and fairly open parameters of interest in recounting any case of developing observation technology.

Already we've seen some appropriation of HM/ND phenomenology into the more familiar scheme of theories, observations, and their relations. To the extent that HM/ND is like theory/observation (and I think there are some strong similarities: ND looks very much like observation; HM looks like a restricted type of theory), other characteristics of HM/ND begin to be suspect. For example, the assumption that HM and ND can exclusively occupy scientific pursuits for extended periods of time and that they may also be exclusive distinguishing characteristics of professional communities might be called into question.

## *Implausibilities of the HM Mode*

I find that HM makes implausible assumptions about how often, even whether, reduction between levels can work in understanding complicated systems. First, at a general level, my own dispositions include a high degree of diversity of modes of scientific study, as marked by Collins' epistemic forms and games and also considering the multiple dimensions of meta-science that I've broken out. This is the "rich and generative" principle in my initial meta-scientific sketch. The extent to which cases can match the HM and ND prototypes will be an issue in some of the details below. In particular, I will show some substantial commonalities between Darwin's characterized-as-ND work and HM work. And, I will also put forward some elements of my own work on p-prims, characterized by Hall et al. as HM, that seem to match elements of what Darwin did.

Let us start by pursuing reduction (or eliminative materialism) in the simple context of clocks as an example that might well inspire the idea of the HM mode more generally. The big picture, which I've already introduced, is that the way Hall et al. portray the HM model appears to me a form of reductionism, or even eliminative materialism. That doesn't work for me.

If clocks represent the HM mode then, we must, as previously noted, take cognizance of the fact that clocks can be built out of very different technologies – gears and springs versus digital electronics. Looking very carefully at gears and springs or other technology may tell you some things about clocks, but there is so much in that level of machinery that it seems plausible that clockness, per se, may always be clouded in the complexities of that underlying level.[12] How do we pick out what is essential for clockness from knowing the implementation technology? In the end, even if we can explain clocks at the implementation level, the (homomorphic) higher-level view of clocks might still be immensely important in sorting out what is clock-relevant about gears or digital electronics and what is not.

Coming at things from the other direction, imagine an alien archeologist from a different universe arriving on Earth after our civilization has gone. They study gears and springs, or digital electronics, and figure out their principles of action. Yet, what do they then know about clocks and whether examples of gears and springs are "the same" in any respect (they might be clocks) as another set of examples of digital electronics?

Here is what I think the alien *should* come to know about clocks.[13] Clocks do chronometry. They should realize that one might want to measure time, or locate oneself in time, and it might also be important to allow easy access to multiple grain-sizes of measurement over which we might need to do chronometry, such as hours, minutes, and seconds. These different scales are implemented as hands on a mechanical clock, and in other ways (e.g., separate displays) on most digital clocks. "Doing chronometry" could be regarded as a functional level for clocks. Then, the technology is at the implementation level, which might be necessary to understand some things about particular clocks (their behavior in varying temperature, for example), but it does not call out the top-level and most important thing about clocks in a perspicuous way, or possibly not in any way.

At this point, I make an observation in anticipation of later discussion. In the case of clocks, the designer intervenes in creating the specifications for clocks (and also, likely, in relevant implementation of these specifications, respecting the characteristics of the implementation systems). This introduces a plainly different causality, a kind of teleological causality, separate from that which one finds in the implementation technology. Now, Darwin's natural selection does not have a designer per se. But, the process (evolution) that results in the creation of a particular "design" (a species) is also at least somewhat independent of the causality within the system as implemented (how the species achieve certain functions). In other places, I call the "design" causality *long-loop causality*, to mark that it is an *extended* process (in time and space) that creates configurations that are locally (in time and space) causal in the "designed" thing that serve the functions at issue.

## *The Problematic Rendering of Visibility in the HM Model*

Hall et al. make the following point about visibility of machinery in the HM model: "[T]here is the expectation that the postulated entities (e.g., electrons, genes) will, eventually, become observable in multiple and independent ways."[14] I do not think this is a good assumption for any decent meta-science. Certainly small (or, in general, hard to see) physical entities may become visible, as they did in the Ramón y Cajal case, but this is a small class of scientific entities. I believe that, even in the Ramón y Cajal case, a lot of importance resides in the underlying "mechanisms" within and between cells, which mechanisms are not visible. The chemical processes in cells or electrical interactions across them are not things that can just be directly seen, like cells themselves. In the final quotation of Ramón y Cajal cited by Hall et al., he seems to make abundantly clear that the importance of seeing actual cells is that the mechanisms of signaling along nerves then must be of a different sort than previously hypothesized. Concerning mechanisms and processes, of course, we can make representations of them, which are visible, but a stronger microscope, per se, doesn't particularly help. Instead, we build firm *inferential pathways* from things we can see (perhaps meter readings or other measurements) to the central entities and processes of our science. In the case of cells, we need to understand diffusion, metabolism, inter-cell electrical influence and the like, and in the relevant inferential pathways, of course, theory is strongly implicated.

One might think that the idea of visibility of underlying mechanisms is inherited from physics: "the clockwork universe." But nothing could be further from modern physics than visibility. No one has ever observed a quantum field, which constitutes the bottom level of explanation for a lot of modern physics. Indeed, because of the nature of quantum mechanics, quantum fields are in principle not directly observable. That is no problem, however, because strong inferential pathways lead us to and from observable things. Quantum fields are consistent with essentially every observation we have been able to make in physics, and they explain some details that are inaccessible to any higher level of explanation. The question of whether electrons (mentioned by Hall et al. in the quote above) are visible might be a boundary case. Electromagnetic waves (visible light, or even X-rays) are too coarse to see even atoms, let alone electrons. One uses "matter" waves (ironically using electrons) to see atoms instead of electromagnetism. But electrons are literally infinitely smaller than atoms, since the best modern theory has electrons as point particles. How can one see that? One can't.[15] One only finds that the assumption of point particles is consistent with other theory, and also consistent with inferred and observable consequences. On the whole, then, I do not think that electrons are visible.[16]

A similar story about visibility can be told about general relativity (and, between quantum fields and general relativity, we've pretty much covered the bottom level of explanatory frameworks in modern physics). My instructor of general relativity in graduate school, a Nobel laureate, gave his last lecture saying that "bent space" was just an effective metaphor, and particle exchange was what is "really" happening: Gravity is a force (particle exchange is *the* modern model of "forces"), after all. One simply cannot observe bent space in order to determine if it is there. One just observes implications of that theoretical construct.

Thinking on a grander scale, one should be skeptical of insisting – or even expecting – that the modality of vision has any claim to exclusivity in defining science. Vision is a very particular, evolutionarily endowed capacity, and one implemented with a very particular and limited technology. The proper replacement is inferential access, as suggested above. I am opposed to insisting on visibility as a basic assumption behind any scientific mode. To the extent such a claim is present in the idea of a HM mode, I consider it suspect.

To sum up, theoretical descriptions often or always do not look like the familiar world of observations we make as humans. Meta-scientific projections that depend on unquestioned observation principles can't take us very far into the secrets of the universe.

## *Implausibilities of the ND Mode*

I continue by considering implausibilities that I see in the ND mode, taking off pretty much at the final point made just above. ND science supposedly enacts an ontologically[17] flat science, one that sits firmly within the level of the "phenomena of interest." Furthermore, Hall et al. seem to insist that this level is mono-ontological. "Explanation remains with *the* observable ontology"[18] (emphasis added). Is this sensible? I previously argued that science rethreads phenomena, so it seems unlikely that scientific scrutiny of a phenomenon can remain ontologically flat. But there is a prior problem. What is the status of observation before and possibly without relevant scientific theory?

Here, we return to Comte's observation and my amendment of it. One cannot observe without a "theory," where "theory" includes implicit and intuitive frameworks that have not had scientific scrutiny. Observation that one might do "within the ontology of the phenomena at issue" is not free from such "theories," and they are almost certainly not mono-ontological. For example, concerning

Hall et al.'s narrative on Goodall, she and her detractors made observations about the spatial locations of particular creatures and other things, such as feeding stations. So far, we may be within one ontological field, having to do with objects in space. But what is the status of other observations that they made? For example, consider this sentence from Hall et al.'s chapter: "Goodall's observations about chimpanzees' aggression have been criticized as a result of feeding stations used at the Gombe Stream Park, suggesting that war-like behaviors observed by Goodall were not 'natural' among chimpanzees." What are "aggression" and "war-like behaviors"? They are certainly not spatial. Instead, these are something like projections of psychological categories that are familiar to humans; so enters another ontology. Things get rapidly more complicated. One imputes psychological states from facial expressions and gestures, so there are "theoretical" links for these things (whatever their ontology) to psychological or bodily states. Relevant "theories" also impute consequences for psychological/bodily states (anger breeds aggression; aggression breeds fear in others; aggression and physical conquest breed status).[19]

I do not believe that *any* theory is mono-ontological. To take a familiar example where we might have a clearer view of theories and ontologies, Newton's laws, $F = ma$, involve both force and acceleration. Acceleration is within the (ontological) category of space-time geometry. Force is quite different. It connects tangentially to space (forces have a place and a direction), but essentially new features get involved, some almost certainly proprioceptively grounded rather than having the dominantly visual grounding of geometric categories. Historically, we can see the important distinctness of these categories. Galileo did quite well with the space-time concepts of speed and acceleration. He did not really get (the ontology of) force figured out.

All in all, I think what Hall et al. describe as mono-ontological levels are better rendered as mono-theoretical levels; they involve all the relevant ontologies from one "causal thread." These are perfectly plausible from my meta-science perspective, but somewhat rare. As I explained, more typically, especially during the scientific development of a phenomenological domain, multiple threads are more likely. The sort of ND "observation" portrayed by Hall et al. may be even more problematic in not recognizing the "theories" behind observations. So, pure ND observation may be "*ragged*," involving an unrecognized collection of observation types and implicit "theories," and it may be *unprincipled* in that no analysis of the relevant ontologies and theories is even broached. Our tendency to naturalize familiar observations as direct and unproblematic hides what we must do as scientists. We must expose our potentially hidden and unrecognized "theories" (whether they are observation theories or more "substantial ones"), and improve or replace them as necessary.

A final note: What can Hall et al. mean by (paraphrase) "bringing to the fore the wider significance of previous observations," which they take to be a typical function of ND research? I think the way that wider implications are created is typically to build a new theory or significantly alter a previous one. So, more or different ontologies are even more likely.

To reprise the argument, the ontologically flat assumption seems to me implausible for any rich set of observations; it is implausible for any theory, even intuitive observation "theories," and it is even more implausible in doing something like "exposing wider impact." The only plausibility I see for ontologically flat observations' building significant scientific results is that for some (few) purposes, implicit and possibly everyday "theories" might be good enough. I believe that sometimes happens, but it is never a "restful" place to remain in scientific inquiry.

## Darwin's Theory

This section backgrounds general concerns about ND, but tries instead to look at what Darwin did with a different eye. I propose that there is a lot in common in his work, characterized as ND by Hall et al., with HM (to the extent that we can ignore some of the inherent difficulties I see in the concept of HM). To anticipate, we will see multiple levels, new ontologies, and even "machinery," all of which are ruled out in a characterization of Darwin's work as ND.

Hall et al. emphasize observations in their account of Darwin's work, and they de-emphasize the nature of his theory. When we look a little more carefully, I think what he did looks very different from ND. This is not to say that Darwin's acuity and breadth of observation do not make him singular. It is just that observation alone is only part of the story.

To embark from a previous point, function is front and center in Darwin's theory of natural selection. The concept of "fitness" of a species to an environment is functional. That is, features or structures of the species serve critical life-sustaining functions…or they don't, which ends in evolution or extinction. As noted before, function is not a material ontology. We can describe it as a homomorphic level above the physical structure (phenotype) of members of the species.

So, Darwin's accomplishment is in this very important way at least bi-ontological in a familiar way: function and structure. But there is another ontological innovation in Darwin's theory that, to me, is even more important. It is an innovation of a type ("species") within the ontological category of "causality."

To my mind, Darwin gave the first account of *ensemble causality* in the history of science. I will sketch what I mean by this, but the ideas, if not the name, should be entirely familiar.

In Darwin's account, species are really an ensemble of individuals, each of which have little or no ability to change; said differently, there is no causal thread of essential change (where "essential" means with respect to heredity) within individuals.[20] Change – in particular, change that might lead to the creation of a new species – enters in at the ensemble level. (Note the level split, here, between individuals and ensembles.) That causal thread is still quite interesting, even if it is now familiar. Individuals differ in many ways from one another, and this diversity is essential to ensemble causality. The fit of each individual to its environment determines its likelihood of survival and procreation. Thus, the future of the ensemble (or, its "average," if one allows that conceit) shifts. The future ensemble is the future of only some individuals, and succeeding generations repeat the process. Succeeding generations start with a different set of variations, around a new "average" (continuing that conceit). In net, over eons, initially unimaginable variation can take place, including the creation of entirely new and apparently essentially distinct species stemming from the same "original." As Darwin (1859, 1976) put it, "natural selection ... accumulate[s] all profitable variations, however slight, until they become plainly developed and appreciable to us." (p. 175)

Deep difficulties of students in grasping ensemble causality echo the incredible novelty of Darwin's creation. One essential difficulty is merely keeping track of the two levels and where change enters in. Another difficulty is in the role of chance and randomness. Yet other difficulties lie in leaving behind (a) "the designer" in this case of natural "design" (to specifications set by the environment), and (b) common tropes of elliptical causality[21] ("ducks have webbed feet *so that* they can swim"), or even agency-based accounts ("ducks change themselves so that they can swim" – like body builders change themselves so that they can lift huge weights).

Ensemble causality constitutes, in my mind, a new and important ontology in the pantheon of science, all by itself. I think it lies manifestly beyond the vocabulary of observation accessible before Darwin created his innovations. It is not the material sort of level imagined by Hall et al., but I have already argued that material reductionism is a simplistic and limited view of multi-level explanation.

With the exception of "containing things that must be directly seen" (as opposed to inferentially accessible), I do not see any objection to referring to ensemble causality as "machinery." It has: a relevant set of things (e.g., individuals and species); a set of parameters of these things (e.g., structural variation, "fit" with the environment); and, most importantly, a dynamic that can be "run" to see how evolution might proceed – taller animals had a great advantage over shorter ones in the savanna, hence giraffes! One doesn't need the implementation level proper, DNA, to imagine roughly how things might develop over time.

The autonomy of the level constituted by ensemble causality is attested to in Darwin's immense accomplishments in understanding the development of individual species. And yet, we know that important implementation-level contributions were to come. DNA, as noted by Hall et al., added some things, most particularly explaining elements of heredity that Darwin knew he could not explain, and also introducing new phenomena, such as genetic drift (understood as a shift in the frequency of a particular allele in a population), the effects of which Darwin did not, and probably could not, notice. The part of diversity of individuals due to sexual procreation also became clearer and more refined. Darwin also could not anticipate genetic engineering, where we can actually intervene at the implementation level (DNA). Yet, natural selection and ensemble causality stand to me as a "substantially autonomous level" (which Hall et al. explicitly and literally rule out of ND inquiries), almost a mathematical one (attested to by how easy it is to write a computer program to demonstrate the essence of natural selection; see "the blind watchmaker algorithm" in Dawkins, 1986).

Two final points: Darwin simultaneously changed the very ontology of species, from an immutable essence explaining similarity to a constantly changing and shifting ensemble. As I do, Darwin himself put this change explicitly at the center of his theoretical innovations. And Darwin explicitly lists in the last paragraph of *The Origin of Species* (1859, 1976) the various threads that he had to discover and intertwine to come up with his theory: growth and reproduction, inheritance, variability and its causes, ratio of increase (geometric growth of unchecked populations), struggle of life, natural selection, divergence of character or extinction. I cannot see these, individually or collectively, as ND accomplishments.

## Natural Selection and P-prims

Since p-prims were explicitly called out by Hall et al. as HM creations, I would like briefly to present my own view. First of all, p-prims are not things we can ever expect to see. Or, at least, I am quite agnostic about their ultimate disposition. At this stage, I offer them as a model, a homomorphic level, that, like natural selection, has its own insights to give (if rather more modest ones than Darwin's). I don't expect that there are necessarily any corresponding "things" at the neural level. However, I am open to the possibility that there might be some semblance of this. I hypothesized that p-prims operate as kinds of recognitions. To the extent that the brain implements recognition in very particular ways, details there may help with understanding the phenomenology connected to p-prims.

P-prims have their functional aspects; they contribute feelings of confidence and naturalness, or, on the contrary, feelings of something's being wrong. Hence, the same non-physical ontology (function) plays a central role. In other corners of my work, function is even more prominent. Coordination classes are in essence completely functional things. To be sure, things like p-prims can play a role in implementing the functions of coordination classes, but the concept of coordination class, itself, is functional. If any part of my work is strictly in HM modes of doing science, I don't see it.

In other things I have written, I have proposed a version of evolution as a general framework for understanding knowledge and intelligence (diSessa, 1994). I begin by rejecting reductionist claims, such as those by Searle, who claims that "brains cause minds" (Searle, 1984, p. 39). I then move to the evolutionary perspective that "the history of their development causes minds." The distinction between local causality (brain mechanisms) of minds and the long-loop causality of evolution is central here. The details are not relevant, but, to the extent that Darwin was doing something different than HM-based science, so am I. Of course, according to my view, neither of us is doing (exclusively) ND- or HM-based science. Within the meta-scientific perspective I have put forward here, it is difficult for me to see any stark differences between us.

While Hall et al. minimize the importance of theory and ontological innovation in Darwin's work, I emphasize it. Theory, per se, is particularly important in my meta-science, and also in the science that I do. Again, I don't believe there is much difference between the way that I work and the way Darwin did, at this level of consideration. In generating the p-prims model, I iterated for several years on a rather large (though puny, in comparison to Darwin's) database of observations, looking for ways to understand it. Here is how Darwin (1859, 1976) describes his process:

> When on board H.M.S. Beagle, as naturalist, I was much struck with certain facts in the distribution of the inhabitants of South America, and in the geological relations of the present to the past inhabitants of that continent. These facts seemed to me to throw some light on the origin of species – that mystery of mysteries, as it has been called by one of our greatest philosophers. On my return home, it occurred to me, in 1837, that something might perhaps be made out of this question by patiently accumulating and reflecting on all sorts of facts which could possibly have any bearing on it. After five years' work I allowed myself to speculate on the subject.
>
> (p. 65)

This does not sound much like the dispassionate ND observer, collecting and dispatching observations for no systematic reason. It sounds like a methodical search for a new theory, which eventually replaced his starting theory. The search was stimulated, in fact, by incongruences he had observed between his expectations (cultivated common sense about the distribution of variations of species) and what he glimpsed might be contained in some of his observations on the *Beagle*. Importantly, Darwin describes that this search for relevant facts began in earnest after he had made all of his observations in the field. Like Comte's "desultory facts," much that he observed in the field was abandoned, and only a select part, suitably refined to best relate to his evolving theory, remained.[22] Darwin, in my eyes, is a grounded theorist through and through, who was patient enough to bother to create new ways of seeing, new ontologies in the form of new concepts (e.g., a new version of "species"), and even a dramatically different "machinery for the universe," which I've called ensemble causality.

Finally, Hall et al. give the impression that individual scientists and communities can get stuck with their predilections to do one kind of science (such as HM-based science) or another. I am more optimistic, based on the "kicking and screaming" phenomenon. In reflecting on the development of the p-prims model (diSessa, 1994), I described myself as a "disappointed physicist" (p. 2). Many of the initial expectations that I had about naive physics turned out not to work. I liked the simplicity of compact and timeless expressions of theories one frequently finds in physics, such as Newton's laws, Einstein's general relativity, or Maxwell's laws. Though "kicking and screaming" is overly dramatic, I nonetheless found myself pulled into a very evolution-like regime, where accidents of history created a wonderful, if essentially complex, variety of species (p-prims) that we need to know individually in order to understand present-day cognitive ecology (diSessa, 2002). I didn't sign up to become a biologist in changing from physics to the learning sciences. But, Nature taught me a relatively painless lesson on fairly short order.

In the last paragraph of his own introduction to his monumental volume, Darwin (1859, 1976) also remarked that he had been dragged "kicking and screaming" to an initially very implausible conclusion:

> I can entertain no doubt, after the most deliberate study and dispassionate judgment of which I am capable, that the view which most naturalists entertain, and which I formerly entertained – namely, that each species has been independently created – is erroneous.
>
> *(p. 69)*

Later work compelled him to an even more counterintuitive conclusion, one against a central fabric of his society, and one with which he struggled himself and within his household: Man descended from apes. Could there be any more graphic illustration that the epistemic forces of science well accomplished can overcome initial predilections, however strong these might be?

## Conclusion: Where Are We? Where Can We Go from Here?

When I read Hall et al., I found myself swamped with intuitive reactions that ranged from puzzlement to feelings of disbelief. "Hidden machineries," which was to describe at least some of my science, entailed a brand of material reductionism that seemed unambiguously outside of my own experience with science and the way I understood parts of the history of science with which I have an acquaintance. "Natural description" seemed to me to focus exclusively on things that can be naively seen, as if to deny that science essentially always uncovers hidden worlds that don't look like the overt one. Natural description seemed to naturalize naive observations and put them into the category of "unencumbered by theory." That struck me as awkwardly naive realist. Descriptions of science that I know something about (Darwin), but also science of which I was only barely aware (Ramón y Cajal), put some phenomena in strange boxes (treating sequences of sciences, which were about different things, as if they were some natural sequence within one domain). And some things that I felt were absolutely central (the essence of Darwin's great theoretical accomplishment) had essentially no analysis.

So, then, this commentary is an attempt to unpack my own intuitive reactions, to systematize them a bit, and to make them sensible to others.

What is the outcome of these efforts? In a certain sense, we have not come very far. I believe my exposition has made clear that there are different predilections concerning "how science works." But, as I said early on, I don't want to go so far as to say mine is a "better" or more faithful to what "really" happens. Meta-science is murky, unsettled, and contested. Furthermore, I don't think we know how my dispositions and those of Hall et al. are distributed across the IA/KA "divide." I am acutely aware that some of my predilections are personal, and I have no real basis to support my feeling that some are very widespread, at least in certain communities.

But, here's the revised generous* inquiry that I offer in reaction to that of Hall et al. I would be interested to understand the distribution of some relatively full range of meta-scientific ideas across the KA/IA "divide" as it now stands. It seems certain that other bases for describing science would need to be added to the list created here. Then, we might be in a better position to find a core out of which we could build a more synthetic view. Or, at least, we could become clear on where we stand and have targets to settle in further progressing toward synthesis. Another potential usefulness would be to look carefully at emerging synthetic research, as represented in quite a number of chapters of this volume, to see how it plays out meta-scientifically. Are we all being dragged "kicking and screaming" toward a more similar view? Or are we, in fact, playing the rapprochement/synthesis game in different ways, depending on our previous dispositions? All of this does pick up the "game" of closely examining cases of the development of science to see what they look like, which was suggested by Hall et al. and which I most heartily endorse. That may be the best game we can play at the present time with respect to meta-scientific issues, and it stands out as a strong commonality across my views as expressed here and those of Hall et al.

I don't know how instrumental this inquiry can be in moving IA and KA toward some more definitive rapprochement than has been achieved. However, "how science works" is certainly an inquiry for the ages. I personally find examining others' science, and my own, infinitely engaging – and at least potentially important in changing and improving what is done under the banner of scientific inquiry concerning learning.

## Cumulative Notes

1 Generous* questions are designed to invite attention to our assumptions and commitments, in ways that make them visible for discussion, further study, refinement, and use.
2 We do not have access to the work of discovery in any of these more recent historical cases, and at this point, the investigators may not either. Still, we offer our understanding of how the interplay of ND and HM approaches might have contributed in each case.

3 Explaining structural regularities in interaction in terms of unobserved mental structures, while backgrounding analysts' work practices that were involved in finding these regularities, may be similar to deleting modalities when claims about Nature are made by scientists in a realist rather than a contingent repertoire (Callon & Latour, 1992). This practice would be consistent with an epistemic framing of natural description as preliminary to hidden mechanism accounts. Explanation and desire go hand in hand.
4 The authors revised their chapter after my commentary was finalized and sent to them. However, I believe that essentially all of my comments remain productive if a few are reinterpreted as "One might think …" explorations, rather than "These authors have committed themselves to …." The logic in the argument stands, independent of who affiliates with what particular ideas. I will add "in-press" notes on relevant points in this contribution.
5 Einstein maintained that in doing science one searches among our everyday ideas (such as rulers, clocks, and measurement) for ones that are suitable for axiomatizing (rulers, clocks, and measurement, it turns out). The resulting axiomatic system, then, is science.
6 The concept of coordination classes was developed in very substantial degree in order to give an account of the underlying "theory" behind many observations, which may not count as scientific theories in any restrictive sense. In coordination class theory, the inferential net is the equivalent of the relevant "theory" for observing particular "things" in the world.
7 I find Lakatos (1970) illuminating on the status and function of observation. However, there is a huge literature on theory and observation that can easily be found online.
8 This essay was written over a few days after a careful reading of Hall et al. I am sure it has many faults for this brevity of consideration.
9 I once tried to convince Jean Lave that she should not care about certain implementation levels at all, at least, as regards social and cultural levels and the sketch of a possible implementation level provided by Newell and Simon's physical symbol systems hypothesis. Her levels of interest were autonomous enough not to need much from this particular potential implementation analysis, or maybe even profit much from it. On the other hand, I stand for the need to incorporate aspects of the knowledge level, where I mostly work, into considerations of culture and activity.
10 I use conventional terminology for function/structure relations even if it is terribly confusing. It should be called something like function/implementation to distinguish between this meaning of structure in "function/structure" and the more generic one, of having a discernable, patterned analysis. Function in itself has "structure" in the more general sense, but its "structure" is, by definition, divorced from implementation.
11 In-press revision (see note 4): The authors added this explicit disavowal to their chapter: "It is key to note that we are not mapping HM approaches to 'theory' and ND approaches to 'observation.' Theorizing and observing are germane to both." As I make clear here in other parts of my commentary, I do not put forward theory and observation as one-for-one replacements for HM and ND. Instead, I think systematic consideration of theory and observation and their role in science can replace – with what I feel are clear improvements – some of the *interpretations* made using the HM/ND language. In addition, I feel that their notion of ND is at least inspired by the category of observation, and the nature and role of theory in ND remains, to me, unclear in their presentation. Similarly, some aspects of HM (not all of them) are, in my view, aspects of essentially all theories, and should thus be found in accounts of ND science, even if we might have to look carefully to see them. In this regard, see my comments in the text proper concerning new ontologies in theories, and, in particular, my later examination of Darwin's characterized-as-ND work.
12 One can ask questions about clocks that are more specific to particular technology. For example, one can ask "what makes the hands go around?" or "what happens when the

hour digit flips from 1 to 2?" with a digital clock. But I will ask a set of questions that better fit later considerations and relevant examples in the history of science.
13 If I thought I could make it comprehensible, this is precisely the description of clocks with which I would start with a young child. All the rest is details, many of them implementation details that have no generality concerning clocks.
14 In-press revision (see note 4): The claim that entities associated with HM typically become visible was removed from the prior version of the chapter. While its removal is quite congenial to my point of view, as expressed just here in my text, issues of visibility – what and how things are observable – remains a core concern that requires more extensive treatment than is given in the HM/ND analytic frame. In addition, the authors retain the claim that, in the natural sciences, hidden machineries usually become "examinable," apparently unlike what has happened in the social sciences. If "examinable" means anything like "visible," then my comments on visibility in physics belie the distinction between social and natural sciences that they tentatively explore. If "examinable" means "inferentially accessible," then the authors appear to be saying merely that theories in the social sciences are not as well developed as in some of the natural sciences (the inferential network involving theoretical terms is less secure). I agree.
15 It's actually easy to "find" invisibility in modern science. Features of the world that are small enough (in a way that is determined by specific physical parameters) are intrinsically quantum mechanical. So, our everyday assumptions about "things that are visible" (our implicit "theories of observation") are inapplicable. There are no things ("particles") that have particular places to which we can point, for example.
16 The history of physics here is illuminating. When electrons began to get traction as particles, a huge furor arose concerning their reality. On one side, august scientists like Robert Millikan maintained that electrons were simply there. Irate in the face of denials, Millikan said (something like), "I can see the little buggers" jumping from oil drop to oil drop (referencing his famous experiment). I take that statement to be metaphorical. On the other side, highly respected scientists like Ernst Mach rejected electrons as "mere mathematical creations." Mach never accepted their reality. As time went on, however, physicists got used to electrons' nature and treated them as "really there." There was no point, in any case, at which electrons were observed – no new type of microscope allowed them to be seen. Reality for such things is all in robust inferential pathways to observations.
17 "Ontology" is, in my view, a seriously problematic term. I don't believe it has any agreed meaning to the point that we will be able to firmly settle the question of whether something constitutes an ontology or not. Nevertheless, I will not give voice to those skepticisms here and, instead, I will try to use the term in a way that I expect those who use it will not find immediately objectionable.
18 In-press revision (see note 4): The revised phrasing is "explanations remain *meshed with* the observable ontology" (emphasis added). This change forestalls the most direct criticism that I had of the former phrasing. However, I do not consider it helpful concerning the principle issues. "Meshed with" is vague. What *else*, beyond the observable ontology, is involved in explanation? Might there be new ontologies, revised causal threads, or even new theories? These are where the action is. That the observable ontology (presumably, unchanged) remains within the larger scientific and explanatory pursuit might well just respect the fact that scientific explanation also retains some common ways of talking about observations. Einstein's views (note 5) would seem to guarantee that everyday ideas (e.g., measurements) would appear in scientific explanation. However, their logical status (they are now axioms) has changed radically.
19 I strongly expect – hope – that ethologists have surpassed common sense and anthropomorphic projection in their study of animals; thus would enter more theory development, which would abrogate, or at least challenge, naïve observation.

20 There is a causal thread of change between generations, via procreation. However, this thread is predominantly random and not specifically directed toward adaptive change.
21 With regard to "elliptical causality," see my micro-essay on modeling and reality (diSessa, this volume).
22 Notice that, in the quotes cited by Hall et al., Darwin makes clear that the importance of the (possibly) ND observations that he made early on is precisely that – suitably refined and augmented by other theoretically related considerations – they eventually became part of the grand theory that he created. Notice that "wider significance" is here critical, and the wider significance came about because of theoretical development entailing, as I see it, ontological innovation and new, "substantially autonomous" levels (ensemble causality).

## Cumulative References

Bateson, G. (1971). Communication. In N. A. McQuown (Ed.), *The natural history of an interview* (pp. 1–40). Microfilm Collection of Manuscripts on Cultural Anthropology, 15th Series. Chicago, IL: University of Chicago. Joseph Regenstein Library, Department of photo duplication.

Beach, K. (1999). Consequential transitions: A sociocultural expedition beyond transfer in education. *Review of Research in Education*, 24, 101–139.

Bowers, J., Cobb, P., & McClain, K. (1999). The evolution of mathematical practices: A case study. *Cognition and Instruction*, 17(1), 25–66.

Callon, M. (1986). Some elements of a sociology of translation: Domestication of the scallops and the fishermen of St. Brieux Bay. In J. Law (Ed.), *Power, action and belief: A new sociology of knowledge?* (pp. 196–229). London: Routledge.

Callon, M. (1991). Techno-economic networks and irreversibility. In J. Law (Ed.), *A sociology of monsters? Essays on power, technology, and domination* (pp. 132–161). London: Routledge.

Callon, M., & Latour, B. (1992). Don't throw the baby out with the Bath School! A reply to Collins and Yearly. In A. Pickering (Ed.), *Science as practice and culture* (pp. 343–368). Chicago, IL: University of Chicago Press.

Carraher, T. N., Carraher, D. W., & Schliemann, A. D. (1987). Written and oral mathematics. *Journal for Research in Mathematics Education*, 18(2), 83–97.

Churchland, P. M. (1981). Eliminative materialism and the propositional attitudes. *The Journal of Philosophy*, 78(2), 67–90.

Cobb, P., Stephan, M., McClain, K., & Gravemeijer, K. (2011). Participating in classroom mathematical practices. In E. Yackel, K. Gravemeijer, & A. Sfard (Eds.), *A journey in mathematics education research* (pp. 117–163). Dordrecht, NL: Springer.

Cohen, I. B. (1994). *Interactions: Some contacts between the natural sciences and the social sciences.* Cambridge, MA: MIT Press.

Collins, A., & Ferguson, W. (1993). Epistemic forms and epistemic games: Structures and strategies for guiding inquiry. *Educational Psychologist*, 28(1), 25–42.

Comte, A. (1855). *The positive philosophy of Auguste Comte.* (Translated and condensed by H. Martineau). New York: Calvin Blanchard.

Darwin, C. (1859, 1976). *The origin of species.* New York: Penguin Books.

Darwin, C. (2006). *Autobiographies.* [Kindle version]. Retrieved from Amazon.com.

Darwin, C. (2009). *The Origin of Species: 150th Anniversary Edition.* [Kindle version]. Retrieved from Amazon.com.

Darwin, C. (2011). *The voyage of the Beagle.* [Kindle version]. Retrieved from Amazon.com.

Dawkins, R. (1986). *The blind watchmaker*. New York: W. W. Norton & Company.

diSessa, A. A. (1994). Speculations on the foundations of knowledge and intelligence. In D. Tirosh (Ed.), *Implicit and explicit knowledge: An educational approach* (pp. 1–54). Norwood, NJ: Ablex.

diSessa, A. A. (2002). Why "conceptual ecology" is a good idea. In M. Limón & L. Mason (Eds.), *Reconsidering conceptual change: Issues in theory and practice* (pp. 29–60). Dordrecht, NL: Kluwer.

diSessa, A. A. (2004). Metarepresentation: Native competence and targets for instruction. *Cognition and Instruction*, 22(3), 293–331.

diSessa, A. A., & Cobb, P. (2004). Ontological innovation and the role of theory in design experiments. *Journal of the Learning Sciences*, 13(1), 77–103.

diSessa, A. A., Hammer, D., Sherin, B., & Kolpakowski, T. (1991). Inventing graphing: Meta-representational expertise in children. *Journal of Mathematical Behavior*, 10(2), 117–160.

Erickson, F. (2004). *Talk and social theory: Ecologies of speaking and listening in everyday life*. Cambridge, UK: Polity Press.

Gardner, H. (1986). *The mind's new science: A history of the cognitive revolution*. New York: Basic Books.

Garfinkel, H. (1967). *Studies in ethnomethodology*. Cambridge, UK: Polity Press.

Gutiérrez, K. D., & Vossoughi, S. (2010). Lifting off the ground to return anew: Mediated praxis, transformative learning, and social design experiments. *Journal of Teacher Education*, 61(1–2), 100–117.

Hall, R. (2000). Video recording as theory. In D. Lesh & A. Kelley (Eds.), *Handbook of research design in mathematics and science education* (pp. 647–664). Mahwah, NJ: Lawrence Erlbaum.

Hall, R. (2011). Cultural forms, agency, and the discovery of invention in classroom research on learning and teaching. In T. Koschmann (Ed.), *Theories of learning and studies of instructional practice* (pp. 359–383). New York: Springer.

Hall, R., Kibler, D., Wenger, E., & Truxaw, C. (1989). Exploring the episodic structure of algebra story problem solving. *Cognition and Instruction*, 6(3), 223–283.

Hall, R, & Leander, K. M. (2010, April). Comparative analyses of spatial thinking in diverse professional practices. In R. Hall & K. Leander (Chairs), *Learning and development of new practices of spatial thinking*. Symposium conducted at the Annual Meeting of the American Educational Research Association, Denver, CO.

Jordan, B., & Henderson, A. (1995). Interaction Analysis: Foundations and practice. *The Journal of the Learning Sciences*, 4(1), 39–103.

Koschmann, T. (Ed.). (2011). *Theories of learning and studies of instructional practice*. New York: Springer.

Lakatos, I. (1970). Falsification and the methodology of scientific research programmes. In I. Lakatos & A. Musgrave (Eds.), *Criticism and the growth of knowledge* (pp. 91–196). London, UK; New York, NY: Cambridge University Press.

Latour, B. (1987). *Science in action: How to follow scientists and engineers through society*. Cambridge, MA: Harvard University Press.

Latour, B. (2005). *Reassembling the social: An introduction to Actor-Network Theory*. New York, NY: Oxford University Press.

Latour, B., & Woolgar, S. (1979). *Laboratory life: The construction of scientific facts*. Princeton, NJ: Princeton University Press.

Lave, J. (2011). *Apprenticeship in critical ethnographic practice*. Chicago, IL: University of Chicago Press.

Lave, J., Murtagh, M., & de la Rocha, O. (1984). The dialectic of arithmetic in grocery shopping. In B. Rogoff & J. Lave (Eds.), *Everyday cognition: Its development in social context*. Cambridge, MA: Harvard University Press.

Lave, J., & Wenger, E. (1991). *Situated learning: Legitimate peripheral participation*. New York, NY: Cambridge University Press.

Law, J. (1992). Notes on the theory of the actor-network: Ordering, strategy, and heterogeneity. *Systems Practice*, 5(4), 379–393.

Law, J. (2004). *After method: Mess in social science research*. New York: Routledge.

Law, J., & Hassard, J. (1999). *Actor network theory and after*. Malden, MA: Blackwell.

Law, J., & Singleton, V. (2005). Object lessons. *Organization*, 12(3), 331–355.

Leeds-Hurwitz, W. (2005). The natural history approach: A Bateson legacy. *Cybernetics and Human Knowing*, 12(1, 2), 137–146.

Marshall, H. (1972). Structural constraints on learning. *American Behavioral Scientist*, 16(1), 35–45.

Midgley, M. (2011). *The myths we live by*. New York: Routledge.

Mol, A. (2002). *The body multiple: Ontology in medical practice*. Durham, NC: Duke University Press.

Pannese, E. (1999). The Golgi stain: Invention, diffusion and impact on neurosciences. *Journal of the History of the Neurosciences*, 8(2), 132–140.

Parnafes, O., & diSessa, A. A. (2013). Microgenetic learning analysis: A methodology for studying knowledge in transition. *Human Development*, 56(5), 5–37.

Ramón y Cajal, S. (1937/1989). *Recollections of my life* (E. H. Craigie & J. Cano, Trans.). Philadelphia, PA: American Philosophical Society.

Reeves, C., & Taylor, D. (2004). A history of the optic nerve and its diseases. *Eye*, 18(11), 1096–1109.

Saxe, G. B. (1991). *Culture and cognitive development: Studies in mathematical understanding*. Hillsdale, NJ: Lawrence Erlbaum Associates.

Scheflen, A. E. (1973). *Communicational structure: Analysis of a psychotherapy transaction*. Bloomington, IN: Indiana University Press.

Scribner, S. (1986). Thinking in action: Some characteristics of practical thought. In R. J. Sternberg & R. K Wagner (Eds.), *Practical intelligence: Nature and origins of competence in the everyday world* (pp. 13–30). Cambridge, UK: Cambridge University Press.

Searle, J. (1980). Minds, brains and programs. *Behavioral and Brain Sciences*, 3(3), 417–457.

Searle, J. (1984). *Minds, brains and science*. Cambridge, MA: Harvard University Press.

Sefton-Green, J. (2013). *Learning at not-school: A review of study, theory, and advocacy for education in non-formal settings*. Cambridge, MA: MIT Press.

Shepherd, G. M. (1991). *Foundations of the neuron doctrine*. Oxford, UK: Oxford University Press.

Sismondo, S. (2004). *An introduction to science and technology studies*. Malden, MA: Blackwell.

Sulloway, F. (1982). Darwin's conversion: The Beagle voyage and its aftermath. *Journal of the History of Biology*, 15(3), 325–396.

Taylor, K. H., & Hall, R. (2013). Counter-mapping the neighborhood on bicycles: Mobilizing youth to reimagine the city. *Technology, Knowledge and Learning*, 18, 65–93.

ter Haar, D., & Wergeland, H. (1966). *Elements of thermodynamics*. Reading, MA: Addison-Wesley.

Yackel, E., & Cobb, P. (1996). Sociomathematical norms, argumentation, and autonomy in mathematics. *Journal for Research in Mathematics Education*, 27(4), 458–477.

Yin, R. K. (2011). *Applications of case study research*. Thousand Oaks, CA: Sage.

# PART IV
# Reflections and Prospects

# 20
# ANOTHER CANDIDATE FOR RELATING KNOWLEDGE ANALYSIS AND INTERACTION ANALYSIS

Mitchell's Integrative Pluralism

*James G. Greeno*

In the introduction to this volume, diSessa, Levin, and Brown discuss six ways in which relations between the research programs of Knowledge Analysis and Interaction Analysis (KA and IA) could be understood. The relation that they label "micro-complementarity" seems promising to them, and I agree. As they wrote, "IA and KA … each has a perhaps critical role in understanding particular and important issues in learning." Examples in this volume include Azevedo and Lee's analysis of cognition and interaction in "how model rocketeers and their communities individually and collectively know the stability of models," diSessa, Greeno, Michaels, and O'Connor's analysis of an episode in a clinical interview, Levin and diSessa's account of disciplined perception, Russ, Sherin, and Lee's account of clinical interviewing, and Umphress' account of epistemic authority.

Another example is an analysis by Greeno, Melissa Sommerfeld (now Melissa Gresalfi), and Muffie Wiebe (now Muffie Waterman) of an interaction involving four middle-school students working on mathematical problems of population biology in a curriculum that included constructing models of population growth and decline. The data considered here were results obtained in a study of learning that focused on students' modeling activities in a project-based middle-school mathematics classroom (Hall, 1999). These data were also included in a report by Stenning, Greeno, Hall, Sommerfeld, and Wiebe (2002).

In this chapter, I focus on two episodes involving the student group known as MLKN (Manuel, Lisa, Kera, and Nick). The first episode occurred as MLKN worked on a problem in the pre-test, before the instructional unit. The question for the group to answer was how many mice would be in a population after two years if the population started with 20 adult mice. The students were directed to set parameters, including the number of seasons per year the mice gave birth (they chose 4), and the number of pups per litter (they chose 4). Manuel proposed a solution involving linear growth. With 10 pairs of adult mice to start, the number of pups in the first breeding season would be 40, and there would be 8 breeding seasons; therefore, we hypothesize Manuel reasoned that the number of pups born during the two-year period would be 320, so the population (including the initial 20 adults) would be 340. As Manuel began to draw a graph to represent the group's answer, Lisa said:

**L:** [*leaning over M's graph*] WAIT a minute! It's forty and then it's like … [*formed a triangle with her hands, with fingertips touching*] like forty, right? [*looked at K*]
**K:** Mm hm.
**L:** And then you have to pair those up [*brought palms together*] and then they have kids [*flattened hands and spread apart over the table*]
**M:** [*looked up at L; his mouth dropped open*]
**K:** Pair the f –
**M:** [*looked at camera, eyes widened*] OH, yeah, huh? [*smiled; looked at L*]
**K:** So //that means
**M** //We were doing it – [*looked at K, smiled*]
**K:** Ok, ok. [*nodded; beat right hand down on table*] That goes <back>
**L:** [*laughed*] That's a lot of mice [*sat back; looked up at camera, smiling*]
**K:** OK, back up
**M:** [*tore the graph sheet off the pad*]
**K:** Gosh, they'd repro – Oh my gosh, that's a lot of nasty mice. Okay.

In a later episode (Day 9 of the 20-day unit) of work by the same group, Manuel again proposed a solution that omitted some calculations. Lisa again questioned Manuel's solution, but she did not assert an alternative understanding of the task. This time, Manuel persisted and Kera supported his proposal.

These two episodes illustrate a contrast. In one episode, actions that Manuel initiated were challenged and halted; in the other, actions that Manuel initiated were questioned, but Manuel was not deterred. An explanation of these two occurrences uses hypotheses from both KA and IA. In terms of interaction, Manuel was positioned as the group leader; he initiated actions in the group's efforts to complete the instructional tasks. Lisa was positioned as a participant who paid attention and commented on the actions that were initiated and carried out by Manuel. Lisa was more insistent in her objection to Manuel's solution in the pre-test episode than she was in the episode of Day 9, including her leaning into Manuel's work space and her gesturing that simulated pairing of mice that had been born previously and their subsequent reproduction. On Day 9, Lisa's questioning was more tentative, saying, "I'm kind of confused," and asking, "But what's that 4%?" (4% was the value that Manuel proposed as a parameter of the model, without justifying it by additional calculations).

In terms of cognition, Lisa's objection to Manuel's action in the pre-test was accompanied by an explanation and an argument that gave an account that invalidated Manuel's action. Her gestures provided persuasive support to Manuel's and Kera's understanding of her objection.

I present this example to support diSessa, Levin, and Brown's concept of a relationship between KA and IA that they called micro-complementarity, which they defined as "each has a perhaps critical role in understanding particular and important issues in learning" (p. 2). In the example of the MKLN group, discussed here and in Stenning et al. (2002), the explanation offered drew significantly on a conceptual resource of *positioning*, developed in IA, as well as hypothesizing a process of mental modeling, developed in KA.

At the same time, because diSessa, Levin, and Brown referred to the relationship as *micro*-complementarity, their concept might be interpreted as involving complementarity mainly at a detailed level of analysis rather than at a relatively global level, and I would disagree with that conceptual expectation. Instead, I expect that complementarity is likely to occur mainly at the level of general conceptualization, such as KA and IA, and that detailed analyses of specific activities will be the locus of integration of resources developed more or less separately in the two research programs. I would be inclined to call the view of a KA–IA relationship that I find in examples *macro-complementarity* and *micro-fusion*.

I believe that this view of the relation between KA and IA as scientific programs is an example of a general meta-scientific conceptualization by Sandra Mitchell, presented in her book *Biological Complexity and Integrative Pluralism* (Mitchell, 2003). Mitchell, a philosopher of biology, argues that the usual scientific effort to construct the one, best, theory is misaligned with current scientific practice, especially in biology.

Mitchell noted that as a consequence of the complexity of biological systems, any single theory abstracts from that complexity, with the result that multiple valid theories are developed, providing multiple perspectives on and alternative explanations of different aspects of phenomena. I propose that Mitchell's observation of biological sciences applies as well – perhaps even more strongly – to the learning sciences. More specifically, I propose that KA and IA are two general research programs that exemplify Mitchell's conceptualization.

Mitchell argues that there are cases in which alternative valid theories have the same level of analysis. Even so, one of the ways in which multiple valid theories can develop is by focusing on different levels of analysis of phenomena in the domain. Research efforts in KA and IA often focus at different levels of analysis – KA by hypothesizing knowledge and cognitive processes of individuals, and IA by hypothesizing practices involving patterns of interaction at the level of activity systems that may include more than one individual person along with other systems that humans use as sources of information and other resources in activity and learning.[1]

While Mitchell (2003) argued for pluralism, in the sense that some alternative theories can be understood as being complementary, she also argued for integrative pluralism, in the sense that integration of theories is an important scientific goal. Mitchell did not encourage efforts to construct globally integrative theories, apparently in agreement with diSessa, Levin, and Brown that "[although] one might imagine a future stage of *fusion*, where distinct perspectives have become merged into an overarching one. We are a long way from that, so speculating about when, how, and even if, is not worth much effort" (p. 6). But developing a single "overarching perspective" is not the only way to achieve significant integration across scientific boundaries. At another (much more micro) level, studies that are focused on specific phenomena or types of activity can include development of explanatory hypotheses that use concepts and principles from both KA and IA research programs. As Mitchell (2003) wrote: "at the theoretical level, pluralism is sanctioned. At the concrete explanatory level, on the other hand, integration is required." Mitchell discussed examples in biology. In our field of the learning sciences, an example is in the analysis I discussed earlier in this chapter, in which an explanation of a change in a group's trajectory of work on a problem either did or did not occur in different episodes.

The integration that I propose is a simple conjunction of hypotheses, each involving attunement to constraints that can be understood either as individual or collective knowing and cognition.[2] One set of constraints applies to the contents of problem-solving activity; the other applies to the ways in which individuals coordinate their respective participation in the activity system. A constraint on contents is that numerical operations should be consistent with properties of quantities in the situation that the numbers in the calculations refer to. A constraint on interpersonal interaction is that participants are positioned to recognize leadership by one of the members when he or she is performing actions that are relevant to making progress on solving the problem that they are working on. In the first episode, when Lisa's presentation led to a change of trajectory, Lisa recognized an inconsistency between the situation after the first season and the number of mice represented in the calculation, and this content of her presentation was accepted and taken up by Manuel and Kera, resulting in a change in the group's trajectory. I also hypothesize that this constraint on propositional content had a higher priority than the interactional constraint of accepting Manuel's leadership. In the other episode considered here, in contrast, Lisa expressed uncertainty about Manuel's assignment of a numerical value, but this was not taken up by Manuel and Kera. According to the hypothesis that I propose, the content of Lisa's questioning in the second episode did not activate the constraint of consistency, which could have taken priority over the constraint of interpersonal coordination, but did not.

More generally, the proposal that I present, following Mitchell (2003), is to treat KA and IA as programs that develop complementary theories at the general level (that is, a version of pluralism) and that theories developed in both of these programs can serve as resources for integration in studies of practices of activity systems and in studies of the knowledge, understanding, and actions of individual persons. It will be valuable to continue to study activities in which individuals participate as members of activity systems,[3] thereby inviting hypotheses about how ways that individuals are positioned in groups (from IA) help frame their contributions to the content of the group's activity (from KA).

## Notes

1 In other writing, especially Greeno (2011), I have labeled these programs as "analysis from cognitive science and psychology" and "situative analysis."
2 Sandra Mitchell (personal correspondence, October 29, 2014) noted that explanations that cross levels of systems in biology also involve hypotheses about constraints. An example involving foraging by individual bees and the amount of nectar stored in a colony's hive was discussed in Mitchell (2012).
3 I believe that Clark and Schaefer's (1989) theory of conversational contributions provides a significant resource for this program.

## References

Clark, H. H., & Schaefer, E. F. (1989). Contributing to discourse. *Cognitive Science*, 13, 259–294.
Greeno, J. G. (2011). A situative perspective on cognition and learning in interaction. In T. Koschmann (Ed.), *Theories of learning and studies of instructional practice* (pp. 41–71). New York: Springer.
Hall, R. (1999). *Case studies of math at work: Exploring design-oriented mathematical practices in school and work settings.* Final report to the National Science Foundation (RED-9553648).
Mitchell, S. D. (2003). *Biological complexity and integrative pluralism.* Cambridge, UK: Cambridge University Press.
Mitchell, S. D. (2012). Emergence: Logical, functional, and dynamical. *Synthese*, 185, 171–186.
Stenning, K., Greeno, J. G., Hall, R., Sommerfeld, M., & Wiebe, M. (2002). Coordinating mathematical with biological multiplication: Conceptual learning as the development of heterogeneous reasoning systems, In P. Brna, M. Baker, K. Stenning, & A. Tiberghien (Eds.), *The role of communication in learning to model* (pp. 3–48). Mahwah, NJ: Lawrence Erlbaum Associates.

# 21
# THAT OLD PROBLEM OF INTERSUBJECTIVITY

*Timothy Koschmann*

As recounted in one of the opening chapters (diSessa, Sherin, & Levin), the current volume has its roots in Andy diSessa's long-standing project to document the development of students' conceptual understandings of physical principles (e.g., diSessa, 1983, 1991, 1993). His approach to studying these matters, what he terms Knowledge Analysis (KA), employs methods appropriate to the fine-grained analysis of interaction. Whereas studies of cognition and studies of interaction are often viewed as disjunct, even oppositional, enterprises, diSessa, in his work, has ambitiously attempted to bridge these two programs. The discussions that eventually led to the production of this volume were undertaken to sort out some of the issues related to this marriage, that is to sort out "the relationship between knowing and interacting" (Enyedy & Danish, commenting on Sherin, this volume, p. 448). This began with an AERA-sponsored workshop that occurred in 2011. Later came two symposia, one at AERA in 2012 and another at ICLS in 2014. Along the way, a number of new voices have joined the conversation, producing the rich collection of contributions that comprise this volume.

As described in the diSessa et al. chapter, the KA program is "unapologetic[ally] cognitivist" (p. 63). KA researchers seek to elucidate "the knowledge that is drawn upon as an individual engages in some task" (Sherin, this volume, p. 430). Researchers working within it seek to construct models of the learner's knowledge which (eventually) will be "computational and runnable" (diSessa et al., this volume, p. 64). Knowledge, we are told, "is constituted in mental representations and processes of individuals – a type of mental stuff" (p. 31). But herein lies the rub; how do we make scientifically grounded claims about mental stuff, stuff that is not available to direct inspection? Let me try to illustrate the problem.

We read what people have in their heads off their conduct – what they say, what they demonstrate they can do, how they do it. When we try to communicate with others, we use words to express ideas, counting on the recipients to understand the words in roughly the same way we do. Here is where problems arise – the words we use may be meaningful to different individuals in different ways. Take the term *force*. Levin and diSessa (this volume) discuss the notion of force as it is applied in simple mechanics. diSessa has studied force as a physicist, taught it, and thought about it for a long, long time. Though I took an introductory course in physics once and can recall some of the basic formulas, my understanding of force will never be precisely the same as his. diSessa's is richly articulated, whereas mine is sketchy and textbook-based. We could attempt to probe each other's understandings and, in so doing, we could increase our confidence that we were achieving some sort of mutual understanding. At no point could we ever achieve a state of absolute certainty. Furthermore, as we explore the topic, our understandings of what we are talking about are subject to modification. This, of course, does not preclude our having a conversation. We proceed *as if* we understand each other. This *as if* clause represents a taken-for-granted presumption in all conversation, not just discussions of physical principles. It gestures in the direction of what has been called the "problem of intersubjectivity" (Heritage, 1984, pp. 27–30).

Intersubjectivity is an issue that has preoccupied epistemologists, philosophers of language, and social theorists for some time. It has to do with how we make assessments of what others really know. For epistemologists, it rests on the deeper and thornier question of what counts as knowing and knowledge. With respect to language, the issue revolves around how words mean; that is, when we use a specific term, how can we be assured that it is understood by our interlocutors in the way in which we intend? Consider our earlier discussion of force. In social theory, intersubjectivity lies at the heart of a larger debate having to do with action recognition. Recall Weber's (1968) example of the wood cutter. We observe a person swinging an axe in the woods, but how can we make objective claims about what that person is actually *doing*, absent some sort of access to the person's motives (e.g., collecting firewood, earning wages, testing a new axe)?

Wittgenstein (1958) argued that a simple referential model of language use, one in which there is a one-to-one correspondence between words and meanings, is not possible. Similarly, Quine (1968) noted that meaning could not be grounded in manual demonstration because even indexical gestures are inherently ambiguous. This calls into question how we can ever achieve mutual understanding. But, at the same time, communication, joint activity, and all other forms of sociality depend crucially upon the achievement of mutual understanding. This, essentially, is the problem of intersubjectivity. Beneath it lurks an assortment of foundational concerns – knowing and the nature of knowledge, meaning, and motives.

Two prominent social theorists of the last century took up the issue of intersubjectivity in quite different ways. Talcott Parsons (1937) and Alfred Schütz (1953) were contemporaries who each developed original and influential theories of social action. Parsons was the architect of what came to be known as the structural-functional approach in American sociology. Schütz's work also had a major impact, inspiring later developments in ethnomethodology (Garfinkel, 1952, 2006; Cicourel, 1964) and phenomenological sociology (Berger & Luckmann, 1966).

Parsons' (1937) "voluntaristic theory of action" was designed to provide a framework within which human action could be studied, rationalized, and rendered predictable. Its purpose was to transform the study of human action into a rigorous science. His proposal was intended not only to unify various strands of classical sociological inquiry but also to bring to bear the contributions of social psychology, anthropology, and psychoanalysis. He wrote, "Action is rational in so far as it pursues ends possible within the conditions of the situation, and by means which, among those available to the actor, are intrinsically best adapted to the end for reasons understandable and verifiable by positive empirical science." (p. 58).

Though Parsons fully appreciated the import of the problem of intersubjectivity for a general theory of action, he believed that the objective causes of human behavior could be determined scientifically. If one accepts this as an article of faith, the problem of intersubjectivity is effectively banished (Heritage, 1984).

Schütz, on the other hand, embraced it. He adopted a scepticist stance with respect to the possibility of our ever fully achieving intersubjectivity. He (1953) began from the premise that each of us occupies a unique position in the world and we do so with a biography that is ours and ours alone. As a consequence, our experiences and understandings are irremediably idiosyncratic; they will never map exactly onto the experiences and understandings of others. Nonetheless, we are able to function *as if* our understanding of the world was shared and stable. We do this, Schütz proposed, employing two presuppositions, or what he termed "idealizations," namely:

> [1] The idealization of the interchangeability of the standpoints: I take it for granted – and assume my fellowman does the same – that if I change places with him so that his "here" becomes mine, I would be at the same distance from things and see them in the same typicality as he actually does; moreover, the same things would be in my reach which are actually in his. (All this vice versa.)
> 
> [2] The idealization of the congruency of the system of relevances: Until counter-evidence, I take it for granted – and assume my fellowman does the same – that the differences in perspectives originating in my and his unique biographical situations are irrelevant for the purpose at hand of either of us and that he and I, that "We" assume that both of us have selected and

interpreted the actually or potentially common objects and their features in an identical manner or at least an "empirically identical" manner, namely, sufficient for all practical purposes.

*(Schütz, 1953, p. 8)*

Taken together, the two presuppositions constitute what he termed the "general thesis of reciprocal perspectives" (p. 8). Much of the time, we bumble along as if intersubjectivity was assured, until we encounter evidence that our understandings are at variance and then we work to repair the differences. So intersubjectivity is for Schütz an endless work in progress. Our grasp of the world is organized in terms of established "typifications" (p. 12), but these are open ended in their definition and are constantly being reassessed and refined with new experience. Schütz's treatment of intersubjectivity, as a result, rests on an entirely different theory of knowledge from that to which Parsons subscribed. His proposal opens the door to a new kind of social science. Rather than orienting to the elucidation of the abstract models and general principles that govern social conduct, he directs our attention to the practical methods through which we build a world held-in-common.[1]

In the remainder of this commentary I would like to explore how the problem of intersubjectivity might factor into our prospects for doing "Knowledge Analysis" within embodied interaction. To make that discussion a bit more concrete, I will examine a data fragment for which an analysis has already been reported (Parnafes, 2007; Parnafes & diSessa, 2013) and which has been held up as a paradigmatic example of a "Knowledge Analysis" (diSessa et al., this volume). It was also reanalyzed in another chapter in this volume, focusing both on knowledge development and interactional processes (Danish, Enyedy, & Parnafes, this volume). The fragment involves an exchange between two high-school students, Robin and Sue, who participated in an instructional activity involving natural harmonic oscillation (Danish et al., this volume; Parnafes, 2007).

## Transcription Issues

Orit Parnafes was kind enough to provide access to the video that was reanalyzed in the Danish et al. chapter (this volume) and that originally appeared in Parnafes (2007). I retranscribed it using the Jeffersonian conventions employed in Conversation Analysis (CA).[2] This was not because I had any reason to distrust the transcript in the Danish et al. chapter, but for other reasons. First, I needed to bring myself in contact with these materials and transcribing is a useful exercise for doing so. Second, Jeffersonian transcripts record not only what was said, but some features of *how* it was said. Two of these features – timing and intonation – are important for understanding how sense was built within the interaction, and so part of my motivation for retranscribing was to add these features to the record. Finally, just as I find it easier to follow the action if the transcript is in a form with which I am familiar, it makes it easier for others to read my transcription when I follow a set of accepted conventions.

When I went to transcribe this fragment I heard a few things a little differently than they are presented in the Danish et al. chapter and this illustrates something about transcribing generally. Transcription is an interpretive act and the transcript is a representation of a particular hearing; it is, in a sense, a theory about what has been or could be heard.[3] So it is not unusual for two transcribers to represent the same materials differently, or even for the same transcriber to hear the same recording differently on different occasions. This is just an unavoidable aspect of the business in which we are all engaged. Orit, however, collected these materials and had personal contact with the participants and so you must take that into consideration in evaluating my version. If this enterprise of documenting emerging understandings is to have any integrity, however, we must ourselves be accountable in our work practices. I am obliged, therefore, to present them as I heard them and that is what I have done.

"Directing the displacement" from Parnafes (2007, pp. 435–436)

```
1   0:00:00;28   R:   So (1.7)⌈these are at the sam::e
                         skinniness level but
2                        they're not as high
3   0:00:03;00   R:      ⌊((points with cursor to velocity
                         vs. time
4                        graph))
5   0:00:06;15   R:      Like remember ⌈when it went this fast?
6   0:00:06;29   S:                    ⌊yeah:
7   0:00:07;26        (0.7)
8   0:00:08;22   R:   =⌈Those things were really high?
9   0:00:08;22   S:   =⌊Yeah.
10  0:00:09;29        (0.4)
11  0:00:10;10   S:   And it (0.2) touches⌈(the axis)      ⌉ at
12                       the same points:.
13  0:00:11;03   R:                        ⌊The ⌈(hats) >are
                         the same<⌋ (0.5)
14                       I think these are the same (1.2)
                         I think
15  0:00:11;07   R:                                    ⌊((points
                         with cursor to
16                       frequency graph))
17  0:00:15;14        (1.0)
18  0:00:16;13   S:   Are they?
19  0:00:16;24        (0.4)
```

```
20  0:00:17;06  R:  Yeah >let's see<
21  0:00:17;23  S:  >°here we go°<
22  0:00:18;06      (6.7)
23  0:00:22;28  R:  ((re-starts simulation))
24  0:00:24;29  R:  No those look (.) closer together
25  0:00:25;29      (1.2)
26  0:00:27;06  S:  No⌈no    (0.5)   ⌈they just started off
                    different=
27  0:00:27;16  R:       ⌊Those are the sa⌊me
28  0:00:29;04  R:  =⌈Those are the same, but ⌈these are
                    higher.
29  0:00:29;04  R:  =⌊((points with cursor to frequency
                    graph))
30  0:00:29;26  R:                          ⌊((points with
                    cursor to
31                  velocity vs. time graph))
32  0:00:30;11  S:  So (0.3)⌈like (0.5) it's moving faster.
                    (1.1) It's:::
33  0:00:30;28  S:         ⌊((points toward the oscillating
                    object with
34                  reversed r. hand))
35  0:00:34;14      (1.9)
36  0:00:36;10  R:  (All/well) the periods are the same
                    (let's)=
37  0:00:37;27  S:  =Yeah ⌈(0.3) but⌉(0.3) in
38  0:00:38;09  R:        ⌊periods  ⌋
39  0:00:39;08      (0.3)
40  0:00:39;16  R:  ⌈It's going far⌈ther
41  0:00:39;16  R:  ⌊((points with cursor at range of
                    movement of
42                  oscillating object))
43  0:00:40;04  S:                  ⌊It's (following)
                    farther in the
44                  ⌈same amount of time
45  0:00:41;14  R:  ⌊So there's more motion in the ⌈same
                    amount of time.
46  0:00:42;27  S:                                 ⌊So
                    it's going
47                  ⌈(to there)
48  0:00:43;29  S:  ⌊((reaching r. hand toward keyboard))
```

The differences in the two transcripts are actually quite modest. Looking at my version, there are some minor wording changes here and there. Where Danish et al. has transcribed Robin as saying, "But these are the same," I hear something different. It's hard to make out, but it sounds something like, "the (hats) are the same" (l. 13), which, of course, does not make sense, but I cannot hear "these are the same.". At the conclusion of the fragment, Susan says something (l. 46) in overlap with Robin that is also hard to make out while reaching with her right hand toward what I take to be the keyboard (l. 48). Danish et al. had her saying something slightly different than what I thought I heard. My transcript includes some manual actions (e.g., lines 15–16, 29, 30–31). The Danish et al. transcript, on the other hand, reveals details of what is happening on the computer screen, something I did not attempt to represent in my transcript, but which is clearly relevant to developing sense. The additions I made to the transcript were simply things I noticed; they were not added in the service of any particular analytic agenda. This illustrates another general observation about transcribing: When constructing a transcript, it is not always possible to tell which details are going to matter.

However, some features of the augmented transcript are quite illuminating. For instance, seeing how the participants' gestures are coordinated with their talk is an important aspect of the general intelligibility of their interaction. Hindmarsh and Heath (2000) described how pointing gestures are "punctuated" by affiliated talk and here we see how Robin's pointing with the cursor in line 3 is precisely coordinated with enunciation of the demonstrative "these." Similarly, Robin's turn in line 8, though not constructed grammatically as a question, is delivered with inquiring intonation. Noting this is helpful in appreciating Sue and Robin's delicate work of collaboratively building a shared understanding.

## A Repair Sequence and a Discovery

Whereas Danish et al. divided the fragment into three parts, I would like to look at the full excerpt as a sequentially unfolding exchange, with special attention paid to a complex turn-at-talk produced by Robin in line 13. Students of communication employ quite different ways of recognizing the boundaries of speaker turns. One relatively simple technique is to use breaks in talk as turn delimiters. Another is to engage in an analysis of syntax and treat each grammatical sentence as defining a turn. In one of CA's seminal articles, Sacks, Schegloff, and Jefferson (1974) argued that the duration of a turn, though sensitive to the features listed above, is delicately negotiated by interlocutors. By the "simplest systematics" algorithm (Sacks et al., 1974), a single turn may include one or more embedded pauses[4] and might consist of multiple "turn construction units" (TCUs) that may take the grammatical form of sentences, clauses, phrases, or isolated lexical elements.

In transcribing this fragment, therefore, I have chosen to represent Robin's talk in the early portion of the fragment not as a series of utterances, but rather as a single complex turn, just as Danish et al. did in their transcript. Presented in this way, Robin's turn includes two embedded pauses, one that is remarkably long (1.2 s.). However, when parties are engaged doing some other activity while talking, such pauses are not uncommon. In this case, Robin and Sue appear to be engaged in observing something and time passes while they study the scene in front of them. Robin's turn is launched in overlap with one being produced by Sue. It begins with something that might be characterized as a noticing. The enunciation of the referential term is not clear, but it is precisely synchronized with Robin's point with the cursor (lines 15–16). The second TCU serves as a "self-initiated self-correction" (Schegloff, Jefferson, & Sacks, 1977); it reasserts the noticing with a "modalizing" (Woolgar, 1988, pp. 69–33) "I think", the effect of which is to downgrade the certainty of the original noticing. The third TCU repeats the second in an abbreviated form. It reinforces rather than corrects.

In Sue's turn that follows (l. 18), we also find evidence of repair. Her "Are they?" calls Robin's noticing into question. Rather than self-repair of a turn in progress, this is a "next-turn repair initiation" (Schegloff et al., 1977). As Schegloff (1991) writes:

> it appears that virtually all efforts to deal with [problems or troubles in speaking, hearing, or understanding the talk], including problems in shared understanding, are initiated either in the turn in which the trouble or potential trouble occurs (as when a speaker stops to clarify a potential ambiguity before or just after finishing that turn at talk), [or] in the next turn by some other participant (a recipient for whom it may be relevant to respond).
> *(pp. 157–158)*

He goes on to say, "The ordinary sequential organization of conversation thus provides for displays of mutual understanding and problems therein, one running basis for the cultivation and grounding of intersubjectivity" (p. 158). In the students' careful negotiation of epistemic status, the hedging, and the ongoing assessment of beliefs, we see some of the practical work of building intersubjectivity on display. In the place where we might expect either a defense or a re-evaluation of the original noticing, we find, instead, Robin making a proposal to re-observe the simulation.

After redoing the simulation, Robin issues another noticing (l. 24), one that contradicts the one she made previously. But, with further scrutiny, Sue contradicts Robin's updated noticing (l. 26), in effect affirming the original. She also adds an additional consideration ("they just started off different"). Simultaneously, Robin affirms the original noticing (l. 27), then repeats her endorsement and offers a new one (l. 28). So, we have a cascade of noticings that highlight different features of the display.

With Sue's next turn (l. 32), however, the action shifts to trying to articulate the upshot of what they have seen. This is cued in part by her prefacing some comments with "so," but also by a shift from describing specific features of the display (e.g., lines 13, 24, 26, 28) to making a more general claim. Parnafes (2007) discusses at length Sue's "it's moving faster." The introduction of the term "faster" at this juncture does seem significant, but there are additional new descriptions advanced in the following turns ("the periods," "going farther," "more motion"). The understandings engendered by these expressions are tightly tied to the context within which they were produced. The sequence displays the sequential organization of an "occasioned discovery" (Koschmann & Zemel, 2009), but the precise nature of the discovery is elusive. Features of the display that may have previously gone unnoticed have been brought to the fore. These features have not changed, but the participants now have new referential resources with which to discuss them. Over the course of the segment, the effort toward building intersubjectivity could not be more striking.

## Studying Situated Understandings

Parsons' (1937) and Schütz's (1953) different responses to the problem of intersubjectivity have bearing on the question of how we might go about documenting students' intuitive notions of physical phenomena. They, of course, were centrally concerned with the study of social action, not developing understandings of physical principles. They did, however, grapple with the problem of finding a way to study how things are understood from the actor's perspective, and this is the same problem with which we are currently struggling. Like Parsons' structural-functional approach in sociology, information-processing theory has adopted a functional approach to studying human problem solving. It seeks to develop functioning models of the competent problem solver. KA, as described in the diSessa et al. chapter (this vol.), pursues the self same ambition. And like the Parsonian model of motivated action, it does not engage the problem of intersubjectivity.

Within actual interaction, intersubjectivity is generally taken for granted and it is only occasionally topicalized. It is anterior to interaction and, yet, always a part of it. An analysis of interaction, then, is an analysis of the continuing, and never quite completed, pursuit of intersubjectivity. Following the insights provided by Schütz, an interaction analysis would involve examining the methods whereby intersubjectivity is negotiated in practical settings with the object of documenting how understandings emerge over time. Sacks et al. (1974) described how conversation, in its organization, provides a form of "proof procedure" for understanding understanding:

> But while understandings of other turns' talk are displayed to co-participants, they are available as well to professional analysts, who are thereby afforded a proof criterion (and a search procedure) for the analysis of what a turn's talk is occupied with. Since it is parties' understandings of prior turns' talk that

is relevant to their construction of next turns, it is THEIR understandings that are wanted for analysis. The display of those understandings in the talk of subsequent turns affords both a resource for the analysis of prior turns and a proof procedure for professional analyses of prior turns – resources intrinsic to the data themselves.

*(p. 729, original authors' emphasis)*

Unlike knowledge representations, such understandings do not need to be inferred, but rather are a part of the conversational record. In studying just how such understandings are produced, we can gain insight into the participants' local sense-making methods.

Shifting focus from knowledge representations to methods of local sense-making would have implications for how we report our findings. In the description of the principles of KA research, we are told, "KA research has documented how a person's intellectual performance is highly contextual, dependent on the particular situation in which one acts" (diSessa, et al., this volume, p. 37). But the local understandings in which we are interested are not only highly contextualized, they are *essentially* contextual. That is to say, they only exist for the parties involved, for present purposes, and only for the moment under study. (Witness the notions of "faster," "farther," and "more motion" in the examined excerpt.)

Understandings, as they develop in particular situations, however, are discoverable for us as observers, just as they are for the local participants. But when we speak of understandings, we are dealing with a delicate phenomenon, one that does not continue to exist shorn of its situational entanglements. Taking its situated character to heart will require developing ways of documenting understanding that preserve these connections. Analysts with special expertise like diSessa may be able to see things in the interaction that may not be apparent to the rest of us,[5] but his observations must be documented in such a way that the rest of us can evaluate them. Analyses, then, are like transcripts, in that they are endlessly open to public critique and revision. Examples of this open-ended mode of working would include Schegloff's (1992) reanalysis of Goodwin's (1987) analysis of a picnic-table conversation, Koschmann and Zemel's (2009) reanalysis of Roschelle's (1992) report of two students doing ballistics experiments at the computer, and the reanalysis of Parnafes (2007) found in Danish et al. (this volume) and in the current commentary.

The question that frames the volume pertains to how we might go about analyzing knowledge displayed within embodied interaction; but perhaps, it is neither knowledge nor interaction per se that we need to be analyzing, but rather deeply situated understandings appreciated from the subject's perspective. And in so doing, we cannot afford to ignore that old problem of intersubjectivity..

## Notes

1  This presentation of the treatments of intersubjectivity in the writings of Parsons and Schütz is, of necessity, cursory. For a critical summary of the two approaches, the interested reader might consult Heritage (1984). Heritage's presentation builds on one originally developed by Garfinkel (1952) (see Koschmann, 2012). One might alternatively consult the correspondence between Parsons and Schütz at the time that they were working out their respective positions (Grathoff, 1978).
2  The full set of conventions is described in Jefferson (2004). In brief, brackets are used to mark talk or other forms of action produced in overlap. Use of standard punctuation marks such as periods and question marks denotes delivery with falling (or rising) intonation resembling that ordinarily heard at the end of a sentence (or question). Numbers enclosed in single parentheses represent periods of silence measured to a tenth of a second. Periods of silence reported at the end of a turn represent time elapsed to the next turn of talk. Colons are used to display sound stretching. Text enclosed between degree signs represents talk delivered at diminished volume. Annotations supplied by the transcriber are enclosed in double parentheses. These are most often used to describe visible action affiliated with the talk. The column appearing on the left side of the transcript presents the time, measured in hours, minutes, seconds, and frames of the onset of the described action or talk. Line numbers are added on the far left to simplify reference in the text.
3  This is a different sense of how a transcript represents a theory about a set of materials than, for example, Ochs (1979) had in mind when she argued that different ways of formatting a transcript represent different theories about what was being transcribed.
4  See their discussion of the distinction between pauses, gaps, and lapses (Sacks et al., 1974, p. 715, Footnote 26).
5  For further discussion on this point, see Garfinkel and Weider (1992) on "vulgar competency" and the "unique adequacy requirement" (pp. 175–206).

## References

Berger, P. L., & Luckmann, T. (1966). *The social construction of reality*. Garden City, NY: Doubleday.
Cicourel, A.V. (1964). *Method and measurement in sociology*. New York: Free Press.
diSessa, A. A. (1983). Phenomenology and the evolution of intuition. In D. Gentner & A. Stevens (Eds.), *Mental models* (pp. 15–33). Hillsdale, NJ: Lawrence Erlbaum.
diSessa, A. A. (1991). Epistemological micromodels: The case of coordination and quantities. In J. Montangero & A. Tryphon (Eds.), *Psychologie génétique et sciences cognitives* (pp. 169–194). (Volume from the Eleventh Advanced Course.) Geneva, CH: Archives Jean Piaget.
diSessa, A. A. (1993). Toward an epistemology of physics. *Cognition and Instruction*, 10, 105–225.
Garfinkel, H. (1952). *The perception of the other: A study in social order*. (Unpublished dissertation), Harvard University, Cambridge, MA.
Garfinkel, H. (1967). *Studies in ethnomethodology*. Englewood Cliffs, NJ: Prentice Hall.
Garfinkel, H. (2002). *Ethnomethodology's program: Working out Durkheim's aphorism*. Lanham, MD: Rowman & Littlefield.
Garfinkel, H., & Weider, D. L. (1992). Two incommensurable, asymmetrically alternate technologies of social analysis. In G. Watson & R. M. Seiler (Eds.), *Text in context* (pp. 175–206). Newbury Park, CA: Sage.

Goodwin, C. (1987). Unilateral departure. In G. Button & J. R. L. Lee (Eds.), *Talk and social organization* (pp. 206–218). Clevedon, UK: Multilingual Matters.
Grathoff, R. (Ed.). (1978). *The theory of social action: The correspondence of Alfred Schütz and Talcott Parsons.* Bloomington, IN: Indiana University Press.
Heritage, J. (1984). *Garfinkel and ethnomethodology.* Cambridge, UK: Polity Press.
Hindmarsh, J., & Heath, C. (2000). Embodied reference: A study of deixis in workplace interaction. *Journal of Pragmatics*, 32, 1855–1878.
Jefferson, G. (2004). Glossary of transcript symbols with an introduction. In G. Lerner (Ed.), *Conversation analysis: Studies from the first generation* (pp. 13–31). Amsterdam, NL: John Benjamins.
Koschmann, T. (2012). Early glimmers of the now familiar ethnomethodological themes in Garfinkel's "The perception of the other." *Human Studies*, 35, 479–504. doi: 10.1007/s10746-012-9243-z.
Koschmann, T., & Zemel, A. (2009). Optical pulsars and black arrows: Discoveries as occasioned productions. *Journal of the Learning Sciences*, 18, 200–246. doi: 10.1080/10508400902797966.
Ochs, E. (1979). Transcription as theory. In E. Ochs & B. B. Schieffelin (Eds.), *Developmental pragmatics* (pp. 43–72). New York: Academic Press.
Parnafes, O. (2007). What does "fast" mean? Understanding the physical world through computational representations. *Journal of the Learning Sciences*, 16, 415–450.
Parnafes, O., & diSessa, A. (2013). Microgenetic learning analysis: A methodology for studying knowledge in transition. *Human Development*, 56, 5–37. doi: 10.1159/000342945.
Parsons, T. (1937). *The structure of social action: A study in social theory with special reference to a group of recent European writers.* Glencoe, IL: The Free Press.
Quine, W. V. O. (1968). Ontological relativity. *Journal of Philosophy*, 65, 185–212.
Roschelle, J. (1992). Learning by collaboration: Convergent conceptual change. *Journal of the Learning Sciences*, 2, 235–276.
Sacks, H., Schegloff, E., & Jefferson, G. (1974). The simplest systematics for the organization of turn-taking for conversation. *Language*, 50, 696–735.
Schegloff, E. (1991). Conversation analysis and socially shared cognition. In L. Resnick, J. Levine, & S. Teasley (Eds.), *Perspectives on socially shared cognition* (pp. 150–171). Washington, DC: American Psychological Association.
Schegloff, E. (1992). In another context. In A. Duranti & C. Goodwin (Eds.), *Rethinking context: Language as an interactive phenomenon* (pp. 191–228). New York: Cambridge University Press.
Schegloff, E., Jefferson, G., & Sacks, H. (1977). The preference for self-correction in the organization of repair in conversation. *Language*, 53, 361–382.
Schütz, A. (1953). Common-sense and scientific interpretation of human actions. *Philosophy and Phenomenological Research*, 14, 1–38.
Weber, M. (1968). *Economy and society: An outline of interpretive sociology.* New York: Bedminster Press.
Wittgenstein, L. (1958). *Philosophical investigations.* Malden, MA: Blackwell.
Woolgar, S. (1988). *Science: The very idea.* Chichester, UK: Ellis Horwood.

# 22
# REFLECTIONS
## The KAIA Project and Prospects

*Andrea A. diSessa, Mariana Levin, and Nathaniel J. S. Brown*

Our goal here is to provide a brief summary and reaction to the overall project that led to this book: seeking to place the study of knowledge and interaction more properly (and, possibly, more positively) with respect to one another.

Those of us who helped instigate and organize this effort did not expect that it would be an easy road. On the contrary, we felt that we were taking on an ambitious agenda that would transcend even the few and mostly perfunctory "compare and contrast" approaches to differing theories and traditions that exist in education. Against difficulties, we held out for serious progress grounded in new studies with tangible new results.

Without declaring overall success, which will be measured mainly by how the field reacts to what was accomplished, we feel that the project has had a great number of positive outcomes. Inter-perspectival teams managed to work together and emerged with results that both the editorial team and authors seem to regard as innovative and scientifically satisfying. Individuals also deliberately took paths that were quite new to them, again with satisfying outcomes. Dialogue was substantial during the whole project, especially at the several follow-up workshops.

One unanticipated development of interaction across communities was a fairly extensive set of meta-scientific discussions and writings. After the fact, however, this seems more than sensible. People in different scientific communities may just have different expectations about how science works, or what constitutes the best science, and these differences might be at the root of – or might express – contrasts and conflicts. On the other hand, some strong meta-scientific commonalities between KA and IA communities also emerged. Early on, we editors noticed that the commitment to detailed interpretations of real-time data might foster bridges. On this, we feel the volume gives more than sufficient affirmation. Cross-paradigm work did not have difficulty with the nature of data each community thought would be interesting. Reanalysis of data collected to serve one perspective proved unproblematic in many instances in serving the other perspective. In addition, both of these communities strongly value theoretical development as well as empirical undertakings. So, neither is satisfied with validating that some instructional treatment works, but they instinctively want to know why, or insist on starting with theoretically motivated learning environments.

The one most powerful and persuasive conclusion one could draw from our efforts is that scientifically productive and important empirical work can be done employing KA and IA jointly. From our perspective, joint work is also the best way to promote rapprochement. Focusing on the concrete task of making sense of data seems to alleviate, for example, meta-scientific or ideological differences. In addition, it seemed to us that younger or, perhaps even more, middle-career researchers worked together best. In any event, continuing work on a joint or merged agenda requires a judgment that the new paradigm is progressing and paying dividends in the concrete form of new and distinctive empirical results.

Towards this end, in what follows we provide a brief description of each of the chapters in Parts II and III of the volume, highlighting the contribution to the agenda of articulating KAIA perspectives.

## Chapter-by-Chapter Description of Advances in the KAIA Agenda

Azevedo and Lee articulate KA and IA by overlaying IA principles and methods on a prior KA-oriented study (Azevedo, 2013), looking to see how cognitive activity unfolds in collective practices that are deeply meaningful to participants. From the perspective of the KAIA agenda, a key contribution of their piece is coordinating individual and social aspects of "practice," a construct that has become ubiquitous in the learning sciences. Using a rich corpus of field data concerning how model rocketeers and their communities individually and collectively know about stability, which is an everyday and salient concern with respect to flying rockets, they map out the "ecology of knowing" and highlight the ways in which it extends beyond individuals' minds.

DeLiema, Lee, Danish, Enyedy, and Brown perform a reanalysis of a data corpus collected and previously analyzed by Brown (2009). This data set was novel in its design of engaging a student in four comparable conversations with three unique conversational partners. DeLiema et al. focused on how the student refined his explanations of a set of chemistry phenomena over multiple days through systematic re-compositions of gesture, speech, representation, and knowledge. Similar to other teams (e.g., Gupta, Elby, and Sawtelle; Danish, Enyedy, and Parnafes), the construct of framing plays an important role in their efforts to integrate KA and IA perspectives. In addition, their chapter makes a methodological contribution toward the KAIA agenda by illustrating the construction and use of multimodal transcripts that make clear the coupled nature of utterances, gestures, and representations.

Danish, Enyedy, and Parnafes make a strong move toward integrating IA and KA, arguably one of the more definitive such moves in this volume. They start with a clear integrative agenda: "Knowledge is not only seen through interaction, but drives interaction and is in turn shaped by interaction in a continuous and dynamic manner. Similarly, interaction originates in, displays, and leads to the transformation of an individual's knowledge" (p. 160). Then, they enact a methodologically precise plan, providing three separate analyses of a small but rich corpus of two students advancing their understanding of the concept of "fast": (a) a KA-oriented analysis, (b) an IA-oriented analysis, and (c) an integrated analysis. The authors make the case that the integrated analysis is, in many ways, superior: it "highlight[s] the process through which interactional choices [IA] both shut down and open up various explorations of knowledge [KA]" (p. 178), while it simultaneously shows how intersubjectivity is deliberately built [IA], and of what it consists [KA]. In this synopsis, we have deliberately marked IA- and KA-typical concerns to emphasize how they are here intertwined.

In commenting on Danish et al.'s work, diSessa makes two general points. First, he elaborates an important point made by the authors: Accomplishing pure and separate IA and KA analyses is difficult, if not impossible. Intuitive analyses of knowledge intrude in analyses of interaction, and vice versa. However, when we integrate analyses intuitively, rather than explicitly, much is lost. diSessa's elaboration involves the idea of a "STEP," a historical landmark when professional but intuitive accomplishments are cleanly surpassed by explicit, scientific work. Then he asks whether we have reached a STEP with regard to professional practices of IA and KA. Have we reached the point where professional analysis of interaction will cleanly surpass the intuitive treatment of interaction by knowledge researchers, and vice versa? diSessa's second point concerns essential commonalities that may exist already between IA and KA. He argues Coordination Class Theory (as used by Danish et al.), while formulated in the KA tradition, already enfolds the capacity to attend to interaction and distributed knowing, and even demands such analyses in certain cases. The point is elaborated by imagining a socio-historical study of a grand scientific accomplishment, the "reading out" of the mass of the Higgs boson.

Levin and diSessa offer a KA perspective in pursuing theoretical and empirical elaboration of some issues present in Stevens and Hall's (1998) original IA analysis of the construct of *disciplined perception*, which cast expertise as a sort of refined vision (perception) and learning as a process of tuning one's vision (disciplining perception) through interaction with others. Levin and diSessa's analysis takes a Coordination Class Theory perspective on the data[1] and augments the notion of disciplined perception without changing the essential idea or most of the insights Stevens and Hall originally gained from using it. Yet, Levin and diSessa's analysis opens up important complexities. These include (a) the very fact of many different forms of disciplining (noted also in the work of Abrahamson and Trninic in this volume), (b) how an instructor's interpretation of a student affects the form of disciplining they use, (c) details about when a newcomer is in the position to have their perception disciplined, and (d) the consideration of the multiple threads and long-term trajectories of developing disciplined perception.

Abrahamson and Trninic contribute to the KAIA agenda without being a priori "affiliated" so to speak with either KA or IA perspectives. Yet their chapter and previous publications make good contact to both perspectives. For example, a study by Abrahamson (Abrahamson, Gutiérrez, Charoenying, Negrete, & Bumbacher, 2012) explicitly builds upon a framework of Goodwin's (1994) to demonstrate the many varied ways that tutors can "discipline" the perception of novices. This point resonates with a central theme of the Levin and diSessa analysis of disciplined perception – that tutors have rich repertoires of professional knowledge that allow them to respond appropriately in the moment to students. Abrahamson and Trninic's chapter in this volume aims to put in dialogue dynamical-systems and sociocultural theories of conceptual genesis. They focus on the relationship between motor-skill development and conceptual development, attending in particular to the way motor-skill development is supported by representational and social infrastructure. In their work, a KA perspective on action-based emergent constructivism is intertwined with an IA perspective of the role social agents serve in guided mediation of culturally meaningful skills.

Kapon reanalyzes the data from a prior KA-oriented (clinical) study (Kapon and diSessa, 2012) using methods and foci of attention from IA. She looks in microscopic detail at gestures and their roles in an interview, and she considers the moves of the interviewer and their effects on the subject. Arguably the most important discovery in the reanalysis was an essentially invisible gesture that seemed initially without communicative intent or effect, but which reappeared regularly in the corpus, eventually transforming into an obvious action with communicative effect. Kapon argues that the gesture originally served the subject as a simulation invoking and allowing the consideration of a non-verbal element of knowledge (a p-prim). Thus, careful analysis of gesture added a new and important dimension to the original Knowledge Analysis (how an idea came into consideration), but also expanded the possible functions of gestures beyond those in the existing (socially oriented) literature: Metaphoric gestures sometimes exist for their powerful and individual epistemic effects. She argues that her analysis was a deep integration, an appropriation of methods from one paradigm (IA) for the goals of another (KA).

In commenting on Kapon's work, Elby highlights the fact that sensitivity to some IA ideas – short of a full adoption of interactionist ontologies, and far short of the denial of the functional role of knowledge – can provide alternative interpretations of subjects' actions that deserve empirical consideration. In particular, Elby introduces "framing" – what a subject believes is going on in an activity. The subject of Kapon's analysis might, for example, frame the interview as "guided sense-making": An interviewer encourages a subject to explore ideas and draw his own conclusions, but, still, she might aim to be helpful, gently pointing out profitable directions. In one case, assuming guided sense-making, the interviewer's actions might seem to favor one particular direction of thinking. In another case, the subject might be confused as to what guidance the interviewer might be providing, which might be difficult to distinguish from confusion about the topic of the interview per se. Elby's analyses are not made to refute Kapon's claims but to extend the list of possible interpretations, which only further analysis could resolve.

Gupta, Elby, and Sawtelle present a reanalysis of an interview Gupta performed and previously analyzed with Elby (Gupta & Elby, 2011) in which a student gets stuck on a physics problem. The original analysis argued that the student's difficulty was not due to a knowledge deficit, but rather that the epistemological stance he took in that context "blocked" him from using relevant knowledge that he demonstrably possessed. Their reanalysis considers key segments of the interview from an IA perspective, attending to turn-by-turn conversational dynamics and focusing on both stabilities and shifts in participants' knowledge activations. Their reanalysis does not merely layer a new IA-based analysis onto their previously published KA-based analysis. Instead, they reconceptualize an epistemological stance previously attributed to an individual (the student) as mutually constructed and sustained by the situated interaction between the student and the interviewer.

Ma explores the phenomenon of what she calls "ensemble learning and knowing" and presents a multimodal analysis from a sociocultural perspective, using the methods of IA. She tracks the learning of three secondary-school students developing a strategy for dilating a large-scale ("walking scale") quadrilateral that was made using everyday materials such as ropes and lawn flags. The strategy, initially proposed by one student, was developed by the group during implementation. In her analysis, knowledge is embedded in ensemble activity that is accomplished in a group. The individuals have access only to partial views and certain physical manipulations of the figure and must complete the task in collaboration with others. Ma is explicit in her attribution of cognitive activity to the level of the ensemble and resists making claims about cognition at the individual level.

In commenting on Ma's work, Conlin and Hammer explore Ma's data with respect to the possibilities of multiple levels of analysis. Aiming to bridge KA and IA, Conlin and Hammer offer strategies for guiding researchers' selections of sensible units of analysis. Their heuristics for attending to the scale of cognitive dynamics have been published elsewhere (Conlin, Gupta, & Hammer, 2010) and in this piece, they apply those heuristics to Ma's data. Their analysis agrees with Ma's central claim that the ensemble learns a strategy for how to dilate the quadrilateral. However, by allowing their attention to shift to individuals, they are able to say more about individual contributions to ensemble learning and knowing.

Umphress proposes that both caregivers – in their everyday interaction with children – and clinical interviewers are Skilled Knowledge Practitioners (SKPs) – "adults whose … work includes understanding and developing children's knowledge and thinking." She provides an analysis of a mother and child working in a garden in which the mother – quite evidently, and using multiple interactional strategies – manipulates her own and her child's "epistemic authority." In particular, the mother, like an interviewer, withholds her own judgment, enhances her daughter's authority, and skillfully provides grounds and encouragement for a joint exploration of the child's ideas. Umphress also describes some differences among various contexts for SKP work, such as teaching, parenting, and interviewing, which lead to expected differences in practices. While her analysis is largely within the IA paradigm, Umphress locates these practices squarely in the intersection of IA and KA, and prepares for KA follow-up: Can SKPs from diverse contexts learn from one another? (Are parents better prepared than most to be good clinical interviewers?) What is the form of knowledge and learning processes involved in becoming a SKP?

diSessa, Greeno, Michaels, and O'Connor take up an analysis of interaction in a context – clinical interviewing – that has been a flashpoint of contention between IA and KA researchers. They do this by reanalyzing a clinical interview that had already been thoroughly analyzed from a KA point of view. They focus specifically on the interactive form called "revoicing," where an interlocutor reframes and repeats something a subject or student has already said. Results indicate massive use of revoicing, and a rather amazing diversity of forms, presumably adapted to local conditions and purposes. Comparison to revoicing in classrooms yields some commonality of forms and functions, but also significant differences. Many of the differences can be traced to different top-level goals: for classrooms, to move students along toward normative understanding; for interviewing, to "make data appear" concerning subjects' thinking. The paper argues that the knowledge of the interviewer (including "knowledge concerning interaction") is a non-negotiable part of understanding the form and function of interactions. Thus, an optimal analysis of interaction also entails an analysis of knowledge.

Russ, Sherin, and Lee also contribute to the enterprise of exploring the properties and challenges of conducting one-on-one clinical interviews. They use methods typical of neither KA nor IA, but try to understand the interplay between knowledge and interaction in clinical interviews. Similar to Umphress and to diSessa et al., Russ et al. start from the assumption that students' ideas are delicate and complex and that substantial skill on the part of an interviewer (a Skilled Knowledge Practitioner) is necessary to surface them. They present two complementary goals of interviews. From a knowledge perspective, they present the challenge of avoiding *knowledge restriction* – that is, interviewers need to conduct the interview in a way that reveals the maximal amount about a student's conceptual ecology and less about his or her reaction to the interviewer's ideas and judgments. From an interactional perspective, the challenge is *interactional interpretation* – the interviewer needs to ensure students interpret the interview as a time for substantial and authentic interaction with the tasks at hand. Russ et al. present a set of codes that flesh out these two dimensions and allow us to learn about how often and in what ways interviewers engage in "knowledge" work and "interactional" work. Like Brown does in his chapter, they acknowledge the substantial effects that even a silent interviewer can have in shaping a discourse interaction. Like diSessa et al., they consider how frequently moves like revoicing occur in clinical interactions.

Brown also takes up issues of knowledge and interaction in interview settings, but makes a more general contribution to the methodological problem of how to interpret the phenomenon of participants revising and reworking their explanations on a moment-by-moment basis. Brown describes a mechanism of interaction by which speakers create opportunities for listeners to provide feedback at specific moments during an explanatory narrative, in order to monitor the success of the explanation as it unfolds. Attention to the design of these moments, called *feedback-relevant places* (FRPs), and how they are taken up or ignored by the listener allows a knowledge analyst to more precisely characterize students' knowledge systems. In particular, by comparing when shifts in explanation occur relative to FRPs, and how successful the explanation is currently positioned by both speaker and listener when the shift occurs, a knowledge analyst can learn more about the reliability priority of knowledge elements. A further methodological contribution of Brown's chapter involves the transcription conventions he employs in the service of rendering interactional detail on paper, in particular prosody (e.g., intonation, volume), rhythm (e.g., silence, tempo), and kinesics (e.g., shifts in gaze, nodding).

Sherin brings yet a different methodological approach to the study of clinical interviews, one that stands in provocative contrast to many of the analyses presented in this volume. He explores to what degree some questions at the core of KA can be addressed with a computational analytic technique that omits all interactional detail and attends only to the words spoken (even ignoring most aspects of word ordering). He applies this method to transcripts of interviews in which students were asked to explain the seasons, showing that aspects of a typical KA analysis can be reproduced by an automated analysis. From the perspective of the KAIA agenda, however, a salient outcome of Sherin's analysis is that such a radical reduction of interview data led him to analyze what special interactional features of his data could have allowed this surprising outcome. For example, he hypothesizes that even if utterances are multimodal, redundancy in channels might obviate using all of them. In addition, the computer program's focus for analysis does not need to include what is required by a person in order to participate successfully in the interaction, per se.

In commenting on Sherin's work, Enyedy and Danish wish to evaluate how Sherin's experiments with radical reductions in data (interviews reduced to collections of words, in order to afford computational efficiency and objectivity) can contribute to a rapprochement of IA and KA. Briefly, they maintain that a joint KAIA program must respect core principles of IA. The elimination of interaction detail is, in their view, unhelpful. Such reduction prematurely forecloses studying key issues, such as what our most basic terms (e.g., "knowledge") should mean. IA maintains an "essentially distributed" view of knowledge. "[K]nowing and interacting [are] fundamentally simultaneous and co-constituting" (p. 448). Another core focus of IA is recovering the perspective of participants, and eliminating interaction radically reduces or eliminates our ability to do that. Enyedy and Danish show instances of removing interaction (e.g., the interviewer's contributions in an interview) and illustrate what they take to be non-negotiably critical things that are also removed. The authors suggest that Sherin's analyses should be supplemented by analyses of the contributions of the interviewer and of the (jointly constructed) perspectives of the participants.

Nemirovsky and Kelton reflect on a central tension that is shared among traditions and practices for studying interaction (as is naturally the case in most of the analyses in the KAIA enterprise). On one hand, there is the goal of avoiding what the authors call theoretical imperialism – force-fitting theoretical frameworks and ignoring endogenous meanings. On the other hand, it is desirable to analyze data in a way that is generalizable and speaks to broader psychological, social, political, and ethical concerns. The authors first trace scholarly debates that put these desiderata in opposition. They then reflect on methodological issues in their research of videotaped interactions recorded during 5th-graders' field trips to the Science Museum of Minnesota, focusing in particular on selected interactions among Hmong children and their classmates as they visit a replica of a traditional Hmong house. They pursue the issue of how to study moment-by-moment production of intersubjective understanding. They point out that studying topics such as kinesthesia or affect is difficult, and lack of relevant methods can render some important questions "less visible" to the research community.

In his suite of micro-essays, diSessa seeks to exemplify and extend informal discussions that occurred during the KAIA project through addressing three points of contention. First, he seeks to defuse the idea that intact and naturally occurring systems have a privileged status compared to "artificial" ones. In this regard, he points out that science seems almost always to cycle back and forth between "natural" and "artificial" environments – and for good reason – to get adequate purchase on focused scientific issues. While connections across different environments of study and relevant real-world "application" are always tricky, scientists are often aware of issues and have proactive strategies to deal with them. Second, he argues that it is a mistake to assume that our models of what happens (e.g., in the mind) should appear to us just like the phenomenology (e.g., thinking) itself. Models are just models, and some of their properties are often or always different from "reality." Third, diSessa summarizes persistent differences between IA and KA communities in construing the viability of interviewing as a scientific method. He concludes that criticisms of interviewing often do not have a firm scientific basis, or they concern difficulties of which interviewers are aware and for which they have compensating strategies.

Hall, Nemirovsky, Ma, and Kelton offer a meta-scientific basis for discussion across paradigms (such as KA and IA). A "hidden machineries" (HM) approach to doing science – perhaps more prominent in KA – focuses on underlying levels (such as mental structures) that explain what happens at a more phenomenological level. In contrast, a "natural descriptive" approach (ND) – perhaps more prominent in IA – seeks to fill out understanding within a single level, that at which a phenomenon of interest appears to us. Both modes of doing science are valid and interactions between them are common, varied, and interesting. The authors offer case studies in the history of science to illustrate. The second half of the paper asks a series of critical (*generous\**) questions with which to interrogate our methodologies and theories, independent of how we affiliate with HM and ND. Two examples: (a) How do we remain open and not become captive to our preconceived ways of understanding things? (b) How do we maximize the impact of our research in terms of human good, equity, and alleviating suffering? Case studies of IA and KA research illustrate how one might approach these questions.

In commenting on Hall et al.'s work, Levin takes a personal approach to openness (generous\* question (a), above). She recounts her experiences of deep commitment to openness from both IA and KA researchers and proposes that deliberate openness might be an especially important commonality across KAIA. Deliberate openness does not just happen; it is an active pursuit. One element of that pursuit is a studied modesty in considering how little we actually understand of knowing and interacting. A second element is an insistent critical attitude toward our theories: Do they really do important work, or are we just "painting the data" with theoretical terms? Finally, since seeing involves being prepared to see, Levin notes that a joint KAIA program combines our different sensitivities to new things.

In commenting on Hall et al.'s work, diSessa examines the constructs of HM and ND frameworks from a different meta-scientific perspective, in which HM and ND appear problematic. For example, he argues (a) HM and ND are not plausibly exclusive modes for any extended scientific inquiry, (b) ND's assumption that science, including theorizing, can progress solely within the level of the investigated phenomena seems doubtful, and, in contrast, (c) multiple levels in science are an unproblematic and common occurrence. A revised look at case studies in the history of science reveals that, for example, Darwin's ND study (as categorized by Hall et al.) is rife with HM earmarks, and that some of diSessa's own work (characterized as HM) appears, meta-scientifically, very much like Darwin's. Finally, diSessa proposes to examine the breadth of meta-scientific principles espoused by researchers across the KA/IA spectrum to see if differences are systematic points of division or if there exists – or is coming to exist – important common ground.

## Synthesis of Empirical and Theoretical Contributions

Thematically, progress was made on several issues. The constructs of "practice" (Azevedo & Lee), "disciplined perception" (Levin & diSessa), "revoicing" (diSessa, et al.), and "intersubjectivity" – typically thought of solely within the sociocultural paradigm – were repositioned as joint cognitive-social phenomena. Creating intersubjectivity in particular became a theme running through several of the pieces (Abrahamson & Trninic; Danish et al.; Levin & diSessa; Russ et al.; Umphress).

Several chapters elaborated on the dynamics of cognitive constructs such as (cognitively construed) resources, p-prims (e.g., Kapon), and coordination classes (Danish et al.; Levin & diSessa), and how, specifically, they are activated and developed in interaction with social and material resources. Several authors proposed the construct of "framing" as useful in KAIA analyses (Danish et al.; DeLiema et al.; Elby; Enyedy and Danish; Gupta et al.). Further, the extensive strand within the volume focused on developing a KAIA perspective on clinical interviewing (Brown; the third micro-essay in diSessa; diSessa et al.; Kapon; Russ et al; Sherin) made strong contributions to the agenda of characterizing the nature, strengths, and limitations of the methodology, while connecting it to other agendas (Umphress) and pointing out directions for further advance.

Within the corpus of empirical chapters, several teams made attempts to represent data in novel ways that facilitated their work on the KAIA agenda (e.g., Brown; DeLiema et al.; Ma) or made methodological contributions in the form of analytic heuristics (Conlin and Hammer). Meta-theoretical and meta-methodological pieces (diSessa; Hall et al.; Nemirovsky & Kelton) served to further the agenda of articulation of perspectives by taking a step back from the nitty-gritty details of joint analysis and allowing for reflection on larger issues related to commonalities and differences in the way we understand our research enterprise, including the kinds of questions we consider researchable and valuable.

While the opening "perspectival" chapters on KA and IA did not intend to make contributions to the synthetic agenda per se, they did set the groundwork for the articulation of perspectives in the empirical chapters. As windows into the state of the art with respect to KA and IA, they should be useful for researchers pursing a synthetic agenda, and also, incidentally, for researchers hoping to pursue either of these perspectives separately.

As evident from the above synopses of the empirical results of the volume, there are many possible kinds of contributions and possibilities for working on the agenda of articulating perspectives. The following list showcases some of this diversity in analytical approaches to the KAIA agenda and can serve as a model for how others wishing to engage in articulating perspectives may proceed. In the following, "borrowing from a perspective" might include the focus for analysis, theory or bits of theories, methodology, or any combination thereof.

- Start with a previously developed IA of data and extend it from a KA perspective (e.g., Levin & diSessa).
- Start with a previously developed KA of data and extend it from an IA perspective, possibly focusing specifically on methodology rather than theory or focus of analysis (e.g., Kapon).
- Develop and present three separate analyses: KA, IA, and integrated (KAIA) (Danish et al.; Gupta et al.).
- Cultivate a new "KAIA" analysis borrowing theoretical constructs and methodological tools from both KA and IA (Azevedo & Lee; DeLiema et al.).
- Develop an analysis from one perspective, but explicitly mark or open up issues that speak to the other perspective (Ma; Sherin).
- Develop an analysis using neither core methods of KA nor of IA, but one that reframes or elaborates constructs or issues of interest to the KAIA enterprise (diSessa et al; Russ et al.).

These patterns generalize straightforwardly to any dialectical or synthetic projects.

## Summing Up

In the introduction, we presented a ladder of kinds of outcomes to our pursuit of a synthetic KAIA agenda:

- Global competition
- Global complementarity
- Micro-complementarity
- Mutually influencing paradigms
- Deep synergy
  - Mutual accountability
  - Deep synergy proper
- Fusion.

The first two possibilities, **global competition** and **global complementarity**, are basically antithetical to the aims of this volume and have little voice here. However, remaining contests and disputes most certainly indicate that a more micro competition – concerning which questions to pursue, how to pursue them, and what our "final" understanding should be – most certainly remains. These smaller contests, in our view, are completely healthy and bespeak a complex and long-term agenda of realizing powerful synthetic possibilities.

**Micro-complementarity** is evident in almost every chapter of this volume. Indeed, it is so pervasive and generally successful that we would judge that at least **shadows of deep synergy** are definitively on the table. Consider the several

IA-inspired theoretical terms (mentioned above) that were developed and resituated within the KAIA agenda: practice, disciplined perception, revoicing, and intersubjectivity. Consider also the KA-characteristic terms (p-prims, coordination classes, etc.) that took on new interactive relevancies and found salient places in analyses of interaction.

Recognizing potentially deep synergies, the larger judgment of **mutually influencing paradigms** seems clearly suggested, if not established. One volume, however, cannot speak for the reactions of the field at large. Contrarily, **fusion** is plainly elusive – but we never expected to get close to that possibly chimeric outcome.

The whole volume represents a kind of **mutual accountability**. All authors here acknowledge, from the beginning, that knowledge and interaction are both worthy pursuits: Analysis of knowledge must always be understood with respect to the material and social conditions that support and constrain its activation and display; analyses of interaction for educational purposes must account for the properties of what is learned, or not, in interaction, and how what is known affects aspects of interaction.

To put things in the smallest possible formulation, this volume demonstrates both a basic mutual respect and intention to capitalize on another perspective's accomplishments, and also genuine successes in explicitly pursuing a synthetic agenda. What could be a better summary for this volume?: Your perspective is insightful; our perspective is insightful; together, we're even better.

## Note

1   Historical note: With regard to the social history of the KAIA project discussed in this volume's preface, it is worth noting that diSessa, Hall, and Stevens discussed the possibility of a coordination class analysis of their data at the early stages of work that led to their disciplined perception paper, nearly 20 years ago.

## References

Abrahamson, D., Gutiérrez, J., Charoenying, T., Negrete, A., & Bumbacher, E. (2012). Fostering hooks and shifts: Tutorial tactics for guided mathematical discovery. *Technology, Knowledge and Learning*, 17(1–2), 61–86.

Azevedo, F. S. (2013). Knowing the stability of model rockets: An investigation of learning in interest-based practices. *Cognition and Instruction*, 31(3), 345–374.

Brown, N. J. S. (2009). *Information performances and illative sequences: Sequential organization of explanations of chemical phase equilibrium* (Doctoral dissertation). Retrieved from https://escholarship.org/uc/item/9zw1p1ps.

Conlin, L., Gupta, A., & Hammer, D. (2010, June). Where to find the mind: Identifying the scale of cognitive dynamics. In *Proceedings of the 9th International Conference of the Learning Sciences-Volume 1* (pp. 277–284). International Society of the Learning Sciences.

diSessa, A. A. (2007). An interactional analysis of clinical interviewing. *Cognition and Instruction*, 25(4), 523–565.

Goodwin, C. (1994). Professional vision. *American anthropologist*, 96(3), 606–633.
Gupta, A., & Elby, A. (2011). Beyond epistemological deficits: Dynamic explanations of engineering students' difficulties with mathematical sense-making. *International Journal of Science Education*, 33(18), 2463–2488.
Kapon, S., & diSessa, A. A. (2012). Reasoning through instructional analogies. *Cognition and Instruction*, 30(3), 261–310.
Stevens, R., & Hall, R. (1998). Disciplined perception: Learning to see in technoscience. In M. Lampert & M. Blunk (Eds.), *Talking mathematics in school: Studies of teaching and learning* (pp. 107–149). Cambridge, UK: Cambridge University Press.

# INDEX

**Introductory Note**

References such as '178–9' indicate (not necessarily continuous) discussion of a topic across a range of pages. Wherever possible in the case of topics with many references, these have either been divided into sub-topics or only the most significant discussions of the topic are listed. Because the entire work is about 'knowledge' and 'interaction', the use of these terms (and certain others which occur constantly throughout the book) as entry points has been restricted. Information will be found under the corresponding detailed topics.

abrupt transitions, 216, 224, 230
abstraction, 57–8
acceleration, 52, 112, 193, 264, 269–72, 539
accountability, mutual, 1, 5, 580–1
accounts, precise and verifiable, 462, 472–3
accuracy, 145, 155, 366, 407
activation, 41–3, 48–50, 239–40, 243–5, 248–9, 251–4, 283–6, 436–8; contextual, 57, 282; of formal knowledge, 267, 285; levels, 436, 438, 441, 446, 455
active engagement, 239, 250, 253
activity: settings, 342–3; systems, 87–8, 517, 555–7
Actor-Network Theory, *see* ANT
actor-networks, 511–12
adaptability, 25–6
adults, 84, 97–9, 215, 327, 398, 554, 575
a-frames, 353–4, 362, 367–8, 372–3
after-the-fact computer analysis, 431, 454
agency, 48, 50, 208, 217–18, 295, 508, 512, 515

agenda, 26, 182, 188, 191, 520, 524–6, 571, 579; synthetic, 26, 186, 579, 581
agents, 48, 216, 220, 320–1; multiple, 321
aggression, 499, 539
air pressure, 113–14
alcohol, 140, 405–6, 415; molecules, 411, 415–16; vapor, 140, 405–6
alignment, 52, 54, 173, 175, 180, 199, 201, 206
ambulatory sequences, 93–4
analogical reasoning, 55–6
analysis: computational, 429, 431–2, 453–6; integrated, 161–2, 166, 175–6, 178, 180–1, 183, 185, 572
analytic techniques, 81–2, 85, 576
analytical innovations, 25
analytical tools, 11, 261, 287–8, 527
answers, 253–6, 268, 279–80, 321–2, 378–9, 384–5, 407–8, 410; right/correct, 134, 139, 147, 155, 268, 302, 398, 407–8
ANT (Actor-Network Theory), 100, 506, 510–12

anthropology, 20, 214, 312, 496, 560; cognitive, 76; linguistic, 2, 409
anticipation frames, *see* a-frames
approximate modularity, 481–4, 530
architectural designs, 84, 88, 102
articulation, 2, 5, 59, 181, 224, 244, 493, 533
artifacts, 19, 212, 216, 219, 230, 237–40, 249, 251; interactional, 348, 488; material, 138, 247; symbolic, 223–4
artificial contexts, 4, 489
artificial intelligence, 33, 64, 183, 260, 484
atoms, 5, 56, 486, 496, 537–8
attraction, 141, 143, 145, 151–3, 157, 216; of gravity, 242–4, 253
attribution, 282, 349, 351, 354, 356, 362, 368, 472–3; of knowledge, 267, 286; problems, 85–6
Australia, 360, 388, 396, 433–4, 440–1, 453
authority, 266–7, 284, 286, 327, 331, 356, 361, 363
automated analysis, 432–3, 435–6, 439, 441–2, 444–6, 454–5, 576
automatisms, 219–20, 226
axioms, naturalized, 57–8
axis, 114–15, 168, 170, 173, 177, 387–8, 434, 440

back-channel feedback, 393–4
Bakhtin, M.M., 480
balls, 14, 17, 133, 154, 179, 265
Bamberger, J., 171, 215, 227, 232
bar representations, 167, 170–1, 173–4, 177
beliefs, 20–1, 38–9, 256, 287, 460, 488, 529, 533; epistemological, 262, 490
Bernstein, N.A., 218–19
best intuitive practitioners, 183–5
bids, 99, 278–9, 308, 313–15
biology, 55, 483, 499, 501, 555–7; intuitive, 63
birds, 192, 499–500
body enactment, 476
boundary markers, 412, 421–2
boundary objects, 74

CA, *see* conversation, analysis
Cajal, Ramón y, 499, 501–4, 525–6, 535, 537, 544
cameras, 53, 73–4, 90, 94, 97, 121, 140, 554; video, 18, 140, 166, 296, 515
capture, 43–5, 52–4, 60–1, 77, 430, 435, 441–2, 444
Carey, S., 20, 34, 237

Cartesian space, 93, 196–7
causal threads, 482–4, 530, 539–40, 547–8
causality, 169, 537, 540; ensemble, 541, 543, 548
CC, *see* coordination class
center of dilation, 296–8, 300–301, 304–7, 319
center of gravity (CG), 113–17, 123–6
center of pressure (CP), 113–17, 122–6
CG, *see* center of gravity
check inference revoicings, 358
chemical phenomena, 133, 139–41, 144–5, 147, 571
chemistry, 5, 55, 139, 363, 378, 403, 405, 407–8
children, 15, 81–3, 212–13, 218, 327–32, 339, 342–4, 575; knowledge, 327–8, 343, 575
chimpanzees, 498–9, 539
choices, 3, 24–5, 197–8, 277–9, 282, 284–5, 449–50, 455–6
civilization, 5, 182, 481, 536
clarification, 278, 329, 335, 363, 372, 389, 391, 396–7; requests, 372, 389–93, 398
classroom: community, 293, 508; instruction, 377, 488; interactions, 128–9, 509; learning, 22, 293, 343, 488; revoicing, 350, 359–63, 365
classrooms, 81–2, 331, 350 1, 361–5, 481–2, 487–90, 507–10, 514–15; mathematics, 507–8
Clement, J., 222, 348, 377, 488
climate, 391, 499–500
clinical context, 188, 361–4, 490–3
clinical interactions, 4, 348, 362, 370, 491, 576
clinical interviewers, 327–9, 331, 339, 341–3, 375, 379, 488, 575; as skilled knowledge practitioners, 328–9
clinical interviewing, 139, 236–7, 262, 329, 342, 451–2, 491–2, 575–6; challenges, 377–99; cognitive, 377, 379, 382, 398–9; revoicing, 348–75; viability, 486–94
clinical methods, 490–1, 493
clockness, 536
clocks, 525, 536, 546–7
closer-farther explanations, 394, 432–3, 440–1
clumps, 145–7, 154
clustering, 51, 312–14, 316, 319–20, 387, 389, 393
Cobb, P., 20, 56, 100, 185, 222, 292–4, 507–9, 513
co-constructed framing, 267–8, 282

codes, 44, 46, 206–7, 352, 354, 364–5, 385–6, 389
coding schemes, 47, 352, 354, 357, 362, 372, 477
cognition, 2, 64, 75–7, 229–30, 238–9, 293, 315–16, 555–6; embodied, 34–6; epistemic, 135; individual, 236, 238, 512, 531; situated, 33–4, 37, 76
cognitive activity, 130, 213, 403–4, 420–1, 571, 574
cognitive anthropology, 76
cognitive clinical interviewing, 377, 379, 382, 398–9
cognitive dynamics, 261, 311, 574
cognitive ecology, 254, 263, 267, 284, 316, 544
cognitive elements, 257, 260–2, 286, 436
cognitive modeling, 35, 37, 39, 43, 262, 266, 436, 438
cognitive perspective, 1, 31, 34, 236
cognitive psychology, 20, 88, 496
cognitive resources, 17, 58, 261, 448
cognitive revolution, 31–3, 503
cognitive science, 34, 62, 76, 85, 193, 293, 312, 533
cognitivists, 6, 22, 36, 83, 194, 260–1, 283–4, 558
co-knowers, 338, 342
commitments, 21–2, 76–7, 81, 88, 447, 450–1, 507, 512; theoretical, 75, 311, 320–1, 449
common ground, 13, 66, 350, 357, 365, 369, 384, 394
common interviewer turns, 383, 385, 393
commonalities, 365, 520, 536, 545, 570, 572, 575, 578–9
communicated information, 431, 444, 450
communicative gestures, 242, 251
communities, 1–2, 23–4, 26, 118, 121, 127–9, 293–4, 570–1; Hmong, 471, 476; professional, 497–8, 526, 534–5; rocketry, 113, 115–16, 125; scientific, 184, 186, 367, 503, 570
comparative analysis, 83–4, 86–7, 90, 514–19
competence, 17–18, 59, 195, 197, 202, 209, 409, 513; disciplinary, 198, 209; meta-representational, 506, 512–15; native, 513–15; reconceived, 11–27
competition, global, 2–3, 580
complementarity, 2–3, 555, 580
complex knowledge system, 20, 41, 49, 209, 237
complex systems, 20, 26, 30, 39, 41, 49, 55, 192

complexity, 23–6, 37, 43, 511, 521, 528, 536, 555
complex-systems approach, 20
comprehension, 16, 404, 411, 413–17
computation, symbolic, 64, 484
computational analysis, 429–56; and interactional detail, 431, 433, 435, 439, 441, 449, 451, 453
computational models, 64, 455, 566
computational representations, 51–3, 167
computer analysis, after-the-fact, 431, 454
computer screens, *see* screens
computer simulations, 161, 165–6, 172
computers, 36, 63, 78, 125, 166, 183, 455, 531–2
concept projections, 58–60, 65
concept-characteristic information, 59, 65, 193
concepts, 38–9, 51, 84–5, 128–31, 161–2, 192–3, 505–11, 516–19; mathematical, 214, 218, 221; normative, 370, 491; statistical, 514–15
conceptual change, 2, 20–1, 40, 145, 156–7, 236–7, 407, 493; research, 37, 133, 488
conceptual development, 51–2, 54, 56, 58, 202, 218, 220, 230
conceptual ecology, 39–40, 111–12, 128–9, 380–1, 384, 386–9, 391, 393–9
conceptual knowledge, 217, 262, 327
conceptual learning, 224, 231, 322
conceptual metaphors, 35, 503
conceptual practices, 73, 89, 91–3, 96–7, 99
conceptual reasoning, 219–20
conceptual resources, 262, 283, 555
conceptual space, 113, 175–6
conceptual understanding, 13, 162, 315, 558
conceptualization, 62, 194, 224, 238, 313, 555
confirmation, 176–7, 276–7, 351–2, 360, 362, 411, 413–14, 419; requests, 340
conflict, 3, 22, 152, 179, 199, 240, 321, 331
confusion, 178, 255, 263, 275, 278, 301, 305, 309
conjecture, 221–2, 237, 249, 505, 513
consequentiality, 18, 79–80; developmental, 79, 86, 100; procedural, 78–9
conservation, 74–5, 91, 102
containers, 101, 405–6, 418–19
content, 36, 39–40, 49–50, 96, 169, 172–3, 175–6, 556–7; disciplinary, 55; mathematical, 223, 508; propositional, 239, 556

context, 11–13, 15–21, 23–6, 82–7, 161–4, 180–3, 236–9, 284–7; artificial, 4, 489; interactional, 81, 112, 133, 138, 366, 449; interview, 264, 286, 381; material, 87, 136; natural, 481, 488; new, 51, 54, 133, 152, 348; performance in, 11, 16, 18, 21, 24; social, 2, 12, 157, 161, 163–4, 181, 349, 492
contextual activation, 57, 282
contextual priority, 238, 243, 245, 249; of dynamic balance, 247, 255–6
contextuality, 12–13, 25–6, 33, 37, 42, 45, 48–9, 52
continuities, 87, 102, 136–7, 197, 200, 210, 486, 502
contradictions, 2, 285, 355–6, 370
conversation, 94–5, 249–51, 327–9, 359–62, 398–9, 480, 505–7, 518–20; analysis, 78, 85, 100, 250–1, 263, 275–6, 459, 562; everyday, 44, 254, 335, 367, 393, 410
conversational dynamics, 255, 263, 284; turn-by-turn, 261, 574
cooking, 358, 360, 362, 366, 379, 514
coordination, 19, 22, 58–9, 188, 202, 205, 366, 369–70; of knowledge, 58, 370
coordination class (CC), 51–4, 58–60, 65–6, 185–9, 191–5, 197, 205–10, 522–3; extension of model, 58–60; model, 58–9; revised terminology, 65–6; state as, 59; theory, 51–2, 54, 162–5, 186–9, 192–4, 199–201, 207–9, 522–3; theory, and disciplined perception, 191–210; theory, and individual illumination, 197–8
coordination clusters, 59
core functions, 350, 361, 373
correct answers, 139, 268, 398
correct explanations, 155, 432, 440
counter-principles, 38–9
coupled gestures, 239, 247, 250–1
CP, *see* center of pressure
critical points of change, 165
cues, 19, 151, 252, 255, 286, 448, 454; interactional, 164, 166, 176, 399, 455; schoolish, 254
cuing, 42, 50, 253, 384, 404, 420
cultural activity, 516, 518
cultural holism, 505
cultural practices, 85, 293, 476, 513, 516
culture, 6, 11, 21, 62–3, 186, 503–5, 531, 533
curation, personal, 96, 102
cycles, 49, 89, 136, 167, 486, 577; day/night, 396, 440

Darwin, Charles, 499–501, 503, 525, 529, 535–7, 540–4, 546, 548
data corpora, 224, 322, 332, 343, 382, 384–5, 393, 432–3
daughters, 94, 326–8, 331–3, 336, 338–9, 341–2
delamination, 149, 154–5
deliberate openness, 578
derivation, 269–72
descriptions, 6–7, 47–9, 73–4, 329–31, 389–90, 435–6, 472–3, 507–8; natural, 496–7, 499–500, 503, 517, 544, 546; structural, 41, 517–18
design, 72–3, 120–6, 128–9, 200–201, 206–7, 213–14, 410–11, 416–17; architectural, 84, 88, 102; embodied, 218, 220; experimental, 77, 221–2; experiments, 294, 507; instructional, 221, 377, 490, 514; objects of, 508–9; rationales, 90–1, 200–201, 206–7; recipient, 240, 250; roadways, 91, 93, 200–202, 204
designed environments, 96, 163, 507
designers, 96, 184, 187, 230, 477, 531, 536–7, 541
development, mechanisms of, 59
developmental consequentiality, 79, 86, 100
developmental study, true, 43–4
diagrams, 140–1, 146, 150, 152–3, 155, 408–9, 433–5, 510–11; visual, 138, 145, 154
dilation, 294, 296–7, 301–7, 309, 316, 319–20, 322, 574; center of, 296–8, 300–301, 304–7, 319; strategy, 296–7, 306, 308, 316–19, 321–2
direct instruction, 343, 487
disciplinary competences, 198, 209
disciplined perception (DP), 84–6, 93, 102, 553, 572–3, 579, 581; and coordination class theory, 191–210; and disciplining perception, 83–8
disciplining perception, 83, 85, 191, 195, 198, 203, 210, 572
discourse, 145, 148, 272, 282, 285, 312, 348, 383–5; analysis, 34, 73, 383
discovery, 73–5, 223, 230, 251, 489, 507, 511–15, 517–18
dissent, 76, 510
distance, 136, 169, 171, 179–80, 225, 296–8, 300–301, 304–7; fixed, 221–2, 226
distributed elements, 58–9
distributed perspectives, 307, 310

distribution, 41, 127–8, 130, 189, 483, 543, 545; social, 186–7
diversity, 198–9, 208–9, 503, 506, 527–8, 540–1, 575, 579
DNA, 503, 526, 535, 541
DP, *see* disciplined perception
dynamic balance, 17, 240, 243–4, 246, 252–4, 256; contextual priority of, 247, 255–6
dynamic equilibrium, 139, 415
dynamics, 41, 44, 260–1, 263, 283–4, 311–13, 321–2, 492; cognitive, 261, 311, 574; conversational, *see* conversational dynamics; cultural, 505; interactional, 166, 261, 283–5; interview, 252–3; of knowledge in use, 260–89

earth, 136, 238, 373, 387–92, 395–6, 432–5, 440–2, 521; orbit, 440–1
ecologies, 23, 316, 380, 483; cognitive, 254, 263, 267, 284, 316, 544; conceptual, 39–40, 111–12, 128–9, 380–1, 384, 386–9, 391, 393–9; of knowing, 111–31; of knowing stability, 113, 121–3, 127, 129–30; material, 112, 292; semiotic, 164
economics, 504–5
edges, 94, 101, 199, 470, 485; fuzzy, 37; ragged, 184–5
education, 11, 13, 23, 31, 81, 139, 231, 342; informal, 515; research, 6, 31, 33, 224, 320, 435, 481, 493; science, 34, 191, 285, 377
elaboration, requests, 390, 393, 395
electrons, 537–8, 547
elementary school students, 13, 15–16
eliminative materialism, 533, 536
elliptical causality, 485, 541, 548
embodied cognition, 34–6
embodied design, 218, 220
embodied interaction, 231, 561, 568
emotions, 75, 249, 262, 460, 472
empirical set-up, 44, 47, 52–3
energy, 14, 186, 363, 411–12, 416; kinetic, 14, 413–14
engagement, 94–6, 161, 250, 294, 309, 518; active, 239, 250, 253; contours, 93–4, 96
engineers, 84–5, 90–1, 93, 194, 200–204, 207–9, 262
ensemble: activity, 292, 574; causality, 541, 543, 548; and individual, 311–22; learning, 97, 292–323, 574; thinking, 313, 318–19

environment, 83–5, 164, 212, 215, 224, 239, 249–51, 540–1; designed, 96, 163, 507; material, 163, 196
environmentally coupled gestures, 239, 247, 250–1
environments, learning, 2, 11, 17–18, 25, 162–3, 218, 220, 343
episodes, 46, 165–7, 169–72, 174–6, 196–200, 239–40, 294–7, 553–4
epistemic authority, 151, 328–9, 331–3, 336, 339–40, 342–3, 553, 575
epistemic cognition, 135
epistemic frame, 135, 137–8, 145, 147–8, 156
epistemic manipulation, 333, 342, 345
epistemic markers, 170, 332, 335, 341
epistemic rights, 327, 332, 340–3
epistemological beliefs, 262, 490
epistemological frames, 111, 312, 314, 523
epistemological framing, 312, 316
epistemological perspective, 54, 58, 237–8
epistemological resources, 263–4, 267–8, 284
epistemological shift, 262–3
epistemological stance, 261–4, 282, 286, 574
epistemology, 55, 158, 187, 313; genetic, 35, 217; intuitive, 312, 352
e-prims, *see* explanatory primitives
equilibrium, dynamic, 139, 415
equivalence: functional, 373; proportional, 222–3
Erickson, F., 81–2, 135, 161, 163, 293, 409, 518
escape, 39, 140–3, 145–6, 149, 156, 415; molecules, 143, 145, 149–52
ethanol molecules, 413, 417–19
ethnomethodology, 2, 81, 85, 100, 102, 194, 348, 368
evaporation, 134, 139, 405–6, 415, 417
events, 45, 47, 77–80, 86–7, 101, 330, 332, 485–6; launch, 118, 121; learning, 206, 487, 522; non-contiguous, 86–7; physical, 42, 461; recorded, 78–80, 83–4; social, 381, 460
everyday conversation, 44, 254, 335, 367, 393, 410
everyday interaction, 32, 184, 329, 344, 369, 575
everyday language, 300, 378
everyday life, 12, 15, 83, 328, 341, 370, 472
everyday materials, 294, 300, 310, 574
everyday thinking, 35, 197, 529

evolution, 41, 55, 102, 330, 500–501, 503, 537, 540–2
expected feedback, 411, 413
experience(s), 218, 249–51, 282–3, 308–9, 379, 450–1, 458–78, 521; perceptual, 163, 266; physical, 63, 251–2, 255, 462
experimental designs, 77, 221–2
expert knowledge, 40, 455
expert practitioners, 182–4
expertise, 39, 41, 50–1, 55, 185, 191, 194, 200–201
experts, 36, 38, 66, 73, 182–4, 191–3, 208–9, 213
explanation change, 144, 148–9, 152, 154–5
explanations: closer-farther, 394, 432–3, 440–1; correct, 155, 432, 440; initial, 391, 434–5; new, 151, 156–7, 396, 433; normative, 139, 147, 156, 158, 161, 175, 416
explanatory narratives, 403–5, 407, 409–10
explanatory power, 238, 252, 286–8
explanatory primitives, 56–8, 237–8, 244–5, 250, 252, 257
explicitness, 60, 330
exploration, 169–71, 173, 176–7, 292, 295, 328, 332–3, 342–3; knowledge, 178, 339–40, 343, 572
external representations, 53, 138, 408
extraction strategies, 163–4, 170
extractions, 51–2, 54, 65, 163, 170, 186, 193–4
eye gaze, *see* gaze

facets, 57–8, 66, 184, 208–9
facing formations, 92–3, 334, 338
familiarity, 82, 130, 202, 204, 209, 273, 407, 462
families, 4, 46, 51, 94, 102, 328, 331–3, 344
family members, 102, 330, 332
fathers, 120, 330, 333; *see also* parents
feedback, 223, 228, 288, 307–10, 404, 410–14, 416–17, 419–20; back-channel, 393–4; expected, 411, 413
feedback-relevant places, *see* FRPs
feeding stations, 499, 539
feelings, 62, 472–3, 542, 544
Feldenkrais, M., 217–18
fine-grained analysis, 134, 243, 250, 558
fixed intervals, 220, 222, 225–8
fixed-interval strategy, 226–7
flagging tape, 294, 296–7, 311, 316
flight, 114–15, 118–19, 188, 477
focal episodes, 200, 263–5, 267–8, 273, 283–4, 286, 288, 294

force, 14, 51–2, 112, 193, 240–4, 246–9, 253–6, 538–9; amount of, 193, 242–3, 253; of gravity, 14, 193, 244, 247; upward, 17, 252–7
formal instruction, 31–2, 84, 377–8, 514, 517
formal knowledge, 32, 266–72, 274, 276, 280, 282–6, 380; activation of, 267, 285
formal physics knowledge, 32, 271–2
formations, facing, 92–3, 334, 338
frames, 134–5, 144–5, 147–8, 152, 154–5, 182, 447–9, 568; change, 147–8, 155; epistemic, 135, 137–8, 145, 147–8, 156; epistemological, 111, 312, 314, 523; social, 135, 141, 145, 147–8, 157
framing, 135, 144, 256–7, 261, 272, 283–4, 312–15, 405–7; co-constructed, 267–8, 282; epistemological, 312, 316; social, 176; unit of, 312–14
friends, 134, 139, 264–5, 268–9, 279–80, 406–7, 417, 461–2
FRPs (feedback-relevant places), 382, 403–23, 576
functional equivalence, 373
functions, 56–8, 350–3, 355–7, 359–61, 363–5, 393–4, 539–40, 542
fusion, 3, 6, 556, 580–1

galleries, 93–4, 462, 465
gaps, 150–1, 153–6, 266, 344, 471, 496, 507, 568
gardening, 332–4, 336, 339, 341
gardens, 4, 326, 333–6, 338–9, 341–3, 345, 575
gaze, 45, 261–3, 269–71, 277–8, 408–9, 411–17, 419, 423; shifts, 409, 411–12, 414–15, 423
genetic epistemology, 35, 217
geometry problem solving, 295, 404
germ theory, 102, 509
gestures, 135–41, 147–57, 236–51, 255–7, 309–10, 423, 429, 571–3; communicative, 242, 251; coupled, 239, 247, 250–1; environmentally coupled, 239, 247, 250–1; indexical, 175, 423, 559; metaphoric, 239, 243–4, 246–8, 573; spinning, 396, 452
global competition, 2–3, 580
goals, 161–2, 165–6, 181–5, 352–5, 357–61, 380–4, 407–9, 447–8; interactive, 459
Goffman, E., 19, 27, 92–3, 135, 261, 263, 312, 409
Goodall, Jane, 498–9, 539

Goodwin, M. H., 93, 137–8, 163–4, 239, 249–50, 330–1, 408–10, 429–31
graphs, 86, 89, 169–74, 176–9, 195, 198–9, 554, 562–3; time, 167, 563
gravity, 14, 17, 133, 244–5, 247, 264–5, 529, 538; attraction of, 242–4, 253; center of, 113–14, 117, 123–6; force of, 14, 193, 244, 247
green tape, 297–300, 303–7, 309–10
grid calculus, 84, 86, 196
gridlines, 202–3, 229
grids, 97–9, 195–6, 199, 202, 223, 227–9, 301, 303
group members, 94, 310, 314

harmonic oscillation, 52, 161, 167
Henderson, A., 7, 13, 24, 72, 111–12, 161, 163, 260–3
heterogeneous assemblages, 510–11
heuristics, 125–6, 128, 312–13, 315–16, 318, 481, 523, 574
hidden machineries, 496–548, 578
Higgs boson, 186–7, 572
high-school students, 52, 237, 294, 489, 561
historical precedents, 73, 75
history, 94, 100–101, 127–8, 477, 484, 516–17, 544, 547; contentious, 23–4, 26; developmental, 57–8, 237; natural, 72–4, 499, 506; shared, 24, 26, 173, 177
Hmong House, 462–3, 466–8, 471–2, 476–8
hobbies, 111–13, 119–20, 122, 128–9
holism, cultural, 505
homes, 82, 330, 332, 344, 485
homomorphic levels, 531, 533, 540, 542
human activity, 86, 88, 97, 100, 512, 516–17, 520, 523
humble theories, 20, 56, 64
Hutchins, E., 76–7, 85–6, 88, 125, 127, 239, 293, 311
hydrostatic pressure equation, 264, 267, 273–4, 280
hypotheses, 46, 49, 165, 229, 255, 263, 554, 556–7

images, 39, 44, 94, 121, 137, 140–1, 143, 149
imperialism: ontological, 227; theoretical, 459, 477, 577
implementation, 213, 308, 532, 536, 546, 574; level, 533, 535–6, 541, 546; relations, 532–3; technology, 536–7
improvisation, representational, 204, 207
incidental features, 148–50

inconsistency, 14–15, 17, 156, 556
indexical gestures, 175, 423, 559
individual cognition, 238, 512, 531; gestures, speech and manipulation of objects as window to, 236–57
individual knowledge, 36, 44, 112, 186, 188, 192, 237–9, 311; systems, 1, 169, 194
infants, 213–17
inferences, 51–2, 161–4, 193–4, 352–3, 355–6, 358–61, 380–2, 516
inferencing, 51, 54, 65
inferential net, 52, 59, 162–3, 170, 186, 189, 193, 546
inferential pathways, 52, 207, 537, 547
inferential relations, 170–1, 179
informal education, 515
informal learning, 295; environments, 87, 224
information, 59, 162–4, 199–202, 206–8, 353, 430–2, 444–5, 450; channels, 431, 450; communicated, 431, 444, 450
infrastructure, 22, 97, 182–4, 484, 530, 534; material, 125, 127; representational, 22, 90, 93, 102, 310
initiation-response-evaluation (IRE) sequence, 81
innovations: analytical, 25; ontological, 512, 540, 543, 548; representational, 206; theoretical, 56–7, 542
inscription devices, 506, 510–12
inscriptions, 19, 295–6, 412, 422–3, 510–11
inspection desk, 116, 118–19
inspectors, 118–19, 122–3, 127–8, 130
instruction, 16, 32, 114–15, 185, 219–20, 300, 487–9, 493–4; classroom, 377, 488; direct, 343, 487; formal, 31–2, 84, 377–8, 514, 517
instructional design, 221, 377, 490, 514
instructional sequences, 237, 240, 250
instructors, 38, 172, 186, 220, 224, 230, 295, 487
instrumented interaction, 219–20
intact systems, 481–3
integrated analysis, 161–2, 166, 175–6, 178, 180–1, 183, 185, 572; of knowledge in interaction, 161, 163, 165, 167, 169, 171, 173, 175
integration, 156–7, 162, 165, 251, 448, 450, 505, 555–7
integrative pluralism, 553–7
integrative theories, 501, 556
intellectual resources, 284, 312

intelligence, 85, 484, 542; artificial, 33, 64, 183, 260, 484
interaction: classroom, 128–9, 509; clinical, 4, 348, 362, 370, 491, 576; everyday, 32, 184, 329, 344, 369, 575; instrumented, 219–20; order, 92, 97, 99, 102; situated, 262, 574; unfolding, 252, 261, 263, 286–7, 294, 297; *see also Introductory Note*
interaction analysis: introduction, 72–103; members' relevance, and methods, 77–80; mobility and studies of knowledge in use, 88–9; multimodal, 73, 292, 294, 310; *see also Introductory Note*
interaction analysts, 23, 251, 257, 421, 431, 450
interactional artifacts, 348, 488
interactional context, 81, 112, 133, 138, 366, 449
interactional cues, 164, 166, 176, 399, 455
interactional detail, 417, 419, 429–56, 576
interactional dynamics, 166, 261, 283–5
interactional interpretation, 382, 384–5
interactional perspectives, 236, 239, 283, 294, 380–1, 384, 392, 398–9
interactional processes, 138, 180, 561
interactionist perspectives, 260–1, 263
interest-based practices, 114–15, 117
interlocutors, 140–1, 145, 160–1, 163–4, 192, 240, 410–12, 453–4
intermolecular attractions, 141, 143, 152–7
intermolecular forces, 141, 144
interpretation, 173–4, 242, 254–6, 384–5, 393–4, 396–9, 420–1, 458–78
intersubjective understanding, 461, 577
intersubjectivity, 166, 172, 174–6, 178, 180–1, 558–68, 579, 581
intervals, 170–1, 173–4, 177–9, 181, 195, 220, 228; fixed, 220, 222, 225–8
interview, context, 264, 286, 381
interview dynamics, 252–3
interviewees, 238, 250, 353–75, 379–81, 403, 445, 452–3, 491–2; responses, 353–4, 357, 372–3
interviewer turn, 384–9, 394–5; common, 383, 385, 393
interviewers, clinical, 327–9, 331, 339, 341–3, 375, 379, 488, 575
interviewing, 354, 361, 364, 375, 382–4, 492, 575, 577; clinical, *see* clinical interviewing
interviews, 237–40, 261–9, 377–87, 396–9, 405–9, 432–6, 441–6, 573–7; cognitive clinical, 377, 379, 398–9; one-on-one, 365, 430, 432; semi-structured, 25, 224, 377, 404, 406–7, 416–17
intonation, 289, 351, 354, 408, 411–13, 415–17, 419, 422; contours, 414, 419, 422
intuition, 39, 55, 57, 77, 285, 287, 379, 381
intuitive knowledge, 30, 32, 36, 49, 56, 264–5, 367, 377
intuitive physics, 36, 50, 382; knowledge system, 50
invention, 188, 504, 514–15, 527; personal, 102, 206

Jefferson, G., 78, 97, 99, 335, 344, 409, 564–5, 568
Jordan, B., 111–12, 161, 163, 260–3, 404, 409, 438, 442
joy, 288, 472–3; personal, 521

KA (Knowledge Analysis): counter-principles, 38–9; evolving theories, 56; future, 60–5; history, 31–3; introduction, 30–66; regimes of study, 42–4; research themes, 54–6; situating, 33–5; systems perspective on change and development, 39–42; theoretical foundations, 35–7; topic distribution, 54–5; *see also Introductory Note*
KAIA (Knowledge Analysis/Interaction Analysis), 186, 311, 392, 489, 520, 524–5, 578, 580; agenda, 182, 188, 523, 571, 573, 576, 579, 581; community, 496, 498, 519–20; Project, 7, 487, 489, 571, 573, 575, 577, 581; Project, and prospects, 570–81
kicking, 527–8, 532, 544–5
kinesics, 19, 24, 417, 423, 576
kinetic energy, 14, 413–14
KiP (Knowledge in Pieces), 30–1, 35, 54–5, 57–8, 64, 237–8, 282, 521–2
knowing, 11–13, 21–6, 111–17, 125–31, 293–5, 328–33, 447–53, 455–6; in families, 329–32
knowing stability, 113, 116, 122, 124–8; ecology of, 113, 121–3, 127, 129–30
knowledge: analysts, 22, 251, 253, 257, 417, 420, 445–6, 576; base, 65, 162–3; children, 327–8, 343, 575; claims, 135, 332, 342, 510, 512; conceptual, 217, 262, 327; development of, 40, 101, 561; elements, 17, 57–8, 237–40, 283, 384, 393–5, 418–20, 439–40; elements, punctual, 484–6; expert, 40,

455; exploration, 178, 339–40, 343, 572; formal, 32, 266–72, 274, 276, 280, 282–6, 380; individual, 36, 44, 112, 186, 188, 192, 237–9, 311; in interaction, 160–89, 365, 449; intuitive, 30, 32, 36, 49, 56, 264–5, 367, 377; mathematical, 76, 213, 220, 508, 510; models of, 2, 30–1, 38–9, 188; naive, 32, 36, 66; nature of, 31, 35, 130, 559; new, 148, 339, 386–9, 392–3, 395–8; perceptual, 266–8, 280–2, 284–6; perspective, 178, 251, 380, 384, 399, 575; physics, 80, 280, 352; prior, 55–6, 133, 135–7, 152, 154, 157, 243, 253; professional, 200, 573; reactive, 37, 368; representations, 566–7; resources, 25, 128, 137, 146, 156–7, 210, 264–5, 430; restriction, 381–2, 384, 575; science, 34, 382–3, 430; structures, 57, 169, 176, 180, 260, 448, 513, 515; student, 145, 195, 200, 370, 380, 387, 389, 418–20; systems, 18, 39, 58, 62–3, 207, 403–4, 417, 419; tacit, 61–3, 392; theories of, 158, 327, 532; types, 42, 57–8, 60, 111, 128; in use, 72–103, 289; in use, comparative analysis, 81–3; in use, dynamics of, 260–89; in use, from natural history to outdoor psychology, 72–7; what counts as, 80–1; *see also Introductory Note*

Knowledge Analysis/Interaction Analysis, *see* KAIA

Knowledge in Pieces, *see* KiP

known-answer questions, 81–2, 453

laboratories, 75–6, 88, 511–12
Lakatos, I., 546
lamination, 135, 137–9, 150, 154–7
language, 48–9, 57, 61–3, 138, 140, 326–7, 341, 559; everyday, 300, 378; mathematical, 300, 309; modeling, 39, 64, 486
latent Dirichlet allocation, *see* LDA
Latour, B., 26, 89, 92, 100, 102, 510–12, 519
launch events, 118, 121
Lave, J., 33–4, 76–7, 87, 96, 100, 112, 514, 516–17
LD, *see* Learning Disabled
LDA (latent Dirichlet allocation), 438–9, 444
learners, 12, 79, 220, 227, 230, 312, 514–15, 517–18; individual, 322, 516
learning, 1–4, 21–6, 30–8, 85–9, 212–18, 236–8, 292–5, 515–19; by/about making things together, 96–9; classroom, 22, 293, 343, 488; conceptual, 224, 231, 322; disability, 13, 15, 404; ensemble, 97, 292–323, 574; environments, 2, 11, 17–18, 25, 162–3, 218, 220, 343; environments, informal, 87, 224; events, 206, 487, 522; informal, 295; machine, 61, 436; mathematics, 212–13, 215, 217, 219, 221, 223, 225, 229–31; motor, 214, 217, 230–1; sciences, 11–12, 18, 100–101, 236–7, 505, 527–8, 530–2, 555–6; sciences, research, 72, 101, 191, 510; skill, 219, 231

Learning Disabled (LD), 15, 18, 83
legitimate peripheral participation, *see* LPP
linguistic anthropology, 2, 409
liquid methanol, 139–40, 405
liquid molecules, 140, 143, 151–2, 157
liquid state, 141, 143, 145–6, 418
listeners, 404, 410–19, 421, 423, 448, 576
locus of stability, 313, 315, 322
logocentric analysis, 430–2, 452; computer-based, 431, 450; extreme, 431, 442, 445
LPP (legitimate peripheral participation), 506, 516–18

McDermott, R., 13, 15–17, 20, 23–7, 81–3, 87, 313–14, 404
machine learning, 61, 436
manipulation, 19, 223, 300, 309, 327–9; epistemic, 333, 342, 345; of epistemic authority, 329, 339; material, 297, 308, 310; of objects, 236–57; physical, 92, 238, 574
Marin, A., 93–4, 96, 101
markers, 140, 149, 173, 175, 177, 351, 354–5, 362; boundary, 412, 421–2; epistemic, 170, 332, 335, 341; so, 351, 354
mass, 52, 113, 156, 186–7, 193, 413–14, 572
material artifacts, 138, 247
material contexts, 87, 136
material ecologies, 112, 292
material environment, 163, 196
material infrastructure, 125, 127
material manipulations, 297, 308, 310
material reductionism, 541, 544
material resources, 144, 155, 292–4, 310, 579
materialism, eliminative, 533, 536
materials, 89–91, 93–4, 114–15, 293–5, 308–14, 316–17, 321–2, 562; everyday, 294, 300, 310, 574

mathematical activity, 310–11, 507, 509
mathematical concepts, 214, 218, 221
mathematical ideas, 462, 471, 504, 507
mathematical knowledge, 76, 213, 220, 508, 510
mathematical language, 300, 309
mathematical reasoning, 230–1
mathematical support, 504
mathematical understanding, 58
mathematics, 84, 197–8, 213–14, 262, 281–2, 293, 504–5, 508; classrooms, 507–8; education, 213, 215; learning, 212–31, 472, 477
mechanisms of development, 59
Mehan, H., 81–2, 342, 350
member relevance, 78–9
member's phenomenon, 100–101
mental activity, 15, 131, 293, 311
mental models, 32, 34, 111, 216, 348
mental representations, 22–3, 31, 36, 558
meta-messages, 389–90
metaphoric gestures, 239, 243–4, 246–8, 573
metaphors, conceptual, 35, 503
meta-representational competence, 506, 512–15
meta-science, 527–48
meta-scientific micro-essays, 480–94
meta-scientific perspective, 7, 525, 543, 578
methodological refinement, 60
methodological tensions, 458–9
methodologies, 18–19, 22–3, 44, 47, 60–2, 348–9, 487, 578–80; preferred, 13, 18
microanalytic study, 42, 47–50
micro-complementarity, 2–4, 553, 555, 580
micro-essays, 530, 548, 577, 579; meta-scientific, 480–94
microgenesis, 22, 37, 41–3, 47, 63, 250
microgenetic study, 42–3, 51
microlatitudinal/microlongitudinal analysis, 133–58
micro-operational study, 43
middle-school students, 84, 87, 102, 378, 383, 430, 432, 553
Minstrell, J., 57, 487, 489
misconceptions, 12, 32, 34, 39, 184, 265, 487, 489; common, 15, 397
Mitchell, S., 137, 553–7
mobility, 87–91, 93, 96–7, 101
mockingbirds, 499–500

model rocket stability, 113–15, 117, 121, 130
model rocketry, 112–18, 127–30
modeling, 42, 55, 73, 89–90, 92, 135, 484–5, 493; cognitive, 35, 37, 39, 43, 262, 266, 436, 438; languages, 39, 64, 486; mathematical, 88; practices, 90–2, 96
models, 30–3, 50–1, 56–7, 89–91, 114–17, 119–28, 438–9, 485–7; of knowledge, 2, 30–1, 38–9, 188; mental, 32, 34, 111, 216, 348; normative, 15, 145, 487
molecular escape, 141, 143–5, 150, 155–6
molecules, 134, 140–1, 143–6, 149–57, 378, 411–12, 415–19, 422; escape, 143, 145, 149–52; ethanol, 413, 417–19; liquid, 140, 143, 151–2, 157; non-escaping, 152, 156–7; single, 140, 143, 145, 153
moment-by-moment basis, 12, 18–19, 21, 403, 409–10, 414, 576
moment-by-moment production, 461, 577
moment-by-moment shifts, 18, 20
mothers, 94, 96, 102, 326–8, 331–4, 337–9, 341–2, 575
motion, 48, 85, 133, 167–9, 171, 173, 180, 435; harmonic, 52; oscillatory, 53–5, 169, 171, 180–1
motivation, 34, 75, 341, 364, 453–4, 490, 562
motor learning, 214, 217, 230–1
motor plans, 215, 218
motor problem solving, 212–31
motor problems, 214–15, 218, 225, 227–9, 231
motor skills, 213–14, 216, 227, 230
motor-skill development, 218, 230, 573
movement, 89, 92, 94–5, 151–3, 217–18, 241, 243, 461; physical, 230, 332; up-down, 242–3
MRC (meta-representational competence), 506, 512–15
multimodal interaction analysis, 73, 292, 294, 310
multimodal transcripts, 140, 572
multiple representations, 45, 167, 194, 208
multiple semiotic fields, 138, 145, 408
muscles, 241, 246–7, 249
museums, 4, 77, 94–6, 102, 344, 462, 471, 516
mutual accountability, 1, 5, 580–1
mutual understanding, 559, 565

mutually influencing paradigms, 4–5, 580–1

naive knowledge, 32, 36, 66
naive physics, 32–3, 543
narratives, 111, 136, 330, 449; explanatory, 403–5, 407, 409–10
native competence, 513–15
natural contexts, 481, 488
natural description, 496–7, 499–500, 503, 517, 544, 546
natural descriptive approaches, 496–548, 578
natural history, 72–4, 499, 506
Natural History of an Interview, *see* NHI
natural selection, 535, 537, 540–2
naturalized axioms, 57–8
negative stability, 116, 122
negotiation, 308, 310, 508, 523, 565
nestings, 41, 482
neuron doctrine, 501, 503
neurosciences, 64, 214
neutral stability, 116, 122
new knowledge, 148, 339, 386–9, 392–3, 395–8
new vertex, 299–300, 306, 308–10, 316, 318–19
NHI (Natural History of an Interview), 73, 81, 102, 506
nodding, 276, 351, 359, 411–17, 419, 421, 423, 576
nodes, 57–8
non-contiguous events, 86–7
non-escaping molecules, 152, 156–7
normative concepts, 370, 491
normative explanations, 139, 147, 156, 158, 161, 175, 416
normative models, 15, 145, 487
normative understanding, 170, 363–5, 491, 575
norms, 115, 122, 181, 295, 314, 449, 459, 560; socio-mathematical, *see* SMNs
nothingness, 150–1
novices, 40, 139, 213, 215, 219, 252, 455, 573
nuances, 36, 61, 181, 219, 378, 454, 478

objectivity, 458–78, 576
observable ontology, 499, 538, 547
observation theories, 530, 535, 539
Ochs, E., 24, 75, 78, 89, 330, 449, 458, 568
one-on-one interviews, 365, 430, 432
ontological imperialism, 227

ontological innovation, 512, 540, 543, 548
ontology, 252–3, 260, 262, 283, 285, 288, 538–42, 547; new, 507, 540, 543, 546–7; observable, 499, 538, 547
openness, 520–3, 578; deliberate, 578
optics, 313, 501, 526, 530, 535
orbits, 193, 355, 364, 388–9, 394, 432, 440, 452; non-circular, 434, 441
organization, 20, 40, 77, 82, 112, 157, 514–15, 517; sequential, 250, 409–10, 566
*Origin of Species, The*, 500, 542–3
oscillation, 52, 54, 162, 167, 169, 171, 178
oscillators, 52–3, 167, 169; physical, 52–3, 167
oscillatory motion, 53–5, 169, 171, 180–1
outdoor psychology, 72, 75–7
overlapping speech, 168, 196, 289, 478

paper-and-pencil tasks, 321, 489
paralinguistics, 417, 421–2
parents, 63, 82, 93, 184, 345, 515, 575; as skilled knowledge practitioners, 326–45; *see also* fathers; mothers
Parsons, T., 21, 560–1, 566, 568
participant frameworks, 349, 492
participants, 46, 77–80, 135, 138–40, 147–9, 405–10, 450–1, 453–6
participation, 113, 127–9, 294–6, 310, 315–16, 334, 336, 518; frameworks, 249–50, 330–2, 334, 339, 341, 350, 454–5, 461; structures, 261, 293
pattern finding, 44, 46–7, 49, 52
patterns, 25, 44, 169–70, 313–14, 317, 319, 464–6, 470–1
pauses, 242–3, 344, 373–4, 411–12, 415–16, 419, 421–2, 434; long, 147, 262, 271, 407, 418; short, 413
pedagogy, 327, 509–10
peers, 16–18, 53, 118, 130, 161, 172, 180, 407–8
perception, 162, 164, 192, 198, 200, 264–7, 281–3, 572–3; disciplined, *see* disciplined perception (DP)
perceptual knowledge, 266–8, 280–2, 284–6
perceptuomotor schemes, 217, 219
performance, 11–12, 16–18, 20–1, 23–6, 86, 124, 214, 404; in context, 11–19, 21, 23–4; intellectual, 37, 567
persistence, 314–15, 317–18
personal curation, 96, 102
personal experience, 281, 331

personal invention, 102, 206
phase change, 133–58
phenomena, 15–17, 44–8, 52–3, 403, 405–8, 486–90, 496–8, 530–1; biological, 500, 509; chemical, 133, 139–41, 144–5, 147, 571; new, 57, 216, 541
phenomenological primitives, 47–52, 56–8, 60–4, 240, 243–4, 251–3, 484–6, 542; extending model, 56
phenomenology, 3–4, 207–8, 365, 493, 525, 542, 577
physical actions, 12, 145, 196, 216, 309
physical events, 42, 461
physical experiences, 63, 251–2, 255, 462
physical manipulations, 92, 238, 574
physical oscillators, 52–3, 167
physical principles, 558–9, 566
physical world, 30, 32–3, 48, 54, 64, 167, 237, 251
physicists, 5, 186–7, 217, 277, 528, 532, 547, 559
physics, 13–14, 31–2, 237, 239–40, 279–80, 352, 531–2, 544; classrooms, 112, 129, 516; intuitive, 36, 50, 382; knowledge, 80, 280, 352; modern, 537–8; naive, 32–3, 543; students, 15, 267, 316
Piaget, J., 35, 40, 216–18, 230, 377, 384, 403, 407
pitch, 113, 263, 275, 289, 412, 422, 472
plants, 89, 93, 333, 335–7, 343, 502, 529
pluralism, integrative, 553, 555–7
pointed questions, 146, 148, 150, 153, 155–7
positionings, 18, 27, 81, 249, 257, 314, 350–1, 419
posture, 225, 271, 313
power, 118, 447, 454–5, 491, 509; structure, 492
p-prims, *see* phenomenological primitives
practices: conceptual, 73, 89, 91–3, 96–7, 99; disciplinary, 85, 230, 322; interest-based, 114–15, 117; scientific, 74, 496–7, 503, 510, 555; technical, 75–6, 100, 514
practitioners, 113, 116, 182, 184, 487, 489–90, 498, 504; best intuitive, 183–5; expert, 182–4; reflective, 343, 367, 370, 375
precise and verifiable accounts, 462, 472–3
preferred methodologies, 13, 18
pressure, 113–14, 125–6, 264–7, 273, 275, 277–81, 283, 286–7; center of, 113–14, 117, 124–6

primitives: explanatory, 56–8, 237–8, 244–5, 250, 252, 257; phenomenological, 47–52, 56–8, 60–4, 240, 243–4, 251–3, 484–6, 542
prior knowledge, 55–6, 133, 135–7, 152, 154, 157, 243, 253
priority: contextual, 238, 243, 245, 249; reliability, 48, 50, 404, 418–20, 576; shifts, 249–51
probabilities, 30, 343, 436, 438–41, 446, 455
problem solving, 15, 55–6, 58–60, 200, 207, 209–10, 286, 292–5; geometry, 295, 404; motor, 212–31
procedural consequentiality, 78–9
professional communities, 497–8, 526, 534–5
professional knowledge, 200, 573
professional practice, 25, 194, 203, 490, 492–3, 572
professionals, 84, 87, 207, 328, 367–8, 490
proficiency, 271, 274, 276
profiles, 86, 90–1, 201–6, 209
pronunciations, 45, 422
proportional equivalence, 222–3
propositional content, 239, 556
prosody, 19, 23–4, 46, 95, 138, 263, 361, 431
protocol requests, 389–90
proxying, 481–3, 532
psychology, 62, 76–7, 503, 557; cognitive, 20, 88, 496; outdoor, 72, 75–7
punctual knowledge elements, 484–6

quadrilateral, 296–302, 304–5, 311–12, 315–18, 320–2, 574; new, 296, 299–300, 304, 306, 308, 317–18, 320
qualitative analyses, 46–7, 436, 441–2
qualitative interviews, 399
quantum mechanics, 5, 529, 531–3, 537–8
questions: initial, 280, 432, 471; known-answer, 81–2, 453; open, 321; pointed, 146, 148, 150, 153, 155–7

ragged edge, 184–5
rational-number problems, 221–2
reactive knowledge, 37, 368
readout, 59, 65, 163, 170, 186–7, 189, 193–4, 210; strategies, 65, 163, 193–4
reanalysis, 255, 257, 262–3, 267, 284–6, 567, 571, 573–4
reasoning: analogical, 55–6; conceptual, 219–20; mathematical, 230–1; student, 222, 455

recipient design, 240, 250
recollection, 77, 173, 178, 353
recorded events, 78–80, 83–4
recordings, 74, 77–8, 83, 100–102, 140, 332–6, 339, 342; video, 18–19, 23–4, 45, 74, 83–4, 102, 420, 459
reduction, 5–6, 44–7, 49, 52, 89, 535–6, 577
reductionism, material, 541, 544
redundancy, 431, 444–5, 450–1, 576; and separability, 431, 444–5, 451
reference models, 47, 51, 57, 523
refinement, 4, 50–1, 362, 372, 382, 515, 518, 527–9
reflective practitioners, 343, 367, 370, 375
reformulation, 209, 351, 354, 356, 359, 373, 520
regimes of study, 42–4
regularities, 48, 459, 473, 478, 509, 512–13, 517, 546; structural, 512–13, 517, 546
relamination, 156–7
reliability priority, 48, 50, 404, 418–20, 576
remnant models, 75, 93
repetitions, 217–18, 356, 359; repetition without, 218
reporting, 44, 47, 50, 52, 162, 313, 501
representation use, 135, 137, 139, 141, 143, 145, 147, 149
representational forms, 195, 203, 206, 209, 514
representational improvisation, 204–7
representational infrastructure, 22, 90, 93, 102, 310
representational innovation, 206
representational practices, 89, 514
representational tools, 293–4
representations, 52–4, 58–9, 137–8, 156–7, 166–9, 171–6, 178–9, 200–207; computational, 51–3, 167; external, 53, 138, 408; knowledge, 566–7; mental, 22–3, 31, 36, 558; multiple, 45, 167, 194, 208; visual, 45, 94, 156, 172
requests: confirmation, 340; elaboration, 390, 393, 395; protocol, 389–90
research settings, 25–6
research themes, 54–6
researchers, 24–5, 45–6, 52–3, 80, 139–41, 144–56, 165, 316–17
resistance, 48, 125, 145, 301, 305, 314–15, 317–19
resources, 58, 136–8, 267–8, 309–10, 316, 320–1, 555, 567; cognitive, 17, 58, 261, 448; conceptual, 262, 283, 555; epistemological, 263–4, 267–8, 284;
intellectual, 284, 312; material, 144, 155, 292–4, 310, 579; semiotic, 84, 137, 149, 239, 250
revoicing, 188, 244–5, 348–67, 369–75, 384, 575–6, 579, 581; check inference, 358; classroom, 350, 359–63, 365
right answers, 134, 139, 147, 155, 268, 302, 398, 407–8
rights, epistemic, 327, 332, 340–3
roadways, 73, 90–1, 200–207, 209; design, 91, 93, 200–202, 204
rocket stability, 118, 121, 126–7
rocketeers, 113–14, 116–19, 121–3, 127–31
rocketry, 113, 120, 126–7, 131; communities, 113, 115–16, 125
rockets, 113–22, 124–9; body tubes, 115–16, 120–6; flying, 113, 118, 121, 128, 571; low-powered, 116, 120–1; stable, 116, 121–2, 130
rotation, 113, 389, 392, 432, 440–2, 453
rulers, 295, 301, 304, 546

Sacks, H., 78–9, 97, 99, 161, 249–50, 409–10, 564–5, 567–8
scaling, 296–7, 309, 316–17
Schegloff, E. A., 20, 78–9, 97, 99, 294, 381, 409–10, 564–5
Scherr, R. E., 111, 135, 261–2, 312–14
schooling, 13, 128, 350, 481–2, 514–17; formal, 292, 518
Schütz, A., 560–1, 566, 568
science education, 34, 191, 285, 377
science knowledge, 34, 382–3, 430
scientific communities, 184, 186, 367, 503, 570
scientific knowledge, 38, 510
scientific practices, 74, 496–7, 503, 510, 555
scientists, 330–1, 497, 501, 511, 521–3, 527–8, 539, 546; social, 460, 560
screens, 53, 85, 89, 221–3, 225–9, 313, 564
Searle, J. R., 21, 350, 484, 542
seasons, 136, 355, 385, 387–8, 392–5, 432–5, 440, 445–6
secrets, 219, 501, 538
selective focus, 23–5
self-correction, system, 165
semantics, 422, 451
semiotic ecology, 164
semiotic fields, 134–5, 138, 146, 149–50, 155, 157, 173–4, 176–7; lamination in interaction, 137–9; multiple, 138, 145, 408

semiotic resources, 84, 137, 149, 239, 250
semi-structured interviews, 25, 224, 377, 404, 406–7, 416–17
sensitivities, 19, 24, 73, 187, 215, 528, 573, 578
separability, 431, 444–5, 450–1; and redundancy, 431, 444–5, 451
sequences, 56, 81, 93, 97–9, 102, 146, 155–7, 410; ambulatory, 93–4; instructional, 237, 240, 250
sequential organization, 250, 409–10, 566
settings, 23–6, 75–7, 89–93, 101–2, 134–5, 292–5, 342–3, 516–18
shamans, 462, 465, 473, 476
shared enterprise, 11–27
shared history, 24, 26, 173, 177
shared representational space, 173, 409, 412, 416, 423
shared understanding, 61, 163, 174, 181, 321, 564–5
shifts, 12, 15–19, 155, 261–2, 312–17, 319, 403–4, 576; epistemological, 262–3; gradual, 216, 316; moment-by-moment, 18, 20; priority, 249–51
signals, 155, 271, 273, 313–14, 327, 329, 335–6, 338
silence, 271, 273, 277–8, 412, 419, 421, 568, 576
simplicity, 39, 47, 172, 189, 287–8, 543
simulation(s), 52–3, 167, 169–70, 172–4, 178, 242–4, 563, 565; computer, 161, 165–6, 172
situated cognition, 33–4, 37, 76
situated learning, 506, 516
skepticism, 38–9, 304, 308–9, 343, 348, 503, 547
skill learning, 219, 231
skilled knowledge practitioners (SKPs), 184, 575; clinical interviewers as, 328–9; parents as, 326–45
skills, 213, 217, 219, 223, 328, 377, 573, 575; physical, 213, 219
skinniness, 170–1, 176, 179; level, 168, 172, 562
SKPs, *see* skilled knowledge practitioners
sleight of hand, 432, 445
slope, 193, 201–2, 204, 206–7
SMNs (socio-mathematical norms), 293, 506–10, 515
smooth transitions, 216, 224
so marker, 351, 354
social context, 2, 12, 157, 161, 163–4, 181, 349, 492

social distribution of knowledge, 186–7
social events, 381, 460
social frames, 135, 141, 145, 147–8, 157
social framing, 176
social history, 57, 100, 187, 581
social interaction, *see* Introductory Note
social sciences, 56, 430, 460, 497, 503–5, 512, 547, 561
social scientists, 460, 560
socialization, 560–1
sociocultural perspectives, 213, 236, 238, 310, 574
sociocultural theories, 164, 238, 496, 573
sociology, 20, 312, 459, 477, 560, 566
socio-mathematical norms, *see* SMNs
socio-physical environment, 260–1
somathics, 220–1
space, 91–4, 145–6, 150–4, 156, 268–70, 417–18, 529–30, 537–9; Cartesian, 93, 196–7; conceptual, 113, 175–6; shared representational, 173, 409, 412, 416, 423
speakers, 81, 404, 409–23, 431, 444, 448, 454, 576
species, 75, 499–500, 537, 540–4
speech, 19, 137–9, 236–9, 249–51, 257, 289, 313–14, 421–3; overlapping, 168, 196, 289, 478; surrounding, 289, 412, 422
spinning, 387–8, 391–2, 396, 434, 440, 452–3; gesture, 396, 452
spokes, 296–7, 319
springiness p-prim, 61–2
stability, 113–14, 116, 121–2, 124–31, 133–4, 261, 283–4, 315; judgments of, 127, 130; locus of, 313, 315, 322; negative, 116, 122; neutral, 116, 122
stabilization, 134, 137–8, 140, 157, 252, 267–8, 283–6
stable models, 114, 117, 122, 124, 126, 128
stable-by-design models, 122, 130
stations, 201, 204–6; feeding, 499, 539
statistical concepts, 514–15
steepness, 201, 204, 206
STEPs, 183–5, 572
strategic levels, 195, 200–203
strategies, 193, 197–9, 201, 297–301, 303–4, 308–12, 315–22, 574
strategy systems, 59–60, 206–7, 210
Streeck, J., 73, 461–2, 472
structural descriptions, 41, 517–18
structural regularities, 512–13, 517, 546
student knowledge, 145, 195, 200, 370, 380, 387, 389, 418–20

student reasoning, 222, 455
student thinking, 57, 377–8, 380, 489
students, 51–4, 161–81, 217–25, 307–13, 349–53, 380–91, 393–4, 485–91; high-school, 52, 237, 294, 489, 561; individual, 82, 176, 295, 314–15, 320–2; middle-school, 84, 87, 102, 378, 383, 430, 432, 553; pre-algebra, 194–5; undergraduate, 13, 48, 139, 405
sub-codes, 386–7, 389–90
subsumption, 5–6
success, 377, 379–81, 398–9, 404, 430, 444, 485, 488
summer, 351–2, 355, 388, 391, 394–6, 432–4, 452–3
sun, 136, 387–9, 391, 394–5, 397, 432–5, 440–2, 452
surprise, 41, 46–7, 178, 229, 237, 304, 338, 340
surrounding speech, 289, 412, 422
symbolic artifacts, 223–4
symbolic computation, 64, 484
symbolic forms, 57–8, 111
symbols, 89, 120, 163, 288, 421
synergies, 2, 4–6, 11, 41, 43, 111, 580–1
synthesis, 7, 26, 161, 166, 360, 371, 478, 545
synthetic agenda, 26, 186, 579, 581
system self-correction, 165
systematicities, 37, 41, 50, 527
systems perspective on change and development, 39–42

tacit knowledge, 61–3, 392
Tannen, D., 252, 261, 263, 312, 381, 389
tape, 78, 123, 296, 298–300, 304–8, 310, 317–19, 322; flagging, 294, 296–7, 311, 316
teachers, 79, 81–2, 343–4, 349–51, 363, 365–8, 507–10, 514–15
technical practices, 75–6, 100, 514
technical vocabulary, 349–50
temperature, 136, 391, 405–6, 413, 536
terminology, 38, 65, 175, 209, 363–4, 407–8, 528, 546
terrain, 76, 201–2, 204–9, 216, 219, 520; representations of, 194, 202
tessellations, 462–6, 468–9, 471–2, 477–8
Thelen, E., 215–17, 321
theoretical commitments, 75, 311, 320–1, 449
theoretical foundations, 35–7
theoretical imperialism, 459, 477, 577

theoretical innovations, 56–7, 542
theoretical orientations, 11, 18, 20–3, 35
theoretical perspectives, 11, 13, 35, 75–6, 134–5, 192, 288, 321
thermodynamics, 55, 531, 533
thinking: ensemble, 313, 318–19; everyday, 35, 197, 529
threads, 187, 204, 482–4, 493, 502, 520, 542, 548; causal, 482–4, 530, 539–40, 547–8; multiple, 539, 573
tilt, 61, 136, 440–1
timescales, 21–2, 27, 37, 40, 42, 134, 286
tone, 19, 23, 263, 269, 275–7, 279, 351, 356
tools, 31, 252–3, 260–1, 263, 334, 338, 502–3, 527–8; analytical, 11, 261, 287–8, 527; representational, 293–4
toon strips, 90, 98–9, 102
topic distribution, 54–5
traditions, 1–2, 11–12, 18–20, 35, 99–100, 429, 448–50, 526
transcribers, 289, 438, 562, 568
transcription, 45, 355, 360, 458, 461, 562; conventions, 257, 263, 288–9, 322, 344, 411–12, 421, 576
transcripts, 24, 77–80, 296–7, 411–23, 438–9, 562, 564–5, 567–8; multimodal, 140, 572
transformations, 34–5, 86, 139, 149, 155, 157, 160, 172
transition-relevant place (TRP), 410
transitions, 52, 225, 227, 230, 314, 319–20, 441–2, 444–5; abrupt, 216, 224, 230; smooth, 216, 224
TRP (transition-relevant place), 410
true developmental study, 43–4
truth, 38–9, 135–6, 145, 147, 251, 257, 264, 446
Turing Test, 183–4
turn*s, 480–1, 484, 487, 493, 520
turn-by-turn conversational dynamics, 261, 574
turns, 240–8, 255–6, 336, 379, 382–94, 398–9, 480, 566–7
turns-at-talk, 383, 385
tutorial groups, 313–14
tutoring sessions, 142, 194, 408, 415
tutors, 83–4, 139, 157, 195, 200, 208, 573

understanding: conceptual, 13, 162, 315, 558; intersubjective, 461, 577; mathematical, 58; mutual, 559, 565;

normative, 170, 363–5, 491, 575; shared, 61, 163, 174, 181, 321, 564–5
unfolding interaction, 252, 261, 263, 286–7, 294, 297
unit of cognition, 312–15
unit of framing, 312–14
urban street grid, 88, 97–9
utility, 213–14, 286, 451
utterances, 269, 274–7, 289, 350–1, 419, 421–2, 431, 450; *see also* speech

validation, 308–9, 356–7, 363, 375; requests, 351, 354, 356–7
velocity, 162, 167, 169–72, 177, 180, 269, 271–2, 562–3
vertices, 296–301, 305–9, 316–19, 322; new, 297, 308, 320
video, 45–6, 72, 79, 97, 102, 120–1, 459, 477; cameras, 18, 140, 166, 296, 515; data, 19, 22, 46, 101, 163, 165, 408, 417; recordings, 18–19, 23–4, 45, 74, 83–4, 102, 420, 459
visibility, 251, 297, 350, 537–8, 547
visitor groups, 93–5, 102
visual diagrams, 138, 145, 154

visual representations, 45, 94, 156, 172
vocabulary, 438–9, 532; technical, 349–50
Vosniadou, S., 31, 34, 237–8, 403
Vygotsky, L. S., 218, 220, 230

Wagner, J. F., 37, 52, 55–6, 58–60, 112, 189, 191, 237
Walking Scale Geometry, *see* WSG
water, 81, 93, 264–7, 273, 276–7, 279–81, 378–9, 397–8
weight, 123, 125–6, 241, 244, 247, 253–5, 278, 287
Wenger, E., 112, 506, 514, 516–17
Wetherell, M., 460, 477
winter, 136, 352, 355, 388, 391, 394–6, 432–4, 452–3
worksheets, 295, 313–15, 462, 464–6, 470, 473
world held-in-common, 560–1
worldviews, 288, 477–8, 526
WSG (Walking Scale Geometry), 294–6, 307–11

yellow ropes, 298, 301, 305–6, 318